CAMBRIDGE GREEK A

THREE HOMERIC HYMNS

TO APOLLO, HERMES, AND APHRODITE

HYMNS 3, 4, AND 5

EDITED BY

NICHOLAS RICHARDSON

Emeritus Fellow of Merton College, Oxford

CAMBRIDGE
UNIVERSITY PRESS

CAMBRIDGE
UNIVERSITY PRESS

University Printing House, Cambridge CB2 8BS, United Kingdom

Cambridge University Press is part of the University of Cambridge.

It furthers the University's mission by disseminating knowledge in the pursuit of education, learning and research at the highest international levels of excellence.

www.cambridge.org
Information on this title: www.cambridge.org/9780521457743

First published 2010
Reprinted 2012

A catalogue record for this publication is available from the British Library

Library of Congress Cataloguing in Publication data
Homeric hymns. Selections.
Three homeric hymns : to Apollo, Hermes, and Aphrodite, hymns 3, 4, and 5 / Nicholas Richardson.
p. cm. – (Cambridge Greek and Latin classics)
Includes index.
ISBN 978-0-521-45158-1 (hardback)
1. Homeric hymns. 2. Hymns, Greek (Classical) 3. Gods, Greek – Poetry.
I. Richardson, N. J. (Nicholas James) II. Title.
PA4023.H8 2010
883′.01 – dc22 2009038169

ISBN 978-0-521-45158-1 Hardback
ISBN 978-0-521-45774-3 Paperback

A.M.D.G.

For
Rachel Chapman,
and to the memory of
Peter Levi

CONTENTS

MAPS AND FIGURE

PREFACE

In August 1992 Pat Easterling wrote to me, suggesting an edition of some of the *Homeric Hymns* for this series. Fortunately the long delay in completing the present volume has not deterred several younger scholars from undertaking more detailed commentaries on each of these three poems. This has made it easier for me to see my own work as a stage in a process, rather than an attempt to offer a final verdict on all the possible questions which might arise.

I have not undertaken a new examination of the manuscripts, but have used the *apparatus criticus* of Càssola. In the Introduction linguistic issues are briefly discussed, and there is still scope for further work in this area. Equally, my suggestions about the dating and provenance of these hymns are very provisional, and I should be only too happy if others can improve on these. I regret that it has not been possible to discuss more extensively the *Nachleben* of the *Hymns*, a subject on which much more remains to be said, or to include some of the shorter ones as I had originally hoped to do.

verum haec ipse equidem spatiis exclusus iniquis
praetereo atque aliis post me memoranda relinquo.

In view of the fact that Andrew Faulkner's major edition of the *Hymn to Aphrodite* is now published, I have also kept my commentary on this poem (which I had drafted first of all) relatively brief, and have paid more detailed attention to the other two hymns.

My main hope is that this edition will enable students of these delightful poems both to understand and to enjoy them more fully.

I am conscious of many debts of gratitude. Several sabbatical terms, generously provided by Oxford University and Merton, gave opportunities for periods of more sustained work, and a British Academy award allowed me an extra term free. The Fondation Hardt, the British School at Rome (together with the library of the German Archaeological Institute), and Stanford University have also offered congenial environments for study at various times. I am especially grateful to Richard Martin and Marsh McCall for enabling me to spend some months at Stanford, and to the members of my graduate class there for their contributions. I also benefited from the classes on the *Hymn to Aphrodite* given some years ago in Oxford by Peter Parsons. Most recently, a conference in

Lyon on Greek hymns in June 2008, organised by Pascale Brillet-Dubois, Richard Bouchon, and Nadine Le Meur, has provided useful new ideas and stimulus.

I have greatly enjoyed and profited from interaction with four scholars working on individual hymns, Mike Chappell, Andrew Faulkner, Oliver Thomas, and Athanasios Vergados. Mike's doctoral thesis ('A Commentary on the Homeric Hymn to Delian Apollo, with Prolegomena', London, 1995) offered much helpful material. Both Andrew and Oliver read drafts of the introduction and made valuable suggestions for improvement, and I have profited from Athanasios' discussion of other versions of the Hermes story in his PhD thesis. In addition, I am grateful for advice or help received from John Boardman, Jim Coulton, Malcolm Davies, Stephen Evans, Helen Hughes-Brock, Barbara Kowalzig, Rachel Maxwell-Hyslop, Douglas Olson, Robert Parker, Natasha Peponi, Simon Pulleyn, William Slater, Martin West, and Nigel Wilson. As editors of the series Pat Easterling and Richard Hunter have been unfailingly patient and supportive, and I have nothing but praise and thanks for the thoroughness with which they have offered suggestions for improvement. The exemplary work of Dr Iveta Adams as copy editor has also done much to improve the form and expression of the final version.

Cecilia Nobili recently sent me a copy of her interesting PhD thesis, 'L'*Inno Omerico a Ermes* e le tradizioni poetiche locali' (Milan, 2008), and I am sorry that I have not been able to take account of this.

Work on two of these hymns, to Apollo and Hermes, really began with classes which Peter Levi and I gave together in the 1970s. I remember Peter saying then that I should do an edition of them. Classes with Peter were always uniquely stimulating and enjoyable, and I much regret that he is no longer with us to see his advice finally followed. This book is dedicated to his memory, and also to Rachel Chapman, who has typed countless drafts of the work over so many years. For her astonishing accuracy and patience I am immeasurably grateful.

N. J. R.

ABBREVIATIONS

Abbreviations for Greek authors usually follow those in LSJ. Periodicals are abbreviated as in *L'Année philologique.*

AHS	Allen, T. W., Halliday, W. R., and Sikes, E. E. (1936) *The Homeric Hymns.* Oxford
Allen and Sikes	Allen, T. W. and Sikes, E. E. (1904) *The Homeric Hymns.* Oxford
ANET	Pritchard, J. B., ed. (1969) *Ancient Near Eastern Texts,* 3rd edn with supplement. Princeton
Arch. Hom.	Metz, F. and Buchholz, H. G., edd. (1969–) *Archaeologia Homerica: die Denkmäler und das frühgriechische Epos.* Göttingen
Càssola	Càssola, F. (1975) *Inni omerici.* Rome
Chantraine, *Dict.*	Chantraine, P. (1968–80) *Dictionnaire étymologique de la langue grecque.* Paris
Chantraine, *GH*	Chantraine, P. (1942–53) *Grammaire homérique.* Paris
Daremberg and Saglio, *Dictionnaire*	Daremberg, C. and Saglio, E. (1877–1919) *Dictionnaire des antiquités grecques et romaines.* 10 vols. Paris
Davies	Davies, M., ed. (1988) *Epicorum Graecorum fragmenta.* Göttingen
Denniston, GP^2	Denniston, J. D. (1950) *The Greek particles,* 2nd edn. Oxford
Farnell, *Cults*	Farnell, L. R. (1896–1909) *Cults of the Greek states.* Oxford
FGrH	Jacoby, F. (1923–58) *Die Fragmente der griechischen Historiker.* Leiden
Gemoll	Gemoll, A. (1886) *Die homerischen Hymnen.* Leipzig
Humbert	Humbert, J. (1936) *Homère, Hymnes.* Paris
LfgrE	Snell, B. and Erbse, H., edd. (1955–) *Lexikon des frühgriechischen Epos.* Göttingen
LIMC	*Lexikon iconographicum mythologiae classicae* (1981–99). Zurich
L–P	Lobel, E. and Page, D. L., edd. (1955) *Poetarum Lesbiorum fragmenta.* Oxford
LSJ	Liddell, H. G., Scott, R., and Jones, H. S. *A Greek–English lexicon,* 9th edn, 1940; Supplement, 1996. Oxford
Monro, HG^2	Monro, D. B. (1891) *A grammar of the Homeric dialect,* 2nd edn. Oxford

M–W	Merkelbach, R. and West, M. L, edd. (1967) *Fragmenta Hesiodea*. Oxford
Nilsson, *GGR* i³	Nilsson, M. P. (1967) *Geschichte der griechischen Religion*, vol. i, 3rd edn. Munich
OCD	Hornblower, S. and Spawforth, A., edd. (1996) *The Oxford classical dictionary*, 3rd edn. Oxford
PCG	Kassel, R. and Austin, C., edd. (1983–) *Poetae comici Graeci*. Berlin
PEG ed. Bernabé	Bernabé, A. (1988) *Poetae epici Graeci: testimonia et fragmenta. Pars* i. Leipzig
PMG	Page, D. L., ed. (1962) *Poetae melici Graeci*. Oxford
Powell, *CA*	Powell, J. U., ed. (1925) *Collectanea Alexandrina*. Oxford
Princeton Encyclopedia	Stilwell, R., ed. (1976) *The Princeton encyclopedia of classical sites*. Princeton
Radermacher	Radermacher, L. (1931) *Der homerische Hermeshymnus*. Vienna
RE	Wissowa, G. *et al.*, edd. (1893–) *Paulys Real-Encyclopädie der classischen Altertumswissenschaft*. Stuttgart and Munich
SH	Lloyd-Jones, H. and Parsons, P. J., edd. (1983) *Supplementum Hellenisticum*. Berlin
TrGF	Snell, B., Kannicht, R., and Radt, S. L., edd. (1971–) *Tragicorum Graecorum fragmenta*. Göttingen
V	Voigt, E.-M., ed. (1971) *Sappho et Alcaeus*. Amsterdam
van Eck	Eck, J. van (1978) 'The Homeric Hymn to Aphrodite'. Diss. Utrecht

Other editions of Homer, *Homeric Hymns*, and Hesiod, referred to by author's name (e.g. Kirk on *Il.* 1.1, etc.):

Kirk, G. S. (1985) *The Iliad: a commentary. Books 1–4*. Cambridge

Kirk, G. S. (1990) *The Iliad: a commentary. Books 5–8*. Cambridge

Hainsworth, J. B. (1993) *The Iliad: a commentary. Books 9–12*. Cambridge

Janko, R. (1992) *The Iliad: a commentary. Books 13–16*. Cambridge

Edwards, M. W. (1991) *The Iliad: a commentary. Books 17–20*. Cambridge

Richardson, N. J. (1993) *The Iliad: a commentary. Books 21–24*. Cambridge

Heubeck, A., West, S., and Hainsworth, J. B. (1988) *A commentary on Homer's Odyssey: books* i–viii. Oxford

Heubeck, A. and Hoekstra, A. (1989) *A commentary on Homer's Odyssey: books* ix–xvi. Oxford

Russo, J., Fernandez-Galiano, M., and Heubeck, A. (1992) *A commentary on Homer's Odyssey: books* xvii–xxiv. Oxford

Richardson, N. J. (1974) *The Homeric Hymn to Demeter*. Oxford

West, M. L. (1966) *Hesiod: Theogony*. Oxford
West, M. L. (1978) *Hesiod: Works and Days*. Oxford
Solmsen, F., Merkelbach, R., and West, M. L. (1990) *Hesiodi opera*, 3rd edn. Oxford

The four major *Homeric Hymns* are referred to as *H. Ap.* (= *Hymn* 3), *H. Aph.* (= *Hymn* 5), *H. Dem.* (= *Hymn* 2), and *H. Herm.* (= *Hymn* 4). The remainder are referred to by their number in Allen's Oxford text (e.g. *H.* 6, etc.).

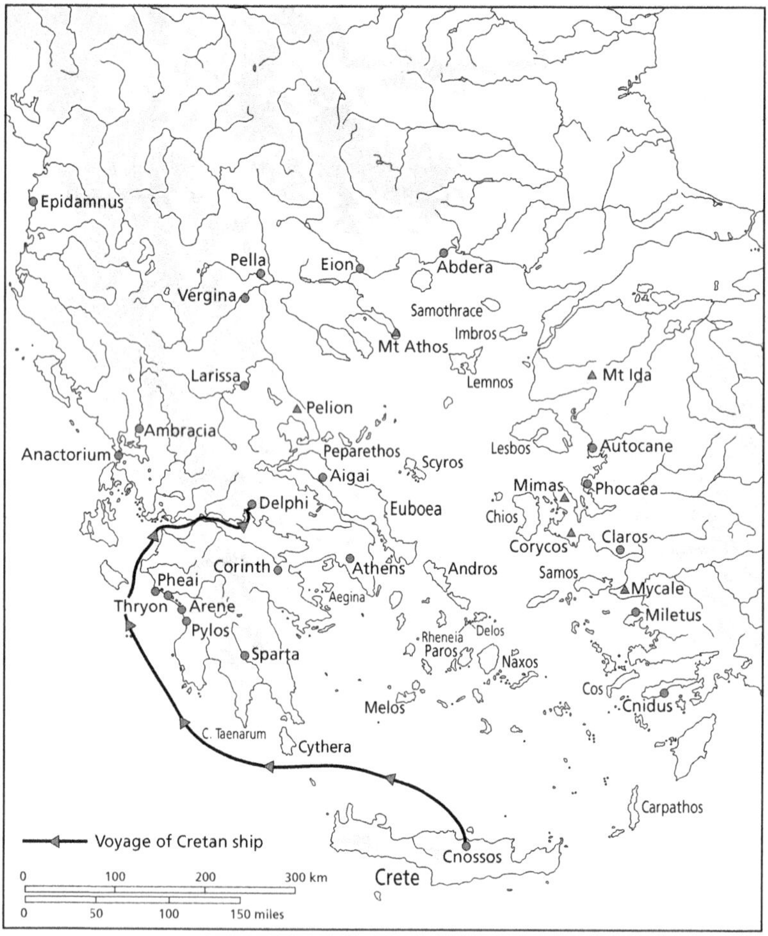

Map 1 Leto's wanderings (lines 30–49) and voyage of Cretan ship (391–523).

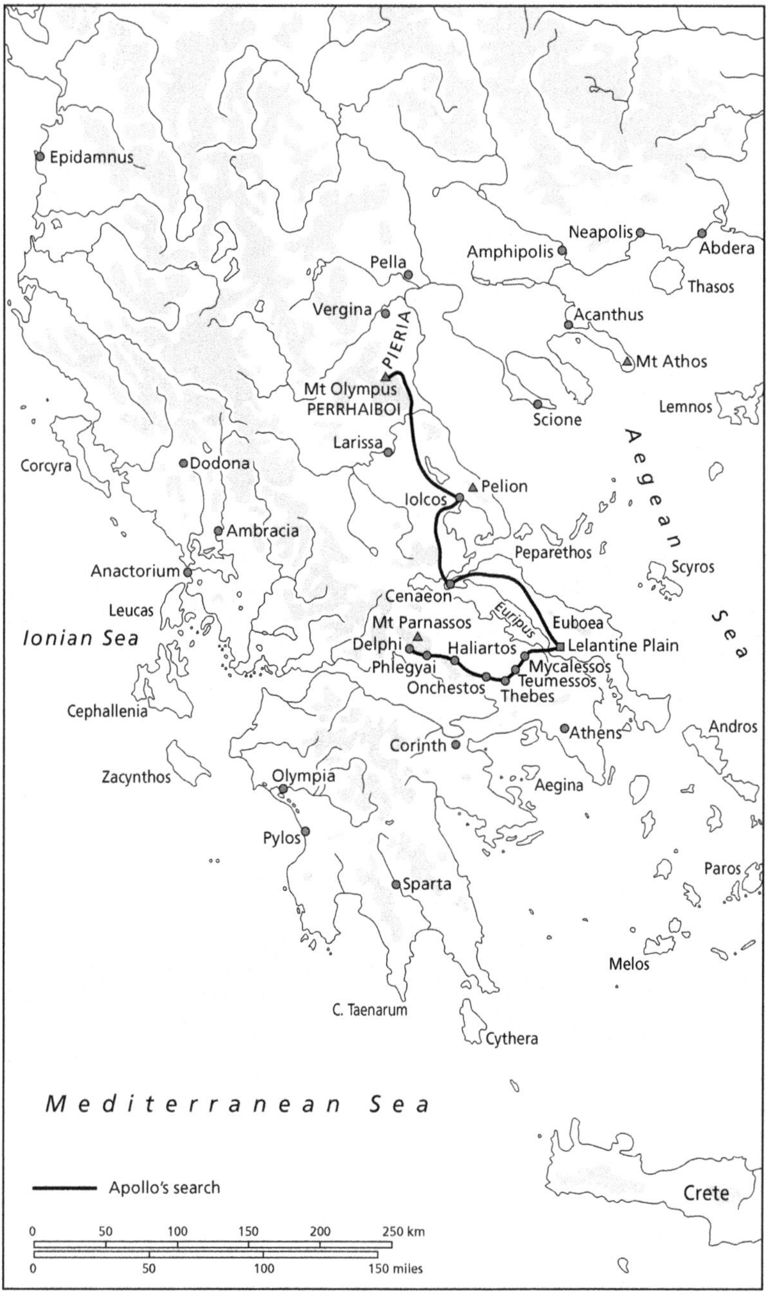

Map 2 Apollo's search for an oracle site (216–86).

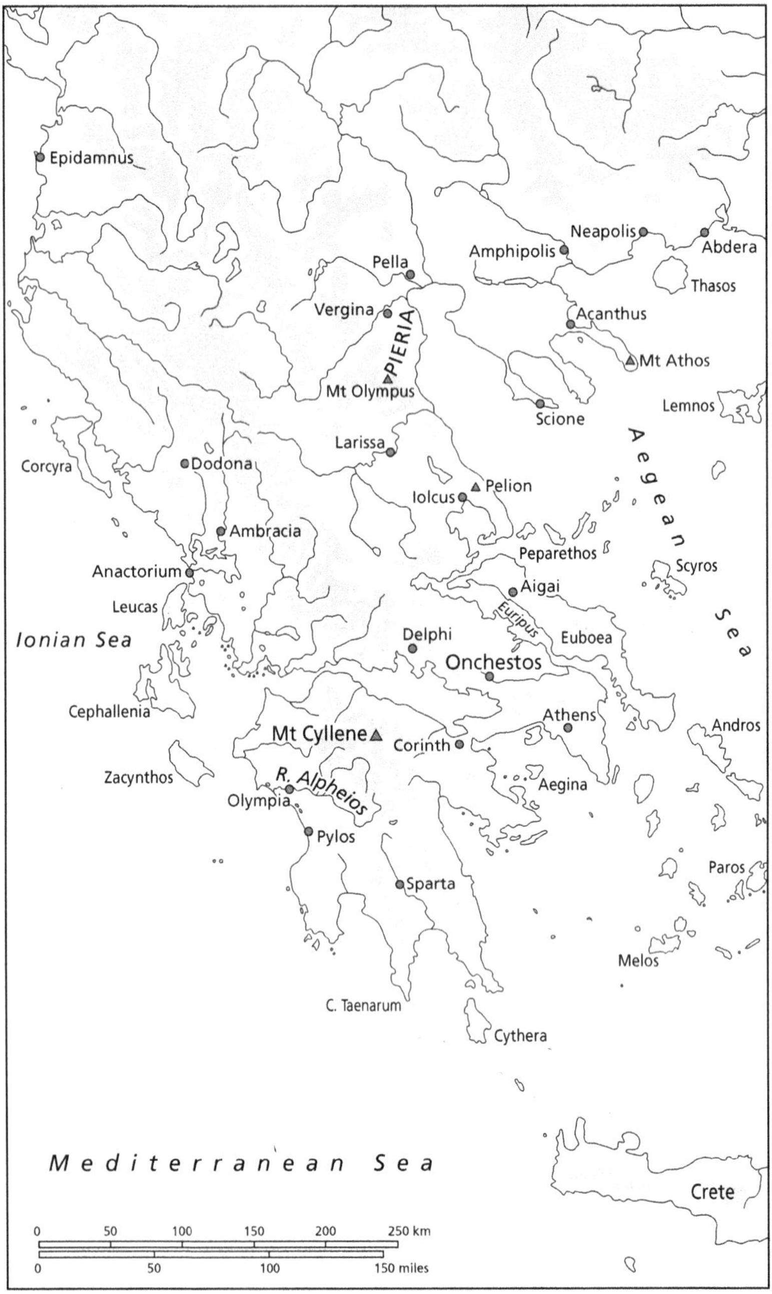

Map 3 Hermes' journeys – Pieria: lines 70–4 etc.; Onchestos: 87–93, 185–212; River Alpheios: 101–2, 139, 397–8; Mt Cyllene: 2, 142, 228, 337.

INTRODUCTION

1 THE HOMERIC HYMNS

(a) Nature and purpose

The three poems studied in this book belong to a collection of thirty-three hymns in hexameter verse, composed in honour of ancient Greek gods and goddesses. Their title in the manuscripts is Ὁμήρου ὕμνοι. They vary considerably in length. In the collection as we have it, the four longest hymns, to Demeter (495 lines), Apollo (546 lines), Hermes (580 lines), and Aphrodite (293 lines), are preceded by the last section of a hymn to Dionysus, which originally must also have been a longer one. (For a possible reconstruction of this hymn see West (2001b); cf. also Dihle (2002) for a contrary view.) Of the others, the longest (*H.* 7, also to Dionysus) is fifty-nine lines, the shortest (*H.* 13, to Demeter) only three. Several deities are the subject of more than one hymn, and a few are short pieces composed of extracts from longer poems (13, 17, and 18 from the longer hymns to Demeter, the Dioscuri, and Hermes, and 25 from Hesiod's *Theogony*).

Most of these poems probably belong to the 'Archaic' period, i.e. between *c.* 700 and 500 BC, but some appear to be later in date. An Attic vase painting of *c.* 470 BC shows a boy holding a papyrus-roll, on which are written what appear to be the opening two words of *Hymn* 18. It has been inferred that some at least of the hymns could have already been used as school texts at this time (cf. *H. Herm.* 1n.). Our earliest explicit reference to one of the hymns is by Thucydides (3.104), who quotes two passages from the *Hymn to Apollo* (146–50 and 165–72), ascribes it to Homer, and calls it a προοίμιον (prelude). Later writers, however, from the second century AD onwards, express doubts about Homer's authorship of the *Hymns*. Athenaeus (22B) attributes the *Hymn to Apollo* to 'Homer or one of the Homeridae', and a scholiast to Pindar, *Nemean* 2.1 ascribes it to a rhapsode named Cynaethus (cf. 2(b) below). *Hymn* 2 is quoted by a scholiast to Nicander (*Alex.* 130) as 'among the hymns ascribed to Homer', and some of the *Lives of Homer* assert that only the *Iliad* and *Odyssey* are definitely Homer's own work (cf. *Vita* v, p. 248.19–24, *Plutarchi Vita* p. 243–4.98–100, *Suda* p. 258.37–8 Allen). Alexandrian scholarship does not often refer to the *Hymns*, and this suggests that by the Hellenistic period, if not before, their authenticity as Homeric was questioned (cf. AHS pp. lxxix–lxxxi).

The passages quoted by Thucydides from the *Hymn to Apollo* describe a Pan-Ionian festival of this god on Delos, and the poet's own request to the Delian girls who are Apollo's attendants, to commemorate him as a blind man who lives in Chios and to praise him as the best of singers (cf. 140–78, 146–72, 165–76nn.). The poem therefore is set dramatically at the festival which is being described, and the poet's claim suggests, as Thucydides infers (3.104.5), performance of this hymn at a poetic contest. In a similar way, *Hymn* 6 closes with a prayer to Aphrodite to grant the singer 'victory in this contest' (19–20), and several others end by asking the deity to grant favour or honour to the poet's song (10.4, 24.5, 25.6). The reference in the *Hymn to Apollo* to the singer's blindness also places him in the tradition of the Homeric bard (such as the blind Demodocus) who composed and performed without a written text.

Thucydides' use of the form προοίμιον has led scholars to conclude that hymns of this kind were (originally at least) composed as preludes to further song. The traditional closing formula αὐτὰρ ἐγὼ καὶ σεῖο καὶ ἄλλης μνήσομ' ἀοιδῆς (*H.* 2.495, 3.546, 4.580, etc.), whatever its precise translation should be, suggests this (cf. *H. Ap.* 546n.), and the close of *Hymn* 5 (293 = *H.* 9.9, 18.11) σεῦ δ' ἐγὼ ἀρξάμενος μεταβήσομαι ἄλλον ἐς ὕμνον is still more explicit. The hymns to Sun and Moon (31 and 32) end by declaring that the singer will go on to tell of the deeds of heroes. These two poems may be composed later than most of the others, but they reflect a tradition that such preludes could be followed by heroic epic narrative. An alternative opening line to the *Iliad* invokes Apollo as well as the Muses (Μούσας ἀείδω καὶ Ἀπόλλωνα κλυτότοξον). In the *Odyssey* Demodocus is said to begin a song 'from the god' (*Od.* 8.499): this has also been taken to indicate an opening invocation or prelude to a deity. Both Hesiod's *Theogony* and *Works and Days* open with hymns, to the Muses and to Zeus respectively, and the one to the Muses is of considerable length (cf. West on *Theogony* 1–115). Pindar (*N.* 2.1–3) speaks of the Homeridae beginning Διὸς ἐκ προοιμίου. This statement occasions a lengthy commentary by a scholiast about the Homeridae, in the course of which Cynaethus is named as author of the *Hymn to Apollo*. Tradition then seems to have associated the *Hymns* with the Homeridae (cf. also Athenaeus above), a group or guild of singers based in Chios, claiming links with Homer either as his descendants or as his followers (cf. Graziosi (2002) 201–34).

Something similar to the practice of singing hexameter hymns as preludes to epic song is described in the *Hymn to Apollo*, when the poet praises the Delian girls' choir. He says that they first sing hymns to Apollo, Leto, and Artemis, and then 'a song in praise of men and women of old' (cf. 158–61n.).

In the case of most of the shorter hymns, their original purpose as preludes has been generally accepted. Scholars have sometimes questioned whether the longer ones were really composed for this purpose, or rather were independent compositions, the term 'prelude' having lost its original meaning (cf. AHS xciii–xcv). But their length is not in itself an argument against their being designed as genuine preludes, if we consider for example the much larger scale of some early epic poems, which could have followed them. The longer hymns may, of course, represent a development from an earlier tradition of short ones. But some of the briefer ones, as mentioned above, are simply abbreviated versions of the longer hymns: so this process could go the other way (cf. also West on Hesiod *Th.* 94–7).

It is reasonable to assume that many at least of these hymns were originally composed for performance at a festival. It is often thought that an individual hymn was designed to honour the god of the festival concerned. This may have been so, but it cannot be proved. In any case, it is clear that these poems continued to be reused over a period of time, since the manuscript tradition contains many variant readings, as with the Homeric epics (see Janko (1982) 2–4). In particular, Thucydides' text of the passages he quotes from the *Hymn to Apollo* differs considerably from that of our medieval manuscripts (see 146–72n.), and there are also cases where lines are quoted which appear to be alternatives (cf. especially on *H. Ap.* 135–9, where some of our texts have marginal signs, probably indicating this). Such re-performances could have been in different types of context from the original ones, as in the case of epic poetry (see Parker (1991) 1–2). Performance at banquets or *symposia* has also been suggested as a possible type of occasion (Clay (2006) 7). The longer *Hymn to Aphrodite* (*H.* 5) could have been composed for performance at the court of a ruler, as in the case of Demodocus' 'Song of Ares and Aphrodite' in *Odyssey* 8.

(b) *Origins of the collection*

We do not know how this collection of hymns came to have its present form. Whereas Thucydides identifies the *Hymn to Apollo* with the name προοίμιον, from at least the first century BC we find quotations from the longer hymns which refer to them as ὕμνοι of Homer (e.g. Diodorus Siculus 1.15.7, 3.66.3, 4.2.4, Philodemus, *On Piety* p. 42, tab. 91, vv. 12ff. Gomperz). This suggests that an edition of these at least was made by some time in the Hellenistic period. At *H. Ap.* 136–9 the marginal signs mentioned above probably derive from Alexandrian scholarship (see *H. Ap.* 135–9n.). Most of the ancient quotations or allusions to the *Hymns* are from the five longer ones. Schol. Pind. *P.* 3.14, however, quotes *H.* 16.1–3 as ἐν τοῖς Ὁμηρικοῖς ὕμνοις. This shows that by the time of this commentator the collection already included this shorter hymn. A second-century AD papyrus commentary on a comedy (*P.Oxy.* 2737, fr. 1.i.19–27) assigns the phrase κύκνος ὑπὸ πτερύγων (*H.* 21.1) to the 'hymns ascribed to Homer', after discussing attributions of it to various lyric poets by Aristarchus and other scholars. Moreover, a papyrus of the third century AD (*P.Oxy.* 4667) contains lines 4–11 of *Hymn* 18 (to Hermes), followed by two lines in prose, the second of which may possibly read εἰς Διόνυ]σον ὕμν[ος, and then lines 1–11 of *Hymn* 7 (to Dionysus). It is not clear why these two hymns are quoted, but the papyrus again shows that some of the shorter hymns were being discussed or quoted by this period. (It is interesting that this papyrus omits line 12 of *Hymn* 18, which had been regarded by some modern editors as a doublet of lines 10–11.)

We can see some principles at work in the ordering of the poems as we have them (cf. Van der Valk (1976), Fröhder (1994) 14–15 n. 1, Torres-Guerra (2003), West (2003) 21). After the first five long hymns comes the second one to Aphrodite (twenty-one lines), evidently as a pendant to the first, and then the second to Dionysus (fifty-nine lines), which contains an extended narrative of

Dionysus' capture by pirates, and so is probably grouped with the other major hymns. *Hymn* 8 to Ares has always been considered as an 'odd one out', since its language and style are completely different. It has been attributed to the fifth-century AD Neoplatonist Proclus (West (1970)), but differs from his hymns in several respects (cf. Devlin (1995) 338–42). But it was clearly composed in the Roman period. At some point the *Homeric Hymns* were combined with the *Orphic Argonautica*, and the *Hymns* of Proclus and Callimachus, in a single edition (cf. 5 below). It is still a matter for debate as to whether the inclusion of the *Hymn to Ares* with the Homeric ones was due to deliberate choice at this stage of editing, or a later accident of transmission (cf. West (1970), Gelzer (1987) and (1994) 125–9).

The shorter hymns (9–33) are ordered to some extent in groups: 9–14 are to goddesses, 15–17 to deified heroes, 18–23 to gods, and 27–30 are for goddesses. *H.* 30 (to Earth) also goes with 31–2 (to Sun and Moon) as hymns to cosmic deities. *H.* 33 (to the Dioscuri) may possibly fit in with this group, as it praises especially their elemental character as the calmers of storms at sea. *H.* 19 (to Pan) is a more elaborate composition of forty-nine lines, which follows directly after 18, the second hymn to Hermes, as Pan is Hermes' son.

For the later transmission of the *Hymns* see 6 below.

(c) *Structure and themes*

The shortest hymn (13) consists of two lines announcing its subject (Demeter and her daughter Persephone), and a closing verse saluting Demeter, and asking her to keep the city safe and begin the poet's song. The two deities are briefly characterised with epithets of praise.

The other short hymns add more information about the deity, often by means of a relative clause. Many of these describe typical activities and attributes in the present tense, but some have a narrative development in past tenses, and in some cases we also find variation between past and present. The enduring character of the god can be linked with certain past actions or events, or alternatively a narrative section can culminate in a description of how he now is, after these developments. Nearly all the hymns end with a closing verse or verses saluting the god, usually coupled with a prayer, and often also a transitional formula to another story.

This simple and basic structure forms the framework in which a longer narrative can be developed, as in *Hymns* 1–7. These poems (with their traditional epic style and language) resemble miniature epics, telling stories about the gods. Foremost among the themes of these is the god's birth, and then often how they acquired their distinctive powers or spheres of action (cf. *H. Hermes* 428 ὡς τὰ πρῶτα γένοντο καὶ ὡς λάχε μοῖραν ἕκαστος). The birth-narrative can be complicated, involving concealment or hostility (as with Apollo, Hermes, or the Dioscuri). It may also have wider or cosmic repercussions, as with Athene's birth fully armed from the head of Zeus (*H.* 28), or when the island of Delos greets Apollo's birth by covering herself in golden flowers (*H. Ap.* 135–9).

Birth can be followed directly by the god's assuming his powers (e.g. *H. Ap.* 127–32), or performing exploits (*H. Herm.* 17–23). It can also lead directly to another major theme, the introduction of the new deity to the company of the gods on Olympus, as for example in the miniature hymn of the nymphs, within the *Hymn to Pan* (19.28–47), where they describe how Hermes immediately takes his newborn son and introduces him to the other gods. This theme can be used in a wider variety of ways. In the short *Hymn to Heracles* (15), since Heracles is a mortal, life on Olympus and marriage come as a reward at the end, after his Labours. In the longer *Hymn to Demeter*, Persephone is picking flowers on earth when she is carried off by Hades, and Demeter deserts Olympus and creates a famine on earth, forcing Zeus to order Persephone's rescue. At the end of the hymn both goddesses go up to Olympus and live there (483–6), but Persephone must still spend part of the year in the Underworld (cf. 393–403). In the *Hymn to Hermes*, by a typically comic twist, Hermes' first entry to Olympus occurs when his brother Apollo takes him there in order to accuse him before Zeus of stealing his cattle (322–96). After the return of the stolen goods and their reconciliation the two brothers go back to Olympus and are welcomed there by Zeus (504–7).

The *Hymn to Apollo* makes a double use of this theme, in an original and powerful way. The poem opens dramatically with the scene of Apollo's entry to Zeus's palace, as an archer with his bow drawn, causing consternation among the gods until Leto unstrings the bow and leads him to a seat (1–13). The theme recurs as a prelude to the account of the founding of the Pythian oracle: here Apollo is portrayed as a god of music, going up to Olympus from Pytho (i.e. Delphi), and leading the gods there in music and dancing (182–206).

Another natural development after birth is the god's nursing or upbringing, usually by other divine beings. Apollo is bathed and wrapped in swaddling-clothes by the goddesses present at his birth, and then fed on nectar and ambrosia by Themis (123–5). Dionysus in *Hymn* 26 (3–6) is nursed by the nymphs in the glens of Nysa, and then roams with them through the wilds. In *Hymn* 6 Aphrodite's birth is suggested, as the sea foam (in which she was traditionally born) carries her to Cyprus, where the Seasons clothe her and adorn her with jewellery, after which she is introduced to the other immortals. By contrast, Hermes does not stay in his cradle after his birth, but immediately sets off in search of Apollo's cattle (*H. Herm.* 20–3). Divine nursing is also a motif transferred to specially favoured mortals, such as Demophon, the nursling of Demeter, whom she tries to immortalise (*H. Dem.* 219–91), and Aeneas, who as Aphrodite's son will be brought up by the nymphs (*H. Aph.* 256–75). Sometimes such divine attendants become the god's habitual companions, as in the case of Dionysus and the nymphs of Nysa, or Pan with his nymphs, who also praise his birth (*H.* 19.19–47), or Persephone picking flowers with the Oceanids when she is carried off (*H. Dem.* 5–18).

The *Hymns* are primarily concerned with the divine world, like Hesiod's *Theogony*. Consequently their portrayal of the world of mortals and of the interaction between gods and men is understandably different in some ways from what we find in the Homeric epics, although broadly speaking the divine society of these epics is the same as that of the *Hymns*. But the gods' interaction with mortals is an important aspect of these poems, especially the longer ones. The *Hymn to Hermes* is unusual in that only one mortal character actually appears in the narrative, an anonymous old farmer, who does however play an important role as the witness of Hermes' cattle-theft (87–94, 185–212, 354–5). The Greek gods were traditionally ambivalent towards mortals, conscious of their own vast superiority but at the same time unable to detach themselves from the human world, and also reliant on their worship and sacrifices, if not physically then at least for prestige and honour. When Demeter's famine robs the gods of sacrifices on earth this creates a crisis in heaven and Zeus is compelled to intervene (*H. Dem.* 305–41).

Naturally also the poets and their audiences who are seeking the favour of the gods will tend to speak of the honours men pay them and of their favourite sanctuaries, as was the case in prayers to the gods from Homer onwards. In several of the *Hymns* the deities are described as visiting their special places of cult. Some take this theme an important stage further, as they tell of how a major cult was first instituted. Much of the *Hymn to Demeter* is concerned with Demeter's favourable reception at Eleusis and its consequences, leading to her command to the Eleusinians to build her a temple and altar there. In this temple she remains until Persephone's return to the upper world, and then at the close of the poem she teaches her secret rites (the Eleusinian Mysteries) to the leaders of the people. The poem thus asserts the special status of Eleusis as a (or the) leading centre for the cult of Demeter and Persephone. In a similar way Leto promises Delos that Apollo will build his first temple on the island, and Delos is said to be his favourite place of worship (49–88, 143–8). This is counterbalanced by the narrative of how he came to choose Pytho as an oracular site, and appoint his first priests there.

This theme of the institution of cult is closely linked to that of the god's epiphany, or his appearance in true form to men, which is often the signal for cult or worship. When Aphrodite comes in disguise to Anchises his first response is to assume (correctly) that she is a goddess, and to promise to set up an altar and make regular sacrifices to her, in return for which he prays for her favour (*H. Aph.* 91–106). Later, after their union, Aphrodite reveals her true identity, but in this case, instead of this leading to cult, she foretells the birth of Aeneas and his future kingship (168–99). Aphrodite wants her liaison to remain a secret (281–8). When Demeter in disguise as an old woman sets foot on the threshold of the palace at Eleusis, her divinity is momentarily revealed in language very similar to that of Aphrodite's epiphany. Queen Metaneira is overcome by awe, reverence, and fear, and the following scene actually foreshadows some of the preliminary rituals of the Mysteries (*H. Dem.* 187–211; cf. Richardson ad loc.). Later Demeter reveals her true identity more explicitly both in words and in action, and this is accompanied by her command to set up her sanctuary and the promise to institute her rites (251–80).

In the *Hymn to Apollo*, the god's birth on Delos is followed by the elaborate description of the Delian festival (146–76), and although this is not portrayed as the direct consequence of his appearance, the association between the two events is evident, since it is because of Delos' reception of Leto and Apollo's birth there that this island has such a special status. The theme of the search for an oracular site later in this hymn is explicitly linked to a series of *aitia* for cults of the god, as Pythios, Telphousios, and Delphinios (cf. 371–4, 375–87, 486–510). The building of Apollo's temple at Delphi (281–99) is directly followed by the narrative of the killing of the Pythian serpent, and this in turn may be connected with the festivals commemorating this event, the Septerion and the Pythian Games (cf. *H. Ap.* 300–74, 357–62nn.). At the end of the poem the god reveals his identity to his future priests, sets up his cult on the shore of Crisa, and leads them in procession to the site of Delphi, where he commands them to take care of his worship (474–544).

Aetiology is a powerful factor in the shaping of these poems, not only on a religious level but also on a wider cultural plane. The *Hymn to Hermes* is rich in this respect, because of the god's ingenuity and inventiveness (see 3(f) below). Equally, it seems probable that a major impetus for the creation of the longer *Hymn to Aphrodite* is the wish to account for the origin of the family of Aeneas as rulers of the Trojans in later times (cf. 4(a) and (b) below, and *H. Aph.* 196–7n.). On a broader level, the *Hymns*, especially the narrative ones, focus on the phase when the current divine order was being established, and help to account for this. They can be fitted in mythologically between the earlier cosmogonic eras which the *Theogony* includes, and the heroic age reflected in the Homeric epics (cf. Clay (2006)).

The *Hymns* also explore the relationship between the divine and human worlds, and they emphasise both the gulf between gods and men, and also their closeness in some ways. Demeter's wish to immortalise the child Demophon is thwarted as a result of human folly, because Metaneira spies on her, although he is promised an annual commemorative festival (*H. Dem.* 242–67). But the gift of the Mysteries offers men the hope of divine favour, both in this life and in life after death (473–82, 486–9). The *Hymn to Aphrodite* describes her power in mixing gods with mortals (34–41), and how she herself fell victim to this. But it also reflects on the limits of mortality. In her long final speech to Anchises the goddess says that his family was always close to the gods, and mentions the examples of Ganymede, who escaped old age and death, and Tithonus, less happy because he became immortal but not ageless. She would not wish such a fate for Anchises. Even the nymphs who will nurse Aeneas will eventually die, as the trees which share their life come to their natural ends (200–72).

The superiority of the gods is shown not only by their power and freedom from age and death, but also because of their greater knowledge of destiny. When Demeter is detected by Metaneira she laments the ignorance of mortals, who cannot foresee the future (*H. Dem.* 256–8), and in the *Hymn to Apollo* the Muses sing of 'the gods' immortal gifts, and the sufferings of men, all that they have at the hands of deathless gods as they live in ignorance and helplessness, and cannot find a remedy for death or defence against old age' (189–93). In these various ways the *Hymns* explore the limitations of mortality, as well as portraying so vividly the nature of the gods.

By contrast, the closeness of men to the gods is beautifully illustrated in those scenes where their worship is described. In the picture of the Delian festival we are told that a spectator would believe the Ionians gathered there to be immortal and ageless (*H. Ap.* 151–2). In this hymn the scenes of music and singing both at Delos and also on the way up to Pytho are linked thematically with the singing and dancing of Apollo and the gods on Olympus (see 2(a) below). Within several of the *Hymns* the praise of the deities concerned is echoed internally by the songs sung either by gods or mortals (cf. *H. Ap.* 158–9, 516–19, *H. Herm.* 54–61, 424–33, *H.* 19.27–47, 27.18–20; cf. also *H.* 21.1–4, 30.13–16). The self-reflexive character of these poems suggests that the *Hymns* themselves, divinely inspired as they are, can bring their audiences closer to the heavenly realm.

In telling stories about the gods the *Hymns* follow many of the traditional conventions used by other early Greek hexameter poetry. But at the same time they show greater freedom when it comes to narrative realism (cf. Parker (1991) 4). For the first time in early poetry we meet a talking island (Delos) and fountain (Telphousa). The *Hymn to Hermes* is full of marvels and oddities, and in *Hymn* 7 to Dionysus, one of the most delightful and picturesque of all, a series of miracles takes place on the pirates' ship which is carrying Dionysus as a prisoner. Wine flows everywhere on board, a vine grows along the sail, ivy twines around the mast, and garlands decorate the rowlocks. The god becomes a roaring lion and creates a bear in the midst of the ship, and the pirates leap overboard and are turned into dolphins (34–53). As Parker says, the *Hymns* 'present divine myths . . . with all the freedom of fantasy that such serious subjects demand' (Parker (1991) 4).

In their richness of ornamental detail and also their language, the *Hymns* may be viewed as similar to some early lyric poetry, and in fact they could be located stylistically between Homeric and Hesiodic poetry on the one hand and lyric on the other. They also can evoke comparison with the Archaic art of the seventh and sixth centuries BC. The famous Exekias vase in Munich (*LIMC* s.v. Dionysus, no. 788, late sixth century), showing Dionysus on a ship beneath two spreading vines, with dolphins sporting in the sea, is a good example of how close the *Hymns* can come to visual art. The vivid description in *H.* 28 of Athena's birth, fully armed and brandishing her spear, from the head of Zeus is well illustrated by another famous early seventh-century amphora from Tenos (*LIMC* s.v. Athena, no. 360; cf. also some black-figure representations, such as nos. 345, 346, and 353). In their mixture of charm and seriousness the *Hymns* brilliantly portray the double character of the Greek gods, as both benevolent and awe-inspiring. Throughout them runs a strong sense of delight and joy in the natural world, of whose powers the gods are the manifestation. For this reason these poems from a remote past still speak to us today so vividly and with so clear a voice.

On structure and themes see also Danielewicz (1973) and (1976), Lenz (1975), Janko (1981), Sowa (1984), Parker (1991), Fröhder (1994), Calame (1995), Devlin (1995) 31–81, Clay (2006). On the theme of epiphany see also Garcia (2002). Narrative technique is discussed by Nünlist (2004). On ancient Greek hymns in general see Devlin (1995), Haubold (2001), and Furley and Bremer (2001).

2 HYMN TO APOLLO

(a) Structure

The hymn tells the story of the birth of Apollo, the god's foundation of his temple and oracle at Delphi, and his choice of Cretan merchants as his first priests there. The narrative is preceded by a dramatic prologue (1–18), which describes Apollo's entry to Zeus's palace on Olympus with his bow drawn, and his welcome by his parents, Zeus and Leto, and the other gods. This also forms a miniature hymn to Leto, as the mother of Apollo and Artemis.

The main narrative opens, after a brief survey of the range of themes for the god's praise, with a catalogue of islands and other landmarks around the Aegean, which were visited by Leto in her search for a birthplace. None would receive her, until she came to Delos, whose initial reluctance was overcome by the promise of a rich and famous cult of the new god (19–88). Because of Hera's jealousy the other goddesses summon Eileithyia secretly, and when she sets foot on Delos Leto gives birth to her son, who is fed on nectar and ambrosia by Themis, and immediately proclaims that he will be a god of the *kitharis*, the bow, and prophecy. Delos is covered in golden growth in response to his birth (89–139).

This opening movement of the narrative ends with a passage in which Apollo's special love of Delos is illustrated by a description of the Ionian festival in his honour there, and the choir of Delian girls who are attendants of the god and whose songs the poet praises. In return he asks them to praise him as the sweetest and best of singers, and proclaims himself as a blind man who lives in rocky Chios (140–78).

The second main theme, Apollo's search for a site for his oracular temple, is preceded (after a brief transitional passage, 179–85) like the first by a prologue which describes Apollo's arrival on Olympus, this time as god of music, and a splendid scene of the gods singing and dancing in response to his arrival, under the admiring eyes of Leto and Zeus (181–206). A short list of Apollo's love affairs is reviewed, only to be passed over in favour of the theme of the search (207–15). This is developed in a second geographical catalogue, describing Apollo's journey through the northern part of mainland Greece from Olympus until he finally reaches Crisa, the site of his future oracle (216–93). In the course of this he is dissuaded by the spring Telphousa from choosing her, because she wants to keep the honour of the place to herself (244–76). The god then founds his temple, kills the serpent of the place, which is called Pytho, and takes the name Pythios (299–374). A parenthetic episode (305–55) describes how this serpent had been the nurse of the monster Typhaon, born to Hera because of her anger with Zeus over Athena's birth. Then Apollo returns to Telphousa, angry with her because she deceived him, covers her spring with rocks, and sets up his own altar there as Apollo Telphousios (375–87).

The third and final movement of the poem again begins with a lengthy geographical catalogue, this time describing the journey of the Cretan merchants round the Peloponnese and through the Gulf of Corinth to Crisa (388–439). Apollo sees their ship on its way from Cnossos to Pylos, appears to them in the form of a dolphin, and guides the ship to Crisa. He announces his arrival by taking the form of a shooting star at midday, and then meets them disguised as a young man and asks where they come from. He reveals his true identity, promises that they will be his priests, and instructs them to set up an altar to him on the shore as Delphinios, which they do (440–512). He then leads them up to Pytho, singing the paean and dancing, and assures them that they will always have an abundance of offerings to live off. He ends with a solemn warning that if they misbehave they will be subjected to others as their governors in future (513–44). The poet closes with a salute to Apollo and a formula of transition to another song (545–6).

Traditionally this hymn has been divided by scholars into two sections, the first describing Apollo's birth and the second being concerned with his oracle, and these have been labelled 'Delian' and 'Pythian'. Since David Ruhnken in 1782, a popular view has been that these were originally separate hymns, which were joined together at some date to form a new whole. It is certainly the case that the passage in which the poet salutes the Delian choir and speaks of himself bears some resemblance to an *envoi*. But it is also possible to see the hymn as falling into three main sections, each one being to some extent articulated by a geographical catalogue. Together these three catalogues make up the Greek world of the Aegean and northern and southern mainland Greece, which represents the range of Apollo's power (as described in 20–4, 140–5, and especially 248–52 and 288–92). It is also clear that there are many motifs which recur at different points, and these recurrent themes help to bind the different sections to one another. This is best illustrated by the following table:

First movement: Birth of Apollo (1–178)

1–18	Proem: Apollo's entry to Zeus's palace (*bow*) Leto's joy, and salute to her as mother of Apollo and Artemis (12–18)	cf. 182–206 cf. 125–6, 204–7
19–29	Choice of theme: birth of Apollo (19 = 207) Priamel: universal worship of the god (20–9)	cf. 207–15 cf. 140–5, 248–52, 288–92

30–50	Leto's journey round the Aegean – catalogue of islands and landmarks Reluctance to accept god (47–50)	cf. 216–93, 388–544 cf. 61–82, 255–76
51–88	Dialogue of Leto and Delos Poverty of site, wealth of sanctuary	 cf. 524–39
89–126	Birth of god. Epiphany Hera's jealousy (92–114) *Ololūgē* (119) Themis (124–5) Leto's joy (125–6)	cf. 399–417, 440–50, 486–510 cf. 305–55 cf. 445–6 cf. 253, 293, 541 cf. 12–18, 204–5
127–39	Growth of god, and response of Delos *Lyre, bow, oracle* (131–2)	 cf. 182–544
140–5	Priamel: range of god's power	cf. 20–9, 248–52, 288–92
146–78	Delian festival General description (146–55) Delian choir, and the poet (156–78)	cf. 182–206, 513–23

Second movement: Founding of the Delphic Oracle (179–387)

179–81	Transitional invocation (Delos, 181)	cf. 140–6
182–5	Journey to Pytho. Music.	cf. 513–23
186–206	Second scene on Olympus. Music and dance. Muses' song: gods and men Joy of Leto and Zeus	cf. 1–18, 146–78, 513–23 cf. 158–64, 532–4 cf. 12–18, 125–6
207–15	Choice of theme: search for oracle-site (207 = 19) Priamel: Apollo's love affairs (208–13)	cf. 19–29
216–93	Apollo's journey through northern Greece Ideal site for cult (214–15, 247–53, 257–74, 287–93) Telphousa (244–76) Reluctance to accept god (255–76) Universal worship of god (248–52, 288–92)	cf. 30–46, 388–544 cf. 51–60, 80–8 cf. 375–87 cf. 47–88 cf. 20–9, 140–5

294–9	Building of temple	
300–4	Apollo kills serpent of Pytho	cf. 305–55 (Python, Typhaon)
305–55	Hera's enmity: Typhaon	cf. 92–114
356–74	Apollo kills serpent: *aition* of Apollo Pythios	
375–87	Telphousa Cult of Apollo Telphousios (379–87)	cf. 244–76

Third movement: Apollo chooses his first ministers at Delphi (388–544)

388–450	Journey round Peloponnese to Crisa Epiphanies: dolphin (399–417, 486–510) star (440–7) young man (448–50)	cf. 30–46, 216–93 445–6 ~ 119 (ritual cry) cf. 134
451–501	Dialogue with Cretans Self-revelation and instructions for cult (474–501)	
502–12	Cult of Apollo Delphinios at harbour of Crisa	
513–23	Procession to Pytho Paean (517–19)	cf. 146–78, 182–206 cf. 300–74 (Python)
524–44	Final dialogue Poverty of site, wealth of sanctuary Warning to god's ministers against *hybris* (540–4) Cf. also *H. Aph.* 286–90 (*Ap.* 544 ~ *Aph.* 289), *H. Dem.* 473–82	 cf. 51–88 cf. 1–88?
545–6	Closing formulae: salute to Apollo	

The opening sections of the first and second movements are closely related. Apollo's entry to Olympus as archer and warrior-god at the beginning (1–18) is complemented by his arrival there as god of music (182–206), and the choice of a subject of song is introduced in the same way, with the initial question (19 = 207) and the priamel-type review of a range of possibilities (20–4, 208–13), followed by the announcement of the subject (25–9, 214–15). But some themes recur in all three movements: for example (apart from the geographical catalogues) the brilliant description of the Delian festival and the choir of Delian girls (146–78) is paralleled not only at 182–206 by Apollo's procession as god of music to Pytho and the following scene on Olympus, but again at 513–23, where he leads his priests from Crisa to Pytho, singing the paean and dancing. Moreover, this paean can also be linked to Apollo's victory over the serpent of Pytho (300–74), since this was traditionally celebrated by a hymn or paean of victory, in which the battle and the serpent's death were described (see 357–62n.). The building of Apollo's temple at Pytho and his killing of the serpent can be seen as the central episodes of the hymn as a whole, preceded by the birth-narrative, and followed by the introduction of his priests to Pytho.

(b) Authorship and date

Thucydides (3.104) quotes lines 146–50 and 165–72 of the hymn as the work of Homer, and calls it a προοίμιον ('prelude'): cf. 146–72, 165–76nn. At the same period Aristophanes may possibly allude to it as Homeric, since at *Birds* 575 the comparison of Iris to a dove is ascribed to Homer (cf. *H. Ap.* 114, with comment). Later authors usually ascribe the hymn to Homer (see AHS pp. lxvii–lxxviii). Athenaeus (22B), however, in the second century AD, quotes it as by 'Homer or one of the Homeridae'. A scholiast on Pindar, *Nemean* 2.1 gives a more detailed account, saying that a Chian rhapsode named Cynaethus was said to have composed the hymn, and that according to Hippostratus (a Sicilian historian, *FGrH* 568 F 5) he was the first to sing the poems of Homer at Syracuse, in the 69th Olympiad (504–501 BC). They also say that Cynaethus and his associates composed many poems and 'added these to the poetry of Homer'. Another tradition, recorded in the *Contest of Homer and Hesiod* (315–21 Allen), describes the poet Homer reciting the *Hymn to Apollo* during the festival on Delos, standing on the altar of horns, and adds that the Delians then inscribed it on a tablet (λεύκωμα), and dedicated this in the temple of Artemis. It may be significant that it is Artemis' temple, and not Apollo's, which was selected for the inscription (cf. Janko (1982) 257). In the Archaic period at least it seems likely that this was the most prominent temple building in the sanctuary. A good deal of the material in the *Contest* derives from traditions about Homer's life which were probably current already in the fifth century BC (cf. Richardson (1981)). Consequently, it is not unreasonable to suggest that the inscription of the hymn might date from a relatively early period.

Scholars have varied considerably in their dating of the hymn as we have it, between the late eighth century BC (AHS 184–6) and the late sixth (Burkert (1979a), Janko (1982) 112–15, West (2003) 9–12). Both Burkert and Janko suggested that the final version was composed in 523 or 522 BC for a festival on Delos instituted by the tyrant Polycrates for Apollo, worshipped as both Delios and Pythios (cf. also Aloni (1989)). From his study of linguistic criteria and other evidence

Janko argued that the first part (1–181) belonged to the early seventh century BC, and the remainder to *c.* 585 BC, both being combined by Cynaethus in the late sixth century (see Janko (1982) 112–15, 200, 228–31). Janko's linguistic arguments have, however, been questioned (2(c) below).

Various pieces of evidence may help to narrow the range of possibilities for dating. The construction of Apollo's temple at Pytho forms the central episode of the poem (285–99). Its 'broad and very long foundations' and 'stone threshold' are described, and the 'well-wrought [*or* well-set] stones' of which either the threshold or the temple itself was composed are also mentioned. The first temple of Apollo at Delphi of which stone foundations can be identified has been dated by archaeologists (on admittedly limited evidence) to the second half of the seventh century BC. This was burnt in 548/7 BC (cf. 294–9, 296nn.). If this was the first large-scale temple with walls of stone (as opposed to less durable materials) its novelty could have helped to give an impetus to the hymn, projecting back its construction into the mythical past, and this would suggest a date after *c.* 650 BC.

Thucydides, when discussing the hymn as evidence for the festival on Delos, says that 'in the past' (πάλαι, 3.104.3 and 6) there must have been 'a great gathering and festival on Delos', as Homer shows, whereas 'later the islanders and the Athenians continued to send choruses with offerings, but most events including the contests were discontinued owing to some adverse circumstances, as one would suppose' (ὡς εἰκός, 3.104.6). He clearly views both the early festival and its decline as belonging to a past period for which he does not have other evidence apart from the hymn, which he ascribes to Homer (see also 146–72n.). Although this does not help us to pin down the date too closely for the description in the hymn, it surely indicates that (for example) the later sixth century BC is most unlikely, since Thucydides knows both about Pisistratus' purification of Delos and also Polycrates' dedication of the island of Rheneia to Delian Apollo (3.104.1–2; cf. Janko (1982) 112).

It is also striking that the hymn speaks of Apollo choosing men as his ministers, 'who perform sacrifices for the Lord and announce the decrees of Phoebus Apollo' (393–5, significantly with the present tenses ῥέζουσι and ἀγγέλλουσι, suggesting reference to the poet's own time: cf. 394n.). There is no mention anywhere of the Pythia, the prophetess whose inspired utterances were later given to inquirers either directly or through the medium of male interpreters, and who is first mentioned in Theognis (807): cf. 389n. Once again this seems to make a later sixth-century date unlikely (cf. Chappell (2006)).

Apollo's final warning to the priests, that if they do not avoid misdemeanours and ὕβρις they will be subjected to the government of others (540–3), has often been taken as a reference (*post eventum*) to the so-called First Sacred War, assigned by Greek tradition to the early sixth century BC (*c.* 594–584), which was supposed to have arisen from the misconduct of the people of Crisa, who taxed or plundered pilgrims to Delphi, and which led to the destruction of Crisa and control of the sanctuary in future by the Amphictionic League of northern Greek states.

Tradition associated the war closely with the institution of the Pythian Games in their classical form. The existence of the war has been questioned, but some aspects of the tradition do seem reliable. If Apollo's warning does indeed refer to those events, then the poem as we have it must be dated to the 580s at the earliest. It is possible that these verses (540–3) are a later addition to the hymn, but the traditional nature of the train of thought in Apollo's speech as a whole (cf. 531–44n.) suggests that they are original. (See further 540–3n.)

Apollo's journey from Olympus to Crisa via Thessaly, Euboea, and Boeotia corresponds quite closely (although not exactly) with the list of northern states of the Amphictionic League (before it was enlarged with the addition of Athens and some Peloponnesian ones), and it has been argued that it reflects the situation after the First Sacred War: cf. 216–86n. Moreover, the language of both 274 and 298 may allude to the League of ἀμφικτίονες (neighbouring or surrounding peoples): cf. 274, 299 + 298nn. An association of communities of this kind may have existed before the War, but these references would have more significance after this date.

It is also possible that the hymn's account of the killing of the serpent of Pytho is linked to the institution of the Pythian Games in their classical form. A major innovation was said to be the aulos-playing contest, first won by Sacadas in 586 BC, in which the god's battle with the dragon was vividly depicted in musical form (the Πυθικὸς νόμος). The hymn's description of Apollo's killing of the serpent and his triumph over her (357–69) has some similarities with what we are told about this composition, although it should be admitted that a triumphal hymn to Apollo celebrating his victory was traditionally seen as an older element in the festival (cf. 300–74, 357–62nn.).

Thus a case can be made on various grounds for linking the hymn as we have it to events early in the sixth century BC. A date later in this century seems less probable. It remains a possibility that the hymn grew out of an earlier composition in praise of Apollo's birth and his Delian festival, which was developed into a longer work charting his institution of the Delphic oracle and priesthood, linked closely to the earlier song by a series of repeated themes. But the poem is designed to be taken as a unified composition, and this is how we ought to read it. Cf. the excellent remarks on this subject by Miller (1986), especially in his Preface and Appendix 1, and Clay (2006) 18–19, who concludes that 'as a whole, the hymn presents a unified and comprehensible progression with a complex but nevertheless linear movement that ends when the new god has established himself and received his full definition within the Olympian order'.

(c) Language and style

The language of the hymn is discussed by Hoekstra (1969) 21–38, and Janko (1982), especially 99–132. Both consider verses 1–181 separately from 182–546. Both base their analyses on assumptions about the way in which the traditional diction of early hexameter poetry was subject to various forms of modification and development over the course of time. Hoekstra found very little in the so-called 'Delian' part to suggest what he considered to be post-Homeric modification of formular diction, except in 140–81, the section leading to and describing the Delian festival, where as he says (25) 'in the personal part of the hymn the poet is seen to compose much more freely than in the story'. Janko identified more evidence of modification throughout, and his own statistical tests suggested to him some advance in the diction by comparison with the *Iliad* and *Odyssey*. In 181–546 Hoekstra concluded that there were a few more examples of post-Homeric (or as he called it 'subepic') composition, but that this 'can hardly be adduced in support of the separatist view' (34). Janko added some more cases of what he saw as post-Homeric developments, but found these combined with examples of 'false archaisms', which he thought were the result of a poet deliberately introducing earlier forms in order to give his composition a more archaic style (cf. 76–8, etc.).

Janko's statistical methods have been criticised (see for example Hoekstra (1986) 162–3, West (1995) 204–5). Other factors apart from chronology may give rise to formular variation, such as regional differences, subject matter, or personal style. Moreover, the concept of 'false archaism' is particularly problematic, since it requires one to distinguish supposedly false from genuine archaic forms.

Another simple test of development of language within the early hexameter tradition is to consider the incidence of words (i.e. lexical items) not found elsewhere in this corpus of poetry (see also Zumbach (1955)). In verses 1–181 there are only 9 or possibly 10 examples, i.e. *c.* 1 in 20 or 18. In verses 182–546 there are *c.* 26, or *c.* 1 in 14. Given the limited size of each section the difference may well not be very significant. It is interesting to compare the frequency in the other three long hymns: in *Aphrodite c.* 1 in 27 (11 in 293 verses), in *Demeter* 1 in 8 (59 in 495 verses: cf. Richardson, *H. Dem.* pp. 43–5), and in *Hermes* 1 in 4 (139 in 580 verses: cf. Vergados (2007a) 32–3 and 35–7). In these terms, then, the whole of the *Apollo* hymn is less traditional than *Aphrodite*, but more so than the other two hymns.

Direct dependence of the hymn on any other early hexameter poem is difficult to detect, with one significant exception. The links with the *Odyssey* in the later parts of the poem could be to a certain extent due to use of common traditional material, but in some cases the correspondence is particularly close and suggests a direct link. This may be the case with Hera's speech at 311–30 (see note on this passage), and again still more probably with the journey of the ship and subsequent scenes, from 409 onwards (see especially 410–21, 412–13, 421–9, 434–5, 438, 452–61, 458–9, 464–6, 466–7, 469–73, 471, 499, 529, 534nn., and also Janko (1982) 129–31). It is notable that in three cases we have possible echoes of the final scenes in the *Odyssey* (see 426, 464–7, 499nn.), a part of this poem which (whatever the truth may be) has since antiquity been suspected as a post-Homeric addition.

On the whole there is not a great deal of linguistic evidence to support the kind of separatist view of the hymn advocated by Janko and others, and equally no very clear pointers in the language towards a date in (say) the sixth rather than the seventh century BC. West (1975) actually thought that the greater neglect of digamma in 1–181 supported his view that this part was a later composition than the rest. This theory has not won support, although it is still advocated by West (2003) 10–12. But it illustrates the kind of difficulties one faces in using such criteria.

Judgements about style and poetic quality are likely to be still more subjective. The poem opens with a scene of powerful dramatic intensity, and the narrative of Apollo's birth is lively and colourful, culminating in the brilliant portrayal of the Delian festival. The proem to the second movement (179–206) is a good match for this last scene, whereas the ensuing description of Apollo's journey to Crisa is more leisurely, taking in various subsidiary episodes, such as those of Onchestus and Telphousa, along the way. All of this seems to be intended as an intensifying build-up to the foundation of the temple at Pytho and killing of the serpent (itself expanded greatly by the inserted Typhaon episode).

The last movement (388–544) is again lively and entertaining like the first, with Apollo's various epiphanies and the reactions of the Cretans effectively portrayed, and it culminates in a brilliant scene of music and dancing as they process up to Pytho, which echoes the earlier scenes of this kind. The final warning to Apollo's ministers forms a powerful closure, whose abruptness mirrors that of the opening scene of his entry to Olympus as a warrior-god.

In terms of its narrative technique this hymn stands out from the others in the corpus in one very significant respect (see Nünlist (2004), especially 40–2). References to the narrator's person ('I'), and to the addressee's ('you'), occur several times in the course of the actual narrative (up to line 282), and in the case of Apollo himself we sometimes find a mixed style, alternating between second- and third-person reference to him (e.g. at 129–30). This gives the poem a more personal character, which is further emphasised by the passage in which the poet addresses the Delian choir and speaks of himself, which is unique in these hymns.

The hymn thus gives us a vivid impression of Apollo as an awe-inspiring and potentially dangerous, but also life-enhancing, deity, the god of archery, music, and prophecy (cf. 131–2).

3 HYMN TO HERMES

(a) Structure

The prologue (1–19) tells of Hermes' birth to Zeus and Maia, and alludes to the two main exploits which will be the subject of the narrative, his invention of the lyre and theft of the cattle of his elder brother Apollo. After his secret birth he leaves his cradle, meets a tortoise, and makes its shell into the first lyre, with which he sings of his own birth (20–61). He then goes at sunset to Pieria, home of Apollo's cattle, and steals fifty of them, which he takes to the river Alpheios in north-western Peloponnese, disguising his tracks by using specially invented shoes and driving them backwards. On his way he is seen by an old farmer at Onchestos, whom he orders not to give him away (62–104). He slaughters and roasts two of the cattle, and returns to his cradle on Mt Cyllene, where his mother scolds him, and he threatens even worse exploits of burglary (105–83).

At dawn Apollo goes to Onchestos in search of the cattle, and meets the old man, who tells him that he saw a boy driving cattle backwards. With the aid of a bird-omen he realises that the thief is Hermes, and goes to Cyllene and accuses him. Hermes denies all knowledge of the cattle, and demands that Apollo should put his case for trial before Zeus (184–312).

They come to Olympus and Apollo again accuses Hermes, who skilfully defends himself. Zeus orders them to be reconciled and Hermes to reveal the cattle to Apollo (313–96). They go to the Alpheios and find the cattle, and Hermes then amazes Apollo by playing his lyre, and singing a theogony. Apollo is enchanted by this new form of music, Hermes offers him the lyre, and in exchange Apollo gives him a share in his own role as god of flocks and herds. Thus reconciled the two brothers return to Olympus (397–512).

The main narrative is now concluded, but in a final episode Hermes swears never to steal from Apollo again, and Apollo gives him a special golden wand, and offers him also ownership of three prophetic sisters who live on Mt Parnassus. After a further list of some of Hermes' attributes the hymn closes with the usual formulae of farewell (513–80).

The general structure of the narrative is clear enough, and a series of parallel motifs helps to bind it together. The central exploit, Hermes' cattle-theft, is framed by the two episodes of the invention of the lyre and the gift of it to Apollo. Both include songs by Hermes, about his own birth and the origin of the gods in general (54–61, 424–33), both of which are compared to the songs of young men at feasts (55–6, 453–4). Hermes' journey with the cattle is counterbalanced by Apollo's search, both including the meetings at Onchestos. The scenes with the cattle at the Alpheios are also balanced. Above all, the two scenes in which Hermes defends himself against Apollo's accusations are complementary, the 'trial scene' being a more formalised version of the one at Cyllene.

In view of this analysis, the final episode concerning the gift of a mantic art to Hermes looks at first sight like an appendix, and it has often been considered to be a later addition. This is certainly possible, but there are close links in the later part of the hymn between the themes of music and prophecy (see 464–89, 482–8, 541–9nn.) which help to bind this episode more closely with what precedes it. It is also theoretically possible that the corruption in line 473 conceals a request by Hermes for a share in Apollo's prophetic skills, answered by him at 533–66 (see 473, 533nn.). Moreover, the final episode restores to Apollo his dignity as the oracular god who interprets the will of Zeus, after his previous deflation by his infant brother, and thereby gives Hermes added status by association.

(b) The hymn as comedy

Although the hymn uses many of the narrative techniques of early hexameter poetry, and the language is based in the epic artificial diction (*Kunstsprache*), it stands out from the other major Homeric hymns in many respects. It has been characterised as 'the most untraditional in its language, with many late words and expressions, and many used in slapdash and inaccurate ways' (West (2003) 12). West adds that 'it is the most incompetent in construction, with many narrative inconsistencies and redundancies, and no command of the even tempo appropriate to epic storytelling'. But as some scholars have realised (Radermacher 216–17, Janko (1982) 148–9), a clue to the distinctive quality of the poem lies in its essentially comic character. If we view it as a forerunner of later comic genres, we can understand why it uses a different style and language, has a looser sequence of narrative, and portrays its leading characters, Hermes and Apollo, as more like ordinary human beings than is normally the case with the description of gods in early epic.

Hermes' exploits are in one sense supernatural, but many of the details, such as the construction of the lyre, the way he disguises his tracks, and so on, are told in a more naturalistic way. There is no indication when Hermes or Apollo meet the old farmer (the only mortal character) that they attempt to disguise their divinity, and yet the old man seems quite unaware of this. Apollo himself, for all his supposed omniscience (cf. 467, 474, 489), is bewildered by Hermes' tricks, asks information of the old man, and needs the help of a bird-omen to track him down. He is constantly made to look ridiculous by his baby brother. There are several allusions to his own greed for wealth, a subject on which he is clearly sensitive (176–81, 330 and 335, 494–5, 546–9). Particularly significant for the hymn's comic register is the episode where Apollo picks up Hermes and his brother 'emitted an omen, an insolent servant of the belly, an unruly messenger' (295–6). This riddling, mock-epic periphrasis for a fart anticipates later occasions in Attic comedy where this is treated as an omen, or a parody of Zeus's thunder (see 293–303, 295–6nn.).

Above all, Apollo appears to know nothing of the use of stringed instruments, before he is introduced to the lyre by Hermes (especially 450–5 and 452n.). This is in marked contrast with the *Hymn to Apollo*, where immediately after his birth he claims the *kitharis* as his attribute (131), and is portrayed as leader of both gods and men in music (182–206, 513–19). The tortoise-shell lyre was a smaller and lighter instrument than the *kitharis* or *phorminx* (used traditionally to accompany epic song), but in the *Hymn to Hermes* it is equated with these instruments (see 47–51n.). The songs of Hermes himself could be classed as hymns, but their style is that of the mocking songs of young men at symposia (55–6, 453–4), which suggests something less elevated. And yet this new music strikes Apollo as wonderfully original and superior to anything he has experienced (434–55). Hermes presents the lyre to Apollo as a sympotic ἑταίρη (475), whose effect is constantly described in the language of erotic love and desire (cf. 31, 421–3, 426, 434, 448–9, and especially 478–88; and see 31, 478–88, 485, 486nn.).

The contrast between the two gods is effectively portrayed in the way they are characterised through speech and action. Hermes operates by night, and is a god of deception and theft, Apollo acts by daylight and is concerned with justice and truth. Apollo's speeches are straightforward and earnest (especially in the trial scene: 334–64n.), Hermes is the master of persuasive rhetoric and special pleading (see 162, 260–77, 366–88, 463nn.). Hermes exploits to the full his status as newborn infant, in contrast to his brother who is presumably already envisaged as adult and mature.

(c) Relationship with the Hymn to Apollo

In view of the way in which Hermes gets the better of Apollo and makes fun of him, it is natural to ask whether the poet has the *Hymn to Apollo* in mind. In the prologue to the *Hymn to Hermes* the rapidity of his prowess is vividly described (17–19):

> Born in the early morning, at midday he was playing the lyre,
> In the evening he stole the cattle of far-shooting Apollo,
> On the fourth day of the month, the day the lady Maia bore him.

Apollo's miraculous growth is also emphasised in the *Hymn to Apollo*, but in a more general way (123–34). It is only after being fed on divine food that he begins his career. Apollo then claims that he will be god of the *kitharis*, the bow, and prophecy of Zeus's will (131–2). As we have seen, the first of these claims is called into question by Hermes' invention of the lyre, and Apollo also says that he is afraid lest Hermes steal his bow, in addition to taking back his lyre (514–15, where 515 may echo *H. Ap.* 131). Hermes is eager for a share in his prophetic art as well, but here Apollo asserts his supremacy, whilst allowing him a minor role in divination.

The surprising choice of Onchestos in Boeotia as the place where Hermes meets the farmer may be due to its being singled out for special attention in the *Hymn to Apollo* (230–8): see 88n. It is not obviously on Hermes' route towards the river Alpheios, whereas in Apollo's case it is part of a detailed itinerary through Boeotia to Delphi. A clue in support of this may be that it is called λεχεποίη (88), a rare word in Homer but one used of Teumessos at *H. Ap.* 224, just before the passage about Onchestos.

If the poet of *Hermes* had the *Apollo* hymn in mind, one might have expected more direct linguistic echoes of this kind (cf. for example *H. Herm.* 17n.). But it remains an attractive possibility that the hymn was intended to form a light-hearted counterpart to the grander and more serious *Hymn to Apollo*. On the relationship between the two hymns see also Radermacher 110–11, 229, Abramowicz (1937) 71–85, Dornseiff (1938) 81–4, Penglase (1994) 184, Vergados (2007a) 54–6, Richardson (2007) 83–91.

(d) Legal aspects

Hermes' cattle-theft leads to a kind of lawsuit between him and his brother, culminating in a mock-trial on Olympus. As comedy this resembles to some extent the situation in Demodocus' Song of Ares and Aphrodite (*Od.* 8.266–366), where Ares' adultery raises questions of compensation, which become a matter for debate among the gods (352, 344–58). In *Hermes* there are many echoes of what seems to be legal terminology, to judge by parallels in later literature: see 246–51, 254, 264, 312, 313, 315–16, 372, 373, 524, 526–8, 528–32nn. On his arrival at Hermes' cave on Cyllene Apollo conducts a search of the premises, and demands information from him (246–59). Hermes' initial defence speech expresses indignation at Apollo's conduct, and uses an argument from probability typical of Greek rhetoric from the fifth century BC onwards. He offers to swear an oath, without actually doing so formally (see 260–77n.). The trial scene itself has a simple formal structure (322–96n.). Apollo's accusation is largely composed of *narratio*, a straightforward account of what happened, in the manner of a plaintiff full of righteous indignation, and with considerable repetition. He adduces the physical evidence of the footprints and the testimony of the old farmer as an eyewitness, and describes his adversary in typically derogatory terms (see 334–64, 338–9, 342–55, 346, 358–60nn.). Hermes' response uses similar techniques to those in his first speech, and in addition stresses the violence of Apollo's conduct and his lack of witnesses at the trial, and appeals to Zeus as his father for support (366–88n.).

The parallels with Greek rhetorical theory and practice are one reason why some scholars have wished to date the hymn to the fifth century BC (see especially Görgemanns (1976)). But we have no way of knowing how early such techniques as the argument from probability might have been used, before being formally analysed by fifth-century rhetoricians. On the other hand, the developed nature of the legal language and structure by comparison with the Homeric epics does seem to support a post-Homeric date.

(e) Music and prophecy

As we have seen, the theme of music frames Hermes' theft, and it is the means by which the reconciliation is achieved. In this way the tortoise he meets at the outset is indeed a σύμβολον μέγ' ὀνήσιμον (30), a 'very useful token', since it will be used to seal the compact between the brothers (see 30, 526–8nn.). Hermes gives back the cattle to Apollo and adds the lyre in compensation. In return, however, Apollo gives him a share in his own pastoral role. Lyre and cattle (the latter being themselves a standard of value in early epic) are the elements in this process of exchange, as in the story of Archilochus' meeting with the Muses, where they give him a lyre in exchange for his cow. Hermes thus becomes the god of commerce, as well as of theft (see 397–512, 437, 576–7nn.).

Apollo claims to be already himself 'a companion of the Olympian Muses, who are concerned with dances and the glorious path of song, and lively music and the desirable sound of pipes', but Hermes' music is something new to him (443–55). This is the music of the λύρη, played at symposia as an accompaniment to the mocking songs of young men (55–6), and associated especially with erotic themes. It is the music of personal lyric song, as it came to prominence in the Archaic period in the poetry of Archilochus (who is probably the first extant writer to mention the λύρη), Sappho and Alcaeus, Ibycus and Anacreon. It involves not only inspiration or innate ability, but also skill and practice (τρίβος, used first here: see 447–8n.). Played with proper expertise the lyre will respond easily and with charm, but an ignorant player will only produce discordant nonsense (482–8). Here again, as in the case of law and rhetoric, we seem to have a reflection of a period when new techniques and musical forms are developing, with an emphasis on learning and practice, and the poet appears to be suggesting that these new forms are in some ways superior to the more traditional genres of music and poetry.

The contrast between the right and wrong uses of the lyre is a motif which recurs in the case of prophecy, in the final section (or epilogue). Apollo declares that he will help some of his consultants who come auspiciously, whereas others will be deceived (541–9), and likewise the three prophetic sisters of Parnassus will sometimes tell the truth and sometimes mislead men (558–63). They are similar to Hesiod's Muses, who know how to utter both truth and falsehood (see also 556–7n.). Hermes himself, in the closing lines of the hymn, is said to have the same gift of helping some but deceiving many mortals (577–8). In this way the poem links together the arts of Apollo and Hermes.

(f) Aetiology

The hymn describes the origin of Hermes himself, and how he acquired his various attributes and powers, as a god of animals, music and prophecy, rhetoric and persuasion, theft and commerce, and as a messenger between heaven, earth, and the underworld. As with many of the other Homeric hymns, it includes his entry to Olympus and reception as a full member of Olympian society. In Hermes' case this occurs in an unusual way, but one which typifies his character, since after the secrecy of his birth his first appearance in heaven is as an infant accused by Apollo of theft. Later, however, the two brothers return to heaven to the sound of the lyre, in an atmosphere of harmony and joy (504–12).

Unlike the hymns to Apollo and Demeter, neither this one nor the longer hymn to Aphrodite includes the institution of a cult of the god with temple and sanctuary, although Anchises does promise a cult on first meeting Aphrodite (*H. Aph.* 100–2). In the case of Hermes, the god kills and roasts two of Apollo's cattle, and divides the meat into twelve portions. It seems probable that this should be associated with the important cult of the 'Twelve Gods' at Olympia, attested already by Pindar, for which this could be the *aition*. The first evidence of such a cult elsewhere is at Athens in the late sixth century BC: see 128–9n. Moreover, he leaves the two hides on a rock, where they are said to be still visible, a clearly aetiological reference (124–6n.), and he also deposits the meat and fat inside a cave, 'as a sign of his recent theft', which again seems to indicate that something may have been on display in later times (see 134–7n.).

Hermes is also an inventor: he creates the lyre, devises special shoes to hide his tracks, invents the art of kindling with fire-sticks (108–11), and also makes the panpipes (511–12). Thus Hermes is distinguished for his technical ingenuity. In this respect the hymn resembles satyric drama, in which such inventions are a common feature (see Seaford (1984) 36–7).

(g) Language and style

As already mentioned above (2(c)), this hymn has a much higher incidence of words not found elsewhere in early hexameter poetry than the other three major hymns, i.e. about 1 in every 4 verses (see Vergados (2007a) 32–7 for detailed lists). The poet uses *c.* 36 words found only here in surviving literature (not counting mentions by lexicographers). About 16 words recur elsewhere before 500 BC in other verse forms, and *c.* 51 are first repeated in fifth-century literature. The remainder of those not in early hexameter verse elsewhere (*c.* 36) occur first after 400 BC. Of these, *c.* 12 are in later hexameter poetry. (Figures are approximate because of textual uncertainties.) The frequency of unique words is high (1 in 16 verses) compared to the *Iliad* and *Odyssey*, where it is 1 in 52 and 1 in 63 respectively. (The Homeric data are taken from Kumpf (1984) 206, who includes proper names, excluded in the count for *H. Herm.*) In *H. Dem.* we only find 12, i.e. 1 in 41 (Richardson, *H. Dem.* pp. 43–5). On the other hand, it is difficult to use such linguistic criteria for absolute dating purposes, except in broad terms. Unique vocabulary may be partly due to subject matter. It may also indicate a poet who is adopting a more liberal attitude towards his tradition in coining new forms on the analogy of existing ones. When surveying the list of words not found elsewhere before 500 BC, we can exclude from significance several compounds (such as καταβλάπτω, ἀνακλέπτω, etc.) of simple words which occurred earlier. Others are natural developments or variants of earlier forms: cf. for example ὁδοιπορίη, Homeric ὁδοιπόρος; ἀμαρυγή, Hesiodic ἀμάρυγμα; σπάργανον, Hesiodic σπαργανίζω, etc. Some recur in later hexameter poetry and could be drawn from the early epic tradition, e.g. ὑψιμέλαθρος, βαθύσκιος, ἀγγελιώτης, ὑπωλένιος. Another class is of words later used in everyday speech or prose literature: e.g. ἀνόητος, μασχάλη, ἀπρεπέως, διαρρήδην, ἄγνος. Such words may reflect the comic or down-to-earth tone and the subject matter (e.g. διαρρήδην in a legal context). At the same time even when the subject matter is coarse the poet still preserves a certain level of 'epic decorum' in the way he describes it, as befits the style of a hymn: cf. especially the riddling language of 294–6 (discussed by Bain (2007) 51–2).

One should also remember that in terms of the total number of words in the poem the untraditional vocabulary only represents about 4 per cent at most. (If we assume *c.* 6 words per verse on average, 1 in 4 verses = 1 in 24 words.) Consequently, the overall linguistic effect is not so different from that of the other hymns, or indeed of early hexameter poetry in general. Even when what is being portrayed is ludicrous the style is still elevated, and it is the combination of the comic and the dignified which gives this hymn its particular piquancy and charm.

(h) Dating, and occasion of first performance

Various considerations mentioned above suggest, although they do not prove, a sixth-century date: the possible influence of the *Hymn to Apollo*, the allusion to the cult of the Twelve Gods at Olympia, the high estimation of a form of music which suggests comparison with personal lyric poetry, and the developed forms of legal procedure and rhetorical technique. The untraditional language would also fit a date in this period. There does not seem to be any compelling reason to date the hymn later than *c.* 500 BC, as some scholars have done (see 3(d) above, and for other examples see Janko (1982) 142). The *Hymn to Pan* (19) is almost certainly influenced by it (see Janko (1982) 185, Fröhder (1994) 329). This hymn, the style of which is very unusual, has been dated to the fifth century, chiefly on the grounds that Pan's cult was not widespread in Greece before *c.* 500 BC (cf. AHS 402–3, Janko (1982) 185, West (2003) 18), but arguments for a later date (Andrisano (1978–9)) are less convincing. It is significant that the syrinx, invented by Hermes in the *Hymn to Hermes* (511–12), appears as an attribute of Hermes from *c.* 580/570 BC onwards in art, but from *c.* 500 onwards it is associated with Pan, and no longer with Hermes (see 511–12n.). It seems reasonable to link its portrayal as Hermes' instrument with the date of the *Hymn to Hermes.*

A further point is that in vase-painting the themes of the baby Hermes as cattle-thief, or simply Hermes together with cattle, are noticeably popular between the mid sixth century and early fifth. Two vases, of *c.* 530 and 480 BC, show him in his cradle, with the cattle, and also Apollo and Maia (see 21, 227–92nn.). Others (*LIMC* s.v. Hermes nos. 245–8), all between *c.* 565 and 490 BC, show him as an adult god, with cattle. The popularity of these themes would again fit well with a sixth-century date for the hymn.

Several scholars have recently suggested that the hymn may have been composed for first performance at Olympia. This is an attractive possibility, in view of the location of Hermes' sacrifice by the Alpheios and its probable connection with the cult of the Twelve Gods at Olympia. See Burkert (1984), Johnston (2002) especially 128–30, West (2003) 14, Thomas (forthcoming).

(i) Relationship with other versions

Another version of the story of Hermes' cattle-theft describes how the god meets a man called Battos in Arcadia, whom he later punishes for betraying the identity of the thief by turning him into a rock (see 87–93n.). This first appears in Ovid's *Metamorphoses*, but the version in Antoninus Liberalis is accompanied by a *scholion* giving a list of sources which includes Hesiod's *Great Ehoiai* (fr. 256 M–W). It is unclear, however, whether the whole story of Battos as told in Antoninus goes back to the Hesiodic poem. The main source is probably Nicander's *Heteroeoumena*. In the hymn the role of the old man at Onchestos, who acts as a witness of Hermes' theft, has seemed to some scholars rather perfunctory, and this has been seen as evidence that the Battos story is earlier and is being adapted by the poet of the hymn. It could, however, equally well be a later elaboration.

Alcaeus' hymn to Hermes, of which we have the first stanza (fr. 308(b) L–P = 308 V), told of Hermes' birth to Zeus and Maia, his theft of Apollo's cattle, and how, when threatened by Apollo, he stole his quiver also (cf. frr. 308(c) and (d), *SLG* 264.11–19, and Schol. AB *Il.* 15.256). The theft of the quiver is mentioned by Apollo as something he fears may occur, at *H. Herm.* 514–15 (see note). If the Homeric hymn is later than Alcaeus' poem, then both may be influenced by an earlier version of the story (cf. West (2002) 217, Liberman (1999) 133). But the relationship of the two versions remains uncertain.

The most important reworking of the whole story is Sophocles' satyr-play *Ichneutai* ('Searchers'), of which we have extensive papyrus fragments (*TrGF* 4.274–308). Doubts have been raised as to whether Sophocles is influenced by the hymn (Steffen (1960) 9), but this seems very probable, and the differences between the two versions are surely due to Sophocles' adaptation of the story for a satyric drama: see Koettgen (1914), Radermacher 183–4, 216, and Lloyd-Jones (2003) 143.

In the play, Hermes has already stolen Apollo's cattle and hidden them in a cave underground in Mt Cyllene, and he has also invented the lyre. Apollo proclaims a reward for anyone who has seen the cattle. He has come to Cyllene (via Thessaly and Boeotia) in search of them. Silenus offers to help with his sons the Satyrs, in return for gold and release from slavery, which Apollo promises. The Chorus of Satyrs discover strange backward-turned prints outside the cave, and from inside there comes a mysterious sound which frightens them. Silenus reproaches them for cowardice, but when he hears the noise he too is terrified. Eventually they disturb the nymph Cyllene by jumping up and down. She appears and tells them that she is secretly nursing a baby son of Zeus and Maia called Hermes, and that the sound they heard is that of the lyre, made from a tortoise shell with an oxhide stretched over it. The Satyrs conclude that Hermes must have stolen the cattle, but Cyllene denies this, arguing that an infant child, and the son of such divine parents, cannot be the thief. The rest of the papyrus is very fragmentary, but Apollo reappears, and there is further mention of a reward and freedom.

There are a good many points of contact between the play and the hymn, both thematically and also verbally. Apollo's journey via Thessaly and Boeotia to Peloponnese parallels in outline that in the hymn. The Satyrs take the place of the old man of Onchestos as his informants. The description of the tracks of the cattle echoes *H. Herm.* 75–8 (see comments). Cyllene's account of Hermes' secret birth (265–71) parallels the hymn's, and the baby is nursed in a λίκνον (275–6; cf. *H. Herm.* 21). His miraculous growth is emphasised (277–82), and he has created the lyre in a single day (284–5). As in the hymn, the paradox is expressed of the dead tortoise acquiring a living voice (299–300 and 328; cf. *H. Herm.* 38, and see 25n.). The lyre's wonderful power to arouse pleasure and cure unhappiness is described (325–300; cf. *H. Herm.* 419–55).

The argument between Cyllene and the Satyrs, in which they accuse Hermes and she contends that he cannot be the thief, resembles Hermes' successive defence speeches in answer to the accusations of Apollo and Zeus (252–80, 333–88). However, Hermes' use of an oxhide to make the lyre leads the Satyrs to infer that he is the cattle-thief (345–6, 371–6), and this suggests that Sophocles made the theft precede the lyre's invention, as in some later accounts (see *H. Herm.* 20–61n.).

Other possible verbal echoes of the hymn have been detected: see Pearson (1917) 228, Vergados (2007a) 70–1. Cf. especially *Ichn.* 340 φιλήτην (perhaps also S. fr. 933 Radt) with *H. Herm.* 67 etc.; *Ichn.* 87 μηνύ[τρον (?) with *H. Herm.* 264, 364; *Ichn.* 188 στίβος, *H. Herm.* 353; *Ichn.* 98 ἔρευναν, *H. Herm.* 176; *Ichn.* 123 βοηλατήν, *H. Herm.* 14; *Ichn.* 143–4 ἐξενίσμεθα ψόφωι τὸν οὐδεὶς π[ώπο]τ' ἤκουσεν βροτῶν, *H. Herm.* 443; *Ichn.* 250 ἐγήρυσε θέσπιν αὐδάν, *H. Herm.* 426, 442.

The *Library* of Pseudo-Apollodorus (3.10.2) summarises the story told in the hymn, but with significant variations. Hermes eats some of the flesh of the two oxen which he kills (contrast *H. Herm.* 130–6). He invents the lyre *after* stealing the cattle rather than before, and uses their entrails to make its strings, whereas he uses sheep-gut in the hymn (51). He also invents the plectrum. Apollo comes to Pylos and questions its inhabitants, rather than interrogating the old man of Onchestos. In the trial on Olympus, Hermes is ordered by Zeus to restore the cattle, but denies possession of them. He is disbelieved, and then he gives them back (contrast *H. Herm.* 327–96, where Hermes' denial is followed by Zeus's order, and this is obeyed by Hermes). After Hermes has invented the syrinx (cf. *H. Herm.* 511–12), he plays it and Apollo, wishing to have it (as well as the lyre), offers him 'the golden wand (ῥάβδον) which he had acquired when tending cattle' (contrast *H. Herm.* 497–8, 528–32). Hermes then gives him the pipes, and, wishing to acquire the art of divination, is given the skill of divining by pebbles (cf. *H. Herm.* 550–66, with comments).

It is not known which source or sources the *Library* is using, where it diverges from the hymn. Vergados (2007a) 79–80 suggests as a possible source the fifth-century mythographer Pherecydes of Athens, who mentioned that Apollo gave Hermes the staff which he used when tending Apollo's cattle (*FGrH* 3 F 131), and who may have systematised earlier versions.

Other authors who give briefer versions of Hermes' birth and exploits, or allude to these, are the fifth-century BC mythographer and chronicler Hellanicus (*FGrH* 4 F 19b; cf. 67n.), the Hellenistic poets Aratus (*Phaen.* 268–9; cf. 41–2n.), Nicander (*Alex.* 559–62; cf. 25, 41–2nn.), and Eratosthenes (*Hermes*, Powell, *CA* 58–63, *SH* frr. 397–8; cf. also Pseudo-Eratosthenes' *Catasterismi*, Olivieri (1897) III (1)), and in the Roman period Lucian (*Dialogues of the Gods* 79.11 Macleod), Philostratus (*Imagines* 1.26), and Hyginus (*Astron.* 2.7.358–64).

For a useful discussion of all of these sources see Vergados (2007a) 59–86.

4 HYMN TO APHRODITE

(a) *Structure and themes*

The structure of this hymn is simple, but untypical. The proem is unusually long (1–44). The poet proclaims as his theme the works of Aphrodite (rather than simply the goddess herself). He describes her power over all living beings, but then adds that three goddesses are not subject to her influence, Athene, Artemis, and Hestia (7–33). Each is given a passage in praise of her nature and powers. He goes on to say that even Zeus himself was led by Aphrodite to fall in love with mortal women, without the knowledge of Hera, who is also given a brief passage of praise. The narrative is then introduced by a short section announcing the main theme, how Zeus made Aphrodite herself fall in love with a mortal man, so that she should not be exempt from this experience, nor be able to boast of how she had mixed gods and goddesses with mortals, and brought about the birth to deities of mortal offspring (45–81).

This general statement leads to the detailed narrative (53–291). Zeus causes her to fall in love with Anchises, and the first part describes her seduction of him and their ensuing union (53–167). Aphrodite visits him at his farmstead on Mt Ida in disguise as a young girl, wearing a beautiful dress and jewellery. Anchises at first thinks that she is a goddess, but she tells him a false tale, that she is a daughter of the Phrygian king Otreus, and was carried off by Hermes to become Anchises' wife. Anchises accepts her story and declares his intention of sleeping with her on the spot. He undresses her and they make love together.

The rest of the narrative concerns the aftermath (168–291). While he is asleep Aphrodite dresses, assumes her true form as a goddess, and wakes him. Anchises is afraid and begs her not to harm him, because he has slept with her in ignorance (168–90).

Aphrodite replies with a long speech (191–291). She promises that he will not come to harm, and tells him that he will have a son who will be called Aeneas. He will rule over the Trojans, and his descendants will continue in future times. She then illustrates how Anchises' family have always been 'close to the gods', by the two stories of Ganymede, carried off to heaven by Zeus to enjoy eternal youth and immortality, and Tithonus, who was loved by Dawn and was given immortality, but without freedom from old age. Since Anchises too will not escape old age, Aphrodite would not wish him to become immortal. Because she will bear a son from a mortal father she will be full of shame in the company of the gods.

As for Aeneas, the nymphs of Mt Ida will be his nurses, and they will bring him to Anchises, when he reaches his prime of youth. Anchises must take him to Troy, and say that he is reputed to be the son of one of these mountain nymphs. But if he should speak the truth about his union with Aphrodite, Zeus will strike him with his thunderbolt.

With this warning she returns to heaven, and the poet bids her farewell and announces that he will go on to another song (292–3).

The scene of Anchises' union with Aphrodite forms the centrepiece of the poem (155–67). But it is unusual for so much of what follows to be taken up by Aphrodite's speech, once she has revealed her identity. The reason is most probably the importance of her prediction about the birth of Aeneas, his kingship, and the continuity of his dynasty in future generations (see 196–7n. for further discussion). This is set in the context of the divine favour enjoyed in the past by Anchises' ancestors. At the same time, her speech dwells on the theme of the boundary between the divine and mortal worlds. The whole of the narrative is concerned with the way in which these two worlds have become intertwined, through the union of gods and mortals. The stories of Ganymede and Tithonus are two contrasting examples of the exceptional treatment of divine favourites who escape death. Anchises will not have this privilege, but can take consolation from the prophecy about Aeneas. Even the mountain nymphs, Aphrodite says, are not immortal, since they are the spirits of the trees, and die with them (264–72).

The hymn as a whole is untypical also in that it does not simply tell of the birth or exploits of a deity. It does exemplify 'the works of Aphrodite', but in an ironic way, since she is herself made a victim of her own power of love, and rather than adding to her glory this is seen by her as a cause for shame. In doing so the poem paradoxically illustrates the way in which the power of love works, its ambiguous quality as something which can have both positive and negative effects. At the same time the narrative does predict a birth, but in this case it is a heroic one. This is another reason to see this as part of the purpose of the hymn, and probably its main impetus. Aphrodite's embarrassment in no way detracts from the heroic status of her offspring Aeneas.

The shorter hymn to Aphrodite, which is placed next in the collection, has a more traditional pattern. It praises her as the goddess of Cyprus, and describes how she arrived there after her birth and was welcomed and dressed by the Horai, and then introduced by them to the Olympian gods. Its positive tone makes it a good counterpart to the bitter-sweet irony of the longer hymn.

(b) Relationship with other early poetry

Of all the *Hymns*, this one is nearest to the Homeric poems in its language, with twenty verses closely resembling or identical with lines in Homer, and many formulaic parallels. As was noted above (2(b)), the frequency of words not found elsewhere in early hexameter poetry is also very low. But both Hoekstra (1969) and Janko (1982) have shown that the hymn contains a good many modifications of Homeric language and formulae. In some cases imitation of particular Homeric passages or scenes is also a possibility. The poem accounts for the birth of Aeneas, the Trojan hero prominent in the *Iliad*, and Aphrodite's prophecy about him and his family is probably modelled on that of Poseidon at *Il.* 20.307–8 (see *H. Aph.* 196–7n.). The portrayal of Anchises' seduction has parallels with Homeric scenes of divine amours, especially the deception of Zeus by Hera in *Iliad* 14, and the song of Demodocus about Ares and Aphrodite in *Odyssey* 8. There are also points of contact with other scenes which make fun of the goddess of love, such as those in *Iliad* 5 and 21, where she is worsted in battle. Direct imitation, rather than use of traditional themes, is less easy to establish in such cases, but they add to the general impression of the poem as Homeric in character.

At the same time, the hymn has some striking parallels with the Hesiodic poems. The portrayal of Hestia follows the *Theogony* closely (see 21–32nn.). The proem of the *Theogony* seems to be echoed at *H. Aph.* 8 and 258–61 (see 8, 256–8, 261nn.), and the passage about the creation of woman (*Th.* 570–612) has parallels with *H. Aph.* 5 and 29 (see 5, 29–32nn.). The closest links are with the description of winter at *Op.* 504–35 (see 1, 6, 9–11, 14–15, 264–5nn.). Here the influence of Hesiod on the hymn seems more likely than the reverse (see Faulkner (2008) 36–8, as against Janko (1982) 165–9).

There are also close links with the *Hymn to Demeter*, and in this case it is probable that *Demeter* is influenced by *Aphrodite* (see 31–2, 81–3, 136, 155–7, 172–5, 205, 256–8, 278–9, 284–5nn., and Richardson, *H. Dem.* pp. 42–3, Janko (1982) 163–5, Faulkner (2008) 38–40).

A number of interesting points of contact can also be detected with the Lesbian poets Sappho and Alcaeus (see 13, 26–8, 155–7, 218–38nn.). In particular, Hestia's oath of virginity, confirmed by Zeus (26–9), is very similar to a fragment of a Lesbian hymn to Artemis, which may be the work of either Sappho or Alcaeus (Sappho 44(A) V = Alc. 304 L–P), and the story of Tithonus is mentioned by Sappho in a poem which has similarities to the passage about him at *H. Aph.* 218–38 (see comments). Such points of contact are also visible in some of the other hymns. Alcaeus' hymn to Hermes has parallels with the Homeric one to this god (cf. 3(i) above). In addition, his hymn to the Dioscuri (fr. 34 L–P = 34 V) resembles *Hymn* 33 in its description of them appearing to rescue sailors who are in danger of shipwreck. Alcaeus seems to have told the story of Hephaestus' capture of Hera and her release by Dionysus (fr. 349 L–P = 349 V), and it has been argued that the first Homeric *Hymn to Dionysus* may have contained this myth (cf. West (2001b)). These parallels suggest that the tradition of the *Hymns* had close links with that of Lesbian lyric hymns. In the case of *Aphrodite* it seems reasonable to assume that the Lesbian poets knew the version which we possess of this hymn, if this was composed before 600 BC (see 4(c) below), although use of common models in earlier tradition cannot be entirely excluded (cf. also West (2002) 216–17, Faulkner (2008) 45–7).

(c) Date and place of composition

As we have seen, the hymn should probably be dated after the *Iliad* and *Odyssey*, and also after the *Theogony* and *Works and Days*, but before the *Hymn to Demeter*. Although there continues to be debate about the chronology of all these works, a seventh-century date for *Aphrodite* seems reasonable, especially if *Demeter* belongs to the seventh rather than the sixth century (see Richardson, *H. Dem.* pp. 5–11, Clinton (1986) 47). If one accepts the more traditional scholarly view that the major Homeric and Hesiodic poems belong to the eighth rather than seventh century, then the hymn could have been composed in the early seventh or even possibly as far back as the late eighth century.

The prominence of the theme of Aeneas' birth, and the prophecy about his future kingship and the continuing success of his descendants, make it likely that the hymn originates from Asia Minor rather than mainland Greece. The reference by Aphrodite to her ability to speak Phrygian as well as Anchises' language could be an indication that the poem was composed in the north-west of Asia Minor (see 113–16n.). The links with Lesbian poetry would fit this hypothesis, although *Hermes* and some of the other hymns show similar links (cf. 4(b) above). Finally, the pronounced Homeric character of the language would also agree with an origin in the Ionian or Aeolic regions of Asia Minor. A popular view in recent scholarship is that the hymn was actually composed to honour an aristocratic family in the Troad which claimed descent from Aeneas. This has been contested (see especially Smith (1981a)), but it seems a reasonable hypothesis and may well be correct. (For further discussion see Faulkner (2008) 3–18).

(d) Style

The narrative flows very smoothly, and has the clarity of Homeric style. But for all its apparent simplicity the hymn is artfully constructed. Elaborate patterns of repetition and variation, which are surely deliberate, help to emphasise the poem's themes: see Porter (1949). This can be illustrated by analysis of the opening sections of the hymn (1–57), leading into the main narrative. The initial proclamation of the theme ('the works of Aphrodite rich in gold') is repeated at line 9, in the passage about Athena, and ἔργον or ἔργα recur at lines 6, 10, and 15. The motif of Aphrodite's persuasion or deception, introduced at 7, recurs at 33 (rounding off 7–33), 36, and 38. 'Rousing sweet longing' (line 2) is echoed at 45 and 53, where Zeus turns the tables on Aphrodite (cf. also 57), and 'overpowering' (3) recurs at 17. In the section praising the three virgin goddesses (7–33), forms of ἁνδάνειν (εὔαδεν, ἅδον, ἅδε, ἅδεν) occur at 9, 10, 18, and 21. Lines 12–15 are composed of two parallel couplets, describing Athene's skills, and 31–2 are also parallel verses in praise of Hestia. 34–5 resume the opening theme of Aphrodite's almost universal power. 37 and 41–3, in praise of Zeus and Hera, have internal repetition or variation. Above all, the motif of the 'mixing' of deities and mortals, fundamental to the poem, is emphasised with complex variation at 39, 46, and 50–2 (see 45–52, 50–2nn.).

The narrative of the seduction is also articulated by the important recurring motif of Aphrodite's adornment. This occurs three times, when she prepares to visit Anchises (61–5), when he first sees her (84–90), and finally when she undresses (161–6). The first is more general, the second (emphasising her effect on Anchises) lists her jewellery in detail, and the final passage is a simpler version of the second.

Other forms of repetition occur at 58–63, 76–9, and 92–9 (especially 97–9). These probably guarantee the text in cases where interpolation has been suspected (e.g. 62–3 and 97–8). In Aphrodite's final speech a recurrent opening phrase is used to emphasise the structure of her argument, at 225, 230, and 237, and again at 256, 274, and 278.

At times also we find a more elaborate periodic (rather than paratactic) form of construction, leading up to a climax. The most dramatic example is Anchises' declaration that, if Aphrodite is telling the truth, then no one will prevent him from making love to her at once, even if he should be killed by Apollo as a result (145–54: see comments). 145–52 are a single sentence, with a four-line conditional clause, followed by the main clause, to which is added a further negative conditional (οὐδ' εἴ κεν . . .). 153–4 then form a climactic development, with asyndeton, confirming what he has declared. The following passage, leading up to the point where Anchises sleeps with Aphrodite, is also elaborately structured. 155–60 consist mainly of a single sentence (after the first half of 155), with several examples of necessary enjambment, and 161–7 also contain successive lines with necessary enjambment at 164–7, culminating in the carefully crafted statement at 166–7 (see 161–7 and 166–7nn.).

It was such forms of repetition and elaboration which led Freed and Bentman (1954) to the extreme view that the hymn must belong to the Hellenistic period. There is no reason why an early hexameter poet should not be capable of such effects. But it remains true that the poem tends towards a richer style than most parts of the *Iliad* and *Odyssey*.

5 THE HOMERIC HYMNS AND HELLENISTIC POETRY

Several features of the *Hymns* proved attractive to Hellenistic and Roman poets: the sense of narrative experimentation and compression, which makes the *Hymns* important forerunners of the shorter hexameter narratives of the later periods ('epyllia'); the light touch of humour which plays over several of the longer hymns; the interest in the birth and childhood of gods, and the emphasis upon divine epiphany (cf. García (2002)) which appealed to important features of Hellenistic cult and religious sensibility; the focus upon modes of divine praise ('How shall I praise you?') which became ever more important in a world in which great men were becoming more and more like gods (cf. Theocritus' *Encomium of Ptolemy*, which adapts the birth narrative of the *Hymn to Apollo* for the birth of Ptolemy Philadelphus on Cos). The *Hymns* have left a much larger footprint in Hellenistic poetry than in Hellenistic scholarship.

All six of Callimachus' *Hymns* are literary reactions to the *Homeric Hymns*; Callimachus' *Hymn to Demeter* explicitly refuses to repeat the story of the archaic hymn (8–17). The Homeric *Hymn to Apollo* is particularly important for Callimachus' hymns to Apollo, Artemis and Delos, the last of which retells and expands the story of Apollo's birth and sets it within the new political frame of Ptolemaic rule; for particular points of contact with Callimachus' *Hymns* see the notes to *H.Ap.* 1, 16–18, 19–24, 19, 25–8, 38, 39, 41, 42, 47–50, 77–8, 92, 102–4, 119, 131–2, 134–9, 158–61, 382–3, and 396. For possible Callimachean echoes of the other two hymns treated in this edition see the notes to *H. Herm.* 17–19, 21, 192, 552–66, and *H. Aph.* 16–20, 19, 20, 26–8, 259–72, 264–72, and for echoes in other Hellenistic poets see the notes to *H. Ap.* 490–6, *H. Herm.* 21, 25, 41–2, 43–6, 45, 55–61, 87–93, 146–7. For Hellenistic echoes of the *Hymn to Aphrodite* cf. Faulkner (2008) 50–1, and for the *Hymn to Demeter* Richardson, *H. Dem.* pp. 68–71.

For further discussion of Hellenistic poetry and the *Homeric Hymns* see Bulloch (1977), Hunter (1992), (1996), especially 46–57, 72–3, and (2003), Bing (1995), Hunter and Fuhrer (2002), Fantuzzi and Hunter (2004) 350–71, Vamvouri-Ruffy (2004), and Faulkner (2009). For Roman poetry and the *Hymns* see especially Hinds (1987) and Barchiesi (1999).

6 TRANSMISSION OF THE TEXT

On the origins of the collection of *Homeric Hymns* see 1(b) above. There is only a small handful of papyri of the *Hymns*. Our medieval manuscripts are all of the fifteenth century. Most of them contain a collection of hexameter hymns, including those of Callimachus, Orpheus, and Proclus, together with the *Orphic Argonautica*. This cannot have been formed earlier than the fifth century AD (the time of Proclus).

The manuscripts all appear to descend from a single original (Ω), but M (Leidensis BPG 33 H) differs significantly from all the others, which must derive from a separate source known as Ψ. M, which was rediscovered in 1777 by C. F. Matthaei in Moscow, is the only one which preserves the last part of *Hymn* 1 and the whole of *Hymn* 2. It was written by Ioannes Eugenikos in the first half of the fifteenth century AD (see Gelzer (1994) 123–5). Unlike most of the other manuscripts, M also contains part of the *Iliad*, but none of the other parts of the hymnic corpus (Callimachus etc.). It probably derives from a source which contained both the *Iliad* and the *Odyssey*, as well as the *Homeric Hymns*, and as it shows some errors due to confusion between uncial letters, this should belong to a period before the change to minuscule script (see Gelzer (1994) 135–6).

Ψ, on the other hand, was probably a twelfth- or thirteenth-century codex, and may possibly be the one mentioned in a letter of 1424 by Ioannes Aurispa, containing a collection of hymns of Homer, Callimachus, and Orpheus, which he had acquired in Constantinople (see Pfeiffer (1949–53) II lxxxi–ii). The manuscripts of the Ψ group fall into three families (*f*, *p*, and *x*).

The *editio princeps* was published in 1488 by Demetrius Chalcondyles in Florence, together with the *Iliad* and *Odyssey*.

In the present edition I have used the sigla of Càssola, and taken his *apparatus criticus* as a base. For the *Hymn to Aphrodite* Faulkner (2008) has collated or consulted all relevant MSS, and made a few minor corrections to the *apparatus* of previous editors.

For more detailed discussion see Breuning (1929), AHS xi–lviii, Humbert 12–15, Càssola lxv–lxvi, 593–613, and Gelzer (1994).

SIGLA
(cf. Càssola)

A	Parisinus Graecus 2763
At	Athous Vatopedi 671
B	Parisinus Graecus 2765
Γ	Bruxellensis 74
D	Ambrosianus 120
E	Mutinensis 164
H	Harleianus 1752
J	Mutinensis 51
K	Laurentianus XXXI 32
L	Laurentianus XXXII 45
M	Leidensis 22 (BPG 33 H)
P	Vaticanus Palatinus 179
Π	Parisinus, suppl. 1095
Q	Ambrosianus 734
T	Matritensis 4562
V	Marcianus 456
x	consentiunt E T L Π
Θ	consentiunt At D *x*
p	consentiunt A Q B Γ P V aut A Q B P V
Ψ	consentiunt Θ_p
A^{ac}	ante correctionem
A^{c}	correxit manus prima
A^{m}	adiecit in margine manus prima
A^{ss}	supra lineam scripsit manus prima
A^{2c}	correxit manus alia
A^{2m}	adiecit in margine manus alia
A^{2ss}	supra lineam scripsit manus alia
v. l.	variae lectiones

THREE HOMERIC HYMNS

TO APOLLO, HERMES, AND APHRODITE

HYMNS 3, 4, AND 5

ΕΙΣ ΑΠΟΛΛΩΝΑ

Μνήσομαι οὐδὲ λάθωμαι Ἀπόλλωνος ἑκάτοιο,
ὅν τε θεοὶ κατὰ δῶμα Διὸς τρομέουσιν ἰόντα·
καί ῥά τ' ἀναΐσσουσιν ἐπὶ σχεδὸν ἐρχομένοιο
πάντες ἀφ' ἑδράων, ὅτε φαίδιμα τόξα τιταίνει.
Λητὼ δ' οἴη μίμνε παραὶ Διὶ τερπικεραύνωι,
ἥ ῥα βιόν τ' ἐχάλασσε καὶ ἐκλήϊσε φαρέτρην,
καί οἱ ἀπ' ἰφθίμων ὤμων χείρεσσιν ἑλοῦσα,
τόξον ἀνεκρέμασε πρὸς κίονα πατρὸς ἑοῖο
πασσάλου ἐκ χρυσέου· τὸν δ' εἰς θρόνον εἷσεν ἄγουσα.
τῶι δ' ἄρα νέκταρ ἔδωκε πατὴρ δέπαϊ χρυσείωι
δεικνύμενος φίλον υἱόν, ἔπειτα δὲ δαίμονες ἄλλοι.
ἔνθα καθίζουσιν· χαίρει δέ τε πότνια Λητώ,
οὕνεκα τοξοφόρον καὶ καρτερὸν υἱὸν ἔτικτεν.
χαῖρε μάκαιρ' ὦ Λητοῖ, ἐπεὶ τέκες ἀγλαὰ τέκνα
Ἀπόλλωνά τ' ἄνακτα καὶ Ἄρτεμιν ἰοχέαιραν,
τὴν μὲν ἐν Ὀρτυγίηι, τὸν δὲ κραναῆι ἐνὶ Δήλωι,
κεκλιμένη πρὸς μακρὸν ὄρος καὶ Κύνθιον ὄχθον,
ἀγχοτάτω φοίνικος ἐπ' Ἰνωποῖο ῥεέθροις.
Πῶς τ' ἄρ σ' ὑμνήσω πάντως εὔυμνον ἐόντα;
πάντηι γάρ τοι, Φοῖβε, νομοὶ βεβλήαται ὠιδῆς,
ἠμὲν ἀν' ἤπειρον πορτιτρόφον ἠδ' ἀνὰ νήσους.
πᾶσαι δὲ σκοπιαί τοι ἅδον καὶ πρώονες ἄκροι
ὑψηλῶν ὀρέων ποταμοί θ' ἅλα δὲ προρέοντες,
ἀκταί τ' εἰς ἅλα κεκλιμέναι λιμένες τε θαλάσσης.
ἦ ὥς σε πρῶτον Λητὼ τέκε χάρμα βροτοῖσι,
κλινθεῖσα πρὸς Κύνθου ὄρος κραναῆι ἐνὶ νήσωι
Δήλωι ἐν ἀμφιρύτηι; ἑκάτερθε δὲ κῦμα κελαινὸν
ἐξήιει χέρσον δὲ λιγυπνοίοις ἀνέμοισιν·
ἔνθεν ἀπορνύμενος πᾶσι θνητοῖσιν ἀνάσσεις.
ὅσσους Κρήτη τ' ἐντὸς ἔχει καὶ δῆμος Ἀθηνῶν
νῆσός τ' Αἰγίνη ναυσικλειτή τ' Εὔβοια
Αἰγαί τ' Εἰρεσίαι τε καὶ ἀγχίαλος Πεπάρηθος
Θρηΐκιός τ' Ἀθόως καὶ Πηλίου ἄκρα κάρηνα

3 ῥά τ' Hermann: ῥά γ' codd. 11 δαίμονες ἄλλοι. Gemoll 18 ἐπ' Ἰνωποῖο Reiz: ὑπ' Ἰνωποῖο codd. 19 τ' ἄρ Barnes (cf. 207): γάρ codd. 20 νομοὶ Barnes: νόμος codd. 21 πορτιτρόφον M Θ: παντότροφον *p* 26 Κύνθου Holstein: κύνθος codd. 28 ἐξήιει codd.: ἐξίει Cantilena 30 τ' add. Hermann 32 ἀγχίαλος *p*: ἀγχιάλη Θ 33 Ἀθόως Barnes: ἄθως codd.

Θρηϊκίη τε Σάμος Ἴδης τ᾽ ὄρεα σκιόεντα
Σκῦρος καὶ Φώκαια καὶ Αὐτοκάνης ὄρος αἰπὺ
Ἴμβρος τ᾽ εὐκτιμένη καὶ Λῆμνος ἀμιχθαλόεσσα
Λέσβος τ᾽ ἠγαθέη Μάκαρος ἕδος Αἰολίωνος
καὶ Χίος, ἣ νήσων λιπαρωτάτη εἰν ἁλὶ κεῖται,
παιπαλόεις τε Μίμας καὶ Κωρύκου ἄκρα κάρηνα
καὶ Κλάρος αἰγλήεσσα καὶ Αἰσαγέης ὄρος αἰπὺ
καὶ Σάμος ὑδρηλὴ Μυκάλης τ᾽ αἰπεινὰ κάρηνα
Μίλητός τε Κόως τε, πόλις Μερόπων ἀνθρώπων,
καὶ Κνίδος αἰπεινὴ καὶ Κάρπαθος ἠνεμόεσσα
Νάξος τ᾽ ἠδὲ Πάρος Ῥήναιά τε πετρήεσσα,
τόσσον ἔπ᾽ ὠδίνουσα Ἑκηβόλον ἵκετο Λητώ,
εἴ τίς οἱ γαιέων υἱεῖ θέλοι οἰκία θέσθαι.
αἱ δὲ μάλ᾽ ἐτρόμεον καὶ ἐδείδισαν, οὐδέ τις ἔτλη
Φοῖβον δέξασθαι καὶ πιοτέρη περ ἐοῦσα
πρίν γ᾽ ὅτε δή ῥ᾽ ἐπὶ Δήλου ἐβήσετο πότνια Λητώ,
καί μιν ἀνειρομένη ἔπεα πτερόεντα προσηύδα·
  Δῆλ᾽ εἰ γάρ κ᾽ ἐθέλοις ἕδος ἔμμεναι υἷος ἐμοῖο
Φοίβου Ἀπόλλωνος, θέσθαι τ᾽ ἔνι πίονα νηόν·
ἄλλος δ᾽ οὔ τις σεῖό ποθ᾽ ἅψεται, οὐδέ σε τίσει,
οὐδ᾽ εὔβων σε ἔσεσθαι ὀΐομαι οὐδ᾽ εὔμηλον,
οὐδὲ τρύγην οἴσεις, οὔτ᾽ ἂρ φυτὰ μυρία φύσεις.
αἱ δέ κ᾽ Ἀπόλλωνος ἑκαέργου νηὸν ἔχῃσθα,
ἄνθρωποί τοι πάντες ἀγινήσουσ᾽ ἑκατόμβας
ἐνθάδ᾽ ἀγειρόμενοι, κνίση δέ τοι ἄσπετος αἰεὶ
δημοῦ ἀναΐξει, βοσκήσεις θ᾽ οἵ κέ σ᾽ ἔχωσι
χειρὸς ἀπ᾽ ἀλλοτρίης, ἐπεὶ οὔ τοι πῖαρ ὑπ᾽ οὖδας.
  Ὣς φάτο· χαῖρε δὲ Δῆλος, ἀμειβομένη δὲ προσηύδα·
Λητοῖ κυδίστη θύγατερ μεγάλοιο Κοίοιο,
ἀσπασίη κεν ἐγώ γε γονὴν ἑκάτοιο ἄνακτος

42 πόλις Θ: πόλεις *p* 44 ῥηναία τε codd.: Ῥήνειά τε Gemoll 45 ἔπ᾽ ὠδίνουσα Barnes: ἐπωδινόυσα codd. 46 εἴ τίς οἱ γαιέων H J T[2c] (Stephanus): εἴ τίς σοι γαιέων Θ: εἴ τις γαιάων *p* θέλοι Matthiae: θέλει codd. 49 ἐβήσετο E T Π p: ἐβήσατο At D: ἐβήσσατο L 51 εἰ γάρ codd.: ἦ ἄρ Matthiae 53 τίσει Ernesti: λίσσει codd.: alii alia 54 οὐδ᾽ . . . οὐδ᾽ codd.: οὐδ᾽ . . . οὔτ᾽ Hermann σε ἔσεσθαι codd.: σε γ᾽ ἔσεσθαι Hermann 59 δημοῦ Baumeister: δηρὸν codd. (μ E[ss]) ἀναΐξει Schneidewin: ἄναξ εἰ codd. βοσκήσεις θ᾽ οἵ κέ σ᾽ ἔχωσιν Stoll: βόσκοις θεοί κέ σ᾽ ἔχωσιν At D Π: βόσκοις περίτας (ss. θ) σ᾽ ἔχωσιν spatio interiecto E T: εἰ βόσκοισθε οἱ κέ σ᾽ ἔχωσιν E[m]: βόσκοις σ᾽ ἔχωσιν spatio interiecto L: βόσκοις spatio relicto *p*: βόσκεις (ss. οι) spatio relicto Γ (θύτας οἵ κέ σ᾽ ἔχωσιν in lac. Γ[2]) 62 μεγάλοιο Κοίοιο vel Κόοιο dubitanter Allen and Sikes: μεγάλοιο Κρόνοιο codd.

δεξαίμην· αἰνῶς γὰρ ἐτήτυμόν εἰμι δυσηχὴς
ἀνδράσιν, ὧδε δέ κεν περιτιμήεσσα γενοίμην.
ἀλλὰ τόδε τρομέω Λητοῖ ἔπος, οὐδέ σε κεύσω·
λίην γάρ τινά φασιν ἀτάσθαλον Ἀπόλλωνα
ἔσσεσθαι, μέγα δὲ πρυτανευσέμεν ἀθανάτοισι
καὶ θνητοῖσι βροτοῖσιν ἐπὶ ζείδωρον ἄρουραν.
τῶι ῥ' αἰνῶς δείδοικα κατὰ φρένα καὶ κατὰ θυμὸν
μὴ ὁπότ' ἂν τὸ πρῶτον ἴδηι φάος ἠελίοιο
νῆσον ἀτιμήσας, ἐπεὶ ἦ κραναήπεδός εἰμι,
ποσσὶ καταστρέψας ὤσει ἁλὸς ἐν πελάγεσσιν.
ἔνθ' ἐμὲ μὲν μέγα κῦμα κατὰ κρατὸς ἅλις αἰεὶ
κλύσσει, ὁ δ' ἄλλην γαῖαν ἀφίξεται ἥ κεν ἅδηι οἱ
τεύξασθαι νηόν τε καὶ ἄλσεα δενδρήεντα·
πουλύποδες δ' ἐν ἐμοὶ θαλάμας φῶκαί τε μέλαιναι
οἰκία ποιήσονται ἀκηδέα χήτεϊ λαῶν·
ἀλλ' εἴ μοι τλαίης γε θεὰ μέγαν ὅρκον ὀμόσσαι,
ἐνθάδε μιν πρῶτον τεύξειν περικαλλέα νηὸν
ἔμμεναι ἀνθρώπων χρηστήριον, αὐτὰρ ἔπειτα
πάντας ἐπ' ἀνθρώπους, ἐπεὶ ἦ πολυώνυμος ἔσται.
Ὣς ἄρ' ἔφη· Λητὼ δὲ θεῶν μέγαν ὅρκον ὄμοσσεν·
ἴστω νῦν τάδε γαῖα καὶ οὐρανὸς εὐρὺς ὕπερθεν
καὶ τὸ κατειβόμενον Στυγὸς ὕδωρ, ὅς τε μέγιστος
ὅρκος δεινότατός τε πέλει μακάρεσσι θεοῖσιν·
ἦ μὴν Φοίβου τῆιδε θυώδης ἔσσεται αἰὲν
βωμὸς καὶ τέμενος, τίσει δέ σέ γ' ἔξοχα πάντων.
Αὐτὰρ ἐπεί ῥ' ὄμοσέν τε τελεύτησέν τε τὸν ὅρκον,
Δῆλος μὲν μάλα χαῖρε γόνωι ἑκάτοιο ἄνακτος,
Λητὼ δ' ἐννῆμάρ τε καὶ ἐννέα νύκτας ἀέλπτοις
ὠδίνεσσι πέπαρτο. θεαὶ δ' ἔσαν ἔνδοθι πᾶσαι
ὅσσαι ἄρισται ἔσαν, Διώνη τε Ῥείη τε
Ἰχναίη τε Θέμις καὶ ἀγάστονος Ἀμφιτρίτη,
ἄλλαι τ' ἀθάναται, νόσφιν λευκωλένου Ἥρης·
ἧστο γὰρ ἐν μεγάροισι Διὸς νεφεληγερέταο.
μούνη δ' οὐκ ἐπέπυστο μογοστόκος Εἰλείθυια·
ἧστο γὰρ ἄκρωι Ὀλύμπωι ὑπὸ χρυσέοισι νέφεσσιν

72 ἀτιμήσας *p*: ἀτιμήσω Θ (ss. η At D) 73 ὤσει Θ: ὤσηι *p* 75 ἅδηι οἱ Hermann: ἀδὴ οἷ *x*: ἀδοίη *p*: ἀΐδης M 81 post hunc versum lacunam statuit Hermann 82 ἔσται M J[ss]: ἔστιν Ψ 90 γονῆι Franke 91 ἀέπτοις Càssola 93 Ῥείη Chalcondyles: Ῥέη codd. 96 om. E T M, seclusit Ruhnken μεγάροις codd.: corr. Chalcondyles

Ἥρης φραδμοσύνῃς λευκωλένου, ἥ μιν ἔρυκε
ζηλοσύνηι ὅ τ᾽ ἄρ᾽ υἱὸν ἀμύμονά τε κρατερόν τε
Λητὼ τέξεσθαι καλλιπλόκαμος τότ᾽ ἔμελλεν.
  Αἳ δ᾽ Ἶριν προὔπεμψαν ἐϋκτιμένης ἀπὸ νήσου
ἀξέμεν Εἰλείθυιαν, ὑποσχόμεναι μέγαν ὅρμον
χρυσείοισι λίνοισιν ἐερμένον ἐννεάπηχυν·
νόσφιν δ᾽ ἤνωγον καλέειν λευκωλένου Ἥρης
μή μιν ἔπειτ᾽ ἐπέεσσιν ἀποστρέψειεν ἰοῦσαν.
αὐτὰρ ἐπεὶ τό γ᾽ ἄκουσε ποδήνεμος ὠκέα Ἶρις
βῆ ῥα θέειν, ταχέως δὲ διήνυσε πᾶν τὸ μεσηγύ.
αὐτὰρ ἐπεί ῥ᾽ ἵκανε θεῶν ἕδος αἰπὺν Ὄλυμπον
αὐτίκ᾽ ἄρ᾽ Εἰλείθυιαν ἀπὸ μεγάροιο θύραζε
ἐκπροκαλεσσαμένη ἔπεα πτερόεντα προσηύδα
πάντα μάλ᾽ ὡς ἐπέτελλον Ὀλύμπια δώματ᾽ ἔχουσαι.
τῆι δ᾽ ἄρα θυμὸν ἔπειθεν ἐνὶ στήθεσσι φίλοισι,
βὰν δὲ ποσὶ τρήρωσι πελειάσιν ἴθμαθ᾽ ὁμοῖαι.
εὖτ᾽ ἐπὶ Δήλου ἔβαινε μογοστόκος Εἰλείθυια,
τὴν τότε δὴ τόκος εἷλε, μενοίνησεν δὲ τεκέσθαι.
ἀμφὶ δὲ φοίνικι βάλε πήχεε, γοῦνα δ᾽ ἔρεισε
λειμῶνι μαλακῶι, μείδησε δὲ Γαῖ᾽ ὑπένερθεν·
ἐκ δ᾽ ἔθορε πρὸ φόως δέ, θεαὶ δ᾽ ὀλόλυξαν ἅπασαι.
ἔνθα σὲ ἤϊε Φοῖβε θεαὶ λόον ὕδατι καλῶι
ἁγνῶς καὶ καθαρῶς, σπάρξαν δ᾽ ἐν φάρεϊ λευκῶι
λεπτῶι νηγατέωι· περὶ δὲ χρύσεον στρόφον ἧκαν.
οὐδ᾽ ἄρ᾽ Ἀπόλλωνα χρυσάορα θήσατο μήτηρ,
ἀλλὰ Θέμις νέκταρ τε καὶ ἀμβροσίην ἐρατεινὴν
ἀθανάτηισιν χερσὶν ἐπήρξατο· χαῖρε δὲ Λητὼ
οὕνεκα τοξοφόρον καὶ καρτερὸν υἱὸν ἔτικτεν.
  Αὐτὰρ ἐπεὶ δὴ Φοῖβε κατέβρως ἄμβροτον εἶδαρ,
οὔ σέ γ᾽ ἔπειτ᾽ ἴσχον χρύσεοι στρόφοι ἀσπαίροντα,
οὐδ᾽ ἔτι δέσματ᾽ ἔρυκε, λύοντο δὲ πείρατα πάντα.
αὐτίκα δ᾽ ἀθανάτηισι μετηύδα Φοῖβος Ἀπόλλων·
  Εἴη μοι κίθαρίς τε φίλη καὶ καμπύλα τόξα,
χρήσω δ᾽ ἀνθρώποισι Διὸς νημερτέα βουλήν.
  Ὣς εἰπὼν ἐβίβασκεν ἐπὶ χθονὸς εὐρυοδείης
Φοῖβος ἀκερσεκόμης ἑκατηβόλος· αἱ δ᾽ ἄρα πᾶσαι

99 φραδμοσύνῃς M: φραδμοσύνηι Ψ   104 ἐερμένον Barnes: ἐεργμένον codd.   110 ἀπὸ M: ἀπὲκ (ἀπ᾽ ἐκ) Ψ   120 λόον Stephanus: λοῦον codd.   122 στρόφον Stephanus: στροφὸν codd. (item 128)   129 οὐδ᾽ ἔτι *p*: οὐδέ τι M Θ Γ   δέσματ᾽ Barnes: δεσμά σ᾽ *p*: δεσμά τ᾽ (vel δέσμα τ᾽) cet.   130 ἀθανάτηισι M *p x*: ἀθανάτοισι At D Γ   133 ἐπὶ Matthiae: ἀπὸ codd.

θάμβεον ἀθάναται, χρυσῶι δ᾽ ἄρα Δῆλος ἅπασα
βεβρίθει καθορῶσα Διὸς Λητοῦς τε γενέθλην,
γηθοσύνηι ὅτι μιν θεὸς εἵλετο οἰκία θέσθαι
νήσων ἠπείρου τε, φίλησε δὲ κηρόθι μᾶλλον.
[ἤνθησ᾽ ὡς ὅτε τε ῥίον οὔρεος ἄνθεσιν ὕλης.]
Αὐτὸς δ᾽ ἀργυρότοξε ἄναξ ἑκατηβόλ᾽ Ἄπολλον,
ἄλλοτε μέν τ᾽ ἐπὶ Κύνθου ἐβήσαο παιπαλόεντος,
ἄλλοτε δ᾽ αὖ νήσους τε καὶ ἀνέρας ἠλάσκαζες.
πολλοί τοι νηοί τε καὶ ἄλσεα δενδρήεντα,
πᾶσαι δὲ σκοπιαί τε φίλαι καὶ πρώονες ἄκροι
ὑψηλῶν ὀρέων, ποταμοί θ᾽ ἅλα δὲ προρέοντες·
ἀλλὰ σὺ Δήλωι Φοῖβε μάλιστ᾽ ἐπιτέρπεαι ἦτορ,
ἔνθα τοι ἑλκεχίτωνες Ἰάονες ἠγερέθονται
αὐτοῖς σὺν παίδεσσι καὶ αἰδοίηις ἀλόχοισιν.
οἱ δέ σε πυγμαχίηι τε καὶ ὀρχηθμῶι καὶ ἀοιδῆι
μνησάμενοι τέρπουσιν ὅταν στήσωνται ἀγῶνα.
φαίη κ᾽ ἀθανάτους καὶ ἀγήρως ἔμμεναι αἰεὶ
ὃς τότ᾽ ἐπαντιάσει᾽ ὅτ᾽ Ἰάονες ἀθρόοι εἶεν·
πάντων γάρ κεν ἴδοιτο χάριν, τέρψαιτο δὲ θυμὸν
ἄνδρας τ᾽ εἰσορόων καλλιζώνους τε γυναῖκας
νῆάς τ᾽ ὠκείας ἠδ᾽ αὐτῶν κτήματα πολλά.
πρὸς δὲ τόδε μέγα θαῦμα, ὅου κλέος οὔποτ᾽ ὀλεῖται,
κοῦραι Δηλιάδες Ἑκατηβελέταο θεράπναι·
αἵ τ᾽ ἐπεὶ ἂρ πρῶτον μὲν Ἀπόλλων᾽ ὑμνήσωσιν,
αὖτις δ᾽ αὖ Λητώ τε καὶ Ἄρτεμιν ἰοχέαιραν,
μνησάμεναι ἀνδρῶν τε παλαιῶν ἠδὲ γυναικῶν
ὕμνον ἀείδουσιν, θέλγουσι δὲ φῦλ᾽ ἀνθρώπων·
πάντων δ᾽ ἀνθρώπων φωνὰς καὶ κρεμβαλιαστὺν

136–8 omittunt codd. plerique: habent in marg E L[1] T D, in textu Π S, nota instar antisigmatis in E T Π apposita ante 136–8 vel 136–7, et verbis ἐν ἑτερω κεῖνται καὶ οὗτοι οἱ στίχοι in E T, ἐν ἑτερω καὶ οὗτοι οἱ στίχοι κεῖνται in L Π praefixis 139 ὅτε τε ῥίον M *p*: ὅτε τε ῥρίον *x*: ὅτε ῥρίον At D 142 αὖ codd.: ἂν D'Orville 146–50 citat Thuc. 3.104.4 146 ἀλλὰ σὺ codd.: ἀλλ᾽ ὅτε Thuc.: ἄλλοτε Camerarius μάλιστ᾽ ἐπιτέρπεαι ἦτορ codd. (ἐπιτέρπεο M): μάλιστά γε θυμὸν ἐτέρφθης Thuc. 148 αὐτοῖς σὺν codd.: αὐτοῖσιν Hermann: αὐτοὶ σὺν Gemoll σὺν σφοῖσιν τεκέεσσι γυναιξί τε σὴν ἐς ἀγυιάν Thuc. 149 ἔνθα σε . . . ὀρχηστυῖ Thuc. 150 στήσωνται codd.: καθέσωσιν Thuc. 151 αἰεὶ M *p* x^{m}: ἀνὴρ Θ: ἄνδρας J K^{2m} 152 ὃς τότ᾽ ἐπαντιάσει᾽ ὅτ᾽ Ilgen: οἳ τότ᾽ ἐπ᾽ ἀντιᾶσι τ᾽ M: οἳ τότ᾽ ἐπαντία σεῖο τ᾽ Θ: οἳ δὴ τότ᾽ ἐπαντία σεῖο τ᾽ *p* 156 ὅου E T B C Γ: θ᾽ οὗ M: ὅ οὐ (vel sim.) cet. 157 Δηλιάδες M: δηλιάδες δ᾽ Ψ 159 αὖτις M Θ: αὖθις *p* 162 βαμβαλιαστὺν E T: κρεμβαλιαστὺν (-σὺν -στὴν) cet.: βαμ corr. $Γ^{2}$ et totum verbum in marg. adscripsit: βαμ ss. L Π

μιμεῖσθ' ἴσασιν· φαίη δέ κεν αὐτὸς ἕκαστος
φθέγγεσθ'· οὕτω σφιν καλὴ συνάρηρεν ἀοιδή.
ἀλλ' ἄγεθ' ἱλήκοι μὲν Ἀπόλλων Ἀρτέμιδι ξύν,
χαίρετε δ' ὑμεῖς πᾶσαι· ἐμεῖο δὲ καὶ μετόπισθε
μνήσασθ', ὁππότε κέν τις ἐπιχθονίων ἀνθρώπων
ἐνθάδ' ἀνείρηται ξεῖνος ταλαπείριος ἐλθών·
ὦ κοῦραι, τίς δ' ὔμμιν ἀνὴρ ἥδιστος ἀοιδῶν
ἐνθάδε πωλεῖται καὶ τέωι τέρπεσθε μάλιστα;
ὑμεῖς δ' εὖ μάλα πᾶσαι ὑποκρίνασθαι ἀφήμως·
τυφλὸς ἀνήρ, οἰκεῖ δὲ Χίωι ἔνι παιπαλοέσσηι,
τοῦ πᾶσαι μετόπισθεν ἀριστεύουσιν ἀοιδαί.
ἡμεῖς δ' ὑμέτερον κλέος οἴσομεν ὅσσον ἐπ' αἶαν
ἀνθρώπων στρεφόμεσθα πόλεις εὖ ναιεταώσας·
οἱ δ' ἐπὶ δὴ πείσονται, ἐπεὶ καὶ ἐτήτυμόν ἐστιν.
αὐτὰρ ἐγὼν οὐ λήξω ἑκηβόλον Ἀπόλλωνα
ὑμνέων ἀργυρότοξον ὃν ἠΰκομος τέκε Λητώ.
ὦ ἄνα, καὶ Λυκίην καὶ Μηιονίην ἐρατεινὴν
καὶ Μίλητον ἔχεις ἔναλον πόλιν ἱμερόεσσαν,
αὐτὸς δ' αὖ Δήλοιο περικλύστου μέγ' ἀνάσσεις.
εἶσι δὲ φορμίζων Λητοῦς ἐρικυδέος υἱὸς
φόρμιγγι γλαφυρῆι πρὸς Πυθὼ πετρήεσσαν,
ἄμβροτα εἵματ' ἔχων τεθυωμένα· τοῖο δὲ φόρμιγξ
χρυσέου ὑπὸ πλήκτρου καναχὴν ἔχει ἱμερόεσσαν.
ἔνθεν δὲ πρὸς Ὄλυμπον ἀπὸ χθονὸς ὥς τε νόημα
εἶσι Διὸς πρὸς δῶμα θεῶν μεθ' ὁμήγυριν ἄλλων·
αὐτίκα δ' ἀθανάτοισι μέλει κίθαρις καὶ ἀοιδή.
Μοῦσαι μέν θ' ἅμα πᾶσαι ἀμειβόμεναι ὀπὶ καλῆι
ὑμνεῦσίν ῥα θεῶν δῶρ' ἄμβροτα ἠδ' ἀνθρώπων
τλημοσύνας, ὅσ' ἔχοντες ὑπ' ἀθανάτοισι θεοῖσι
ζώουσ' ἀφραδέες καὶ ἀμήχανοι, οὐδὲ δύνανται
εὑρέμεναι θανάτοιό τ' ἄκος καὶ γήραος ἄλκαρ·
αὐτὰρ ἐϋπλόκαμοι Χάριτες καὶ ἐΰφρονες Ὧραι
Ἁρμονίη θ' Ἥβη τε Διὸς θυγάτηρ τ' Ἀφροδίτη

163 μιμεῖσθ' Barnes: μιμεῖσθαι codd. 165 ἀλλ' ἄγεθ' ἱλήκοι μὲν Thuc.: ἀλλά γε Λητὼ μὲν καὶ M: ἀλλ' ἄγε δὴ Λητὼ μὲν Ψ 168 ταλαπείριος ἄλλος ἐπελθών Thuc. 171 ὑποκρίνασθε Ψ: ὑποκρίνεσθ' M: ὑποκρίνασθαι δ' Thuc.: ἀποκρίνασθε (-αι) Aristid. (34.35) ἀφ' ὑμῶν *p*, Aristid. codd. plerique: ἀφ' ὑμέων E T: ἀφ' ἡμέων cet. (Aristid. R^2 ἀφ' ἡμῶν): ἀφήμως Thuc. codd. plerique: εὐφήμως Thuc. H^{1c}, J^{2c} (Aristid. R^1 **φ**ως): ἀμφ' ἡμέων Marx: ὑποκρίνασθε σαφηνέως Carey 184 τεθυωμένα Barnes: τεθυώδεα codd.: εὐωδέα Pierson 192 ἀφραδέες M Γ^{2m}: ἀμφαδέες Ψ

ὀρχεῦντ᾽ ἀλλήλων ἐπὶ καρπῶι χεῖρας ἔχουσαι·
τῆισι μὲν οὔτ᾽ αἰσχρὴ μεταμέλπεται οὔτ᾽ ἐλάχεια,
ἀλλὰ μάλα μεγάλη τε ἰδεῖν καὶ εἶδος ἀγητὴ
Ἄρτεμις ἰοχέαιρα ὁμότροφος Ἀπόλλωνι.
ἐν δ᾽ αὖ τῆισιν Ἄρης καὶ ἐΰσκοπος Ἀργειφόντης
παίζουσ᾽· αὐτὰρ ὁ Φοῖβος Ἀπόλλων ἐγκιθαρίζει
καλὰ καὶ ὕψι βιβάς, αἴγλη δέ μιν ἀμφὶ φαεινὴ
μαρμαρυγαί τε ποδῶν καὶ ἐϋκλώστοιο χιτῶνος.
οἱ δ᾽ ἐπιτέρπονται θυμὸν μέγαν εἰσορόωντες
Λητώ τε χρυσοπλόκαμος καὶ μητίετα Ζεὺς
υἷα φίλον παίζοντα μετ᾽ ἀθανάτοισι θεοῖσι.
πῶς τ᾽ ἄρ σ᾽ ὑμνήσω πάντως εὔυμνον ἐόντα;
ἠέ σ᾽ ἐνὶ μνηστῆισιν ἀείδω καὶ φιλότητι
ὅππως μνωόμενος ἔκιες Ἀζαντίδα κούρην
Ἴσχυ᾽ ἅμ᾽ ἀντιθέωι Ἐλατιονίδηι εὐίππωι;
ἢ ἅμα Φόρβαντι Τριοπέωι γένος, ἢ ἅμ᾽ Ἐρευθεῖ;
ἢ ἅμα Λευκίππωι καὶ Λευκίπποιο δάμαρτι
πεζός, ὁ δ᾽ ἵπποισιν; οὐ μὴν Τρίοπός γ᾽ ἐνέλειπεν.
ἢ ὡς τὸ πρῶτον χρηστήριον ἀνθρώποισι
ζητεύων κατὰ γαῖαν ἔβης ἑκατηβόλ᾽ Ἄπολλον;
Πιερίην μὲν πρῶτον ἀπ᾽ Οὐλύμποιο κατῆλθες·
Λέκτον τ᾽ ἠμαθόεντα παρέστιχες ἠδ᾽ Αἰνιῆνας
καὶ διὰ Περραιβούς· τάχα δ᾽ εἰς Ἰαωλκὸν ἵκανες,
Κηναίου τ᾽ ἐπέβης ναυσικλειτῆς Εὐβοίης·
στῆς δ᾽ ἐπὶ Ληλάντωι πεδίωι, τό τοι οὐχ ἅδε θυμῶι
τεύξασθαι νηόν τε καὶ ἄλσεα δενδρήεντα.
ἔνθεν δ᾽ Εὔριπον διαβὰς ἑκατηβόλ᾽ Ἄπολλον
βῆς ἀν᾽ ὄρος ζάθεον χλωρόν· τάχα δ᾽ ἷξες ἀπ᾽ αὐτοῦ
ἐς Μυκαλησσὸν ἰὼν καὶ Τευμησσὸν λεχεποίην.
Θήβης δ᾽ εἰσαφίκανες ἕδος καταειμένον ὕληι·
οὐ γάρ πώ τις ἔναιε βροτῶν ἱερῆι ἐνὶ Θήβηι,
οὐδ᾽ ἄρα πω τότε γ᾽ ἦσαν ἀταρπιτοὶ οὐδὲ κέλευθοι

198 ἀγητὴ Ψ: ἀγαυὴ M 200 ἐν δ᾽ αὖ τῆισιν Matthiae: ἔνθ᾽ αὖ τῆισιν Ψ: ἐν δ᾽ αὐτῆσιν M 202 ἀμφὶ φαεινή codd. aliqui: ἀμφιφαείνει cet. 208 ὅππως Wolf: ὁππόσ᾽ Ψ: ὁππόταν M μνωόμενος Martin: ἀνωόμενος Ψ: ἱέμενος M Ἀζαντίδα Ψ: ἀτλαντίδα M 211 Τριοπέωι Allen: τριόπω,τριοπῶ, τριοπόω codd. ἅμ᾽ ἐρευθεῖ Ψ: ἅμ᾽ ἐρεχθεῖ M: ἀμαρύνθω L[m] Π[m] 212 lacunam post hunc versum statuit Hermann 217 ἠδ᾽ Αἰνιῆνας Fick: ἠδ᾽ ἀγνιῆνας M: ἢ μαγνηίδας, ἢ μαγνιῆνας cet. 223 ἀπ᾽ M: ἐπ᾽ cet.

Θήβης ἂμ πεδίον πυρηφόρον, ἀλλ' ἔχεν ὕλη.
ἔνθεν δὲ προτέρω ἔκιες ἑκατηβόλ' Ἄπολλον,
Ὀγχηστὸν δ' ἷξες Ποσιδήϊον ἀγλαὸν ἄλσος·
ἔνθα νεοδμὴς πῶλος ἀναπνέει ἀχθόμενός περ
ἕλκων ἅρματα καλά, χαμαὶ δ' ἐλατὴρ ἀγαθός περ
ἐκ δίφροιο θορὼν ὁδὸν ἔρχεται· οἱ δὲ τέως μὲν
κείν' ὄχεα κροτέουσιν ἀνακτορίην ἀφιέντες.
εἰ δέ κεν ἅρματ' ἀγῆισιν ἐν ἄλσεϊ δενδρήεντι,
ἵππους μὲν κομέουσι, τὰ δὲ κλίναντες ἐῶσιν·
ὣς γὰρ τὰ πρώτισθ' ὁσίη γένεθ'· οἱ δὲ ἄνακτι
εὔχονται, δίφρον δὲ θεοῦ τότε μοῖρα φυλάσσει.
ἔνθεν δὲ προτέρω ἔκιες ἑκατηβόλ' Ἄπολλον·
Κηφισὸν δ' ἄρ' ἔπειτα κιχήσαο καλλιρέεθρον,
ὅς τε Λιλαίηθεν προχέει καλλίρροον ὕδωρ·
τὸν διαβὰς Ἑκάεργε καὶ Ὠκαλέην πολύπυργον
ἔνθεν ἄρ' εἰς Ἁλίαρτον ἀφίκεο ποιήεντα.
βῆς δ' ἐπὶ Τελφούσης· τόθι τοι ἅδε χῶρος ἀπήμων
τεύξασθαι νηόν τε καὶ ἄλσεα δενδρήεντα.
στῆς δὲ μάλ' ἄγχ' αὐτῆς καί μιν πρὸς μῦθον ἔειπες·
Τελφοῦσ' ἐνθάδε δὴ φρονέω περικαλλέα νηὸν
ἀνθρώπων τεῦξαι χρηστήριον, οἵ τέ μοι αἰεὶ
ἐνθάδ' ἀγινήσουσι τεληέσσας ἑκατόμβας,
ἠμὲν ὅσοι Πελοπόννησον πίειραν ἔχουσιν
ἠδ' ὅσοι Εὐρώπην τε καὶ ἀμφιρύτας κατὰ νήσους,
χρησόμενοι· τοῖσιν δέ τ' ἐγὼ νημερτέα βουλὴν
πᾶσι θεμιστεύοιμι χρέων ἐνὶ πίονι νηῶι.
Ὣς εἰπὼν διέθηκε θεμείλια Φοῖβος Ἀπόλλων
εὐρέα καὶ μάλα μακρὰ διηνεκές· ἡ δὲ ἰδοῦσα
Τελφοῦσα κραδίην ἐχολώσατο εἶπέ τε μῦθον·
Φοῖβε ἄναξ ἑκάεργε ἔπος τί τοι ἐν φρεσὶ θήσω,
ἐνθάδ' ἐπεὶ φρονέεις τεῦξαι περικαλλέα νηὸν
ἔμμεναι ἀνθρώποις χρηστήριον, οἵ δέ τοι αἰεὶ
ἐνθάδ' ἀγινήσουσι τεληέσσας ἑκατόμβας·
ἀλλ' ἔκ τοι ἐρέω, σὺ δ' ἐνὶ φρεσὶ βάλλεο σῆισι·
πημανέει σ' αἰεὶ κτύπος ἵππων ὠκειάων

228 ὕλη Barnes: ὕλην codd. 235 ἀγῆισιν Cobet: ἄγησιν codd. 243 ἁλίαρτον Γ[2c] (Casaubon): ἅμαρτον codd. 244 Τελφούσης Baumeister: δελφούσης codd. τοι ΜΓ[2ss]: οἱ Ψ 247 Τέλφουσ' Μ: δέλφουσ' Ψ 249 ἐνθάδ' Ψ: πολλοὶ Μ 251 ἀμφιρύτας Ψ: ἀμφιρύτους Μ (cf. 291) 252 τ' codd.: κ' Ilgen 255 ἡ δὲ ἰδοῦσα Hermann: ἡ δ' ἐσιδοῦσα codd. 259 οἱ δέ codd.: οἵ τε Wolf

ἀρδόμενοί τ' οὐρῆες ἐμῶν ἱερῶν ἀπὸ πηγέων·
ἔνθα τις ἀνθρώπων βουλήσεται εἰσοράασθαι
ἅρματά τ' εὐποίητα καὶ ὠκυπόδων κτύπον ἵππων
ἢ νηόν τε μέγαν καὶ κτήματα πόλλ' ἐνεόντα.
ἀλλ' εἰ δή τι πίθοιο, σὺ δὲ κρείσσων καὶ ἀρείων
ἐσσὶ ἄναξ ἐμέθεν, σεῦ δὲ σθένος ἐστὶ μέγιστον·
ἐν Κρίσηι ποίησαι ὑπὸ πτυχὶ Παρνησοῖο.
ἔνθ' οὔθ' ἅρματα καλὰ δονήσεται, οὔτε τοι ἵππων
ὠκυπόδων κτύπος ἔσται ἐΰδμητον περὶ βωμόν.
ἀλλά τοι ὣς προσάγοιεν Ἰηπαιήονι δῶρα
ἀνθρώπων κλυτὰ φῦλα, σὺ δὲ φρένας ἀμφιγεγηθὼς
δέξαι' ἱερὰ καλὰ περικτιόνων ἀνθρώπων.
Ὣς εἰποῦσ' Ἑκάτου πέπιθε φρένας, ὄφρα οἱ αὐτῆι
Τελφούσηι κλέος εἴη ἐπὶ χθονὶ μηδ' Ἑκάτοιο.
ἔνθεν δὲ προτέρω ἔκιες ἑκατηβόλ' Ἄπολλον,
ἷξες δ' ἐς Φλεγύων ἀνδρῶν πόλιν ὑβριστάων,
οἳ Διὸς οὐκ ἀλέγοντες ἐπὶ χθονὶ ναιετάασκον
ἐν καλῆι βήσσηι Κηφισίδος ἐγγύθι λίμνης.
ἔνθεν καρπαλίμως προσέβης πρὸς δειράδα θύων,
ἵκεο δ' ἐς Κρίσην ὑπὸ Παρνησὸν νιφόεντα
κνημὸν πρὸς ζέφυρον τετραμμένον, αὐτὰρ ὕπερθεν
πέτρη ἐπικρέμαται, κοίλη δ' ὑποδέδρομε βῆσσα
τρηχεῖ'· ἔνθα ἄναξ τεκμήρατο Φοῖβος Ἀπόλλων
νηὸν ποιήσασθαι ἐπήρατον εἶπέ τε μῦθον·
Ἐνθάδε δὴ φρονέω τεῦξαι περικαλλέα νηὸν
ἔμμεναι ἀνθρώποις χρηστήριον οἵ τέ μοι αἰεὶ
ἐνθάδ' ἀγινήσουσι τεληέσσας ἑκατόμβας,
ἠμὲν ὅσοι Πελοπόννησον πίειραν ἔχουσιν,
ἠδ' ὅσοι Εὐρώπην τε καὶ ἀμφιρύτας κατὰ νήσους,
χρησόμενοι· τοῖσιν δ' ἂν ἐγὼ νημερτέα βουλὴν
πᾶσι θεμιστεύοιμι χρέων ἐνὶ πίονι νηῶι.
Ὣς εἰπὼν διέθηκε θεμείλια Φοῖβος Ἀπόλλων
εὐρέα καὶ μάλα μακρὰ διηνεκές· αὐτὰρ ἐπ' αὐτοῖς
λάϊνον οὐδὸν ἔθηκε Τροφώνιος ἠδ' Ἀγαμήδης
υἱέες Ἐργίνου, φίλοι ἀθανάτοισι θεοῖσιν,

269 Κρίσηι M: κρισση Ψ   272 τοι M: καὶ Ψ   276 Τελφούση M: δελφούση Ψ (T L^{ss})   278 Κρίσην M: Κρίσσην Ψ   287 τεῦξαι Abel: τεύξειν codd.   291 ἀμφιρύτας Barnes: ἀμφιρύτους codd.   292 ἂν Ψ: ἄρ' M   295 μακρὰ Ψ: καλὰ M   διηνεκὲς M: διαμπερὲς Ψ

κτιστοῖσιν λάεσσιν ἀοίδιμον ἔμμεναι αἰεί·
ἀμφὶ δὲ νηὸν ἔνασσαν ἀθέσφατα φῦλ' ἀνθρώπων.
ἀγχοῦ δὲ κρήνη καλλίρροος ἔνθα δράκαιναν
κτεῖνεν ἄναξ Διὸς υἱὸς ἀπὸ κρατεροῖο βιοῖο
ζατρεφέα μεγάλην τέρας ἄγριον, ἣ κακὰ πολλὰ
ἀνθρώπους ἔρδεσκεν ἐπὶ χθονί, πολλὰ μὲν αὐτοὺς
πολλὰ δὲ μῆλα ταναύποδ' ἐπεὶ πέλε πῆμα δαφοινόν.
καί ποτε δεξαμένη χρυσοθρόνου ἔτρεφεν Ἥρης
δεινόν τ' ἀργαλέον τε Τυφάονα πῆμα βροτοῖσιν,
ὅν ποτ' ἄρ' Ἥρη ἔτικτε χολωσαμένη Διὶ πατρὶ
ἡνίκ' ἄρα Κρονίδης ἐρικυδέα γείνατ' Ἀθήνην
ἐν κορυφῆι· ἡ δ' αἶψα χολώσατο πότνια Ἥρη
ἠδὲ καὶ ἀγρομένοισι μετ' ἀθανάτοισιν ἔειπε·
 κέκλυτέ μευ πάντες τε θεοὶ πᾶσαί τε θέαιναι,
ὡς ἔμ' ἀτιμάζειν ἄρχει νεφεληγερέτα Ζεὺς
πρῶτος, ἐπεί μ' ἄλοχον ποιήσατο κέδν' εἰδυῖαν·
καὶ νῦν νόσφιν ἐμεῖο τέκε γλαυκῶπιν' Ἀθήνην,
ἣ πᾶσιν μακάρεσσι μεταπρέπει ἀθανάτοισιν·
αὐτὰρ ὅ γ' ἠπεδανὸς γέγονεν μετὰ πᾶσι θεοῖσι
παῖς ἐμὸς Ἥφαιστος ῥικνὸς πόδας ὃν τέκον αὐτή·
ῥίψ' ἀνὰ χερσὶν ἑλοῦσα καὶ ἔμβαλον εὐρέϊ πόντωι·
ἀλλά ἑ Νηρῆος θυγάτηρ Θέτις ἀργυρόπεζα
δέξατο καὶ μετὰ ᾗσι κασιγνήτῃσι κόμισσεν·
ὡς ὄφελ' ἄλλο θεοῖσι χαρίσσασθαι μακάρεσσι.
σχέτλιε ποικιλομῆτα τί νῦν μητίσεαι ἄλλο;
πῶς ἔτλης οἷος τεκέειν γλαυκῶπιν Ἀθήνην;
οὐκ ἂν ἐγὼ τεκόμην; καὶ σὴ κεκλημένη ἔμπης
ἦα ῥ' ἐν ἀθανάτοισιν οἳ οὐρανὸν εὐρὺν ἔχουσι.
φράζεο νῦν μή τοί τι κακὸν μητίσομ' ὀπίσσω· 325a
καὶ νῦν μέν τοι ἐγὼ τεχνήσομαι ὥς κε γένηται
παῖς ἐμὸς ὅς κε θεοῖσι μεταπρέποι ἀθανάτοισιν,

298 ἔνασσαν codd.: ἔλασσαν Roux 298 post 299 transposuit von Blumenthal 308 ἡνίκ' ἄρα Ruhnken: ἥνεκ' ἄρα M: εὖτ' ἄρα δὴ Ψ: εἵνεκ' ἄρα Pfeiffer 309 ἐκ κορυφῆς Γ², V²: ἐν κορυφῆι cet. 313 ποιήσατο Stephanus: ἐποιήσατο codd. 317 ὃν τέκον codd.: ὅν τέ κεν Barnes: ὅν γε μὲν Ruhnken: ὅν τέ ποτ' Gemoll: post hunc versum lacunam statuit Chalcondyles 318 ῥίψ' ἀνὰ codd. (δὲ Γ²ˢˢ): ῥίψα δὲ Abel ἔμβαλον M: ἔμβαλεν Ψ 320 κόμισσεν Stephanus: κόμισεν codd. 321 χαρίσσασθαι Allen: χαρίσασθαι M: χαρίζεσθαι Ψ 322 μητίσεαι M: ἔτι μήσεαι *p*: μήσεαι Θ 323 γλαυκῶπιν Abel: γλαυκῶπιδ' codd. 325 ἦα ῥ' ἐν Matthiae: ἤ ἄρ' ἐν S: ἦ (ἥ) ῥ' ἐν cet.: ἦν ἄρ' ἐν Chalcondyles 325a habet in marg. *x*, om. cet. μήτι τοι *x* (om. τοι E): μή τοί τι Schneidewin 326 μέν τοι M: τοι γὰρ *p*: μέν τοι γὰρ Θ

οὔτε σὸν αἰσχύνασ᾽ ἱερὸν λέχος οὔτ᾽ ἐμὸν αὐτῆς,
οὐδέ τοι εἰς εὐνὴν πωλήσομαι, ἀλλ᾽ ἀπὸ σεῖο
τηλόθεν οὖσα θεοῖσι μετέσσομαι ἀθανάτοισιν.
  Ὣς εἰποῦσ᾽ ἀπονόσφι θεῶν κίε χωομένη περ.
αὐτίκ᾽ ἔπειτ᾽ ἠρᾶτο βοῶπις πότνια Ἥρη,
χειρὶ καταπρηνεῖ δ᾽ ἔλασε χθόνα καὶ φάτο μῦθον·
κέκλυτε νῦν μοι Γαῖα καὶ Οὐρανὸς εὐρὺς ὕπερθεν,
Τιτῆνές τε θεοὶ τοὶ ὑπὸ χθονὶ ναιετάοντες
Τάρταρον ἀμφὶ μέγαν, τῶν ἐξ ἄνδρες τε θεοί τε·
αὐτοὶ νῦν μευ πάντες ἀκούσατε καὶ δότε παῖδα
νόσφι Διός, μηδέν τι βίην ἐπιδευέα κείνου·
ἀλλ᾽ ὅ γε φέρτερος ἔστω ὅσον Κρόνου εὐρύοπα Ζεύς.
  Ὣς ἄρα φωνήσασ᾽ ἵμασε χθόνα χειρὶ παχείηι·
κινήθη δ᾽ ἄρα γαῖα φερέσβιος, ἡ δὲ ἰδοῦσα
τέρπετο ὃν κατὰ θυμόν, ὀΐετο γὰρ τελέεσθαι.
ἐκ τούτου δὴ ἔπειτα τελεσφόρον εἰς ἐνιαυτὸν
οὔτε ποτ᾽ εἰς εὐνὴν Διὸς ἤλυθε μητιόεντος,
οὔτε ποτ᾽ εἰς θῶκον πολυδαίδαλον ὡς τὸ πάρος περ
αὐτῶι ἐφεζομένη πυκινὰς φραζέσκετο βουλάς·
ἀλλ᾽ ἥ γ᾽ ἐν νηοῖσι πολυλλίστοισι μένουσα
τέρπετο οἷς ἱεροῖσι βοῶπις πότνια Ἥρη.
ἀλλ᾽ ὅτε δὴ μῆνές τε καὶ ἡμέραι ἐξετελεῦντο
ἂψ περιτελλομένου ἔτεος καὶ ἐπήλυθον ὧραι,
ἡ δ᾽ ἔτεκ᾽ οὔτε θεοῖς ἐναλίγκιον οὔτε βροτοῖσι
δεινόν τ᾽ ἀργαλέον τε Τυφάονα πῆμα βροτοῖσιν.
αὐτίκα τόνδε λαβοῦσα βοῶπις πότνια Ἥρη
δῶκεν ἔπειτα φέρουσα κακῶι κακόν, ἡ δ᾽ ὑπέδεκτο·
ἣ κακὰ πόλλ᾽ ἔρδεσκε κατὰ κλυτὰ φῦλ᾽ ἀνθρώπων.
ὃς τῆι γ᾽ ἀντιάσειε, φέρεσκέ μιν αἴσιμον ἦμαρ
πρίν γέ οἱ ἰὸν ἐφῆκεν ἄναξ ἑκάεργος Ἀπόλλων
καρτερόν· ἡ δ᾽ ὀδύνῃσιν ἐρεχθομένη χαλεπῆισι
κεῖτο μέγ᾽ ἀσθμαίνουσα κυλινδομένη κατὰ χῶρον.
θεσπεσίη δ᾽ ἐνοπὴ γένετ᾽ ἄσπετος, ἡ δὲ καθ᾽ ὕλην
πυκνὰ μάλ᾽ ἔνθα καὶ ἔνθα ἑλίσσετο, λεῖπε δὲ θυμὸν

329 ἀλλ᾽ ἀπὸ σεῖο codd.: οὐδ᾽ ἀπὸ σεῖο Heyne 330 μετέσσομαι codd.: ἀπέσσομαι Groddeck: κοτέσσομαι Gemoll ἀθανάτοισιν codd.: Οὐρανίωσιν West 335 ναιετάοντες codd.: ναιετάουσιν Ilgen 339 ἔστω ὅσον Allen: ἔστιν ὅσον M: ἦ πόσσον Θ: ἦ παρόσον *p*: εἴη ὅσον Hermann 341 ἡ δὲ ἰδοῦσα M: ἡ δ᾽ ἐσιδοῦσα Ψ 349 μῆνες M: νύκτες Ψ 352 βροτοῖσιν Ψ: θεοῖσιν M 353 τόνδε codd.: τόν γε West 355 ἣ Wolf: ὃς codd. 355 delendum putavit Ernesti 356 τῆι γ᾽ Ψ: τῶ γ᾽ M

φοινὸν ἀποπνείουσ', ὁ δ' ἐπηύξατο Φοῖβος Ἀπόλλων·
  ἐνταυθοῖ νῦν πύθευ ἐπὶ χθονὶ βωτιανείρηι,
οὐδὲ σύ γε ζωοῖσι κακὸν δήλημα βροτοῖσιν
ἔσσεαι, οἳ γαίης πολυφόρβου καρπὸν ἔδοντες
ἐνθάδ' ἀγινήσουσι τεληέσσας ἑκατόμβας,
οὐδέ τί τοι θάνατόν γε δυσηλεγέ' οὔτε Τυφωεὺς
ἀρκέσει οὐδὲ Χίμαιρα δυσώνυμος, ἀλλὰ σέ γ' αὐτοῦ
πύσει γαῖα μέλαινα καὶ ἠλέκτωρ Ὑπερίων.
  Ὣς φάτ' ἐπευχόμενος, τὴν δὲ σκότος ὄσσε κάλυψε.
τὴν δ' αὐτοῦ κατέπυσ' ἱερὸν μένος Ἠελίοιο·
ἐξ οὗ νῦν Πυθὼ κικλήσκεται, οἱ δὲ ἄνακτα
Πύθιον καλέουσιν ἐπώνυμον οὕνεκα κεῖθι
αὐτοῦ πῦσε πέλωρ μένος ὀξέος Ἠελίοιο.
  Καὶ τότ' ἄρ' ἔγνω ᾗσιν ἐνὶ φρεσὶ Φοῖβος Ἀπόλλων
οὕνεκά μιν κρήνη καλλίρροος ἐξαπάφησε·
βῆ δ' ἐπὶ Τελφούσηι κεχολωμένος, αἶψα δ' ἵκανε·
στῆ δὲ μάλ' ἄγχ' αὐτῆς καί μιν πρὸς μῦθον ἔειπε·
  Τελφοῦσ', οὐκ ἄρ' ἔμελλες ἐμὸν νόον ἐξαπαφοῦσα
χῶρον ἔχουσ' ἐρατὸν προρέειν καλλίρροον ὕδωρ.
ἐνθάδε δὴ καὶ ἐμὸν κλέος ἔσσεται, οὐδὲ σὸν οἴης.
  Ἦ καὶ ἐπὶ ῥίον ὦσεν ἄναξ ἑκάεργος Ἀπόλλων
πέτρηισι προχυτῆισιν, ἀπέκρυψεν δὲ ῥέεθρα,
καὶ βωμὸν ποιήσατ' ἐν ἄλσεϊ δενδρήεντι
ἄγχι μάλα κρήνης καλλιρρόου· ἔνθα δ' ἄνακτι
πάντες ἐπίκλησιν Τελφουσίωι εὐχετόωνται
οὕνεκα Τελφούσης ἱερῆς ἤισχυνε ῥέεθρα.
  Καὶ τότε δὴ κατὰ θυμὸν ἐφράζετο Φοῖβος Ἀπόλλων
οὕς τινας ἀνθρώπους ὀργείονας εἰσαγάγοιτο
οἳ θεραπεύσονται Πυθοῖ ἔνι πετρηέσσηι·
ταῦτ' ἄρα ὁρμαίνων ἐνόησ' ἐπὶ οἴνοπι πόντωι
νῆα θοήν· ἐν δ' ἄνδρες ἔσαν πολέες τε καὶ ἐσθλοί,
Κρῆτες ἀπὸ Κνωσοῦ Μινωΐου, οἵ ῥά τ' ἄνακτι
ἱερά τε ῥέζουσι καὶ ἀγγέλλουσι θέμιστας
Φοίβου Ἀπόλλωνος χρυσαόρου, ὅττι κεν εἴπηι

363 βωτιανείρηι M *p* *x*: πουλυβοτείρη At D 364 γε ζωοῖσι codd.: γ' ἐν ζωοῖσι West 371 ἱερὸν Casaubon: ἵμερον codd. 373 πύθιον codd.: Πυθεῖον Schulze: Πυθῷιον Bergk: Πύθιον <αὖ> West 391 ἐπὶ codd.: ἐνὶ West 392 νῆα θοήν Chalcondyles: ἠμαθόην codd. 393 Κνωσοῦ Baumeister: κνώσσου, κνωσσοῦ codd. 394 ῥέζουσι Stephanus: ῥρέζουσι E T: (ρ)ρέξουσι cet. ἀγγέλλουσι M At D L Π: ἀγγέλουσι E T: ἀγγελέουσι *p*

χρείων ἐκ δάφνης γυάλων ὕπο Παρνησοῖο.
οἱ μὲν ἐπὶ πρῆξιν καὶ χρήματα νηῒ μελαίνηι
ἐς Πύλον ἠμαθόεντα Πυλοιγενέας τ' ἀνθρώπους
ἔπλεον· αὐτὰρ ὁ τοῖσι συνήντετο Φοῖβος Ἀπόλλων·
ἐν πόντωι δ' ἐπόρουσε δέμας δελφῖνι ἐοικὼς
νηῒ θοῆι, καὶ κεῖτο πέλωρ μέγα τε δεινόν τε·
τῶν δ' ὅς τις κατὰ θυμὸν ἐπιφράσσαιτο νοήσας
πάντοσ' ἀνασσείασκε, τίνασσε δὲ νήϊα δοῦρα.
οἱ δ' ἀκέων ἐν νηῒ καθήατο δειμαίνοντες,
οὐδ' οἵ γ' ὅπλ' ἔλυον κοίλην ἀνὰ νῆα μέλαιναν,
οὐδ' ἔλυον λαῖφος νηὸς κυανοπρώροιο·
ἀλλ' ὡς τὰ πρώτιστα κατεστήσαντο βοεῦσιν
ὣς ἔπλεον· κραιπνὸς δὲ νότος κατόπισθεν ἔπειγε
νῆα θοήν· πρῶτον δὲ παρημείβοντο Μάλειαν,
πὰρ δὲ Λακωνίδα γαῖαν ἁλιστέφανον πτολίεθρον
ἷξον καὶ χῶρον τερψιμβρότου Ἠελίοιο
Ταίναρον, ἔνθα τε μῆλα βαθύτριχα βόσκεται αἰεὶ
Ἠελίοιο ἄνακτος, ἔχει δ' ἐπιτερπέα χῶρον.
οἱ μὲν ἄρ' ἔνθ' ἔθελον νῆα σχεῖν ἠδ' ἀποβάντες
φράσσασθαι μέγα θαῦμα καὶ ὀφθαλμοῖσιν ἰδέσθαι
εἰ μενέει νηὸς γλαφυρῆς δαπέδοισι πέλωρον,
ἢ εἰς οἶδμ' ἅλιον πολυΐχθυον ἀμφὶς ὀρούσει·
ἀλλ' οὐ πηδαλίοισιν ἐπείθετο νηῦς εὐεργής,
ἀλλὰ παρὲκ Πελοπόννησον πίειραν ἔχουσα
ἤϊ' ὁδόν, πνοιῆι δὲ ἄναξ ἑκάεργος Ἀπόλλων
ῥηϊδίως ἴθυν'· ἡ δὲ πρήσσουσα κέλευθον
Ἀρήνην ἵκανε καὶ Ἀργυφέην ἐρατεινὴν
καὶ Θρύον Ἀλφειοῖο πόρον καὶ ἐΰκτιτον Αἶπυ
καὶ Πύλον ἠμαθόεντα Πυλοιγενέας τ' ἀνθρώπους·
βῆ δὲ παρὰ Κρουνοὺς καὶ Χαλκίδα καὶ παρὰ Δύμην
ἠδὲ παρ' Ἤλιδα δῖαν ὅθι κρατέουσιν Ἐπειοί·
εὖτε Φεὰς ἐπέβαλλεν ἀγαλλομένη Διὸς οὔρωι
καί σφιν ὑπὲκ νεφέων Ἰθάκης τ' ὄρος αἰπὺ πέφαντο,

398 Πυλοιγενέας Fick: πυληγενέας codd. 402 τῶν codd.: τὸν Weiher ὅστις Ψ: εἴ τις Ilgen: οὔτις M $Γ^{2m}$ ἐπιφράσσαιτο *p*: ἐπιφράσσατο *x*: ἐπεφράσσατο At D: ἐπεφράσατο M νοήσας Richardson: νοῆσαι codd. 403 πάντοσ' *p*: πάντοθ' M Θ ἀνασσείασκε M: ἀνασ(σ)είσασκε Ψ 404 ἐν M *p*: ἐνὶ Θ καθήατο Abel: καθείατο codd. 407 ὡς τὰ πρώτιστα M: ὡς τὰ πρῶτα Ψ 408 ἔπειγε Ruhnken: ἔγειρε codd. 410 Ἕλος τ' ἔφαλον Matthiae 420 ἤϊ' M: ἦεν, ἦεν, ἥεν cet. 423 ἐΰκτιτον M $Γ^{2m}$: ἐυκτίμενον Ψ 424 Πυλοιγενέας Fick: πυληγενέας codd. 427 Φεὰς Eberhard: φερὰς codd.

Δουλίχιόν τε Σάμη τε καὶ ὑλήεσσα Ζάκυνθος.
ἀλλ᾽ ὅτε δὴ Πελοπόννησον παρενίσατο πᾶσαν,
καὶ δὴ ἐπεὶ Κρίσης κατεφαίνετο κόλπος ἀπείρων
ὅς τε διὲκ Πελοπόννησον πίειραν ἐέργει,
ἦλθ᾽ ἄνεμος ζέφυρος μέγας αἴθριος ἐκ Διὸς αἴσης
λάβρος ἐπαιγίζων ἐξ αἰθέρος, ὄφρα τάχιστα
νηῦς ἀνύσειε θέουσα θαλάσσης ἁλμυρὸν ὕδωρ.
ἄψορροι δὴ ἔπειτα πρὸς ἠῶ τ᾽ ἠέλιόν τε
ἔπλεον, ἡγεμόνευε δ᾽ ἄναξ Διὸς υἱὸς Ἀπόλλων.
ἶξον δ᾽ ἐς Κρίσην εὐδείελον ἀμπελόεσσαν
ἐς λιμέν᾽, ἡ δ᾽ ἀμάθοισιν ἐχρίμψατο ποντοπόρος νηῦς.
ἔνθ᾽ ἐκ νηὸς ὄρουσεν ἄναξ ἑκάεργος Ἀπόλλων
ἀστέρι εἰδόμενος μέσωι ἤματι· τοῦ δ᾽ ἀπὸ πολλαὶ
σπινθαρίδες πωτῶντο, σέλας δ᾽ εἰς οὐρανὸν ἶκεν·
ἐς δ᾽ ἄδυτον κατέδυσε διὰ τριπόδων ἐριτίμων.
ἐν δ᾽ ἄρ᾽ ὅ γε φλόγα δαῖε πιφαυσκόμενος τὰ ἃ κῆλα,
πᾶσαν δὲ Κρίσην κάτεχεν σέλας· αἱ δ᾽ ὀλόλυξαν
Κρισαίων ἄλοχοι καλλίζωνοί τε θύγατρες
Φοίβου ὑπὸ ῥιπῆς· μέγα γὰρ δέος ἔμβαλ᾽ ἑκάστωι.
ἔνθεν δ᾽ αὖτ᾽ ἐπὶ νῆα νόημ᾽ ὣς ἆλτο πέτεσθαι
ἀνέρι εἰδόμενος αἰζηῶι τε κρατερῶι τε
πρωθήβηι, χαίτηις εἰλυμένος εὐρέας ὤμους·
καί σφεας φωνήσας ἔπεα πτερόεντα προσηύδα·
ὦ ξεῖνοι τίνες ἐστέ; πόθεν πλεῖθ᾽ ὑγρὰ κέλευθα;
ἤ τι κατὰ πρῆξιν, ἦ μαψιδίως ἀλάλησθε
οἷά τε ληϊστῆρες ὑπεὶρ ἅλα, τοί τ᾽ ἀλόωνται
ψυχὰς παρθέμενοι κακὸν ἀλλοδαποῖσι φέροντες;
τίφθ᾽ οὕτως ἧσθον τετιηότες, οὐδ᾽ ἐπὶ γαῖαν
ἔκβητ᾽, οὐδὲ καθ᾽ ὅπλα μελαίνης νηὸς ἔθεσθε;
αὕτη μέν γε δίκη πέλει ἀνδρῶν ἀλφηστάων
ὁππόταν ἐκ πόντοιο ποτὶ χθονὶ νηῒ μελαίνηι
ἔλθωσιν καμάτωι ἀδηκότες, αὐτίκα δέ σφεας
σίτοιο γλυκεροῖο περὶ φρένας ἵμερος αἱρεῖ.
Ὣς φάτο καί σφιν θάρσος ἐνὶ στήθεσσιν ἔθηκε.
τὸν καὶ ἀμειβόμενος Κρητῶν ἀγὸς ἀντίον ηὔδα·

430 παρενίσατο M: παρενίσσετο Ψ 431 ἐπεὶ Ψ, praeter At Π: ἐπὶ M At Π 436 ἄψορροι Ψ: ἄψορρον M 442 ἶκεν Barnes: ἧκεν codd. 444 φλόγα δαῖε Ψ: φλόγ᾽ ἔδαιε M 446 Κρισαίων Wolf: κρισ(σ)αγῶν codd. 447 ἔμβαλ᾽ ἑκάστωι M: εἷλεν ἕκαστον Ψ 452 τίνες ἐστέ Chalcondyles: πόθεν ἐστέ codd. 459 ποτὶ χθονὶ codd.: ποτὶ χθόνα Matthiae

ξεῖν᾿, ἐπεὶ οὐ μὲν γάρ τι καταθνητοῖσιν ἔοικας,
οὐ δέμας οὐδὲ φυήν, ἀλλ᾿ ἀθανάτοισι θεοῖσιν,
οὖλέ τε καὶ μέγα χαῖρε, θεοὶ δέ τοι ὄλβια δοῖεν.
καί μοι τοῦτ᾿ ἀγόρευσον ἐτήτυμον ὄφρ᾿ εὖ εἰδῶ·
τίς δῆμος; τίς γαῖα; τίνες βροτοὶ ἐγγεγάασιν;
ἄλληι γὰρ φρονέοντες ἐπεπλέομεν μέγα λαῖτμα
εἰς Πύλον ἐκ Κρήτης, ἔνθεν γένος εὐχόμεθ᾿ εἶναι·
νῦν δ᾿ ὧδε ξὺν νηῒ κατήλθομεν οὔ τι ἑκόντες
νόστου ἱέμενοι ἄλλην ὁδὸν ἄλλα κέλευθα·
ἀλλά τις ἀθανάτων δεῦρ᾿ ἤγαγεν οὐκ ἐθέλοντας.
Τοὺς δ᾿ ἀπαμειβόμενος προσέφη ἑκάεργος Ἀπόλλων·
ξεῖνοι, τοὶ Κνωσὸν πολυδένδρεον ἀμφινέμεσθε
τὸ πρίν, ἀτὰρ νῦν οὐκ ἔθ᾿ ὑπότροποι αὖθις ἔσεσθε
ἔς τε πόλιν ἐρατὴν καὶ δώματα καλὰ ἕκαστος
ἔς τε φίλας ἀλόχους, ἀλλ᾿ ἐνθάδε πίονα νηὸν
ἕξετ᾿ ἐμὸν πολλοῖσι τετιμένον ἀνθρώποισιν·
εἰμὶ δ᾿ ἐγὼ Διὸς υἱός, Ἀπόλλων δ᾿ εὔχομαι εἶναι,
ὑμέας δ᾿ ἤγαγον ἐνθάδ᾿ ὑπὲρ μέγα λαῖτμα θαλάσσης
οὔ τι κακὰ φρονέων, ἀλλ᾿ ἐνθάδε πίονα νηὸν
ἕξετ᾿ ἐμὸν πᾶσιν μάλα τίμιον ἀνθρώποισι,
βουλάς τ᾿ ἀθανάτων εἰδήσετε, τῶν ἰότητι
αἰεὶ τιμήσεσθε διαμπερὲς ἤματα πάντα.
ἀλλ᾿ ἄγεθ᾿ ὡς ἂν ἐγὼ εἴπω πείθεσθε τάχιστα·
ἱστία μὲν πρῶτον κάθετον λύσαντε βοείας,
νῆα δ᾿ ἔπειτα θοὴν ἐπὶ ἠπείρου ἐρύσασθε,
ἐκ δὲ κτήμαθ᾿ ἕλεσθε καὶ ἔντεα νηὸς ἐΐσης,
καὶ βωμὸν ποιήσατ᾿ ἐπὶ ῥηγμῖνι θαλάσσης,
πῦρ ἐπικαίοντες ἐπί τ᾿ ἄλφιτα λευκὰ θύοντες·
εὔχεσθαι δὴ ἔπειτα παριστάμενοι περὶ βωμόν.
ὡς μὲν ἐγὼ τὸ πρῶτον ἐν ἠεροειδέϊ πόντωι
εἰδόμενος δελφῖνι θοῆς ἐπὶ νηὸς ὄρουσα,
ὣς ἐμοὶ εὔχεσθαι Δελφινίωι· αὐτὰρ ὁ βωμὸς
αὐτὸς δελφίνιος καὶ ἐπόψιος ἔσσεται αἰεί.
δειπνῆσαί τ᾿ ἄρ᾿ ἔπειτα θοῆι παρὰ νηῒ μελαίνηι,
καὶ σπεῖσαι μακάρεσσι θεοῖς οἳ Ὄλυμπον ἔχουσιν.

468 ἐγγεγάασιν Ilgen: ἐκγέγαασιν codd. 475 κνωσὸν A Q: κνωσσὸν cet. 479 πολλοῖσι M At D Π *p*: λλοῖσι L spatio interiecto: καλλοῖσι E T τετιμένον codd.: τετιμένοι Hermann 488 ἐπὶ Ψ: ἐπ᾿ M 496 δελφίνιος M: δέλφιος At D A Q P: δέλφειος B Γ V *x*

αὐτὰρ ἐπὴν σίτοιο μελίφρονος ἐξ ἔρον ἧσθε,
ἔρχεσθαί θ' ἅμ' ἐμοὶ καὶ ἰηπαιήον' ἀείδειν
εἰς ὅ κε χῶρον ἵκησθον ἵν' ἕξετε πίονα νηόν.
  Ὣς ἔφαθ'· οἱ δ' ἄρα τοῦ μάλα μὲν κλύον ἠδ' ἐπίθοντο.
ἱστία μὲν πρῶτον κάθεσαν, λῦσαν δὲ βοείας,
ἱστὸν δ' ἱστοδόκηι πέλασαν προτόνοισιν ὑφέντες,
ἐκ δὲ καὶ αὐτοὶ βαῖνον ἐπὶ ῥηγμῖνι θαλάσσης,
ἐκ δ' ἁλὸς ἤπειρον δὲ θοὴν ἀνὰ νῆ' ἐρύσαντο
ὑψοῦ ἐπὶ ψαμάθοις, παρὰ δ' ἕρματα μακρὰ τάνυσσαν,
καὶ βωμὸν ποίησαν ἐπὶ ῥηγμῖνι θαλάσσης·
πῦρ δ' ἐπικαίοντες ἐπί τ' ἄλφιτα λευκὰ θύοντες
εὔχονθ' ὡς ἐκέλευε παριστάμενοι περὶ βωμόν.
δόρπον ἔπειθ' εἵλοντο θοῆι παρὰ νηῒ μελαίνηι,
καὶ σπεῖσαν μακάρεσσι θεοῖς οἳ Ὄλυμπον ἔχουσιν.
αὐτὰρ ἐπεὶ πόσιος καὶ ἐδητύος ἐξ ἔρον ἕντο
βάν ῥ' ἴμεν· ἦρχε δ' ἄρα σφιν ἄναξ Διὸς υἱὸς Ἀπόλλων
φόρμιγγ' ἐν χείρεσσιν ἔχων ἐρατὸν κιθαρίζων
καλὰ καὶ ὕψι βιβάς· οἱ δὲ ῥήσσοντες ἕποντο
Κρῆτες πρὸς Πυθὼ καὶ ἰηπαιήον' ἄειδον,
οἷοί τε Κρητῶν παιήονες οἷσί τε Μοῦσα
ἐν στήθεσσιν ἔθηκε θεὰ μελίγηρυν ἀοιδήν.
ἄκμητοι δὲ λόφον προσέβαν ποσίν, αἶψα δ' ἵκοντο
Παρνησὸν καὶ χῶρον ἐπήρατον ἔνθ' ἄρ' ἔμελλεν
οἰκήσειν πολλοῖσι τετιμένος ἀνθρώποισι·
δεῖξε δ' ἄγων ἄδυτον ζάθεον καὶ πίονα νηόν.
τῶν δ' ὠρίνετο θυμὸς ἐνὶ στήθεσσι φίλοισι·
τὸν καὶ ἀνειρόμενος Κρητῶν ἀγὸς ἀντίον ηὔδα·
  ὦ ἄν' ἐπεὶ δὴ τῆλε φίλων καὶ πατρίδος αἴης
ἤγαγες· οὕτω που τῶι σῶι φίλον ἔπλετο θυμῶι·
πῶς καὶ νῦν βιόμεσθα; τό σε φράζεσθαι ἄνωγμεν.
οὔτε τρυγηφόρος ἥδε γ' ἐπήρατος οὔτ' εὐλείμων,
ὥς τ' ἀπό τ' εὖ ζώειν καὶ ἅμ' ἀνθρώποισιν ὀπηδεῖν.
  Τοὺς δ' ἐπιμειδήσας προσέφη Διὸς υἱὸς Ἀπόλλων·
νήπιοι ἄνθρωποι δυστλήμονες οἳ μελεδῶνας

505 βαίνον Ψ: βῆσαν M 507 παρὰ δ' ἕρματα Ψ: περὶ δ' ἔργματα M 510 περὶ Π^{2m}: παρὰ codd. 515 ἐρατὸν M: ἀγατὸν At D: ατὸν spatio interiecto *x*: χρυσῆν *p*: χαρίεν Athenaeus (22C) 516 ῥήσσοντες M: φρίσσοντες Ψ 521–2 ἔμελλεν . . . τετιμένος codd.: ἔμελλον . . . τετιμένοι Pierson 523 ἄδυτον ζάθεον E T L^{m} Π^{m}: αὐτοῦ δάπεδον cet. 528 βιόμεσθα codd.: βώμεσθα Janko 529 ἥδε codd.: οὔτε D'Orville

βούλεσθ᾽ ἀργαλέους τε πόνους καὶ στείνεα θυμῶι·
ῥηΐδιον ἔπος ὔμμ᾽ ἐρέω καὶ ἐπὶ φρεσὶ θήσω.
δεξιτερῆι μάλ᾽ ἕκαστος ἔχων ἐν χειρὶ μάχαιραν
σφάζειν αἰεὶ μῆλα· τὰ δ᾽ ἄφθονα πάντα παρέσται,
ὅσσα ἐμοί κ᾽ ἀγάγωσι περικλυτὰ φῦλ᾽ ἀνθρώπων·
νηὸν δὲ προφύλαχθε, δέδεχθε δὲ φῦλ᾽ ἀνθρώπων
ἐνθάδ᾽ ἀγειρομένων καὶ ἐμὴν ἰθύν τε μάλιστα
. . .
ἠέ τι τηΰσιον ἔπος ἔσσεται ἠέ τι ἔργον,
ὕβρις θ᾽, ἣ θέμις ἐστὶ καταθνητῶν ἀνθρώπων,
ἄλλοι ἔπειθ᾽ ὑμῖν σημάντορες ἄνδρες ἔσονται,
τῶν ὑπ᾽ ἀναγκαίηι δεδμήσεσθ᾽ ἤματα πάντα.
εἴρηταί τοι πάντα, σὺ δὲ φρεσὶ σῆισι φύλαξαι.
Καὶ σὺ μὲν οὕτω χαῖρε Διὸς καὶ Λητοῦς υἱέ·
αὐτὰρ ἐγὼ καὶ σεῖο καὶ ἄλλης μνήσομ᾽ ἀοιδῆς.

ΕΙΣ ΕΡΜΗΝ

Ἑρμῆν ὕμνει Μοῦσα Διὸς καὶ Μαιάδος υἱόν,
Κυλλήνης μεδέοντα καὶ Ἀρκαδίης πολυμήλου,
ἄγγελον ἀθανάτων ἐριούνιον, ὃν τέκε Μαῖα
νύμφη ἐϋπλόκαμος Διὸς ἐν φιλότητι μιγεῖσα
αἰδοίη· μακάρων δὲ θεῶν ἠλεύαθ᾽ ὅμιλον
ἄντρον ἔσω ναίουσα παλίσκιον, ἔνθα Κρονίων
νύμφηι ἐϋπλοκάμωι μισγέσκετο νυκτὸς ἀμολγῶι,
ὄφρα κατὰ γλυκὺς ὕπνος ἔχοι λευκώλενον Ἥρην,
λήθων ἀθανάτους τε θεοὺς θνητούς τ᾽ ἀνθρώπους.
ἀλλ᾽ ὅτε δὴ μεγάλοιο Διὸς νόος ἐξετελεῖτο,
τῆι δ᾽ ἤδη δέκατος μεὶς οὐρανῶι ἐστήρικτο,
εἴς τε φόως ἄγαγεν, ἀρίσημά τε ἔργα τέτυκτο·
καὶ τότ᾽ ἐγείνατο παῖδα πολύτροπον, αἱμυλομήτην,
ληϊστῆρ᾽, ἐλατῆρα βοῶν, ἡγήτορ᾽ ὀνείρων,
νυκτὸς ὀπωπητῆρα, πυληδόκον, ὃς τάχ᾽ ἔμελλεν

534 ῥηΐδιον Ψ: ῥηϊδίως M 537 ὅσσα Ψ: αἰὲν M ἐμοί κ᾽ codd.: τ᾽ ἐμοί κ᾽ Hermann: κ᾽ ἐμοι West 538 νηὸν δὲ Ernesti: νηόν τε codd. 539 καὶ ἐμὴν ἰθύν τε μάλιστα codd.: κατ᾽ ἐμὴν ἰθύν γε μάλιστα Matthiae: καὶ ἐμὴν ἴθυντε θέμιστα Baumeister lacunam post 539 statuit Wolf 540 ἠέ τι τηΰσιον Ψ: ἠέ τ᾽ ἐτήσιον M: εἰ δέ τι τηΰσιον Reiz
11 μεὶς M[c] *p x* (Parisiensis): μὴς M[ac] μεῖς At D 13 τοτ᾽ ἐγείνατο At D: τότε γείνατο M *p x*

ἀμφανέειν κλυτὰ ἔργα μετ᾽ ἀθανάτοισι θεοῖσιν.
ἠῶιος γεγονὼς μέσωι ἤματι ἐγκιθάριζεν,
ἑσπέριος βοῦς κλέψεν ἑκηβόλου Ἀπόλλωνος,
τετράδι τῆι προτέρηι τῆι μιν τέκε πότνια Μαῖα.
ὃς καὶ ἐπεὶ δὴ μητρὸς ἀπ᾽ ἀθανάτων θόρε γυίων
οὐκέτι δηρὸν ἔκειτο μένων ἱερῶι ἐνὶ λίκνωι,
ἀλλ᾽ ὅ γ᾽ ἀναΐξας ζήτει βόας Ἀπόλλωνος
οὐδὸν ὑπερβαίνων ὑψηρεφέος ἄντροιο.
ἔνθα χέλυν εὑρὼν ἐκτήσατο μυρίον ὄλβον·
Ἑρμῆς τοι πρώτιστα χέλυν τεκτήνατ᾽ ἀοιδόν,
ἥ ῥά οἱ ἀντεβόλησεν ἐπ᾽ αὐλείηισι θύρηισι
βοσκομένη προπάροιθε δόμων ἐριθηλέα ποίην,
σαῦλα ποσὶν βαίνουσα· Διὸς δ᾽ ἐριούνιος υἱὸς
ἀθρήσας ἐγέλασσε καὶ αὐτίκα μῦθον ἔειπε·
  Σύμβολον ἤδη μοι μέγ᾽ ὀνήσιμον, οὐκ ὀνοτάζω.
χαῖρε φυὴν ἐρόεσσα χοροιτύπε δαιτὸς ἑταίρη,
ἀσπασίη προφανεῖσα· πόθεν τόδε καλὸν ἄθυρμα;
αἰόλον ὄστρακόν ἐσσι, χέλυς ὄρεσι ζώουσα.
ἀλλ᾽ οἴσω σ᾽ εἰς δῶμα λαβών· ὄφελός τί μοι ἔσσηι,
οὐδ᾽ ἀποτιμήσω· σὺ δέ με πρώτιστον ὀνήσεις.
οἴκοι βέλτερον εἶναι, ἐπεὶ βλαβερὸν τὸ θύρηφιν·
ἦ γὰρ ἐπηλυσίης πολυπήμονος ἔσσεαι ἔχμα
ζώουσ᾽· ἢν δὲ θάνηις τότε κεν μάλα καλὸν ἀείδοις.
  Ὣς ἄρ᾽ ἔφη· καί χερσὶν ἅμ᾽ ἀμφοτέρηισιν ἀείρας
ἂψ εἴσω κίε δῶμα φέρων ἐρατεινὸν ἄθυρμα.
ἔνθ᾽ ἀναπηλήσας γλυφάνωι πολιοῖο σιδήρου
αἰῶν᾽ ἐξετόρησεν ὀρεσκώιοιο χελώνης.
ὡς δ᾽ ὁπότ᾽ ὠκὺ νόημα διὰ στέρνοιο περήσει
ἀνέρος ὅν τε θαμιναὶ ἐπιστρωφῶσι μέριμναι,
ἢ ὅτε δινηθῶσιν ἀπ᾽ ὀφθαλμῶν ἀμαρυγαί,
ὣς ἅμ᾽ ἔπος τε καὶ ἔργον ἐμήδετο κύδιμος Ἑρμῆς.
πῆξε δ᾽ ἄρ᾽ ἐν μέτροισι ταμὼν δόνακας καλάμοιο
πειρήνας διὰ νῶτα διὰ ῥινοῖο χελώνης.
ἀμφὶ δὲ δέρμα τάνυσσε βοὸς πραπίδεσσιν ἑῆισι,
καὶ πήχεις ἐνέθηκ᾽, ἐπὶ δὲ ζυγὸν ἤραρεν ἀμφοῖν,

37 ἔχμα Ruhnken: αἶχμα, αἰχμά, αἰχμά, αἰγχμά codd. 38 θάνηις M At D: θάνοις *p x* τότε κεν Hermann: τότε ἂν codd. 42 ἀναπηλήσας codd.: ἀναπηδήσας Barnes: alii alia 43 περήσει codd: περήσηι B 45 ἢ ὅτε M Γ[2m]: αἳ ὅτε Θ: ἃς ὅτε *p*

ἑπτὰ δὲ συμφώνους ὀΐων ἐτανύσσατο χορδάς.
αὐτὰρ ἐπεὶ δὴ τεῦξε φέρων ἐρατεινὸν ἄθυρμα
πλήκτρωι ἐπειρήτιζε κατὰ μέλος, ἣ δ᾽ ὑπὸ χειρὸς
σμερδαλέον κονάβησε· θεὸς δ᾽ ὑπὸ καλὸν ἄειδεν
ἐξ αὐτοσχεδίης πειρώμενος, ἠΰτε κοῦροι
ἡβηταὶ θαλίηισι παραιβόλα κερτομέουσιν,
ἀμφὶ Δία Κρονίδην καὶ Μαιάδα καλλιπέδιλον
ὡς πάρος ὠρίζεσκον ἑταιρείηι φιλότητι,
ἥν τ᾽ αὐτοῦ γενεὴν ὀνομακλυτὸν ἐξονομάζων·
ἀμφιπόλους τε γέραιρε καὶ ἀγλαὰ δώματα νύμφης,
καὶ τρίποδας κατὰ οἶκον ἐπηετανούς τε λέβητας.
καὶ τὰ μὲν οὖν ἤειδε, τὰ δὲ φρεσὶν ἄλλα μενοίνα.
καὶ τὴν μὲν κατέθηκε φέρων ἱερῶι ἐνὶ λίκνωι
φόρμιγγα γλαφυρήν· ὁ δ᾽ ἄρα κρειῶν ἐρατίζων
ἆλτο κατὰ σκοπιὴν εὐώδεος ἐκ μεγάροιο,
ὁρμαίνων δόλον αἰπὺν ἐνὶ φρεσὶν οἷά τε φῶτες
φιλῆται διέπουσι μελαίνης νυκτὸς ἐν ὥρηι.
Ἠέλιος μὲν ἔδυνε κατὰ χθονὸς ὠκεανὸν δὲ
αὐτοῖσίν θ᾽ ἵπποισι καὶ ἅρμασιν, αὐτὰρ ἄρ᾽ Ἑρμῆς
Πιερίης ἀφίκανε θεῶν ὄρεα σκιόεντα,
ἔνθα θεῶν μακάρων βόες ἄμβροτοι αὖλιν ἔχεσκον
βοσκόμεναι λειμῶνας ἀκηρασίους ἐρατεινούς.
τῶν τότε Μαιάδος υἱὸς ἐΰσκοπος Ἀργειφόντης
πεντήκοντ᾽ ἀγέλης ἀπετάμνετο βοῦς ἐριμύκους.
πλανοδίας δ᾽ ἤλαυνε διὰ ψαμαθώδεα χῶρον
ἴχνη ἀποστρέψας· δολίης δ᾽ οὐ λήθετο τέχνης
ἀντία ποιήσας ὁπλάς, τὰς πρόσθεν ὄπισθεν,
τὰς δ᾽ ὄπιθεν πρώτας, κατὰ δ᾽ ἔμπαλιν αὐτὸς ἔβαινε.
σάνδαλα δ᾽ αὐτίκα ῥιψὶν ἐπὶ ψαμάθοις ἁλίηισιν
ἄφραστ᾽ ἠδ᾽ ἀνόητα διέπλεκε, θαυματὰ ἔργα,
συμμίσγων μυρίκας καὶ μυρσινοειδέας ὄζους.
τῶν τότε συνδήσας νεοθηλέος ἀγκαλὸν ὕλης

51 συμφώνους: ϑηλυτέρων Antigonus Carystius *de mirab.* 7 53 κατὰ μέλος Allen: κατὰ μέρος codd. 54 κονάβησε M: κονάβι(σ)σε cet. 58 ὡς Γ[2c] Ernesti: ὃν codd.: ante 58 lacunam statuit Radermacher 65 ἆλτο At D M: ὧρτο *p*: ὦτο *x* 67 φιληταὶ M V: φηληταὶ Θ *p* (praeter V): φιλῆται Radermacher 70 ϑέων At D: ϑεῶν M *p x* 76 ἴχνη codd.: ἴχνι᾽ Hermann 78 πρώτας M: προσϑεν cet. 79 αὐτίκα ῥιψὶν Postgate: αὐτίκ᾽ ἔριψεν M At D Π *p*: αὐτίκα om. E T: κ᾽ ἔριψεν L 82 νεοϑηλέος ἀγκαλὸν ὕλης Ψ: νεοϑηλέαν ἀγκαλωρήν M: ἄγκαλον Stephanus: νεοϑηλἕ ἀν᾽ ἄγκαλον ὥρην Radermacher (*CQ* 27 (1933) 156–7): νεοϑηλέαν ἀγκάλωι ὥρην Allen (*CQ* 27 (1933) 200)

ἀβλαβέως ὑπὸ ποσσὶν ἐδήσατο σάνδαλα κοῦφα
αὐτοῖσιν πετάλοισι, τὰ κύδιμος Ἀργειφόντης
ἔσπασε Πιερίηθεν ὁδοιπορίην ἀλεείνων,
οἷά τ᾽ ἐπειγόμενος δολιχὴν ὁδόν, αὐτοτροπήσας·
τὸν δὲ γέρων ἐνόησε δέμων ἀνθοῦσαν ἀλωὴν
ἱέμενον πεδίον δὲ δι᾽ Ὀγχηστὸν λεχεποίην·
τὸν πρότερος προσέφη Μαίης ἐρικυδέος υἱός·
Ὦ γέρον ὅς τε φυτὰ σκάπτεις ἐπικαμπύλος ὤμους,
ἦ πολυοινήσεις εὖτ᾽ ἂν τάδε πάντα φέρησι·
καί τε ἰδὼν μὴ ἰδὼν εἶναι καὶ κωφὸς ἀκούσας,
καὶ σιγᾶν, ὅτε μή τι καταβλάπτῃ τὸ σὸν αὐτοῦ.
Τόσσον φὰς συνέσευε βοῶν ἴφθιμα κάρηνα.
πολλὰ δ᾽ ὄρη σκιόεντα καὶ αὐλῶνας κελαδεινοὺς
καὶ πεδί᾽ ἀνθεμόεντα διήλασε κύδιμος Ἑρμῆς.
ὀρφναίη δ᾽ ἐπίκουρος ἐπαύετο δαιμονίη νὺξ
ἡ πλείων, τάχα δ᾽ ὄρθρος ἐγίγνετο δημιοεργός·
ἡ δὲ νέον σκοπιὴν προσεβήσατο δῖα Σελήνη
Πάλλαντος θυγάτηρ Μεγαμηδείδαο ἄνακτος·
τῆμος ἐπ᾽ Ἀλφειὸν ποταμὸν Διὸς ἄλκιμος υἱὸς
Φοίβου Ἀπόλλωνος βοῦς ἤλασεν εὐρυμετώπους.
ἀδμῆτες δ᾽ ἵκανον ἐς αὔλιον ὑψιμέλαθρον
καὶ ληνοὺς προπάροιθεν ἀριπρεπέος λειμῶνος.
ἔνθ᾽ ἐπεὶ εὖ βοτάνης ἐπεφόρβει βοῦς ἐριμύκους
καὶ τὰς μὲν συνέλασσεν ἐς αὔλιον ἀθρόας οὔσας
λωτὸν ἐρεπτομένας ἠδ᾽ ἑρσήεντα κύπειρον,
σὺν δ᾽ ἐφόρει ξύλα πολλά, πυρὸς δ᾽ ἐπεμαίετο τέχνην.
δάφνης ἀγλαὸν ὄζον ἑλὼν ἐπέλεψε σιδήρωι
ἄρμενον ἐν παλάμηι, ἄμπνυτο δὲ θερμὸς ἀϋτμή·
Ἑρμῆς τοι πρώτιστα πυρήϊα πῦρ τ᾽ ἀνέδωκε.
πολλὰ δὲ κάγκανα κᾶλα κατουδαίωι ἐνὶ βόθρωι

83 ἀβλαβέως codd.: ἀσφαλέως Hermann: εὐλαβέως Schneidewin 85 ἀλεείνων codd.: ἀλεγύνων Windisch 86 αὐτοτροπήσας M *p* L[m] Π[m]: αὐτοπρεπὴς ὥς At D L Π: αὐτοτροπήσας ὥς E T 87 δέμων ἀνθοῦσαν M: δόμων αἴθουσαν Ψ 90 ἐπικαμπύλος ὤμους Ψ: ἐπικαμπύλα ξύλα M 91 πολυοινήσεις Ilgen: πολὺ οἰνήσεις M: πολὺ οἰμήσεις Ψ post hunc versum lacunam statuit Groddeck 94 φὰς συνέσευε Chalcondyles: φασὶν ἔσ(σ)ευε codd. 99 σκοπιὴν M *p x*: σκοπιῆι At D 100 μεγαμηδείδαο *p*: μέγα μηδείδαο M: μεγαμηδείαο At D: μέγα μηδείδιο Π: μεγαμηδείδοιο L: μεγαμηδείοιο E T: μέγα μηδομένοιο Càssola 103 ἀδμῆτες codd.: ἀκμῆτες Ilgen 109 ἐπέλεψε Ψ: ἐνίαλλε M: ἐν δ᾽ ἴλλε σιδείωι Radermacher lacunam post hunc versum statuit Schneidewin, sed fortasse post ἄρμενον ἐν παλάμηι statuenda est 110 ἄμπνυτο δὲ M: ἀνὰ δ᾽ ἄμπνυτο Ψ 112 κᾶλα *p*: κάλα Θ: καλὰ M κατουδαίωι Barnes: κατ᾽ οὐδαίωι codd.

οὖλα λαβὼν ἐπέθηκεν ἐπηετανά· λάμπετο δὲ φλὸξ
τηλόσε φῦσαν ἱεῖσα πυρὸς μέγα δαιομένοιο.
ὄφρα δὲ πῦρ ἀνέκαιε βίη κλυτοῦ Ἡφαίστοιο,
τόφρα δ' ὑποβρυχίας ἕλικας βοῦς ἕλκε θύραζε
δοιὰς ἄγχι πυρός, δύναμις δέ οἱ ἔπλετο πολλή·
ἀμφοτέρας δ' ἐπὶ νῶτα χαμαὶ βάλε φυσιοώσας·
ἐγκλίνων δ' ἐκύλινδε δι' αἰῶνας τετορήσας,
ἔργωι δ' ἔργον ὄπαζε ταμὼν κρέα πίονα δημῶι·
ὤπτα δ' ἀμφ' ὀβελοῖσι πεπαρμένα δουρατέοισι,
σάρκας ὁμοῦ καὶ νῶτα γεράσμια καὶ μέλαν αἷμα
ἐργμένον ἐν χολάδεσσι, τὰ δ' αὐτοῦ κεῖτ' ἐπὶ χώρης.
ῥινοὺς δ' ἐξετάνυσσε καταστυφέλωι ἐνὶ πέτρηι,
ὡς ἔτι νῦν τὰ μέτασσα πολυχρόνιοι πεφύασι
δηρὸν δὴ μετὰ ταῦτα καὶ ἄκριτον. αὐτὰρ ἔπειτα
Ἑρμῆς χαρμόφρων εἰρύσσατο πίονα ἔργα
λείωι ἐπὶ πλαταμῶνι καὶ ἔσχισε δώδεκα μοίρας
κληροπαλεῖς· τέλεον δὲ γέρας προσέθηκεν ἑκάστηι.
ἔνθ' ὁσίης κρεάων ἠράσσατο κύδιμος Ἑρμῆς·
ὀδμὴ γάρ μιν ἔτειρε καὶ ἀθάνατόν περ ἐόντα
ἡδεῖ'· ἀλλ' οὐδ' ὥς οἱ ἐπεπείθετο θυμὸς ἀγήνωρ
καί τε μάλ' ἱμείροντι περᾶν ἱερῆς κατὰ δειρῆς.
ἀλλὰ τὰ μὲν κατέθηκεν ἐς αὔλιον ὑψιμέλαθρον,
δημὸν καὶ κρέα πολλά, μετήορα δ' αἶψ' ἀνάειρε,
σῆμα νέης φωρῆς· ἐπὶ δὲ ξύλα κάγκαν' ἀείρας
οὐλόποδ' οὐλοκάρηνα πυρὸς κατεδάμνατ' ἀϋτμῆι.
αὐτὰρ ἐπειδὴ πάντα κατὰ χρέος ἤνυσε δαίμων
σάνδαλα μὲν προέηκεν ἐς Ἀλφειὸν βαθυδίνην,
ἀνθρακιὴν δ' ἐμάρανε, κόνιν δ' ἀμάθυνε μέλαιναν
παννύχιος· καλὸν δὲ φόως κατέλαμπε Σελήνης.
Κυλλήνης δ' αἶψ' αὖτις ἀφίκετο δῖα κάρηνα

114 φύσαν E: φύζαν cet. (σ Γ[2ss]) 116 ὑποβρυχίας codd.: ὑποβρύχους Ludwich: ἐριβρύχους Barnes: ὑποβροχίους Thomas 119 ἐγκλίνων Ψ: ἐκκρίνας M: ἐγκλίνας Ilgen αἰῶνας MΘ: αἰῶνος *p* 120 πίονα M: πίονι Ψ 124 κασαστυφέλωι At *x*: κατὰ στυφέλω D *p*: κατὰ στυφελῆ M ἐνὶ codd.: ἐπὶ Burkert (cf. 404) 125 τὰ μέτασσα M: τὰ μετ' ἄσσα (ἅσσα) Ψ 126 ἄκριτον codd.: ἄκριτοι West 127 χαρμόφρων Stephanus: χαρμοφέρων MΘ: χάρμα φέρων *p* εἰρύσσατο M *p*: εἰρύσατο Θ 132 ἐπεπείθετο M: οἱ ἐπείθετο Ψ 133 περᾶν Barnes: περῆν M: πέρην' Θ Γ: πέρην *p*: περῆν' Radermacher: παρεῖν' Tucker 136 om. M: σῆμα νεῆς φωνῆς Ψ: σῆμα νεῆς φωρῆς Hermann: σήματα ἧς φωρῆς Gemoll: σῆμαθ' ἑῆς φωρῆς Burkert: σῆμα νεῆς θοίνης Cusset (1997) ἐπὶ δὲ codd.: τὰ δ' ἐπὶ Thomas 138 ἐπειδὴ M: ἐπεὶ Ψ: ἐπεί τοι Chalcondyles 141 παννύχιος Ψ: παννύχιον M κατέλαμπε M: ἐπέλαμπε Ψ

ὄρθριος, οὐδέ τίς οἱ δολιχῆς ὁδοῦ ἀντεβόλησεν
οὔτε θεῶν μακάρων οὔτε θνητῶν ἀνθρώπων,
οὐδὲ κύνες λελάκοντο· Διὸς δ' ἐριούνιος Ἑρμῆς
δοχμωθεὶς μεγάροιο διὰ κλήϊθρον ἔδυνεν
αὔρηι ὀπωρινῆι ἐναλίγκιος ἠΰτ' ὀμίχλη.
ἰθύσας δ' ἄντρου ἐξίκετο πίονα νηὸν
ἦκα ποσὶ προβιβῶν· οὐ γὰρ κτύπεν ὥς περ ἐπ' οὔδει.
ἐσσυμένως δ' ἄρα λίκνον ἐπώιχετο κύδιμος Ἑρμῆς·
σπάργανον ἀμφ' ὤμοις εἰλυμένος ἠΰτε τέκνον
νήπιον ἐν παλάμηισι περ' ἰγνύσι λαῖφος ἀθύρων
κεῖτο, χέλυν ἐρατὴν ἐπ' ἀριστερὰ χειρὸς ἐέργων.
μητέρα δ' οὐκ ἄρ' ἔληθε θεὰν θεός, εἶπέ τε μῦθον·
Τίπτε σὺ ποικιλομῆτα πόθεν τόδε νυκτὸς ἐν ὥρηι
ἔρχῆι ἀναιδείην ἐπιειμένε; νῦν σε μάλ' οἴω
ἢ τάχ' ἀμήχανα δεσμὰ περὶ πλευρῆισιν ἔχοντα
Λητοΐδου ὑπὸ χερσὶ διὲκ προθύροιο περήσειν,
ἢ σὲ φέροντα μεταξὺ κατ' ἄγκεα φιλητεύσειν.
ἔρρε πάλιν· μεγάλην σε πατὴρ ἐφύτευσε μέριμναν
θνητοῖς ἀνθρώποισι καὶ ἀθανάτοισι θεοῖσι.
Τὴν δ' Ἑρμῆς μύθοισιν ἀμείβετο κερδαλέοισι·
μῆτερ ἐμὴ τί με ταῦτα δεδίσκεαι ἠΰτε τέκνον
νήπιον, ὃς μάλα παῦρα μετὰ φρεσὶν αἴσυλα οἶδε,
ταρβαλέον καὶ μητρὸς ὑπαιδείδοικεν ἐνιπάς;
αὐτὰρ ἐγὼ τέχνης ἐπιβήσομαι ἥ τις ἀρίστη
βουκολέων ἐμὲ καὶ σὲ διαμπερές· οὐδὲ θεοῖσι
νῶϊ μετ' ἀθανάτοισιν ἀδώρητοι καὶ ἄλιστοι
αὐτοῦ τῆιδε μένοντες ἀνεξόμεθ', ὡς σὺ κελεύεις.
βέλτερον ἤματα πάντα μετ' ἀθανάτοις ὀαρίζειν
πλούσιον ἀφνειὸν πολυλήϊον ἢ κατὰ δῶμα
ἄντρωι ἐν ἠερόεντι θαασσέμεν· ἀμφὶ δὲ τιμῆς
κἀγὼ τῆς ὁσίης ἐπιβήσομαι ἧς περ Ἀπόλλων.
εἰ δέ κε μὴ δώηισι πατὴρ ἐμός, ἤ τοι ἔγωγε

148 ἰθύσας M: ἰθύνας Ψ   152 περ' ἰγνύσι Θ: περιγνύσι M: παρ' ἰγνύσι *p*: περὶ γνυσὶ Forssmann   155 τόδε Wolf: τάδε codd.   157 ἢ τάχ' Ψ: δύσαχ' M: ἢ τάχ' Barnes: δύσμαχ' (i.e. δύσμαχε) Radermacher   159 φέροντα M: λαβόντα Ψ   μεταξὺ codd.: μέταζε Schmitt   φιλητεύσειν M Θ: φηλητεύσειν *p*   163 δεδίσκεαι Pierson: τιτυσκέαι codd.: πινύσκεις Ruhnken   164 παῦρα μετὰ φρεσὶν αἴσυλα Ψ: πολλὰ ἐνὶ φρεσὶν ἄρμενα M   167 βουλεύων codd.: βουκολέων Ludwich: βουκολέειν Gemoll   168 ἄλιστοι E T: ἄπαστοι M At D L Π Γ P V (ss. λι L Π P): ἄπλιστοι A Q: ἄπ στοι B   172 τιμῆς codd.: τιμῆις Gemoll

πειρήσω, δύναμαι, φιλητέων ὄρχαμος εἶναι.
εἰ δέ μ᾽ ἐρευνήσει Λητοῦς ἐρικυδέος υἱός,
ἄλλο τί οἱ καὶ μεῖζον ὀΐομαι ἀντιβολήσειν.
εἶμι γὰρ εἰς Πυθῶνα μέγαν δόμον ἀντιτορήσων·
ἔνθεν ἅλις τρίποδας περικαλλέας ἠδὲ λέβητας
πορθήσω καὶ χρυσόν, ἅλις τ᾽ αἴθωνα σίδηρον
καὶ πολλὴν ἐσθῆτα· σὺ δ᾽ ὄψεαι αἴ κ᾽ ἐθέλῃσθα.
  Ὣς οἱ μέν ῥ᾽ ἐπέεσσι πρὸς ἀλλήλους ἀγόρευον
υἱός τ᾽ αἰγιόχοιο Διὸς καὶ πότνια Μαῖα.
Ἠὼς δ᾽ ἠριγένεια φόως θνητοῖσι φέρουσα
ὤρνυτ᾽ ἀπ᾽ Ὠκεανοῖο βαθυρρόου· αὐτὰρ Ἀπόλλων
Ὀγχηστόν δ᾽ ἀφίκανε κιὼν πολυήρατον ἄλσος
ἁγνὸν ἐρισφαράγου Γαιηόχου· ἔνθα γέροντα
†κνώδαλον† εὗρε δέμοντα παρὲξ ὁδοῦ ἕρκος ἀλωῆς.
τὸν πρότερος προσέφη Λητοῦς ἐρικυδέος υἱός·
  Ὦ γέρον Ὀγχηστοῖο βατοδρόπε ποιήεντος
βοῦς ἀπὸ Πιερίης διζήμενος ἐνθάδ᾽ ἱκάνω
πάσας θηλείας, πάσας κεράεσσιν ἑλικτάς,
ἐξ ἀγέλης· ὁ δὲ ταῦρος ἐβόσκετο μοῦνος ἀπ᾽ ἄλλων
κυάνεος, χαροποὶ δὲ κύνες κατόπισθεν ἕποντο
τέσσαρες ἠΰτε φῶτες ὁμόφρονες· οἱ μὲν ἔλειφθεν
οἵ τε κύνες ὅ τε ταῦρος, ὃ δὴ περὶ θαῦμα τέτυκται·
ταὶ δ᾽ ἔβαν ἠελίοιο νέον καταδυομένοιο
ἐκ μαλακοῦ λειμῶνος ἀπὸ γλυκεροῖο νομοῖο.
ταῦτά μοι εἰπὲ γεραιὲ παλαιγενὲς εἴ που ὄπωπας
ἀνέρα ταῖσδ᾽ ἐπὶ βουσὶ διαπρήσσοντα κέλευθον.
  Τὸν δ᾽ ὁ γέρων μύθοισιν ἀμειβόμενος προσέειπεν·
ὦ φίλος ἀργαλέον μὲν ὅσ᾽ ὀφθαλμοῖσιν ἴδοιτο
πάντα λέγειν· πολλοὶ γὰρ ὁδὸν πρήσσουσιν ὁδῖται,
τῶν οἱ μὲν κακὰ πολλὰ μεμαότες, οἱ δὲ μάλ᾽ ἐσθλὰ
φοιτῶσιν· χαλεπὸν δὲ δαήμεναί ἐστιν ἕκαστον.
αὐτὰρ ἐγὼ πρόπαν ἦμαρ ἐς ἠέλιον καταδύντα
ἔσκαπτον περὶ γουνὸν ἀλωῆς οἰνοπέδοιο·
παῖδα δ᾽ ἔδοξα φέριστε, σαφὲς δ᾽ οὐκ οἶδα, νοῆσαι,
ὅς τις ὁ παῖς ἅμα βουσὶν ἐϋκραίρῃσιν ὀπήδει

175 δύναμαι Chalcondyles: δύναμαι δὲ codd. φιλητέων Wolf: φιλητεύων Ψ: φιλητέον M 183 Μαῖα Ψ: μήτηρ M 188 κνώδαλον codd.: κώκαλον Stahl: νωχαλόν Hermann, West: alii alia δέμοντα Barnes: νέμοντα codd.: λέγοντα Schneidewin: alii alia 202 ἴδοιτο Ψ: ἴδοιμι M: ἴδοι τις Barnes: ἴδοιο Ernesti 205 φοιτῶσιν Ψ: πρήσσουσιν M 208 νοῆσαι Ψ: νοήσας M 209 ἐϋκραίρῃσιν M Θ: ἐϋκραίροισιν *p*

νήπιος, εἶχε δὲ ῥάβδον, ἐπιστροφάδην δ' ἐβάδιζεν,
ἐξοπίσω δ' ἀνέεργε, κάρη δ' ἔχεν ἀντίον αὐτῶι.
  Φῆ ῥ' ὁ γέρων· ὁ δὲ θᾶσσον ὁδὸν κίε μῦθον ἀκούσας·
οἰωνὸν δ' ἐνόει τανυσίπτερον, αὐτίκα δ' ἔγνω
φιλήτην γεγαῶτα Διὸς παῖδα Κρονίωνος.
ἐσσυμένως δ' ἤϊξεν ἄναξ Διὸς υἱὸς Ἀπόλλων
ἐς Πύλον ἠγαθέην διζήμενος εἰλίποδας βοῦς,
πορφυρέηι νεφέληι κεκαλυμμένος εὐρέας ὤμους·
ἴχνιά τ' εἰσενόησεν Ἑκηβόλος εἶπέ τε μῦθον·
  "Ὢ πόποι ἦ μέγα θαῦμα τόδ' ὀφθαλμοῖσιν ὁρῶμαι·
ἴχνια μὲν τάδε γ' ἐστὶ βοῶν ὀρθοκραιράων,
ἀλλὰ πάλιν τέτραπται ἐς ἀσφοδελὸν λειμῶνα·
βήματα δ' οὔτ' ἀνδρὸς τάδε γίγνεται οὔτε γυναικὸς
οὔτε λύκων πολιῶν οὔτ' ἄρκτων οὔτε λεόντων·
οὔτε τι κενταύρου λασιαύχενος ἔλπομαι εἶναι
ὅς τις τοῖα πέλωρα βιβᾶι ποσὶ καρπαλίμοισιν·
αἰνὰ μὲν ἔνθεν ὁδοῖο, τὰ δ' αἰνότερ' ἔνθεν ὁδοῖο."
  Ὣς εἰπὼν ἤϊξεν ἄναξ Διὸς υἱὸς Ἀπόλλων,
Κυλλήνης δ' ἀφίκανεν ὄρος καταείμενον ὕληι
πέτρης εἰς κευθμῶνα βαθύσκιον, ἔνθα τε νύμφη
ἀμβροσίη ἐλόχευσε Διὸς παῖδα Κρονίωνος.
ὀδμὴ δ' ἱμερόεσσα δι' οὔρεος ἠγαθέοιο
κίδνατο, πολλὰ δὲ μῆλα ταναύποδα βόσκετο ποίην.
ἔνθα τότε σπεύδων κατεβήσατο λάϊνον οὐδὸν
ἄντρον ἐς ἠερόεν ἑκατηβόλος αὐτὸς Ἀπόλλων.
  Τὸν δ' ὡς οὖν ἐνόησε Διὸς καὶ Μαιάδος υἱὸς
χωόμενον περὶ βουσὶν ἑκηβόλον Ἀπόλλωνα,
σπάργαν' ἔσω κατέδυνε θυήεντ'· ἠΰτε πολλὴν
πρέμνων ἀνθρακιὴν ὕλης σποδὸς ἀμφικαλύπτει,
ὣς Ἑρμῆς Ἑκάεργον ἰδὼν ἀνεείλε' ἓ αὐτόν.
ἐν δ' ὀλίγωι συνέλασσε κάρη χεῖράς τε πόδας τε
φή ῥα νεόλλουτος προκαλεύμενος ἥδυμον ὕπνον,
ἐγρήσσων ἐτεόν γε· χέλυν δ' ὑπὸ μασχάληι εἶχε·

211 ἔχεν codd.: ἔχον Hermann 212 μῦθον ἀκούσας M x^{m}: φοῖβος ἀπόλλων Ψ 214 φιλητὴν M Θ: φηλωτὴν *p* 218–19 om. M 224 ἔλπομαι εἶναι M E Γ L^{m} Π^{m}: ἔστιν ὁμοῖα At D *p*: ἤστιν ὁμοῖα L Π 238 ὕλης σποδὸς Ψ: ὁλοσποδὸς M ἀμφικαλύπτει At D: ἀμφικαλύπτοι M *p* *x* 239 ἀνέειλε' Postgate: ἀλέεινεν codd. 241 φή ῥα Hermann: δή ῥα codd.: θῆρα x^{m} νεόλλουτος codd.: νέον λοχάων x^{m} ἥδυμον M Θ: νήδυμον *p* 242 ἐγρήσσων ἐτέον γε Hermann: ἄγρης εἰνετεόν τε (vel sim.) codd.: ἐγρήσσων ἐρατήν τε Martin <δ'> addidit Hermann

γνῶ δ' οὐδ' ἠγνοίησε Διὸς καί Λητοῦς υἱὸς
νύμφην τ' οὐρείην περικαλλέα καὶ φίλον υἱόν,
παῖδ' ὀλίγον δολίῃς εἰλυμένον ἐντροπίῃσι.
παπτήνας δ' ἀνὰ πάντα μυχὸν μεγάλοιο δόμοιο
τρεῖς ἀδύτους ἀνέωιγε λαβὼν κληῖδα φαεινὴν
νέκταρος ἐμπλείους ἠδ' ἀμβροσίης ἐρατεινῆς·
πολλὸς δὲ χρυσός τε καὶ ἄργυρος ἔνδον ἔκειτο,
πολλὰ δὲ φοινικόεντα καὶ ἄργυφα εἵματα νύμφης,
οἷα θεῶν μακάρων ἱεροὶ δόμοι ἐντὸς ἔχουσιν.
ἔνθ' ἐπεὶ ἐξερέεινε μυχοὺς μεγάλοιο δόμοιο
Λητοΐδης μύθοισι προσηύδα κύδιμον Ἑρμῆν·
  Ὦ παῖ ὃς ἐν λίκνωι κατάκειαι, μήνυέ μοι βοῦς
θᾶσσον· ἐπεὶ τάχα νῶϊ διοισόμεθ' οὐ κατὰ κόσμον.
ῥίψω γάρ σε βαλὼν ἐς Τάρταρον ἠερόεντα,
εἰς ζόφον αἰνόμορον καὶ ἀμήχανον· οὐδέ σε μήτηρ
ἐς φάος οὐδὲ πατὴρ ἀναλύσεται, ἀλλ' ὑπὸ γαίῃ
ἐρρήσεις ὀλίγοισι μετ' ἀνδράσιν ἡγεμονεύων.
  Τὸν δ' Ἑρμῆς μύθοισιν ἀμείβετο κερδαλέοισι·
Λητοΐδη τίνα τοῦτον ἀπηνέα μῦθον ἔειπας
καὶ βοῦς ἀγραύλους διζήμενος ἐνθάδ' ἱκάνεις;
οὐκ ἴδον, οὐ πυθόμην, οὐκ ἄλλου μῦθον ἄκουσα·
οὐκ ἂν μηνύσαιμ', οὐκ ἂν μήνυτρον ἀροίμην·
οὔτε βοῶν ἐλατῆρι κραταιῶι φωτὶ ἔοικα.
οὐκ ἐμὸν ἔργον τοῦτο, πάρος δέ μοι ἄλλα μέμηλεν·
ὕπνος ἐμοί γε μέμηλε καὶ ἡμετέρης γάλα μητρός,
σπάργανά τ' ἀμφ' ὤμοισιν ἔχειν καὶ θερμὰ λοετρά.
μή τις τοῦτο πύθοιτο πόθεν τόδε νεῖκος ἐτύχθη·
καί κεν δὴ μέγα θαῦμα μετ' ἀθανάτοισι γένοιτο
παῖδα νέον γεγαῶτα διὰ προθύροιο περῆσαι
βουσὶ μετ' ἀγραύλοισι· τὸ δ' ἀπρεπέως ἀγορεύεις.
χθὲς γενόμην, ἁπαλοὶ δὲ πόδες, τρηχεῖα δ' ὑπὸ χθών.
εἰ δ' ἐθέλεις πατρὸς κεφαλὴν μέγαν ὅρκον ὀμοῦμαι·
μὴ μὲν ἐγὼ μήτ' αὐτὸς ὑπίσχομαι αἴτιος εἶναι,
μήτε τιν' ἄλλον ὄπωπα βοῶν κλοπὸν ὑμετεράων,
αἵ τινες αἱ βόες εἰσί· τὸ δὲ κλέος οἷον ἀκούω.

Il. ii.486
catalogue of ships

246 ἀνὰ M: ἄρα Ψ 248 ἐμπλείους Barnes: ἐκπλείους codd. 254 λίκνωι M E T L^m Π^m *p*: κλίνῃ At D L Π κατάκειαι M Θ: κατακήαι *p* 255 θᾶσσον Ilgen: θᾶττον codd. 259 ὀλίγοισι μετ' M: ὀλίγοισιν ἐν Ψ 261 ἔειπας M *p* L Π T: ἔειπες At D 272 ἀγραύλοισι Ψ: ἀγραύλῃσι M 274 δ' ἐθέλεις Ilgen: δὲ θέλεις codd.

Ὣς ἄρ' ἔφη καὶ πυκνὸν ἀπὸ βλεφάρων ἀμαρύσσων
ὀφρύσι ῥιπτάζεσκεν ὁρώμενος ἔνθα καὶ ἔνθα,
μάκρ' ἀποσυρίζων, ἅλιον ὡς μῦθον ἀκούων.
τὸν δ' ἁπαλὸν γελάσας προσέφη ἑκάεργος Ἀπόλλων·
Ὦ πέπον ἠπεροπευτὰ δολοφραδὲς ἦ σε μάλ' οἴω
πολλάκις ἀντιτοροῦντα δόμους εὖ ναιετάοντας
ἔννυχον οὐ χ' ἕνα μοῦνον ἐπ' οὔδεϊ φῶτα καθίσσαι
σκευάζοντα κατ' οἶκον ἄτερ ψόφου, οἷ' ἀγορεύεις.
πολλοὺς δ' ἀγραύλους ἀκαχήσεις μηλοβοτῆρας
οὔρεος ἐν βήσσῃς, ὁπόταν κρειῶν ἐρατίζων
ἀντήσῃς ἀγέλῃσι βοῶν καὶ πώεσι μήλων.
ἀλλ' ἄγε, μὴ πύματόν τε καὶ ὕστατον ὕπνον ἰαύσῃς,
ἐκ λίκνου κατάβαινε μελαίνης νυκτὸς ἑταῖρε.
τοῦτο γὰρ οὖν καὶ ἔπειτα μετ' ἀθανάτοις γέρας ἕξεις·
ἀρχὸς φιλητέων κεκλήσεαι ἤματα πάντα.
Ὣς ἄρ' ἔφη καὶ παῖδα λαβὼν φέρε Φοῖβος Ἀπόλλων.
σὺν δ' ἄρα φρασσάμενος τότε δὴ κρατὺς Ἀργειφόντης
οἰωνὸν προέηκεν ἀειρόμενος μετὰ χερσί,
τλήμονα γαστρὸς ἔριθον ἀτάσθαλον ἀγγελιώτην.
ἐσσυμένως δὲ μετ' αὐτὸν ἐπέπταρε, τοῖο δ' Ἀπόλλων
ἔκλυεν, ἐκ χειρῶν δὲ χαμαὶ βάλε κύδιμον Ἑρμῆν.
ἕζετο δὲ προπάροιθε καὶ ἐσσύμενός περ ὁδοῖο
Ἑρμῆν κερτομέων, καί μιν πρὸς μῦθον ἔειπε·
Θάρσει σπαργανιῶτα Διὸς καὶ Μαιάδος υἱέ·
εὑρήσω καὶ ἔπειτα βοῶν ἴφθιμα κάρηνα
τούτοις οἰωνοῖσι· σὺ δ' αὖθ' ὁδὸν ἡγεμονεύσεις.
Ὣς φάθ'· ὁ δ' αὖτ' ἀνόρουσε θοῶς Κυλλήνιος Ἑρμῆς
σπουδῇ ἰών· ἄμφω δὲ παρ' οὔατα χερσὶν ἐώθει,
σπάργανον ἀμφ' ὤμοισιν ἐελμένος, εἶπε δὲ μῦθον·
Πῇ με φέρεις Ἑκάεργε θεῶν ζαμενέστατε πάντων;
ἦ με βοῶν ἕνεχ' ὧδε χολούμενος ὀρσολοπεύεις;
ὢ πόποι εἴθ' ἀπόλοιτο βοῶν γένος· οὐ γὰρ ἐγώ γε
ὑμετέρας ἔκλεψα βόας, οὐδ' ἄλλον ὄπωπα,

279 ὀφρύσι codd.: ὀφρῦς Hermann 280 ὡς M: τὸν At D E T: ὡς τὸν *p*: τὸν ὡς Π: ὡς (ss. τὸν) L 284 οὔ χ' ἕνα A Q L: οὐδ' ἕνα M: οὐχ ἕνα cet. καθίσσαι *p x*: καθίσαι M At D 287 κρειῶν Ψ: μήλων M 288 ἀντήσεις At D E T: ἀντήσῃς M L Π *p*: ἄντην x^{m} ἀγέλῃσι βοῶν καὶ πώεσι μήλων codd.: βουκολίοισι καὶ εἰροπόκοις ὀΐεσσιν x^{m} 289 ἰαύσῃς Ψ: ἰαύσεις M 292 φιλητέων M Θ B Γ: φηλίτεων A Q P V 306 ἐελμένος M: ἑλιγμένος Θ: ἑλιγμένος *p*: ἐελμένον Schneidewin

αἵ τινές εἰσι βόες· τὸ δὲ δὴ κλέος οἷον ἀκούω.
δὸς δὲ δίκην καὶ δέξο παρὰ Ζηνὶ Κρονίωνι.
 Αὐτὰρ ἐπεὶ τὰ ἕκαστα διαρρήδην ἐρέεινον
Ἑρμῆς τ' οἰοπόλος καὶ Λητοῦς ἀγλαὸς υἱὸς
ἀμφὶς θυμὸν ἔχοντες· ὁ μὲν νημερτέα φωνῶν
οὐκ ἀδίκως ἐπὶ βουσὶν ἐλάζυτο κύδιμον Ἑρμῆν,
αὐτὰρ ὁ τέχνῃσίν τε καὶ αἱμυλίοισι λόγοισιν
ἤθελεν ἐξαπατᾶν Κυλλήνιος Ἀργυρότοξον·
αὐτὰρ ἐπεὶ πολύμητις ἐὼν πολυμήχανον εὗρεν
ἐσσυμένως δἤπειτα διὰ ψαμάθοιο βάδιζε
πρόσθεν, ἀτὰρ κατόπισθε Διὸς καὶ Λητοῦς υἱός.
αἶψα δὲ τέρθρον ἵκοντο θυώδεος Οὐλύμποιο
ἐς πατέρα Κρονίωνα Διὸς περικαλλέα τέκνα·
κεῖθι γὰρ ἀμφοτέροισι δίκης κατέκειτο τάλαντα.
†εὐμιλίη† δ' ἔχ' Ὄλυμπον ἀγάννιφον, ἀθάνατοι δὲ
ἄφθιτοι ἠγερέθοντο μετὰ χρυσόθρονον ἠῶ.
ἔστησαν δ' Ἑρμῆς τε καὶ ἀργυρότοξος Ἀπόλλων
πρόσθε Διὸς γούνων· ὁ δ' ἀνείρετο φαίδιμον υἱὸν
Ζεὺς ὑψιβρεμέτης καί μιν πρὸς μῦθον ἔειπε·
 Φοῖβε πόθεν ταύτην μενοεικέα ληΐδ' ἐλαύνεις
παῖδα νέον γεγαῶτα φυὴν κήρυκος ἔχοντα;
σπουδαῖον τόδε χρῆμα θεῶν μεθ' ὁμήγυριν ἦλθε.
 Τὸν δ' αὖτε προσέειπεν ἄναξ ἑκάεργος Ἀπόλλων·
ὦ πάτερ ἦ τάχα μῦθον ἀκούσεαι οὐκ ἀλαπαδνὸν
κερτομέων ὡς οἶος ἐγὼ φιλοληΐος εἰμι.
παῖδά τιν' εὗρον τόνδε διαπρύσιον κεραϊστὴν
Κυλλήνης ἐν ὄρεσσι πολὺν διὰ χῶρον ἀνύσσας
κέρτομον, οἷον ἐγώ γε θεῶν οὐκ ἄλλον ὄπωπα
οὐδ' ἀνδρῶν, ὁπόσοι λησίμβροτοί εἰσ' ἐπὶ γαῖαν.
κλέψας δ' ἐκ λειμῶνος ἐμὰς βοῦς ᾤχετ' ἐλαύνων
ἑσπέριος παρὰ θῖνα πολυφλοίσβοιο θαλάσσης
εὐθὺ Πύλον δ' ἐλάων· τὰ δ' ἄρ' ἴχνια δοιὰ πέλωρα
οἷά τ' ἀγάσσασθαι καὶ ἀγαυοῦ δαίμονος ἔργα.

313 ἐρέεινον *p*: ἐρέεινεν M Θ 315 φωνῶν Wolf: φωνὴν codd. lacunam statuit Allen post hunc versum 322 δὲ τέρθρον ἵκοντο M At D L Π: δ' ἵκοντο κάρηνα E T L^m Π^m *p* 325 εὐμιλίη M: εὐμυλίη Ψ: εὐωχίη West: alii alia 326 μετὰ χρυσόθρονον ἠῶ E T L^m Π^m: ποτὶ πτύχας Οὐλύμποιο M At D L Π *p* 339 γαῖαν M: γαίῃ Ψ 342 εὐθὺ Πύλονδ' Clarke: εὐθύπυλονδ' M: εὐθυπόρονδ' Ψ δῖα *p*: δοιά cet. 343 ἀγάσσασθαι Ilgen: ἀγάσασθαι M: ἀγάσσεσθαι Ψ

τῆισιν μὲν γὰρ βουσὶν ἐς ἀσφοδελὸν λειμῶνα
ἀντία βήματ᾽ ἔχουσα κόνις ἀνέφαινε μέλαινα·
αὐτὸς δ᾽ οὗτος ἄδεκτος ἀμήχανος, οὔτ᾽ ἄρα ποσσὶν
οὔτ᾽ ἄρα χερσὶν ἔβαινε διὰ ψαμαθώδεα χῶρον·
ἀλλ᾽ ἄλλην τινὰ μῆτιν ἔχων διέτριβε κέλευθα
τοῖα πέλωρ᾽ ὡς εἴ τις ἀραιῆισι δρυσὶ βαίνοι.
ὄφρα μὲν οὖν ἐδίωκε διὰ ψαμαθώδεα χῶρον,
ῥεῖα μάλ᾽ ἴχνια πάντα διέπρεπεν ἐν κονίηισιν·
αὐτὰρ ἐπεὶ ψαμάθοιο μέγαν στίβον ἐξεπέρησεν,
ἄφραστος γένετ᾽ ὦκα βοῶν στίβος ἠδὲ καὶ αὐτοῦ
χῶρον ἀνὰ κρατερόν· τὸν δ᾽ ἐφράσατο βροτὸς ἀνὴρ
εἰς Πύλον εὐθὺς ἐλῶντα βοῶν γένος εὐρυμετώπων.
αὐτὰρ ἐπεὶ δὴ τὰς μὲν ἐν ἡσυχίηι κατέερξε
καὶ διαπυρπαλάμησεν ὁδοῦ τὸ μὲν ἔνθα τὸ δ᾽ ἔνθα,
ἐν λίκνωι κατέκειτο μελαίνηι νυκτὶ ἐοικὼς
ἄντρωι ἐν ἠερόεντι κατὰ ζόφον, οὐδέ κεν αὐτὸν
αἰετὸς ὀξὺ λάων ἐσκέψατο· πολλὰ δὲ χερσὶν
αὐγὰς ὠμόργαζε δολοφροσύνην ἀλεγύνων.
αὐτὸς δ᾽ αὐτίκα μῦθον ἀπηλεγέως ἀγόρευεν·
οὐκ ἴδον, οὐ πυθόμην, οὐκ ἄλλου μῦθον ἄκουσα,
οὐδέ κε μηνύσαιμ᾽, οὐδ᾽ ἂν μήνυτρον ἀροίμην.
  Ἦ τοι ἄρ᾽ ὣς εἰπὼν κατ᾽ ἄρ᾽ ἕζετο Φοῖβος Ἀπόλλων·
Ἑρμῆς δ᾽ ἄλλον μῦθον ἐν ἀθανάτοισιν ἔειπε,
δείξατο δ᾽ εἰς Κρονίωνα θεῶν σημάντορα πάντων·
  Ζεῦ πάτερ ἦ τοι ἐγώ σοι ἀληθείην ἀγορεύσω·
νημερτής τε γάρ εἰμι καὶ οὐκ οἶδα ψεύδεσθαι.
ἦλθεν ἐς ἡμετέρου διζήμενος εἰλίποδας βοῦς
σήμερον ἠελίοιο νέον ἐπιτελλομένοιο,
οὐδὲ θεῶν μακάρων ἄγε μάρτυρας οὐδὲ κατόπτας.
μηνύειν δ᾽ ἐκέλευεν ἀναγκαίης ὑπὸ πολλῆς,
πολλὰ δέ μ᾽ ἠπείλησε βαλεῖν ἐς Τάρταρον εὐρύν,
οὕνεχ᾽ ὁ μὲν τέρεν ἄνθος ἔχει φιλοκυδέος ἥβης,
αὐτὰρ ἐγὼ χθιζὸς γενόμην – τὰ δέ τ᾽ οἶδε καὶ αὐτός –

346 οὗτος ἄδεκτος AHS: οὗτος ὅδ᾽ ἐκτὸς codd.: οὐϑ᾽ ὁδοῦ ἐκτὸς West 352 μέγαν Ψ: πολὺν M 356 κατέερξε *p*: κατέρεξε Θ: κατέρεξεν M 357 διαπυρπαλάμησεν Ilgen: διαπῦρ παλάμησεν M: διὰ πῦρ μάλ᾽ ἄμησεν Ψ 360 λάων, ss. βλέπων E L 361 ὠμόργαζε Ilgen: ὠμάρταζε codd. plerique (ὠμ- L *p*): ὠμόρταζε T ἀλεγύνων Θ: ἀλεγίζων M: ἀλεείνων *p* 366 Ἑρμῆς δ᾽ ἄλλον μῦϑον ἐν ἀϑανάτοισιν ἔειπεν E T L^m^ Π^m^: Ἑρμῆς δ᾽ αὖϑ᾽ ἑτέρωϑεν ἀμειβόμενος ἔπος ηὔδα M At D L Π *p* 368 ἀγορεύσω M: καταλέξω Ψ 371 νεόν γ᾽ *p* (praeter A Q) D^m^: νεὸν cet.

οὔ τι βοῶν ἐλατῆρι κραταιῶι φωτὶ ἐοικώς.
πείθεο, καὶ γὰρ ἐμεῖο πατὴρ φίλος εὔχεαι εἶναι,
ὡς οὐκ οἴκαδ' ἔλασσα βόας, ὣς ὄλβιος εἴην,
οὐδ' ὑπὲρ οὐδὸν ἔβην· τὸ δέ τ' ἀτρεκέως ἀγορεύω.
Ἠέλιον δὲ μάλ' αἰδέομαι καὶ δαίμονας ἄλλους,
καὶ σὲ φιλῶ καὶ τοῦτον ὀπίζομαι· οἶσθα καὶ αὐτὸς
ὡς οὐκ αἴτιός εἰμι· μέγαν δ' ἐπιδώσομαι ὅρκον·
οὐ μὰ τάδ' ἀθανάτων εὐκόσμητα προθύραια.
καί ποτ' ἐγὼ τούτωι τείσω ποτὶ νηλέα φωρὴν
καὶ κρατερῶι περ ἐόντι· σὺ δ' ὁπλοτέροισιν ἄρηγε.
  Ὣς φάτ' ἐπιλλίζων Κυλλήνιος Ἀργειφόντης,
καὶ τὸ σπάργανον εἶχεν ἐπ' ὠλένηι οὐδ' ἀπέβαλλε.
Ζεὺς δὲ μέγ' ἐξεγέλασσεν ἰδὼν κακομηδέα παῖδα
εὖ καὶ ἐπισταμένως ἀρνεύμενον ἀμφὶ βόεσσιν.
ἀμφοτέρους δ' ἐκέλευσεν ὁμόφρονα θυμὸν ἔχοντας
ζητεύειν, Ἑρμῆν δὲ διάκτορον ἡγεμονεύειν,
καὶ δεῖξαι τὸν χῶρον ἐπ' ἀβλαβίηισι νόοιο
ὅππηι δὴ αὖτ' ἀπέκρυψε βοῶν ἴφθιμα κάρηνα.
νεῦσεν δὲ Κρονίδης, ἐπεπείθετο δ' ἀγλαὸς Ἑρμῆς·
ῥηϊδίως γὰρ ἔπειθε Διὸς νόος αἰγιόχοιο.
τὼ δ' ἄμφω σπεύδοντε Διὸς περικαλλέα τέκνα
ἐς Πύλον ἠμαθόεντα ἐπ' Ἀλφειοῦ πόρον ἶξον·
ἀγροὺς δ' ἐξίκοντο καὶ αὔλιον ὑψιμέλαθρον
ἧχοῦ δὴ τὰ χρήματ' ἀτάλλετο νυκτὸς ἐν ὥρηι.
ἔνθ' Ἑρμῆς μὲν ἔπειτα κιὼν παρὰ λάϊνον ἄντρον
εἰς φῶς ἐξήλαυνε βοῶν ἴφθιμα κάρηνα·
Λητοΐδης δ' ἀπάτερθεν ἰδὼν ἐνόησε βοείας
πέτρηι ἐπ' ἠλιβάτωι, τάχα δ' ἤρετο κύδιμον Ἑρμῆν·
  Πῶς ἐδύνω δολομῆτα δύω βόε δειροτομῆσαι,
ὧδε νεογνὸς ἐὼν καὶ νήπιος; αὐτὸς ἐγώ γε
θαυμαίνω κατόπισθε τὸ σὸν κράτος· οὐδὲ τί σε χρὴ
μακρὸν ἀέξεσθαι Κυλλήνιε Μαιάδος υἱέ.

380 τὸ δέ τ' Hermann: τόδε δ' codd. 381 δὲ μάλ' αἰδέομαι M: μάλ' αἰδέομαι Ψ 383 ἐπιδώσομαι Barnes: ἐπιδεύομαι M: ἐπιδαίομαι Ψ 385 καί ποτ' codd.: οὔ ποτ' Ilgen: μή ποτ' West: καί ποῦ Hermann τείσω West: τίσω codd. ποτὶ M: ποτὲ Ψ φωρὴν Hermann: φώρην M: φωνὴν Ψ 397 σπεύδοντε M *p*: σπεύδοντο Θ 398 ἠμαθόεντα ἐπ' M *p*: ἠμαθόεντα δ' ἐπ' Θ 400 ἧχου δὴ Fick: ἦχ' (ἧχ') οὐ (οὗ) δὴ Ψ: ὅχου δὲ M χρήματ' ἀτάλλετο Chalcondyles: χρήματ' ἀτιτάλλετο Ψ (ἀντιτάλλετο T: ἀντιβάλλετο E): χρήματα τιτάλλετο M: κτήνε' ἀτάλλετο Allen and Sikes 401 παρὰ Ψ: ἐς M 402 φῶς codd.: φάος Hermann 403 ἀπάτερθεν Ψ: ἀπάνευθεν M 408 ἀέξεσθαι Ψ: ἀέξασθαι M

Ὣς ἄρ' ἔφη, καὶ χερσὶ περίστρεφε καρτερὰ δεσμὰ
ἄγνου· ταὶ δ' ὑπὸ ποσσὶ κατὰ χθονὸς αἶψα φύοντο
αὐτόθεν ἐμβολάδην ἐστραμμέναι ἀλλήλῃσι
ῥεῖά τε καὶ πάσῃισιν ἐπ' ἀγραύλοισι βόεσσιν
Ἑρμέω βουλῇσι κλεψίφρονος· αὐτὰρ Ἀπόλλων
θαύμασεν ἀθρήσας. τότε δὴ κρατὺς Ἀργειφόντης
χῶρον ὑποβλήδην ἐσκέψατο πῦρ ἀμαρύσσων
ἐγκρύψαι μεμαώς· Λητοῦς δ' ἐρικυδέος υἱὸν
ῥεῖα μάλ' ἐπρήϋνεν ἑκηβόλον, ὡς ἔθελ' αὐτός,
καὶ κρατερόν περ ἐόντα· λύρην δ' ἐπ' ἀριστερὰ χειρὸς
πλήκτρωι ἐπειρήτιζε κατὰ μέλος· ἣ δ' ὑπὸ χειρὸς
σμερδαλέον κονάβησε, γέλασσε δὲ Φοῖβος Ἀπόλλων
γηθήσας, ἐρατὴ δὲ διὰ φρένας ἤλυθ' ἰωὴ
θεσπεσίης ἐνοπῆς, καί μιν γλυκὺς ἵμερος ἥιρει
θυμῶι ἀκουάζοντα· λύρηι δ' ἐρατὸν κιθαρίζων
στῆ ῥ' ὅ γε θαρσήσας ἐπ' ἀριστερὰ Μαιάδος υἱὸς
Φοίβου Ἀπόλλωνος, τάχα δὲ λιγέως κιθαρίζων
γηρύετ' ἀμβολάδην, ἐρατὴ δέ οἱ ἕσπετο φωνή,
κραίνων ἀθανάτους τε θεοὺς καὶ γαῖαν ἐρεμνὴν
ὡς τὰ πρῶτα γένοντο καὶ ὡς λάχε μοῖραν ἕκαστος.
Μνημοσύνην μὲν πρῶτα θεῶν ἐγέραιρεν ἀοιδῆι
μητέρα Μουσάων, ἡ γὰρ λάχε Μαιάδος υἱόν·
τοὺς δὲ κατὰ πρέσβιν τε καὶ ὡς γεγάασιν ἕκαστος
ἀθανάτους ἐγέραιρε θεοὺς Διὸς ἀγλαὸς υἱὸς
πάντ' ἐνέπων κατὰ κόσμον, ὑπωλένιον κιθαρίζων.
τὸν δ' ἔρος ἐν στήθεσσιν ἀμήχανος αἴνυτο θυμόν,
καί μιν φωνήσας ἔπεα πτερόεντα προσηύδα·

Βουφόνε μηχανιῶτα πονεύμενε δαιτὸς ἑταῖρε
πεντήκοντα βοῶν ἀντάξια ταῦτα μέμηλας.
ἡσυχίως καὶ ἔπειτα διακρινέεσθαι ὀΐω.
νῦν δ' ἄγε μοι τόδε εἰπὲ πολύτροπε Μαιάδος υἱὲ
ἦ σοί γ' ἐκ γενετῆς τάδ' ἅμ' ἕσπετο θαυματὰ ἔργα
ἦέ τις ἀθανάτων ἠὲ θνητῶν ἀνθρώπων
δῶρον ἀγαυὸν ἔδωκε καὶ ἔφρασε θέσπιν ἀοιδήν;

411 ἐμβολάδην Ψ: ἀμβολάδην M 412 ἀγραύλοισι *p*: ἀγραύλῃσι M Θ 415 post hunc versum lacunam statuit Baumeister 416 post hunc versum lacunam statuit Radermacher 418 post hunc versum lacunam statuit Hermann 418 λύρην Stephanus: λαβὼν codd. χειρὸς Ψ: λύρην M 422 om. Ψ: habet M 423 θυμῶι codd.: θυμὸν West 431 πρέσβιν Matthiae: πρέσβην codd. ἕκαστος Ψ: ἅπαντες M 433 ὑπωλένιον Barnes: ἐπωλένιον codd. 437 μέμηλας codd.: μέμηδας Page 440 γενετῆς M: γενεῆς Ψ

θαυμασίην γὰρ τήνδε νεήφατον ὄσσαν ἀκούω,
ἣν οὔ πώ ποτέ φημι δαήμεναι οὔτε τιν' ἀνδρῶν,
οὔτε τιν' ἀθανάτων οἳ Ὀλύμπια δώματ' ἔχουσι,
νόσφι σέθεν φιλῆτα Διὸς καὶ Μαιάδος υἱέ.
τίς τέχνη, τίς μοῦσα ἀμηχανέων μελεδώνων,
τίς τρίβος; ἀτρεκέως γὰρ ἅμα τρία πάντα πάρεστιν
εὐφροσύνην καὶ ἔρωτα καὶ ἥδυμον ὕπνον ἑλέσθαι.
καὶ γὰρ ἐγὼ Μούσῃσιν Ὀλυμπιάδεσσιν ὀπηδός,
τῇσι χοροί τε μέλουσι καὶ ἀγλαὸς οἶμος ἀοιδῆς
καὶ μολπὴ τεθαλυῖα καὶ ἱμερόεις βρόμος αὐλῶν·
ἀλλ' οὔ πώ τί μοι ὧδε μετὰ φρεσὶν ἄλλο μέλησεν
οἷα νέων θαλίῃς ἐνδέξια ἔργα πέλονται·
θαυμάζω Διὸς υἱὲ τάδ' ὡς ἐρατὸν κιθαρίζεις.
νῦν δ' ἐπεὶ οὖν ὀλίγος περ ἐὼν κλυτὰ μήδεα οἶδας,
ἷζε πέπον καὶ μῦθον ἐπαίνει πρεσβυτέροισι.
νῦν γάρ τοι κλέος ἔσται ἐν ἀθανάτοισι θεοῖσι
σοί τ' αὐτῷ καὶ μητρί· τὸ δ' ἀτρεκέως ἀγορεύσω·
ναὶ μὰ τόδε κρανάϊνον ἀκόντιον ἦ μὲν ἐγώ σε
κυδρὸν ἐν ἀθανάτοισι καὶ ὄλβιον ἡγεμονεύσω,
δώσω τ' ἀγλαὰ δῶρα καὶ ἐς τέλος οὐκ ἀπατήσω.
Τὸν δ' Ἑρμῆς μύθοισιν ἀμείβετο κερδαλέοισιν·
εἰρωτᾷς μ' Ἑκάεργε περιφραδές· αὐτὰρ ἐγώ σοι
τέχνης ἡμετέρης ἐπιβήμεναι οὔ τι μεγαίρω.
σήμερον εἰδήσεις· ἐθέλω δέ τοι ἤπιος εἶναι
βουλῇ καὶ μύθοισι, σὺ δὲ φρεσὶ πάντ' εὖ οἶδας.
πρῶτος γὰρ Διὸς υἱὲ μετ' ἀθανάτοισι θαάσσεις
ἠΰς τε κρατερός τε· φιλεῖ δέ σε μητίετα Ζεὺς
ἐκ πάσης ὁσίης, ἔπορεν δέ τοι ἀγλαὰ δῶρα
καὶ τιμάς· σὲ δέ φασι δαήμεναι ἐκ Διὸς ὀμφῆς
μαντείας, Ἑκάεργε, Διὸς πάρα θέσφατα πάντα·
τῶν νῦν αὐτὸς ἔγωγε †παῖδ' ἀφνειὸν δεδάηκα.†
σοὶ δ' αὐτάγρετόν ἐστι δαήμεναι ὅττι μενοινᾷς.
ἀλλ' ἐπεὶ οὖν τοι θυμὸς ἐπιθύει κιθαρίζειν,

446 φιλῆτα Aldina: φιλητὰ M Θ: φηλητὰ *p* 449 ἥδυμον MΘ: νήδυμον *p* 451 οἶμος Ψ: ὕμνος M x^{m} 453 ἄλλο μέλησεν M: ὧδε μέλησεν Ψ 456 οἶδας Ψ: οἶσθα M 457–8 om. Ψ 457 μῦθον Ruhnken: θυμὸν M 459 τὸ δ' Hermann: τόδ' codd. 460 κρανάϊνον A At Γ: κρανάϊον cet. ἐγώ σε M At D Π *p*: ἔγωγε E T L 468 θαάσσεις Ψ: θοάσσεις M 471 σὲ δέ M: σέ γέ Ψ 472 μαντείας, Ἑκάεργε Matthiae: μαντείας θ' (vel τ') Ἑκάεργε codd. πάρα Stephanus: παρὰ, παρα codd. 473 τῶν E T L^{m} Π^{m}: καὶ cet. ἔγωγε παῖδ' ἀφνειὸν δεδάηκα codd.: ἐγώ σε Hermann: μάλ' ἀφνειὸν Evelyn-White: alii alia 474 αὐταγρετόν Chalcondyles: αὖτ' ἄγρετόν codd.

μέλπεο καὶ κιθάριζε καὶ ἀγλαΐας ἀλέγυνε
δέγμενος ἐξ ἐμέθεν· σὺ δ᾽ ἐμοὶ φίλε κῦδος ὄπαζε.
εὐμόλπει μετὰ χερσὶν ἔχων λιγύφωνον ἑταίρην
καλὰ καὶ εὖ κατὰ κόσμον ἐπισταμένην ἀγορεύειν.
εὔκηλός μιν ἔπειτα φέρειν εἰς δαῖτα θάλειαν
καὶ χορὸν ἱμερόεντα καὶ ἐς φιλοκυδέα κῶμον,
εὐφροσύνην νυκτός τε καὶ ἤματος. ὅς τις ἂν αὐτὴν
τέχνηι καὶ σοφίηι δεδαημένος ἐξερεείνηι
φθεγγομένη παντοῖα νόωι χαρίεντα διδάσκει
ῥεῖα συνηθείηισιν ἀθυρομένη μαλακῆισιν,
ἐργασίην φεύγουσα δυήπαθον· ὃς δέ κεν αὐτὴν
νῆϊς ἐὼν τὸ πρῶτον ἐπιζαφελῶς ἐρεείνηι,
μὰψ αὔτως κεν ἔπειτα μετήορά τε θρυλίζοι.
σοὶ δ᾽ αὐτάγρετόν ἐστι δαήμεναι ὅττι μενοινᾶις.
καί τοι ἐγὼ δώσω ταύτην Διὸς ἀγλαὲ κοῦρε·
ἡμεῖς δ᾽ αὖτ᾽ ὄρεός τε καὶ ἱπποβότου πεδίοιο
βουσὶ νομοὺς Ἑκάεργε νομεύσομεν ἀγραύλοισιν.
ἔνθεν ἅλις τέξουσι βόες ταύροισι μιγεῖσαι
μίγδην θηλείας τε καὶ ἄρσενας· οὐδέ τί σε χρὴ
κερδαλέον περ ἐόντα περιζαμενῶς κεχολῶσθαι.
  Ὣς εἰπὼν ὤρεξ᾽, ὁ δ᾽ ἐδέξατο Φοῖβος Ἀπόλλων,
Ἑρμῆι δ᾽ ἐγγυάλιξεν ἔχων μάστιγα φαεινήν,
βουκολίας τ᾽ ἐπέτελλεν· ἔδεκτο δὲ Μαιάδος υἱὸς
γηθήσας· κίθαριν δὲ λαβὼν ἐπ᾽ ἀριστερὰ χειρὸς
Λητοῦς ἀγλαὸς υἱὸς ἄναξ ἑκάεργος Ἀπόλλων
πλήκτρωι ἐπειρήτιζε κατὰ μέλος, ἡ δ᾽ ὑπὸ νέρθεν
ἱμερόεν κονάβησε, θεὸς δ᾽ ὑπὸ καλὸν ἄεισεν.
  Ἔνθα βόας μὲν ἔπειτα ποτὶ ζάθεον λειμῶνα
ἐτραπέτην· αὐτοὶ δὲ Διὸς περικαλλέα τέκνα
ἄψορροι πρὸς Ὄλυμπον ἀγάννιφον ἐρρώσαντο
τερπόμενοι φόρμιγγι, χάρη δ᾽ ἄρα μητίετα Ζεύς,
ἄμφω δ᾽ ἐς φιλότητα συνήγαγε. καὶ τὸ μὲν Ἑρμῆς

477 δ᾽ ἐμοὶ Radermacher: δέ μοι codd. 478 γλυκύφωνον E T: λιγύφωνον cet. ἑταῖρον *p*: ἑταίρην cet. 479 ἐπισταμένην Barnes: ἐπισταμένως codd. 480 εὔκηλός μιν Ilgen: εὔκηλος μὲν codd. 481 χορὸν M Θ: χῶρον *p* φιλοκυδέα M Θ: φιλομειδέα *p* 486 φεύγουσα M: φθέγγουσα Ψ 487 ἐρεείνηι M: ἐρέεινε Ψ 488 θρυλίζοι Schneidewin: θρυαλίζοι codd. 489 αὐτάγρετόν Aldina: αὖτ᾽ ἄγρετόν codd. 497 ἔχων codd.: ἔχειν D'Orville: ἑκὼν Martin 501 ὑπὸ νέρθεν M: ὑπὸ καλὸν Ψ 502 ἱμερόεν Ψ: σμερδαλέον M καλὸν M: μέλος (μέλλος) Ψ 503 ἔνθα Ψ: καί ῥα M βόας M: βόες Ψ ποτὶ Ψ: κατὰ M 507 καὶ τὸ Ψ: καὶ τὰ M

Λητοΐδην ἐφίλησε διαμπερὲς ὡς ἔτι καὶ νῦν,
. . .
σήματ', ἐπεὶ κίθαριν μὲν Ἑκηβόλωι ἐγγυάλιξεν
ἱμερτὴν δεδαώς, ὁ δ' ὑπωλένιον κιθάριζεν·
αὐτὸς δ' αὖθ' ἑτέρης σοφίης ἐκμάσσατο τέχνην·
συρίγγων ἐνοπὴν ποιήσατο τηλόθ' ἀκουστήν.
καὶ τότε Λητοΐδης Ἑρμῆν πρὸς μῦθον ἔειπε·
Δείδια Μαιάδος υἱὲ διάκτορε ποικιλομῆτα
μή μοι ἀνακλέψηις κίθαριν καὶ καμπύλα τόξα·
τιμὴν γὰρ πὰρ Ζηνὸς ἔχεις ἐπαμοίβιμα ἔργα
θήσειν ἀνθρώποισι κατὰ χθόνα πουλυβότειραν.
ἀλλ' εἴ μοι τλαίης γε θεῶν μέγαν ὅρκον ὀμόσσαι,
ἢ κεφαλῆι νεύσας ἢ ἐπὶ Στυγὸς ὄβριμον ὕδωρ,
πάντ' ἂν ἐμῶι θυμῶι κεχαρισμένα καὶ φίλα ἔρδοις.
Καὶ τότε Μαιάδος υἱὸς ὑποσχόμενος κατένευσε
μή ποτ' ἀποκλέψειν ὅσ' Ἑκηβόλος ἐκτεάτισται,
μηδέ ποτ' ἐμπελάσειν πυκινῶι δόμωι· αὐτὰρ Ἀπόλλων
Λητοΐδης κατένευσεν ἐπ' ἀρθμῶι καὶ φιλότητι
μή τινα φίλτερον ἄλλον ἐν ἀθανάτοισιν ἔσεσθαι,
μήτε θεὸν μήτ' ἄνδρα Διὸς γόνον· ἐκ δὲ τέλειον
σύμβολον ἀθανάτων ποιήσομαι, ἠδ' ἅμα πάντως
πιστὸν ἐμῶι θυμῶι καὶ τίμιον· αὐτὰρ ἔπειτα
ὄλβου καὶ πλούτου δώσω περικαλλέα ῥάβδον
χρυσείην τριπέτηλον, ἀκήριον ἥ σε φυλάξει
πάντας ἐπικραίνουσα θεμοὺς ἐπέων τε καὶ ἔργων
τῶν ἀγαθῶν ὅσα φημὶ δαήμεναι ἐκ Διὸς ὀμφῆς.
μαντείην δὲ φέριστε διοτρεφὲς ἣν ἐρεείνεις
οὔτε σε θέσφατόν ἐστι δαήμεναι οὔτε τιν' ἄλλον
ἀθανάτων· τὸ γὰρ οἶδε Διὸς νόος· αὐτὰρ ἐγώ γε
πιστωθεὶς κατένευσα καὶ ὤμοσα καρτερὸν ὅρκον
μή τινα νόσφιν ἐμεῖο θεῶν αἰειγενετάων
ἄλλον γ' εἴσεσθαι Ζηνὸς πυκινόφρονα βουλήν.
καὶ σὺ κασίγνητε χρυσόρραπι μή με κέλευε

post 508 lacunam statuit West, e.g. <Λητοΐδης δὲ κασιγνήτου φιλότητος ἀνέγνω> σήματ', 510 ὑπωλένιον codd.: ἐπωλένιον Ilgen (cf. 433) 515 ἀνακλέψηις Ψ: ἅμα κλέψηις M 516 ἐπαμοίβιμα Wolf: ἐπ' ἀμοίβια Ψ: ἐπ' ἀμοίβημα M 526 post hunc versum lacunam statuit Allen 527 πάντως Richardson: πάντων codd. post hunc versum lacunam statuit Radermacher 531 θεμοὺς Ludwich: θεοὺς codd.: alii alia 533 διοτρεφὲς Θ: διαμπερὲς M ἣν ἐρεείνεις codd.: ἣν ἐρεείνῃς Hermann 534 ἄλλον Ψ: ἄλλων M

θέσφατα πιφαύσκειν ὅσα μήδεται εὐρύοπα Ζεύς.
ἀνθρώπων δ' ἄλλον δηλήσομαι, ἄλλον ὀνήσω,
πολλὰ περιτροπέων ἀμεγάρτων φῦλ' ἀνθρώπων.
καὶ μὲν ἐμῆς ὀμφῆς ἀπονήσεται ὅς τις ἂν ἔλθηι
φωνῆι τ' ἠδὲ ποτῆισι τελήεντων οἰωνῶν·
οὗτος ἐμῆς ὀμφῆς ἀπονήσεται οὐδ' ἀπατήσω.
ὃς δέ κε μαψιλόγοισι πιθήσας οἰωνοῖσι
μαντείην ἐθέληισι παρὲκ νόον ἐξερεείνειν
ἡμετέρην, νοέειν δὲ θεῶν πλέον αἰὲν ἐόντων,
φήμ' ἁλίην ὁδὸν εἶσιν, ἐγὼ δέ κε δῶρα δεχοίμην.
ἄλλο δέ τοι ἐρέω Μαίης ἐρικυδέος υἱὲ
καὶ Διὸς αἰγιόχοιο, θεῶν ἐριούνιε δαῖμον·
σεμναὶ γάρ τινες εἰσὶ κασίγνηται γεγαυῖαι
παρθένοι ὠκείηισιν ἀγαλλόμεναι πτερύγεσσι
τρεῖς· κατὰ δὲ κρατὸς πεπαλαγμέναι ἄλφιτα λευκὰ
οἰκία ναιετάουσιν ὑπὸ πτυχὶ Παρνησοῖο
μαντείης ἀπάνευθε διδάσκαλοι ἣν ἐπὶ βουσὶ
παῖς ἔτ' ἐὼν μελέτησα· πατὴρ δ' ἐμὸς οὐκ ἀλέγιζεν.
ἐντεῦθεν δὴ ἔπειτα ποτώμεναι ἄλλοτε ἄλληι
κηρία βόσκονται καί τε κραίνουσιν ἕκαστα.
αἱ δ' ὅτε μὲν θυίωσιν ἐδηδυῖαι μέλι χλωρὸν
προφρονέως ἐθέλουσιν ἀληθείην ἀγορεύειν·
ἢν δ' ἀπονοσφισθῶσι θεῶν ἡδεῖαν ἐδωδὴν
ψεύδονται δήπειτα δι' ἀλλήλων δονέουσαι.
τάς τοι ἔπειτα δίδωμι, σὺ δ' ἀτρεκέως ἐρεείνων
σὴν αὐτοῦ φρένα τέρπε, καί εἰ βροτὸν ἄνδρα δαείης
πολλάκι σῆς ὀμφῆς ἐπακούσεται αἴ κε τύχηισι.
ταῦτ' ἔχε Μαιάδος υἱὲ καὶ ἀγραύλους ἕλικας βοῦς,
ἵππους τ' ἀμφιπόλευε καὶ ἡμιόνους ταλαεργούς·
καὶ χαροποῖσι λέουσι καὶ ἀργιόδουσι σύεσσι
καὶ κυσὶ καὶ μήλοισιν, ὅσα τρέφει εὐρεῖα χθών,
πᾶσι δ' ἐπὶ προβάτοισιν ἀνάσσειν κύδιμον Ἑρμῆν,
οἶον δ' εἰς Ἀΐδην τετελεσμένον ἄγγελον εἶναι,

540 μήδεται M *p* *x*: βούλεται At D 543 ὅς τις ἂν ἔλθηι Θ: ὅστις ἂν ἔλθοι *p*: οὐδ' ἀπατήσω M A[ac] 544 φωνῆι τ' ἠδὲ ποτῆισι Ruhnken: φωνῆι τ' ἠδεπότηισι M: φωνῆι καὶ πτερύγεσσι Ψ 547 ἐθέληισι *p*: ἐθελήσει M Θ 552 σεμναὶ M: μοῖραι Ψ 557 ἀλέγιζεν Hermann: ἀλέγυνεν M Θ: ἀλέγεινεν *p* 558 ἄλλοτε ἄλληι Schneidewin: ἄλλοτ' ἐπ' ἄλληι codd. 560 θυίωσιν M: θύσωσιν *p*: θυίσωσιν Θ 561 ἐθέλουσιν M At D *p*: ἐθέλωσιν *x* 563 ita *x*[m] (δένεουσαι, corr. Baumeister): πειρῶνται δ' ἤπειτα παρὲξ ὁδὸν ἡγεμονεύειν MΨ 565 εἰ M *p* *x*: ἢν At D ἄνδρα δαείης Ψ: ἄνδρ' ἀδαῆ M 568 post hunc versum lacunam statuit Wolf

ὅς τ' ἄδοτός περ ἐὼν δώσει γέρας οὐκ ἐλάχιστον.
  Οὕτω Μαιάδος υἱὸν ἄναξ ἐφίλησεν Ἀπόλλων
παντοίηι φιλότητι, χάριν δ' ἐπέθηκε Κρονίων.
πᾶσι δ' ὅ γε θνητοῖσι καὶ ἀθανάτοισιν ὁμιλεῖ·
παῦρα μὲν οὖν ὀνίνησι, τὸ δ' ἄκριτον ἠπεροπεύει
νύκτα δι' ὀρφναίην φῦλα θνητῶν ἀνθρώπων.
  Καὶ σὺ μὲν οὕτω χαῖρε Διὸς καὶ Μαιάδος υἱέ·
αὐτὰρ ἐγὼ καὶ σεῖο καὶ ἄλλης μνήσομ' ἀοιδῆς.

ΕΙΣ ΑΦΡΟΔΙΤΗΝ

  Μοῦσά μοι ἔννεπε ἔργα πολυχρύσου Ἀφροδίτης
Κύπριδος, ἥ τε θεοῖσιν ἐπὶ γλυκὺν ἵμερον ὦρσε
καί τ' ἐδαμάσσατο φῦλα καταθνητῶν ἀνθρώπων,
οἰωνούς τε διιπετέας καὶ θηρία πάντα,
ἠμὲν ὅσ' ἤπειρος πολλὰ τρέφει ἠδ' ὅσα πόντος·
πᾶσιν δ' ἔργα μέμηλεν ἐϋστεφάνου Κυθερείης.
τρισσὰς δ' οὐ δύναται πεπιθεῖν φρένας οὐδ' ἀπατῆσαι·
κούρην τ' αἰγιόχοιο Διὸς γλαυκῶπιν Ἀθήνην·
οὐ γάρ οἱ εὔαδεν ἔργα πολυχρύσου Ἀφροδίτης,
ἀλλ' ἄρα οἱ πόλεμοί τε ἅδον καὶ ἔργον Ἄρηος,
ὑσμῖναί τε μάχαι τε καὶ ἀγλαὰ ἔργ' ἀλεγύνειν.
πρώτη τέκτονας ἄνδρας ἐπιχθονίους ἐδίδαξε
ποιῆσαι σατίνας καὶ ἅρματα ποικίλα χαλκῶι·
ἡ δέ τε παρθενικὰς ἁπαλόχροας ἐν μεγάροισιν
ἀγλαὰ ἔργ' ἐδίδαξεν ἐπὶ φρεσὶ θεῖσα ἑκάστηι.
οὐδέ ποτ' Ἄρτεμιδα χρυσηλάκατον κελαδεινὴν
δάμναται ἐν φιλότητι φιλομμειδὴς Ἀφροδίτη·
καὶ γὰρ τῆι ἅδε τόξα καὶ οὔρεσι θῆρας ἐναίρειν,
φόρμιγγές τε χοροί τε διαπρύσιοί τ' ὀλολυγαὶ
ἄλσεά τε σκιόεντα δικαίων τε πτόλις ἀνδρῶν.
οὐδὲ μὲν αἰδοίηι κούρηι ἅδεν ἔργ' Ἀφροδίτης
Ἱστίηι, ἣν πρώτην τέκετο Κρόνος ἀγκυλομήτης,
αὖτις δ' ὁπλοτάτην, βουλῆι Διὸς αἰγιόχοιο,
πότνιαν, ἣν ἐμνῶντο Ποσειδάων καὶ Ἀπόλλων·
ἡ δὲ μάλ' οὐκ ἔθελεν ἀλλὰ στερεῶς ἀπέειπεν,

576 ἀθανάτοισιν ὁμίλει Ψ (ὁμιλεῖ Stephanus): ἀθανάτοισι νομίζων M   8 γλαυκῶπιν M : γλαυκώπιδ' Ψ   13 σατίνας τε Barnes : σατίνα M *p x* : σκυτίνα At D   18 καὶ γὰρ τῆι (τοι A Q, τοῖ B) ἅδε Ψ : πουλύχρυσα δὲ M   20 πτόλις Γ marg., ed. pr. : πόλις Θ : πόλεις M : πόνος *p*   22 Ἱστίηι *p x* Chalcondyles : ἑστίη At D M

ὤμοσε δὲ μέγαν ὅρκον, ὃ δὴ τετελεσμένος ἐστίν,
ἁψαμένη κεφαλῆς πατρὸς Διὸς αἰγιόχοιο
παρθένος ἔσσεσθαι πάντ' ἤματα, δῖα θεάων.
τῆι δὲ πατὴρ Ζεὺς δῶκε καλὸν γέρας ἀντὶ γάμοιο,
καί τε μέσωι οἴκωι κατ' ἄρ' ἕζετο πῖαρ ἑλοῦσα.
πᾶσιν δ' ἐν νηοῖσι θεῶν τιμάοχός ἐστι
καὶ παρὰ πᾶσι βροτοῖσι θεῶν πρέσβειρα τέτυκται.
τάων οὐ δύναται πεπιθεῖν φρένας οὐδ' ἀπατῆσαι·
τῶν δ' ἄλλων οὔ πέρ τι πεφυγμένον ἔστ' Ἀφροδίτην
οὔτε θεῶν μακάρων οὔτε θνητῶν ἀνθρώπων.
καί τε παρὲκ Ζηνὸς νόον ἤγαγε τερπικεραύνου,
ὅς τε μέγιστός τ' ἐστί, μεγίστης τ' ἔμμορε τιμῆς·
καί τε τοῦ εὖτ' ἐθέληι πυκινὰς φρένας ἐξαπαφοῦσα
ῥηϊδίως συνέμειξε καταθνητῆισι γυναιξὶν
Ἥρης ἐκλελαθοῦσα κασιγνήτης ἀλόχου τε,
ἣ μέγα εἶδος ἀρίστη ἐν ἀθανάτηισι θεῆισι,
κυδίστην δ' ἄρα μιν τέκετο Κρόνος ἀγκυλομήτης
μήτηρ τε Ῥείη· Ζεὺς δ' ἄφθιτα μήδεα εἰδὼς
αἰδοίην ἄλοχον ποιήσατο κέδν' εἰδυῖαν.
Τῆι δὲ καὶ αὐτῆι Ζεὺς γλυκὺν ἵμερον ἔμβαλε θυμῶι
ἀνδρὶ καταθνητῶι μιχθήμεναι, ὄφρα τάχιστα
μηδ' αὐτὴ βροτέης εὐνῆς ἀποεργμένη εἴη
καί ποτ' ἐπευξαμένη εἴπηι μετὰ πᾶσι θεοῖσιν
ἡδὺ γελοιήσασα φιλομμειδὴς Ἀφροδίτη
ὥς ῥα θεοὺς συνέμειξε καταθνητῆισι γυναιξὶ
καί τε καταθνητοὺς υἱεῖς τέκον ἀθανάτοισιν,
ὥς τε θεὰς ἀνέμειξε καταθνητοῖς ἀνθρώποις.
Ἀγχίσεω δ' ἄρα οἱ γλυκὺν ἵμερον ἔμβαλε θυμῶι,
ὃς τότ' ἐν ἀκροπόλοις ὄρεσιν πολυπιδάκου Ἴδης
βουκολέεσκεν βοῦς δέμας ἀθανάτοισιν ἐοικώς.
τὸν δήπειτα ἰδοῦσα φιλομμειδὴς Ἀφροδίτη
ἠράσατ', ἐκπάγλως δὲ κατὰ φρένας ἵμερος εἷλεν.
ἐς Κύπρον δ' ἐλθοῦσα θυώδεα νηὸν ἔδυνεν
ἐς Πάφον· ἔνθα δέ οἱ τέμενος βωμός τε θυώδης·
ἔνθ' ἥ γ' εἰσελθοῦσα θύρας ἐπέθηκε φαεινάς.

38 εὖτ' ἐθέληι M : εὖτ' ἐθέλοι At D : εὖτε θέλοι *p x* 39 συνέμειξε West (2003) : συνέμιξε codd. κατὰ θνητῆσι At : καταθνηιτῆσι M D *x* : καταθνητοῖσι *p* 50 συνέμειξε West : συνέμιξε Ψ : σύμμιξε M κατὰ θνητῆσι M Θ : κατὰ θνητοῖσι *p* 51 υἱεῖς codd. : υἱέας Faulkner τέκον M : τέκεν Ψ 52 ἀνέμειξε West: ἀνέμιξε codd. 56 δήπειτα Càssola : δ' ἤπειτα codd.

ἔνθα δέ μιν Χάριτες λοῦσαν καὶ χρῖσαν ἐλαίωι
ἀμβρότωι, οἷα θεοὺς ἐπενήνοθεν αἰὲν ἐόντας,
ἀμβροσίωι ἑδανῶι, τό ῥά οἱ τεθυωμένον ἦεν.
ἑσσαμένη δ᾿ εὖ πάντα περὶ χροῒ εἵματα καλὰ
χρυσῶι κοσμηθεῖσα φιλομμειδὴς Ἀφροδίτη
σεύατ᾿ ἐπὶ Τροίης προλιποῦσ᾿ εὐώδεα Κύπρον
ὕψι μετὰ νέφεσιν ῥίμφα πρήσσουσα κέλευθον.
Ἴδην δ᾿ ἵκανεν πολυπίδακα, μητέρα θηρῶν,
βῆ δ᾿ ἰθὺς σταθμοῖο δι᾿ οὔρεος· οἱ δὲ μετ᾿ αὐτὴν
σαίνοντες πολιοί τε λύκοι χαροποί τε λέοντες
ἄρκτοι παρδαλιές τε θοαὶ προκάδων ἀκόρητοι
ἤϊσαν· ἡ δ᾿ ὁρόωσα μετὰ φρεσὶ τέρπετο θυμὸν
καὶ τοῖς ἐν στήθεσσι βάλ᾿ ἵμερον, οἱ δ᾿ ἅμα πάντες
σύνδυο κοιμήσαντο κατὰ σκιόεντας ἐναύλους.
αὐτὴ δ᾿ ἐς κλισίας εὐποιήτους ἀφίκανε·
τὸν δ᾿ εὗρε σταθμοῖσι λελειμμένον οἶον ἀπ᾿ ἄλλων
Ἀγχίσην ἥρωα θεῶν ἄπο κάλλος ἔχοντα.
οἱ δ᾿ ἅμα βουσὶν ἕποντο νομοὺς κάτα ποιήεντας
πάντες, ὁ δὲ σταθμοῖσι λελειμμένος οἶος ἀπ᾿ ἄλλων
πωλεῖτ᾿ ἔνθα καὶ ἔνθα διαπρύσιον κιθαρίζων.
στῆ δ᾿ αὐτοῦ προπάροιθε Διὸς θυγάτηρ Ἀφροδίτη
παρθένωι ἀδμήτηι μέγεθος καὶ εἶδος ὁμοίη,
μή μιν ταρβήσειεν ἐν ὀφθαλμοῖσι νοήσας.
Ἀγχίσης δ᾿ ὁρόων ἐφράζετο θάμβαινέν τε
εἶδός τε μέγεθός τε καὶ εἵματα σιγαλόεντα.
πέπλον μὲν γὰρ ἕεστο φαεινότερον πυρὸς αὐγῆς,
εἶχε δ᾿ ἐπιγναμπτὰς ἕλικας κάλυκάς τε φαεινάς,
ὅρμοι δ᾿ ἀμφ᾿ ἁπαλῆι δειρῆι περικαλλέες ἦσαν
καλοὶ χρύσειοι παμποίκιλοι· ὡς δὲ σελήνη
στήθεσιν ἀμφ᾿ ἁπαλοῖσιν ἐλάμπετο, θαῦμα ἰδέσθαι.
Ἀγχίσην δ᾿ ἔρος εἷλεν, ἔπος δέ μιν ἀντίον ηὔδα·
    Χαῖρε ἄνασσ᾿, ἥ τις μακάρων τάδε δώμαθ᾿ ἱκάνεις,
Ἄρτεμις ἢ Λητὼ ἠὲ χρυσῆ Ἀφροδίτη
ἢ Θέμις ἠϋγενὴς ἠὲ γλαυκῶπις Ἀθήνη
ἤ πού τις Χαρίτων δεῦρ᾿ ἤλυθες, αἵ τε θεοῖσι

63 ἑδανῶι Clarke : ἑανῶ Θ : ἐανῶ M *p*   66 Τροίης M : Τροίην Ψ   Κύπρον Ψ : κῆπον M   67 *νέφεσι ῥίμφα* M : *νεφέεσσι θοῶς* Ψ : *νέφεσιν ῥίμφα* Allen   71 παρδάλιες Θ A Q V : πορδάλιες B L P   82 καὶ Θ P^{ac} V : τε καὶ A Q B Γ P^{2c} 84 θάμβαινέν *p* : θαύμαινέν Θ   87 ἐπιγναμπτὰς B Γ *x* : ἐπὶ γναμπτὰς At D *p* (praeter B Γ) : ἔπι γναμπτὰς Barnes

πᾶσιν ἑταιρίζουσι καὶ ἀθάνατοι καλέονται,
ἤ τις νυμφάων αἵ τ' ἄλσεα καλὰ νέμονται,
ἢ νυμφῶν αἳ καλὸν ὄρος τόδε ναιετάουσι
καὶ πηγὰς ποταμῶν καὶ πίσεα ποιήεντα.
σοὶ δ' ἐγὼ ἐν σκοπιῇι, περιφαινομένωι ἐνὶ χώρωι,
βωμὸν ποιήσω, ῥέξω δέ τοι ἱερὰ καλὰ
ὥρηισιν πάσηισι· σὺ δ' εὔφρονα θυμὸν ἔχουσα
δός με μετὰ Τρώεσσιν ἀριπρεπέ' ἔμμεναι ἄνδρα,
ποίει δ' εἰσοπίσω θαλερὸν γόνον, αὐτὰρ ἔμ' αὐτὸν
δηρὸν ἐῢ ζώειν καὶ ὁρᾶν φάος ἠελίοιο
ὄλβιον ἐν λαοῖς καὶ γήραος οὐδὸν ἱκέσθαι.
Τὸν δ' ἠμείβετ' ἔπειτα Διὸς θυγάτηρ Ἀφροδίτη·
Ἀγχίση, κύδιστε χαμαιγενέων ἀνθρώπων,
οὔ τίς τοι θεός εἰμι· τί μ' ἀθανάτηισιν ἐΐσκεις;
ἀλλὰ καταθνητή τε, γυνὴ δέ με γείνατο μήτηρ.
Ὀτρεὺς δ' ἐστὶ πατὴρ ὄνομα κλυτός, εἴ που ἀκούεις,
ὃς πάσης Φρυγίης εὐτειχήτοιο ἀνάσσει.
γλῶσσαν δ' ὑμετέρην τε καὶ ἡμετέρην σάφα οἶδα·
Τρωιὰς γὰρ μεγάρωι με τροφὸς τρέφεν, ἣ δὲ διάπρο
σμικρὴν παῖδ' ἀτίταλλε φίλης παρὰ μητρὸς ἑλοῦσα.
ὣς δή τοι γλῶσσάν γε καὶ ὑμετέρην εὖ οἶδα.
νῦν δέ μ' ἀνήρπαξε χρυσόρραπις Ἀργειφόντης
ἐκ χοροῦ Ἀρτέμιδος χρυσηλακάτου κελαδεινῆς.
πολλαὶ δὲ νύμφαι καὶ παρθένοι ἀλφεσίβοιαι
παίζομεν, ἀμφὶ δ' ὅμιλος ἀπείριτος ἐστεφάνωτο·
ἔνθεν μ' ἥρπαξε χρυσόρραπις Ἀργειφόντης,
πολλὰ δ' ἔπ' ἤγαγεν ἔργα καταθνητῶν ἀνθρώπων,
πολλὴν δ' ἄκληρόν τε καὶ ἄκτιτον, ἣν διὰ θῆρες
ὠμοφάγοι φοιτῶσι κατὰ σκιόεντας ἐναύλους,
οὐδὲ ποσὶ ψαύειν ἐδόκουν φυσιζόου αἴης·
Ἀγχίσεω δέ με φάσκε παραὶ λέχεσιν καλέεσθαι
κουριδίην ἄλοχον, σοὶ δ' ἀγλαὰ τέκνα τεκεῖσθαι.
αὐτὰρ ἐπεὶ δὴ δεῖξε καὶ ἔφρασεν ἦ τοι ὅ γ' αὖτις
ἀθανάτων μετὰ φῦλ' ἀπέβη κρατὺς Ἀργειφόντης·
αὐτὰρ ἐγώ σ' ἱκόμην, κρατερὴ δέ μοι ἔπλετ' ἀνάγκη.

97 om. E T   98 del. Ruhnken   99 πίσεα Ruhnken : πείσεα (ss. βη) L : βήσεα cet.   105 ἐῢ ζώειν Barnes : ἐϋζώειν codd.   110 τε codd. : γε Gemoll   113 ὑμετέρην τε Wolf : ὑμετέρην codd.   114 Τρωιὰς M : Τρωὸς Ψ   116 γε Hermann : τε codd.   123 ἄκτιτον M D L : ἄκτιστον At E T : ἄτικτον *p*   125 ψαύειν Ψ : ψαύσειν M   ἐδόκουν codd. : δόκεον La Roche

ἀλλά σε πρὸς Ζηνὸς γουνάζομαι ἠδὲ τοκήων
ἐσθλῶν· οὐ μὲν γάρ κε κακοὶ τοιόνδε τέκοιεν·
ἀδμήτην μ' ἀγαγὼν καὶ ἀπειρήτην φιλότητος
πατρί τε σῶι δεῖξον καὶ μητέρι κεδνὰ ἰδυίηι
σοῖς τε κασιγνήτοις οἵ τοι ὁμόθεν γεγάασιν·
οὔ σφιν ἀεικελίη νυὸς ἔσσομαι, ἀλλ' εἰκυῖα.
πέμψαι δ' ἄγγελον ὦκα μετὰ Φρύγας αἰολοπώλους
εἰπεῖν πατρί τ' ἐμῶι καὶ μητέρι κηδομένηι περ·
οἱ δέ κέ τοι χρυσόν τε ἅλις ἐσθῆτά θ' ὑφαντὴν
πέμψουσιν, σὺ δὲ πολλὰ καὶ ἀγλαὰ δέχθαι ἄποινα.
ταῦτα δὲ ποιήσας δαίνυ γάμον ἱμερόεντα
τίμιον ἀνθρώποισι καὶ ἀθανάτοισι θεοῖσιν.
Ὣς εἰποῦσα θεὰ γλυκὺν ἵμερον ἔμβαλε θυμῶι.
Ἀγχίσην δ' ἔρος εἷλεν, ἔπος τ' ἔφατ' ἔκ τ' ὀνόμαζεν·
Εἰ μὲν θνητή τ' ἐσσί, γυνὴ δέ σε γείνατο μήτηρ,
Ὀτρεὺς δ' ἐστὶ πατὴρ ὄνομα κλυτός, ὡς ἀγορεύεις,
ἀθανάτου δὲ ἕκητι διακτόρου ἐνθάδ' ἱκάνεις
Ἑρμέω, ἐμὴ δ' ἄλοχος κεκλήσεαι ἤματα πάντα·
οὔ τις ἔπειτα θεῶν οὔτε θνητῶν ἀνθρώπων
ἐνθάδε με σχήσει πρὶν σῆι φιλότητι μιγῆναι
αὐτίκα νῦν, οὐδ' εἴ κεν ἑκηβόλος αὐτὸς Ἀπόλλων
τόξου ἀπ' ἀργυρέου προϊῆι βέλεα στονόεντα·
βουλοίμην κεν ἔπειτα, γύναι εἰκυῖα θεῆισι,
σῆς εὐνῆς ἐπιβὰς δῦναι δόμον Ἄϊδος εἴσω.
Ὣς εἰπὼν λάβε χεῖρα· φιλομμειδὴς δ' Ἀφροδίτη
ἕρπε μεταστρεφθεῖσα κατ' ὄμματα καλὰ βαλοῦσα
ἐς λέχος εὔστρωτον, ὅθι περ πάρος ἔσκεν ἄνακτι
χλαίνηισιν μαλακῆις ἐστρωμένον· αὐτὰρ ὕπερθεν
ἄρκτων δέρματ' ἔκειτο βαρυφθόγγων τε λεόντων,
τοὺς αὐτὸς κατέπεφνεν ἐν οὔρεσιν ὑψηλοῖσιν.
οἱ δ' ἐπεὶ οὖν λεχέων εὐποιήτων ἐπέβησαν,
κόσμον μέν οἱ πρῶτον ἀπὸ χροὸς εἷλε φαεινόν,
πόρπας τε γναμπτάς θ' ἕλικας κάλυκάς τε καὶ ὅρμους.
λῦσε δέ οἱ ζώνην ἰδὲ εἵματα σιγαλόεντα
ἔκδυε καὶ κατέθηκεν ἐπὶ θρόνου ἀργυροήλου

132 οὐ μὲν γάρ κε M : οὐ γάρ τε Ψ praeter V : οὐ γάρ τοι V post 136 add. εἴ τοι ἀεικελίη γυνὴ ἔσσομαι ἠὲ καὶ οὐκί M Θ : pro 136, 136a οὔ σφιν ἀεικελίη γυνὴ ἔσσομαι ἠὲ καὶ οὐκὶ *p* 139 οἱ δέ κέ <τοι> χρυσόν τε Matthiae : οἱ δέ κε χρυσόν τε M : οἱ δέ τε χρυσόν κεν Ψ (οὐδέ τε A Q) 147 ἀθανάτου δὲ ἕκητι Hermann : ἀθανάτοιο δ' ἕκητι Ψ: ἀθανάτου δ' ἕκατι M 152 προϊῆι Gemoll : προίη M Θ : προίοι *p*

Ἀγχίσης· ὁ δ' ἔπειτα θεῶν ἰότητι καὶ αἴσηι
ἀθανάτηι παρέλεκτο θεᾶι βροτός, οὐ σάφα εἰδώς.
Ἦμος δ' ἂψ εἰς αὖλιν ἀποκλίνουσι νομῆες
βοῦς τε καὶ ἴφια μῆλα νομῶν ἐξ ἀνθεμοέντων,
τῆμος ἄρ' Ἀγχίσηι μὲν ἐπὶ γλυκὺν ὕπνον ἔχευε
νήδυμον, αὐτὴ δὲ χροῒ ἕννυτο εἵματα καλά.
ἑσσαμένη δ' εὖ πάντα περὶ χροῒ δῖα θεάων
ἔστη ἄρα κλισίηι, εὐποιήτοιο μελάθρου
κῦρε κάρη, κάλλος δὲ παρειάων ἀπέλαμπεν
ἄμβροτον, οἷόν τ' ἐστὶν ἰοστεφάνου Κυθερείης.
ἐξ ὕπνου τ' ἀνέγειρεν, ἔπος τ' ἔφατ' ἔκ τ' ὀνόμαζεν·
Ὄρσεο Δαρδανίδη· τί νυ νήγρετον ὕπνον ἰαύεις;
καὶ φράσαι εἴ τοι ὁμοίη ἐγὼν ἰνδάλλομαι εἶναι
οἵην δή με τὸ πρῶτον ἐν ὀφθαλμοῖσι νόησας;
Ὣς φάθ'· ὁ δ' ἐξ ὕπνοιο μάλ' ἐμμαπέως ὑπάκουσεν.
ὡς δὲ ἴδεν δειρήν τε καὶ ὄμματα κάλ' Ἀφροδίτης
τάρβησέν τε καὶ ὄσσε παρακλιδὸν ἔτραπεν ἄλληι.
ἂψ δ' αὖτις χλαίνηις ἐκαλύψατο καλὰ πρόσωπα,
καί μιν λισσόμενος ἔπεα πτερόεντα προσηύδα·
Αὐτίκα σ' ὡς τὰ πρῶτα θεὰ ἴδον ὀφθαλμοῖσιν
ἔγνων ὡς θεὸς ἦσθα· σὺ δ' οὐ νημερτὲς ἔειπες.
ἀλλά σε πρὸς Ζηνὸς γουνάζομαι αἰγιόχοιο
μή με ζῶντ' ἀμενηνὸν ἐν ἀνθρώποισιν ἐάσηις
ναίειν, ἀλλ' ἐλέαιρ'· ἐπεὶ οὐ βιοθάλμιος ἀνὴρ
γίγνεται ὅς τε θεαῖς εὐνάζεται ἀθανάτηισι.
Τὸν δ' ἠμείβετ' ἔπειτα Διὸς θυγάτηρ Ἀφροδίτη·
Ἀγχίση, κύδιστε καταθνητῶν ἀνθρώπων,
θάρσει, μηδέ τι σῆισι μετὰ φρεσὶ δείδιθι λίην·
οὐ γάρ τοί τι δέος παθέειν κακὸν ἐξ ἐμέθεν γε
οὐδ' ἄλλων μακάρων, ἐπεὶ ἦ φίλος ἐσσὶ θεοῖσι.
σοὶ δ' ἔσται φίλος υἱὸς ὃς ἐν Τρώεσσιν ἀνάξει
καὶ παῖδες παίδεσσι διαμπερὲς ἐκγεγάονται.
τῶι δὲ καὶ Αἰνείας ὄνομ' ἔσσεται οὕνεκά μ' αἰνὸν
ἔσχεν ἄχος ἕνεκα βροτοῦ ἀνέρος ἔμπεσον εὐνῆι
ἀγχίθεοι δὲ μάλιστα καταθνητῶν ἀνθρώπων

174 κῦρε M : βύρε E T : ηὗρε L Π *p* : ἧρε At D 175 ἰοστεφάνου M : ἐϋστεφάνου Ψ 178 εἴ τοι M : εἴ τι Ψ 179 τὸ om. Hermann, με om. La Roche 183 χλαίνηις ἐκαλύψατο Van der Ben : χλαίνηι τ' ἐκαλύψατο codd. 197 ἐκγεγάονται codd. : ἐκγεγάοντες Baumeister

αἰεὶ ἀφ᾽ ὑμετέρης γενεῆς εἶδός τε φυήν τε.
ἦ τοι μὲν ξανθὸν Γανυμήδεα μητίετα Ζεὺς
ἥρπασεν ὃν διὰ κάλλος ἵν᾽ ἀθανάτοισι μετείη
καί τε Διὸς κατὰ δῶμα θεοῖς ἐπιοινοχοεύοι,
θαῦμα ἰδεῖν, πάντεσσι τετιμένος ἀθανάτοισι,
χρυσέου ἐκ κρητῆρος ἀφύσσων νέκταρ ἐρυθρόν.
Τρῶα δὲ πένθος ἄλαστον ἔχε φρένας, οὐδέ τι ᾔδει
ὅππηι οἱ φίλον υἱὸν ἀνήρπασε θέσπις ἄελλα·
τὸν δὴ ἔπειτα γόασκε διαμπερὲς ἤματα πάντα.
καί μιν Ζεὺς ἐλέησε, δίδου δέ οἱ υἷος ἄποινα
ἵππους ἀρσίποδας, τοί τ᾽ ἀθανάτους φορέουσι.
τούς οἱ δῶρον ἔδωκεν ἔχειν· εἶπέν τε ἕκαστα
Ζηνὸς ἐφημοσύνηισι διάκτορος Ἀργειφόντης,
ὡς ἔοι ἀθάνατος καὶ ἀγήραος ἶσα θεοῖσιν.
αὐτὰρ ἐπεὶ δὴ Ζηνὸς ὅ γ᾽ ἔκλυεν ἀγγελιάων
οὐκέτ᾽ ἔπειτα γόασκε, γεγήθει δὲ φρένας ἔνδον,
γηθόσυνος δ᾽ ἵπποισιν ἀελλοπόδεσσιν ὀχεῖτο.
ὣς δ᾽ αὖ Τιθωνὸν χρυσόθρονος ἥρπασεν Ἠὼς
ὑμετέρης γενεῆς ἐπιείκελον ἀθανάτοισι.
βῆ δ᾽ ἴμεν αἰτήσουσα κελαινεφέα Κρονίωνα
ἀθάνατόν τ᾽ εἶναι καὶ ζώειν ἤματα πάντα·
τῆι δὲ Ζεὺς ἐπένευσε καὶ ἐκρήηνεν ἐέλδωρ.
νηπίη, οὐδ᾽ ἐνόησε μετὰ φρεσὶ πότνια Ἠὼς
ἥβην αἰτῆσαι, ξῦσαί τ᾽ ἄπο γῆρας ὀλοιόν.
τὸν δ᾽ ἦ τοι εἵως μὲν ἔχεν πολυήρατος ἥβη,
Ἠοῖ τερπόμενος χρυσοθρόνωι ἠριγενείηι
ναῖε παρ᾽ Ὠκεανοῖο ῥοῆις ἐπὶ πείρασι γαίης·
αὐτὰρ ἐπεὶ πρῶται πολιαὶ κατέχυντο ἔθειραι
καλῆς ἐκ κεφαλῆς εὐηγενέος τε γενείου,
τοῦ δ᾽ ἦ τοι εὐνῆς μὲν ἀπείχετο πότνια Ἠώς,
αὐτὸν δ᾽ αὖτ᾽ ἀτίταλλεν ἐνὶ μεγάροισιν ἔχουσα
σίτωι τ᾽ ἀμβροσίηι τε καὶ εἵματα καλὰ διδοῦσα.
ἀλλ᾽ ὅτε δὴ πάμπαν στυγερὸν κατὰ γῆρας ἔπειγεν
οὐδέ τι κινῆσαι μελέων δύνατ᾽ οὐδ᾽ ἀναεῖραι,

203 ἥρπασεν ὃν Hermann : ἥρπασ᾽ ἑὸν At D *p* : ἥρπασ᾽ ἐνὸν *x* : ἥρπασ᾽ αἰνὸν M   204 ἐπιοινοχοεύοι At D : ἐπὶ οἰνοχοεύοι Γ *x* (-ει, ss. -οι E) : ἐποινοχοεύοι *p* : ἐπιοινοχοεύειν M   205 τετιμένος At D *p* : τετιμένον M : τετιμένονος *x*   206 κρητῆρος M : κρατῆρος Ψ   ἀφύσσειν M : ἀφύσσων Ψ   212 τε codd. : δὲ Wolf   214 ἀγήραος At D : ἀγήρως M *p* *x*   ἶσα θεοῖσιν M : ἶσα θεοῖσι E T L[m] Π[m] : ἤματα πάντα At D L Π *p*   229 εὐηγενέος M : εὐγενέος Ψ

ἥδε δέ οἱ κατὰ θυμὸν ἀρίστη φαίνετο βουλή·
ἐν θαλάμωι κατέθηκε, θύρας δ᾽ ἐπέθηκε φαεινάς.
τοῦ δ᾽ ἤ τοι φωνὴ ῥεῖ ἄσπετος, οὐδέ τι κῖκυς
ἔσθ᾽ οἵη πάρος ἔσκεν ἐνὶ γναμπτοῖσι μέλεσσιν.
οὐκ ἂν ἐγώ γε σὲ τοῖον ἐν ἀθανάτοισιν ἑλοίμην
ἀθάνατόν τ᾽ εἶναι καὶ ζώειν ἤματα πάντα.
ἀλλ᾽ εἰ μὲν τοιοῦτος ἐὼν εἶδός τε δέμας τε
ζώοις, ἡμέτερός τε πόσις κεκλημένος εἴης,
οὐκ ἂν ἔπειτά μ᾽ ἄχος πυκινὰς φρένας ἀμφικαλύπτοι.
νῦν δέ σε μὲν τάχα γῆρας ὁμοίιον ἀμφικαλύψει
νηλειές, τό τ᾽ ἔπειτα παρίσταται ἀνθρώποισιν,
οὐλόμενον καματηρόν, ὅ τε στυγέουσι θεοί περ.
αὐτὰρ ἐμοὶ μέγ᾽ ὄνειδος ἐν ἀθανάτοισι θεοῖσιν
ἔσσεται ἤματα πάντα διαμπερὲς εἵνεκα σεῖο,
οἳ πρὶν ἐμοὺς ὀάρους καὶ μήτιας, αἷς ποτε πάντας
ἀθανάτους συνέμειξα καταθνητῆισι γυναιξί,
τάρβεσκον· πάντας γὰρ ἐμὸν δάμνασκε νόημα.
νῦν δὲ δὴ οὐκέτι μοι στόμα τλήσεται ἐξονομῆναι
τοῦτο μετ᾽ ἀθανάτοισιν, ἐπεὶ μάλα πολλὸν ἀάσθην
σχέτλιον οὐκ ὀνόμαστον, ἀπεπλάγχθην δὲ νόοιο,
παῖδα δ᾽ ὑπὸ ζώνηι ἐθέμην βροτῶι εὐνηθεῖσα.
τὸν μὲν, ἐπὴν δὴ πρῶτον ἴδηι φάος ἠελίοιο,
νύμφαι μιν θρέψουσιν ὀρεσκῶιοι βαθύκολποι,
αἳ τόδε ναιετάουσιν ὄρος μέγα τε ζάθεόν τε·
αἵ ῥ᾽ οὔτε θνητοῖς οὔτ᾽ ἀθανάτοισιν ἕπονται·
δηρὸν μὲν ζώουσι καὶ ἄμβροτον εἶδαρ ἔδουσι,
καί τε μετ᾽ ἀθανάτοισι καλὸν χορὸν ἐρρώσαντο.
τῆισι δὲ Σιληνοί τε καὶ εὔσκοπος Ἀργειφόντης
μίσγοντ᾽ ἐν φιλότητι μυχῶι σπείων ἐροέντων.
τῆισι δ᾽ ἅμ᾽ ἢ ἐλάται ἠὲ δρύες ὑψικάρηνοι
γεινομένηισιν ἔφυσαν ἐπὶ χθονὶ βωτιανείρηι
καλαὶ τηλεθάουσαι ἐν οὔρεσιν ὑψηλοῖσιν.
ἑστᾶσ᾽ ἠλίβατοι, τεμένη δέ ἑ κικλήσκουσιν
ἀθανάτων· τὰς δ᾽ οὔ τι βροτοὶ κείρουσι σιδήρωι.
ἀλλ᾽ ὅτε κεν δὴ μοῖρα παρεστήκηι θανάτοιο

250 συνέμειξα West : συνέμιξα codd. 252 στόμα τλήσεται Matthiae : στοναχήσεται codd. : στόμα χείσεται Martin 254 ὀνότατον codd. : ὀνομαστόν Martin 255 ζώνηι Ψ : ζώνην M 262 σιληνοὶ M At D L Π : σειληνοὶ *p* : σεληνοὶ E T 269 παρεστήκηι Stephanus : παρεστήκει M Θ : παρεστήκοι *p*

ἀζάνεται μὲν πρῶτον ἐπὶ χθονὶ δένδρεα καλά,
φλοιὸς δ' ἀμφιπεριφθινύθει, πίπτουσι δ' ἄπ' ὄζοι,
τῶν δέ θ' ὁμοῦ ψυχὴ λείποι φάος ἠελίοιο.
αἳ μὲν ἐμὸν θρέψουσι παρὰ σφίσιν υἱὸν ἔχουσαι.
τὸν μὲν ἐπὴν δὴ πρῶτον ἕληι πολυήρατος ἥβη
ἄξουσίν τοι δεῦρο θεαί, δείξουσί τε παῖδα·
[σοὶ δ' ἐγώ, ὄφρα κε ταῦτα μετὰ φρεσὶ πάντα διέλθω,
ἐς πέμπτον ἔτος αὖτις ἐλεύσομαι υἱὸν ἄγουσα.]
τὸν μὲν ἐπὴν δὴ πρῶτον ἴδηις θάλος ὀφθαλμοῖσι,
γηθήσεις ὁρόων· μάλα γὰρ θεοείκελος ἔσται·
ἄξεις δ' αὐτίκα μιν ποτὶ Ἴλιον ἠνεμόεσσαν.
ἢν δέ τις εἴρηταί σε καταθνητῶν ἀνθρώπων
ἥ τις σοὶ φίλον υἱὸν ὑπὸ ζώνηι θέτο μήτηρ,
τῶι δὲ σὺ μυθεῖσθαι μεμνημένος ὥς σε κελεύω·
φασίν τοι νύμφης καλυκώπιδος ἔκγονον εἶναι
αἳ τόδε ναιετάουσιν ὄρος καταειμένον ὕληι.
εἰ δέ κεν ἐξείπηις καὶ ἐπεύξεαι ἄφρονι θυμῶι
ἐν φιλότητι μιγῆναι ἐϋστεφάνωι Κυθερείηι,
Ζεύς σε χολωσάμενος βαλέει ψολόεντι κεραυνῶι.
εἴρηταί τοι πάντα· σὺ δὲ φρεσὶ σῆισι νοήσας
ἴσχεο μηδ' ὀνόμαινε, θεῶν δ' ἐποπίζεο μῆνιν.
Ὣς εἰποῦσ' ἤϊξε πρὸς οὐρανὸν ἠνεμόεντα.
Χαῖρε θεὰ Κύπροιο ἐϋκτιμένης μεδέουσα·
σεῦ δ' ἐγὼ ἀρξάμενος μεταβήσομαι ἄλλον ἐς ὕμνον.

271 ἄπ' ὄζοι Hermann : ἀπ' ὄζοι Ψ : ἄποζοι M 272 δέ θ' Hermann : δέχ' vel δ' ἔχ' codd. : δε γ' Van Eck 274–7 274–5 seclusit Matthiae, 276–7 Gemoll 275 τοι M, Hermann: σοι Ψ 276 ὄφρα ταῦτα codd. : ὄφρα κε ταῦτα E (secundum Gemoll), et coniecerat Barnes : ὄφρ' ἂν ταῦτα Van Eck : ὄφρα τοι αὖ τὰ Kamerbeek (*Mnem.* 1967, 363), Càssola 280 μιν Hermann : νιν Ψ : νυν M 284 φασίν codd. : φάσθαι Matthiae, fortasse recte ἔκγονον Barnes: ἔγγονον codd. 290 ὀνόμαινε Hermann : ὀνόμηνε codd.

COMMENTARY

To Apollo

Title. Some manuscripts have the title (τοῦ αὐτοῦ) Ὁμήρου ὕμνοι εἰς Ἀπόλλωνα, others the singular ὕμνος. But the plural occurs at the head of some other hymns, and is simply a general title of this collection, not evidence that this hymn was regarded in antiquity as two separate poems.

1–18 *Prelude.* I shall sing of Apollo, whose entry to Zeus's house causes the gods to spring up in fear, as he draws his shining bow. Leto alone remains beside Zeus. She unstrings his bow, closes his quiver, and taking it from his shoulders she hangs bow and quiver against a pillar of Zeus's hall, and leads him to his seat. Zeus offers him nectar and greets him, and the other gods do likewise. Then they take their seats again. And Leto rejoices to have borne a son who is so mighty an archer. Greetings to you, blessed Leto, because you bore such glorious children as Apollo and Artemis! To her you gave birth in Ortygia, to him in Delos, as you leaned against Mount Cynthus, close to the palm tree, by Inopus' streams.

These lines form a self-contained prelude, and could easily stand on their own as a hymn to Apollo, complete with his parents Zeus and Leto, and his sister Artemis. They announce the subject of the hymn, and immediately continue with a relative clause describing Apollo's entry to Zeus's palace on Olympus and his reception by the other gods, especially his parents Leto and Zeus. This leads on to a short passage addressing Leto and praising her as the mother of two such great deities, which also refers briefly to the legends of their birth in Ortygia and Delos. The prelude therefore neatly introduces the main narrative theme of the first Movement of the hymn, the birth of Apollo, before the poet has actually announced his intention to sing of this event.

The praise of Leto and her children is also a theme of the more extended closing section of this Movement (140–78) (cf. Introduction 2(a)). Moreover, the dramatic portrayal of Apollo's entry to Zeus's palace as the mighty archer-god is paralleled in the opening section of the second Movement, where he goes up from Delphi to Olympus as god of music (182–206). Here too Artemis is singled out for special praise (197–9), and Leto and Zeus rejoice at the sight of their son (204–6). This scene, with its emphasis on the joy occasioned by Apollo, both echoes and contrasts with the opening scene where his appearance evokes both fear and delight. These aspects of the god will be fundamental to the narratives which follow.

The sudden epiphany of the god is powerful, and the contrast with the courtly scene of calm which follows is effective. Yet many modern critics have been dissatisfied with these opening lines. The alternation between present and past tenses in 1–13 has raised the question whether they describe Apollo's first appearance in heaven or his habitual one: if the latter, why do the gods still react in terror?

The opening lines, with their present tenses and generalising use of ὅν τε . . . καί ῥά τε . . . , and the closing sentence (χαίρει δέ τε . . .), show that the description is of the god's characteristic activity, and not intended to refer to a single event. (The first entry to Olympus in any case should normally follow the birth narrative.) The shift to aorist and past tenses is paralleled elsewhere in opening or closing scenes of hymnic type. For example, cf. Hes. *Th.* 1–21, with West on *Th.* 7, p. 155, Richardson on *H. Dem.* 483–9, p. 315, West (1989) 135–8, and Faulkner (2005). The purpose of the scene is to portray the god's awe-inspiring character at the outset: his role as archer can inspire even the gods with fear.

The contrast between fear and joy is similar to that described in *H.* 27, to Artemis, Apollo's sister. There the whole narrative describes the effect on the natural world of her appearance as an archer (4–6 ἣ . . . παγχρύσεα τόξα τιταίνει . . . τρομέει δὲ . . . , etc.), followed by her entry to Apollo's house at Delphi, where she leads the gods in dance and song. The motifs of unstringing the bow and hanging up bow and arrows also recur (12, 16). In the *Hymn to Apollo* this sequence is compressed into a single scene on Olympus, which increases its force. This dramatic compression is paralleled still more closely in the *Hymn to Athena* (28), where the gods' amazement and the violent cosmic reactions to her birth, fully armed and brandishing her spear from Zeus's head, are followed by the removal of her armour and the joy of Zeus (4–16). Cf. Fröhder (1994) 189–91, 244–7.

The scene is analogous to the 'Visit' scenes in Homeric epic where someone arrives, reactions are described, and he is welcomed (see Arend (1933) 34ff.). The closest parallels for the arrival of a god on Olympus are those of Zeus at *Il.* 1.533–43 (where all the gods rise when he enters, and he then sits down and is addressed by Hera), and Hera's entry at 15.84–6, where they all rise and greet her with their cups (see Arend (1933) 56). But it also fits into the pattern of Epiphany scenes, such as that of Demeter at *H. Dem.* 188–211, where a god's or hero's appearance arouses fear and astonishment, followed by welcome (see Richardson on *H. Dem.* 180ff., 188–211, etc.). For further discussion see Miller (1986) 12–17, Clay (2006) 19–33.

1 μνήσομαι οὐδὲ λάθωμαι 'may I call to mind and not forget'. μνήσομαι is probably a short-vowel subjunctive rather than a future: for the subjunctive in such contexts cf. Hes. *Th.* 1 ἀρχώμεθ' ἀείδειν (West ad loc.). This opening suggests the need to keep the god in mind not only now but always: cf. at the end of the Delian part of the hymn (177–8) αὐτὰρ ἐγὼν οὐ λήξω . . . ὑμνέων ἀργυρότοξον ὃν ἠΰκομος τέκε Λητώ. For μνήσομαι at the opening cf. *H.* 7.2. Usually it occurs at the end (*H. Ap.* 546 etc.). 'Not forgetting' is also a motif at beginning and end, as at *H.* 1.17–19, 7.58–9, Theognis 1–4. The need to keep the deity in mind is stressed by Callimachus in his hymns (3.1–2, 4.7–8). For a parallel motif in the Vedic hymns see West (2007) 306.

Ἀπόλλωνος ἑκάτοιο: cf. *Il.* 7.83 etc. The traditional epithet, usually interpreted in antiquity as referring to Apollo as archer ('far-shooting'), is glossed in a typical way by the following relative clause.

This line is cited as by Homer in the *Certamen Homeri et Hesiodi* (316), where the poet recites this hymn standing on the altar of horns on Delos and it is then inscribed on a tablet and dedicated in the temple of Artemis (cf. Introduction 2(b)).

2–4 Cf. *Il.* 1.533–5 θεοὶ δ' ἅμα πάντες ἀνέσταν | ἐξ ἑδέων . . . οὐδέ τις ἔτλη | μεῖναι ἐπερχόμενον, ἀλλ' ἀντίον ἔσταν ἅπαντες. This unusual portrayal of Apollo drawing his bow as he enters, and its fearsome effect, have been compared to near-eastern descriptions of Babylonian or Hittite warrior gods and the terror which they instil in their divine colleagues, especially Syrian Rešef, who is actually identified with Apollo in Cyprus in some later inscriptions from Idalion and Tamassos as god of war and plague. Rešef was frequently portrayed as stepping forward with right arm brandishing a weapon, and is described as the archer-god in Ras Shamra and Cyprus: see Kroll (1956) 181–91, Guida (1972) 7–25, Burkert (1975) 51–79, and Penglase (1994) 98–9. The scene has also been compared to one in a Sumerian hymn to Ninurta, where Ninurta's appearance causes alarm to the gods, but he is persuaded to lay aside his weapons, the gods bow before him as he enters Enlil's house, and his mother Ninlil soothes him with praise: see Penglase (1994) 99, West (1997) 355.

5–9 Leto remains unalarmed, seated as she is by Zeus, although we must assume that she then comes forward to disarm her son. She is here the πάρεδρος of Zeus, a position of honour: cf. *Il.* 24.100 where Athena yields this place to Thetis. The object of ἑλοῦσα in 7 must be φαρέτρην, with a comma at the end of the line: cf. Forderer (1971) 63, 166 n. 17, Clay (2006) 21–2. τόξον (8) probably refers to bow and arrows together, as at *Il.* 21.490–2, 502–3 (τόξα), where this must refer to the bow-case containing bow and arrows.

8–9 A bow is hung on a peg, as at *Il.* 5.209, *Od.* 21.53–4, here golden as it is in heaven. The courteous reception resembles Telemachus' welcome for the disguised Athena (*Od.* 1.103–31): she stands in the doorway, holding her spear, and Telemachus grasps her right hand, takes the spear, and sets it against a pillar in a spear-stand, leads her to a seat (130 αὐτὴν δ' εἰς θρόνον εἷσεν ἄγων), and gives her food and drink (139–43). Cf. also *Od.* 8.65–70: Demodocus is given a seat (πρὸς κίονα), his lyre is taken from its peg, and he is offered food and wine. πρὸς κίονα πατρὸς ἑοῖο means 'on a pillar of his father's house'.

10–12 Traditionally, welcome is followed by the offer of food or drink, or both. Cf. especially *Il.* 15.85–8, where the gods rise and greet Hera with their cups (86 δεικανόωντο δέπασσιν), and she takes a cup from Themis. Here Zeus himself serves his son, an unusual honour. δεικνύμενος ('pledging') is used here as at *Il.* 9.196, *Od.* 4.59, as if it were a participial form related to δε(ι)δίσκετο, δεικανόωντο, etc., like δειδισκόμενος. Cf. S. West on *Od.* 3.41, Russo on *Od.* 18.121.

11–12 ἔπειτα δὲ δαίμονες ἄλλοι. | ἔνθα καθίζουσιν: 'and next the other gods (greet him). Then they sit down.' With this punctuation the gods follow Zeus's example and greet Apollo whilst still standing, as at *Il.* 15.85–6 (cf. also *Il.* 9.671). ἔνθα καθίζουσιν rounds off the action which began at 3–4, with the gods leaping to their feet. ἔνθα can be used without any other particle. West (2003) has no punctuation after 11, and translates 'and then the other gods do likewise, from where they sit'. But we have not been told that they sat down, and this anyway weakens the effect of the whole scene. Moreover, 'from where' is not what ἔνθα means. Allen and Sikes take ἔνθα as 'then and not till then', with ἔπειτα... καθίζουσιν as a single clause ('and next the other gods finally sit down'), but this is awkward, and ἔνθα should come first in the clause, rather than following ἔπειτα δέ (cf. Gemoll). The same applies to AHS (and Càssola): 'and next the other gods sit down there'.

12–13 The reference to the joy of Leto closes the scene, as in those Homeric similes where the reaction of an onlooker is described at the end. Cf. especially *Od.* 6.102–6, where Nausicaa is compared to Artemis at sport among the nymphs, γέγηθε δέ τε φρένα Λητώ (106). But in the hymn χαίρει is echoed by the singer's own greeting to Leto (14–18). 12–13 recur like a refrain at 125–6, at the end of the birth-narrative (13 = 126), and are echoed again at the end of the prelude to the second Movement (204–6). Moreover, 12–13 introduce the main theme of the Birth, repeated again twice (at 14–18 and 25–8), before the actual narrative gets under way.

The sequence of divine rejoicing followed by the singer's greeting closes the *Hymn to Athena* (28.16–17), where the narrative sequence is similar to that of *H. Ap.* 1–13. Cf. also the end of the *Hymn to Pan*, Πᾶνα δέ μιν καλέεσκον ὅτι φρένα πᾶσιν ἔτερψε (19.47). τοξοφόρος occurs in Homer only at *Il.* 21.483 (of Artemis).

14–18 The wording of 14 closely echoes that of 12–13, and the poet achieves an effect of spontaneity: 'And lady Leto rejoices, because she bore . . . Rejoice indeed, O blessed Leto, because you have borne . . .' The focus is widened, however, to include Apollo's sister; and the elegant chiastic order of 15–16 pays honour to them both.

14 μάκαιρ' ὦ Λητοῖ: for this type of word order cf. *Od.* 4.26 διοτρεφὲς ὦ Μενέλαε, etc., and later Eur. *Ba.* 565 μάκαρ ὦ Πιερία, Ar. *Nub.* 1205, Orph. *H.* 3.12, *AP* 6.239.1.

15 This line resembles Hes. *Th.* 14 Φοῖβόν τ' Ἀπόλλωνα καὶ Ἄρτεμιν ἰοχέαιραν.

16 = Orph. *H.* 35.5. The name Ortygia ('Quail-island') occurs twice in the *Odyssey* (5.123, 15.406), but its location is unclear; in 15.403–6 it is 'beyond the island Syrie, where are the turnings of the sun'. Strabo (486) says that it was the ancient name of Rheneia, and this identification has been advocated by Tréheux (1946) 560–76 and Bruneau (1970) 189–91. The name Ortygia occurs several times in Hellenistic inscriptions from Delos as that of a local cult-site, and this supports the view that Artemis' birthplace in the hymn is local, i.e. on one of the islands next to Delos. Rheneia is named at *H. Ap.* 44, but it remains possible that Ortygia refers to a place or area of this island. Later, however, the name was given to various islands or places: (a) Delos itself (Pindar, *Paean* VIIb, fr. 52 h 48 Snell–Maehler, Call. *H.* 2.59, etc.); (b) the island next to Syracuse (probably already in Hes. fr. 150.26, Pindar *P.* 2.6–7, *N.* 1–4, etc.); (c) a place at Ephesus (Strabo 639, Tac. *Ann.* 3.61, etc.); or elsewhere. Strong claims were made by Syracusan and Ephesian Ortygia to be Artemis' birthplace. Pindar actually calls the Syracusan island δέμνιον Ἀρτεμίδος, Δάλου κασιγνήτα (*N.* 1.3–4), and Aristarchus understood this as a reference to Artemis' birth there (Schol. Pi. *N.* 1.3). On Ephesus see Kowalzig (2007) 103–10.

16–18 Apollo's birth on Delos is first mentioned here, but Homer surely knows the legend, as Odysseus compares Nausicaa's beauty to that of the palm tree by Apollo's altar on Delos, and implies that this was a special place of pilgrimage (*Od.* 6.162–9). Palm trees seem to have been rare in ancient Greece and so regarded as special: cf. Paus. 9.19.8, and Murr (1890) 48. The Delian palm tree was famous later because of the birth-story: cf. Theognis 5–6 Φοῖβε ἄναξ ὅτε μέν σε θεὰ τέκε πότνια Λητὼ | φοίνικος ῥαδινῆς χερσὶν ἐφαψαμένη (echoing *Ap.* 117, and Theognis 9–10 echoes 118); Call. *H.* 4.209–10 ἀπὸ δ' ἐκλίθη ἔμπαλιν ὤμοις | φοίνικος ποτὶ πρέμνον, etc. Olive and bay were also later associated with these birth-legends of Apollo and Artemis (Eur. *IT* 1097 etc.).

Leto leans against Mt Cynthus when giving birth because she is a goddess, and so of supernatural size. (Cynthus is actually more of a hill than a mountain, 368 feet high.) πρὸς μακρὸν ὄρος καὶ Κύνθιον ὄχθον is a hendiadys, i.e. both phrases together describe the same hill, and ὄχθος occurs only here before fifth-century BC literature. In the classical period there was a temple of Zeus at the top. Inopus is the only stream on Delos, and is now a dry watercourse for much of the year. In Call. *H.* 4.206–8 it is fed by water from the Nile in flood. For the location of Cynthus and Inopus see Bruneau and Ducat (2005) 273–4, 283–9. Theognis (7) mentions the 'circular lake' in relation to Apollo's birth, and this too was a landmark: cf. A. *Eum.* 9, Hdt. 2.170, etc., Bruneau and Ducat (2005) 227.

18 ἀγχοτάτω occurs only here in early epic, but is used by Herodotus; cf. Homeric ἑκαστάτω, τηλοτάτω. The MS reading ὑπ' Ἰνωποῖο ῥεέθροις is unsatisfactory, since ὑπό does not seem to be used to mean 'by' rather than 'under' (cf. Richardson on *Il.* 21.87).

19–50 How shall I praise you, since your praises are so widespread? Shall I sing of your birth in Delos? From there your power extends all over mankind. All islands and places in the Aegean sea were visited by Leto, when looking for a home for her son, but all were afraid to receive him, until she came to Delos and asked her aid.

Having already anticipated his theme in the prelude, the poet breaks off to express the range of possible subjects of praise open to him, and sketches briefly the universality of Apollo's power and influence, in order to focus on the birth-story once again (25–8). The question at 25–7 is left unanswered, and we move once more from Delos (in the centre of the Aegean) outwards to a view of the god's empire over all men. This in turn is developed in the following extended geographical catalogue of the Aegean world (30–44), the first of several in the hymn as a whole, which in the end turns into a list of places visited by Leto in her search for a birthplace, culminating in Delos once again (45–50). The song thus advances through a series of repetitions, at once broadening and narrowing its viewpoint. The types of places mentioned also suggest Apollo's various cult-epithets, such as Nomios (cf. 21 πορτιτρόφον), Nasiotas, Aktaios, Ekbasios, etc.: cf. Farnell, *Cults* IV, 145 etc.

19–24 The expression of *aporia* when confronted with such a wealth of material for praise is a typical rhetorical and narrative device. Cf. already in Homer *Od.* 9.14–15 τί πρῶτόν τοι ἔπειτα, τί δ' ὑστάτιον καταλέξω, | κήδε' ἐπεί μοι πολλὰ δόσαν θεοὶ οὐρανίωνες; and Bundy (1972) 57–77, Miller (1986) 20–31. Here 19 is repeated at 207, the same structural point in the second Movement (see Introduction 2(a)). In both cases the actual subject is announced at 25 and 214, with ἢ ὥς σε πρῶτον Λητὼ τέκε... and ἢ ὡς τὸ πρῶτον χρηστήριον... But in 20–4 the poet explains his *aporia* by Apollo's universality, whereas in 208–13 a series of possible alternative themes is catalogued. Both may be viewed as types of *priamel*, where a range of possibilities is seen as the setting or foil for the one selected by the poet. The device is imitated by Callimachus in his Delian hymn (4.28–33). For parallels in the Vedic hymns see West (2007) 307.

19 τ' ἄρ is the reading at 207 and is probably right here.

εὔυμνος occurs first here; cf. Call. *H.* 2.31, 4.4, etc., and πολύυμνος *H.* 26.7, πολυύμνητος Pi. *N.* 2.5.

20 'For everywhere for you, Phoebus, the fields of song are laid out.' The reading νόμος (or νομός) is not grammatically possible if we keep the plural verb βεβλήαται. νομοί ('pastures') implies the fields open to the singer, although he may also have in mind the musical sense of νόμος ('melody', with paroxytone accent). Cf. *Il.* 20.249 ἐπέων δὲ πολὺς νομὸς ἔνθα καὶ ἔνθα, and Hes. *Op.* 403. βάλλεσθαι is used by Pindar of laying down a foundation of song (*P.* 4.138, 7.4). For the contracted form ὠιδῆς cf. *H. Dem.* 494, *H.* 30.18, etc.

21 Cf. *H. Aph.* 5 ἠμὲν ὅσ' ἤπειρος πολλὰ τρέφει ἠδ' ὅσα πόντος. The colourful πορτιτρόφος ('calf-rearing') recurs only at Bacchylides 11.30.

22–4 The general statement of 20–1 is explained in more detail, as the poet moves from the high points of the mainland to rivers running seawards, and hence to coastal places, anticipating the catalogue of 30–44 with its many islands and mountains. Rubensohn (1962) 39–42 observes that many of the sites of temples dedicated to Apollo Delios in the Aegean area lie on high points, outside the cities, overlooking the sea or on the coast. Cf. *H. Ap.* 143–6, where the *reprise* of 22–4 culminates in praise of Delos itself. For 22 cf. *Il.* 8.557, 16.299 πᾶσαι σκοπιαὶ καὶ πρώονες ἄκροι; for ποταμοί θ' ἅλαδε προρέοντες cf. *Il.* 5.598, *Od.* 10.351; and for 24 cf. *Od.* 13.234–5 ἠέ τις ἀκτὴ | κεῖθ' ἁλὶ κεκλιμένη.

25–8 The description of the birth echoes 14–18 (especially 16–17). For 25 cf. *Il.* 14.325 ἡ δὲ Διώνυσον Σεμέλη τέκε, χάρμα βροτοῖσιν, *H.* 16.4 (Asclepius, born to Apollo and Coronis), and *H. Dem.* 269 (with Richardson's comment). The emendation Κύνθου is necessary as the name is not used as a neuter. For 27 cf. *Od.* 1.50 (etc.) νήσωι | Δίηι ἐν ἀμφιρύτηι. 27–28 develop the idea contained in this epithet, of the waves driven by the winds onto the shore all round the island. λιγύπνοιος is only found here; cf. *Od.* 4.567 Ζεφύροιο λιγὺ πνείοντος ἀήτας, and λιγύπνοος in late epic. Call. *H.* 4.11–14 echoes these lines.

29–46 29 echoes 20–4, but it also looks forward to the following list of peoples. The asyndeton at 30 is paralleled in the catalogues at *Il.* 12.19–24 (ὅσσοι . . . τῶν πάντων . . .) and 24.544–6 (ὅσσον . . . τῶν σε . . .), where *H. Ap.* 30 and 37 both echo 24.544. But this catalogue serves a dual purpose, since it becomes the narrative of Leto's wanderings in search of a birthplace. It follows a circular course around the Aegean, moving westwards from Crete to Athens, then north up the coast of the mainland, east across the sea to the Asia Minor coast and islands, and finally west to Rhenaia and Delos (at 49). Thus the places which reject Leto later become parts of Apollo's Aegean empire. But the list is not intended as a complete catalogue of cult-centres. It is carefully organised in triplets of verses: 33–5, and 39–41 each end with three references to mountains; 30–2, 33–5, and 42–4 all end with a verse containing three names, whereas the other verses have two names; and the central triplet ends with the whole-line praise of Chios, the poet's home (Miller (1986) 34). Moreover, there is parallelism in 33–4, and the epithets at the end of 43–4 are balanced. For cults of Apollo Delios on both the Ionian and Dorian islands see Kowalzig (2007) 72–80. This catalogue is complemented by the list of places visited by Apollo in his search for an oracle at 214–93, culminating in Delphi, and the narrative of Apollo's sea journey with the Cretan sailors around the south and west coasts of the Peloponnese and through the Corinthian Gulf to Crisa and hence up to Delphi (388–523). Cf. Baltes (1982) 25–43, and see Introduction 2(a) and Maps 1 and 2.

30 We begin with Crete and Athens, two major cult-centres connected closely in legend with Delos. For Athens see Parker (2005) 80–2, Kowalzig (2007) 83–6. Theseus was said to have instituted Apollo's Delian festival on his way back from Crete to Athens (Plut. *Thes.* 21 etc.), and Apollo's Delphic priests and paean will come from Crete (*H. Ap.* 388ff. and 516–19). For the expression ὅσσους . . . ἐντὸς ἔχει cf. *Il.* 2.616–17, 845, 24.544. δῆμος means 'land' here.

31 On Aegina Apollo had a prominent cult as Delphinios (Farnell, *Cults* IV 147), and in Euboea he was Daphnephoros at Eretria, Delphinios at Chalcis. Carystos was on the route of the Hyperborean offerings (Hdt. 4.33.2). Cf. Farnell IV 437. 'Famed for ships' (cf. 219) does not occur in Homer as an epithet of Euboea, although it certainly fits the period from the eighth century onwards when the

Euboeans were so active as seafarers and traders. The line is wholly spondaic (see Pye (1964) 2–6).

32 Aigai is mentioned three times in Homer, as one of Poseidon's chief cult-sites (*Il.* 8.203), or as his home (*Il.* 13.21, *Od.* 5.381), but its location was disputed in antiquity. The place on the north-west coast of Euboea would be a possible candidate here, even though Euboea as a whole has just been mentioned. Alternatively, ancient tradition identified Homer's Aigai with an island near Euboea (Hesychius s.v., Schol. bT *Il.* 8.203, b 13.21, etc.). Eiresiai may be the island mentioned by Pliny (Irrhesia) on the Thermaic gulf (*NH* 4.72). Peparethos is the island north-east of Euboea, so the other two places are presumably somewhere in this general area. ἀγχίαλος (literally 'near the sea') is used in Homer of coastal places, but here and later (A. *Pers.* 889 etc.) of islands, as if it meant 'surrounded by sea'. ἀγχίαλος (*p*'s variant for ἀγχιάλη) is probably right, as the word is two-termination in Homer (*Il.* 2.640, 697, etc.).

33 Pliny (*NH* 4.37) mentions a place called Apollonia on Mt Athos.

34 Samothrace, Ida, and Aigai all occur together in *Il.* 13.11–22.

35 With Phocaea and Autocane we are on the eastern side of the Aegean. Autocane is the mountain range opposite the southern end of Lesbos, usually called Κάνη. ΑΥΤΟΚΑΝΑ occurs on coins, once at least with Apollo's head (see Head (1911) 552, Oldfather, *RE* s.v. Kanai). The island of Scyros on the other hand takes us back to the western Aegean. Wilamowitz (1916) 445–6 suggested that the name here may refer to a place in Asia Minor; cf. Schol. A *Il.* 9.668, where it is located in 'Phrygia, previously Cilicia', and *IG* 12 (2) 504.8 for a group of Scyrians on Lesbos. (Homer's Cilicians live in the Troad: *Il.* 6.397, 415.) This is ingenious, but it is much more natural that the poet should be referring to the well-known island. The geographical order is not so tight here. In fact we move north again from Phocaea and Autocane in 36, and then south in 37–43.

36 In *Il.* 9.129, *Od.* 4.342 Lesbos is εὐκτιμένη. Cf. *Il.* 24.753 ἐς Σάμον ἔς τ' Ἴμβρον καὶ Λῆμνον ἀμιχθαλόεσσαν. The epithet ἀμιχθαλόεσσα is not found elsewhere in early epic poetry. Hellenistic and later poets may have interpreted it as meaning 'misty' (cf. Call. fr. 18.8 Pf., Colluthus 208), but the sense is uncertain. See Richardson on *Il.* 24.753 for various other ancient views.

37 Cf. *Il.* 24.544 ὅσσον Λέσβος ἄνω, Μάκαρος ἕδος, ἐντὸς ἐέργει. Macar ('Blessed One') was a legendary colonist of Lesbos, which was named Macaria after him (see Richardson on *Il.* 24.543–6). Apollo was worshipped there as Maloeis: Thuc. 3.3 etc., Farnell, *Cults* IV 445.

38 Chios, the home of this poet (cf. 172), is given a whole verse, praising it as the most rich or flourishing of the islands. For the language cf. *Od.* 9.25 πανυπερτάτη εἰν ἁλὶ κεῖται, Call. *H.* 4.3 αἳ νήσων ἱερωτάται εἰν ἁλὶ κεῖνται. For cults of Apollo there see Farnell, *Cults* IV 445.

39 Mimas and Corycos are mountains opposite Chios on the Erythraean peninsula. In Call. *H.* 4.157–8 Iris watches from Mimas to stop the islands from accepting Leto.

40 Claros had a temple and oracle of Apollo, which the Colophonians claimed to be very ancient, and in *H.* 9.4–6 it is to this sanctuary that Artemis drives her chariot, in order to visit her brother there. Cf. also Hes. fr. 278, *Epigoni* (?) fr. 3 Davies. αἰγλήεσσα (only of Olympus in Homer) suggests its importance in the Archaic period, when remains include an altar of Apollo (late seventh century), temple of Apollo, altar of Artemis, and *kouroi* and *korai* (see De la Génière (1998) 235–43). Epigraphically it has left its most profuse record in the Roman period: see Parke (1985) 112–70.

Aisagea recurs (as a 'strong headland') only in the local poet Nicander of Colophon's *Theriaca* (218), together with Cercaphos, a mountain near Colophon (Schol. Lyc. 424). The Chian poet's knowledge of landmarks on the coast south of his homeland is thus detailed and extensive: between Chios and Samos he names four separate places.

41 For 'watery Samos' cf. Call. *H.* 4.48–9 νήσοιο διάβροχον ὕδατι μαστὸν | Παρθενίης (οὔπω γὰρ ἔην Σάμος), perhaps echoing this verse. For cults of Apollo there cf. *Vita Herodotea Homeri* 462–82 (*Homeri Opera* v 213–15 Allen), Farnell, *Cults* IV 446. Μυκάλης τ' αἰπεινὰ κάρηνα occurs at *Il.* 2.869, with Miletus in 868.

42 Miletus had a sanctuary of Apollo Delphinios (cf. 493–6) by the harbour, although the surviving remains date only from the fifth century BC (see Kleiner (1968) 32–5). This was the starting point of the annual procession to Didyma, 10 miles to the south, where lay the famous oracular sanctuary controlled by Miletus and administered by the Branchidae, whose antiquity and widespread importance in the Archaic period is attested by Herodotus (1.92.2, 157–60, 2.159.3). It was 'used by all the Ionians and Aeolians', and dedications were made by Necho II and Croesus there. The earliest evidence for an enclosed sanctuary there dates from the eighth or seventh century BC, and the first large-scale building from the mid sixth. The shrine was destroyed in 494 BC by Darius I and the Branchidae were exiled; it was only refounded in the time of Alexander the Great. Miletus is mentioned again, this time as one of Apollo's chief places of worship, at *H. Ap.* 180. See Parke (1985) 1–111.

The Meropes were the legendary ancient inhabitants of Cos: cf. Pi. *N.* 4.26 etc., and especially Call. *H.* 4.160. The expression πόλις Μερόπων ἀνθρώπων is probably influenced by Homeric πόλις μερόπων ἀνθρώπων (*Il.* 20.217; cf. 18.342, 498), where μερόπων is an epithet. In Homer ἄνδρες is sometimes added to proper names (*Il.* 1.594 etc.). For Apolline cults on Cos see Farnell, *Cults* IV 446, Sherwin-White (1978), especially 299–303, Kowalzig (2007) 77, 97–8.

43 Cnidos had a sanctuary of Triopian Apollo (on the peninsula at Triopion), and this was the site of the major festival of the Dorian Hexapolis (which included Cos, the three Rhodian cities, and Halicarnassus). Apollo was also worshipped as Carneios in Cnidos. See Farnell, *Cults* IV 365, 449–50. The territory of Cnidos is largely mountainous, and ends in the steep Triopian promontory, justifying the epithet used here: see Newton (1865) 168ff., Bean and Cook (1952) 171–212 (and 208–10 on the location of Triopion), Bean (1971) 135–52.

44 We now move westwards towards Delos. Apollo's cult was widespread on Naxos: cf. Ananius fr. 1 West, *RE* XVI 2086–7 s.v. Naxos (5), N. M. Kontoleon in *Princeton encyclopedia* 611–12, Farnell, *Cults* IV 444. For Paros cf. Farnell IV 444 and Kontoleon, *Princeton encyclopedia* 678, Rubensohn (1962). Rhenaia (or Rheneia), the rocky island next door to Delos (cf. 16n.), was dedicated to Delian Apollo by Polycrates in the late sixth century (Thuc. 1.13.6, 3.104.2). The form Ῥήναια recurs in Theocr. 17.70 (perhaps echoing our hymn: 'Apollo loves Rhenaia no less than Delos'), and in Stephanus of Byzantium and *Suda* s.v., for the more usual Ῥήνεια, which is also normal in inscriptions: see Dittenberger (1906) 172.
45–6 After the long roll-call of names we finally reach what is really the opening of the detailed narrative. The hiatus after ὠδίνουσα reflects the original digamma of Ἑκηβόλον.
46 γαιέων: the plural of γαῖα is used in the *Odyssey* (γαιάων 3×). The variant εἴ τις γαιάων would be possible, but the addition of οἱ ('on behalf of herself') is more idiomatic, and a corruption to the rarer form γαιέων seems unlikely.
47–50 We are not told yet why the lands are afraid to receive Apollo. A special reason is revealed by Delos at 67–78: fear of the new god's might, and the danger that he may despise her poverty. The reference to the greater fertility of some of the other islands (48) seems to anticipate this: the others fear him, despite being less barren. In later versions it is fear of Hera's anger which prevents them: Call. *H.* 4.68–196, Apollod. 1.4.1, Ovid *Met.* 6.332–6. This motif is alluded to at 97–107, where Hera tries to prevent Eileithyia from assisting the birth, but it is not given full prominence.
47 = *Il.* 7.15 (οἱ δὲ ...).
49 ἐβήσετο is the form preferred by Aristarchus to ἐβήσατο in Homer: see Chantraine, *GH* I 416–17.
51–88 Leto promises that if Delos receives Apollo, then, despite her natural poverty, she will prosper through the sacrifices he will receive. In reply Delos expresses her willingness, but also her fear that the god will despise her and thrust her down into the depths of the sea. She asks Leto to swear an oath that he will make his first temple on her island, and Leto does so.

The dramatic personification of the eponymous nymph or deity of a place (with dialogue) occurs first here, although Achilles and the river Scamander already converse and fight in *Il.* 21.212–382. There is a contrast here between the future greatness of the god and the lowliness of the island. Delos picks up Leto's allusion to this, and vividly elaborates it, in order to extract a firm assurance of future favour. There is also a parallel with the scene at the end of the hymn, where the sailors ask Apollo how they will live in the rocky landscape of Delphi, and he promises them wealth from his cult (526–37).
51–60 'If you would be willing ... (since you have no other means of support): but if you *will* be the home of Apollo's temple, then ...' The opening εἰ γάρ κ' ἐθέλοις could be viewed as a separate wish, but it can also be regarded as

a protasis anticipating the conditional clause in 56, which is then answered by 57–60. However, the conditional request clause in 79–82 again has no apodosis. Denniston (*GP*[2] 94) comments that 'Hom. *h.Ap.* 51 stands apart from all other examples of εἰ γάρ, in that the particles occur at the opening of a conversation, without any obvious logical connection'. But Matthiae's ἦ ἄρ, as a question (cf. 50 ἀνειρομένη, and *Od.* 18.357 ξεῖν', ἦ ἄρ κ' ἐθέλοις . . . ;), seems unnecessary.

52 'To create a (rich etc.) temple' is a leitmotif of this hymn (cf. 76, 80, 221, etc.). For πίονα νηόν cf. *Od.* 3.46 (τεύξομεν), *H. Ap.* 478, etc. The first temple dedicated to Apollo on Delos for which we have definite evidence is the so-called *Porinos Naos*, built in the second half of the sixth century BC (see Bruneau and Ducat (2005) 182). Candidates for an earlier temple of Apollo proposed by the archaeologists include the building later known as the 'Oikos of the Naxians', which probably dates from the early sixth century BC (Bruneau and Ducat (2005) 171–6), and the so-called 'Temple Γ', a smaller building which probably belongs to the Geometric period (Bruneau and Ducat (2005) 176). For further discussion see Courbin (1980) 11–41, Picard (1992) 232–47, and Gruben (1997) 261–416, especially 270, 292–3, 407–14, and 416 (summary).

53–5 The cumulative negatives underline the hopelessness of Delos' situation if left to herself.

53 Ernesti's τίσει (cf. 88) makes better sense than the MS reading λίσσει.

54–5 Cf. 529–30 (of Delphi), and *Od.* 15.406 εὔβοτος, εὔμηλος, οἰνοπληθής, πολύπυρος. εὔβως occurs only here, and τρύγη nowhere else in early epic. For the hiatus after σε cf. *Il.* 19.288, *Od.* 6.15, Hes. *Th.* 549, and perhaps *H. Ap.* 88.

56–60 Cf. 535–7 (Delphi). Apollo was worshipped at Athens as Ἑκατόμβαιος (Hesychius s.v. Ἑκατομβαίων), also on Myconos, and doubtless in other Ionian communities, where there was a month Hecatombaion (including Delos): cf. *RE* VII 2785–6 s.v. Hekatombaion, Hekatombaios.

58 ἐνθάδ' ἀγειρόμενοι: cf. *Od.* 16.390, 17.379.

59 The text as transmitted is thoroughly corrupt, but the conjectures of Baumeister (and also Cobet) and of Stoll make good sense. Formular usage offers no obvious parallels, but the general sense must be similar to the point of 535–7.

δημοῦ means 'fat' here.

60 Cf. *Il.* 14.455, 23.843 χειρὸς ἀπὸ στιβαρῆς, *Od.* 9.535, 11.115 νηὸς ἐπ' ἀλλοτρίης, and *Od.* 9.135 ἐπεὶ μάλα πῖαρ ὑπ' οὖδας. πῖαρ is a noun: 'since there is no richness below the ground'. The custom of making offerings from all over the Greek world on Delos should probably be linked to the famous tradition of the Hyperborean offerings, brought (supposedly) from the distant north via Greece (cf. Hdt. 4.33–5, Call. *H.* 4.278–99, Paus. 1.31.2). In later inscriptions we find a range of valuable objects (especially φιάλαι) recorded as having been offered by various cities or rulers: see Bruneau (1970) 93–114. These θεωρίαι (official delegations) are closely associated with the choir of Delian girls (Δηλιάδες), who seem often to have made the dedications on their behalf (cf. on *H. Ap.* 156–7). See also Tréheux (1953) 758–74, Kowalzig (2007) 120–4.

61–82 Delos' reply is tripartite: (a) joyful acceptance; (b) fearful anxiety; (c) request for an oath. Her fear that Apollo will prove ἀτάσθαλος has puzzled critics: how could the god who was later viewed as a paradigm for Greek morality be described by a word indicating excessive and hybristic behaviour? But Apollo has his violent and dangerous side, which strikes terror even among the Olympians (cf. 2–4): cf. his later treatment of Telphousa, for example (375–87). On Apollo as a god of violence see Detienne (1998). Moreover, what we have here is not a characterisation of Apollo by the poet, rather it is Delos' report of her anxiety about what people predict that his character will be. She is emphasising the extreme contrast between her own insignificance and his future grandeur, together with her fear of his potential violence, in order to ensure that Leto's promise will really be secure.

61 Cf. *Od.* 2.35 ὣς φάτο, χαῖρε δὲ φήμηι . . . , and *Il.* 14.270 ὣς φάτο, χήρατο δ' Ὕπνος, ἀμειβόμενος δὲ προσηύδα, where the neat tripartite structure is the same (see Janko ad loc.).

62 In Hesiod's *Theogony* (404–8) and elsewhere Leto is the daughter of the Titan Coios. The verse Ἥρη, πρέσβα θεά, θυγάτηρ (-ερ) μεγάλοιο Κρόνοιο occurs four times in the *Iliad* (5.721 etc.), and reminiscence of this may have led to corruption here.

63 ἐγώ γε anticipates the following reservation: 'Personally I should be delighted, but . . .'

64 δυσηχής ('ill-sounding') in Homer is used of war and death (*Il.* 2.686 etc.), always in genitive formulae. The original derivation was probably from ἄχος, but the poet may have connected it with ἠχέω.

αἰνῶς . . . ἐτήτυμον adds double emphasis to her self-deprecation.

65 **περιτιμήεσσα:** περιτιμήεις occurs only here.

67 **ἀτάσθαλον:** ἀτάσθαλος is normally used in early epic in a pejorative sense, of excessively violent characters or behaviour. In *H.* 15.6, however, it is applied to Heracles (πολλὰ μὲν αὐτὸς ἔρεξεν ἀτάσθαλα), who is called 'best of men on earth' and now lives in heaven (15.1, 7–8). In *H. Herm.* 296 it is used of Hermes' fart, in a comic passage. Here what Delos fears is the potential violence of the god.

68 **πρυτανευσέμεν:** πρυτανεύειν occurs first here, but Πρύτανις is a proper name of a Lycian at *Il.* 5.678. The noun is often used of deities in later poetry, and is very probably a loan word from Asia Minor (cf. Chantraine, *Dict.* s.v.). There is no need to assume any pejorative sense (as Clay (1989), 37–8 does).

69 = *Od.* 3.3, 12.386.

70 Cf. *Il.* 1.555 etc.

72 κραναήπεδος occurs only here.

Jacoby (1933) thought that 72 was a variant version (with ἀτιμήσηι) for 73. But the combination of participles in 72–3 is not unusual. Allen and Sikes compared *Il.* 12.113–14 (with aorist and present participles), and examples in classical Greek (Ar. *Nub.* 937–8 etc.).

73 καταστρέψας probably means 'overturning' rather than 'trampling on' (as LSJ suggest). It occurs first here.

ὤσει with short-vowel subjunctive actually represents the original form in Chios and other Ionic-speaking areas, as shown by later inscriptions: see Schulze (1885) 491–4, Marx (1907) 620. The line dramatically suggests the ease with which the god could sink the island under the sea. In later legend Delos was originally a floating island, but became fixed in the sea at the birth of Apollo (cf. Pindar, frr. 33d, 52h.49 Snell–Maehler, Call. *H.* 4.30–54).

ἁλὸς ἐν πελάγεσσιν: cf. *Od.* 5.335.

74–8 Delos switches to direct prediction, with a graphic picture of her future plight.

75 κλύσσει 'will wash over'.

76 = 221, 245 (in a similar context of the god's pleasure). Cf. ἐν ἄλσεϊ δενδρήεντι at *Od.* 9.200, *H. Ap.* 235, 384.

77–8 This vivid motif of sea creatures making their homes in Delos adds pathos and perhaps also humour to her plea. The polypus ('many-footer') and its 'chamber' (θαλάμη) appear in the simile at *Od.* 5.432, and Hesiod speaks of the 'boneless one' (octopus, probably) and its 'fireless home and miserable haunts' in *Op.* 524–5. Seals are mentioned in Odysseus' wanderings in Egypt (*Od.* 4.404ff.), and again at 15.480. The only type of seal found in Mediterranean waters is the Mediterranean monk seal (S. West on *Od.* 4.404). They must have been commoner in antiquity in the Aegean than they are now (cf. Steier, *RE* s.v. Phoke). Here they are described as black. Call. *H.* 4.242–3 must be a reminiscence of this passage, where Hera contemptuously says that Leto may give birth ὅθι φῶκαι | εἰναλίαι τίκτουσιν, ἐνὶ σπιλάδεσσιν ἐρήμοις. ἀκηδέα is also a graphic touch ('carefree' or 'uncaring'): cf. *Il.* 21.122–3, where the fish which Achilles says will lick Lycaon's wounds are ἀκηδέες. For οἰκία ποιήσονται in the context of non-human creatures cf. *Il.* 12.168, where it is used of wasps.

79–88 The motif of asking a deity to swear a solemn oath, and its ratification by cosmic powers, is Homeric: cf. *Il.* 14.271–9, *Od.* 177–87, 10.342–5, and for similar oaths *Il.* 15.36–44, *H. Dem.* 259–61, *H. Herm.* 518–23, with Arend (1933) 122–3.

79–82 The conditional clause has no apodosis and is equivalent to a request: 'If only you would...', i.e. 'please will you...?' The line resembles *Od.* 5.178, 10.343, and especially *H. Herm.* 518 (with θεῶν instead of θεά), but in all these cases there is an apodosis. 80–1 are echoed by 258–9, 287–8 (with ἀνθρώποις); cf. also 247–8. The sense is 'please promise that Apollo will build a temple *first* here, and (only) *afterwards* throughout the rest of the world'. There is no need to assume a lacuna after 81. For πάντας ἐπ' ἀνθρώπους cf. *Od.* 1.299 etc. πολυώνυμος implies that he will have many cults (cf. Hes. *Th.* 685, of Styx; *H. Dem.* 18, 32). χρηστήριος or χρηστήριον are not found in Homer; cf. 248, 259, 288, and Hes. fr. 240.6.

There is virtually no evidence in later archaeological sources for an oracle of Apollo on Delos. Only one inscription refers to a μαντεῖον (*IG* XI 2165.44, early third century BC), but we do not know whose this was. In literature, cf. possibly Pindar fr. 140a.58–9 (Snell–Maehler) of Heracles, ἀρχαγέται τε Δάλου πίθετο, which has been taken as indicating a Delian oracle: Kowalzig (2007) 81–102, especially 95–6. A story told by Semos of Delos (*FGrH* 396 F12) has been interpreted as referring to an oracle, but may only concern interpretation by local seers of unusual omens at a sacrifice. There are a number of later references in literary sources to Delos as a centre of prophecy, but most of these refer back to the mythical past. Lucan (6.425), however, speaks of Sextus Pompeius as *not* consulting the tripods of Delos, and Theodoret (*Hist. Eccl.* 3.16) refers to consultation by the Emperor Julian of an oracle on Delos amongst other Apolline centres. Much of the other evidence simply assumes oracular activity in general terms for the island. It would be odd if Apollo's supposedly oldest sanctuary did not originally have some oracular functions, but presumably these were eclipsed by the rise of Delphi and other centres in the historical period. For discussion of the evidence see Bruneau (1970) 142–60.

83–6 For θεῶν μέγαν ὅρκον cf. *Od.* 2.377 (and 378 = *H. Ap.* 89), *H. Herm.* 519, Hes. *Th.* 784. The form of the oath, by Earth, Heaven, and Styx, is that used in *Il.* 15.36–8 and *Od.* 5.184–6, in both cases by a goddess. Hesiod describes in great detail the procedure when a god swears by Styx (*Th.* 775–806). Cf. also Janko on *Il.* 14.271–9, 15.36–46. In 85–6 Styx is herself the ὅρκος, i.e. the object by which the oath is sworn, as in *Il.* 2.755, Hes. *Th.* 400, 784, etc.

87 ἦ μήν introduces the oath: cf. ἦ μέν *Il.* 1.77, *Od.* 14.160, and for ἦ μήν A. *Th.* 531 etc.; and Denniston, GP^2 351, 389.

θυώδης . . . βωμὸς καὶ τέμενος: cf. *H. Aph.* 59, and with θυήεις *Il.* 8.48 etc. The fact that Leto does not mention the oracular temple is not significant. She has already offered a temple (51–60), and χρηστήριον does not need to be repeated, since Apollo is by nature an oracular god. For the probable location of the altar, and its identification with the altar known later as the κεράτινος βωμός, see Bruneau and Ducat (2005) 201–2.

88 τίσει δέ σέ γ' ἔξοχα πάντων: the promise of exceptional honour confirms the suggestion in 53–60 (with τίσει 53) and 65.

89–126 *The birth of Apollo.* Delos rejoiced, but Leto was pierced by bitter labour-pangs for nine days. All the major goddesses were there, except Hera, and Eileithyia, whom Hera kept in ignorance on Olympus out of jealousy of Leto. But the others sent Iris to summon her, promising a large gold necklace, without letting Hera notice. So Iris and Eileithyia came down to Delos, and Leto gave birth to the god, clasping the palm tree in her arms. The goddesses washed him and wrapped him in fine baby clothes. His mother did not nurse him, but Themis gave him nectar and ambrosia. And Leto rejoiced at his birth.

After the slow pace of the introductory narrative, with its emphasis on reluctance and delay, the imminent birth is further postponed through Hera's jealousy. But events move more quickly from 102 onwards: Iris' rapid journey to fetch Eileithyia, who is easily persuaded, and their descent on Delos occupy only thirteen lines, and (in contrast to 50–88) there is no direct speech. The moment Eileithyia begins to set foot on Delos (ἔβαινε, 115), the birth starts to take place. This climactic event occurs within five lines (115–19), and another seven describe the care of the newborn god and Leto's joy. We have here the familiar technique of the build-up of suspense, itself contributing to the sense of the momentous character of what is to come, followed by rapid action. This part of the narrative is framed by the references to the joy of Delos and of Leto at the birth (90, 125–6). This theme contrasts sharply with Leto's suffering in delayed labour (91–2) and Hera's jealousy because Leto's son will be so great (99–107). 117–18 (Apollo's birth) and 125–6 (joy at the event) also repeat themes of the prologue (12–13, 14–18). Moreover the narrative, like the prologue, moves from fear of Apollo to joy at his appearance, and as in the opening scene he is greeted by his father with a cup of nectar (10–11), so too after his arrival on earth he is fed on nectar and ambrosia by Themis (124–5). Thus the narrative elaborates themes already present in the opening of the poem. See Forderer (1971) 86–7.

89 = *Il.* 14.280 etc.

90 This line recalls 63, with γόνος instead of γονή. In Homer γόνος normally means 'offspring' or 'race, stock', but it is unnecessary to emend to γονῆι (Franke). Both words are probably used to mean 'engendering' or 'birth' here (cf. A. *Supp.* 173, etc.).

91–2 For 'nine days and nights' cf. *Od.* 10.28 ἐννῆμαρ... νύκτας τε καὶ ἦμαρ. Nine days is a conventional period in early epic (see Kirk on *Il.* 1.53–4, Richardson on 24.660–7), and ἐννῆμαρ is presumably expanded to 'nine days and nine nights' for greater emphasis. ἀελπτός is not Homeric; cf. *H. Dem.* 219 and Hes. fr. 204.95, where it means 'unexpected'. Here it perhaps means 'hopeless', i.e. 'desperate'. The epithet is placed emphatically at the end of the line with necessary enjambment. Birth-pangs are compared to the sharp pains caused by a spear-wound at *Il.* 11.269–72: so here πέπαρτο. Cf. also *Il.* 5.399 ὀδύνῃσι πεπαρμένος. In later accounts of the birth of Apollo and Artemis cf. Simon. fr. 519.32–4 ἐβάρυνον ὠδῖνες, Pi. fr. 33d.3–4 ὠδίνεσσι ἀγχιτόκοις, and Kowalzig (2007) 63.

92–5 Leto is assisted at the birth by other goddesses, just as women came to help with a birth in human society: cf. Ar. *Eccl.* 526–34, and Garland (1990) 61–4. The goddesses named here presumably represent primarily the generation of the older or Titan deities. Dione (mother of Aphrodite in Homer) is named with Themis and other deities at Hes. *Th.* 17, Themis and Rhea together at *Th.* 135. Amphitrite, however, is a Nereid at *Th.* 243. In the *Odyssey* she represents the sea, and is perhaps present because Delos is a 'sea-girt' island. Themis, however, will also play the important role of feeding the infant Apollo on divine food (123–5), and this is symbolic in terms of his future association with morality. But the list is only a selection of the most important among the goddesses, as 95 shows.

92 ἔνδοθι means 'at home with Leto' here, i.e. on Delos. Cf. *Od.* 5.58 τὴν δ' ἔνδοθι τέτμεν ἐοῦσαν, Hes. fr. 205.4 ἔνδοθι νήσου, Call. *H.* 4.222 Λητώ τοι μίτρην ἀναλύεται ἔνδοθι νήσου.

93 Cf. *Il.* 17.377 ὅσσοι ἄριστοι ἔσαν. Dione usually has a short opening syllable (*Il.* 5.370 etc.), but variation of scansion is common in proper names (cf. *Il.* 5.31, 455 Ἄρες, Ἆρες, etc.).

94 There was a cult of Themis at Ichnae in Thessaly, in the region of Thessaliotis (Strabo 9.5.14, 435). Stephanus of Byzantium and Hesychius connect the title with Ichnae in Macedonia (near Pella), and Hesychius (s.v. Ἰχναίη) says that there was an oracle of Apollo there. Themis' cult is well attested in Thessaly (Vos (1956) 45–7, and K. Latte, *RE* VA 1628 s.v. Themis). Cf. Lycophron 129, and *AP* 9.405, where Nemesis is called ἰχναίη πάρθενος. 'Tracker' is a suitable epithet for deities of justice, and the title seems to have been interpreted in this way (Schol. Lyc. 129). For ἀγάστονος ('loud-moaning') Ἀμφιτρίτη cf. *Od.* 12.97 and Quintus of Smyrna 14.644 (πολυστόνου).

95–101 96 is omitted by some MSS, and has been regarded as a variant for 98, or as an interpolation. West (1975) 169–70 argued that the original version lacked the theme of Hera's opposition, and wished to remove 95, 98–101, 105–6 (cf. also West (2003) 11). But all these lines can be defended. It is arbitrary to cut Hera's role out of the poem. The repetition between 96 and 98, although not elegant, is paralleled elsewhere (e.g. 351–2, 537–8). The important point is that Hera is detaining Eileithyia within Zeus's palace on Olympus (cf. 110–11), and thereby preventing her from learning about Leto's labour. 98 elaborates this point: Hera is in the palace (96), and Eileithyia is also there (on Olympus etc.). See also 109–12n. For the first half of 96 cf. *Od.* 1.114 ἧστο γὰρ ἐν μνηστῆρσι, for Διὸς νεφεληγερέταο *Il.* 5.631 etc.

97–101 These lines resemble *Il.* 13.521–5, where Ares is kept on Olympus by Zeus, in ignorance of his son's death at Troy (cf. 521 οὐδ' ἄρα πώ τι πέπυστο . . . 523 ἀλλ' ὅ γ' ἄρ' ἄκρωι Ὀλύμπωι ὑπὸ χρυσέοισι νέφεσσιν | ἧστο, Διὸς βουλῆισιν ἐελμένος . . .). Hera's detention of the goddess of childbirth is similar to the story of the births of Eurystheus and Heracles at *Il.* 19.114–24, where Hera checks the Eileithyiai, and so delays Heracles' arrival in the world. Eileithyia, or Eileithyiai, are in fact Hera's daughters (*Il.* 11.270–1, Hes. *Th.* 922–3), and the name could be used as a cult title of Hera (cf. Farnell, *Cults* II 608ff.). For μογοστόκος Εἰλείθυια cf. *Il.* 16.187, 19.193, and in the plural 11.270. The epithet means something like '(goddess of) birth-pangs' (cf. LSJ), although here the pangs have come without the goddess, and it is she who brings them to an end. Essentially this is her main function, as her name (cf. ἐλυθ-, ἐλευθ-) means 'the one who comes to one's aid' (cf. Hainsworth on *Il.* 11.270).

Eileithyia had an important cult on Delos, because of her role in Apollo's birth. In the hymn for the Delians by the Lycian poet Olen she was brought from the Hyperboreans to assist, and her worship was associated with that of the Hyperborean maidens, Hyperoche and Laodice: cf. Hdt. 4.35, Paus. 1.18.5, 8.21.3, 19.27.2. Olen calls her older than Cronos, and mother of Eros, and Pausanias interprets him as equating her with Destiny and adds that the Athenians regarded Delos as the place from which her cult originated. Her temple (*Eileithyiaion*) and annual festival are several times mentioned on Delian inscriptions. See Bruneau (1970) 212–19.

99 φραδμοσύνηις: not Homeric, but cf. Hes. *Th.* 626 Γαίης φραδμοσύνηισιν, etc. The plural is always used in Hesiod (4×), but the singular, which is a variant reading, would also be possible; cf. A.R. 2.647 φραδμοσύνηι.

100–1 ζηλοσύνηι: ζηλοσύνη occurs only here, for ζῆλος. For the rest of 100–1 cf. 13 etc.

100 ὅ τ' = ὅτι τε (Chantraine, *GH* II 288f.).

υἱὸν . . . κρατερόν τε is formulaic (*Il.* 4.89 etc.).

102–14 The mission of Iris to fetch Eileithyia resembles Homeric divine messenger scenes, but the type is here abbreviated, to include only the essential points: the promise of a gift, the need to avoid Hera's notice, Iris' journey and delivery of her message, and the descent to Delos. See Arend (1933) 54–61.

102–4 Iris was worshipped by the Delians on the 'island of Hecate' (Semos of Delos, *FGrH* 396 F 5), but this may not be directly connected with her role here. In Call. *H.* 4.66ff. she is the agent of Hera, preventing other islands from aiding Leto. Hera sends her on a secret errand at *Il.* 18.166–8. The promise of a necklace resembles the scene in *Iliad* 14 where Hera enlists the aid of Sleep, offering him first a golden throne and footstool, and then, when he shows reluctance, adding one of the Charites as a prospective wife (238–41, 267–8). The description is similar to *Od.* 18.295–6 ὅρμον . . . | χρύσεον, ἠλέκτροισιν ἐερμένον . . . ; cf. 15.460 χρύσεον ὅρμον ἔχων, μετὰ δ' ἠλέκτροισιν ἔερτο.

103 ὅρμον: Lawler (1948) 2–6 suggests that ὅρμος means a garland (as perhaps in Alcman, *PMG* 91). She gives examples from later festivals of garlands of several cubits in length (e.g. Ath. 678AB), but her argument that in the Delian inventories there are garlands dedicated to Eileithyia which are called ὅρμοι is not supported by the evidence to which she refers (ὅρμος is distinguished from στέφανος and στεφανῶμα in these inscriptions). It is possible that the nine-cubit necklace is mentioned as an *aition* for an actual necklace dedicated to Eileithyia in her sanctuary before the hymn was composed. In later legend (Hdt. 4.35) Eileithyia is rewarded with tribute from the Hyperboreans (see 115–16n.).

104 λίνοισιν: It is not clear whether λίνα are gilded threads, or made of gold wire combined with thread to strengthen it, or gold wire on its own. Gold thread, composed of 'threads of silver-gilt metal strip wound directly on a core' of silk or linen, has been found in pieces of embroidery from Koropi, near Athens, probably of the late fifth century BC (J. Beckwith in *The Illustrated London News*, 23 January 1954, p. 114), and these have been compared to a small number of surviving examples from later periods found near Kertch (third century BC), at Dura-Europus, Palmyra, and elsewhere. This seems an attractive solution. On the other hand, wire made of gold or other metals was used in the ancient Near East and Greece in the Bronze Age and classical times, to make chains for necklaces and other jewellery: cf. Schliemann (1878) 120–1, Higgins (1961)

13–16, 82, 99 (with plate 13F), 128, etc., Moorey (1985) 85–7, Bielefeld, *Arch. Hom.* C 54 ('Schmuck'). λίνα are mentioned quite often in later inventories, e.g. from Delos itself: cf. *IG* XI.2 208–22 ἄλλα παντόδαπα χρυσᾶ ἀνηρμένα ἐπὶ λίνου and other references in AHS on *H. Ap.* 104 (but read *BCH* x 464, and *IG* XI.2 162B.18 etc.). A gold necklace in *IG* XI.2 162B.17–18 has its weight recorded σὺν τοῖς λίνοις: this may imply that the λίνα themselves had some weight, i.e. included some metal.

ἐερμένον, from εἴρω, means 'strung with'. In both these cases there are variants ἐεργμένον, ἔερκτο, as here, which would have to derive from ἔρδω, meaning 'worked with'. Wilamowitz (1916) 447 n. 4 keeps ἐεργμένον here, translating 'made out of golden threads' (or 'golden wires').

ἐννεάπηχυν ('nine cubits long') is a vast length for a necklace, even that of a goddess (*c.* 13.6 ft). Such a ὅρμος would have been wound several times round the neck, and worn loosely, by contrast with the more tight-fitting single ἴσθμιον ('neck-band'): cf. Schol. *Od.* 18.300, Eust. 1847.49–50, Helbig (1887) 268–71, and Bielefeld, *Arch. Hom.* C 18. Nevertheless, the size seems absurdly exaggerated. But there is no obvious reason to suspect parody or humour (as Janko does in the similar case of *Il.* 14.233–41). ἐννεάπηχυς in Homer is used of a 'yoke-binding' (*Il.* 24.270) and of the breadth of the giants Otus and Ephialtes (*Od.* 11.311).

105–8 The use of indirect speech here and at 111–12 resembles that of *H. Dem.* 314–16, where again Iris is sent as a messenger, and *H. Ap.* 108 is similar to *H. Dem.* 317. See Richardson on *H. Dem.* 314–23, where other examples of indirect speech in epic are discussed. It is commoner in the *Hymns* than in Homer: see Nünlist (2004) 38–9. For νόσφιν . . . λευκωλένου Ἥρης cf. *H. Ap.* 95. 107 is formulaic (107a: *Il.* 20.318 etc.; 107b: *Il.* 5.368 etc.). For 108 cf. *Il.* 2.183 etc. βῆ δὲ θέειν; *Od.* 17.517 διήνυσε, and ῥίμφα . . . διήνυσαν of a journey at *H. Dem.* 380; *H. Dem.* 317 (Iris) μεσσηγὺ διέδραμεν ὦκα πόδεσσιν. The dactylic rhythm of 107–8 is characteristic in such descriptions of swift movement: see examples given by Richardson on *Il.* 24.691, together with *Od.* 2.406, and (most famous of all) *Od.* 11.598, where Dionysius of Halicarnassus *Comp.* 20, comments: 'Does not the speed of the narration outstrip the rush of the stone?'

109–12 The normal pattern of Messenger or Visit scenes is varied here. Instead of entering the house, Iris asks Eileithyia to step outside in order to escape Hera's notice. This incidentally proves that the theme of Hera's jealousy is not a later addition (see 95–101n.). Cf. *Od.* 2.399–406, where Athene (Mentor) calls Telemachus out of the palace in order to address him in secret (400 ἐκπροκαλεσσαμένη). ἔπεα . . . προσηύδα is used only here without a speech following.

114 This line resembles *Il.* 5.778 (Athena and Hera) αἱ δὲ βάτην τρήρωσι πελείασιν ἴθμαθ' ὁμοῖαι. Aristophanes (*Birds* 575) quotes 'Homer' as comparing Iris to a τρήρωνι πελείῃ, perhaps referring to this passage (as one scholiast on *Birds* suggests). Cf. 443, echoed in *Knights* 1016. The point of the comparison is uncertain. The Homeric scholia suggested either rapidity and flight, or that they move delicately in order to escape notice. The latter fits well here, though less obviously so in *Iliad* 5 where there is no need for secrecy. τρήρων probably originally meant 'timid', but could be used as a noun denoting the genus pigeon, with πέλεια for a particular type, e.g. the rock dove (cf. Dunbar on *Birds* 575).

115–16 As Eileithyia sets foot on Delos (ἔβαινε), the actual birth begins. The asyndeton at 115 is normal with εὖτε first in the sentence (cf. 427, *Il.* 6.392, etc.). It is also effective here dramatically, and the moment of setting foot in a place or on its threshold was often seen as a significant one in antiquity (see Richardson on *H. Dem.* 188).

116 τόκος εἷλε is a vivid expression for the onset of birth. In Hdt. 4.35 the Hyperborean girls Hyperoche and Laodice bring Eileithyia tribute ἀντὶ τοῦ ὠκυτόκου ('in return for the speed of the delivery').

117–19 The event is described in a series of five brief and powerful clauses, with necessary enjambment at 117–18. For the palm tree see 16–18n. Lengthening of the final iota of the dative *in arsi* (i.e. when it coincides with the verse beat) is common in Homer.

To give birth kneeling seems to have been common in Greek antiquity: see Samter (1911) 6ff., and Frazer on Paus. 8.48.7. In epic cf. *Il.* 19.110, Hes. *Th.* 460, and more generally see Garland (1990) 59ff.

118 λειμῶνι μαλακῶι: cf. Hes. *Th.* 279, *H. Dem.* 7, *H.* 19.25, etc.

μείδησε δὲ γαῖ' ὑπένερθεν: Earth smiles in response to this cosmic event. Cf. the more developed version of this theme at 135–9, and Theognis 5–10 Φοῖβε ἄναξ, ὅτε μέν σε θεὰ τέκε πότνια Λητώ, | φοίνικος ῥαδίνης χερσὶν ἐφαψαμένη, | ἀθανάτων κάλλιστον ἐπὶ τροχοειδέϊ λίμνηι, | πᾶσα μὲν ἐπλήσθη Δῆλος ἀπειρεσίη | ὀδμῆς ἀμβροσίης, ἐγέλασσε δὲ Γαῖα πελώρη, | γήθησεν δὲ βαθὺς πόντος ἁλὸς πολιῆς. Cf. also Limenius, *Paean* 5–10 (Powell, *CA* p. 149), and for this theme of cosmic joy at a divine birth or epiphany see other examples quoted by Richardson on *H. Dem.* 13. Here Earth participates in the birth, perhaps herself as a goddess of fertility.

119 ἐκ δ' ἔθορε πρὸ φόωσδε: cf. *H. Herm.* 20 ἀπ' ἀθανάτων θόρε γυίων; *Il.* 16.188 ἐξάγαγε πρὸ φόωσδε, and similarly 19.118, *H. Herm.* 12.

θεαὶ δ' ὀλόλυξαν ἅπασαι: the ὀλολυγή (a women's ritual cry) marks the moment of relief after the tension of the birth: Wilamowitz (1916) 448, and Deubner (1941) 5. Cf. *H. Ap.* 445–7 (αἱ δ' ὀλόλυξαν at Apollo's power), and Pindar, *Paean* 12 (fr. 52m) 14–17 (of the birth of Apollo and Artemis): ἔλαμψαν δ' ἀελίου δέμας ὅπω[ς | ἀγλαὸν ἐς φάος ἰόντες δίδυμοι | παῖδες, πόλυν ῥόθο[ν] ἵεσαν ἀπὸ στομ[άτων | Ἐ]λείθυιά τε καὶ Λά[χ]εσις. Callimachus (*H.* 4.255–8) expands the theme; cf. also Theocr. 17.64. In *Paean* 12 and also Simonides, *PMG* 519 fr. 55, this ritual cry is taken up or echoed by the local women of Delos: cf. Kowalzig (2007) 63–5.

120–2 After the birth the child is washed and wrapped in swaddling-clothes, like any other newborn baby, although what follows is definitely not a matter of routine. The first bath was also a standard feature of divine birth-stories (cf. Parker (1983) 50). It is appropriate that this is the first moment at which the poet actually addresses Apollo in the narrative part of the hymn. This hymn is unique among the long ones in its use of apostrophe within the narrative (cf. Introduction 2(c)). In ἤιε Φοῖβε (cf. *Il.* 15.365, 20.152) the epithet ἤϊος derives from the ritual cry to the god ἰή or ἰὴ ἰέ (see on 272, and Janko on *Il.* 15.365).

For ἁγνῶς καὶ καθαρῶς ('in purity and cleanness') cf. Hes. *Op.* 337. Purification after a mortal birth was essential, but Apollo himself is also a god of purity, whose name Φοῖβος was actually interpreted as meaning 'pure' (cf. Hesychius, LSJ s.v.). His swaddling-clothes are described as shining white (λευκῶι), fine, brand-new (?), and they are bound with a golden band, all suitable to this deity. Cf. *Il.* 18.353 φάρεϊ λευκῶι, and 14.185 καλῶι νηγατέωι· | λευκὸν δ' ἦν ἠέλιος ὥς. νηγάτεος probably means 'unworn, new' (see Janko ad loc.). See also 200–3, 440–7nn.

123–6 Infant gods and heroes are entrusted to special divine nurses (see on *H. Aph.* 256–80), and given ambrosia and/or nectar. The result is miraculous growth and strength: cf. especially *H. Dem.* 233–41, and Richardson on *H. Dem.* 231–55, 235, 236, 237. 123–5 resemble *H. Dem.* 236 οὔτ' οὖν σῖτον ἔδων, οὐ θησάμενος . . . Δημήτηρ χρίεσκ' ἀμβροσίηι.

123 χρυσάορα: χρυσάωρ and χρυσάορος are formular epithets for Apollo (*Il.* 5.509 etc.; cf. *H. Ap.* 395 χρυσαόρου). There was dispute in antiquity as to whether ἄορ meant simply 'sword' or could refer to any weapon, e.g. Apollo's bow: see Richardson on *H. Dem.* 4, Janko on *Il.* 15.254–9.

θήσατο: θῆσθαι is only used here of the mother, elsewhere of the baby who is being suckled.

124 Themis (cf. 94) was associated with Apollo at Delphi in later literature, or regarded as oracular: cf. especially A. *Eum.* 2–4, where she occupies Delphi before Apollo does, and E. *IT* 1259–69. At *H. Ap.* 253 (and later) θεμιστεύειν is used of Apollo delivering his oracular judgements. Cf. also Pi. *P.* 11.9–10 θέμιν ἱερὰν Πυθῶνά τε καὶ ὀρθοδίκαν γᾶς ὀμφαλόν. In a later legend Themis acts as a nurse to Zeus, with Amaltheia: Hyginus *Astr.* 2.13 ('Musaeus'), Schol. AD *Il.* 15.229. On Themis and Apollo see also Detienne (1998) 150–74.

125 **ἐπήρξατο:** ἐπάρχεσθαι in Homer (*Il.* 1.471 etc.) is used only with δεπάεσσιν, to describe the ritual of pouring a little wine into cups for a libation; cf. Mazon (1937) 319–25. Here the sense must be something like 'offered a first taste of' (*LfgrE* s.v. ἄρχω p. 1390).

125–6 **χαῖρε . . . ἔτικτεν:** this echoes 12–13, again after a scene in which Apollo makes a dramatic epiphany and is served with nectar. The repetition closes the narrative of the birth. What follows describes the first exploits of the new god, although 134–9 are still concerned with the response of goddesses and nature to the event.

127–39 When Apollo had eaten immortal food he immediately broke free of his golden bands, and proclaimed himself god of music, archery, and prophecy. He began to walk over the earth, all the goddesses were amazed, and Delos was filled with gold, rejoicing to be chosen as his home.

After the birth-narrative the god's growth and habitual activities or haunts may be described: cf. for example *H.* 26.3–10, where Dionysus is nurtured by the nymphs and then roams through the woodlands with them. Apollo's growth is miraculously swift, and he then announces his main spheres of activity, which anticipate his exploits later in the poem. His haunts will be described in 140–2, after we have heard of the reactions of the other participants in assisting his birth.

127–9 Cf. *H. Aph.* 260 ἄμβροτον εἶδαρ ἔδουσι (ἀμβρόσιον εἶδαρ *Il.* 2×). For 129 cf. *H.* 7.13 (Dionysus) τὸν δ' οὐκ ἴσχανε δεσμά, | λύγοι δ' ἀπὸ τηλόσ' ἔπιπτον. The form δέσματα is used in Homer and often later, δέσμα in *H. Herm.* 157, 409, *H.* 7.12, 13. πείρατα means 'ropes' here.

The tricolon of 128–9 underlines the miraculous power of the god, breaking all his bonds. Hermes likewise begins to perform his exploits on the day of his birth: cf. *H. Herm.* 17–23, and 21 οὐκέτι δηρὸν ἔκειτο μένων ἱερῶι ἐνὶ λίκνωι. See also Richardson on *H. Dem.* 235 for other examples of this theme, and West (2007) 149–50.

130–50 These lines are echoed by Virgil in the famous simile at *Aen.* 4.143–9: *qualis ubi hibernam Lyciam Xanthique fluenta* | *deserit ac Delum maternam invisit Apollo* (~ 146–50) | *instauratque choros, mixtique altaria circum* | *Cretesque Dryopesque fremunt pictique Agathyrsi:* | *ipse iugis Cynthi graditur* (~ 141) *molli que fluentem* | *fronde premit crinem fingens* (~ 136) *atque implicat auro* (~ 135), | *tela sonant umeris* (~ 131).

130–2 Apollo's music is described in 182–206 and 514–16, his use of the bow in 1–13 and in the story of the killing of the dragon (300–74), and his oracular character is the main theme of the later part of the hymn.

131 Cf. *Il.* 5.891 αἰεὶ γάρ τοι ἔρις τε φίλη πόλεμοί τε μάχαι τε, and similarly Hes. *Th.* 917, *H.* 14.3–4. At *H.* 11.2–4 there is a combination of nouns and a verbal clause describing the deity's activities. The tricolon crescendo structure of 131–2, with the third element taking up a whole line, and the shift from impersonal optative to the emphatic first person singular future tense, all bring out the importance of Apollo's oracular powers. 132 is echoed at *H. Ap.* 252, 292. Callimachus imitates 131–2 at *H.* 2.42–6, adding medicine as his fourth art. In Pindar (*P.* 5.63–9) he is god of medicine, music, and prophecy.

133–4 'So saying he began to walk on the broad-wayed earth.' ἐβίβασκε should mean 'he began to walk': cf. the verb βιβάω (and related forms) in Homer, and for this form cf. παρέβασκε *Il.* 11.103. With the manuscript reading ἀπό the sense must be that Apollo began to leave the earth (for heaven), but βιβάω usually denotes stepping or striding, and it would be odd not to say where he is going (cf. 186–7 where he goes from earth to heaven). With ἐπί Apollo begins to move over the earth and this fits well with 140–2, describing the places he likes to visit. The corruption may have arisen because ἀπὸ χθονὸς εὐρυοδείης is formulaic in Homer and Hesiod.

134 This unusual combination of epithets dignifies Apollo at the start of his activity. When he appears in disguise at 449–50 his hair covers his shoulders.

Cf. *LIMC* II.1 185 s.v. Apollon, for other literary references to his long hair, and for examples from visual art, *LIMC* II.2 s.v. Apollon.

134–9 Wonder is a usual response to a divine epiphany (cf. Richardson on *H. Dem.* 188–90, p. 208, and especially *H.* 28.6 where again it is all the gods who are seized with σέβας). The miraculous response of Delos is also characteristic of epiphanies (see *H. Ap.* 118n.): cf. *H.* 28.9–13. At Dionysus' appearance especially, natural miracles occur as in *H.* 7.34–42 (θαύματα ἔργα), E. *Ba.* 704–11, 726–7, etc. This gilding of the whole island, however, goes beyond what we find elsewhere in early epic. Callimachus develops it further at *H.* 4.260–73, and seems to echo and expand *H. Ap.* 137–8 in 264–73, where Delos rejoices because she will be loved by Apollo more than any other land. For parallels in Vedic hymns to the theme of divine rejoicing at the birth of a deity see West (2007) 313.

135–9 Most MSS omit 136–8, leaving 135 and 139 as a simple description of Delos' response. Six MSS have 136–8 either in the text or the margin, in some cases with a comment and marginal sign (*antisigma*), which seems to indicate that they existed as an alternative reading, or as an additional passage. (The *antisigma* could be used for a number of reasons in ancient texts: cf. McNamee (1992) 14–15.) It seems best to view 135–8 and 135 + 139 as variant versions of this passage. Callimachus echoes 137–8 (see 134–9n.), and therefore must have known these lines.

135–6 χρύσωι . . . βεβρίθει: βρίθειν is commonly used of vegetation (*Il.* 8.307 etc.). Cf. especially *H. Dem.* 472–3 πᾶσα δὲ φύλλοισίν τε καὶ ἄνθεσιν εὐρεῖα χθὼν | ἔβρισ'. So here the idea is presumably of the island bursting out in golden vegetation. This might be seen as support for transposing 139 to follow 135 and reading βεβρίθηι in 136 (Gemoll). Bruneau (1970) 89 linked the scene to the sudden growth of flowers in springtime on Delos, the time (probably) of the celebration of Apollo's birthday, in the Delian month Hieros (February–March).

136 γενέθλην: this word in the meaning 'offspring' is paralleled by *Il.* 5.270, Hes. fr. 204.57, and in tragedy S. *El.* 129, 226, etc. For γηθοσύνηι (in this position) cf. *Il.* 13.29, 21.390; for οἰκία θέσθαι *H. Ap.* 46 (in same position).

137–8 θεὸς εἵλετο . . . ἠπείρου τε means 'the god chose to make her his home out of all the islands and the mainland'. For νήσων ἠπείρου τε cf. 21.

138 φίλησε δὲ κηρόθι μᾶλλον: cf. *Od.* 15.370 φιλεῖ δέ με κηρόθι μᾶλλον (and κηρόθι μᾶλλον 9× *Il.* and *Od.*).

139 For ῥίον οὔρεος ἄνθεσιν ὕλης cf. *H.* 1.8 ὄρος ἀνθέον ὕληι, and *H. Dem.* 386, *H. Aph.* 285. ὡς ὅτε τε can stand without a verb, as at *Il.* 12.232.

140–78 Apollo sometimes set foot on Mt Cynthus and sometimes wandered elsewhere, for he has many places dear to him. But he loves Delos most, where the Ionians gather for his festival. A visitor would think they were immortal when he saw them there. A special marvel are the Delian girls who are the god's attendants. They sing in praise of Apollo, Leto, and Artemis, and then they sing in honour of men and women of the past, and they can imitate the voices of all men wonderfully well.

May Apollo and Artemis be favourable, and to all you girls also I bid farewell. Remember me in time to come, and if a stranger asks you who is the sweetest singer, tell him it is the blind man who lives in Chios whose songs are best of all. In return, I shall spread your fame throughout the world. But I shall not cease to praise Apollo, whom Leto bore.

Apollo's travels over the world (cf. 133–4) close the narrative of the first part of the hymn, which moves imperceptibly back to the present tense to describe again (as in 20–4) the range of the god's influence. This whole passage in turn acts as introduction (or *priamel*) to the extended praise of Delos which follows. This takes the form of a vivid description of the great Ionian festival of Apollo and its participants (146–55), and the focus of this general scene is then narrowed to the praise of the Delian girls and their extraordinary songs (156–64).

The following passage (165–76) resembles the closing section of other hymns in its threefold themes. Conventionally, a hymn closed with salutation of the deity, a request for favour, and a promise in return, usually to praise the god in future. Cf. *H. Dem.* 490–5, *H.* 6.19–21, 10.4–6, etc. This form is adapted here to a double purpose, honour to the gods and to the Delian girls, and it is they who, unusually, occupy the front of the stage, and with whose favour the poet is chiefly concerned. Moreover, what appears to be the closure of the hymn eventually becomes a transition to other themes, as the poet declares his intention of continuing his praise of Apollo (177–8), instead of (as usual) moving on to a separate song (see Richardson on *H. Dem.* 495). Cf. Miller (1986) 60–6, against the view that 177–8 are actually a closing formula.

Thus, as the text stands, the first part of the hymn acts as a large-scale introduction to the longer narrative which follows about the foundation of the Delphic oracle (207–544). In between, we have a prelude to this narrative similar to that at the opening of the hymn (1–18, 179–206).

140 αὐτός may be used of Apollo by contrast with Delos, but it is quite often applied to this god in an honorific way: cf. 181, *H. Herm.* 234, *H. Aph.* 151, *Il.* 1.47, 17.322, and Richardson on *H. Dem.* 371–2.

Here the god is addressed with a whole-verse formula, for the first time in the hymn. In fact, the references to him have become progressively grander, starting with simple name + epithet or name formulae, and then going on to name + two epithets (134), and so to this whole verse. This particular combination of epithets occurs nowhere else, but cf. ἀργυρότοξε (4× *Il.*), ἄναξ ἑκατηβόλ' Ἄπολλον (*Od.* 8.339). There is also marked assonance of initial vowels, making an euphonious effect. See also Bergren (1982) 92.

141–2 There could be an allusion to the cult of Apollo on the top of Mt Cynthus (see on 16–18). The reference to Cynthus anticipates the praise of Delos at 146–64, framing the intervening passage. For ἄλλοτε . . . ἄλλοτε in this context of the god's haunts cf. especially *H.* 19.8–11, and see Miller (1986) 56–7 on the *priamel* technique used here.

142 There is no need to emend αὖ to ἄν (i.e. ἀνά), since ἠλασκάζειν takes a direct accusative at *Od.* 9.457 (where it means 'flee from' or 'avoid'), and the related ἀλᾶσθαι is used with direct object later; cf. also *H. Ap.* 175 στρεφόμεσθα πόλεις.

νήσους τε καὶ ἀνέρας is similar to ἤπειρον . . . νήσους (21) and νήσων ἠπείρου τε (138), and must mean 'islands and mankind elsewhere'.

143–5 143 means 'Many are your temples (etc.)', and 144–5 are a separate sentence which repeats 22–3 (with τε φίλαι for τοι ἅδον). For 143 cf. 76 etc.

146–72 Thucydides (3.104.3–6) quotes 146–50 and 165–72, with variant readings, as evidence that there used in earlier times to be a festival on Delos, which included musical and athletic contests (cf. Introduction 2(b)). He ascribes the hymn to Homer, and calls it προοίμιον Ἀπόλλωνος. He also quotes 165–72 as evidence of a musical contest, in other words, he seems to see this passage as a plea by the poet for victory on this occasion. Thus he evidently thought that the poem was composed to be sung at the Delian festival. Aristides (34.35) also cites 169–71, probably echoing Thucydides' quotation.

Thucydides' text is too different to be entirely due to misquotation from memory, and therefore may be taken as further evidence (together with 136–9) that the text of this hymn was subject to variation in the classical period. This in its turn suggests its relative popularity, which is also indicated by the frequency with which it was quoted and imitated by other writers.

The antiquity of the Delian festival is indicated by the tradition that Eumelos of Corinth (late eighth century BC?) composed a processional hymn for the Messenians on the first occasion when they sent a sacrifice and chorus to Delos (Paus. 4.1.1; cf. *PMG* 696). That Delos was an important place of pilgrimage by the time of the *Odyssey* is suggested by *Od.* 6.162–9, where Odysseus speaks of visiting the island and admiring the palm tree by Apollo's altar. Moreover, an Athenian regulation concerning the Deliastai (the Attic mission to Delos) probably dates from Solon's time (Ath. 234EF): see Parker (1996) 87–8. Athenian tradition connected the festival's foundation, or the sending of the first Attic *theoria* to Delos, with either Theseus or Erysichthon (Plut. *Thes.* 21, Paus. 1.31.2, 8.48.3, Phanodemus, *FGrH* 325 F 2, etc.). Thucydides says that after the time of the *Hymn to Apollo* the islanders and Athenians continued to send choirs to the festival, but the other contests and most of the activities were probably brought to an end by adverse circumstances, until Athens restored the festival with the addition of horse races after purifying the island in 426–425 BC. The revived festival was four-yearly: it is not clear from Thucydides whether the earlier one was annual or less frequent. For the later history of the festival (including the problems of its name(s) and time of year) see Th. Homolle in Daremberg and Saglio, *Dictionnaire* s.v. Delia (pp. 55–60), Nilsson (1906) 144–9, Gallet de Santerre (1958) 243–9, Bruneau (1970) 65ff., Parker (1996) 151. The festival described in the hymn probably took place in spring, in the month Hieros, as did the later Apollonia (see 135–9n.).

146–8 Thucydides' text (with ἀλλ' ὅτε) would mean 'but when you most rejoiced in Delos, then [*or* there] the Ionians gather', which does not fit the context. West (1975) 170 suggested that Thucydides' quotation began at 141, and a scribe's eye jumped from ἀλλότε there to ἀλλὰ σύ in 146. But it is unlikely that Thucydides would have quoted 141–5.

147 The Ionians with trailing chitons are mentioned at *Il.* 13.685; for the form Ἰάονες see Janko ad loc. Their trailing robes continued to be famous later: cf. Asius of Samos fr. 13.3 Davies χιονέοισι χιτῶσι πέδον χθονὸς εὐρέος εἶχον, and Thuc. 1.63 etc.

148 Cf. *Od.* 3.381 αὐτῶι καὶ παίδεσσι καὶ αἰδοίηις ἀλόχοισιν. The emphatic αὐτοῖς is unexpected here, and Gemoll's αὐτοί could be right. αὐτῆι σὺν πήληκι κάρη (*Il.* 14.498) is different: 'head, helmet, and all'. Thucydides' σὴν ἐς ἀγυιάν is a strange variant, as ἀγυιά always seems to mean 'street, highway'. Càssola thinks it refers to the Sacred Way leading to Apollo's temple, which was built in the second half of the sixth century BC; cf. also Aloni (1989) 116–18.

149–50 Cf. *Od.* 8.62–384, where the Phaeacians honour Odysseus with song, athletic contests, and dancing. The combination in one line of boxing, dancing, and singing is not Homeric, although each noun occurs separately in Homer (as does the variant ὀρχηστύς). Boxing comes first in the short lists of sports at *Il.* 23.621–3 and 634–7, and so may be named here as representative of sports in general. For the second half of 149 cf. Theognis 79 φόρμιγγι καὶ ὀρχηθμῶι καὶ ἀοιδῆι; *Od.* 8.253, 17.605 ὀρχηστυῖ καὶ ἀοιδῆι. For singing contests on Delos cf. also Hes. (?) fr. 357 M–W (Homer and Hesiod compete there).

150 The general pleasure which Apollo takes in Delos is particularly embodied in this great festival, where delight is one of the keynotes, together with wonder (153, 156, 169–70).

μνησάμενοι has the connotation of commemorating the god by celebrating his festival, of which the contests held in his honour are an essential part.

ἀγῶνα: ἀγών has its basic sense here of a gathering, and especially one for games, as in *Il.* 23.258 etc.

151–2 The imaginary spectator from elsewhere (introduced with vivid asyndeton) is appropriate to a scene where spectacle is so important, like the spectators in the Games in *Iliad* 23 (448ff. etc.). Cf. also the imaginary stranger of *H. Ap.* 167–8. The poet cannot see all this himself, and uses another's eyes to do so. For φαίη or φαίης ('one would think that') in this context cf. *H. Ap.* 163–4, *Il.* 3.220, etc.; for ἀθανάτους καὶ ἀγήρως cf. *Od.* 7.94.

152 ἐπαντιάσειε is a conjecture, but seems very likely to be right, although this particular compound of Homeric ἀντιάζειν occurs only here (cf. ἀν-/ἐν-/ὑπαντιάζω). In Homer individual heroes or heroines are often compared to gods, but it is unusual to describe a whole assembly of people in this way, and this extravagant praise of the godlike Ionians looks like a *captatio beneuolentiae* on the part of this singer, eager for victory in his own contest.

154–5 For 'men and fair-girdled women' cf. *Il.* 7.139 etc.

155 κτήματα πολλά (*H. Ap.* 266 etc.) might suggest not only wealth, but also that the festival had a commercial aspect. Delos was to become a major commercial centre in the Hellenistic period, thanks to its central position in the Aegean and the popularity of its cults.

156–64 The climax of the poet's catalogue of praise is the choir of Delian girls, who are themselves 'a great marvel'. Although some of the details remain unclear, he gives us an invaluable vignette of their activity and their art. They are attendants of Apollo. They sing in praise of the Delian triad of deities, and then go on to praise men and women of old. We have a similar sequence to that of epic recitation: the hymn to a god or gods as prelude to heroic narrative. We are not told what metrical form their songs take, but as they are a choir it seems probable that this is lyric rather than hexameters. We are also not told whether they dance or not, although this seems most probable. Their artistic effect is described in traditional terms: like the singers in Homer they have power to charm men's hearts. But they also possess the gift of μίμησις. Exactly what this involves is uncertain, but it is seen as something wonderful, and its vivid realism appeals directly to all men individually. This achievement is closely associated with the skill with which their song is 'fitted together', i.e. dramatic quality and good composition go together. Cf. the praise of Demodocus by Odysseus at *Od.* 8.487–91, where his ability to sing λίην κατὰ κόσμον is associated with the directness of his tale 'as though you yourself were an eyewitness or heard it from another'. Finally, 'the fame of these singers will never perish' (156): as with epic song, so here, immortal κλέος is the result. Cf. 174–5 where the girls are promised fame throughout the world by the poet in return for their favour.

156–7 πρὸς δέ means 'and in addition', and τόδε... θαῦμα 'there is the following wonder'; cf. ἦ μέγα θαῦμα τόδ' *Il.* 13.99 etc., and for ὅδε looking forward see Ebeling, *Lexicon Homericum* s.v. II. For ὅου κλέος οὔποτ' ὀλεῖται cf. *Il.* 2.325. ὅου must have originally been ὅο, subsequently contracted to οὗ in colloquial speech and so pronounced ὅου in epic with *diectasis.*

157 This is a dignified four-word verse, with the grandiose epithet Ἑκατηβελέταο. θεράπνη occurs first here in literature, then in tragedy and later poetry, but it was the name of a Laconian town, the home of the Dioscuri. Euripides (*HF* 687–90) speaks of the Delian girls as singing a paean to Apollo as noble son of Leto, with lovely dancing, near the gates (of the temple). Cf. also E. *Hec.* 462–5 (praise of Artemis by the Delian girls), with discussion in Henrichs (1996). Cratinus wrote a play called Δηλίαδες (*PCG* frs. 24–37) in which the Hyperborean offerings were mentioned. All these may have been stimulated by the Athenian revival of the festival in 426/5 BC. Inscriptions from the Hellenistic period refer to a choir of women which took part in the Apollonia and several other festivals, and used torches: see Bruneau (1970) 35–7 etc. Cf. also perhaps the women's dances mentioned by Callimachus, together with male singers (*H.* 4.302ff.). They are especially associated with the θεωρίαι which came from all over Greece to make dedications on Delos (see on 60). Delos was the centre by the classical period of a whole network of cults of Apollo Delios, especially in the Aegean islands, and the Deliades could have been a focus for interaction between the local cult and this wider Greek community: on this see Kowalzig (2007) 56–128.

158–61 158–9 seem to indicate a hymn to Apollo followed by one or two to Leto and Artemis. For 160–1 cf. *H.* 31.18–19 and 32.18–20, where the poet explicitly declares that he will follow his prelude with praise of the deeds of the heroes. Cf. also the Muses' songs at *H. Ap.* 189–93 and Hes. *Th.* 43–52. Wilamowitz (1916) 451–2 suggested that this song was the ancient hymn ascribed to Olen, mentioned by Herodotus (4.35.3), in which the Hyperborean maidens Arge and Opis were honoured: cf. also Sale (1961) 87. Both Herodotus (4.33.3) and Callimachus (*H.* 4.291–5) speak of men as well as the legendary girls among those bringing the Hyperborean offerings, and receiving cults in Delos. The fact that the poet uses the singular ὕμνον here might suggest that one particular hymn could be meant, and this could be Olen's. But the language is too general to be sure of this.

161 θέλγουσι: θέλγειν and similar words are commonly used of the power of song or story-telling in early epic (and later): cf. *Od.* 1.337, 11.334 = 13.2, 12.40, 44 (Sirens), 14.387, 17.514–24; later Pi. *P.* 1.12, *N.* 4.2–3, etc., and Walsh (1984), Parry (1992) 149ff.

162–4 'And they know how to imitate the voices and rhythms (?) of all men: each individual would suppose that he himself were speaking. So well-constructed is their lovely song.'

κρεμβαλιαστύν is the reading of most MSS. This word occurs only here. κρέμβαλα were a type of instrument described by Athenaeus (636CD), quoting Dicaearchus, who says that they were once extremely popular for women as an accompaniment to song and dance, and 'when one touched them with the fingers this produced a ringing sound'. He cites as evidence a song to Artemis (*PMG* 955), which describes them as 'bronze-cheeked, gold-shining'. The verb κρεμβαλιάζειν is also quoted from Hermippus (*PCG* fr. 31); cf. Hesychius s.v., and Photius s.v., who explains κρεμβαλιάζειν by ἐλεφαντίνοις τισὶ (κροτάλοις? Cobet) κροταλίζειν, which suggests that they could also be made of ivory. They are usually translated as 'castanets', but they may have been different from the κρόταλα ('clappers') more often mentioned in literature (first in *H.* 14.3) and shown on vases, where they are used by women to produce a rattling sound, as these were usually made of wood. But the exact distinction between these instruments, and also κύμβαλα, is not clear: West (1992) 122–6.

A number of Geometric vases show musical scenes, with a phorminx-player, dancers, and men clapping their hands in time with the music, and in other cases it is possible that rattles or wooden clappers are being used: cf. M. Wegner, *Arch. Hom.* U (*Musik und Tanz*) 22–4, 38–40. In one of the dancing scenes in *Odyssey* 8 the young men who are spectators accompany the two solo dancers with what is probably rhythmic hand-clapping: cf. 379–80 κοῦροι δ' ἐπελήκεον ἄλλοι | ἑσταότες κατ' ἀγῶνα, πόλυς δ' ὑπὸ κόμπος ὀρώρει. If κρεμβαλιαστύν is the correct reading, it should refer to the use of κρέμβαλα to create a rhythmic sound as an accompaniment to singing, or (by metonymy) to the variety of rhythms created in this way. Greek dancing was seen as using rhythms for mimetic purposes: cf. Plato, *Laws* 655d–e, Arist. *Poet.* 1447a26–8.

A few MSS read βαμβαλιαστύν, which also occurs nowhere else, and is presumably an onomatopoeic word meaning 'chatter, babble'. Cf. βαμβαίνειν (*Il.* 10.375 etc., 'stutter'), and similar words such as βαμβάλειν, βαμβακύζειν, βαμβαλύζειν, βαμβαλίζειν. This would refer to some aspect of the various types of speech imitated, whether speech-patterns in general, or dialects, or different languages. Cf. for example Theocr. 15.87–8, where someone complains about the 'ceaseless chattering' and the broad vowel-sounds of the Syracusan ladies in Alexandria. With this reading, φαίη δέ κεν αὐτὸς ἕκαστος φθέγγεσθ' follows naturally. On the other hand, it is hard to see how a word which would most naturally denote inarticulate or confused sounds can be used in this context, where the Delian girls' songs are so highly praised. The same objection would apply to Bing's interpretation (1993, 196) of κρεμβαλιαστύν as meaning 'chatter', by analogy with the metaphorical use of κρόταλον of a talkative speaker. In addition, κρεμβαλιαστύν is the *lectio difficilior*, and it is less easy to see why the change was made to this word than vice versa. One should then take the whole phrase φωνὰς καὶ κρεμβαλιαστύν together, denoting the voices and their rhythmic or musical accompaniment as a single whole.

The best parallel in early epic for the idea of imitation of voices is *Od.* 4.277–9, where Helen imitates the voices of the wives of the Greeks inside the Wooden Horse, in order to try to trick them into answering (πάντων Ἀργείων φωνὴν ἴσκουσ' ἀλόχοισιν). The poet presumably implies that divine inspiration is the cause of the Delian girls' wonderful gift. Herodotus tells how the oracle of Apollo at Ptoion in Boeotia answered the Carian Mys in what Mys claimed to be his own tongue, to the amazement of the Greeks who were with him (8.135 θῶμα μέγιστον; cf. variant versions in Plutarch, *Aristides* 19, *Mor.* 412A). The account in the *Acts of the Apostles* of the scene at Pentecost where the disciples begin to 'speak with tongues' has also been compared (2.1–12). Cf. *Reallexikon für Antike und Christentum* s.v. Glossolalie.

Later we know that the Delian choir was asked by visiting θεωρίαι to make dedications on their behalf (see on 60), and their contact with these and with other visiting choirs, together with the Panhellenic character of Delos in general, could have helped them to assimilate local styles of speech and music. On the other hand, it is possible that the *mimesis* described here is on a broader level, and closer to the kind of dramatic impersonation discussed by later literary critics. Cf. for example Lucian *Salt.* 81, where a dancer is praised when 'each of those who behold him recognises his own traits, or rather sees in the dancer as in a mirror his very self, with his customary feelings and actions. Then people cannot contain themselves for pleasure, and with one accord they burst into applause, each seeing the reflection of his own soul and recognising himself.'

See also Bing (1993) 194–6, Stehle (1997) 182–5, Papadopoulou-Belmehdi and Papadopoulou (2002) 172–5, and Peponi (2009).

164 συνάρηρεν: this compound occurs only here in early epic, later in Apollonius Rhodius etc. The metaphor of 'fitting together' the song anticipates later expressions which emphasise the craftsmanship of poetry.

165–76 The poet's farewell to Apollo and Artemis, and to the Delian choir, leads into an elaborate passage about himself. This *sphragis* (as it is sometimes called in modern scholarship, after the use of the word σφρηγίς meaning 'seal' in Theognis 19) is unique in these hymns, although some do close with brief requests to the deity for favour in the singing-contest (6.19–20) or as a singer (10.5, 24.5, 25.6). Our poet does not actually name himself, unlike, for example, Hesiod or Theognis: this looks deliberate, but it remains unclear what exactly is the point of this. However, he gives us a certain amount of information: he is a visitor to Delos (169–70), blind, living in rugged Chios, and he is evidently used to travelling to various Greek communities, although we cannot tell how wide his geographical range is. He claims to be the sweetest and best of singers, not only now, but in time to come (169–70, 173), a grand boast indeed.

Those like Thucydides who believed Homer to be the author of this poem would have had no quarrel with this claim. In the *Contest of Homer and Hesiod* Homer is given special honours in Delos because of this hymn: *Certamen* 315–21. The traditions about Homer's blindness, and his association with Chios, would also have fitted, although it is possible that these derive precisely from this passage, together with the depiction of the blind bard Demodocus in the *Odyssey*. It has also been suggested that the poet is a later rhapsode (e.g. Cynaethus), who is claiming to sing the work of Homer himself: see Burkert (1979a) 53–62, Janko (1982) 114–15, West (1999) 368–72, and Graziosi (2002) 62–6. See also Introduction 2(b).

We cannot know the answer to the puzzle which this bard has set us. But if what he says of himself is actually true, then he is our best piece of early evidence for a so-called 'oral' poet: a blind singer in antiquity can hardly have written down his own poems. Moreover, he is also, as Homer was thought to be, a travelling singer. He portrays himself as a visitor to the Delian festival, and he is surely asking for victory in the singing contest on this occasion (cf. on 151–2), although his request to the Delian girls is apparently primarily concerned with his future fame. His praise of their song (155–64, 174–6) will be answered by their praise of him, in a fair exchange of favours.

165–6 The Delian girls are coupled closely with the Delian gods here, and χαίρειν is elsewhere in these hymns reserved for deities. See Bundy (1972) 49 on the parallel usage of χαῖρε and ἵληθι (e.g. *H.* 15.9 and 20.8).

165 ἀλλ' ἄγεθ' ἱλήκοι: cf. *H. Dem.* 490 ἀλλ' ἄγ(ε); *Od.* 3.380 ἀλλὰ ἄνασσ' ἵληθι, and *Od.* 16.184, *H.* 20.8.

Ἀπόλλων Ἀρτέμιδι ξύν: cf. *Od.* 15.410. The coupling of Apollo and his sister echoes 15, and in this context reflects their close association in cult on Delos itself.

166–8 The chiastic ordering of χαίρετε δ' ὑμεῖς πᾶσαι· ἐμεῖο δὲ καὶ... μνήσασθ'... emphasises the parallelism between the choir and the poet. In 168 the ξεῖνος ταλαπείριος resembles the imaginary spectator of 151–5. The phrase is used by Odysseus of himself at *Od.* 7.24 (cf. 17.84, 19.379).

169 ὔμμιν means 'in your view'.

ἥδιστος occurs elsewhere in early epic only at *Od.* 13.80 and possibly *H. Dem.* 13.

170 πωλεῖται indicates that singers regularly visited Delos.

171 **ὑποκρίνασθαι ἀφήμως:** this text follows the reading of most of the MSS of Thucydides here. The infinitive is imperatival (Chantraine, *GH* II 316–17), and ἀφήμως may be translated 'with one voice, in unison'. The scholiast on the Thucydides passage gives the senses σιγῆι, ἡσύχα, and ἀθρόως, whereas Hesychius s.v. offers ἐν κόσμωι, ἡσυχῆι. The word occurs nowhere else, although Hesychius also has ἄφημοι, ἀφήμονες in the senses of 'nameless, unspoken'. εὖ μάλα πᾶσαι emphasises ἀφήμως, 'all together with full accord': cf. Theocr. 25.19 εὖ μάλα πᾶσι. Burkert reads ἀφήμως, but in the sense 'anonymously', i.e. they do not identify the singer by his name (1979a, 61).

The other readings of MSS of the hymn, ἀφ' ἡμέων, ἀφ' ὑμ(έ)ων, do not make sense, and the conjecture ἀμφ' ἡμέων has little point. εὐφήμως, the variant reading in Thucydides and possibly Aristides, cannot easily mean 'in words of praise' (as taken by Ruhnken ad loc., Wilamowitz (1916) 454, and Càssola). 'Propitiously' or 'auspiciously' would be better, and could be taken as implying a discreet reserve over the poet's name (cf. Graziosi (2002) 65). But ἀφήμως is the *lectio difficilior* and closer to the other readings, and εὐφήμως could be an ancient or early Byzantine conjecture. Carey's σαφηνέως would also be possible: (1980) 288–90.

172 Cf. *Od.* 3.170 Χίοιο... παιπαλοέσσης. The poet has praised Chios in 38. Homer is already called Χῖος ἀνήρ in Simonides fr. 19 West, quoting *Il.* 6.146. Cf. later Theocr. 7.47, 22.218 for Χῖος ἀοιδός. The guild of singers known as Ὁμηρίδαι, who claimed descent from him, were based in Chios: cf. Acusilaus, *FGrH* 2 F 2, Hellanicus, *FGrH* 4 F 20, *Certamen* 13–15, Strabo 14.1.35, Schol. Pind. *N.* 2 (init.), etc. Later traditions often said that Homer was born in Smyrna or elsewhere and then lived in Chios: see Graziosi (2002) 51–89.

173 'Whose songs, in after-time, are all the best.' The present tense with μετόπισθεν seems illogical, but what he is claiming is presumably that his songs are now the best, and will continue to be in future; not only 'as soon as he has sung them', as AHS say, but in time to come as well. This suggests that the songs will be preserved and performed in future (cf. also 174–7). 'The hymn, which celebrates a universally Panhellenic Apollo, likewise declares itself to be Panhellenic' (Clay (2006) 52).

174–5 The change to first person plural is taken as referring to a group of singers (e.g. the Homeridae) by Aloni (1989) 127–8, who compares *H.* 1.17–19, 26.11–13,

32.17–20. This seems less probable than reference to the poet, since he has only spoken about himself.

175 στρεφόμεσθα: this verb is used only here with accusative, but cf. *Od.* 13.326 γαῖαν ἀναστρέφομαι, 17.326 ἐπιστρωφῶσι πόληας.

176 This statement rounds off the poet's assertions, perhaps as much about his own prowess as about the achievements of the Delian choir.

177–8 For the transitional character of these lines see 140–78n. They echo the proem, and close the theme of Apollo's birth, whilst looking forward to future song. For ὃν ... Λητώ cf. *Il.* 1.36 (τὸν) etc. As the god is not addressed directly the lines cannot be a closing formula.

179–206 The poet invokes Apollo as lord of Lycia, Maeonia, Miletus, and Delos, and then describes how he goes up to Pytho, playing his lyre, and from there to Olympus. Here he accompanies the singing of the Muses and dancing of other deities, whilst Leto and Zeus look on with joy.

179–81 As they stand, these lines act as a brief introduction, or *priamel*, to the rest of the hymn, invoking the god again as lord of various places, culminating in Delos, before moving on to his association with Delphi. They resemble (in shorter form) 140–6, and indeed Van Groningen regarded them as a variant on that passage: (1958) 311–12. The change from third to second person and back to third at 182 is paralleled at 119–34, where it occurs four times: cf. 120–2n., and Introduction 2(c).

For ὦ ἄνα cf. 526, Theognis 1 ὦ ἄνα, Λητοῦς υἱέ. The vocative ἄνα is only used of Zeus in Homer (*Il.* 3.351 etc.). καὶ ... καὶ ... hardly occurs in Homer (*Il.* 13.260?): cf. Denniston, *GP*[2] 323–4. Maeonia was later identified with Lydia (not mentioned in Homer): *RE* XIV.582–3 s.v. For Μηονίην ἐρατεινήν cf. *Il.* 3.401, 18.291. For Apollo's cults in Lycia, Lydia, and Miletus see on 42, and Farnell, *Cults* IV 224–31. The eponymous founder of Maeonia was a son of Apollo (Apollod. 3.1.2 etc.). ἔναλος occurs here in early epic, and must mean 'by the sea' (cf. E. *Hel.* 1130, Timotheus, *PMG* 791.98). ἱμερόεσσαν is rarely used of places in epic (Hes. fr. 43a.62 M–W). For περίκλυστος cf. Hes. *Th.* 199.

179–81 are carefully composed: there is a progression from simple name to name plus epithet, to name plus extended phrase (180), and finally to the whole verse describing Delos, αὐτὸς δ' αὖ ... μέγ' ἀνάσσεις (181). For αὐτός of Apollo in a similar context see 140 (with comment). 181 echoes 29. See also Miller (1986) 66.

182–206 Apollo's journey to Pytho marks the introduction of the theme of Delphi, and is repeated near the end of the hymn, when he leads his new priests up to Pytho with dancing and song (514–23). Here, however, Pytho is juxtaposed with Delos, and then the scene shifts rapidly northwards to Mt Olympus. The elaborate description of celebration mirrors the scene of the Delian festival. It also marks a contrast with the opening of the hymn (1–18), whilst itself forming the prelude to the following narrative. At the opening Apollo was god of archery, here of music. (For parallels see on 1–18.) The scene is similar to the accounts of habitual divine activity in *Hymns* 19, 26, and 27 (11–20), with music, song, and dancing.

182–5 The stately description of Apollo's musical progress is dignified by a series of epithets. For Λητοῦς ἐρικυδέος υἱός cf. *H. Herm.* 176, 189, and *Il.* 14.327 (Λητοῦς ἐρικυδέος). φόρμιγγα γλαφυρήν occurs 3× in *Od.* (8.257 etc.), also at *H. Herm.* 64, and in genitive at *Od.* 17.262. For Πυθὼ πετρήεσσαν cf. *Il.* 2.519 Πυθῶνά τε πετρήεσσαν, and *H. Ap.* 390 (dative). For εἵματα τεθυωμένα cf. *Cypria* fr. 4 Davies τεθυωμένα εἵματα ἕστο. The plectrum is first mentioned here, and at *H. Herm.* 53 etc. For καναχὴν ἔχει cf. *Il.* 16.105, 794.

186–206 Apollo's journey to Olympus is 'swift as thought' and it creates an immediate effect (αὐτίκα), as in the opening scene. In what follows there is careful grouping of figures, as in visual art. The action is divided between choral song (189–93), dancing (194–201), and solo lyre-playing (201–3). The nine Muses singing (189–93) are balanced by nine dancers, the two triads of Charites and Horai, plus Harmonia, Hebe, and Aphrodite. Among the dancers Artemis stands out (as in *Od.* 6.102–8 and Verg. *A.* 1.498–502), as Apollo's sister. There follows a trio of male gods, Ares and Hermes, who are perhaps dancing in the centre of the ring (200 balancing 197), and Apollo, who as lyre-player and dancer is the leading figure of the whole composition. Meanwhile his parents look on with joy (cf. *Od.* 6.106 γέγηθε δέ τε φρένα Λητώ, Verg. *A.* 4.502 *Latonae tacitum pertemptant gaudia pectus*). Their pleasure recalls not only Leto's at 12–13 and 14–18, but also the delight of the human spectator at the Delian festival in 151–5, and the Muses' song picks up the theme of the Delian choir: both sing of gods and men, although the Muses see men from a divine perspective, as helpless in face of age and death, by contrast with 151–3. The procession to Delphi at 513–23 resumes these themes. As often, mortal music and celebration echo those of the gods. Cf. Kakridis (1937), Förstel (1979) 44, Miller (1986) 67–9, Evans (2001) 86–8.

186–8 The gods traditionally moved as swift as thought: cf. *Il.* 15.80–3 (Hera), and Janko ad loc., and for ὥς τε νόημα *H. Ap.* 448, *Od.* 7.36, Hes. *Sc.* 222, Theognis 985, and *H. Herm.* 43–6. Διὸς πρὸς δῶμα echoes 2 (κατὰ δῶμα Διός). For 187 cf. *Il.* 20.142 (*H. Dem.* 484) ἄψ (βάν ῥ') ἴμεν Οὔλυμπόνδε θεῶν μεθ' ὁμήγυριν ἄλλων.

188 μέλει κίθαρις καὶ ἀοιδή: cf. *Od.* 1.159.

189–93 The Muses sing of the 'immortal gifts of the gods and the sufferings of men', their helplessness in face of old age and death. The gifts of the gods are usually what they bestow on men for good or ill, and are closely linked to the themes of men's endurance (τλημοσύνη) and helplessness: see Richardson on *H. Dem.* 147f., and 256ff. δῶρ' ἄμβροτα in this passage has been taken by some scholars as divine privileges (e.g. immortality), thus giving a stronger contrast between gods and men. But more probably ἄμβροτα simply qualifies δῶρα because these are divine gifts. Then ὅσ' ἔχοντες ὑπ' ἀθανάτοισι θεοῖσι picks up this theme again, and θεῶν . . . τλημοσύνας all go closely together, as two sides of the same coin.

For 189 cf. *Il.* 1.604 Μουσάων, αἳ ἄειδον ἀμειβόμεναι ὀπὶ καλῆι (with Apollo as lyre-player), and *Od.* 24.60. The phrase suggests a form of responsion by the Muses, with alternate voices or semi-choirs. Cf. Verg. *Ecl.* 3.59 *alternis dicetis; amant alterna Camenae.* Fernandez-Galiano, on *Od.* 24.60, suggests that in *Iliad* 1 Apollo leads the singing, as well as playing the φόρμιγξ, and the Muses respond. Cf. also Pulleyn (2000) 275, for a similar view. But this does not seem to fit the passage in the hymn so well, as the Muses' singing is mentioned first. For δῶρ' ἄμβροτα cf. *Il.* 18.191. τλημοσύνη occurs first here (and only here in plural), and then at Archil. fr. 14.6, as a divinely given palliative for incurable troubles, and Plutarch *Crass.* 26. It combines the two ideas of suffering and endurance. These themes of men's ignorance and helplessness are traditional in Greek literature: see Richardson on *H. Dem.* 256ff. In 192–3 the reduplicated alpha privative (ἀφραδέες καὶ ἀμήχανοι) is glossed by οὐδὲ . . . ἄλκαρ. For 193 cf. *Il.* 9.250 κακοῦ ἔστ' ἄκος εὑρεῖν. The phrase γήραος ἄλκαρ occurs only here.

190–3 are echoed by Apollo himself in his address to his Cretan priests at 532–3 (νήπιοι ἄνθρωποι δυστλήμονες, etc.). It is one of the benefits of his oracular power that he will help men in future to cope better with these deficiencies.

193–6 The Charites are closely associated with the Muses (cf. *H.* 27.15, and West on Hes. *Th.* 64), and with Apollo (e.g. Pi. *O.* 14.1–12, Call. fr. 114.8–9, etc.), and the Horai and Charites often go together (West on *Th.* 901). Here the parallel epithets underline their association. Cf. Panyassis fr. 13.1 Davies Χάριτές τ' ἔλαχον καὶ ἐΰφρονες Ὧραι. Harmonia is daughter of Ares and Aphrodite and wife of Cadmus at Hes. *Th.* 933–7. For Harmonia and the Muses cf. E. *Med.* 831–2. For 196 cf. *Il.* 18.594 (with ὠρχεῦντ'). The Charites are often shown in art as dancers in a line holding each other's hands, and in modern Greece dancers still hold each other's hands or wrists as they move in a line or circle.

197–9 The stately three-line description effectively portrays Artemis' prominence and dignity. Cf. the simile at *Od.* 6.102–9, of Artemis and her nymphs, especially πασάων δ' ὑπὲρ ἥ γε κάρη ἔχει ἠδὲ μέτωπα | ῥεῖά τ' ἀριγνώτη πέλεται, καλαὶ δέ τε πᾶσαι. The litotes of 197 is balanced by 198, where beauty and size recur in chiastic order, and the closing four-word line (199) neatly places sister and brother at beginning and end. For μεταμέλπεται cf. *Il.* 16.182–3 μετὰ μελπομένηισιν | ἐν χορῶι Ἀρτεμίδος. The compound verb occurs only here, unless one chooses to read μέτα μέλπεται, taking μέτα with τῆισι. Aristarchus distinguished the Homeric use of μέλπεσθαι for play in general, including dance and music, from its later restriction to song (cf. Lehrs (1882) 138ff., Janko on *Il.* 13.636–9). Here it must refer to dancing. ὁμότροφος occurs first here and at *H.* 9.2 ὁμότροφον Ἀπόλλωνος.

200–1 Ares and Hermes are dancing as a duo in the midst of the goddesses, perhaps like the acrobatic dancers in *Il.* 18.604–5. Ares as a dancer is unexpected, but 'music has charms to soothe a savage breast'. Cf. Pi. *P.* 1.10–12, where he is spell-bound by the music of Apollo and the Muses. The mention of Harmony and

Aphrodite may also have brought him to the poet's mind (cf. 193–6n.). ἐΰσκοπος Ἀργειφόντης ('keen-sighted Argos-slayer') recurs at *H. Herm.* 73, *H. Aph.* 262, and 4× in Homer. The etymology of Ἀργειφόντης is discussed by S. West, on *Od.* 1.37ff.

201 ἐγκιθαρίζει: this verb occurs only here and at *H. Herm.* 17.

202 καλὰ καὶ ὕψι βίβας is repeated at 516 (Apollo's procession to Delphi). The high-stepping dance may be specifically Cretan: cf. Ar. *Eccl.* 1163–6 Κρητικῶς οὖν τὼ πόδε | καὶ σὺ κίνει, and Lawler (1951) 62–70.

202–3 αἴγλη . . . χιτῶνος: 'and radiance is bright around him, and [bright too is] the sparkling of his feet and well-spun tunic'. Apollo was worshipped as Aigletes on the island of Anaphe, near Thera: cf. Call. fr. 7.19ff., A.R. 4.1714–18, etc. For Apollo as god of purity and radiance see also 120–2, 440–7nn. The variant ἀμφιφαείνει cannot be ruled out.

203 μαρμαρυγαί τε ποδῶν: cf. *Od.* 8.265 μαρμαρυγὰς θηεῖτο ποδῶν, of the Phaeacian dancers.

ἐϋκλώστοιο: this adjective occurs only here in early hexameter poetry and later in an epigram (first century AD?) of Maecius. Cf. *Il.* 18.595–6 χιτῶνας . . . ἐϋννήτους etc.

204–6 Cf. Leto's pride in Apollo at 12–13, 125–6, and in Artemis at *Od.* 6.106. χρυσοπλόκαμος occurs first here; cf. Timotheus, *PMG* fr. 791.127.

207–15 The poet again asks how he should praise Apollo, and lists some of his love affairs, as a prelude to his choice of theme, the god's search for the site of an oracular shrine. Local legends are passed over, in favour of one with Panhellenic significance. The passage is designed to mirror 19–29 (19 ~ 207, 25 ~ 214), and is similar to a *priamel*, reviewing a series of options before focusing on the main subject.

208–13 'Or am I to sing of you amongst the girls whom you courted and your love affairs, how you went as a suitor after the daughter [*or* descendant] of Azan, together with the godlike Ischys, famed for his horsemanship, offspring of Elatus? Or with Phorbas, of the family of Triops, or with Ereutheus? Or with Leucippus and the wife of Leucippus, you on foot and he with horses? Indeed he did not fall short of Triops.' The poet is summarising legends, and text and interpretation are unclear at several points.

208–10 Apollo and Ischys, son of Elatus, were rival suitors of Coronis, the mother of Asclepius according to the story told by Pindar (*P.* 3). In the usual tradition Coronis was daughter of Phlegyas (*H.* 16 etc.; see also on *H. Ap.* 278–80), and Ἀζαντίδα is a puzzle. Azan was an early Arcadian hero, and brother of Elatus (Paus. 8.4), and Pindar makes Ischys come from Arcadia, but not Coronis. Possibly, however, an earlier version made them cousins. Some scholars have preferred M's reading Ἀτλαντίδα, and connected this with the rival genealogy of Asclepius which made him son of Arsinoe, a descendant of Atlas (cf. Hes. fr. 50 etc.): see Bodson (1971) 12–20, and also Latte (1968) 729–30.

211 Phorbas, son of Triops or Triopas, appears to be a rival of Apollo here, whereas he is sometimes portrayed later as beloved by him (cf. Hyginus *Astr.* 2.14, Plutarch, *Numa* 4). However, the name was also given to one of the Phlegyae (cf. 278–80n.), a mythical robber who attacked travellers on the road to Delphi, and was killed by Apollo (cf. *EGF* ed. Davies, p. 74 fr. 3, *RE* xx 529–30 s.v. Phorbas). Ereutheus is unknown, apart from a very late mention of the name in Quintus of Smyrna 2.239. The variant names Amarynthus and Erechtheus cannot be directly linked to known myths of Apollo's love affairs, unless Erechtheus is named here as father of Creusa, who bore Ion to Apollo, but this seems unlikely.

212–13 The best explanation of these lines is that Leucippus, son of Perieres, is meant, since he and Apollo shared a claim to be the father of Phoebe and Hilaeira (*Cypria* fr. 9 Davies). 213 suggests a bride-race in which Apollo competed on foot against his rival in a chariot. But the allusion to Triopas is unexplained, unless this Leucippus was related to him (cf. Càssola on 213), and a line or lines may be missing after 212, as Hermann thought.

214 τὸ πρῶτον does not mean that this is Apollo's first oracular shrine, but is adverbial, i.e. the poet will tell how he originally went in search of a site for what will later be his most important oracle.

215 ζητεύων: ζητεύειν is not Homeric: cf. Hes. *Op.* 400, *H. Herm.* 391.

216–86 Apollo's route from Olympus through northern Greece to Delphi is described. He moves south-east through Thessaly, crosses from Iolcus to the north end of Euboea, and then back from Chalcis to Boeotia. His route through Boeotia is given in more detail, including a description of a ritual in honour of Poseidon at Onchestus, and an extended episode in which Telphousa dissuades him from setting up his shrine there. See Map 2.

Did this route have a religious significance? It certainly includes a number of places later associated with Apollo. It does not correspond exactly with the list of states in the Amphictionic League which controlled Delphi after the first Sacred War (see 540–3n.), nor with the route followed by the Delphic delegation returning from Tempe after the eight-yearly festival of the Septerion, which commemorated Apollo's purification after killing the serpent. But it does overlap with both of these to a considerable extent, and it is possible that the journey may reflect the religious association of various northern Greek communities with Delphi: cf. Kolk (1963) 9–23, Nilsson, *GGR* I^3 550–1, 554. At the same time, Apollo's preference of Delphi over other possible sites for his oracle (e.g. 220–1, 244ff.) emphasises Delphi's pre-eminence. There are also several references to the wild or uncivilised nature of the terrain which Apollo traverses (cf. 223, 225–8, 277–85).

The journey 'is punctuated by a series of pauses of steadily increasing length' (Miller (1986) 72). As with Odysseus' journeys (*Od.* 9–12), a formulaic line three times marks the god's progression from place to place (229 = 239, 277). It is narrated throughout (apart from 254) as an address to the god ('du-Stil'), up to 282, when he arrives at his ultimate goal (cf. Introduction 2(c)), and with deliberate variation in the verbs of movement used. There is a marked contrast between Apollo's journey and Leto's (30–50). There the places visited all rejected Leto and her son, except Delos: here Apollo rejects them, except for Delphi. Cf. Baltes (1982) 31–4.

216–18 Pieria is the area just north of Mt Olympus. The poet may be influenced by journeys such as Hera's at *Il.* 14.225–30, where she is heading for Lemnos: cf. *Il.* 14.225 Πιερίην δ' ἐπιβᾶσα καὶ Ἠμαθίην ἐρατεινήν, which may have led to the use of ἠμαθόεντα here (cf. Aloni (1989) 98). Lectos is unknown. The Ainianes or Enienes and Perrhaebi are listed together in the Catalogue of Ships (*Il.* 2.749), where they belong with the region of Dodona, in the far north-west of Thessaly. Later, however, the Perrhaebi were located south of Olympus, and the Ainianes moved right down to the upper valley of the river Spercheios. A quadrennial θεωρία of the Ainianes to offer a hecatomb at the tomb of Pyrrhos, during the Pythian festival, is attested by Heliodorus (*Aith.* 2.34–3.6, 3.10f.), and may be ancient: see Fontenrose (1960) 195–8.

218 Ἰαωλκόν: Iolcos' chief fame was in heroic times, in connection with Argonautic saga. There was certainly a cult of Artemis Iolcia here in the historic period (cf. *RE* IX 1853 s.v. Ἰωλκός).

219 From Iolcos Apollo crosses to cape Cenaeon, at the north-west tip of Euboea. For ναυσικλειτῆς Εὐβοίης see 31n.

220–1 The Lelantine plain, first mentioned here, was the site of a famous war (or series of conflicts) in the eighth or seventh centuries BC between Chalcis and Eretria. The important late Bronze and early Iron Age site of Lefkandi is located here. Chalcis and Eretria both had cults of Apollo and Artemis (cf. Farnell, *Cults* II 605, IV 437). At Eretria the earliest temple of Apollo Daphnephoros dates from the eighth century BC (cf. Schefold and Auberson (1972) 113–21), and the temple of Artemis Amarousia, about 10 miles east of Eretria, was also important (cf. Knoepfler (1988) 382–421).

222–4 The Euripus (the narrow strait separating Euboea from Boeotia) is first mentioned here. The 'holy, green mountain' is Messapion, above Anthedon on the coast of Boeotia. Mycalessos is listed in the Catalogue of Ships (*Il.* 2.498), and seems to have flourished in the Archaic and early Classical periods (*New Pauly* VIII, 570–1 s.v.). Teumessos (first here) is a hill and settlement between Mycalessos and Thebes (cf. Paus. 9.19.1). The hill is rocky and barren, and λεχεποίην must refer to the land to the south of the hill. 224 is quoted by Stephanus of Byzantium (s.v. Τευμησσός), and ascribed to 'Homer in his hymn to Apollo'.

225–8 The poet emphasises the priority of the Delphic cult over the important one of Apollo Ismenios at Thebes, by stressing that the Theban site was still uninhabited and covered in woodland, although he calls it 'holy'.

229–38 Apollo's arrival at the grove of Poseidon is the occasion for a detailed account of what appears to be a ritual in honour of this god. The poet is paying special tribute to Apollo's uncle, whose cult is already established here. Cf. the tributes paid to three virgin goddesses and to Hera at *H. Aph.* 7–44.

229 = 239, 277. Cf. *Od.* 9.62 etc. ἔνθεν δὲ προτέρω πλέομεν, as a transitional formula.

230 Onchestus is situated west of Thebes, and south of lake Copais. The sanctuary lay on top of a ridge, over which the road from Thebes to Delphi passes. It is mentioned already at *Il.* 2.506 Ὀγχηστόν θ' ἱερὸν Ποσιδήϊον ἀγλαὸν ἄλσος, and again at *H. Herm.* 186–7 (cf. 87–8). It was inhabited in the Mycenaean period, and remains of what was probably a temple on the ridge date from the sixth century BC. It was also later the centre of a Boeotian federal league. Cf. Schachter (1981–94) II 207–21.

231–8 A literal translation might be: 'There a newly tamed colt draws breath, distressed as it is from drawing a fine chariot, and the driver, excellent as he is, leaps down from the chariot and goes on his way. Meanwhile they (i.e. the horses) rattle an empty car, being relieved of his control. But if a chariot is broken in the wooded grove, they attend to the horses, but they prop up the chariot and leave it. For that is how the rite came about to begin with. And they pray to the lord, and then the god's portion preserves the chariot.'

There is no agreement as to what is being described here. A useful survey of earlier views is given by Schachter (1976) 102–14; cf. also Burkert (1979b) 113 and 199, Schachter (1981–94) II 219, and Teffeteller (2001) 159–66.

Most scholars think that the custom concerns normal travellers, visiting Poseidon's sanctuary as they pass along the road. Burkert objected that chariots were not used for ordinary travelling. But they are so used in the *Odyssey*, and the poet is employing traditional epic language, even if he is speaking of a contemporary custom. Burkert thought of chariot races, which are attested for Poseidon's festival at Onchestus (cf. Pi. *I.* 1.32–5, 52–4, fr. 94b.42–6 Snell–Maehler). In races at some festivals a charioteer dismounted and ran beside the chariot (cf. Paus. 5.9.2). A custom of this kind could be referred to: but would the races be in the actual grove of the god, rather than in a separate racecourse? Surely also one would expect a more specific description of running on foot (see 233n.).

The description refers specifically to young horses who have been newly broken (231). The driver of such a horse (or horses) must leave his chariot as he reaches the sanctuary, thereby giving the horse(s) a respite. It is possible that this is not simply to rest one's horses, but also because it is prohibited to drive through the precinct. In many sanctuaries such traffic was forbidden: cf. Sokolowski (1960) 376–80, arguing for this here also. However, it is not stated that the horses should not enter the grove at all, and 235 seems to suggest that this was allowed. If a driverless colt runs away and breaks its chariot, a special procedure seems to be prescribed: this is suggested by 237 ὡς γὰρ . . . ὁσίη γένεθ', which surely refers to 235–6, as well as to 237–8 οἱ δὲ . . . φυλάσσει.

Most scholars have thought that a broken chariot had to be left in the possession of Poseidon: i.e. ἐῶσιν means 'leave permanently', and δίφρον . . . φυλάσσει indicates that the god keeps the chariot. Roux, however (1964, 6–22), objected that φυλάσσειν in Homer and Hesiod always means 'guard, preserve', never 'keep'. Consequently he argued that the process here is a simple one of leaving one's chariot temporarily, whilst calming a disturbed horse, and then praying for divine favour, a prayer which guarantees protection against future accidents. One then continues on one's way. This, however, involves taking ὣς . . . γένεθ' as only looking forward to 237–8, not back to 236, and in view of οἱ δέ (237) this can hardly be right. Probably then the chariot does have to be left behind, and θεοῦ μοῖρα may here refer specifically to the fact that it becomes the 'portion' of the god. This gives more point to the phrase than if one takes it as simply referring to the god's power. (Roux, *loc. cit.*, conjectured φυλάσσειν: 'it is the god's part to preserve the chariot', but this seems unlikely.) Normally it was customary to dedicate a victorious and unbroken chariot after a race (e.g. Epicharmus, *PCG* fr. 68, Pi. *P.* 34–53, Paus. 6.10.8). But objects involved in a breach of a *lex sacra* concerning a sanctuary would become the god's property (see Sokolowski (1960) 379); and something similar may be envisaged here, if a chariot involved in an accident within the precinct were seen as a sign of divine disfavour.

Whatever the right explanation, it is striking that the poet should give this custom such attention. Aetiological detail is a feature of this hymn in general. Moreover, a similar theme, concerning the disturbance of the peace of a sanctuary by chariots and horses, recurs in the episode of Telphousa (261–71). The remoteness of Delphi will preserve Apollo against such disturbance, and contrasts it with other shrines which were on or near a main highway (cf. also Miller (1986) 73–4).

There is another possible link between Onchestus and Delphi, in the myth of Clymenus, king of the Minyans of Orchomenus. He was killed in a fight at the festival of Onchestian Poseidon by a man or men of Thebes, and his eldest son Erginus attacked Thebes in revenge (cf. Commentary on Pindar in *P. Ox.* 2442 fr. 29, Apollodorus 2.4.11, Paus. 9.37.1). Erginus in turn was the father of Trophonius and Agamedes, the legendary architects of Apollo's first temple at Delphi (*H. Ap.* 294–9). Erginus is also the name of an Argonaut who was Poseidon's son (A.R. 1.185–8 etc.). This suggests an aetiological myth connected with the origin of the Orchomenian festival, at which Clymenus was associated with Poseidon as hero of the games. In one version Clymenus was killed by Menoeceus' charioteer Perieres: Apollod. 2.4.11. This could be linked to a prohibition on driving chariots in the precinct: cf. Burkert (1979b) 113, 199 n. 20, although he is wrong to say that Clymenus was killed in a chariot race. Apollodorus says he was wounded by a stone thrown by Perieres in Poseidon's precinct, and died later in Orchomenus.

231 νεοδμής occurs first here; cf. E. *Med.* 1366, and νεόδμητος (Euripides etc.).

231–2 περ in both 231 and 232 may be either concessive ('although') or intensifying. Cf. Denniston, GP^2 481–6.

233 **ὁδὸν ἔρχεται:** 'goes on his way'. This probably refers simply to going along the road, as in 420 etc. *LfgrE* (s.v. ὁδός p. 495) considers that it could refer to a race. Certainly ὁδός is used in such a context (cf. *Il.* 23.330, and frequently in that episode), but one expects a more explicit indication that a race is intended.

234 Cf. *Il.* 11.159–62, 15.452–3, both referring to horses rattling empty chariots whose drivers have been killed. ἀνακτορίην occurs first here; cf. A.R. 1.839.

236 κλίναντες ἐῶσιν: in Homer a chariot is 'parked' by leaning it vertically against a wall (*Il.* 8.435, *Od.* 4.42): see also Teffeteller (2001) 163–4. Presumably here too it is left stationary, although no wall is mentioned, but the phrase does not make it clear whether this is temporary or permanent.

237 For ὁσίη meaning 'rite' see Richardson on *H. Dem.* 211, and cf. also *H. Herm.* 130n.

238 θεοῦ . . . μοῖρα: this phrase is used in the *Odyssey* of the destiny imposed on someone by a god (11.292), and similarly μοῖρα θεῶν (3.269, 22.413). But here it probably has the more fundamental sense of the god's portion or share, i.e. the chariot becomes his property from then onwards.

239–76 Apollo crosses the river Cephisus, passes through Ocalea and Haliartus, and comes to the spring Telphousa. He tells her that he intends to build his temple there and begins to do so, but Telphousa dissuades him by saying that he will be disturbed by the noise of horses and by mules watering at her spring, and the traffic will distract visitors from paying due honour to the god. She advises him to choose the site of Crisa, where he will be free of such disturbance, although her real motive is to keep honour for herself rather than the god.

240–4 The Cephisus was later identified with a river which flowed into the Copaic Lake from the north-west, and Lilaea was in Phocis, north of Parnassus. Here the name seems to be given to the river which flowed into the lake from the south between Onchestus and Haliartus. Moreover, Strabo locates Ocalea half-way between Haliartus and Alalcomenae, which he places near the spring Telphousa (9.2.26, 36), whereas our poet clearly puts Ocalea before Haliartus. On the geography see AHS on *H. Ap.* 240–2, Hope Simpson and Lazenby (1970) 20, 25–6, 28–9, and Wallace (1979) 72–5, 79, 108, 117–20 with Maps V–VI.

240–1 καλλιρέεθρον . . . καλλίρροον: elegant variation rather than mere repetition.

241 This line is attributed to Hesiod by the scholia to *Il.* 2.522 (with προΐει) and Eustathius (with προχέει): cf. Hes. fr. 70.18. Cephisus and Lilaea occur in the Catalogue of Ships (*Il.* 2.522–3); cf. Hope Simpson and Lazenby (1970) 44. 241 also resembles *Il.* 2.752 ὅς ῥ' ἐς Πηνειὸν προΐει καλλίρροον ὕδωρ, and cf. *H. Ap.* 380.

242 Ὠκαλέην πολύπυργον: Ocalea is mentioned at *Il.* 2.501, but πολύπυργος occurs nowhere else; cf. εὔπυργος (*Il.* 7.71, etc.).

243 Ἁλίαρτον . . . ποιήεντα: cf. *Il.* 2.503 ποιήενθ' Ἁλίαρτον. Archaeological evidence suggests an extensive settlement here already in the late Bronze Age, and it remained a prominent city in later times. Cf. Hope Simpson and Lazenby (1970) 28–9.

244 The site of Telphousa remains uncertain: two main candidates are at the foot of a hill called Petra, on the south edge of Lake Copais, and *c.* 3 km south of the convent of Hagios Nikolaos, near Ypsilanti: cf. Schachter (1981–94) 1 76–7. Telphousa is mentioned first here and then by Pindar, who praises μελιγαθὲς ἀμβρόσιον ὕδωρ | Τιλφώσσας ἀπὸ καλλικράνου (fr. 198b). There was a tradition that Teiresias died here after Thebes was captured by the Epigonoi, as a result of drinking the water of the spring which was too cold for him, and his tomb was shown there (Aristophanes of Boeotia, *FGrH* 379 F 4, etc.). Since Apollo returns later to set up his cult here (375–87), the myth of Teiresias suggests a mantic shrine, similar to a group of others around Lake Copais, associated with a male prophet, and nymph of a spring: cf. Schachter (1967) 1–16. The similarity of name with Delphi suggests close links. The name varies in the MS tradition of the hymn between τελφοῦσα and δελφοῦσα (244, 247, 256, 276), and there were various other spellings later (cf. AHS on 244). Telphousa may have originally been another chthonic opponent of Apollo, like the Delphic dragon: see Fontenrose (1959) 366–74.

244–5 τόθι . . . δενδρήεντα: cf. 220–1 τό τοι οὐχ ἅδε θυμῶι . . . δενδρήεντα.

244 χῶρος ἀπήμων: this motif of freedom from trouble, tranquillity, is picked up by Telphousa in her speech to Apollo (262, πημανέει σ᾽. . .).

246–76 This diplomatic exchange between Apollo and the nymph is reminiscent of Leto's exchange with Delos (cf. Förstel (1979) 246–7, Miller (1986) 76–80). In both cases the major deity politely indicates their wish to the spirit of the place, who expresses her concerns about the new cult which will result. But Telphousa is more devious than Delos, pretending to have Apollo's interests at heart, whereas she is really thinking of herself. The reason she gives to put him off is rather unconvincing, since one might have expected that a sanctuary would gain from being in a busy place. But it suits the theme of the remoteness and natural poverty of Apollo's two main shrines of Delos and Delphi. There is also probably an implied link between Telphousa and the serpent of Pytho, which Apollo must kill (like the explicit link between Pytho and Typhaon). This is suggested by the fact that Apollo's anger at his realisation of Telphousa's deception of him follows directly on his killing of the dragon (375–87). The charming *naïveté* of Apollo here is a far cry from his usual omniscience, and closer to Apollo's character in the *Hymn to Hermes.*

247–55 These lines are closely echoed at 287–95; cf. also 56–7, 80–2, 132, 258–60. Apollo stresses the universally Hellenic character his cult will have at 250–1, as at 20–4 etc. His speech has been considered abrupt and insensitive, by contrast with Leto's request to Delos, and he does not wait for the nymph's consent before acting (254–5). But this indicates his power and decisiveness.

250–1 The three-fold division of Greece here roughly corresponds with the three catalogues of 30–44, 216–86, and 409–39.

250 Πελοπόννησον: not in Homer, but known to 'Hesiod' (fr. 189); cf. also *Cypria* fr. 11.3–4 Allen = 13.3–4 Davies νῆσον . . . Πέλοπος, Tyrtaeus fr. 2.15 West εὐρεῖαν Πέλοπος νῆσον.

251 Εὐρώπην: cf. Hes. *Th.* 357 as the name of an Oceanid, and fr. 140, 141.8. The name is first used here in a geographical sense, and must refer to central and northern Greece. Later it was gradually extended to cover an ever-widening area.

ἀμφιρύτας: in Homer this epithet is three-termination, and also at *H. Ap.* 27, and so this form seems preferable here and at 291. It is two-termination at Hes. *Th.* 983, and later.

252–3 τοῖσιν δέ τ' . . . νηῶι: θεμιστεύειν is used of giving judgements in Homer (*Od.* 9.114, 11.569), later of proclaiming oracles (E. *Ion* 371). See also on *H. Ap.* 123–6, and cf. in 394 θέμιστας of the god's decrees. νημερτέα βούλην is most naturally taken as the object of χρέων, as in 132 (χρήσω). Cf. Himerius 18.1 θεμιστεύειν ἐκεῖθεν τοῖς Ἕλλησιν, of Delian Apollo.

254 διέθηκε: this verb is used first here; cf. Hdt. etc.

255 διηνεκές replaces the Homeric form διηνεκέως; cf. epic διαμπερές, which is read by most MSS at 295 and could be correct there, as such variation between repeated passages is not uncommon.

257 Cf. *Il.* 19.121 ἔπος τί τοι ἐν φρεσὶ θήσω; similarly *Od.* 11.146, *H. Ap.* 534.

262–6 This must surely refer to the noise of traffic on a busy road, rather than to horse or chariot races. 264–6 suggest the kind of admiration by visitors expressed in 151–64. Cf. the wonder of the chorus at Apollo's temple in Delphi in Euripides' *Ion* 184–218, and similarly Theocr. 15.78–86, Herodas 4.20–78 (with more examples in Cunningham's edition p. 128).

262 κτύπος ἵππων: repeated again for emphasis at 265 and 270–1.

263 ἀρδόμενοι: this verb occurs first here, and at *H.* 9.3; cf. Pindar etc.

264–5 εἰσοράασθαι . . . κτύπον: a zeugma, i.e. where the verb goes with the first of two objects, and another verb has to be understood with the second. Cf. *Od.* 9.166–7 ἐλεύσσομεν . . . καπνόν τ' αὐτῶν τε φθογγὴν . . .

265 ἅρματά τ' εὐποίητα is not a Homeric formula, but cf. *Od.*13.369 εἵματα τ' εὐποίητα.

267–8 Telphousa disingenuously adopts a subservient attitude: cf. the more genuine apprehension of Delos at 66–78.

269 Crisa is mentioned at *Il.* 2.520 (Κρῖσάν τε ζαθέην). The acropolis of the Homeric settlement is usually identified with a Mycenaean site at Hagios Georgios below Delphi, on a rocky spur above the Pleistos valley. This settlement was destroyed around the end of the LH III B period (*c.* 1200 BC), and seems to have been completely deserted thereafter until the Byzantine period. See Hope Simpson and Lazenby (1970) 41, Kirk on *Il.* 2.520. For an alternative view, however, see Skorda (1992) 50–3, 62–5, who identified Crisa with Agia Varvara, just east of Hagios Georgios. Here the name is used in a general sense, for the area in which Apollo's sanctuary is to be founded. At 281–6 the description could fit the actual Mycenaean site identified as Crisa, but more probably refers to that of Delphi. At 430–47 the name is used for the harbour site (438–9 ἐς Κρίσην . . . ἐς λιμέν᾽. . .), which in later times was called Κίρρα. Originally, however, the two names Crisa and Cirrha may well have been dialect variants for the same place. Pindar uses both interchangeably, and cf. also Paus. 10.37.5.

270–1 This need not mean that there would be no chariot or horse races (cf. 262–6n.). Consequently it cannot be used as evidence to date the poem before the introduction of these events, as some scholars have argued. In any case, the races took place in the plain below Delphi, not near the sanctuary itself.

272 With ἀλλά τοι ὥς the sense is presumably 'but for this reason (because people are not distracted by other sights) men would bring gifts to you, lord of the paean'. Càssola reads ἀλλά τοι ὡς, taking it as a wish, as at *Il.* 18.107, but this seems unnecessary. The variant ἀλλὰ καὶ ὥς would imply, 'but even so (although the place is so quiet), you could still receive gifts'.

Ἰηπαιήονι: this name (first here) is used as a title of Apollo, as perhaps at A.R. 2.702–3, whereas in 500 and 517 it refers to the song (paean) in honour of the god. As with Iacchus, Linus, etc., a ritual cry is identified with the god or hero. Cf. Rutherford (2001) 10–17 on the complex development of this term and the paean, the song to which it relates. In Homer Apollo is not necessarily god of the paean (see Richardson on *Il.* 22.391–4), whereas here it is clear that he is. See also 357–62, 500, 514–19nn.

273 ἀμφιγεγηθώς: the compound occurs only here, and one could also read φρένας ἄμφι, 'in his heart'.

274 περικτιόνων ἀνθρώπων: this may well suggest the idea of an association of neighbouring peoples, as with the later ἀμφικτίονες, ἀμφικτύονες, the Amphictionic League which administered Delphi. Cf. perhaps 298 (if this should follow 299: see comments), and see 540–3n.

277–98 Apollo passes the home of the Phlegyae, and comes to Crisa. Here he again announces his intention of founding his oracular shrine, and lays the foundations of a temple, which is built by Trophonius and Agamedes.

278–80 The Phlegyae are located here in Phocis, near the Cephisian lake, i.e. Copais, into which the river Cephisus flowed. They are mentioned at *Il.* 13.302, where Ares and Phobos join a conflict involving them and the Ephyrians. Phlegyas was himself a son of Ares, and father of Ixion the Lapith (cf. Janko on *Il.* 13.301–3), as well as of Coronis (see on *H. Ap.* 209–10). Their hybristic nature and arrogance towards Zeus recalls the Giants and the Cyclopes: cf. *Od.* 11.275 οὐ γὰρ Κύκλωπες Διὸς αἰγιόχου ἀλέγουσιν. They were said to have attacked travellers to Delphi, or Delphi itself, until they were more or less wiped out by Apollo (see on *H. Ap.* 211, and Paus. 9.36.2–3, etc.). They were settled at Panopeus (Paus. 10.4.1), and it was here that Tityus attacked Leto on her way to Delphi (*Od.* 11.580–1). See also Fontenrose (1959) 22–7, 46–69.

280 Lake Copais is so called at *Il.* 5.709; cf. Paus. 9.24.1 etc.

281 δειράδα: first here, and later in Pindar etc., of a ridge of hills. It presumably refers to Parnassus, which is due west of Panopeus.

θύων perhaps means 'with eager haste' here, rather than 'in anger' (as Càssola assumes). Apollo's pace quickens as he nears his goal.

282–6 'And you came to Crisa below snowy Parnassus, a mountain-spur facing westwards: above a rock overhangs it, and a deep, rugged glen runs below. Here the lord Phoebus Apollo determined to make his lovely temple, and made this speech.' The description is vivid and the language untraditional (see 284 and 285nn.). It surely refers to the site of Delphi itself (see Robertson (1978) 42–3, Miller (1986) 72), rather than to the Mycenaean site at Hagios Georgios, as Hope Simpson and Lazenby assume (1970, 41).

At Delphi there was a late Mycenaean settlement in the area near the later temple of Apollo, and numerous votive objects were found in the region of the sanctuary of Athena Pronaia, suggesting a cult there. After this there is little evidence until the late Geometric period, but from then onwards its importance is evident. Cf. Hope Simpson and Lazenby (1970) 40–1.

282 Παρνησὸν νιφόεντα: cf. Panyassis fr. 15 Davies, S. *OT* 473–5, Call. *H.* 4.93.

283 Cf. *Od.* 12.81 πρὸς ζόφον . . . τετραμμένον.

284 ἐπικρέμαται: first here; cf. (perhaps) Theognis 206, then Simonides etc.

ὑποδέδρομε: only here in this topographical sense.

285 τεκμήρατο: this verb is not used elsewhere in early epic with the infinitive; cf. A.R. 4.559.

287–95 Cf. 247–55. In 287 τεῦξαι is probably correct, as at 245 and 258.

294–8 The earliest temple to Apollo at Delphi for which possible material evidence (stone blocks and roof tiles) has been identified is usually thought to date to some time between *c.* 650 and 600 BC: cf. Morgan (1990) 132–4, Bommelaer (1991) 183–4, Jacquemin (1993) 217–25 (especially 222–3). This temple was burnt in 548/7 BC, and rebuilt by the Alcmaeonidae (cf. Hdt. 2.180, Paus. 10.5.13). Later legend told of four early temples, the first a hut of branches of bay, the second made of beeswax and feathers, the third made by Hephaestus of bronze, and the fourth of stone by Trophonius and Agamedes (cf. Pi. fr. 52.i, Paus. 10.5.9–13, with Sourvinou-Inwood (1991) 192–216, Rutherford (2001) 209–32). According to Pausanias it was the fourth one which was burnt in 548 BC. Our hymn, however, speaks of this as the original building on the site. Strabo (9.3.9) also thought that there were only two temples, the one built by Trophonius and Agamedes, and the one built after 548 BC. The fact that it is said to be ἀοιδίμον . . . αἰεί (299) makes better sense if the passage was composed before 548 BC, although it does not prove this point. See also Introduction 2(b).

294–5 θεμείλια . . . εὐρέα καὶ μάλα μακρὰ διηνεκές: the supporting terrace of the later (fourth-century BC) temple is 60 metres long and 3 to 4.5 metres in height, and the temple itself measures 60.32 × 23.82 metres.

296 λάϊνον οὐδόν: cf. *Il.* 9.404–5 οὐδ' ὅσα λάϊνος οὐδὸς ἀφήτορος ἔντος ἐέργει, | Φοίβου Ἀπόλλωνος, Πυθοῖ ἔνι πετρηέσσῃ (of the wealth of Apollo at

Delphi), and *Od.* 8.79–81 ὣς γάρ οἱ χρείων μυθήσατο Φοῖβος Ἀπόλλων | Πυθοῖ ἐν ἠγαθέηι, ὅθ' ὑπέρβη λάϊνον οὐδὸν | χρησόμενος . . . (of Agamemnon's consultation of the oracle).

Clearly the λάϊνος οὐδός was a distinctive feature. The phrase should mean a stone threshold, and this must be the case in *Od.* 8.79–81. In the *Iliad* it has been explained as the stone socle on which could be built walls of mud-brick (Von Blumenthal (1927–8) 220–4). But it is more likely that it is the threshold in both the *Iliad* and the hymn. In the first monumental temples built of stone the threshold was a major feature, often monolithic and the largest single block in the building. The fourth-century BC temple of Apollo has a threshold measuring 5.9 × 2 metres, and at least 30 cm in depth (i.e. *c.* 3.5 cubic metres). An inscription of 277–6 BC honours a certain Menedemus because he had 'conveyed the threshold for the god', i.e. had brought it up to the sanctuary. See Roux (1966) 1–5.

If the Homeric passages refer to a building, as they surely must, and if they belong to poems composed before the construction of a seventh-century temple, it would follow that this must have had a predecessor, not necessarily all of stone, but whose threshold was grand enough to deserve special mention. The threshold was also a place of religious and symbolic significance, and crossing or stepping on it was an important moment (cf. Richardson on *H. Dem.* 188). Cf. also Hdt. 1.90, where Croesus orders his shackles to be deposited 'on the threshold of the temple' at Delphi.

296–7 Trophonius and Agamedes were legendary master-builders, to whom various temples, treasuries, and other buildings were attributed. The gods' love for them (297) was demonstrated by their being rewarded with an early death by Apollo ([Pl.], *Axiochus* 367c etc.). Trophonius became a famous oracular hero, in an underground chamber at Lebadeia (Paus. 9.37.5). One tradition made him a son of Apollo. On these legends and Trophonius' cult see Schachter (1981–94) III 66–89. The two heroes were mentioned also in the *Telegony* (p. 109.11 Allen = p. 72 Davies), and Trophonius probably in the Hesiodic *Catalogue* (Schachter (1981-94) III 72). For Erginus, son of Clymenus, see 231–8n. (last paragraph). His name is suitable for the father of two legendary builders.

299 + 298 'With well-wrought [*or* well-set] stones, to be sung of for ever. And around the temple dwelt the countless tribes of men.' With Von Blumenthal's transposition of 298 and 299 (1927–8, 223), the passage as a whole describes the building of the stone threshold. It is the threshold of Apollo's temple at Delphi which is singled out in the two Homeric passages referring to the sanctuary (see 296n.). With this reading, the actual construction of the temple is taken for granted. This is not altogether satisfactory, but if the original order of the lines is kept, 298 ought to mean 'and countless tribes . . . dwelt around the temple', or 'and they settled countless tribes . . . around the temple'. In that case, κτιστοῖσιν λάεσσιν is left hanging. Consequently, 298–9 have been taken as 'and the countless tribes constructed the temple around (the threshold) from well-worked stones . . .'

However, ναίειν nowhere else means 'to construct', and it is hard to see how it can acquire this sense. (It is probably actually related to νηός, ναός, meaning 'dwelling-place'.) Càssola gives examples for the sense 'found', but this refers to founding a settlement. Roux suggested reading ἔλασσαν, which is often used in Homer and later of building, e.g. *Od.* 6.9 ἀμφὶ δὲ τεῖχος ἔλασσε πόλει, and especially 7.86–7 χάλκεοι μὲν γὰρ τοῖχοι ἐλήλεατ' ἔνθα καὶ ἔνθα, | ἐς μυχὸν ἐξ οὐδοῦ... It is quite often combined with ἀμφί or περί also. This is a simple emendation, but ἀμφὶ... ἐλαύνειν seems less suitable for building a temple 'around a threshold' than (say) a wall round a city. As no better solution has been put forward, Von Blumenthal's suggestion is adopted here. In this case, 298 may allude to the idea of an Amphictiony, as in 274.

298 κτιστοῖσιν λάεσσιν: κτιστός as an epithet seems to occur only here in literature, although κτιστόν is used to mean a 'building' in some papyri. It probably means 'well-wrought' ('des pierres appareillées', Roux (1966) 4–5), or 'well-set'. Cf. the use of κτίζειν to mean 'make, produce'.

ἀοίδιμον ἔμμεναι αἰεί: the universal character of Apollo's sanctuary is extended here to future generations, encompassing the poet's own song itself (cf. also 177–8). For ἀοίδιμος in this context cf. *Il.* 6.357–8 (the only other early epic use of the word).

300–74 Nearby was the spring where Apollo killed the serpent with his bow, a terrible monster which used to cause great harm to men and flocks.

She had also been the nurse of Typhaon, Hera's offspring, whom Hera bore in her anger at the birth of Athene from the head of Zeus. Hera protested at Zeus's neglect of her, and the weakness of her own son Hephaestus. She withdrew from the gods and prayed to the elemental powers of Earth, Heaven, and the Titans, that she should bear a fatherless child, who would be more powerful than Zeus. A year later she produced Typhaon, whom she gave to the serpent to rear. Apollo shot the serpent, and with agonised cries she died. He exulted over her death, and the Sun rotted her corpse: hence the place is named *Putho*, and men invoke Apollo as *Puthios* (cf. πύθειν = 'to rot').

The killing of the serpent is the next act in the Pythian drama. One might have expected it to come before the building of the temple, and in fact the temporal sequence is perhaps deliberately left indefinite at 300ff. The poet wanted to concentrate first on the choice of Delphi for the god's shrine, and the serpent-killing also leads us back at 375–87 to Telphousa, since after that Apollo realised that Telphousa had deceived him (see 246–76n.).

The narrative of the killing (300–4, 357–74) broadly follows the pattern of Homeric scenes where minor warriors are slain: details of the victim's origins (etc.), the fight and killing (sometimes with graphic description of death), speech of victor (cf. Förstel (1979) 258–9).

Apollo's slaying of the dragon at Delphi was seen as a major exploit by the god, and it was later commemorated in the Delphic ritual of the Septerion. This eight-yearly festival was also said to re-enact the purification of Apollo after this event (cf. Plut. *Mor.* 293B–C, 418A–D, Aelian *VH* 3.1). In the hymn, however, there is no mention of the need for purification. Later tradition also usually held that the Pythian Games were originally instituted by Apollo as a funeral celebration after the killing (cf. Frazer on Paus. 10.7.2). In 586 BC Sacadas was the first victor in the aulos-playing contest, with a tune which was said to represent the fight and the serpent's death, the Πυθικὸς νόμος: see 357–62n. The serpent was later sometimes seen as the original guardian of the oracle at Delphi (e.g. Eur. *IT* 1245–9), and in Aeschylus' *Eumenides* (1–19) Apollo succeeds a series of female deities (Earth, Themis, and Phoebe) as possessor of the site. Cf. also AHS (on *H. Ap.* 300–74), Fontenrose (1959) especially 13–22, 396–7, 453–61, Kolk (1963) 24–7, 41–51, and Sourvinou-Inwood (1991) 217–43. For discussion of parallels to the dragon-slaying myth in ancient Greek and other traditions see Fontenrose (1959) *passim*, Watkins (1995) 297–544, West (2007) 255–9.

Into this story of dragon-slaying is inserted a parallel myth, that of Typhaon (or Typhoeus): 305–55. This occupies fifty lines, and much of it is taken up by the description of Hera's anger, dramatically evoked in her speech at 311–30. The parallelism of Typhaon with the serpent is emphasised: both are monsters, and a terrible pest for mankind (302–4, 354–5, etc.). It is possible, in fact, that Python and Typhon (and their related forms) were originally 'doublets', as the name of an archetypal opponent of the gods (cf. Fontenrose (1959), especially 91–2, Watkins (1995) 462). It is their similarity which makes the serpent a suitable nurse for Hera's child. Moreover, the fearsome nature of Typhaon (an arch-enemy of Zeus and opponent of divine order in Hesiod's *Theogony*) adds to the deadly character of the dragon, justifying Apollo's killing even more and underlining its significance (cf. Miller (1986) 82–8, Sourvinou-Inwood (1991) 228–30). Another myth (Apollod. 1.6.3) told how Typhaon cut out the sinews of Zeus and hid them in the Corycian cave, setting the dragon Delphune to guard them (cf. West on Hes. *Th.* 853).

The Typhaon episode has been considered as an addition to the original version of the hymn, partly because of its disproportionate scale, and also because the join between this and the dragon-slaying is awkward at 353–8 (with an abrupt change of reference at 355–6). This however can be avoided by reading ἣ κακά etc. at 355 (see 355–6n.). The allusion to Typhoeus by Apollo at 367–8 might also be thought to guarantee its genuineness (cf. Förstel (1979) 261–2).

300 ἀγχοῦ δὲ κρήνη καλλίρροος: for the wording cf. 241, 376, 380, 385. It is unclear whether the spring is Castalia, or Cassotis, which is nearer to Apollo's temple, or indeed another source (cf. Paus. 10.8.9, 12.1, 24.7, with Frazer's notes).

δράκαιναν: this feminine form of δράκων ('snake') occurs first here, later in Aeschylus etc. She is nameless here, but later is called Python (masculine), or Delphune(s) (fem. or masc.): see Fontenrose (1959) 14–15.

302 ζατρεφέα μεγάλην τέρας ἄγριον: the accumulation of epithets stresses her monstrosity.

304 δαφοινόν 'blood-red'. Cf. *Il.* 2.308 δράκων ἐπὶ νῶτα δαφοινός, of a terrible portentous snake.

305–55 The motif of Hera's anger and jealousy echoes the theme of her hostility to Leto in the Delian hymn (92–101, 105–6), and develops it on a much larger scale. In Hesiod's *Theogony*, however, Typhoeus is the offspring of Earth and Tartarus (820–2). Here he is a son of Hera, but Hera invokes Earth and Tartarus in praying for a child (334–9). Stesichorus followed the genealogy of the hymn (*PMG* 239). Hera also nursed the Lernaean hydra and Nemean lion, because of her anger with Zeus over Heracles (Hes. *Th.* 313–15, 326–9). In the *Theogony* (820–80) Typhoeus is a hundred-headed dragon (824–6). His battle with Zeus, described in vivid detail, is the last challenge to the establishment of Zeus as ruler of the world (836–7), a motif picked up by Hera in her speech at *H. Ap.* 337–9.

The passage has a ring-structure, returning to the theme of Typhaon's birth and upbringing at the end (305–7, 351–4; 352 = 306). This is enclosed within the ring of 300–4, 356–74 (death of serpent), and the reprise of the Telphousa theme at 375–87 closes the whole section.

306 Τυφάονα: he is Τυφωεύς at 367, a variation also found in Hes. *Th.* 306, 821, 860.

πῆμα βροτοῖσιν: he is the parent of evil winds at Hes. *Th.* 869–80.

308–9 That Athena was the child of Zeus alone may be implied already at *Il.* 5.875–80, especially 880 ἐπεί αὐτὸς ἐγείναο παῖδ' ἀΐδηλον. In the *Theogony* (886–900) the birth of Athena is the result of Zeus's union with Metis, whom he swallows, because Earth and Heaven have warned him that otherwise she would produce a son who would supplant him as king of the gods. She is born from his head, a warrior goddess, and Hera then produces Hephaestus in revenge, without intercourse, because of her anger with Zeus (*Th.* 924–9). Another version of Athena's birth was ascribed to Hesiod by Chrysippus (Hes. fr. 343): here, strife between Hera and Zeus leads first to her producing Hephaestus on her own, and then to Zeus producing Athena, after having swallowed Metis. Athena is born armed for war (19).

H. 28 describes her birth, again fully armed (5–6), and the powerful impact which this has on the whole universe. Stesichorus was later said to have been the *first* author who described how Athena sprang fully armed from the head of Zeus, and a line is quoted from his version in a papyrus (*PMG* 233, and Schol. A.R. 4.1310). The reference must be to the detail of her birth 'fully armed', and the commentator either ignores the Hesiodic fragment and *H.* 28, or regards Stesichorus as earlier than these. It is possible that Stesichorus combined the two themes of Athena's and Typhoeus' births, as in the *Hymn to Apollo*.

The motif of Hera's anger and subsequent production of a son on her own is reduplicated, in the myths of Hephaestus' birth and that of Typhoeus (*H. Ap.* and Stesichorus, *PMG* 239, where again this is 'due to her grudge against Zeus').

The theme of a son who would overthrow Zeus also recurs in the myths of both Typhoeus and Athena (who herself is predicted to be 'equal in might and wisdom to her father' at *Th.* 896).

In art, Athena's birth from Zeus's head was already portrayed from at least the late seventh century BC, and possibly as early as *c.* 680 BC, if the famous representation on a relief *pithos* from Tenos is of this event, as seems likely (cf. H. Cassimatis, *LIMC* II.1 985–8 and 1021–3, and II.1, figures 360–4, etc.).

On the literary evidence for this and the other myths discussed here see also Kauer (1959), and West on Hes. *Th.* 820–80, 886–900, 924–9.

308 ἦνίκ' ἄρα 'at the time when': the variant reading εὖτ' ἄρα δή is also possible. Pfeiffer's conjecture εἵνεκ' ἄρα ('because') would be parallel to the use of ἕνεκα at *H. Aph.* 199 (where see n.).

309 ἐν κορυφῆι: the variant ἐκ κορυφῆς is what we find at Hes. *Th.* 924, *H.* 28.5; cf. Hes. fr. 343.12 πὰρ κορυφήν.

311–30 Hera's powerful speech of injured pride is very much in accord with the way she is portrayed in the *Iliad* (1.540–3 etc.). The themes of Hera's dishonour and Hephaestus' deformity (311–21) have an interesting parallel at *Od.* 8.306–12, where Hephaestus protests to the gods about Aphrodite's adultery and rejection of him as deformed: cf. 308 ὡς ἐμὲ χωλὸν ἐόντα . . . | αἰὲν ἀτιμάζει . . . | . . . αὐτὰρ ἐγώ γε | ἠπεδανὸς γενόμην . . . ; and 312 . . . τὼ μὴ γείνασθαι ὄφελλον is parallel to Hera's wish at *H. Ap.* 321. Does our poet have this passage in mind?

Hera's complaint seems to be echoed directly by Ovid at *Fasti* 5.239–44, where she then gives birth alone to Mars in retaliation for Minerva's birth. In *Aeneid* 7 Juno's speech expressing her rage at Aeneas' success is followed by her recourse to chthonic aid (286–340): cf. 312 *flectere si nequeo superos, Acheronta mouebo.*

311 = *Il.* 8.5, 19.101.

312–15 Hera accuses Zeus of having 'started it', after he had made her his wife. καὶ νῦν in 314 taken literally would suggest that Athena's birth is not his first act of infidelity towards her. In the *Theogony* Metis is his first wife, and Hera the last divine one (886, 921), but he actually gives birth to Athena *after* his marriages to Hera and other goddesses (924–6).

317–18 As the text stands, there is an abrupt asyndeton after 317, which Càssola defends, because it is a feature of agitated speech, such as Hera's. However, the text may be corrupt, or a verse may be lost here, as most previous editors have assumed.

317 ῥικνός 'withered, shrivelled' occurs first here; cf. A.R. 1.669 ῥικνοὶ πόδες etc.

ὃν τέκον αὐτή: in Homer Hephaestus is son of both Zeus and Hera, and it would not make sense to assume here that the poet is referring to the Hesiodic version where Hera is his sole parent, since the birth of Typhaon is designed by Hera to get even with Zeus after that of Athena. The point is that he is not the son of another wife of Zeus, but of Hera herself.

318–20 At *Il.* 18.394–405 Hephaestus is cast from heaven by Hera, in disgust at his lameness, and rescued by Thetis and Eurynome. Another fall from heaven is described by Hephaestus at *Il.* 1.590–4, where cf. 591 (Zeus) ῥίψε ποδὸς τεταγών.
319 Cf. *Il.* 1.538, 556 ἀργυρόπεζα Θέτις, θυγάτηρ ἁλίοιο γέροντος. The epithet is applied only to Thetis in Homer.
321 'How I wish that she had done something else as a favour for the blessed gods!' A particularly bitter remark.
322–3 Cf. *Od.* 13.293 σχέτλιε, ποικιλομῆτα, δόλων ἄτ(ε)..., addressed by Athena to Odysseus. Here, as there, we have word-play on the theme of μῆτις (or Μῆτις): cf. *Od.* 13.299, 303, and *H. Ap.* 325a, 326, 344. 322–3 also resemble *Od.* 11.474–5 (to Odysseus) σχέτλιε, τίπτ' ἔτι μεῖζον ἐνὶ φρεσὶ μήσεαι ἔργον; | πῶς ἔτλης...
323 γλαυκῶπιν is probably right here, as at 314, *Od.* 1.156, *H. Aph.* 8, *Th.* 13, 888.
324–5 With Matthiae's reading this means 'Could I not have (also) given birth (to her)? And yet after all I was called your wife...' Cf. *Il.* 4.60–1, 18.365–6 καὶ οὕνεκα σὴ παράκοιτις | κέκλημαι... Chalcondyles' text is supposed to mean 'And even so she would after all have been called your daughter...', but this would require ἄν or κεν, which (*pace* Càssola) can hardly be understood from the preceding οὐκ ἂν ἐγὼ τεκόμην;
325a This line was omitted from the MSS, but added in the margins of one group (*x*), probably because of the similarity of νῦν μή τοί and νῦν μέντοι in 326. This helps to guarantee M's reading in 326. Cf. *Il.* 22.358 φράζεο νῦν μή τοί τι θεῶν μήνιμα γένωμαι, and 24.436 μή μοί τι κακὸν μετόπισθε γένηται.
326–30 Cf. Ovid, *Fasti* 5.241–2 (Juno) *cur ego desperem fieri sine coniuge mater | et parere intacto, dummodo casta, uiro?*
327 echoes 315: Typhaon will be her answer to Athena.
329–30 In 329–48 Hera withdraws from the Olympian gods in general, not only from Zeus, and stays in her temples on earth, just as Demeter does at *H. Dem.* 302–4 (303 μακάρων ἀπὸ νόσφιν ἁπάντων; cf. 92–3, 354–6). She does, however, associate herself with the chthonic powers (334–6). West's conjecture (330) Οὐρανίωσιν (i.e. the Titans) is designed to make this more explicit: cf. *Il.* 5.898 where the Titans are thus described, in a speech by Zeus to Ares, which refers also to Hera's enmity. But it seems doubtful whether the word on its own here would be understood in this way.
330 **οὖσα:** for this form instead of ἔουσα see *H. Herm.* 106n.
332–9 Hera prays to Earth, Sky, and the Titans who dwell in Tartarus. Cf. *Il.* 14.270–9, where Sleep asks Hera to swear an oath by Styx, placing one hand on Earth, the other on the Sea, with the Titans as her witnesses, and she does so. Her prayer and gesture of striking the earth are similar to *Il.* 9.566–72, where Althaea beats the earth with her hands and invokes Hades and Persephone, and the Erinys hears her. Striking the earth in invocation was often mentioned in later literature: cf. A. *Pers.* 683, Eur. *Tro.* 1306, etc.

333 χειρὶ καταπρηνεῖ δ' ἐλάσε χθόνα: 'she beat the ground with the flat of her hand'. This powerful gesture is ascribed especially to gods in Homer: cf. *Il.* 15.113–14, where it indicates Ares' grief, and 16.791–2, *Od.* 13.164, where it has a physical effect.

334–5 The Titans are the children of Earth and Heaven (Hes. *Th.* 132–8 etc.). Their relegation to Tartarus is described at *Th.* 717–819, and alluded to at *Il.* 14.273–4, 278–9.

335 τοὶ . . . ναιετάοντες: 'those who dwell below the earth'. If the MS reading is correct, τοί must be the article here, as at *Il.* 24.687: cf. Allen (1931) 146.

336 τῶν ἐξ ἄνδρες τε θεοί τε: the Titans are parents or grandparents of the Olympian gods, but not specifically described elsewhere in early epic as ancestors of mankind, although Zeus is called 'father of gods and men'. Hesiod (*Op.* 108) says that 'gods and mortals have a common origin (ὁμόθεν γεγάασι)', and the Olympian gods, or Zeus, create the successive generations of men (109–201). Cf. Pi. *N.* 6.1–2: 'Single is the race of men, single of gods: from a single mother we both draw our breath.'

A myth ascribed to Orpheus described how mankind came into being from the soot created when Zeus blasted the Titans with his thunderbolt, because they had killed and eaten Dionysus: cf. Orph. *H.* 37.1–2 Τιτῆνες Γαίης τε καὶ Οὐρανοῦ ἀγλαὰ τέκνα | ἡμετέρων πρόγονοι πατέρων, with Orph. fr. 220 Kern, and West (1983) 164–6. Just when this myth was first formulated in a Greek context remains uncertain. The Titans Prometheus and Epimetheus also sometimes seem to feature as ancestors of mankind: cf. Currie (2007) 178–81.

337–9 See 305–55, 308–9nn. The motif of a child who will be stronger than Zeus, and by implication would succeed him as Zeus succeeded Cronos, occurs also in the story of Zeus's pursuit of Thetis, and Prometheus' ultimate revelation that their son would overthrow him.

339 ἔστω is a conjecture based on M's reading. Hermann's εἴη would also be possible, but is further from the readings in the MSS.

340 ἵμασε χθόνα χειρὶ παχείηι echoes 333, closing the speech and leading on to its effects on Earth. Cf. *Il.* 2.781–3 γαῖα δ' ὑπεστενάχιζε Διὶ ὣς τερπικεραύνωι | χωομένωι, ὅτε τ' ἀμφὶ Τυφωέϊ γαῖαν ἱμάσσηι | εἰν Ἀρίμοις, ὅθι φασὶ Τυφωέος ἔμμεναι εὐνάς, and Hes. *Th.* 857–8 (of Zeus's defeat of Typhoeus) αὐτὰρ ἐπεὶ δή μιν δάμασε πληγῆισιν ἱμάσσας, | ἤριπε γυιωθείς, στενάχιζε δὲ γαῖα πελώρη. Since both concern Typhoeus, there seems to be a thematic link with this passage of the hymn.

341 φερέσβιος is not in Homer, but occurs five times in the *Hymns*, and at Hes. *Th.* 693. Apollodorus quotes it as 'Homeric': see Richardson on *H. Dem.* 450.

345–6 The word order is rather complex, by Homeric standards. εἰς θῶκον goes with ἐφεζομένη, αὐτῶι with φραζέσκετο.

345 εἰς θῶκον πολυδαίδαλον: this phrase occurs only here, but cf. *Il.* 8.439 θεῶν δ' ἐξίκετο θώκους, *Od.* 5.30 οἱ δὲ θεοὶ θῶκόνδε καθίζανον.

347–8 Cf. *H. Dem.* 27–9 ὁ δὲ νόσφιν | ἧστο θεῶν ἀπάνευθε πολυλλίστωι ἐνὶ νηῶι | δέγμενος ἱερὰ καλὰ παρὰ θνητῶν ἀνθρώπων, and *H. Dem.* 355–6 (of Demeter) ἀλλ᾽ ἀπάνευθε θυώδεος ἔνδοθι νηοῦ | ἧσται.

349–50 = *Od.* 11.294–5, 14.293–4.

351 δέ is 'apodotic' here, i.e. it introduces the main clause after ἀλλ᾽ ὅτε . . . This use after a temporal clause is 'by far the commonest form of apodotic δέ in Homer' (Denniston, *GP*[2] 179).

The negative expression in 351 is a way of indicating the portentous character of this offspring. Cf. (for example) *H. Herm.* 219–25, where Hermes' footprints are unlike those of man or woman, various wild beasts, or even a centaur.

352 = 306, emphasising the ring-structure. Despite the repetition of βροτοῖσι(ν) in 352–3, this reprise makes it likely that this, rather than M's θεοῖσιν, is correct here, even though Typhaon really was a bane to the gods in the first place.

353–4 We return to the Delphic dragon, whose similarity to Typhaon is emphasised (κακῶι κακόν).

353 **τόνδε:** West conjectured τόν γε (and at *H.* 26.7), because ὅδε in epic narrative is normally only used in a prospective sense. Cf. however *Il.* 9.77, *H. Dem.* 480, and other examples in Ebeling, *Lexicon Homericum* s.v. ὅδε IIIB.

355–6 If we read ἥ in 355, then 356 follows on naturally: 'Whenever anyone encountered that pest (τῆι γ᾽), his day of doom would carry him off.' Cf. the image of men being carried off by their κῆρες: *Il.* 2.302 etc. With the MS reading ὅς at 355, the line refers to Typhaon, and there is then an abrupt change to the dragon in 356. The corruption could have been caused by reminiscence of *Il.* 9.540 (of the Calydonian boar) ὃς κακὰ πολλ᾽ ἔρδεσκεν (or ἔρρεξεν, ἔρρεζεν).

357–62 The actual killing is described very briefly, but great attention is paid to the dragon's death-throes. There may be links with the Pythian *nomos* (see 300–74n.), which was a vivid musical representation of the fight and death, played on the flute. In Pollux' version (4.84) this included:

(1) πεῖρα, where Apollo inspects the site for battle;
(2) κατακελευσμός, his challenge to fight;
(3) ἰαμβικόν, the fight, which included trumpet blasts, and ὀδοντισμός (representing the dragon grinding its teeth);
(4) σπονδεῖον, the victory;
(5) καταχόρευσις, the god's dance to celebrate his victory.

Different versions are given by the scholiast to Pindar's *Pythians* (Arg. 1, II 2.8ff. Drachmann) and by Strabo (9.3.10). These include abuse of the dragon (ἴαμβος), and the hissing of the dying snake (σύριγμα, σύριγγες), and elements connected with Dionysus, Zeus (Κρητικόν), and Mother Earth. Clearly the different parts and their symbolic interpretation varied, but there was a basic pattern, at least from 586 BC onwards, and quite possibly earlier. The oldest form of the Pythian contest was a hymn or paean to Apollo (Paus. 10.7.2, Strabo 9.3.10). The legendary poet Olympus was said to have first played a dirge for the dragon on his aulos in the Lydian mode, and Apollo himself to have sung a funerary song over it (Fontenrose (1959) 457–8). There is a parallel legend in the invention of aulos-playing, or specifically the so-called 'many-headed tune' by Athena (or Athena and Olympus), as a representation of Perseus' killing of the Gorgon (Pindar *P.* 12 etc.).

Strabo describes the Pythian *nomos* as being prescribed for *kitharis* also. The paean sung by Apollo and his first ministers at 514–19 can be linked to the καταχόρευσις of the *nomos*. The two surviving Delphic paeans refer to the killing of the serpent, and mention its 'hissing', with suitable musical *mimesis*. See Kolk (1963) 41–7, West (1992) 212–15, 279–80, 292, 298, and on other Delphic paeans see Rutherford (2001) 27–9.

One tradition about the origin of the paean refrain, and Apollo's invocation as Ἰηπαιήων etc., derived these from a cry encouraging him in his battle with the dragon, e.g. ἵει, παῖ, ἰόν ('shoot, child, your arrow'). There are no explicit references to this or related etymologies before the fourth century BC (see Rutherford (2001) 25–7), but it is just possible that line 357 (πρίν γέ οἱ ἰὸν ἐφῆκεν . . .) of our hymn might allude to this. The paean is derived from Crete in 516–19, but a double derivation is not impossible. See also Strunk (1959) 79–82 for similar word-play on ἰήιος etc. in Pi. *Paean* 6.121–2 and Call. *H.* 2.97–104.

357–62 The mainly dactylic rhythm suits the rapidity of the actions described.

357 πρίν γέ . . . ἐφῆκεν: this is the first example of πρίν used with the indicative, as in fifth century BC and later authors. Homer uses πρίν γ' ὅτε δή.

ἑκάεργος is apt in this context, in view of its traditional association with Apollo's archery.

358–9 ὀδύνῃσιν ἐρεχθομένη χαλεπῇσι . . . κεῖτο: the exact sense of ἐρέχθω is uncertain, but it indicates strong distress or trouble, physical or mental: see Richardson on *Il.* 23.317, and *LfgrE* s.v. Cf. *Il.* 5.354 ἀχθομένην ὀδύνῃσι etc., and Archil. fr. 193 West δύστηνος ἔγκειμαι πόθωι, | ἄψυχος, χαλεπῇσι θεῶν ὀδύνῃσιν ἕκητι | πεπαρμένος δι' ὀστέων.

359 μέγ' ἀσθμαίνουσα κυλινδομένη: cf. *Il.* 5.585 etc., and 8.86, for these words applied to stricken warriors or horses.

360 θεσπεσίη δ' ἐνοπὴ γένετ' ἄσπετος: cf. *H. Herm.* 422 θεσπεσίης ἐνοπῆς of the lyre; ἐνοπή also of pipes at *Il.* 10.13, *H. Herm.* 512, which would be appropriate if there is a link here with Pythian music (see 357–62n.).

καθ' ὕλην: cf. Hes. fr. 204.131 (of a snake?) ἀνὰ δρυμὰ πυκνὰ καὶ ὕλην.

361–2 λεῖπε δὲ θυμὸν | φοινὸν ἀποπνείουσ' 'and she gave up her spirit, breathing it out blood-red'. Cf. *Il.* 4.524, 13.654 θυμὸν ἀποπνείων. φοινός occurs only at *Il.* 16.159 παρήϊον αἵματι φοινόν, and in Hellenistic poetry (see Janko's comment on *Il.* 16.159). Cf. Pi. *P.* 3.101 τόξοις ἀπὸ ψυχὰν λιπών, Verg. *A.* 9.349 *purpuream uomit ille animam*. λεῖπε . . . θυμόν has been thought odd, as in Homer a person's θυμός normally leaves him at death, but cf. λείπειν φάος ἠελίοιο (etc.), of dying, and see Hoekstra (1969) 30–1.

362–70 Apollo's speech of triumph is modelled on those of Homeric victors (see Förstel (1979) 259, 470 n. 675, Miller (1986) 89). These often declare that the victim's body will not be buried, but will be left as prey to birds and dogs. Especially close, however, is Achilles' boast over Lycaon (*Il.* 21.121–35). Cf. 21.122 ἐνταυθοῖ νῦν κεῖσο..., 123–5 οὐδέ σε μήτηρ |... γοήσεται... ἀλλὰ Σκάμανδρος | οἴσει..., 130–3 οὐδ' ἡμῖν πόταμός περ... | ἀρκέσει... ἀλλὰ καὶ ὧς ὀλέεσθε κακὸν μόρον... Cf. 11.449–54, 16.836–42, and the frequent occasions when a victor declares that other victims' deaths have been avenged (13.414–16 etc.); also 20.388–93 (where 393 = *H. Ap.* 370).

363 πύθευ ἐπὶ χθονὶ βωτιανείρῃ: the etymology (πύθειν) is introduced emphatically at the start of Apollo's speech and again at its close (369), and repeated four times in 371–4. There is an implied contrast in 'the earth which gives men life' and the rotting of the serpent on the same earth (cf. 369), and this motif is echoed in 364–8, which play on the words for life and death and the life-giving earth. 369, 371, and 374 also have an elegant variation of phrases to describe the Sun-god's power.

364–7 οὐδὲ σύ γε ζωοῖσι... οὐδέ τί τοι θάνατόν γε: life and death are contrasted in the parallel phrasing. West's γ' ἐν ζωοῖσι would bring this out more clearly, but is not strictly needed.

364–6 Apollo declares that his sanctuary will now be free of the troubles which beset it, leaving men to make their offerings undisturbed. Cf. Menander Rhetor's encomium of Apollo, where this theme is developed (pp. 215.16–216.1 Russell and Wilson).

364 δήλημα: once in Homer (*Od.* 12.286); cf. Homeric δηλήμων.

367–8 οὔτε Τυφωεὺς... οὐδὲ Χίμαιρα 'neither Typhoeus... nor indeed Chimaera'. This is progressive: cf. Denniston, *GP*² 193. The mention of Typhoeus here neatly echoes the theme of 305–54. Chimaera is the daughter of Typhoeus and Echidna in Hes. *Th.* 319–25.

367 θάνατόν γε δυσηλεγέ' 'painful death': the phrase occurs at *Od.* 22.325.

369 ἠλέκτωρ Ὑπερίων: cf. *Il.* 19.398 (and 6.513 ἠλέκτωρ alone). ἠλέκτωρ is usually taken to mean 'shining', though the derivation is uncertain, and Ὑπερίων here must be the Sun (371), as at *Il.* 8.480 and usually in the *Odyssey*. In the *Theogony* and other Homeric hymns Hyperion is Helios' father (see West on Hes. *Th.* 134).

370 = *Il.* 20.393.

371–4 This is the first of three *aitia* for Apolline cult titles: cf. 386–7 (Τελφούσιος) and 493–6 (Δελφίνιος).

371 ἱερὸν μένος Ἠελίοιο: cf. ἱερὸν μένος (*Od.* 7.167 etc.), and μένος Ἠελίοιο *Il.* 23.190 (in a similar context), *Od.* 10.160.

372 Πυθώ: this is the name given to the site of Apollo's sanctuary in Homer and Hesiod. Δελφοί first occurs at *H.* 27.14. The etymology is given as 'the usual tradition' by Pausanias (10.6.5).

373 Πύθιον: this (the MS reading) is the usual form of Apollo's title, and we may assume that the iota is scanned long here as a metrical licence. Such variation in scansion of names is quite common: cf. 496n. The proposed emendations Πυθεῖος and Πυθῷιος are forms which have little or no support elsewhere.

374 μένος ὀξέος Ἠελίοιο: cf. Hes. *Op.* 414. This acts as a metrical variant with ἱερὸν μένος Ἠελίοιο (after an elision) in 371.

375–87 Apollo now realises that Telphousa has deceived him, and returning to her he tells her that he will have his fame at this place, and not she alone. He then hides her stream with a shower of rocks and makes an altar near her spring, where men pray to him as Telphousios.

This brief passage closes the whole section from 244 to 387, and the second *aition* follows closely on the previous one, forming 'a kind of conceptual refrain', so that 'in combination with the ring-form itself this refrain effect creates a strong sense of closure' (Miller (1986) 91).

376 ἐξαπάφησε: this aorist form recurs only in late epic.

379 'Telphousa, so after all you were not going to get away with deceiving my mind.' For this use of ἄρα with imperfect of a situation long true but now realised, cf. *Od.* 9.475 Κύκλωψ, οὐκ ἄρ' ἔμελλες . . . , and similarly 11.553, 13.293 (of Odysseus' deceits).

380 προρέειν καλλίροον ὕδωρ: προρέειν is transitive only here in early epic, but cf. A.R. 3.225, Orph. *A.* 1132.

381 οὐδὲ σὸν οἴης: this implies that Apollo will not take all the glory, but leave some for Telphousa, i.e. she will share in his cult. Equally, 382–5 suggest that her spring was still visible, flowing from under the rocks.

382–3 Cf. Call. *H.* 4.133–5 ἀλλά οἱ Ἄρης | Παγγαίου προθέλυμνα καρήατα μέλλεν ἀείρας | ἐμβαλέειν δίνῃσιν, ἀποκρύψαι δὲ ῥέεθρα.

383 πέτρῃσι προχυτῇσιν 'with a shower of stones'. προχυτός occurs only here, but cf. Προχυτή as the name of the volcanic island Procida in the Gulf of Naples.

384–7 Strabo mentions τὸ τοῦ Τιλφωσσίου Ἀπόλλωνος ἱερόν, near the tomb of Teiresias (9.2.27). See 244n., and Lycophron *Alex.* 562, where Apollo is called Τιλφούσιος.

387 ᾔσχυνε: the emphasis is on the 'disfigurement' or 'dishonouring' of Telphousa, i.e. her loss of κλέος as punishment.

388–439 Then Apollo began to consider what men he should choose as his ministers. He saw a ship in which were Cretan merchants from Cnossos, bound for Pylos, and he met them disguised as a great dolphin. This leapt onto the ship, shaking it and causing amazement and terror. The south wind carried the ship round the Peloponnese, and then a west wind blew them into the Gulf of Corinth, until they arrived at the harbour of Crisa, where the boat ran ashore.

This episode, and the following ones, in which Apollo first appears like a star, and then as a young man on the shore at Crisa (440–50), have thematic links with *Hymn* 7. There Dionysus appears on the seashore as a young man, and is seized by pirates. The miracles which follow on board their ship include the god's transformation into a series of wild beasts (44–8), and it is the pirates who are turned into dolphins (51–3). Both episodes involve unheroic types (merchants and pirates) and have a semi-comic character (see Garcia (2002), especially 16–22).

Plutarch refers to the story in the *Hymn to Apollo* (*Mor.* 984AB), ascribing it to 'the mythographers', although here the god is said to lead the ship, in the form of a dolphin. He rejects this version in favour of one where the god sends a dolphin to guide them to Cirrha, and mentions a parallel legend about how some people sent by Ptolemy Soter to Sinope were driven off course by a storm, which carried them round the Peloponnese to Cirrha, where they offered a sacrifice. Cf. also the myth of Apollo's son Icadius, rescued by a dolphin from a shipwreck and carried by it to near Parnassus, where he built a temple and altars at Delphi to Apollo (Servius on Verg. *A.* 3.332). The hymn's version, or variants of this, are mentioned by several later sources: see *RE* IV 2514.32–41 s.v. Delphinios.

389 ὀργείονας 'ministers'. This ought to be the early epic spelling of this word (Attic ὀργέων): cf. Janko (1982) 123. The word occurs first here, and is rare in later literature, although it also appears in cultic inscriptions, for members of a religious group or association. The lexicographers give examples from poetry where they say that it has the more general sense of 'priests'.

In the hymn we only hear of male ministers of Apollo at Delphi (391–6, 481–4, 535–9), and they are said both to offer sacrifices and to announce the god's decrees. From Theognis (807) onwards we hear of an inspired woman, the Pythia, who utters the responses: cf. Amandry (1950) 115–23, Parke and Wormell (1956) I 17–45, Maurizio (1995) 69–86. It seems that at Dodona the prophets of Zeus were originally male (*Il.* 16.233–5), and later female (Parke (1967b) 52–79). The hymn may reflect a tradition that the Pythia was not part of the original cult, or it may have been composed before her introduction. Cf. Chappell (2006), especially 343–8, Clay (2009), and see Introduction 2(b).

393 Κρῆτες ἀπὸ Κνωσοῦ Μινωΐου: Minos is mentioned as a past ruler at Cnossos in *Od.* 19.178–9. This derivation of Apollo's priests from Cnossos may reflect a historical reality. At *H. Ap.* 516–19 the paean sung by these men is said to be the type of song sung by Cretans, and the cult of Apollo Delphinios was important in Crete (see on 493–6 and 517–19). Pindar (*P.* 5.39–42) mentions an ancient wooden statue offered by Cretans at Delphi, most probably in Apollo's temple. Archaeological evidence indicates contacts between Crete and Delphi especially in the eighth and seventh centuries BC: see Guarducci (1943–6), Forrest (1956) 34–5, Defradas (1972) 26, 72–3, Rolley (1977) especially 145–6. See also Huxley (1975), Rutherford (2001) 24–5, 205–7, for other traditions connecting Delphi with Crete; for a more sceptical view see Morgan (1990) 142–6. The name Crisa may have been thought to be linked etymologically with Crete (Κρῖσα and Κρῆσσα πόλις): cf. Servius on Verg. *A.* 3.332, Fontenrose (1960) 322, Kolk (1963) 34 n. 33, *RE* XI.2 1890.3–12 s.v. Krisa.

394 ῥέζουσι . . . ἀγγέλλουσι: the present tenses (if correct) are an anticipation of what is to come later, the situation in the poet's own time. ῥέξουσι and ἀγγελέουσι are variants (the former in most MSS), but they would not follow so naturally after the simple statement of 392 as the future tense in 390 does after 388–9.

θέμιστας: see 123–6, 252–3nn.

395 Φοίβου Ἀπόλλωνος χρυσαόρου = *Il.* 5.509. See 123n.

396 χρείων ἐκ δάφνης: the bay (or sweet laurel) tree was later the symbol of Delphi *par excellence.* But it is not clear what this phrase means. Callimachus echoes it (*H.* 4.94): ἀλλ' ἔμπης ἐρέω τι τομώτερον ἢ ἀπὸ δάφνης, i.e. Apollo says that he will 'make an utterance which is clearer than (one spoken) from the bay tree'. The tree and the tripod are linked together by Lucretius (1.739): *Pythia quae tripode a Phoebi lauroque profatur.*

Some authors speak of the Pythia shaking the tree (Ar. *Plut.* 213, etc.), and the scholia on this passage in Aristophanes say that the tree stood near the tripod. Callimachus makes the tree herself claim that 'the Pythia is seated on bay, | bay she sings, and bay she has for her couch' (fr. 194.26–7). There too, however, it is unclear what δάφνην δ' ἀείδει means (cf. Kerkhecker (1999) 91–2). Some later authors speak of Apollo's seers as chewing bay leaves, others of burning them, in place of incense.

It has also been suggested (e.g. by Parke and Wormell (1956) 3) that the procedure described in the hymn was similar to that of Dodona, 'where the god spoke from the oak tree and the Selli expounded his oracles', and that the priests would claim to recognise the god's utterances in the rustling of the leaves (cf. *Il.* 16.233–5, *Od.* 14.327–30, and Parke (1967b) esp. 1–33). There is no other evidence of this, however, at Delphi. A related suggestion is that the leaves were used for a form of cleromancy, or interpretation by drawing lots: see Amandry (1950) 132–3. For a review of the evidence see Amandry (1950) 126–34, and cf. also Chappell (2006) 343–4.

γυάλων ὕπο Παρνησοῖο: cf. Hes. *Th.* 499 γυάλοις ὕπο Παρνησοῖο.

397 ἐπὶ πρῆξιν: cf. *Od.* 3.72, 9.253 ἤ τι κατὰ πρῆξιν . . .

398 Cf. 424, where the order of names in 421–6 suggests that Pylos is here located in Triphylia, near to the river Alpheios, rather than in Messenia at the site usually identified as 'Nestor's Pylos' (the palace at Ano Englianos). There was a controversy already in antiquity about this question: cf. Hope Simpson and Lazenby (1970) 82. The Pylos of *H. Herm.* 398 is also located 'by the ford of Alpheios'. At the same time, the fact that Cretans from Minoan Cnossos are sailing to Pylos suggests a tradition here which could have survived from the late Bronze Age.

For Πυλοιγενής cf. *Il.* 2.54, 23.303. Πυληγενής is a variant at *Il.* 2.54; cf. Euphorion fr. 63.

400 ἐν πόντωι: ἐκ πόντου has been suggested by Agar, but cf. 493–4 which echo these lines.

402–3 'And whoever of them noticed and observed, it shook him to and fro in all directions, and made the ship's timbers shiver.' The text is not certain, and has been variously emended. The underlying formula may be ἐπεφράσατ' ἦδ' ἐνόησεν (*Od.* 8.94, 533, and with negative *Il.* 5.665). ἐπιφράζεσθαι can be used with infinitive, but ἐπιφράσσαιτο νοήσας is a very simple change. For ὅστις instead of εἴ τις cf. Hes. *Th.* 783–4 καί ῥ' ὅστις ψεύδηται . . . | Ζεὺς δέ τε Ἶριν ἔπεμψε . . . , and *H. Herm.* 482–8 etc. The motif of observing the portent is repeated more clearly at 414–17, which to some extent supports the interpretation given here.

403 ἀνασσείασκε: for such frequentative forms cf. κρύπτασκε (*Il.* 8.272) etc. For ἀνασείειν cf. Hes. *Sc.* 344 etc.

404 Silence and fear are common reactions to divine signs, or epiphanies. See Richardson on *H. Dem.* 188–211, 188–90, 275ff., 478–9 (especially p. 306).

405–9 The sailors are too terrified to take any action to stop the ship (cf. 414), which sails on of its own accord, aided by a strong south wind.

406 λαῖφος: first here in the sense 'sail'; cf. Alc. 326.7 L–P etc.

407 κατεστήσαντο βοεῦσιν 'they had fixed it down with the halyards'. Cf. *Od.* 2.426 = 15.291, and Morrison and Williams (1968) 55–6.

408 ἔπλεον must be scanned either ⏑ ⏑ – or – – (with synizesis). For the former cf. 388 ἐφράζετο. Correption of a vowel before a consonant plus liquid is commoner in the *Hymns* than in Homer: see Monro, HG^2 p. 344.

ἔπειγε: this is Ruhnken's emendation (for ἔγειρε). ἐπείγειν is commonly used of a wind driving a ship, e.g. *Il.* 15.382, *Od.* 12.167, Soph. *Ph.* 1450–1, A.R. 4.1769. No satisfactory parallel for ἔγειρε exists, and the corruption is an easy one.

409–39 The ship's journey is the third geographical catalogue of the poem, and it takes the form of a *periplous*. It complements the journeys at 30–49 and 216–86, and between them they encompass most of the Greek world, i.e. the Aegean, the northern mainland, and the Peloponnese. It may also be significant that both the first and third catalogues have Crete as their starting point. Apollo's power is manifested in the final parts of the hymn most clearly, involving the response of nature (cf. already the reactions to his birth at 117–39). Moreover, whereas in 216–86 the second-person address of 207 is continued right up to the god's arrival at Crisa (282), in 388–544 the god is always in the third person.

There is considerable variety in the details of the *periplous*, both in the verbs used, and in the length of the passages. As with 216–86, some places are given special attention (e.g. 411–18, describing the cattle of Helios at Taenarum, where the sailors want to stop, or the vivid glance at Odysseus' homeland in 428), and the pace quickens towards the end (433–5), as at 281. The moment of arrival is also expressed in parallel form, but with elegant variation (282–5 ~ 438–9).

There are more points of contact in this catalogue with the geographical information in the *Iliad* and *Odyssey* than in the case of the other two. On the other hand, some of the language of 410–21 is un-Homeric. See also Map 1, and Baltes (1982) 25–43 (especially 35ff.).

410–21 There may be direct echoes here of the episode about the island of the Sun in *Odyssey* 12: cf. 411 τερψιμβρότου Ἠελίοιο, which recurs in early epic only at

Od. 12.269, 274, the motif of the Sun-god's flocks, and the use of παρὲκ . . . ἔχουσα in 419, paralleled at *Od.* 12.276.

410–12 As it stands we should translate the text: 'And along the Laconian land they came to the sea-crowned settlement and country of Helios who cheers men's heart, to Taenarum . . .' It seems impossible to take ἁλιστέφανον πτολίεθρον in apposition to Λακωνίδα γαῖαν, with πὰρ . . . ἶξον as a *tmesis* (as AHS do), since a country cannot be called a πτολίεθρον. So it must go with what follows. There was an ancient settlement at Cape Taenarum: cf. Frazer on Paus. 3.25.4, III p. 398, and *RE* IVA 2037 s.v. Tainaron. ἁλιστέφανος could certainly be applied to this area, and the epithet recurs a couple of times in late poetry; cf. ἁλιστεφής, commoner in late verse. The order of words is unusual, however, and the ingenious conjecture of Matthiae Ἕλος τ' ἔφαλον πτολίεθρον may be correct. Cf. *Il.* 2.584, where this half-line occurs in the catalogue of Menelaus' kingdom. Helos is probably the modern Agios Stephanos, near the sea south of Sparta, a Bronze Age site. Cf. Hope Simpson and Lazenby (1970) 78.

412–13 Taenarum (or Taenarus) is first mentioned here. The sacred flocks of the Sun-god at Taenarum appear nowhere else, but resemble the sacred flocks and herds of Helios on Thrinacia in the *Odyssey* (11.104–15, 12.127–41, etc.). There were also flocks sacred to Apollo at Apollonia in Epirus (Hdt. 9.93), and in the *Hymn to Hermes* his cattle are in Pieria. As in the passage about Poseidon at Onchestus (230–8), the poet here pays tribute to another god in passing.

412 βαθύτριχα: only here in early epic; cf. Oppian, and βαθυχαίτης in Hesiod, etc.

413 ἐπιτερπέα: also only here in early poetry; cf. Plato etc.

414–21 The unsuccessful attempt to find a stopping-place is a similar motif to Apollo's abortive plan to set up his temple at Telphousa's spring (244–76).

416 δαπέδοισι: this word (always singular in Homer) is not elsewhere found referring to a ship's deck.

417 πολυΐχθυον: a *hapax legomenon*, but cf. πολύϊχθυς (Strabo).

ἀμφὶς ὀρούσει 'would leap away (from the ship)'. Cf. *Il.* 23.393 ἀμφὶς ὁδοῦ δραμέτην 'they ran off the track', and *Od.* 19.221, 24.218 ἀμφὶς ἐόντα, 'being apart (away)'.

418 οὐ πηδαλίοισιν ἐπείθετο: cf. Theognis 458 πηδαλίωι πείθεται. In Homer (*Odyssey*) only one πηδάλιον is mentioned, whereas two steering oars are normal for later ships, and two are already shown on some late Bronze Age and Geometric depictions. See D. Gray, *Arch. Hom.* (Seewesen) G102 and illustrations, Casson (1971) 46 and n. 26, 224–8, Morrison and Williams (1968) 53 and Index s.v. steering oar. However, it may be significant that οἰήϊον ('tiller') is used once in Homer in the plural, of a single ship (*Od.* 12.218).

419 παρὲκ . . . ἔχουσα 'keeping on past'. Cf. *Od.* 3.182 Πύλονδ' ἔχον, 12.276 παρὲξ τὴν νῆσον ἐλαύνετε νῆα μέλαιναν.

Πελοπόννησον πίειραν: see 250n.

420 ἤϊ' ὁδόν: see 232n.

421–9 The geography of this passage has points of contact with the description of Nestor's kingdom (*Il.* 2.591–4), and Telemachus' journey from Pylos to Ithaca (*Od.* 15.295–8; cf. also *H. Ap.* 434–5n.), together with references to the Ionian islands (*Od.* 1.246 etc.). There was debate in antiquity about the location of some of the places named. Argyphea is not mentioned elsewhere. The sequence of places is not in exact order going from south to north, but we move up the west coast past Triphylia and Elis.

422 Ἀρήνην: cf. *Il.* 2.591, 11.723. It was usually identified in antiquity with later Samicon in Triphylia (Strabo 8.3.19, Paus. 5.6.2–3). The epithet ἐρατεινήν is given to Arene at *Il.* 2.591, here to the unknown Argyphea.

423 = *Il.* 2.592. Thruon is called Thruoessa at *Il.* 11.711, and described there as 'a steep hill, far away by the Alpheios, on the borders of sandy Pylos'; it was identified by Strabo (8.3.24) with the later Epitalion. Strabo (8.3.24) is unsure whether Aipu was a noun or an adjective, and its location is quite uncertain. On the places in 422–3 see Hope Simpson and Lazenby (1970) 83–4.

424 See 398n. for the location of Pylos in Triphylia.

425–7 These verses are close to *Od.* 15.295 + 297–8 βὰν δὲ παρὰ Κρουνοὺς καὶ Χαλκίδα καλλιρέεθρον, and ἡ δὲ Φεὰς ἐπέβαλλεν ἐπειγομένη Διὸς οὔρωι, | ἠδὲ παρ' Ἤλιδα δῖαν, ὅθι κρατέουσιν Ἐπειοί. 295 is not in our MSS, but is quoted by Strabo as part of this passage (8.3.26; again at 10.1.9 with πετρήεσσαν at the end of the line). Since the preceding lines (293–4) are virtually identical to *H. Ap.* 434–5, it seems probable that our poet had the *Odyssey* in mind here.

425 Strabo (8.3.13, 27) puts the river Chalcis and spring Crounoi together with a settlement called Chalcis all just north of Samicon. Dume, first mentioned here, was further north, in Achaea. But Hecataeus (*FGrH* 1 F 121) and Antimachus of Colophon (fr. 27 Wyss) both seem to have thought that there was another Dume in Triphylia: see Matthews (1996) 131–4, and Càssola on *H. Ap.* 425.

426–7 These lines occur in reverse order in *Od.* 15.297–8, where Aristarchus and Strabo read Φεαῖς or Φεάς, for Φεράς in our MSS. Here too Φεάς, or Φεαῖς, is probably correct. AHS think Pherae is the same as later Pharae in Achaea, but this was inland, its position does not fit 428–9, and *Phar-* has a long alpha. Pheai is actually at the south end of Elis, but the point is that the Ionian islands (428–9) begin to appear at this point in Elean territory. 426 also closely resembles *Od.* 24.431: see 466–7, 499nn. for other links with this *Odyssey* scene, Janko (1982) 130–1, and Introduction 2(c).

426 Ἐπειοί: as in Homer (*Il.* 2.619 etc.) the Epeans are the inhabitants of Elis.

427–8 εὖτε . . . καὶ . . . : for this use of asyndetic εὖτε followed by the apodosis with καί cf. *Od.* 13.78–9 (and see *H. Ap.* 115n.).

427 Φεάς: ἐπιβάλλειν in the sense of 'approach' or 'set course towards' takes the dative later, and Φεαῖς may be the right reading here, as at *Od.* 15.295.

ἀγαλλομένη: this more lively word than ἐπειγομένη at *Od.* 15.297 suits the tone of this passage, where the ship seems to speed on of her own accord.

428–9 The sudden appearance of the islands (visible in the distance from high points on this coast) is effective, with Mt Neriton on Ithaca glimpsed amid the clouds.

429 = *Od.* 1.246 etc. Doulichion's identity is disputed: candidates since antiquity have been Leucas, Dolicha (one of the Echinades, but too small), part of Cephallenia, Same being the other part of this island, or even present-day Ithaca. That Same is all or part of Cephallenia seems fairly certain. See S. West on *Od.* 1.246–7. Bittlestone, Diggle, and Underhill (2005) discuss the identity of these islands afresh, but their views are controversial.

430–9 We come to the final stage of the journey, marked by the appearance of the Gulf of Corinth, after the whole Peloponnese has been passed. Here a strong west wind at once begins to carry the Cretans swiftly through the Gulf to their journey's end. There is a sense of urgency in this passage which is dramatically effective.

430 παρενίσατο: in Homer the aorist of νίσομαι is not used, and it is rarely found later, but it is more appropriate here than the variant reading of the imperfect. παρεμείψατο would have been possible (cf. 409 etc.).

431 ἐπεί is preferable to the variant ἐπί, and καὶ δὴ ἐπεί parallels ἀλλ' ὅτε δή in 430. The Gulf is called 'of Crisa', and was still so called by both Thucydides and Strabo: see Robertson (1978) 43. It is 'vast', like Ἑλλήσποντος ἀπείρων (*Il.* 24.545), and πόντος ἀπείρων (Hes. *Th.* 678). καταφαίνειν/-εσθαι is used first here; cf. Pindar, Herodotus, etc.

432 'Which separates off the rich Peloponnese.' διὲκ . . . ἐέργει is a *tmesis*.

433–4 The great west wind is dignified by an extensive descriptive phrase. αἴθριος is first used here, and later is applied to a wind which clears the sky (especially the north wind). In Homer cf. αἰθρηγενής (*Il.* 15.171), αἰθρηγενέτης (*Od.* 5.296), both of Boreas.

433 ἐκ Διὸς αἴσης: only used here, but cf. Διὸς αἶσαν/-ῃ in *Il.* 9.604, 17.321. Zeus's will and Apollo's coincide (cf. 420–1, 437), and Zeus is also god of the weather, as at 427.

434–5 This resembles *Od.* 15.292–4, where Athene sends a fair wind for Telemachus: λάβρον ἐπαιγίζοντα δι' αἰθέρος, ὄφρα τάχιστα | νηῦς ἀνύσειε θέουσα θαλάσσης ἁλμυρὸν ὕδωρ (see 425–7n.). λάβρος ἐπαιγίζων is also used of Ζέφυρος at *Il.* 2.147–8.

438–9 ἐς Κρίσην . . . ἐς λιμέν': i.e. to the harbour of Crisa, which gave access to the settlement inland.

438 εὐδείελον: this epithet of places occurs several times in the *Odyssey*, and was probably taken as meaning 'easily visible': see Chantraine, *Dict.* s.v. δῆλος, and S. West on *Od.* 2.167.

439 ἐχρίμψατο: in Homer this verb occurs only at *Od.* 10.516 χριμφθείς, but forms of ἐγχρίμπτεσθαι occur more often.

ποντοπόρος νηῦς: the ship runs aground 'with a rhythmically audible bump' (Miller (1986) 93).

440–73 Apollo left the ship, like a star at midday, and entered his inner sanctum, kindling a fire there, and lighting up all of Crisa with its radiance, and the women of Crisa gave a ritual cry in response to his presence. Then he flew back to the ship and appeared as a young man. He asked the sailors who they were, and why they were so frightened, and had not disembarked. Their leader replied, and asked what land they had reached.

440–7 The arrival at Crisa is followed at once by the first manifestation of the god's presence. His appearance like a star in full daylight, and the divine radiance which fills Crisa, are similar to the sudden radiance of Demeter as she enters the palace at Eleusis (*H. Dem.* 188–9), or the radiant splendour of Aphrodite's appearance when she enters Anchises' farmstead (*H. Aph.* 81–90). The ritual cry of the Crisaean women is paralleled by the response of the goddesses to Apollo's birth (119). Cf. also the series of ritual actions instituted by the response of Metaneira and Iambe at *H. Dem.* 191–211, and Anchises' promise to set up a cult and his prayer at *H. Aph.* 92–106. Apollo's presence evokes fear, as at *H. Dem.* 190, and the Cretan leader also senses Apollo's divinity (464–6; cf. 473).

In all these cases, this ritual revelation is the prelude to the full self-revelation of the god to follow: cf. *H. Ap.* 475–501, *H. Dem.* 256–74, *H. Aph.* 172–290. In the parallel story of Dionysus and the pirates also, the helmsman already realises that he is a god when it is impossible to bind him (*H.* 7.13–24), in anticipation of his self-identification at the end (55–7). But in Apollo's case, there may be a particular point in his divine radiance, since he is a god of purity and light (see 120–2 and 202–3nn.), just as his appearance as an ephebe at 449–50 reminds us of his role as patron of young men (κοῦροι).

440–2 This is close to the description of Athene's descent from Olympus at *Il.* 4.75–9: οἷον δ' ἀστέρα ἧκε Κρόνου πάϊς ἀγκυλομήτεω, | ἢ ναύτῃσι τέρας ἠὲ στρατῶι εὐρέϊ λαῶν, | λαμπρόν· τοῦ δέ τε πολλοὶ ἀπὸ σπινθῆρες ἵενται· | τῶι ἐϊκυῖ' ἤϊξεν ἐπὶ χθόνα Παλλὰς Ἀθήνη, | κὰδ δ' ἔθορ' ἐς μέσσον· θάμβος δ' ἔχεν εἰσορόωντας... There too this is followed by her appearance in disguise as a man (86–7). The description in both cases suggests a shooting star or meteor, or perhaps a comet (see Kirk on *Il.* 4.75–8). Here however the appearance of this in full daylight makes it even more portentous.

443 ἐς δ' ἄδυτον κατέδυσε διὰ τριπόδων ἐριτίμων: there seems to be word-play in ἄδυτον κατέδυσε – Apollo enters where no ordinary mortal may. Some have thought that a cult is envisaged as already existing at Crisa (see Picard (1938) 97–9). But it seems more likely that the poet is thinking of the new temple at Pytho.

Tripods were very closely associated with Apollo's cult, both at Delphi and elsewhere. Apollo himself, or the Pythia, was supposed to prophesy seated on a sacred tripod (cf. Amandry (1950) 140–8, Parke and Wormell (1956) I 24–6). Tripods dedicated at Delphi are among the objects listed by Hermes as possible plunder at *H. Herm.* 178–81, and they were an important form of offering later:

cf. especially the golden ones set up outside the temple by Gelon and Hieron (Bacchylides 3.17–21).

Aristophanes echoes this line at *Knights* 1015–16, in a comic oracle: φράζευ, Ἐρεχθεΐδη, λογίων ὁδόν, ἥν σοι Ἀπόλλων | ἴαχεν ἐξ ἀδύτοιο διὰ τριπόδων ἐριτίμων. Cf. the echo at *Birds* 575 of *H. Ap.* 114. Here the oracular voice resounds from the inner sanctum, 'through the tripods'. Cf. Aristonous' *Paean* 9–13 (Powell, *CA* p. 163) ἔνθ' ἀπὸ τριπόδων θεο|κτήτων, χλωρότομον δάφναν | σείων, μαντοσύναν ἐποι|χνεῖς, ἰὴ ἰὲ Παιάν, | φρικώεντος ἐξ ἀδύτου . . . ('where, from divinely owned tripods, shaking freshly-cut laurel, you practise your oracular art, Lord Paean, from your dread inner sanctum'). Cf. also Corinna, *PMG* 654 col. iii.32–4 (of a Boeotian oracular cult) πράτοι [μὲν] γὰ[ρ Λατ]οΐδας | δῶκ' Εὐωνούμοι τριπόδων | ἐσς ἰῶν [χρε]ισμὼς ἐνέπειν ('for the son of Leto granted first Euonymus to utter prophecies from his tripods'). Pindar describes the wealth of tripods dedicated in the temple of Apollo Ismenios in Thebes (*P.* 11.5–6): χρυσέων ἐς ἄδυτον τριπόδων | θησαυρόν, ὃν περίαλλ' ἐτίμασε Λοξίας. This suggests (whether ἄδυτον is an epithet or a noun) that they were kept within the ἄδυτον of this shrine. At the Boeotian sanctuary of Apollo Ptoios (and the hero Ptoios) there was an alley flanked by lines of tripods. See Guillon (1943) II especially 57–62, and Schachter (1981–94) I 52–73.

444 Apollo kindles a flame within the ἄδυτον, 'making manifest his signs of divine power'; πιφαυσκόμενος τὰ ἃ κῆλα is used of snowflakes sent by Zeus at *Il.* 12.280. κῆλα is often translated 'arrows' or 'missiles', but West (on Hes. *Th.* 708) argues that it is only used of manifestations of divine power, as in the case of Apollo's plague-bearing arrows at *Il.* 1.53 and 383, or Zeus's thunder and lightning at *Th.* 707–8. Pindar (*P.* 1.12) uses it metaphorically of the sounds of the lyre which charm even the gods. The scholia there suggest that he has in mind a connection with κηλήματα (etc.) meaning 'charms'. Popular etymology quite possibly also connected it with καίειν meaning 'burn' (cf. πυρὶ κηλέωι). The fire at the sacred hearth of Delphi was later seen as especially holy. It was used, for example, to purify the altars of Greece after the Persian Wars: cf. Plut. *Aristides* 20.4–5, Malkin (2002) 77.

445–6 Cf. *Od.* 3.450–1 αἱ δ' ὀλόλυξαν | θυγατέρες τε νυοί τε καὶ αἰδοίη παράκοιτις (at a sacrifice). See also *H. Ap.* 119n.

447 Φοίβου ὑπὸ ῥιπῆς: ῥιπή can be used of a violent movement or 'onrush' of some kind, e.g. of a weapon or warrior, or of strong wind or fire, and then sometimes later metaphorically of 'winds of passion' (S. *Ant.* 137, 930) or the power of Aphrodite (*Orph. H.* 4.141). So here it could refer to the fire kindled by Phoebus, or to the inspiration which this creates, or both at once.

448–512 The following scene has structural parallels with other 'scenes of meeting', involving a disguised deity, and more generally with those episodes where a character arrives at a new place by sea and encounters someone there (divine or human). See Richardson on *H. Dem.* 98ff. (and Appendix III there).

448 νόημ' ὥς: see 186–8n.

ἆλτο πέτεσθαι: cf. *H. Dem.* 389 ἆλτο θέειν, and the similar Homeric formula βῆ δὲ θέειν.

449–50 Cf. *Il.* 16.715–16, where Apollo comes to Hector, ἀνέρι εἰσάμενος αἰζηῶι τε κρατερῶι τε, and *H.* 7.3–6, where Dionysus appears νεηνίηι ἀνδρὶ ἐοικὼς | πρωθήβηι· καλαὶ δὲ περισσείοντο ἔθειραι | κυάνεαι. Hermes and Athene also take the disguise of a young man at *Od.* 10.277–9 and 13.221–4. But long hair is especially characteristic of Dionysus, and of Apollo ἀκερσεκόμης (*H. Ap.* 134), who is also a patron of ephebic youths (κοῦροι). Cf. Burkert (1985) 144–5, and see *H. Ap.* 134, 493–6nn.

451–73 Apollo's dialogue with the sailors marks 'a distinct slowing down of narrative tempo', by contrast with the 'high-pitched excitement of the preceding fifty lines' (Miller (1986) 94).

452–61 The opening questions are those asked by Nestor of Telemachus and his companions on their arrival at Pylos, and by Polyphemus of Odysseus and his men (452–5 = *Od.* 3.91–4, 9.252–5; see below 469–73n.). What comes next, however, is an ironic comment on the abnormality of the situation: these sailors are not following the usual epic conventions of 'arrival scenes'. In fact, it is only after Apollo's revelation of his identity and instructions to them that the 'normal' narrative thread will be resumed (503–12).

453–5 On piracy in the Homeric poems see Souza (1999) 17–22.

456 ἧσθον: it is odd that we suddenly find three cases of the dual used instead of plural here, at 487 (κάθετον λύσαντε), and at 501 (ἵκησθον). The dual was probably no longer used in the spoken Ionic of the time of the *Iliad*, and there are a number of cases where it is used instead of plural in the text of that poem as we have it: cf. 4.407, 5.487, 8.74, 9.182–98 (seven times); cf. also *H. Herm.* 504. The cases in the *Hymn to Apollo* may be due to modification of formulaic prototypes, such as (for 456) τίφθ' οὕτως ἕστητε τεθηπότες (*Il.* 4.243), τίφθ' οὕτω τετίησθον, Ἀθηναίη τε καὶ Ἥρη (*Il.* 8.447), etc.; cf. Hoekstra (1969) 28–9.

458–9 Cf. *Od.* 11.218 ἀλλ' αὕτη δίκη ἐστὶ βροτῶν, ὅτε . . . , 19.43 αὕτη τοι δίκη ἐστὶ θεῶν, etc. (This use of δίκη to mean 'mark' or 'manner' does not occur in the *Iliad*.)

458 ἀνδρῶν ἀλφηστάων: cf. *Od.* 6.8 (again not an Iliadic use). ἀλφηστής probably means 'grain-eating': see S. West on *Od.* 1.349.

460 καμάτωι ἀδηκότες 'overcome by weariness'. The derivation of ἀδηκότες is uncertain: see Hainsworth on *Il.* 10.98.

461 = *Il.* 11.89 (σίτου τε . . .).

462 After the fear and astonishment evoked by a divine epiphany, the god often reassures those affected, as Apollo does here. See *H. Aph.* 192–5n.

463 Κρητῶν ἀγός: he is nameless in our hymn. Later sources call him Castalius (*Et. M.* 255.17–18, Orion 46.22, Tzetzes *in Lycophr.* 208), or Icadius (Servius on *Aen.* 3.332).

464–73 The Cretan leader's reply is built from a series of traditional or Odyssean elements, but in his businesslike and mundane way he expresses their bewilderment at an extraordinary situation.
464–6 This courteous form of greeting to a stranger, admiring his noble or godlike appearance, and expressing a wish or prayer for his well-being, belongs to a conventional pattern: cf. for example *Od.* 6.149–85 (a highly elaborate development), and for variant forms see Richardson on *H. Dem.* 135ff., 213ff. Sometimes it is coupled, as here, with a request for information about the place where one has arrived: cf. *Od.* 13.228–35 (and similarly *H. Dem.* 133–4). Where the addressee is really a god, there is also irony in the recognition of his godlike qualities.
464 ἐπεὶ οὐ μὲν γάρ τι: 'since in fact (γάρ) in no way...' The combination ἐπεὶ... γάρ is unusual, and perhaps arises from coalescence of epic οὐ μὲν γάρ and ἐπεὶ οὐ μέν τι.
466–7 = *Od.* 24.402–3. The archaic form οὖλε (literally 'be healthy': cf. Latin *salue*) seems to occur only in these two cases in literature. Influence from this part of *Odyssey* 24 is possible: see 426–7, 499nn., Introduction 2(c).
468 = *Od.* 13.233.
469–73 Cf. *Od.* 9.259–63 (in reply to Polyphemus' questions, which are repeated at *H. Ap.* 452–5): Ἡμεῖς... ἀποπλαγχθέντες Ἀχαιοὶ |... ὑπὲρ μέγα λαῖτμα θαλάσσης, | οἴκαδε ἱέμενοι, ἄλλην ὁδόν, ἄλλα κέλευθα | ἤλθομεν· οὕτω που Ζεὺς ἤθελε μητίσασθαι. | λαοὶ δ' Ἀτρεΐδεω Ἀγαμέμνονος εὐχόμεθ' εἶναι. The coincidences with Apollo's speech and the Cretan's reply are close enough to suggest direct influence from the *Odyssey*. νόστου ἱέμενοι (472) may be due to reminiscence of the Odyssean passage (οἴκαδε ἱέμενοι). Verdenius (1969) 195 takes νόστος as simply meaning 'journey's goal' here, as sometimes later. But 476–8 suggest rather that he is expressing his men's desire to return home, which will be unfulfilled.
471 Cf. *Od.* 1.182 νῦν δ' ὧδε ξὺν νηῒ κατήλυθον.
474–523 Apollo declares his true identity, and tells the sailors that they are to take care of his temple. He instructs them to disembark, build an altar on the shore, make an offering, and pray to him there as Delphinios. They should next have a meal and offer libations to the gods, and then accompany him, singing a paean in his honour, until they reach his temple. They obey his orders, and after the ritual is complete, he leads them with his lyre in dancing and singing up the hill to his temple at Pytho.

Once again, epiphany here is followed by ritual: first the institution of a cult at the place of the god's revelation, and then a processional hymn, with Apollo himself as leader, from the altar by the shore to the god's chief sanctuary. Apollo's instructions here, and (still more) his final speech at 531–44, can be viewed as his first oracular pronouncements in his new role as the god of Delphi: see Leclerc (2002) 159–60.
475–85 The long, elaborate opening address prepares the way for the climax of 480. The powerfully enjambed τὸ πρίν of 476 modifies 475, and this suggests a

sense of the loss of all they hold most dear, to be replaced by their future role as servants of the god. They have no choice in the matter (as with their journey), but Apollo implies the degree of honour which this will bestow: cf. 478–9, echoed by 482–3, and 484–5.

479 Cf. 483 and 522.

480 The form of self-revelation is conventional: see Richardson on *H. Dem.* 268. But the fact that Apollo introduces himself first as 'son of Zeus' may be significant, as implying Zeus's backing for the whole enterprise.

485 The redundancy of 'always, continually, for all days' is not untypical of expressions of permanence: cf. (e.g.) *H. Herm.* 125–6.

τιμήσεσθε: the future middle of τιμᾶν (always with passive sense) does not occur elsewhere in early epic, but is common later.

486 A variant of the formular ἀλλ' ἄγεθ', ὡς ἂν ἐγὼ εἴπω, πειθώμεθα πάντες (*Il.* 2.139 etc.).

487–9 The actions prescribed are typical of scenes of arrival by sea (see 503–7n.), although the language is not formulaic. 487 describes 'the operation of lowering sailyard and sail (after furling) by letting go the leathers by which both had been hoisted to the top of the mast': Morrison and Williams (1968) 62–3. The ship is then drawn up on the beach, and possessions and equipment are disembarked. For arrival scenes see also Arend (1933) 79–81.

487 For the duals see 456n.

488 Cf. *Il.* 1.485 = *Od.* 16.325 (and cf. 16.359) νῆα μὲν οἵ γε μέλαιναν ἐπ' ἠπείροιο ἔρυσσαν. The hiatus in ἐπὶ ἠπείρου is paralleled by *Il.* 22.206, 23.274, and should not be emended. It is probably due here to adaptation of the Homeric formular verses just quoted.

489 Cf. *Od.* 13.120 (arrival in Ithaca) ἐκ δὲ κτήματ' ἄειραν.

ἔντεα: in early epic this is normally used of weapons, once of utensils for a meal (*Od.* 7.232), and only here of ship's tackle (instead of ὅπλα); cf. Pi. *N.* 4.70.

490–6 Sacrifice and prayer to Apollo on the seashore take place in the scene of Chryseis' return to her father at *Il.* 1.438–74, following the ship's arrival at 432–9, which resembles *H. Ap.* 503–7. When Telemachus arrives at Pylos he also finds the Pylians sacrificing by the sea to Poseidon (*Od.* 3.4–66). In the *Iliad* scene an altar already exists (440), whereas here it must be built, as a new cult is being set up. Cf. A.R. 2.669–719, where the Argonauts have a vision of Apollo on a deserted island, set up an altar on the shore, and sacrifice to him, and Orpheus sings a paean about his defeat of the serpent of Delphi (with some probable echoes of our hymn). Malkin (2002) 76 sees the scene in the hymn as similar to the practice of Greek colonists, setting up an altar to Apollo as ἀργηχέτης on first landing in a new country.

490 **καὶ βωμὸν ποιήσατ':** cf. 384.

491 **ἐπί τ' ἄλφιτα λευκὰ θύοντες:** sprinkling barley-grains over the victim was a standard feature of Homeric sacrifice (οὐλυχύτας): cf. Kirk on *Il.* 1.447–68. Here there is no animal to be offered, and they simply offer barley. Cf. the offerings to the dead (*Od.* 10.520, 11.28), which include sprinkling ἄλφιτα λευκά, and Eumaeus' meal at *Od.* 14.77, where barley-grains are sprinkled over the roasted pigs.

493–6 This is the third *aition* of a cult-title of the god: cf. 372–4 (Πύθιος), 385–7 (Τελφούσιος). Apollo's cult as Delphinios was common throughout the Aegean area, but especially in Crete. It is not attested at Delphi itself, where Δελφαῖος or Βελφαῖος are found, but the site of the cult in the hymn is by the sea, i.e. at the harbour-site of Crisa. Pausanias (10.37.8) attests a later temple to Apollo, Artemis, and Leto here.

In Crete, Athens, and elsewhere Apollo Delphinios was closely associated with central civic institutions, and in particular with the ephebes, for whom he acted as patron or Κουροτρόφος. His appearance as a young man with flowing hair at 448–50 suits this association. He also has a moral role, as in the use of the Delphinion at Athens as a court for justifiable homicide. In the hymn the title is 'explained' by his appearance as a dolphin, and it used to be thought that this indicated a maritime aspect to this cult (e.g. Farnell, *Cults* IV 145–8). Some of Apollo's other titles imply this (e.g. Ἀκταῖος, Ἐκβάσιος, Ἐμβάσιος, etc.), but the evidence does not seem to show this for Delphinios. Later tradition associated the name Delphi with the dolphin, and this appears as a symbol on Delphic coins from the late sixth century BC onwards (cf. Förstel (1979) 220). On Apollo Delphinios see especially Graf (1979) 2–22.

496 'And the altar will be (called) Delphinian, and will be conspicuous for all time to come.' With M's reading we must scan δε̄λφῐνῑο̄ς, or perhaps rather as three syllables, with synizesis of the final one, in contrast to Δε̄λφῑνῐ́ῳ in 495. For such variation see 373n., and cf. Hopkinson (1982) 162–77. For similar examples of variation cf. *H. Ap.* 9–10 χρυσέου . . . χρυσείωι, *H. Aph.* 97–8 νυμφάων . . . νυμφῶν, *H. Herm.* 92 τε ἰδὼν μὴ ἰδών. This is surely the right reading here, rather than δέλφ(ε)ιος. Ἐπόψιος is also a title given to Apollo and Zeus (Hesychius s.v.), in the sense of 'Overseer'. The word occurs first here (apart from a variant at *Il.* 3.42).

499–501 The sequence of a meal followed by music (song and dance) forms the traditional template for this pattern here.

499 Cf. *Od.* 24.489 οἱ δ' ἐπεὶ οὖν σίτοιο μελίφρονος ἐξ ἔρον ἕντο. σίτοιο μελίφρονος is an unusual metrical variant of the common πόσιος καὶ ἐδητύος (cf. *H. Ap.* 513). See also 466–7n.

500 ἰηπαιήον' ἀείδειν: 'sing the paean-song [*or* refrain]'. On this see 272, 357–62nn.

502–23 The execution of the god's orders about beaching the ship etc. is described in a passage of a relatively formulaic type, echoing 487–501 with variations. 500–1, however, are developed into an elaborate description of the procession to Pytho at 514–23.

503–7 503 echoes 487, and is probably a formular prototype for that verse, with its awkward duals. 504–7 are formulaic: 504 = *Il.* 1.434, 505 = *Il.* 1.437, *Od.* 15.499 (cf. *Od.* 9.150 etc.); 506–7 resemble the landing at *Il.* 1.485–6 (507 = *Il.* 1.486).

The variant version of *Il.* 1.484–6 in a papyrus (pap. 53 Allen = West) has extra lines which resemble 505–6.

504 'They lowered the mast on to the crutch, letting it down with the forestays.' The ἱστοδόκη is a crutch on the stern, into which the mast was lowered. See Kirk on *Il.* 1.434, and Morrison and Williams (1968) 62–3.

505 ἐκ δὲ καὶ αὐτοὶ βαῖνον: καὶ αὐτοί is less appropriate here than at either *Il.* 1.437 or *Od.* 15.499, suggesting the formular character of this line. βαῖνον is the reading at *Il.* 1.437 (where it is necessary, to distinguish this from the transitive βῆσαν in 438), and at *Od.* 15.499. M's reading βῆσαν is also possible here: cf. *Od.* 9.150 βῆμεν etc.

506–7 The ship is drawn up on the beach, and wooden props (ἕρματα) fixed to hold it upright. See Kirk on *Il.* 1.485–6.

508–13 Cf. 490–2, 497–9.

514–19 The procession, with song and dance accompanied by Apollo's lyre, echoes or parallels the first reference to Apollo going up to Pytho at 182–5, and the following scene of celebration on Olympus (516 ~ 202 καλὰ καὶ ὕψι βίβας). But here the song is identified as a paean, sung by the first pilgrims ever to make the journey from the harbour of Crisa up to Delphi. Many later paeans were processional, and some could be classed by ancient writers as either paean or prosodion ('processional song'). Some songs were also classified as consisting of paean followed by prosodion: cf. Rutherford (2001) 33–6, 104–8, 306–7, 323–4, 329–31, etc. Here the scene must surely be aetiological, giving mythical authority to later Delphic practice. The Pythian *nomos* also ended with celebratory dancing by the god (καταχόρευσις), possibly including cretic rhythms. The earliest form of Pythian contest was in singing a hymn or paean to Apollo after his victory (Paus. 10.7.2, Str. 9.3.10). See 357–62n.

514 Cf. *Il.* 14.384 βάν ῥ' ἴμεν· ἦρχε δ' ἄρα σφι Ποσειδάων ἐνοσίχθων (and 14.134).

515 ἐρατὸν κιθαρίζων: cf. *H. Herm.* 423, 455. Athenaeus cites 514–16 (Ἀπόλλων . . . βίβας) with χαρίεν for ἐρατόν.

516 καλὰ καὶ ὕψι βίβας: see 202n.

οἱ δὲ ῥήσσοντες ἕποντο: cf. *Il.* 18.571–2 τοὶ δὲ ῥήσσοντες ἁμαρτῇ | . . . ποσὶ σκαίροντες ἕποντο. ῥήσσοντες means 'stamping, beating the ground'. Cf. A.R. 1.539 πέδον ῥήσσωσι πόδεσσι, in the context of dances by young men to Apollo at Pytho and other sanctuaries.

517–19 The close association of Crete and Delphi is emphasised by the wording (Κρῆτες πρὸς Πυθώ), and also the Cretan origin or character of the paean-song. For this association see 393n. The Cretan origin of the paean was suggested by some ancient traditions making Thaletas of Gortyn the inventor of paeans (Strabo 10.4.16, citing Ephorus), and the story of his having cured a plague or *stasis* at Sparta with his songs (Pratinas, *PMG* 713 (iii), Paus. 1.14.4, etc.). The paeon (long plus three shorts) can be defined as a resolved cretic (-⏑⏑-), again suggesting a Cretan link. Paiawon occurs as a divine name on the Linear B tablets of Cnossos. See Rutherford (2001) 24–5, 76–7.

518–19 'Like the paeans of the Cretans, in whose breasts the divine Muse has set honeysweet song.' This is the usual interpretation, taking παιήονες as 'paeans'. It has, however, been argued that both οἷοί τε and οἷσί τε must refer to persons, and therefore the word must mean 'paean-singers': Huxley (1975) 119–24; cf. Rutherford (2001) 24. But there do not seem to be any other examples of this sense, and it is possible to interpret οἷοί τε . . . παιήονες as referring to the songs (sung by) Cretans, and οἷσί τε as referring to Κρητῶν. This is also better than assuming that the τε in οἷσί τε means 'and', introducing a second class of inspired singers (as Evelyn White's Loeb translation and Huxley (1975) 124 n. 23 do). For the description of poetic inspiration cf. *Od.* 22.347–8 θεὸς δέ μοι ἐν φρεσὶν οἴμας | παντοίας ἐνέφυσεν, and for μελίγηρυν ἀοιδήν cf. *Od.* 12.187 μελίγηρυν . . . ὄπα, of the Sirens, Hes. *Th.* 83–4, 96–7, of speech or song inspired by the Muses.

520–2 The ease and speed with which the dancers climb the hill is a sign of their divine possession, as (for example) with the Dionysiac inspiration of Cadmus and Teiresias in Euripides' *Bacchae* 187–94 etc.

520 ἄκμητοι: this form, for Homeric ἀκμής, only recurs at Nicander *Ther.* 737.

523 ἄδυτον ζάθεον: the ἄδυτον is emphasised again as at 443.

524–44 The Cretan leader asks Apollo how they are to live in such a rugged place. Apollo, pitying his men's human ignorance, reassures them, replying that if they continue to make their sacrifices, pilgrims will always come and give them offerings in plenty. He ends by warning them against any rash word or deed, or insolent action, whose result will be that other men will become their masters for all time to come.

The Cretans' anxiety and Apollo's reassurance echo Delos' concern about her poverty and Leto's promise of rich offerings and honours (57–88). Thus one of the opening themes of the poem's narrative is resumed at the end.

On Apollo's warning see 540–3n.

524 = *Od.* 20.9 (τοῦ); cf. *Il.* 9.595, *Od.* 24.318.

526–7 Cf. 476–8.

528 'How are we actually now to live? This is what we tell you to consider.' This seems to be echoed at A.R. 1.685 πῶς τῆμος βώσεσθε δυσάμμοροι; and 693 τάδε φράζεσθαι ἄνωγα. βιόμεσθα is unusual as a form of the verb βιόω, and has been variously explained. Janko (1979) argues that the echo in Apollonius guarantees his conjecture βώμεσθα, and that βιόω means 'pass one's life', as opposed to ζάω 'exist'. He therefore regards βώμεσθα as derived from βόσκω, which is also used in the parallel episode at 59. See Janko (1979) 215–16 and (1982) 123–4. This could be right: but βιόμεσθα is an explicable form, as Janko himself says, and since βίος can mean 'livelihood', the use of βιόω in this context seems justifiable.

ἄνωγμεν: an athematic perfect form, like εἰλήλουθμεν etc.; cf. Chantraine, *GH* I 424–5.

529–30 Delphi's natural barrenness was later proverbial, and became a standard reproach against the priests. They were said to have been mocked for their complete dependence on the pilgrims by Aesop, who was killed by the Delphians as a result (Schol. Ar. *Vesp.* 1446, *P.Oxy.* 1800 col. ii.2.30–63, Call. fr. 192.15–17, etc.). Lucian may have these verses in mind, as well as *Iliad* 2.519 and 9.405, at *Phalaris* 2.8, where a citizen of Delphi mentions the rocky site of Delphi and their dependence on the sanctuary and its revenues as a Homeric theme.

529 'This (land) is neither desirable for vine-bearing nor good for pasture.' Cf. 54–5 οὐδ' εὔβων σε ἔσεσθαι ὀΐομαι οὐδ' εὔμηλον, | οὐδὲ τρύγην οἴσεις, οὔτ' ἂρ φύτα μυρία φύσεις, *Od.* 13.246 αἰγίβοτος δ' ἀγαθὴ καὶ βούβοτος, 9.27 τρηχεῖ' ἀλλ' ἀγαθὴ κουροτρόφος, Hes. *Op.* 783 ἀνδρογόνος δ' ἀγαθή. Càssola prefers to interpret 'this desirable (land) is not vine-bearing, nor good for pasture'. The site has just been described by the poet as χῶρον ἐπήρατον (521), but Càssola's interpretation sounds less appropriate in the mouth of the anxious Cretan leader, and is a less natural way of construing the line. There may also be a reminiscence of *Od.* 4.605–7 ἐν δ' Ἰθάκηι οὔτ' ἂρ δρόμοι εὐρέες οὔτε τι λείμων· | αἰγίβοτος, καὶ μᾶλλον ἐπήρατος ἱπποβότοιο. | οὐ γάρ τις νήσων ἱππήλατος οὔτ' εὐλείμων . . . (εὐλείμων only recurs at Hes. fr. 240.1 in early epic.)

τρυγηφόρος occurs only here.

530 καὶ ἅμ' ἀνθρώποισιν ὀπηδεῖν: 'and at the same time to minister to mankind'. As the god's servants they will also 'attend' his pilgrims. ἅμα implies that there is not enough both to support them and also to enable them to have leisure to attend to their public duties (cf. Miller (1986) 100).

531–44 Apollo's reply begins with a gentle reproach, and his smile suggests divine amusement at human weakness. The contrast between men's anxiety for the future and the ease and abundance of divine provision is a typical theme. The message of the Gospels, to 'take no thought for the morrow, what you shall eat' (etc.), could be viewed as a Jewish–Christian development of the same motif. In the hymn, however, the promise is specifically linked to the assurance that the piety of visitors will always be sufficient to supply the needs of the god's ministers. The final warning comes at first sight as something of a shock after the tone of the rest of the speech. It is paralleled by Aphrodite's closing warning to Anchises (*H. Aph.* 286–8), after she has predicted the divine favours in store for their child. But this arises more naturally from Aphrodite's own distress at what has happened and her desire for secrecy. (Notice also that *H. Ap.* 544 closely resembles *H. Aph.* 289.) However, the sequence of Apollo's speech fits into the traditional pattern of ὄλβος leading to excess (κόρος), ὕβρις, and finally ἄτη, and agrees with the Delphic maxim μηδὲν ἄγαν. Cf. Janko (1982) 120, and Miller (1986) 100–10.

531 Cf. *Il.* 4.356 etc. τὸν δ' ἐπιμειδήσας προσέφη . . .

532–3 Cf. *H. Dem.* 257–8 νήϊδες ἄνθρωποι καὶ ἀφράδμονες οὔτ' ἀγαθοῖο | αἶσαν ἐπερχομένου προγνώμεναι οὔτε κακοῖο, and the 'Orphic' version of this (Orph. fr. 49.95–6) ἄφρονες ἄνθρωποι δυστλήμονες etc. For the traditional nature of this 'derogatory address to mankind by a deity or prophet', in both Greek and

Jewish literature, see Richardson on *H. Dem.* 256ff., and cf. also the Muses' song at *H. Ap.* 189–93. In the present passage, however, men are actually said to 'go looking for' (βούλεσϑ') cares, troubles, and anxieties themselves. This idea that they bring their sufferings on themselves, at least to some extent, is similar to that of the 'theodicy' at the opening of the *Odyssey*, where Zeus complains of how men blame the gods unfairly for their troubles, whereas οἱ δὲ καὶ αὐτοὶ | σφῇσιν ἀτασϑαλίῃσιν ὑπὲρ μόρον ἄλγε' ἔχουσιν (1.32–4).

532 μελεδῶνας: in *Od.* 19.517 most MSS have the first declension form μελεδῶναι, and μελεδώνας may be correct here. Cf. West on Hes. *Op.* 66, for the view that the third-declension form is late.

533 στείνεα: in Homer this is used literally, of a narrow or tight space. For the metaphorical use cf. Aesch. *Eum.* 520 σωφρονεῖν ὑπὸ στένει, and Latin *angustiae*, but also *Od.* 9.445, where στεινόμενος is used of the ram distressed by its fleece and the burden of Odysseus.

534 Cf. *Od.* 11.146 ῥηΐδιόν τι ἔπος ἐρέω καὶ ἐνὶ φρεσὶ ϑήσω. For the gods all things can be easy, and this divine facility is offset against mortal difficulties. Apollo will lighten their labour, as at 520–1.

535–7 The abundance of sheep sacrificed at Delphi was later proverbial: cf. Pi. *P.* 3.27 μηλοδόκῳ Πυϑῶνι, Bacchyl. 8.17 Πυϑῶνα μηλοϑύταν, etc. In some versions of the killing of Neoptolemus at Delphi he was said to have quarrelled with the attendants over the division of sacrificial meats, and to have been killed by 'a man with a knife': Pi. fr. 52f. 117–20, *N.* 7.42. The story of Aesop's death is similar (see 529–30n.): in the version in *P. Oxy.* 1800 col. ii.2.32–46 'the Delphians stand around the altar ὑφ' ἑαυτοῖς μαχαίρας κομίζοντες, and each cuts and carries away whatever portion of the meat he can obtain, often leaving the sacrificer to go away without any share'. The Δελφικὴ μάχαιρα was a special kind of knife of an archaic type used at Delphi, and became a proverbial expression for greed, as ascribed to the Delphians. Hence the killer of Neoptolemus was sometimes identified as a priest called Machaireus, son of Daitas: cf. Sophocles, *TrGF* IV p. 192 Radt, Apollodorus, *Ep.* 6.14, Strabo 9.3.9, and *RE* s.v. Machaireus. On these legends see Fontenrose (1960) especially 219–25, Wiechers (1961), Detienne (1998) especially 175–94, Rutherford (2001) 313–15, Kowalzig (2007) 188–201.

536 ἄφϑονα: this epithet is not found in Homer, but cf. Hes. *Op.* 118, Solon 33.5 etc.

537 ὅσσα ἐμοί κ': the hiatus in this position is unusual, and has been variously emended. West's conjecture ὅσσα κ' ἐμοί is a simple solution.

περικλυτὰ φῦλ' ἀνϑρώπων: not an epic formula, but cf. 273, 355, and 298. The repetition in 537–8 led to omission of 538 by some MSS.

538 προφύλαχϑε: the verb occurs first here; cf. Herodotus etc. The form is also unusual, and may be a metrical modification of the perfect form (προπεφύλαχϑε): see Janko (1982) 124.

539 ἐνϑάδ' ἀγειρομένων: cf. 58 ἐνϑάδ' ἀγειρόμενοι, in the parallel passage about Delos.

καὶ ἐμὴν ἰθύν τε μάλιστα: ἰθύς as a noun occurs in Homer only in the accusative, either in the phrase ἀν' ἰθύν ('straight onwards'), or in the sense of 'initiative, enterprise' (from 'direction'). But the text and interpretation are quite uncertain here. If the transmitted text is correct, there must be a lacuna, and one expects 'and moreover above all <observe> both my direction <and also my . . . >', followed by a conditional clause, either in the missing line(s), or introduced by emending 540 to εἰ δέ . . . Janko (1982) 120 argues for καὶ ἐμὴν ἴθυντε θέμιστα. εἰ δέ . . . , and compares Hes. *Op.* 9 δίκηι δ' ἴθυνε θέμιστας.

540–3 The warning against ὕβρις presumably follows an injunction to act in accordance with the god's will (ἰθύν). It also develops out of the preceding emphasis on wealth and abundance (see on 531–44). It could be taken simply as a general warning clause of an ominous kind, and oracular pronouncements often did contain warnings. However, 542–3 seem too specific for this, and so it has been taken as a *post eventum* prophecy, referring to a particular event. Delphic greed was a traditional theme, and so was the motif of conflict over the distribution of the wealth which Apollo predicts for the sanctuary (see 529–30, 535–7nn.). 542–3 imply that some conflict of this kind will lead to the Cretan priests or their successors losing control of the shrine. This has often been interpreted as an allusion to the so-called 'First Sacred War' (a modern term), an event or series of events which later Greek tradition, from the fourth century BC onwards, assigned to the first part of the sixth century (*c.* 594–584 BC). This was supposed to have arisen from misconduct by the people of Crisa (or Cirrha), who behaved arrogantly or greedily, and in one version taxed or plundered pilgrims to Delphi, and it led to the destruction of their town and consecration of the plain of Crisa as sacred land by the Amphictionic League. This group of Greek states subsequently controlled the sanctuary, whether or not they had done so previously. The war was closely associated by tradition with the institution of the Pythian Games in their classical form from 586 or 582 BC onwards. It has been argued that the war never actually took place, and that the tradition was invented in the fourth century BC: see Robertson (1978). But the consecration of the plain of Crisa does seem to have been a historical event, and so does the institution or reorganisation of the Games. Cf. Davies (1994) 193–212, Lefèvre (1998) 13–16, Sanchez (2001) 58–60, 63–79, and Kowalzig (2007) 195–201.

The war was usually seen as intended to liberate Delphi from oppression by its neighbour Crisa, and at first sight this does not seem to agree with the view that it is misbehaviour by the ministers of the god which will lead to their losing control of the sanctuary. Moreover, some of the sources for the war seem to assume that the League was already in control before the war (e.g. Aeschines 3.107–12, Strabo 9.3.4, etc.). If, however, the tradition about the war is linked to *H. Ap.* 540–3, this must imply a close association of Crisa with the sanctuary of Delphi, and this is indeed what is suggested by lines 269–74, 282–6, and 438–47. In the Catalogue of Ships Pytho and Crisa are listed together as Phocian towns (*Il.* 2.519–20). See also 393n. for possible linking of Crisa and Crete. From this point of view then, the supposed 'liberation' of Delphi from Crisaean control was a propagandist way of seeing the war, put about by the Amphictionic allies: cf. for example Forrest (1956) 45 for this interpretation.

It has alternatively been suggested that the new masters envisaged in 542–3 are actually the Crisaeans, and that the poet refers to an earlier takeover of Delphic control by them. But such a statement is unlikely to have survived in later tradition if Crisa was subsequently destroyed by the League. Clay (1989) 90–1 revives an old suggestion that the 'other leaders' are the *Hosioi*, a group of officials later attested at Delphi, who may have had some oversight of the god's ministers, and who seem to have decided whether a sacrifice or consultation of the oracle was acceptable. But we do not know enough of their functions to assess whether this could be right: cf. Amandry (1950) 123–5, 249–52, Roux (1976) 59–63.

It is also theoretically possible that the lines are a later addition to the hymn, in which case they could not be used to date the rest of the poem. But the traditional character of the train of thought in 531–44 does suggest that the lines are integral. (See also Introduction 2(b).)

540 τηΰσιον: cf. *Od.* 3.316 = 15.13 τηΰσίην ὁδόν. The etymology is uncertain, but it seems to mean 'vain, pointless', like μάταιος.

541 These words must surely be deliberately paradoxical, since θέμις would normally refer to conventional conduct which is morally appropriate (see Kirk on *Il.* 2.73–5). There is a similarly paradoxical use of δίκη at *Od.* 4.690–2, where the word is used as elsewhere in the *Odyssey* of habitual behaviour, but refers in this passage to actions or words which show prejudice and favouritism. Cf. Miller (1986) 104, 107–8.

542–3 Apollo's words indicate a strong and permanent form of overlordship, of an unwelcome kind. If the First Sacred War is envisaged, one can compare the fact that the defeated Crisaeans were said to have been enslaved and dedicated to Pythian Apollo (Aeschines *In Ctesiph.* 108).

544 Cf. *H. Aph.* 289 (νοήσας).

545–6 Apollo's speech closes the narrative, and the poet ends with a final salutation to the god as son of Zeus and Leto and the traditional formula indicating another song to follow.

545 καὶ σὺ μὲν οὕτω χαῖρε: cf. *H.* 1.20, *H. Herm.* 579 = *H.* 18.10, 21.5, 26.11, 28.17. οὕτω suggests that the deity should be pleased because of the preceding song.

546 Literally 'but I shall remember both you and also another song', i.e. presumably in moving on to a further song the poet promises not to forget the deity whom he has just celebrated. The ἀοιδή could in theory be either another hymn (as for example at *H. Ap.* 158–9), or a song of another kind, such as heroic narrative. Cf. Introduction 1(a), and for further discussion of this traditional closing formula and its possible interpretation see Richardson on *H. Dem.* 495. For parallels in other forms of poetry and prose see De Martino (1980) 232–40.

To Hermes

1–19 *Prologue: the birth of Hermes.* The poet asks the Muse to sing of Hermes, son of Zeus and Maia, ruler of Cyllene and Arcadia, and messenger of the gods. The nymph Maia used to sleep with Zeus secretly in a shadowy cave. She bore him a son who was a sly brigand, a cattle-rustler and master of dreams, who would soon perform famous deeds: born at dawn, at midday he was playing the lyre, in the evening he stole Apollo's cattle, on the fourth day of the month, the day that Maia bore him.

After the invocation of the Muse, this hymn immediately signals the opening theme of Hermes' parentage and birth, which is then described. The brief reference to parentage is quite common at the start (*H.* 7, 12, etc.), but the birth-narrative occurs at this point less often than one might have expected: cf. *H.* 15.1–3, 16.1–4, 17.1–4, 18.1–9, 28.1–16, 31.1–7. Most of these are brief, but here the special character of Hermes is already anticipated by the extended emphasis on the absolute secrecy of his parents' affair and its context (a shadowy cave at dead of night). Hermes is already at his birth given his attributes as a trickster-god (13–15), and the speed with which he manifests these powers is vividly portrayed: his first exploits are achieved that very day. Thus this prologue has already announced the main themes which are to follow.

1–9 *H.* 18.1–9 repeats these lines, with variations, and then closes with three farewell lines, of which 579 = *H.* 18.10.

1 **Ἑρμῆν ὕμνει Μοῦσα:** *H.* 18.1 has Ἑρμῆν ἀείδω, i.e. without the more traditional request to the Muse. An Attic *lekythos* of *c.* 470 BC shows a boy holding a papyrus-roll on which is written Ἑρμῆ(ν) ἀείδω. This suggests that the *Hymns*, or some of them, may have been used as school texts at this period: cf. Beazley (1948) 336–40, (1950) 318–19, and Immerwahr (1964) 17–48.

Ἑρμῆν: this contracted form of the name is used throughout this hymn, and occasionally in Homer (*Il.* 20.72, 4× *Od.*), Hesiod and other hymns. By contrast *H.* 19 only uses the uncontracted forms Ἑρμείας or Ἑρμείης. See Janko (1982) 133–4.

Διὸς καὶ Μαιάδος υἱόν: cf. *Od.* 14.435 Ἑρμῆι, Μαιάδος υἱεῖ. Hermes' mother's name has the variant forms Μαιάς and Μαῖα. She is a daughter of Atlas (*H.* 18.4, Hes. *Th.* 938), and later one of the Pleiades (Hes.(?) fr. 169, Simon, *PMG* fr. 555, etc.).

2 Mt Cyllene in Arcadia is Hermes' birthplace in the hymn (142) and was generally accepted as such later. In *H.* 19.28–31 he has a τέμενος there, and Pausanias describes a temple to Hermes on its summit (8.17.1–2). There was an annual procession to this sanctuary (Geminos 17.3, first century BC). On this and other local cults of Hermes see Jaillard (2007) 57–62.

3 **ἄγγελον ἀθανάτων ἐριούνιον:** after parentage and home comes Hermes' chief attribute as divine messenger, a function performed by him in the *Odyssey*, whereas Iris has this role in the *Iliad*. Cf. *H. Dem.* 407 ἄγγελος . . . ἐριούνιος etc. The prevalent modern view is that ἐριούνιος originally meant 'good runner', on the basis of a series of Arcadian and Cypriote words οὔνιος, οὔνης, etc., meaning 'runner': see Latte (1968) 690–3. The word could well be an ancient title, like several other divine epithets, surviving from late Bronze Age Greek. But its association with Arcadia might also suggest that it was especially used of Hermes there. In *H.* 19.28–31 we again find him called ἐριούνιον ἔξοχον ἄλλων, which is glossed by ὡς ὅ γ' ἅπασι θεοῖς θοὸς ἄγγελός ἐστι, and immediately afterwards his association with Arcadia and his τέμενος on Cyllene is mentioned.

ὃν τέκε Μαῖα: the relative switches the song to narrative mode, as is usual at the beginning of epic songs: cf. Richardson on *H. Dem.* 1–3.

4 νύμφη ἐϋπλόκαμος: in the *Hymns* this phrase only recurs in association with Hermes (in dative, at line 7 = *H.* 18.7 and 19.34), and in the Homeric poems it is only used in the singular of Calypso (*Od.* 1.86, 5.30, 57–8), and always in connection with Hermes' mission to her. Otherwise cf. *Od.* 12.132, Hes. fr. 304.5, for the nominative plural. For other possible links with the episode in *Odyssey* 5 cf. 154, 227–34nn. Like Maia, Calypso is a daughter of Atlas, and her cave resembles Maia's in various respects: see Shelmerdine (1986) 55–7, Jaillard (2007) 29–40. *H.* 18.4 replaces this formula with Ἄτλαντος θυγατήρ.

Διὸς ἐν φιλότητι μιγεῖσα: cf. *H.* 7.57, and Hes. *Th.* 920 Διὸς φιλότητι μιγεῖσα.

5 αἰδοίη: the emphatic runover word is probably explained by the following sentence, and would then mean 'shy' as at *Od.* 17.578, rather than 'revered'.

5–9 Secrecy is often a motif of divine unions, but it is especially emphasised here. Zeus hides the birth of Dionysus from Hera (*H.* 1.6–7), and Apollo's birth is kept secret from her (*H. Ap.* 92–114). Cf. *H.* 17.3–4 (Dioscouroi), and Hes. *Th.* 56–7, where Zeus's affair with Mnemosyne is νόσφιν ἀπ' ἀθανάτων. Hera herself withdraws from the gods before the birth of Typhaon (*H. Ap.* 326–52). Cf. S. *Ichneutai* fr. 314.265–6 Radt: καὶ γὰρ κέκρυπται τοὔργον ἐν θεῶν ἕδραις, | Ἥραν ὅπως μὴ πύστις ἵξεται λόγου, and 270 λήθηι τῆς βαθυζώνου θεᾶς.

5 μακάρων δὲ θεῶν ἠλεύαθ' ὅμιλον: cf. *Od.* 17.67 ἀλεύατο πουλὸν ὅμιλον, and *H.* 18.5 (with ἀλέεινεν).

6 ἄντρον ἔσω ναίουσα παλίσκιον: ναίουσα governs the accusative ἄντρον (as at *H.* 29.9), and ἔσω is adverbial ('within'). In *H.* 18.6 the dative is used. For παλί(ν)σκιος ('thickly shaded') cf. Archil. fr. 36 West etc. Caves are places for seduction of nymphs in *Od.* 1.71–3 and *H. Aph.* 262–3. Zeus is concealed in a cave after his birth and brought up by Gaia (Hes. *Th.* 477–84) and Dionysus is nursed in a cave by nymphs (*H.* 26.3–6). Cf. also Antim. fr. 3 West, where Zeus creates a shadowy cave in which to hide Europa from the view of the gods (perhaps echoing our hymn).

7 μισγέσκετο: 'used to have intercourse'. For the frequentative form cf. ὠρίζεσκον, *Od.* 18.325, of Melantho sleeping with Eurymachus, and *Il.* 9.450–2.

νυκτὸς ἀμολγῶι: 'at dead of night' is perhaps the best equivalent of this obscure phrase, whose original sense may have been forgotten by Homer's time.

It occurs four times in the *Iliad* and once in the *Odyssey*: cf. Richardson on *Il.* 22.27–8.

8 ὄφρα . . . ἔχοι: *H.* 18.8 has εὖτε . . . ἔχοι. ὄφρα must mean 'while, so long as' here. For the optative with the frequentative μισγέσκετο cf. *Od.* 7.138 ᾧι πυμάτωι σπένδεσκον, ὅτε μνησαίατο κοίτου. The emphasis on the duration of Zeus's affair distinguishes it from his more cursory amours.

9 Cf. *Il.* 14.296 εἰς εὐνῆν φοιτῶντε, φίλους λήθοντε τοκῆας. ἀθανάτους . . . ἀνθρώπους is a Hesiodic formula (*Th.* 588 etc.).

10–12 11 is probably part of the subordinate clause, and the main clause is at 12, with τε . . . τε meaning 'both . . . and'. Cf. *Il.* 19.117–18 ἡ δ' ἐκύει φίλον υἱόν, ὁ δ' ἕβδομος ἑστήκει μείς· | ἐκ δ' ἄγαγε πρὸ φόωσδε . . . The subject of 118 is Hera, causing the premature birth of Eurystheus, and here too the subject of ἄγαγεν is probably Zeus, rather than Maia or δέκατος μείς, although the latter is possible.

10 Cf. *Il.* 1.5 Διὸς δ' ἐτελείετο βουλή and similar expressions, and especially Hes. *Th.* 1002 μεγάλου δὲ Διὸς νόος ἐξετελεῖτο, of the birth of Medeios.

11 μείς is used both of the moon and of the month, and hence 'was set in the sky'. The 'tenth month' refers to sidereal months (of *c.* $27^{1}/_{2}$ days), i.e. the average interval between returns of the moon to the same fixed star. Cf. Verg. *Ecl.* 4.61 *matri longa decem tulerunt fastidia menses*, of the normal length of pregnancy, and Neugebauer (1963) 64–5.

12 ἀρίσημά τε ἔργα τέτυκτο: ἀρίσημος is only here in early epic; cf. Tyrtaeus 12.29 etc. The phrase introduces what follows (14–19): 'then indeed she bore a son . . . who was soon destined to manifest glorious deeds . . .'

13–15 The catalogue of epithets resembles the style of later hymns, such as the Orphic ones, or *H.* 8 to Ares. In this case it elevates the status of this newborn deity in a semi-comic way (e.g. the juxtaposition of 'driver of cattle, leader of dreams') and anticipates his exploits. The language is unusual. αἱμυλομήτης occurs only here, a variation of epic ἀγκυλομήτης, ποικιλομήτης (cf. 155, 514, and of Odysseus in Homer). ὀπωπητήρ recurs only (as restored) in a late hymn to Hermes Trismegistos, probably echoing our hymn (Kaibel, *Epigr. Gr.* 1032); cf. ὀπτήρ *Od.* 14.261. πυληδόκος is only found here; cf. later ὁδοιδόκος of a robber, Homeric πυλαωρός, etc. The balanced contrast of ἐλατῆρα βοῶν, ἡγήτορ' ὀνείρων is combined with chiasmus in ἡγήτορ' . . . ὀπωπητῆρα.

13 παῖδα πολύτροπον: cf. 439, and *Od.* 1.1 ἄνδρα . . . πολύτροπον. The sense of the Odyssean epithet was disputed in antiquity: 'turning many ways, ingenious' or 'much wandering', and both senses could fit Hermes' activities in this poem. The first, however, can include the second, and the more general sense seems better here. Cf. S. West on *Od.* 1.1.

αἱμυλομήτην: cf. ποικιλομήτης of Hermes at 155, 514, and epic ἀγκυλομήτης, αἰολομήτης. This compound form perhaps stresses especially Hermes' verbal dexterity.

14 ἐλατῆρα βοῶν: ἐλατήρ is elsewhere in early epic used of a driver of horses or charioteer.

'of winning wiles'

ἡγήτορ' ὀνείρων: Hermes brings sleep with his wand (*Il.* 24.343–4 etc.), receives a last libation before sleep (*Od.* 7.136–8), and sends dreams (A.R. 4.1732–3, Apollodorus 244 F 129, Heliodorus 3.5.1). His dual roles as ψυχοπομπός and ὀνειροπομπός are closely related, since both concern εἴδωλα (cf. *Od.* 24.1–5). See also 146–7n., and Jaillard (2007) 207–12.

15 νυκτὸς ὀπωπητῆρα, πυληδόκον: 'watcher by night, waiting in gateways'. The first phrase can refer both to his quality as a thief and also to Hermes as guardian against nocturnal hazards. The thief works in darkness, and lurks in doorways waiting for his prey. Cf. Ar. *Birds* 496–7, where Euelpides has just put his head outside the city wall when he is mugged, and ὁδοιδόκος ('highwayman'). Hermes is also Προπύλαιος or Πυλαῖος (Farnell, *Cults* v 19), a god whose effigy (or herm) stood outside the door, and πυληδόκος may allude to this too.

17–19 Hermes' early career is elegantly described in three clauses of ascending length, leading up to his major exploit, the theft of Apollo's cattle, each clause being prefaced by the time-marker. 19 emphasises that this all occurred on a single day, the fourth of the month, and τῆι . . . Μαῖα closes the narrative which began at 3, signalling the end of the prologue. Hermes' precocity is paralleled by Apollo's (*H. Ap.* 127–39), and in fact he goes further than Apollo in the rapidity of his achievements. For this motif applied to other gods and heroes see Richardson on *H. Dem.* 235. Callimachus may have *H. Herm.* 17–18 in mind in his praise of Ptolemy's decisiveness (*H.* 1.87): ἑσπέριος κεῖνός γε τελεῖ τά κεν ἦρι νοήσηι. In Apollo's case it is his strength which is emphasised, whereas in Hermes' it is primarily his rapid mobility and ingenuity: cf. also *H. Herm.* 43–6 etc. Later he also reveals superhuman strength: 116–19, 405–8. In Sophocles' *Ichneutai* Cyllene says that the baby Hermes is growing wonderfully within the first few days since his birth (fr. 314.277–82 Radt).

17 ἠῷος: cf. Hes. *Op.* 548, *Sc.* 396, etc. The Homeric form is ἠοῖος (*Od.* 4.447, 8.29). However, we cannot be sure which pronunciation was actually used by Hesiod and others: cf. West on *Op.* 548.

γεγονώς: for this form of the participle, instead of γεγαώς (usual in early hexameter verse) cf. Alc. fr. 72.11 L–P = V ἐκγεγόνων.

ἐγκιθάριζεν: strictly speaking ἐγ- implies an audience, as at *H. Ap.* 201, but although attendants are mentioned at 60, the compound may be used without special reference. The compound occurs only in these two instances, and μέσωι ἤματι also recurs at *H. Ap.* 441. It is possible that influence from the *Hymn to Apollo* has played a part here (cf. Vergados (2007a) 58).

19 τετράδι τῆι προτέρηι: this is the same as Hesiod's τετρὰς ἱσταμένου, the fourth day of the waxing moon, but προτέρη implies a simple division of the month into two parts (waxing and waning), whereas some early Greek calendars used a tripartite division: cf. West on Hes. *Op.* 765–828 (pp. 349–50). Hesiod mentions the fourth as a sacred day (*Op.* 770), and also one on which to avoid being unhappy (797–9), but not that it was Hermes' birthday. Cf. Philochorus 328 F 85, Plut. *Mor.* 738F, etc.

20–61 Hermes set off in search of Apollo's cattle, and came upon a tortoise. He scooped out its marrow and invented a lyre, using its shell as the sounding board. He then sang in praise of his parents Zeus and Maia, their love affair, and his own birth and home.

The reason for Hermes' quest for Apollo's cattle is not explained at this point, but later it is said to be due to his hunger for meat (64). However, he is immediately diverted by meeting the tortoise, and this leads to his first invention. In later versions (S. fr. 314.372–6 Radt, Apollod. 3.10.2) the theft of the cattle comes first, and he uses their entrails for its strings, or an oxhide to cover the shell (cf. *H. Herm.* 49, 51). This order seems more natural and could be older, modified by the poet of the hymn for his own narrative purposes. For Hermes and the tortoise in art cf. Settis (1966) especially 82–7, Dumoulin (1994), and Chamoux (2000).

20–3 These lines continue the theme of the rapidity of Hermes' early exploits. Like Apollo (*H. Ap.* 119) he 'sprang' from his mother's body at birth, but whereas Apollo is first washed, swaddled, and fed by the goddesses present at his birth, before embarking on his career as a god, Hermes is off almost at once on his travels (cf. Introduction 1(c)).

21 λίκνωι: λίκνον occurs first here; it is a winnowing basket, here used as a cradle. Cf. S. fr. 314.275 Radt, where Maia provides λικνῖτιν τροφήν to the baby god, and Aratus *Phaen.* 268–9 καὶ χέλυς ἐστ' ὀλίγη· τὴν δ' ἄρ' ἔτι καὶ παρὰ λίκνωι | Ἑρμείης ἐτόρησε, Λύρην δέ μιν εἶπε λέγεσθαι. Zeus is also cradled thus in Call. *H.* 1.47–8, and Dionysus was especially worshipped as Liknotes: cf. Harrison (1903) 292–324. Hermes is shown in his λίκνον, with his stolen cows, on a black-figure Caeretan hydria *c.* 530 BC (Louvre E 702 = *LIMC* s.v. Hermes no. 241), and a red-figure kylix by the Brygos Painter, *c.* 490/480 BC (*ARV*² 246.6 = *LIMC* s.v. Hermes no. 242a). The scholia to the above passages of Callimachus and Aratus say that it was an ancient custom to place babies after birth in a λίκνον, as an omen of wealth and fruitfulness.

23 Cf. *Il.* 9.582 οὐδοῦ ἐπεμβεβαὼς ὑψηρεφέος θαλάμοιο. Maia's cave is described throughout this hymn as if it were a grandiose building, with threshold, courtyard doors (26), etc. By 148 and 246–51 it has become almost a temple or sanctuary, with three treasure-chambers.

24 Hermes comes upon the tortoise by chance as he crosses the threshold (26–8): she is a ἕρμαιον or lucky find by the god of luck, and brings good fortune. The first thing or person one meets on leaving or entering the house can be significant or ominous, and so here she is called a σύμβολον (30), or omen met on one's way. Cf. Ar. *Frogs* 196 with Dover's comments. Later the lyre which Hermes makes will help in reconciling him to Apollo and assure him all the favours bestowed as a result (416–578).

χέλυν: the tortoise must be *testudo marginata*, which is native to Greece. The first occurrences of χέλυς are here and at Sappho fr. 118 L–P = V ἄγι δὴ χέλυ δῖα †μοι λέγε† φωνάεσσα †δὲ γίνεο†.

25 This is the first of a series of aetiological statements about Hermes' inventions. For the phrasing cf. 111, of the art of kindling fire. The asyndeton, with τοι, draws attention in both cases to these remarkable events. Cf. also the hymn of the Delphic poet Boeo quoted by Pausanias (10.5.7): πρῶτος δ' [i.e. Olen] ἀρχαίων ὕμνων τεκτάνατ' ἀοιδάν. There is a paradox in the idea of the voiceless tortoise becoming a singer. Cf. *H. Herm.* 38, Sappho fr. 58.12 L–P = V φιλάοιδον λιγύραν χελύνναν (and fr. 118), S. fr. 314.299–300 Radt καὶ πῶς πίθωμαι τοῦ θανόντος φθέγμα τοιοῦτον βρέμειν; | πιθοῦ· θανὼν γὰρ ἔσχε φωνήν, ζῶν δ' ἄναυδος ἦν ὁ θήρ, 328 οὕτως ὁ παῖς θανόντι θηρὶ φθέγμ' ἐμηχανήσατο, Nicander *Alex.* 560–2 ἄλλοτε δ' οὐρείης κυτισηνόμου, ἥν τ' ἀκάκητα | αὐδήεσσαν ἔθηκεν ἀναύδητόν περ ἐοῦσαν | Ἑρμείης ('or else with those of the mountain tortoise that feeds on tree-medick, the creature that Hermes the Gracious endowed with a voice though voiceless'), and Horace, *Odes* 3.11.5 (*testudo*) *nec loquax olim neque grata* (with Nisbet and Rudd's comments).

26 **ἐπ' αὐλείῃσι θύρῃσι** refers to the outer gateway of the courtyard of a house, as at *Od.* 18.239, 23.49. Cf. the courtyard outside Polyphemus' cave (*Od.* 9.462).

28 **σαῦλα ποσὶν βαίνουσα:** σαῦλος occurs only here in early epic, and σαῦλα βαίνειν is used elsewhere of a lightly stepping, prancing, or effeminate way of walking. Cf. Semonides 18 West (like a horse), Anacreon 411 (of Bacchants), 458 (like a courtesan), etc. Here it describes the awkward, waddling gait of the tortoise, but it also anticipates Hermes' vision of her as the 'hetaera' she will become (31).

29 **ἐγέλασσε:** Hermes' delight is paralleled by Apollo's on hearing the lyre (420–1).

30 **σύμβολον:** not elsewhere in early epic; cf. 527. ὀνήσιμος also first occurs here, then in Aeschylus and later. σύμβολον probably refers to a sign or omen, as at Archilochus 218 (etc.), perhaps especially something one meets or encounters (συμβάλλειν). Cf. Müri (1931), and Gauthier (1972) 62–73 (especially 71 n. 26). But at the same time the word could allude to Hermes' commercial role, since it was later used particularly of physical tokens of contracts between two parties. He will indeed use the lyre later as a bargaining counter in his suit with Apollo.

οὐκ ὀνοτάζω means that Hermes does not reject this piece of luck. ὀνοτάζειν ('scorn') is a rare variant of the usual epic ὄνεσθαι, which also occurs at Hes. *Op.* 258. There seems to be word-play in the echo of ὀνήσιμον . . . ὀνοτάζω.

31 This ironic address, anticipating the transformation of tortoise to lyre, dignifies her in hymnic style with a series of epithets which suggest that she is a hetaera or dancing-girl (see also 478–88n.). ἐρόεσσα (not Homeric) is used of nymphs by Hesiod (*Th.* 245, 251, 357, fr. 169.1), and of a girl at *H. Dem.* 109. It is used of an instrument also by Anacreon (fr. 373). χοροιτύπε (cf. Pindar etc.) means 'beating (time in) the dance', and δαιτὸς ἑταίρη is probably a traditional description of the lyre (cf. *Od.* 8.99, 17.271). Later δαιτὸς ἑταῖρε will be applied to Hermes himself as player of the lyre, by Apollo (436). Cf. Horace, *Odes* 3.11.6 of the lyre, *diuitum mensis et amica templis*.

32–3 'From where (is) this beautiful plaything? A patterned shell you are, mountain-dwelling tortoise.' With this punctuation, 33 stands in contrast to what follows: i.e. 'but I shall take you home and make you into something useful' (cf. Gemoll).

33 **ὄστρακον** occurs first here; cf. Sophocles etc.

34–5 These lines echo 30 (μέγ' ὀνήσιμον, οὐκ ὀνοτάζω ~ οὐδ' ἀποτιμήσω· σὺ δέ . . . ὀνήσεις).

35 **ἀποτιμήσω:** ἀποτιμᾶν occurs first here; cf. Hdt. 5.77 (in middle), etc.

πρώτιστον is adverbial.

36 'It's better to stay at home, for the outside world is harmful!' This verse occurs at Hes. *Op.* 365, and was probably proverbial, like 'East, west, home's best.' In Hesiod the context refers to the advantages of keeping one's property at home, and this could be the point here too. Later, however, the tortoise was proverbially considered to be a stay-at-home creature, as she carries her house with her, and the saying οἶκος φίλος, οἶκος ἄριστος was applied to her: cf. *Aesopica* pp. 362–3, no. 106 Perry, Cercidas fr. 2 Powell. Plutarch (*Mor.* 142D, 381E) explains Pheidias' statue of Aphrodite Ourania standing on a tortoise as symbolising the need for married women to stay at home and keep silence. This would make Hermes' address to the tortoise as a ἑταίρη more ironic, since Pheidias' statue was later contrasted with one of Aphrodite Pandemos by Scopas (Paus. 6.25.1). The children's refrain χελιχελώνη, τί ποῖεις ἐν τῶι μέσωι; (*PMG* 876(c)) implies the same idea of the tortoise's place being at home, not out of doors. There is thus a *double entendre* here: home is usually safest for the tortoise, but in this case taking her home will be good for Hermes, but will mean death for her. Crudden (1994) compares a fable quoted by Radin (1956, 72) where the Trickster Hare invites some crabs to help him cross a river, and then skins one and uses its shell as a boat.

37–8 'For surely you will be a protection against hurtful magic in life, and if you die then you would sing most beautifully.' As Van Nortwick says (1975, 70), there is a certain grim humour in ζώουσ', which is underlined by its prominent position as a runover word.

For ἐπηλυσίης πολυπήμονος cf. *H. Dem.* 230. ἐπηλυσίη refers to the attack of some demonic or magical source, causing pain or illness. Pliny (*NH* 32.33–40) lists all the cures for poison, magic spells, or diseases involving use of parts of the land tortoise, and it was also thought to protect vines from hail (*Geoponica* 1.14.8). Cf. *RE* I 77.28–42.

38 See on 25, and cf. Burkert (1984) 39, on the common motif that music is created through the death of a living creature.

41–2 'Then tossing it up (?) he scooped out the marrow of the mountain-haunting tortoise with a knife of grey iron.' ἀναπηλεῖν occurs only here and has been explained as a variant form of ἀναπάλλειν ('to toss up, throw up'). Shelmerdine (1981, 74) compares vase paintings which show a child playing with a tortoise which is suspended by a string (cf. Dumoulin (1994) 137, Abb. 48). However, Nicander uses ἀνακύπωσας ('turning over') of the tortoise (*Ther.* 703), which is the sense one would have liked here. γλύφανος is first used here (cf. Theocr. 1.28 etc.). αἰών means 'marrow' here: cf. Hesychius s.v., quoting Hippocrates, and perhaps *Il.* 19.27, Pind. fr. 111.5. ἐκτορεῖν ('bore out, scoop out') occurs only here, and χελώνη first here; cf. Herodotus etc. The language is echoed by 118–19, where Hermes throws the oxen on their backs and bores through their marrow. Cf. also Aratus *Phaen.* 268–9 καὶ χέλυς ἐστ' ὀλίγη· τὴν δ' ἄρ' ἔτι καὶ παρὰ λίκνωι | Ἑρμείης ἐτόρησε, Λύρην δέ μιν εἶπε λέγεσθαι.

43–6 Similes expressing rapidity, especially of divine movement, by comparison with thought are common in early epic: cf. *Il.* 15.80–3, and briefer expressions such as ὡς εἰ πτέρον ἠὲ νόημα (*Od.* 7.36). This appears to be the first example of an extended double comparison with ὡς ὅτε... ἢ ὅτε... For this cf. A.R. 4.1298–1304, 1452–6. There is a threefold negative simile at *Il.* 14.394–401.

44 resembles *Od.* 19.516–17 πυκιναὶ δέ μοι ἀμφ' ἀδινὸν κῆρ | ὀξεῖαι μελεδῶναι ὀδυρομένην ἐρέθουσιν. θαμινός is first used here, for Homeric θαμειός, and later in Pindar etc. μέριμνα is first used by Hesiod (*Op.* 178).

45 'Or as when glances whirl from the eyes.' The Greeks sometimes thought of sight as caused by rays of light emanating from the eyes (cf. the discussion by Aristotle, *De Sensu* 437a19ff.). For the simile cf. A.R. 4.847–50 (of Thetis) αὐτὴ δ' ὠκυτέρη ἀμαρύγματος ἠὲ βολάων ἠελίου... σεύατ' ἴμεν λαιψηρά..., and 1 Cor. 15.52 ἐν ῥιπῆι ὀφθαλμοῦ. ἀμαρυγή (Aristophanes etc.) occurs first here: cf. ἀμάρυγμα in Hes. fr. 43a4 (etc.), ἀμαρύσσειν in Hes. *Th.* 827, *H. Herm.* 278, 415, and ἀμάρυχμα λάμπρον of the eyes, Sappho fr. 16.18. δινηθῶσιν must refer to the rapid and frequent rays or glances here.

46 Cf. *Il.* 19.242 αὐτίκ' ἔπειθ' ἅμα μῦθος ἔην τετέλεστο δὲ ἔργον, Hdt. 3.134.6, A.R. 4.103. ἅμ' ἔπος ἅμ' ἔργον was proverbial ('no sooner said than done'): cf. Zenobius 1.77 (*Paroemiographi Graeci* I p. 27).

κύδιμος Ἑρμῆς: this is a Hesiodic formula (*Th.* 938, 958), used frequently in this hymn. κῦδος is what Hermes is aiming to acquire by his exploits: cf. Jaillard (2007) 76–80.

47–51 'Then he fixed stalks of reed, cutting them in measured lengths, piercing the back of the tortoise, through its shell. And with the aid of his wits he stretched the hide of an ox around, inserted arms, fitted a crossbar to both of them, and stretched seven harmonious strings of sheep-gut.'

The tortoise-shell lyre whose construction is described here first appears in Greek art around the end of the eighth century BC. The word λύρη is mentioned in literature from the seventh century BC (cf. Archilochus fr. 93a5 West, *Margites* fr. 1.3 West, etc.). κάλαμος occurs first here (cf. Hdt. etc., and καλάμη Hom.). Stalks of reed are mentioned as being 'under a lyre' (ὑπολύριον) in Ar. *Frogs* 233, and also in a fragment of Sophocles as a support for the instrument (36 Radt). These may have formed a frame to prevent the shell from buckling under the strain, and perhaps were also used to fix the arms firmly within the sound-box. In two surviving examples of tortoise-shell lyres holes are cut in the shell, which could be for these reeds. See Roberts (1981) 308–9, Maas and Snyder (1989) 36, 39, 95. The oxhide was stretched over the shell to make the sounding-board, and two arms (πήχεις) fitted into the shell and then joined by a crossbar (ζύγον). The

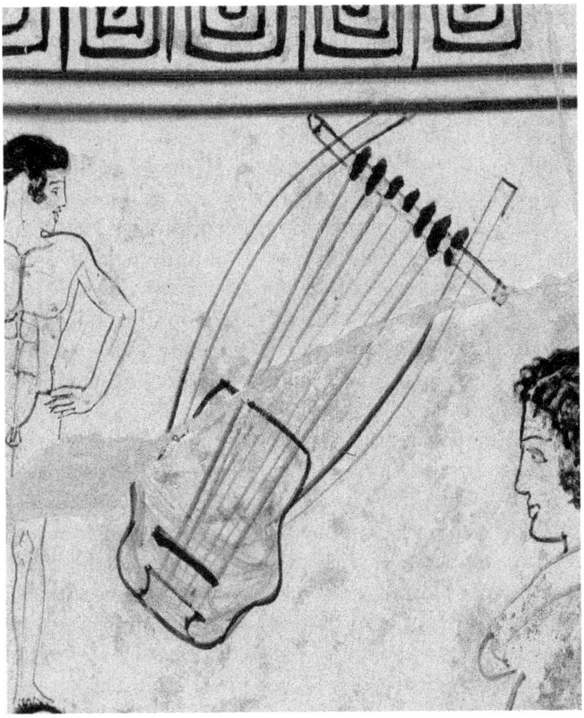

Figure 1 *White ground lekythos (detail showing a lyre)* by the Thanatos Painter. © 2010 Museum of Fine Arts, Boston.

arms were probably originally made of horns, but later could also be wooden. The strings were attached to the crossbar, and at the bottom stretched over the bridge and fastened to the sound-box. For detailed discussion and illustrations see Shelmerdine (1981) 78–86, Roberts (1981) 303–12, Maas and Snyder (1989) 34–9, 42–52, 79–112; cf. also West (1992) 56–7, Landels (1999) 61–6, Evans (2001) 124–7. See also Figure 1.

In this hymn the instrument is called λύρη at 418(?) and 423, but also φόρμιγξ (64, 506) and κίθαρις (509, 515), and the verb (ἐγ)κιθαρίζειν is used (17, 423, etc.), so that it is not clearly distinguished from the instrument (or instruments) traditionally used for epic song. Later, the tortoise-shell λύρα, which was smaller and lighter than the φόρμιγξ or κίθαρις, was the normal instrument which amateurs learnt to play, as opposed to professional singers and musicians. In implying identity with the κίθαρις our poet seems to be competing with the *Hymn to Apollo*, where this god claims the κίθαρις as his own after *his* birth (131): see Introduction 3(b)–(c).

48 πειρήνας διὰ νῶτα διὰ ῥινοῖο χελώνης: πειρήνας διά is probably to be taken as a tmesis, for διαπειρήνας, as in such cases as ἶνα τάμηι διὰ πᾶσαν (*Il.* 17.522).

The sense 'piercing through' is unique, as πε(ι)ραίνειν usually means 'bring to an end'; but later it is sometimes used intransitively, meaning 'penetrate' (A. *Ch.* 57 etc.).

49 πραπίδεσσιν ἐῆισιν: cf. Homeric ἰδυίῃισι πραπίδεσσι, regularly applied to Hephaestus' craftsmanship (*Il.* 1.608 etc.).

51 The ascription of the seven-stringed lyre to Hermes suggests that at the time of our hymn this was thought to be an ancient design. Seven strings seem to have been the normal number for stringed instruments in late Bronze Age Greece, and again the norm from the seventh century onwards. In the Geometric period, however, artistic evidence suggests that some instruments may have had only four. In later tradition one of the innovations credited to Terpander in the seventh century was to increase the *kithara*'s number to seven. This could be connected with the development of a more varied and complex style of music, in comparison with that of earlier epic song (West (1992) 52, 329–30).

συμφώνους: 'sounding in harmony with one another'. The word occurs first here, then in Pi. *P.* 1.70. Cf. S. *Ichneutai* fr. 314.327 (of Hermes' lyre) ξύμφωνον ἐξαίρει γὰρ αὐτὸν αἰόλισμα τῆς λύρας ('for the harmonious variety of the lyre arouses him'). The variant θηλυτέρων is given in a quotation of this line by Antigonus of Carystus, which he cites to show that the guts of female sheep are tuneful, whereas those of rams are soundless. This suggests that he may have been using an alternative text here, rather than simply misquoting from memory. It seems unlikely that συμφώνους was originally a gloss, i.e. that it came into the text as an explanation of θηλυτέρων . . . χορδάς, as argued by Vergados (2007b).

52 αὐτὰρ ἐπεὶ δὴ τεῦξε: cf. *Il.* 18.601, *Od.* 8.276. The participle φέρων adds little to the sense, as at 63, and in some later examples (cf. LSJ A s.v. X.2). φέρων ἐρατεινὸν ἄθυρμα is repeated from 40, framing this passage.

53–4 Cf. 419–20, 501–2. The plectrum (cf. *H. Ap.* 185) was attached by a cord to the base of the lyre, and 'had a comfortable handle and a short, pointed blade of ivory, horn, bone or wood' (West (1992) 65). Later evidence suggests that whereas the left hand plucked the strings, picking out a melody, the plectrum in the right hand was used for 'strumming' (West, *ibid.* 65–9). Here the plectrum seems to be testing the tuning of the strings. Cf. *Od.* 21.410, where Odysseus tests the bowstring and it sings out, Ovid *Met.* 5.339 *praetentat pollice chordas*, Statius *Ach.* 1.187 *leuiterque expertas pollice chordas*, and Borthwick (1959) 27 n. 3.

κατὰ μέλος 'in a tuned scale' (West). Allen's reading makes the text match 419 and 501. μέλος is only used of limbs in Homer; the musical sense occurs at *H.* 19.16 ἐν μελέεσσιν, Theognis 761, etc. This musical use may have developed from the sense 'limb': cf. LSJ s.v. B 'musical member, phrase'.

ἡ δ' ὑπὸ χειρὸς | σμερδαλέον κονάβησε: 'and beneath his hand it resounded tremendously'. σμερδαλέον is often used (with κονάβησε etc.) in epic of awe-inspiring sounds.

ὑπὸ καλὸν ἄειδεν: ὑπο- means 'in accompaniment'. Cf. *Il.* 18.570 ἱμέροεν κιθάριζε, λίνον δ' ὑπὸ καλὸν ἄειδε.

55–61 In Homer αὐτοσχέδιος and αὐτοσχεδόν are only used of close or hand-to-hand fighting. The sense 'improvised' occurs first here; cf. later αὐτοχεδιάζω (etc.). However, σχεδίη is used of a make-shift or improvised boat (*Od.* 5.33 etc.). Hermes' first song is an improvisation, something put together on the spur of the moment. The subject (57–61) is the love affair of his own parents, his birth, and his mother's home: it is a hymn of self-praise, like a miniature hymn within the *Hymn to Hermes* itself, and it also aggrandises the situation of his birth. Cf. *H. Herm.* 424–33, where Hermes sings a theogony; the songs in the *Hymn to Apollo*; *H.* 19.27–47, where the nymphs sing of Hermes and the birth of Pan; *H.* 27.11–20, where Artemis leads the chorus of Muses and Charites at Delphi as they sing in praise of Leto and her children Apollo and Artemis; and Hesiod's opening hymn to the Muses, which portrays them singing in praise of the gods and of their own father Zeus (*Th.* 9–21, 43–79).

Hermes' song is compared to the mocking songs of young men at feasts (55–6): cf. 454 οἷα νέων θαλίηις ἐνδέξια ἔργα πέλονται. The chief point of comparison is probably its improvisatory character, but the description could also suggest its humorous or *risqué* tone (cf. Radermacher ad loc.). Cf. already in the *Odyssey* 14.462–6, where wine is said to prompt a man to sing, laugh, dance, and utter things which are better not said. The practice alluded to in the hymn is that of capping songs in an impromptu and witty way in a sympotic context, with a mockery which could, if uncontrolled, easily slide into abuse. Cf. A.R. 1.457–9 (where the heroes are feasting) μετέπειτα δ' ἀμοιβαδὶς ἀλλήλοισιν | μύθευνθ', οἷά τε πολλὰ νέοι παρὰ δαιτὶ καὶ οἴνωι | τερπνῶς ἑψιόωνται, ὅτ' ἄατος ὕβρις ἀπείη ('and afterwards they told one another stories, such as young men often tell when they merrily take pleasure in feasting and wine, and insatiable insolence is far away'). Such sympotic jesting is described by Demetrius, *On style* 170, and how to do this in a civilised way is discussed by Plutarch in his *Table-Talk* (2.1, *Moralia* 629E–634F). Cf. also Isocrates, *Against Nicocles* 47, Alexis, *PCG* fr. 160, and Reitzenstein (1893) 26 n. 2, West (1974) 16–17, Ford (2002) 35–9.

56 ἡβηταί: first here. Cf. κοῦροι | πρωθῆβαι at *Od.* 8.262–3 of young men dancing in accompaniment to Demodocus' song. ἡβατάς, ἡβητής recur in the fifth century (E. *Heracl.* 858 etc.). ἡβᾶν is used in sympotic contexts, e.g. Theognis 877 ἥβα μοι, φίλε θυμέ, etc.; cf. Hesychius s.v. ἡβᾶν· εὐωχεῖσθαι.

παραιβόλα κερτομέουσιν: cf. *Il.* 4.5–6 αὐτίκ' ἐπειρᾶτο Κρονίδης ἐρεθιζέμεν Ἥρην | κερτομίοις ἐπέεσσι, παραβλήδην ἀγορεύων. The meaning of παραβλήδην there is uncertain, but Leaf's 'provokingly' would suit both the Homeric context and this passage well. Later (Hdt. etc.) παράβολος means 'hazardous' or 'reckless', and παραβάλλεσθαι in Homer means 'to risk'.

κερτομέουσιν: this verb is usually taken to mean 'mock, provoke, taunt, jest', and 'jest' would fit here. The etymology is most probably from κέαρ + τομεῖν, 'to cut the heart', but there is uncertainty about the application of this metaphor and its range of usage in early epic: see Clarke (2001) 329–38, Lloyd (2004) 75–89.

κερτομεῖν and κέρτομος recur at *H. Herm.* 300, 335, and 338, and the popularity of these words in this hymn suits the comic tone of the narrative and the god's tricky nature.

57 **ἀμφί** is a traditional introductory word for a hymnic narrative: cf. *Od.* 8.267, *H.* 7.1, 19.1, 22.1, 23.3, and ἀμφιανακτίζειν used of the traditional opening of a dithyramb and supposedly derived from Terpander's preludes (Schol. Ar. *Nub.* 595).

καλλιπέδιλον occurs nowhere else; cf. however Homeric χρυσοπέδιλος, καλλιπάρηιος, etc.

58 **ὡς πάρος ὠρίζεσκον:** for ὀαρίζειν in the context of love cf. *Il.* 6.156, 22.127, and 14.216 ὀαριστύς. The frequentative form implies habitual activity, as at 7. The contracted imperfect form ὠρ- is only used here. The manuscripts read ὅν rather than ὡς. This could only be explained as an internal accusative with ὠρίζεσκον (i.e. ὄαρον; cf. *H.* 23.3 ὀάρους ὀαρίζει), but this seems unlikely.

ἑταιρείηι φιλότητι: the epithet ἑταιρεῖος occurs first here; cf. Hdt. 1.44 (of Zeus) etc., and the classical use of ἑταίρα meaning courtesan. The Ionic form ἑταρήϊος would not fit in hexameter verse. Cf. ἐρατῆι φιλότητι in Hesiod (*Th.* 970 etc.).

59 Hermes' praise of his own 'renowned origin' is ironic, given the circumstances of his birth. This god has a high opinion of his own value. For the repetition in ὀνομακλυτὸν ἐξονομάζων cf. *Od.* 4.278 ὀνομακλήδην . . . ὀνόμαζες.

60–1 Maia's cave is described by her son as fully furnished with maids (like Calypso's in *Od.* 5.199), and with other equipment (see 23n.). Despite this, Hermes declares his intention of stealing some of Apollo's tripods and cauldrons from Delphi (178–81).

62–86 While singing, Hermes is already planning his theft. He goes to Pieria and steals fifty of Apollo's cattle, which he drives backwards, disguising his own tracks with special sandals.

On the general motif of cattle-raiding as an exploit of adolescent or young men in Indo-European cultures see Johnston (2002).

62–6 The light-hearted rapidity of Hermes is again suggested by the fact that he has his next exploit already in mind. Cf. *Od.* 2.92 (etc.) νόος δέ οἱ ἄλλα μενοινᾶι (of Penelope's deceptions of the suitors). In 63–6 echoes of 20–4 mark the transition to this next episode, with cradle, lyre, the quest for cattle, and Hermes' rapid movement as he leaves the cave all again emphasised.

63–4 **καὶ τὴν μὲν . . . ὁ δ'** 'and the lyre he laid down . . . , but he . . . ' The subject of ὁ δ' is still Hermes.

64 **κρειῶν ἐρατίζων** is used of a lion at *Il.* 11.551, 19.660. In the event, despite his great desire, Hermes does not allow himself to share in the meat (130–3).

65 **ἆλτο κατὰ σκοπιήν:** 'he rushed off to a place of vantage' (or 'to put himself on the lookout'). Cf. *Od.* 14.261 ὀπτῆρας δὲ κατὰ σκοπιὰς ὄτρυνα νέεσθαι, and 17.430.

εὐώδεος: not in Homer. Cf. *H. Aph.* 66, and possibly Hes. fr. 26.21.

66 ὁρμαίνων δόλον αἰπὺν ἐνὶ φρεσίν: cf. *Od.* 4.843 φόνον αἰπὺν ἐνὶ φρεσὶν ὁρμαίνοντες, and Hes. *Th.* 589, *Op.* 83 δόλον αἰπύν. In these contexts αἰπύς means 'sheer, downright'.

67 φιλῆται: 'thieves'. The word first occurs in Hesiod (*Op.* 375), replacing Homeric ληιστήρ. The spelling φῑλήτης (with iota rather than eta) is supported by the ancient etymology which explained it as derived from Zeus's making love to Maia: cf. Hellanicus 4 F 19 (b) τ[ῆι] (or τ[ῶν]) δὲ γίγνεται Ἑρμ[ῆς] φιλήτης, ὅτι αὐτῆι φιλησίμ[ως] συνεκοιμ[ᾶτο, and West on Hes. *Op.* 375. Hellanicus is probably using the Hesiodic *Catalogue of Women* here: see Thomas (2007).

Hermes will become the 'leader of thieves' (175, 292): cf. E. *Rh.* 217 φιλητῶν ἄναξ, *Epigr. Gr.* 1108 τῶν φιλητέων ἄνακτα. For φῶτες φιλῆται cf. A. *Ch.* 987 φιλήτης ἀνήρ, S. fr. 933 Radt.

μελαίνης νυκτὸς ἐν ὥρηι: the whole of the following episode (68–141), including the theft of cattle, Hermes' journey, and his activities by the Alpheios, will take place during the night.

68–9 This description of sunset is un-Homeric. Cf. *H.* 31.15–16 ἔνϑ' ἄρ' ὅ γε στήσας χρυσόζυγον ἅρμα καὶ ἵππους | ϑεσπεσίους πέμπηισι δι' οὐρανοῦ ὠκεανόνδε. The Sun's chariot first appears in seventh-century literature and art: cf. Richardson on *H. Dem.* 63. The avoidance of normal epic formulae for sunsets may be partly due to the fact that the poet wants to indicate that the sun is just beginning to set at this point. When he reaches Onchestos (86–7) the old farmer is still at work outside. Cf. Shelmerdine (1982) 102–3.

70 Pieria in Thessaly is the first stopping-place on the way down from Olympus (cf. *H. Ap.* 216 etc.). In *Il.* 2.766 it is where Apollo breeds the mares of Admetus (unless the right reading there is Πηρείηι). It is also the birthplace of Apollo's companions the Muses (Hes. *Th.* 53–5). In Antoninus Liberalis' version of Hermes' theft (23), Apollo's cattle graze with those of Admetus (see 87–93n.).

ϑέων: 'in haste'. The variant ϑεῶν ('of the gods', with ὄρεα) may be due to ϑεῶν in 71.

71–2 The cattle are called immortal, although they are later killed, because they belong to a god. Cf. e.g. κρήδεμνον ἄμβροτον, *Od.* 5.346–7. The meadows in which they pasture are also ἀκηράσιοι, like the meadow of purity described by Hippolytus, from which he offers a garland to Artemis (E. *Hipp.* 73–8). Land consecrated to the gods could not normally be cultivated or pastured by ordinary flocks. In Homer ἀκηράσιος means 'unmixed' (*Od.* 9.205). See also 221n.

73 ἐΰσκοπος Ἀργειφόντης 'the keen-sighted Argos-slayer'. Cf. *H. Ap.* 200n.

74 πεντήκοντ' ἀγέλης: cf. *Od.* 12.128–30, where each of Helios' herds numbers fifty, and similar phrasing at *Il.* 11.678 πεντήκοντα βοῶν ἀγέλας.

75–8 'And he drove them by a wandering route through the sandy territory, turning their footprints round; he did not forget his crafty skill, reversing their hooves, the front ones behind, and the back ones in front, and he himself walked the opposite way [i.e. facing them].'

The backward-facing tracks are vividly described by the chorus of satyrs in Soph. *Ichneutai*, fr. 314.117–23: ἔα μάλα· | παλινστραφῆ τοι ναὶ μὰ Δία τὰ βήματα | εἰς τοὔμπαλιν δέδορκεν· αὐτὰ δ' εἴσιδε. | τί ἐστὶ τουτί; τίς ὁ τρόπος τοῦ τάγματ[ος; | εἰς τοὐπίσω τὰ πρόσθεν ἤλλακται, τὰ δ' αὖ | ἐνάντι' ἀλλήλοισι συμβ[εβλη]μένα· | δεινὸς κυκησμὸς εἶχ[ε τὸν βοη]λάτην, 'Good gracious! the footprints are reversed! They point backwards! ... The front marks have shifted to the rear, while some are entangled in two opposite directions! A strange confusion must have possessed their driver!' (tr. Lloyd-Jones).

Later versions drop this rather naïve device: in Apollodorus Hermes actually puts shoes on the cattle's hooves to disguise their footprints (3.10.2), and in Antoninus Liberalis (23) he ties brushwood to their tails to wipe away the traces. Herodotus (4.183.2) and Aelian (*NA* 16.33) both know of the cattle of the Lotophagoi, which graze backwards (ὀπισθονόμοι) because their horns curve downwards. Hermes' trick of driving the cattle backwards is imitated in the story of Cacus' cattle-theft: Livy 1.7.5, Virgil *A.* 8.209–12, etc.

75 πλανοδίας: this occurs only here, but cf. Hesychius πληνοδίαι· παρανόμωι ... τῆι πεπλανημένηι τῆς ὀρθῆς ὁδοῦ, τουτέστιν ἀδίκωι. It probably means 'by a wandering route', as in 210 ἐπιστροφάδην.

ψαμαθώδεα: only here and at 347, 350 in early epic; cf. A.R. 4.1376 etc.

76 ἴχνη: elsewhere the hymn has ἴχνια (218 etc.), but ἴχνος also occurs in early epic, and the contracted neuter plural is found at line 95 (ὄρη), and elsewhere in the *Hymns* (19.2, 27.4, 28.15); see Janko (1982) 144. ἀποστρέψας probably means that he turned the tracks round, with δολίης ... ἔβαινε explaining this in more detail.

δολίης δ' οὐ λήθετο τέχνης is used of Prometheus at Hes. *Th.* 547; cf. similar phrases at *Od.* 4.455, *Il.* 23.725, etc.

77–8 The language is deliberately complex and chiastic here, mirroring the ingenuity of the stratagem. M's reading πρώτας in 78 seems preferable, as it adds variation, and πρόσθεν could easily have replaced it. For the chiasmus between lines cf. 14–15, 193–4.

78 κατὰ δ' ἔμπαλιν αὐτὸς ἔβαινε 'and he himself walked the opposite way'. Cf. 211, where Hermes is said to keep the cattle's heads facing him. He could only drive them properly if he did so, and he disguises his own tracks with his special shoes. Some scholars take it as meaning that he himself also walked backwards: cf. εἰς τοὔμπαλιν in Soph. *Ichneutai*, fr. 314.119 (quoted in 75–8n.).

79–86 'And at once he wove sandals with plaited branches, on the sands of the seashore, not seen and not known before, wondrous works, mixing together tamarisks and myrtle shoots, from which then he bound together a bundle of fresh-sprouting brushwood, and securely (?) he tied beneath his feet light sandals, with their leaves still on them, which famous Argeiphontes snatched from Pieria, avoiding making a track, as though hastening on a long road, improvising in a unique manner.'

The poet is using extraordinary language here in order to describe Hermes' invention, and the length and complexity of this sentence is also clearly intended to emphasise the uniqueness of what is portrayed. It is hardly surprising that the manuscripts are in some confusion, and the right reading and interpretation are difficult to recover. The description which Apollo gives of Hermes' tracks at 222–6 indicates that they are extraordinary, very large, and suggest someone moving quickly. In 342–9 he again says that they were huge, and looked as if one were walking on two thin planks (349). This sounds like our earliest depiction in European literature of skis. In 79–86 they seem more like large snowshoes (or sandshoes). 86 also suggests that they enable Hermes to move fast. At the same time, their odd nature is designed to prevent Apollo from discovering who the thief is.

79 σάνδαλα: first here, and σάμβαλα in Eumelus *ap.* Paus. 4.33.2, and Sappho fr. 110 (a) L–P = 110 V. In Homer the normal words for footwear are πέδιλα or ὑποδήματα. Hermes' own πέδιλα enable him to move with divine speed (*Il.* 24.340–2, *Od.* 5.44–6), but what he invents here is something different, designed for this particular occasion. In later magical texts σάνδαλον (bronze or golden) and κηρύκειον are both symbols of underworld deities such as Hecate or Persephone: see Wortmann (1968) 155–60.

ῥιψίν 'with wicker branches'. Cf. *Od.* 5.256 ῥίπεσσι, Hdt. 4.71 ῥιψί. This emendation seems the best way of making sense of the text, since the manuscript's ἔριψεν would give us two verbs without a connective.

ἐπὶ ψαμάθοις ἁλίῃσιν: cf. *Od.* 3.38 (at Pylos).

80 Apart from ἔργα the language of this verse is un-Homeric. ἄφραστος recurs at 353, where it means 'impossible to see'. Cf. Hes. fr. 239.4, Hom. *Epigr.* 3.2 ('strange, inexpressible'). ἀνόητος occurs only here in early epic, and in this sense ('unthought of') in Parmenides and Philolaus. It usually means 'unthinking' in later literature. The use of repeated epithets with negative prefix is a common device for emphasis: cf. 168, 346, and Richardson on *H. Dem.* 200 (p. 221). διαπλέκειν is first used at Alcman fr. 1.38. For θαυματὰ ἔργα cf. 440, *H.* 7.34, Hes. *Sc.* 165, fr. 204.45. θαῦμα and cognate words are frequently used in this hymn, in relation to Hermes' exploits: cf. Jaillard (2007) 82–3.

81 Cf. *Il.* 10.467 συμμάρψας δόνακας μυρίκης τ' ἐριθηλέας ὄζους. μυρσινοειδής occurs first here (cf. Galen etc.), and μυρσίνη first in Archilochus. See also 134–7n.

82 νεοθηλέος ἀγκαλὸν ὕλης: ἀγκαλός (or ἀγκαλόν) is found nowhere else except at *P.Oxy.* 3354.9 (AD 257). It should mean 'armful', as ἀγκαλίς and ἀγκάλη sometimes do later.

83 ἀβλαβέως: 'harmlessly', i.e. perhaps without hurting his tender feet? ἀβλαβής is first in Sappho, and cf. the noun ἀβλαβίῃσι at 393. The nearest parallel is in Arrian (156 F 153), where after fitting snowshoes on their feet people walked ἀβλαβέως on the snow. But εὐλαβέως ('carefully') may be right.

ὑπὸ ποσσὶν ἐδήσατο σάνδαλα κοῦφα: cf. *Il.* 24.340 = *Od.* 5.44 (Hermes) αὐτίκ' ἔπειθ' ὑπὸ ποσσὶν ἐδήσατο καλὰ πέδιλα.

84 αὐτοῖσιν πετάλοισι: 'with leaves still on them'.

85 ὁδοιπορίην ἀλεείνων: if ἀλεείνων is correct this means 'avoiding making a track', or 'concealing his track'. Cf. Hesychius s.v. ἀλεάζειν· κρύπτειν, and

LfgrE s.v. ἀλεείνω. ὁδοιπορίη occurs first here; cf. *Il.* 24.375 ὁδοιπόρος, and ὁδοιπορίη in Herodotus etc.

86 οἷα τ' ἐπειγόμενος δολιχὴν ὁδόν: for the construction cf. 549, *H. Ap.* 233, and Xen. *Anab.* 1.5.91 σπεύδων πᾶσαν τὴν ὁδόν, *AP* 9.83.1 νηὸς ἐπειγομένης ὠκὺν δρόμον.

αὐτοτροπήσας: this occurs nowhere else, and the variant αὐτοπρεπὴς ὥς is also unique. αὐτοτροπεῖν is usually taken as 'to act in a unique way (like no one else)', but a better interpretation might be 'acting in an improvisatory way', like αὐτοσχεδιάζειν; cf. 55 ἐξ αὐτοσχεδίης. Hermes' invention is a brilliant piece of ad hoc ingenuity.

87–93 As Hermes goes through Onchestos he is observed by an old farmer who is working on his vineyard, and Hermes curtly orders him to pretend that he has seen and heard nothing, promising him a good vintage if he keeps quiet.

This brief episode introduces the only human character to appear in the hymn, and he is anonymous. Later (185–212) Apollo meets and interrogates him, and after a lengthy preamble the farmer rather evasively says that he thinks he did notice a small boy of some kind driving cattle backwards. This piece of information is immediately followed by a bird-omen which tells Apollo who the thief is (213–14). When Apollo brings him before Zeus, he again mentions the old man, who (he says) saw Hermes driving the cattle towards Pylos, after the point where their tracks were no longer visible on the harder ground (352–5). Thus the old man plays a part in the progression of the story, especially by being mentioned at the trial as a witness, to contradict Hermes' outright denial of guilt.

In another version of the myth, the witness is a man called Battos ('Stammerer' or 'Blabberer'). In Antoninus Liberalis' account (23) Hermes, who is not a child, meets him in Arcadia at a place called βάττου σκοπίαι. The story is an *aition* for a rock of this name, as Battos is punished for betraying the secret, in this case to Hermes himself in disguise, by being turned to stone. Ovid tells a similar tale (*Met.* 2.685–707). The version of Antoninus is prefaced by a scholion listing earlier authors who are said to have told the story, Nicander in his *Heteroioumena*, Hesiod in the *Great Ehoiai* (fr. 256 M–W), and other later ones. It seems that Nicander was Antoninus Liberalis' main source, and how much can be ascribed to the Hesiodic poem is unclear. The origin could be as the *aition* for a wayside stone herm of a particular shape. Holland (1926, 156–83) argued that the story of Battos was probably a development from the simpler version in our hymn (see especially pp. 173–5). Others, however, have thought it more likely that the Battos story is older and has been simplified by our poet for his own narrative purposes. The hymnic poet's plot would not allow Hermes to return and punish the old man for more or less giving him away, but the story is still effective, especially in the portrayal of the old man, who is caught between these two powerful gods, struggling not to betray Hermes altogether but also wishing to oblige Apollo.

The description of the farmer working on his vineyard resembles that of Laertes in *Od.* 24.220ff. Laertes' servants have gone to gather stones for a wall to the vineyard (*Od.* 24.224), and this may be echoed here at *H. Herm.* 87 and 188 (see below 87n.). Laertes also digs his vineyard, with bowed head (*Od.* 24.242 ~ *H. Herm.* 90), and the later description of the old man of Onchestos at *H. Herm.* 207 may echo *Od.* 1.193 and 11.193 of Laertes. Both are addressed as ὦ γέρον (*Od.* 24.244, *H. Herm.* 90, 190), and Apollo later addresses the old man as βατοδρόπε ('bramble-picker', 190), just as Laertes is wearing gloves to protect his hands from thorns (*Od.* 24.230). It seems likely that our poet has this Odyssean episode specifically in mind: see Shelmerdine (1986) 59–60.

The motif of the old man as a witness is parallel to that of the witnesses of the rape of Persephone in various versions of this myth (cf. Richardson on *H. Dem.* 24–6 and 75ff.). A similar motif recurs in other tales, such as that of Apollo and Coronis.

87 δέμων ἀνθοῦσαν ἀλωήν 'constructing [*or* working on] a flourishing vineyard'. Cf. 188, where δέμοντα . . . ἕρκος ἀλωῆς is again a possible conjecture. In *Odyssey* 24 Odysseus does not find Laertes' household at home because they have gone off αἱμασίας λέξοντες ἀλωῆς ἔμμεναι ἕρκος (224), and at *Od.* 18.359 the basic work of a farm labourer includes collecting stones and planting trees (αἱμασίας τε λέγων καὶ δένδρεα μακρὰ φυτεύων). Preparation of a vineyard would include terracing and building dry-stone walls, and ἐϋκτιμένη is regularly applied to ἀλωή (*Il.* 20.496 etc.). In 90 and 227, however, he is said to be digging (round) his plants, like Laertes (*Od.* 24.227). Cf. Hesiod's σκάφος οἰνέων (*Op.* 572). Columella (4.28.1–2) says that this can be done when the plants are already in bloom.

88 δι' Ὀγχηστὸν λεχεποίην: why Onchestos should be selected as the place of this encounter is unclear. One possibility is because of influence from the *Hymn to Apollo* (230–8), where it is singled out for special attention on Apollo's journey from Pieria (see *H. Herm.* 69–72) to Pytho: see Dornseiff (1938) 82, Janko (1982) 148–9, Schwabl (1986) 155–6. In that hymn it fits into a detailed itinerary through Boeotia, whereas in the case of Hermes its selection seems quite arbitrary. λεχεποίη is applied to Teumessos at *H. Ap.* 224, just a few lines before the passage about Onchestos. This strengthens the case for association between the two hymns. The epithet otherwise only recurs twice in Homer, at *Il.* 2.697, 4.383. See also Introduction 3(c) and Map 3.

89 Cf. 189 τὸν πρότερος προσέφη Λητοῦς ἐρικυδέος υἱός, in the parallel scene of Apollo and the old man. The first hemistich is not formular and recurs nowhere else in early Greek hexameter poetry. The structural parallelism may have suggested this repetition: see Van Nortwick (1975) 31–2, 123. For Μαίης ἐρικυδέος υἱός cf. 550, and *Od.* 11.576 Γαίης ἐρικυδέος υἱόν.

90 Cf. *Od.* 24.244 (to Laertes) ὦ γέρον, 227 λιστρεύοντα φυτόν (Laertes).

σκάπτεις: σκάπτειν is first used here; cf. Herodotus etc., and Hesiodic σκάφος.

ἐπικαμπύλος ὤμους: the epithet recurs only at Hes. *Op.* 427 ἐπικαμπύλα κᾶλα ('curved timbers'), which may explain M's reading, if a reminiscence of this phrase or a marginal gloss is responsible. In the scene with Laertes cf. *Od.* 24.242 ἤτοι ὁ μὲν κατέχων κεφαλὴν φυτὸν ἀμφελάχαινε, and cf. also Lucian *Tim.* 7 σκάπτει δὲ οἶμαι ἐπικεκύφως.

91–3 Hermes is promising the farmer a good vintage, but adds as an implied condition the warning not to betray him. The sequence of thought is abrupt, and some editors have assumed a lacuna after 91. But what he is saying is 'and just make sure you mind your own business'. The infinitives in 92–3 are used as imperatives.

91 **πολυοινήσεις:** this compound (conjectured by Ilgen) occurs only here, but cf. πολύοινος, πολυοινία, and εὐοινεῖν etc., in classical and later Greek.

92 For this proverbial form of expression cf. Dem. 25.89 οἱ μὲν οὕτως ὁρῶντες . . . ὥστε, τὸ τῆς παροιμίας, ὁρῶντες μὴ ὁρᾶν καὶ ἀκούοντες μὴ ἀκούειν, A. *PV* 447–8, *Sept.* 246, etc., and in Hebrew literature Isaiah 6.9–10 'Listen and listen, but never understand! Look and look, but never perceive!' The chiastic order of ἰδὼν μὴ ἰδὼν and κωφὸς ἀκούσας is elegant. The metrical variation of καί τε ἰδὼν μὴ ἰδών, with digamma observed and then neglected, shows the flexibility of the epic *Kunstsprache*. See Hopkinson (1982) 162–77 on such metrical variants, and *H. Ap.* 496n. κωφός means 'deaf' first here and in Heraclitus, as opposed to 'dumb'.

If the story of Battos was already known, there could possibly be an ironic echo of this here, since Battos was indeed silenced permanently because of his chattering.

93 καὶ σιγᾶν makes explicit the message of 92.

ὅτε μή τι καταβλάπτηι τὸ σὸν αὐτοῦ: 'in a case where nothing harms your own interest', i.e. where there is no personal incentive for you to do otherwise. Cf. E. *Ph.* 990 μὴ τὸ σὸν κωλυέτω, Aristides 49.360 εἰ μὴ τὸ σὸν κωλύει. καταβλάπτω is first used here, and recurs in Plato etc.

94–141 Hermes arrived at the river Alpheios with the cattle as the moon was rising before dawn, and after penning them in a stable and feeding them he prepared a fire. To do this he invented the art of kindling fire with a drill, and lit a great heap of logs. He then killed two of the cattle, roasted them, and spread their hides out on a rock, where they still remain today. He divided the meat into twelve portions, but despite his hunger did not taste any himself. He put all the meat away high up in the cave, burned the remainder (heads and feet), threw his sandals into the Alpheios, and put out and levelled the fire.

If Hermes is aiming for Mt Cyllene (cf. 142) this visit to the Alpheios marks a significant detour, since it is well to the west of this mountain. This surely confirms that the whole episode is intended to be aetiological, explaining the origin of a particular ritual or rituals practised there in later times. This is also made explicit by the preservation of the hides (124–6). Most scholars have linked the episode to the cult of the group of deities known as the Twelve Gods at Olympia (see 128–9n.). What Hermes seems to be doing is to institute a sacrificial feast for them, including himself, and the reason why he does not actually eat any of the meat is probably because the gods normally only receive the savour (cf. 130–4). Many of the details of his actions can be paralleled in later rituals, but the whole description is quite different from the usual Homeric scene of sacrifice. There however it is mortals who are performing these rites, whereas here it is a god. It remains paradoxical that Hermes' original motive for this theft of the cattle was said to be hunger. In later legends the Twelve Gods were arbiters in divine disputes, and Long (1987, 156–7) suggests that Hermes' action here is designed to gain the favour of the gods in his coming dispute with Apollo. This, however, is not made explicit. For further discussion see Burkert (1984), Clay (1989) 116–26, Leduc (2005) 141–66, Jaillard (2007) 101–64, Thomas (forthcoming).

94 τόσσον φάς: Homer uses ὣς εἰπών, and this phrase occurs only here in early epic.

συνέσευε: this compound verb (a virtually certain conjecture) is used first here, and recurs at Orph. *A.* 982. Cf. 106 συνέλασσεν.

βοῶν ἴφθιμα κάρηνα: once in Homer at *Il.* 23.260; cf. *H. Herm.* 302, 394, 402.

95 ὄρη σκιόεντα: cf. *Il.* 1.157 οὔρεά τε σκιόεντα.

αὐλῶνας κελαδεινούς 'echoing valleys'. αὐλών occurs first here (cf. Aeschylus etc.), and κελαδεινός elsewhere in early hexameter poetry is always used of Artemis, except *Il.* 23.208 (Zephyros).

97–8 Night is an accomplice of thieves like Hermes: cf. 15, Hes. *Op.* 605 ἡμερόκοιτος ἀνήρ, etc.; and for the contrast with daylight as the time for normal work cf. Hes. *Op.* 578–81, Call. *Hecale* fr. 74.22–8 Hollis, etc.

ὀρφναίη δ'... ἡ πλείων: cf. Homeric νύκτα δι' ὀρφναίην (*Il.* 10.83 etc., *H. Herm.* 578). For ἐπαύετο... νὺξ | ἡ πλείων ('the greater part') cf. *Il.* 10.252–3 παροίχωκεν [*or* παρῴχηκεν] δὲ πλέων νὺξ | τῶν δύο μοιράων. δαιμόνιος is only used in the vocative in Homer and Hesiod, but more generally of wonderful or divine things from Pindar onwards. Cf. Homeric ἀμβροσίη νύξ, which would not fit the verse here.

98 ὄρθρος... δημιοεργός: ὄρθρος is not Homeric, but occurs at Hes. *Op.* 577. The poet may have this passage (*Op.* 576–81) in mind here, as it describes how dawn advances men's work and progress. δημιοεργός is very effective as an epithet for dawn as the 'creator of public business'. Later δημιουργός will often be used metaphorically ('maker, creator'). Hesychius s.v. says that it can be used of the sun, which ripens and warms all things: ὁ ἥλιος, ὅτι πάντα πέσσει καὶ θέρει.

99–102 Hermes steals the cattle at sunset, is already at the Alpheios before dawn, and will be back at Cyllene as the day is actually dawning (142–3). Selene rises conveniently in time to illuminate his killing of the cattle and all that follows this. The elaborate description of the moon rising marks the beginning of the episode at the Alpheios, and is echoed at the end (141). Cf. also 98 and 143 ὄρθρος, ὄρθριος. The emphasis on the moon could be connected with the date of the ritual instituted here. At Olympia the main festival of Zeus took place at the full moon: the date of the monthly sacrifices to all the gods is unknown, but was possibly the first of the month (cf. Weniger (1920) 13–14).

99–100 In Hesiod (*Th.* 371–4) Selene is daughter of Theia and Hyperion, and Pallas is son of Kreios and Eurybie (375–8). Another genealogy of Sun, Moon, and Dawn is given by *H.* 31.2–7, where they are children of Euryphaessa and Hyperion. Megamedes ('Mighty Counsellor') does not occur elsewhere in such a mythical context. Ovid also calls Aurora a daughter of Pallas (*Met.* 9.421 etc.). The structure of the line is traditional for such genealogies: cf. *Il.* 2.566 etc.

102–3 The poet is here applying formulae to Hermes which are reserved in the Hesiodic poems solely for Heracles: (Διὸς) ἄλκιμος υἱός Hes. *Th.* 526, 950, fr. 35.5, 43 (a) 61, *Sc.* 320, and βοῦς ἤλασεν εὐρυμετώπους Hes. *Th.* 291, of the theft of Geryon's cattle. This may be significant in view of Heracles' association also with Olympia and the cult of the Twelve Gods there (see 128–9n.). Διὸς ἄλκιμος υἱός is a doublet of Διὸς ἀγλαὸς υἱός (432), and ἄλκιμος is specially appropriate here to Hermes' achievement.

103 **ἀδμῆτες** 'still innocent of the yoke' (West). This perhaps implies 'of their own accord', a feature which is often mentioned in later literature, e.g. Theocr. 11.12 ταὶ ὄϊες ποτὶ τὠλίον αὐταὶ ἀπῆνθον, *AP* 7.173 αὐτόμαται δείλῃ ποτὶ ταὐλίον αἱ βόες ἦλθον, etc. Kahn (1978, 48) compares the Homeric practice of sacrificing calves which are untamed and unyoked (*Il.* 10.292–3, *Od.* 3.382–3, Schol. *Od.* 12.353), and the poet may be influenced by the formula in these passages βοῦν εὐρυμέτωπον . . . | ἀδμήτην.

103–4 The description of this rustic setting is grandiose, signalling that it will be the place of a major event. αὔλιον and ληνός both occur first here. The former is described as a stone cavern (λάϊνον ἄντρον) at 401 (cf. Soph. *Ph.* 19 etc. where αὔλιον means a cave). ληνός ('water trough') recurs in Hippocrates, Theocritus, etc. ὑψιμέλαθρος is rare, recurring only in late hexameter poetry (Orphic hymns, Nonnus).

105 **ἐπεφόρβει:** pluperfect of φέρβω. The present tense occurs at Hes. *Op.* 377, *H.* 30.2, 4, etc.

106–8 **καὶ τὰς μὲν . . . σὺν δ' ἐφόρει:** καί here may be emphatic ('then') as in Homeric καὶ τότε introducing the main clause. Alternatively the δέ in 108 marks the start of the main clause. Where μέν is used like μήν with καί for emphasis, one usually has καὶ μέν, rather than καὶ . . . μέν as here (Denniston, *GP*² 390–1), and so the second alternative would be abnormal. But the run of the sentence seems to support it, since the main point ought to come at 108, the rest being preparatory to this.

106 **ἀθρόας:** the short-vowel first-declension accusative plural (ἀθρόᾰς) occurs quite often in Hesiod, and sometimes in later poetry (mostly Doric): cf. West, *Theogony* p. 85, *Works and Days* pp. 31–2. ἀθρόας would not fit into hexameter verse, unless scanned thus (¯ ˘˘), or ἄθρŏᾱς, which is abnormal, since a vowel before θρ is usually long in early hexameter verse. For further discussion see Edwards (1971) 141–65, Janko (1982) 58–62, 144–5.

οὔσας: this form, for normal epic ἐούσας, is paralleled by *Od.* 7.94 (ὄντας), *H. Ap.* 330 (οὖσα), and *H.* 19.32, 29.10, Hes. fr. 204.91. See Janko (1982) 117, 144–5, who notes the modification of ἄθροοι ἦσαν (*Od.* 1.27)/εἶεν (*H. Ap.* 152).

107 Cf. *Il.* 2.776, *Od.* 9.97 λωτὸν ἐρεπτόμενοι, 14.348 λωτόν ϑ' ἐρσήεντα, and for λωτός and κύπειρον together *Il.* 21.351, *Od.* 4.603.
108 πυρός δ' ἐπεμαίετο τέχνην 'and he was eager for the art of fire'. In Homer ἐπιμαίεσϑαι is used with the genitive, when it means 'strive after, seek to obtain', and with the accusative in the sense 'grasp, touch'. But cf. 511 σοφίης ἐκμάσσατο τέχνην (from ἐκμαίομαι), Bion 1.2 σοφὰν δ' ἐπεμαίετο τέχναν, and Aratus 89.
109–11 Hermes invents firesticks (πυρήϊα), the art of kindling fire by rotating a wooden drill in a second piece of wood. This is discussed in detail by Theophrastus (*HP* 5.9.6–7), who recommends bay (δάφνη) as the best wood to use for the drill, and various others for the wooden base. (Neither he nor any other author mentions pomegranate, which should rule out σιδείωι in 109, conjectured by Radermacher and Ludwich.) See also Morgan (1890) 13–64, and AHS on 108. If we keep the reading ἐπέλεψε σιδήρωι this ought to refer to trimming the leaves and bark of the drill, and ἄρμενον ἐν παλάμηι is best taken as referring to the drill, rather than to the wooden base (as AHS assume): cf. *Od.* 5.234, where the phrase is used of an axe, and *Il.* 18.600, of a potter's wheel rotated by the hands. This makes it less likely that there is a lacuna after 109. The description, however, is elliptical, since there is no mention of the second piece of wood or the action of kindling by friction. Possibly a line or lines have been lost after the first half of 110.

In connection with the following scene of sacrifice, the emphasis on Hermes' invention of this art of kindling fire suggests comparison with the story of another divine trickster and thief, Prometheus. In the *Theogony* the theft of fire follows after the institution of sacrificial ritual (535–69): see Burkert (1984). Burkert also suggests (836–7) that Hermes' action here can be compared to rituals where new fire is kindled, either from the light of the sun or by friction (cf. also Burkert (1985) 61–2). This was especially the case in the Roman cult of Vesta, where if the fire ever went out it had to be rekindled in such a way. Myths about the origin of fire are collected from across the world by Frazer (1930).
109–10 δάφνης . . . παλάμηι: for the language cf. Hes. *Th.* 30 δάφνης . . . ὄζον, and Achilles' oath by the σκῆπτρον at *Il.* 1.236–8 . . . περὶ γάρ ῥά ἑ χαλκὸς ἔλεψε | φύλλα τε καὶ φλοιόν· νῦν αὖτέ μιν υἷες Ἀχαιῶν | ἐν παλάμηις φορέουσι . . . ἐπιλέπειν occurs only here. For ϑερμὸς ἀϋτμή cf. Hes. *Th.* 696. Similar examples of masculine epithet with feminine noun are *Od.* 12.369 ἡδὺς ἀϋτμή, 6.122 ϑῆλυς ἀϋτή; cf. Chantraine, *GH* I 252.
111 Cf. 25 Ἑρμῆς τοι πρώτιστα . . . πυρήϊα πῦρ τ' should perhaps be taken together, to mean 'the art of making fire by firesticks'. πυρήϊα occurs first here, later (πυρεῖα) in Sophocles etc. ἀναδιδόναι is also a new compound in epic, but cf. Asius fr. 8 etc. It suggests that Hermes' invention will be a gift for others, i.e. for mankind, like Prometheus' gift of fire to men. The invention of firesticks was also ascribed to Prometheus later as a rationalisation of the older myth of his theft of fire (Diod. 5.67.2).
112–13 Cf. *Il.* 21.364, *Od.* 18.308 ξύλα κάγκανα, and Hes. *Op.* 427 πολλ' ἐπικαμπύλα κᾶλα. On the origin and use of the word κᾶλα see West on Hes. *Op.*

427, Janko (1982) 145–6. The word has its original sense of 'wood for burning' here. There is strong alliteration of kappa in 112.

112 κατουδαίωι: cf. Hes. fr. 150.9 and 18 Κατουδαῖοι, as a proper name. The word is not Homeric.

113 οὖλα . . . ἐπηετανά: in Homer οὖλος means 'thick, close', or 'woolly', but it is used by Theophrastus of wood to mean 'close-grained, tough'. ἐπηετανά is scanned with synizesis (⏑ – ⏑ ⏑), as at Hes. *Op.* 607, and sometimes later. As often in this hymn, an accumulation of epithets is used where Homeric epic would normally be more sparing.

114 φῦσαν: this is the early epic and classical form of the word, with φύζαν as a much later and perhaps also dialect form. In Homer φῦσαι refers to Hephaestus' bellows (*Il.* 18.372 etc.).

115 βίη κλυτοῦ Ἡφαίστοιο: cf. Hes. *Sc.* 244 κλυτοῦ Ἡφαίστοιο.

116–18 The resistance of the cattle and the superhuman strength of the infant god are vividly emphasised. Cf. also 405–8. Burkert (1984, 837) compares the exploits of ephebes at Eleusis and elsewhere in 'lifting the cattle' for sacrifice.

116 τόφρα δ': the δέ is apodotic here ('then indeed . . .').

ὑποβρυχίας 'bellowing': cf. βρυχάομαι ('bellow') etc. The second upsilon ought to be long, and the scansion may be ὑποβρῡχίας with synizesis of -ιας. In Homer this occurs mainly with proper names, but cf. *Il.* 3.414 σχετλίη, 2.811 πόλιος, *Od.* 8.560, 574 πόλιας. ὑποβρῠ́χιος with short vowel normally means 'underwater' (*H.* 33.12 etc.); cf. *Od.* 5.319 ὑπόβρυχα.

118–19 Cf. 41–2, where Hermes treats the tortoise in a similar way. Here he bores through the spines of the oxen, rather than cutting their throats (as would be usual in a sacrifice).

119 ἐγκλίνων δ' ἐκύλινδε 'and leaning on them he rolled them over'. ἐγκλίνων is probably intransitive, rather than 'turning them'. It occurs first here, then in fifth-century and later literature.

δι' αἰῶνας τετορήσας: cf. 42 αἰῶν' ἐξετόρησεν. δι' . . . τετορήσας should be taken together as a *tmesis*. τετορήσας appears to be a reduplicated aorist form of τορέω: cf. *Il.* 5.337 ἀντετόρησεν. At 178 and 283, however, we have ἀντιτορήσων and ἀντιτοροῦντα, as at *Il.* 10.267 ἀντιτορήσας. It looks as if a compound ἀντιτορέω has been created through misunderstanding of the reduplicated form.

120 ἔργωι δ' ἔργον ὄπαζε 'and he followed one job with another'. Cf. Hes. *Op.* 382 ἔργον ἐπ' ἔργωι ἐργάζεσθαι.

πίονα δημῶι: *Il.* 23.750, *Od.* 9.464 support M's reading πίονα rather than the variant πίονι.

121–3 After cutting up the meat Hermes roasts it on spits in the normal Homeric manner, and then leaves it in its place while he attends to the hides.

121 δουρατέοισι: in Homer this is only used of the Wooden Horse, at *Od.* 8.493, 512.

122 νῶτα γεράσμια: the saddles or back-portions are special honorific cuts (cf. 129 τέλεον δὲ γέρας). γεράσμιος occurs first here.

122–3 **μέλαν αἷμα | ἐργμένον ἐν χολάδεσσι** 'the black blood enclosed within the guts'.

123 **τὰ δ' αὐτοῦ κεῖτ' ἐπὶ χώρης** 'and the remaining parts lay there on the ground'.

124–6 It was common in sacrificial ritual for the hides to be set aside for special treatment. Sometimes they were dedicated: cf. Dio Chrys. 1.53 (a rustic shrine to Heracles near the Alpheios), Schol. T *Il.* 22.159 (to Heracles), Longus 2.30.5, 31.3 (rural offerings). Sometimes they were given to the priests, or sold for expenses. Hermes spreads them on a rock, and there they remain as relics of this event. The poet is giving an *aition* for what was still on display, whether some actual hides or a rock-formation. Similarly, the skin of Marsyas was on display, turned to stone, at Kelainai (Hdt. 7.26, Xen. *Anab.* 1.2.8). See also Burkert (1972) 7, 14–16, 127, and for such relics in general Boardman (2002).

124 **καταστυφέλωι:** the feminine form read by M may be correct. Cf. epic ἀθανάτη etc.

ἐνὶ πέτρηι: Burkert (1972, 15 n. 13) suggested ἐπί as at 404, but ἐνί is also possible.

125–6 **τὰ μέτασσα . . . πολυχρόνιοι . . . | δηρὸν δὴ μετὰ ταῦτα καὶ ἄκριτον:** the repeated emphasis on the lapse of time is not impossible in this poet's rather full style (cf. 113n.), and here it is surely designed to give special weight to this aetiological point. τὰ μέτασσα is adverbial; cf. μέτασσαι as an adjective at *Od.* 9.221. ἄκριτον is also adverbial, meaning 'endlessly'; cf. 577, and *H.* 19.26 (ἄκριτα). πολυχρόνιος occurs only here in early epic poetry; cf. Hdt. etc.

127 **χαρμόφρων** 'with joyful spirit'. This occurs only here in literature. Cf. Hesychius χαρμόφρων· ὁ Ἑρμῆς, perhaps quoting the hymn. Other deities are described as 'a joy to mortals': cf. *H. Dem.* 269 with Richardson's note.

πίονα ἔργα 'the rich works (of cooking)'. This is used of farmland in Homer (*Il.* 12.283, *Od.* 4.318). For its use to refer to sacrificial meat cf. ἔρδειν meaning 'to sacrifice'.

128 **λείωι ἐπὶ πλαταμῶνι** 'on a smooth slab'. The phrase recurs in A.R. 1.365. πλαταμών is first used here, then in Aristotle and later literature. Hermes spreads out the meat in order to cut it up.

128–9 **καὶ ἔσχισε δώδεκα μοίρας | κληροπαλεῖς . . . ἑκάστηι:** cf. *Od.* 14.434–8, where Eumaeus divides the meat of a pig into seven portions, offering one to Hermes and the Nymphs, and giving Odysseus the back-portions as a special honour (γέραιρεν). For γέρας προσέθηκε cf. A. *PV* 82–3 θεῶν γέρα | συλῶν ἐφημέροισι προστίθει (of Prometheus). Here προσέθηκεν indicates that Hermes *adds* to each portion (ἑκάστηι) a special honorific cut. No explanation of this twelve-fold division is offered, but the language seems to imply that the portions are intended as offerings to important persons. Most scholars have assumed that this should be connected to the cult of the Twelve Gods, widely attested later in Greece as a group of deities, whose names varied from place to place. A cult of this kind is otherwise first attested at Athens in the late sixth century, when the younger Pisistratus, son of Hippias, as archon in 522–1 BC instituted the altar of the Twelve Gods in the Agora (Th. 6.54.6). Pindar (*O.* 5.5, 10.48–9) ascribes to Heracles the foundation of six double altars to twelve gods at Olympia. Herodorus (*FGrH* 31 F 34, *c.* 400 BC) says that one of these double altars is dedicated to Apollo and Hermes, and Pausanias (5.14.8) that they share a single altar because Hermes invented the lyre and Apollo the *kithara*. Moreover, another of these altars was assigned to Alpheios and Artemis. Since Hermes is at the river Alpheios, it is reasonable to assume that the narrative is related to the institution of sacrifice to the Twelve Gods at Olympia, and may be intended as an *aition* for this cult. At 398–400 the cattle are in Pylos, at the ford of the Alpheios (cf. *H. Ap.* 398, 423nn.). The exact geography is uncertain, but a reference to the cult at Olympia looks probable. In this case the reason why the poet is not more explicit could be that (mythologically speaking) the Olympic Games have not yet been founded when Hermes makes his sacrifice, since they were ascribed in the first instance to Heracles. On cults of the Twelve Gods see Long (1987) especially 154–7, Georgoudi (1996), and Johnston (2002) 125–6. See also Jaillard (2007) 114–18, on the analogy between Hermes' actions and the later rituals of τραπεζώματα and θεοξένια, i.e. special feasts offered to the gods.

129 κληροπαλεῖς: 'distributed by lot'. This occurs nowhere else. Hermes is himself the god of allotment (cf. Ar. *Pax* 365 etc.), and so appropriately uses this method, but in this case each portion is a τέλεον γέρας, which suggests some equalisation (cf. Burkert (1984) 838–9).

τέλεον . . . γέρας: in Homer only τέλειος is used (cf. *H. Herm.* 526); τέλεος is used in fifth-century and later literature. The word is applied technically to sacrificial animals (e.g. *Il.* 1.66 etc. and in inscriptions), meaning 'perfect, without blemish', or more generally to sacrifices (e.g. Th. 5.47 ἱερὰ τέλεα). γέρας also continued to be used of a privileged portion of a sacrifice later: cf. LSJ s.v., Stengel (1920) 32, 40, 106. Hermes is also the patron god of heralds, and it was one of the roles of the κῆρυξ to perform a sacrifice: cf. *Il.* 18.558–9, *Od.* 15.319–24, Ath. 160A, and Farnell, *Cults* v 36–7, Stengel (1920) 50.

130–2 Hermes is very hungry, but still refrains from eating. The best explanation of this is that he does so as a god, since the gods enjoy only the savour of the sacrificial meat. It cannot be an allusion to a ritual of bloodless sacrifice to Hermes (which sometimes occurred: Farnell, *Cults* v 30), since the cattle have been killed. Burkert also compares other rituals where those who are making the sacrifice do not themselves share in the meat (1984, 837).

130 ὁσίης κρεάων: 'the holy rite of the meat', or possibly 'his own due of the meat' (West). It may be unwise to try to draw too many implications from the use of ὁσίη here. Clearly it indicates that what is done has a 'ritual' significance, and that it is ὅσιον, i.e. justified from a religious viewpoint, to eat the meat. The word recurs at 173 and 470: see nn., and Richardson on *H. Dem.* 211, and cf. also Jaillard (2007) 107–8. κρεάων is a unique instance in early poetry instead of the usual metrically equivalent κρειῶν: see Janko (1982) 137.

131–2 ὀδμὴ γάρ μιν ἔτειρε . . . | ἡδεῖ': cf. *Od.* 4.441–2 τεῖρε γὰρ αἰνῶς | . . . ὀδμή, and (in the episode of the Cattle of the Sun) 12.332 ἔτειρε δὲ γαστέρα λιμός, 369 κνίσης . . . ἡδὺς ἀϋτμή.

132 ἐπεπείθετο θυμὸς ἀγήνωρ: this formula is used twelve times in the *Odyssey* (*Od.* 2.103 etc.), which supports M's reading.

133 περᾶν ἱερῆς κατὰ δειρῆς 'to pass it down his sacred throat'. The transitive use of περάω seems to be unique, but cf. perhaps forms of πέρνημι, meaning originally 'transport for sale'. The reading περῆν' for περῆναι (from περαίνω) is not acceptable because this infinitive form is not elided.

134–7 This is usually taken to mean that Hermes puts the meat and fat away in the cave, leaving them in a high place, as 'evidence of his recent theft', and then piles more wood on the fire and burns all the heads and feet. This would again suggest (as at 123) that some relics may have been preserved later, which were said to represent Hermes' sacrifice. However, the text and interpretation of 135–7 remain uncertain. In 136 φωρῆς is supported by 385, where M alone has φωρήν, the other MSS φωνήν. φωρή occurs first here and at 385, then in Hellenistic and later literature.

Hermes' action may be compared to that of hunters who display trophies of their kills, as he does with the hides. Crudden (1994, 150) compares *Il.* 10.458–68, where Odysseus takes the spoils of Dolon, holds them up high (ὑψόσ' ἀνέσχεθε) as an offering to Athena, and then again lifting them up (ὑψόσ' ἀείρας) sets them on a tamarisk bush, and makes a sign (σῆμα) of reeds and tamarisk to mark the spot. On his return from his mission he sets them on the prow of his ship. It may be relevant that *Il.* 10.467 συμμάρψας δόνακας μυρίκης τ' ἐριθηλέας ὄζους resembles *H. Herm.* 81, suggesting possible reminiscence. Cf. also Leduc (2005) 159, on Hermes' use of the meat as ἀναθήματα, testifying to his exploits.

137 οὐλόποδ' οὐλοκάρηνα: οὐλόπους occurs only here, and οὐλοκάρηνος at *Od.* 19.246 is an epithet, meaning 'with curly hair'. They can hardly go with τὰ μέν, as Hermes would then wipe out the σῆμα he has just created, and they do not fit well with ξύλα. Either we must take them substantivally, as a ritual formula meaning 'heads and hooves, whole and entire' (cf. ὁλοκαύτωμα, οὐλοθυσία), or else the text needs correction. Cf. Thomas (forthcoming), who reads τὰ δ' ἐπὶ in 136 ('and the rest . . .').

Heads and feet of sacrificial animals were often given separate treatment, being reserved for the deity or for the priests, or alternatively burnt: cf. Stengel (1910) 85–91, Meuli (1946) 261–2, Burkert (1984) 837–8.

κατεδάμνατ': this compound form of the verb occurs only here.

138 ἐπειδή: M's reading is preferable to the conjecture ἐπεί τοι, since ἐπεί τοι is causal, whereas a temporal sense is needed here (cf. Denniston, *GP*² 545–6).

κατὰ χρέος 'in due manner' (cf. Latin *rite*), or 'as was required'.

δαίμων: it may be significant that Hermes is first referred to as a god here, after his sacrificial ritual. Cf. also 154 θεός.

139–41 Hermes seems to be carefully obliterating traces of his crime, and yet he has apparently left the hides and meat behind. Burkert (1984, 838) compares rituals where traces of the sacrifice must afterwards be concealed, but this does not seem to fit here so well.

140 ἀνθρακιὴν δ' ἐμάρανε: cf. *Il.* 9.213 ἀνθρακιὴν στορέσας. ἐμαράνε is aorist of μαραίνω, as in *Il.* 21.347 ἀγξηράνῃ.

ἀμάθυνε: 'levelled'. Cf. *Il.* 9.593 πόλιν δέ τε πῦρ ἀμαθύνει.

141 παννύχιος: presumably 'in the dead of night', rather than 'all night long'. This might be the sense also at *Il.* 23.105.

κατέλαμπε: this is better here than the variant ἐπέλαμπε, which is used of the sun 'shining forth' or 'coming out' from a cloud or darkness (*Il.* 17.650). The compound occurs first here, then in fifth-century and later literature.

142–83 Hermes returns to Mt Cyllene near dawn and stealthily goes back to his cradle, but his mother sees him and scolds him. Hermes however proclaims to her that he intends to obtain the same privilege and honour as Apollo, and that if Zeus will not grant this he will become the leader of all thieves. If Apollo tracks him down he also intends to go and raid his temple at Pytho and carry off his wealth.

143–5 The sequence 'neither gods nor men met him, nor did even the dogs bark' resembles *H. Dem.* 44–6 ('neither gods nor men, nor birds'). Dogs were thought to be especially sensitive to the supernatural: cf. *Od.* 16.162–3 where they see Athene before Telemachus is able to do so, with Hoekstra's comment.

143 ὄρθριος: this strictly speaking means 'at cock-crow', hence while it is still dark (155). Dawn comes only at 184. The adjective occurs first here and at Theognis 863.

οὐδέ τίς οἱ: cf. *Il.* 6.101 for this phrase with neglect of the digamma of οἱ, and Chantraine, *GH* I 147–8.

δολιχῆς ὁδοῦ 'in the course of his long journey'.

144 = *Od.* 9.521, *H. Aph.* 35.

145 Διὸς δ' ἐριούνιος Ἑρμῆς: for this genitive cf. *Il.* 2.527 Ὀϊλῆος τάχυς Αἴας, and later examples of Μαιάδος Ἑρμῆς, e.g. Hipponax fr. 35 West, *AP* 6.334.3, *APl* 1.11.3.

146–7 Hermes slips sideways through the keyhole of his mother's μέγαρον, like an autumn breeze or mist. For δοχμωθείς cf. Hes. *Sc.* 389. κλήϊθρον occurs first here, for Homeric κληΐς, meaning 'keyhole', whereas later κλῆιθρον is usually used in Attic Greek for the bar of a door. Hermes' clandestine entry resembles the dream image in *Od.* 4.795–841, which enters Penelope's chamber παρὰ κληῗδος ἱμάντα (802) and leaves the same way (836). In *Od.* 6.20 Athene comes to Nausicaa in a dream: ἡ δ' ἀνέμου ὡς πνοιὴ ἐπέσσυτο. Cf. also *Il.* 1.359, where Thetis is ἠΰτ' ὀμίχλη, and for the double simile cf. A.R. 4.877 (Thetis) αὐτὴ δὲ πνοιῇι ἰκέλη δέμας ἠΰτ' ὄνειρος. Hermes is himself god of dreams (14), but also a closed door cannot keep a thief out. Thieves are credited with magic powers, such as the ability to pass through keyholes, in other popular traditions. See Bloomfield (1923) 97–133 (especially 118–19), and Radermacher 102.

148 Either 'going straight on he reached the rich sanctuary of the cavern', or 'making straight for the cave he reached its rich inner sanctum' (cf. *Il.* 15.693 etc. for the genitive).

νηόν: νηός originally meant the 'dwelling place' (cf. ναίω) of a deity, and so can be used of Maia's home. It can also later refer to the inner part of a temple (cf. perhaps Hdt. 1.183.1, 6.19.3, etc.). But the use of πίονα νηόν here may be a further sign of Hermes' recent assertion of his divinity, like δαίμων (138) and θεός (154).

149 προβιβῶν: cf. Homeric προβιβῶντι/-ος (*Il.* 13.807, 16.609) as if from προβιβάω, but κοῦφα ποσὶ προβιβάς *Il.* 13.18 etc.

ὥς περ ἐπ' οὔδει 'as (one would) on the ground'.

150–4 There must be an asyndeton at some point after 150. There are several other examples in this hymn (17, 25, 111, 237, 438, 447, 478, 482, 512), but in most cases the reason is more obvious. The nearest parallel to this is at 235–9, where a simile with ἠΰτε is involved, describing Hermes curled up in his baby clothes. ἠΰτε is used with asyndeton in Homer when it begins a sentence (*Il.* 2.455, 469, etc.), and at 237 it introduces the new sentence. Given the similarity of these two passages, punctuation after εἰλυμένος would be possible. But strictly speaking εἰλυμένος should go with κεῖτο, and describe Hermes as he is in his cradle. It is best, therefore, to begin the new sentence with σπάργανον.

151 σπάργανον: first here, but cf. Hes. *Th.* 485 σπαργανίσασα.

152 περ' ἰγνύσι: 'around his haunches'. ἰγνύς is a variant form of the more usual ἰγνύη (cf. *Il.* 13.212, Hippocrates, and later). It probably does not recur before Nicander (*Ther.* 278). This is the earliest example of elision of περί, which is found also in Pindar (*O.* 6.38 etc.). In compound forms, however, it occurs at Hes. *Th.* 678 (περίαχε), and in Aeschylus (*Ag.* 1147, *Eum.* 634). Forssmann (1964, 28–31) conjectured περὶ γνύσι, by analogy with forms such as γνύξ, γνύπετος etc. But his objection to ἰγνύς on the grounds that it does not occur elsewhere in early Greek is not cogent. περ' ἰγνύῃσι in Theocr. 25.242 could, if correct, be due to early epic influence (cf. Gow ad loc.). The variant παρ' ἰγνύσιν is also possible, but may be due to an early conjecture.

λαῖφος ἀθύρων: λαῖφος refers to the clothing or blanket in which Hermes is wrapped, and ἀθύρων, meaning 'toying with', is used with an internal accusative, as at *H.* 19.15. Cf. also Pi. *N.* 3.44 (ἔργα) etc., and ἀθυρομένη passive at *H. Herm.* 485.

153 ἐπ' ἀριστερὰ χειρός 'on his left-hand side', as at *Od.* 5.277; cf. Pi. *P.* 6.19 ἐπὶ δεξιὰ χειρός etc. This description of Hermes again behaving like a baby culminates with him still secretly holding onto the lyre, his prize toy.

154–83 This comic exchange between Hermes and Maia is the first of three confrontations which articulate the central part of the hymn, the others being those of Hermes with Apollo and Zeus (Clay (2006) 127). Both speakers are well characterised, Maia as the angry mother scolding her precocious and undisciplined child, Hermes boisterous and unrepentant, asserting his claim to divine honour equal to that of his grown-up half-brother Apollo, and threatening even worse crimes to come.

154 **θεὰν θεός:** cf. *Od.* 5.97 θεὰ θεόν, of Calypso and Hermes. For other parallels with the meeting of Hermes and Calypso cf. 4, 227–34nn.

155–61 Maia's style and language are colloquial and comic in tone.

155 **τίπτε . . . πόθεν:** cf. Homeric τίς πόθεν.

ποικιλομῆτα: cf. 514, and 13 αἱμυλομήτην, etc.

τόδε: 'hither', as at *Il.* 14.298, *Od.* 1.409, etc.

156 **ἀναιδείην ἐπιειμένε:** cf. *Il.* 1.149, 9.372, in both cases used by Achilles of Agamemnon. The poet may have Achilles' speech in book 9 in mind: cf. also 160–1n.

157–9 **ἤ . . . ἤ:** this probably means 'surely . . . rather than . . .', i.e. Maia predicts Hermes' punishment as certain (cf. Càssola). This makes better sense than ἤ . . . ἤ as two equal alternatives, and the repetition of σε in 159 also supports the first view. For ἤ meaning 'rather than' without an explicit comparative cf. *H. Ap.* 264–6, LSJ s.v. B I. The threat is typical of punishments meted out to insubordinate deities.

157 **ἀμήχανα:** this poet is fond of ἀμήχανος and ἀμηχανίη: cf. 257, 295, 346, 434, 447.

δεσμά: the Homeric form is δέσματα: cf. 409, and *H. Ap.* 129, *H.* 7.13.

158 **Λητοΐδου:** this matronymic form is used seven times in this hymn, and nowhere in Homer or the other *Hymns*. It recurs at Hes. *Sc.* 479, fr. 51.3, Alc. fr. 67.3, *CEG* 302.1 (sixth century BC), and in Pindar. In this hymn, the use of the matronymic could be favoured as a way of distinguishing the two sons of Zeus, Apollo and Hermes, as with Μαιάδος υἱός (73 etc.), Μαίης ἐρικυδέος υἱός (89 etc.).

διὲκ προθύροιο περήσειν: cf. 271 διὰ προθύροιο περῆσαι, *Od.* 18.101 ἕλκε διὲκ προθύροιο λαβὼν ποδός (of Odysseus and the defeated beggar Iros).

159 **φέροντα** 'plundering'. Cf. ἄγειν καὶ φέρειν, and φέρειν on its own at E. *Hec.* 804, Ar. *Eq.* 205, etc.

μεταξύ: if this has a temporal sense it should be 'in the mean time'. However, Radermacher takes it with κατ' ἄγκεα, i.e. 'in the glens amid (the mountains)'. Neither seems entirely natural, and Càssola adopts the conjecture μέταζε, meaning 'in future, afterwards', as in Hes. *Op.* 394 τὰ μέταζε, where again τὰ μεταξύ is a variant.

φιλητεύσειν: the verb occurs only here. For the spelling see 67n.

160–1 **ἔρρε πάλιν:** a very strong expression, like 'to Hell with you!' Cf. ἐρρέτω in *Il.* 9.377 etc. Maia's final sentence however is somewhat less extreme, expressing exasperation at her impossible child.

160 **μέριμναν:** see on 44 (43–6n.).

162 **μύθοισιν . . . κερδαλέοισι** 'with crafty speech'. Hermes' reply is not so much deceitful, but rather concerned to assert his potential role as a master of trickery and theft. The verse (with τὸν δ') is repeated at 260 and 463 and is unique to this hymn. Cf. τὸν δ'... μύθοισι προσηύδα μειλιχίοισι (*Il.* 6.343). It is clearly specific to the context of Hermes' verbal skill. See Van Nortwick (1975) 46–7, 124.

163–5 Cf. *Il.* 20.200–2 = 20.431–3: Πηλεΐδη, μὴ δή μ' ἐπέεσσί γε νηπύτιον ὣς | ἔλπεο δειδίξεσθαι, ἐπεὶ σάφα οἶδα καὶ αὐτὸς | ἠμὲν κερτομίας ἠδ' αἴσυλα μυθήσασθαι. The similarities with 163–5 make Pierson's conjecture δεδίσκεαι in 163 (meaning 'you frighten') very probable (cf. also 165), and support αἴσυλα in 164 as against the variant ἄρμενα. The form δεδίσκομαι for the commoner δε(ι)δίσσομαι is supported by the imperfect ἐδεδίσκετο at Ar. *Lys.* 564, and could have arisen by analogy with the Homeric forms δειδίξεσθαι, δειδίξασθαι. The poet has adapted the sense of the Homeric passage (formulaic perhaps in such contexts) to this situation. There is unusual interlacing of the main and relative clauses, with ταρβαλέον (165) sandwiched in the middle of the latter. It is parallel to νήπιον and has the same emphatic position in the verse.

165 ταρβαλέον: This rare word occurs first here and later in Sophocles etc.

ὑπαιδείδοικεν is a variant form of the usual Homeric ὑποδδειδ-, where the reduplicated delta replaces original digamma (-δϝ-).

166–7 Cf. 464–5 αὐτὰρ ἐγώ σοι | τέχνης ἡμετέρης ἐπιβήμεναι οὔ τι μεγαίρω. There Hermes speaks of sharing his musical skill with Apollo. Here the reference is vague, and he does not specify what kind of skill he has in mind.

167 βουκολέων 'tending, looking after'. This is a conjecture, but makes reasonable sense. From the basic meaning 'herd (cattle)' βουκολεῖν comes to be used more generally to mean 'tend' in classical and later Greek: cf. Gutzwiller (2006) 381–90 for examples and discussion. The MSS reading βουλεύων can hardly be right, since it would need to be followed by dative rather than accusative, and ἐπιβήσομαι cannot take a direct object.

168 ἀδώρητοι καὶ ἄλιστοι: both epithets occur first here, ἀδώρητος next in Euripides, ἄλλιστος in Euphorion. The variant ἄπαστοι ('without tasting food'), which occurs at *H. Dem.* 200, is read by Radermacher, who argues that its comic exaggeration suits Hermes better. But his chief concern is for the honours due to him as a god, and gifts and prayers go better in this case. For this reduplication of negative epithets cf. 80, with comment.

169 αὐτοῦ τῇδε: again emphatic ('on this very spot') as in Hdt. 7.141.2 αὐτοῦ τῇδε μενέομεν, ἔστ' ἂν καὶ τελευτήσωμεν, and αὐτοῦ τῇδε μένουσα in the Homeric epigram at *Vita Herodotea Homeri* 139 Allen etc.

170–2 Hermes forcefully expresses the alternatives, a life of perpetual leisure and prosperity in heaven or one of inactivity in this gloomy cavern. ὀαρίζειν has implications of easy and pleasurable familiarity and social (or sometimes sexual) intercourse, whereas θαασσέμεν is probably here like ἧσθαι, which can be used in a pejorative sense of useless inactivity. At 468 however θαάσσεις is applied to Apollo's seat of honour in heaven. The triple epithets with asyndeton in 171 are a further rhetorical flourish, especially as they are all more or less equivalent in sense.

172 ἀμφὶ δὲ τιμῆς: cf. *H. Dem.* 85 ἀμφὶ δὲ τιμήν, where again this introduces a new sentence, closing the verse with enjambment, 'but as for honour...' (cf. Richardson ad loc.). The dative plural τιμῆις is an attractive suggestion ('privileges'), but the genitive is used at *Il.* 16.285, *Od.* 8.267.

173 κἀγώ: this crasis is un-Homeric. Cf. Hes. *Th.* 284 χὠ, *H. Dem.* 227 κοὐ, and West, *Theogony* p. 100.

τῆς ὁσίης ἐπιβήσομαι ἧς περ Ἀπόλλων: 'I shall acquire [*lit.* set foot upon] the same divine worship as Apollo has'. ὁσίη (cf. 130, 470) must here refer to all the rites or honours due to him as a god. The form of expression echoes 166. For the first time Hermes openly declares his real aim, to put himself on the same level as Apollo.

174–5 Cf. *Il.* 1.324 εἰ δέ κε μὴ δώῃσιν ἐγὼ δέ κεν αὐτὸς ἕλωμαι. Hermes answers Maia's assertion that he will not be allowed to practise as a thief (see 157–9n.). This is ironic, since Hermes will indeed become the prince of thieves anyway (292).

175 δύναμαι: best taken as parenthetic ('as I can'): cf. (εἰ) δύνασαι addressed to a god in prayer (e.g. *Il.* 1.393, 16.515), or parenthetic δύνασαι γάρ at *Od.* 5.25, addressed to Athene. The alternative is to punctuate after πειρήσω, understanding 'to gain the same honour', and then take δύναμαι... εἶναι as an explanatory sentence in asyndeton; but this seems much less natural.

176–81 Hermes' speech ends in a resounding climax, with the boldest threat of all, to rob the sacred temple of Apollo itself. The catalogue of its treasures alludes to the proverbial wealth of Delphi: cf. 335, where Apollo refers to the traditional taunt that he is φιλολήϊος (and 494–5, 549). For this theme, and the reputation for greed of the Delphic priests, see *H. Ap.* 535–7, 540–3nn., and *Il.* 9.404–5.

177 Literally this means 'I think that something else even greater (i.e. worse) will befall him.'

178 ἀντιτορήσων: cf. *Il.* 10.267 ἐξέλετ' Αὐτόλυκος πυκινὸν δόμον ἀντιτορήσας. Autolycus was Hermes' pupil in the art of deception, or Hermes' son: *Od.* 19.395–6, Hes. fr. 65.15. Cf. also 283 ἀντιτοροῦντα δόμους. Hermes has already twice demonstrated his skill in drilling through things (42, 119). For the form of ἀντιτορήσων (etc.) see 119n. The verbal echo of the final words of 177–8 is striking.

179–81 For this list of goods cf. *Od.* 13.217 τρίποδας περικαλλέας ἠδὲ λέβητας, 5.38 etc. χαλκόν τε χρυσόν τε ἅλις, ἐσθῆτά τε (δόντες/ὑφαντήν).

181 σὺ δ' ὄψεαι αἴ κ' ἐθέλῃσθα: cf. Homeric ὄψεαι ἢν (αἴκ') ἐθέλῃσθα (*Il.* 4.353 etc.). At the end of Hermes' speech this has a defiant ring, like 'Just you see!' and similar phrases.

182–3 These formal-sounding lines round off this heated exchange. 182 is a unique variant of the usual Homeric ὣς οἱ μὲν τοιαῦτα πρὸς ἀλλήλους ἀγόρευον.

184–226 As dawn rose Apollo came to Onchestos and asked the farmer about his lost cattle. The old man was evasive, but admitted that he had seen a small boy driving some cattle backwards. Apollo saw a bird of omen and realised that the thief was a son of Zeus. He headed for Pylos, and found the tracks of his cattle and those made by Hermes, which utterly bewildered him.

The poet concentrates on the meeting at Onchestos and the comic reactions of Apollo on seeing the tracks. Apollo's discovery of the theft and the beginning of his journey from Pieria are indicated in his speech to the old man (191–8). We are not told how he knows that Onchestos is on Hermes' route, and the first mention of his seeing the tracks is at 218–26.

184–5 Dawn, heralded already at 98 and 143, comes at last. This is an adaptation of Homeric formulae for dawn. Cf. ἠριγένεια . . . Ἠώς (*Il.* 1.477 etc.), and especially *Il.* 19.1–2 Ἠὼς μὲν κροκόπεπλος ἀπ' Ὠκεανοῖο ῥοάων | ὄρνυθ', ἵν' ἀθανάτοισι φόως φέροι ἠδὲ βροτοῖσιν, and βαθυρρόου Ὠκεανοῖο (*Il.* 7.422 etc.). Van Nortwick (1975, 42–3) suggests that the poet may have been influenced by the wish to keep Ἀπόλλων in his usual position at the end of the verse, and hence created this extended sentence for dawn. Apollo operates by day as a god of light, Hermes by night.

185–7 Cf. *H. Ap.* 230 Ὀγχηστὸν δ' ἵξες Ποσιδήϊον ἀγλαὸν ἄλσος. ἐρισφάραγος is un-Homeric. It is used by Pindar and Bacchylides; cf. also Hes. *Th.* 815 ἐρισμαράγοιο Διός. The sanctuary of Poseidon, Apollo's uncle, is dignified with an elaborate phrase, including three descriptive epithets.

187–8 ἔνθα . . . ἀλωῆς 'there he found an old man working on the enclosure of his vineyard, just off the road'. δέμοντα, for νέμοντα in the MSS, is supported by 87 δέμων ἀνθοῦσαν ἀλωήν. κνώδαλον ('beast') can be applied to both wild and domestic animals, and is later used as a term of abuse in Attic drama (A. *Eu.* 644 etc.), but would make no sense here if applied to the old man. If we read δέμοντα an epithet with γέροντα is needed. Stahl's κώκαλον ('ancient', according to Hesychius s.v.) is possible: for the reduplication of sense cf. for example γεραιὲ παλαιγενές in 199. But the correct reading remains uncertain. AHS keep the text of the MSS, and take it as 'there he found an old man grazing a beast alongside the road, the stay of his vineyard'. They argue that κνώδαλον refers to the farmer's donkey, comically called 'stay of his vineyard', a parody of Homeric ἕρκος Ἀχαιῶν. But this is far-fetched, and nothing is heard of the donkey elsewhere. Radermacher takes the transmitted reading as 'there he found a brutish old man, dwelling in the enclosure of his vineyard beside the road'. But νέμοντα meaning 'dwelling in' is a weak descriptive term in this context, and ἕρκος ἀλωῆς is not a natural way of referring to his farmstead. It normally refers to the hedge or enclosure round a vineyard or orchard: cf. *Il.* 5.90, 18.561–5, and see 87n.

189–212 In this hymn, unlike those to Demeter, Apollo, Aphrodite, and Dionysus, no reference is made to any attempt by Apollo (or for that matter Hermes) to disguise themselves when they meet a human being. Both seem to appear in human form and converse in a natural way with the old man, who addresses Apollo as ὦ φίλος (202), and speaks simply of having seen a small boy (208–10). This is quite unlike the normal epic convention for such encounters. It may be due to the comic and more everyday character of this poem, where Apollo is cut down to size and made to look ridiculous by Hermes. The fact that Apollo also has to go to a mortal for information is a further aspect of this comic treatment of him. Cf. Pindar, *Pythian* 9, where Chiron teases him for asking questions about Cyrene, when he is supposed to be omniscient (29–49). Apollo's speech is, however, dignified and carefully composed, with elegant repetition in 192, chiasmus in 193–5, and euphony in 197–8. By contrast the old man's reply is much more gnomic and matter-of-fact, suiting his rustic character.

190 Apollo politely honours the old man with a whole-line address, although the charming βατοδρόπε ('bramble-picker', only here) has a comic tone. It may be inspired by *Od.* 24.230 (see 87–93n.).

192 This type of repetition is favoured by Hellenistic and Roman poets, especially the Roman elegists. Cf. Call. *H.* 3.14 πάσας εἰνετέας, πάσας ἔτι παῖδας ἀμίτρους, *Coll. Alex.* p. 186.9.2 Powell παίσαι παρθενικαί, παίσαι καλὰ ἔμματα ἐχοίσαι, Theocr. 15.6, Verg. *A.* 6.787, and for other examples of parallel half-lines cf. Wills (1996) 414–18.

κέραεσσιν ἑλικτάς: ἑλικτός occurs first here, then in Attic tragedy and later. Cf. 116, 567 ἕλικας βοῦς. In 220 βοῶν ὀρθοκραιράων does not contradict this, since it may mean that the horns curve upwards, rather than forwards or downwards.

193–6 The details about the single bull and four guard-dogs add conviction to Apollo's report, and also emphasise the puzzling nature of the theft: why were they left behind (and why did the dogs not give the alarm? Cf. 145.) At the same time, the vivid epithets in 194 add colour to the description.

194 **χαροποί** 'fierce-eyed' (?). In early epic this is otherwise exclusively applied to lions (569, *Od.* 11.611, *H. Aph.* 70, *H.* 14.4, Hes. *Th.* 321, *Sc.* 177), but sometimes later to dogs (*Lyr. Adesp.* 101, X. *Cyn.* 3.3, etc.). The original sense is uncertain, but it may have meant 'with ravenous eyes': cf. Latacz (1966) 38–43. However, it later came to be used as a colour word of eyes, and it is possible that the poet had this in mind here, in juxtaposing κυάνεος χαροποὶ δέ. Cf. (for example) on the Shield of Achilles *Il.* 18.562 χρυσείην μέλανες δ', and especially 548–9 ἡ δὲ μελαίνετ'. . . | χρυσείη περ ἐοῦσα, τὸ δὴ περὶ θαῦμα τέτυκτο (cf. *H. Herm.* 196). Examples of χαροπός are collected by Maxwell-Stuart (1981); but see Davies (1982) 214–16 for criticism of his views.

195 **ἠΰτε φῶτες ὁμόφρονες:** as guardians of the herd the dogs are trained to work together. Contrast *Il.* 22.263 οὐδὲ λύκοι τε καὶ ἄνδρες ὁμόφρονα θυμὸν ἔχουσιν.

196 **ὃ δὴ . . . τέτυκται:** cf. *Il.* 18.549 τὸ δὴ περὶ θαῦμα τέτυκτο (the only early epic parallel).

197–8 The description is again elaborate and perhaps deliberately euphonious, with strong assonance of the genitive endings and frequent juxtaposition of vowels and soft consonants, mirroring the sense of softness and sweetness (μαλακοῦ, γλυκεροῖο). Cf. Demetrius *Eloc.* 69–71 on the euphony of ἠέλιος and similar words.

197 **καταδῡομένοιο:** the long upsilon of καταδύω is paralleled in Hellenistic and later poetry, whereas it is short in Homer.

199 The asyndeton suggests a note of urgency, after the long preamble. Cf. Hes. *Th.* 114 ταῦτά μοι ἔσπετε Μοῦσαι, although there ταῦτα is resumptive, whereas here it is prospective.

γεραιὲ παλαιγενές: cf. *Il.* 17.561 Φοῖνιξ, ἄττα γεραιὲ παλαιγενές, where the tone is respectful and familiar.

200 ἀνέρα: Apollo naturally assumes the thief to be an adult man.

202–11 The farmer takes his time to come to the point, beginning with a protracted preamble about the general difficulty of giving any useful information, plus the fact that he was busy all day. When he does address the question his answer is at first vague and evasive (208–9), but then becomes more precise about what he saw, although still in halting style.

202 ὦ φίλος: for this address to a stranger cf. *Od.* 13.229 to Athene in disguise, 15.260. But here 'my friend' is in keeping with the farmer's general moralising tone, in contrast to the more respectful φέριστε (208).

ἴδοιτο: 'one might see'. For the omission of τις cf. *Il.* 13.287, 22.199, etc. But M's ἴδοιμι (or Ernesti's ἴδοιο) could be right here.

203 πάντα λέγειν: the emphasis is on giving information by speech, and hence πάντα λέγειν is to be preferred to πάντ' ἀλέγειν.

204–5 He means that it is hard to distinguish among passers-by whether anyone might be up to no good or not. We should understand μεμαότες with ἐσθλά. M's πρήσσουσιν may be simply repetition from 203, or else an attempt to give ἐσθλά a verb.

207 γουνὸν ἀλωῆς οἰνοπέδοιο: cf. *Od.* 1.193, 11.193, in both cases of Laertes (see 87–93n.).

208 παῖδα: in contrast to Apollo's ἀνέρα (200) and so emphatic.

ἔδοξα is paralleled in this sense ('I thought') in epic at *Il.* 7.192, *H. Aph.* 125, but the Homeric form is δόκησα. The form ἔδοξα recurs in *IG* I³ 1 (*c.* 510–500 BC) and then Pindar and other fifth-century literature.

σαφὲς δ' οὐκ οἶδα is a parenthesis which breaks the sense in a natural way, indicating the old man's hesitation and reluctance. The adjective σαφής does not occur in Homer, who has only σάφα, and otherwise appears in the fifth century, but cf. *H. Dem.* 149 σαφέως.

209 ὅς τις ὁ παῖς 'whoever the child (might be)', as in 277 and 311, *H. Dem.* 119 (with Richardson's comment).

ἐϋκραίρῃσιν: first here, and then at A. *Supp.* 300 ἐϋκραίρωι βοΐ. Homeric ὀρθοκραιράων (cf. 220) supports the feminine form of the adjective here.

210–11 The information continues to emerge in a broken, piecemeal style, a succession of short phrases. νήπιος in runover position is emphatic, as often in Homer (cf. Van Nortwick (1975) 69–70).

210 ἐπιστροφάδην 'from side to side', i.e. in a rambling way. Cf. 75 πλανοδίας, and 226.

ἐβάδιζεν: only here and at 320 in early hexameter poetry, common from the fifth century onwards.

211 'And he drove them backwards, and kept their heads facing him.' In *Il.* 17.752 μάχην ἀνέεργον ὀπίσσω means 'they checked the battle from behind', but here ἐξοπίσω should mean 'backwards', as at *Il.* 11.461, 13.436. If κάρη δ' ἔχεν ἀντίον αὐτῶι is the correct text, κάρη is either an accusative plural or a collective accusative singular. For the former, instead of normal epic καρήατα, cf. *H. Dem.* 12 κάρα as nominative plural (with Richardson's comment). In *Il.* 10.259 (ῥύεται δὲ κάρη θαλερῶν αἰζηῶν) it is probably singular, and possibly also at S. *Ant.* 291 (κάρα σείοντες). With Hermann's ἔχον, the text would mean 'and they kept their heads facing him' (cf. West). One could also read αὐτός or αὐτοῖς: 'he (himself) kept his head facing them', i.e. he walked forwards himself.

212–14 Apollo hurries on without further delay, and the old man's testimony is confirmed by a bird-omen, which enables him to identify the criminal as Hermes. Διὸς παῖδα must imply this here, and the point of using this formula may be to stress that Hermes is his own brother. Cf. Apollod. 3.10.2, where Apollo discovers the truth about Hermes ἐκ τῆς μαντικῆς, and Schol. AB *Il.* 15.256. In a similar way Apollo hears of the love affair of Coronis and Ischys from the raven (Hes. fr. 60), a version rejected by Pindar, who says that it was thanks to his own omniscient mind (*P.* 3.27–9).

216 ἐς Πύλον: i.e. the district near the river Alpheios. Cf. 101, 354–5, and 128–9n. In Antoninus Liberalis' version (23) the southern (Messenian) Pylos is the scene.

217 Cf. *Il.* 5.186 (a god) νεφέληι εἰλυμένος ὤμους, 17.551 (Athene) πορφυρέηι νεφέληι πυκάσασα ἓ αὐτήν, 16.790 (Apollo) ἠέρι γὰρ πολλῆι κεκαλυμμένος ἀντεβόλησε. Apollo does not need to conceal himself in this case, and the description must be designed to emphasise his menacing power, as in *Il.* 1.47 ὁ δ' ἤϊε νυκτὶ ἐοικώς.

218–26 Apollo's complete bewilderment is comically absurd in view of his supposed powers of divination. The soliloquy builds up to a climax with the catalogue of creatures in 222–5, culminating in the most outlandish of all, the centaur. Cf. his description of the tracks at 342–9 (where 344–5 echo 220–1), and the puzzlement of the satyrs in *Ichneutai* (see 75–8n.).

219 = *Il.* 13.99 etc.

221 ἐς ἀσφοδελὸν λειμῶνα: cf. 344. In Homer the meadow of asphodel appears only in the Underworld: cf. *Od.* 11.539, 573, 24.13. Here it refers to the god's pasture, as in the elaborate descriptions at 72 and 198. For Hesiod (*Op.* 41) asphodel is symbolic of the simplest and cheapest form of diet.

222–5 For this catalogue of creatures, with οὔτε . . . οὔτε (etc.), cf. *Il.* 17.20–2 οὔτ' οὖν παρδάλιος τόσσον μένος οὔτε λέοντος | οὔτε συὸς κάπρου ὀλοόφρονος etc., and *H. Dem.* 44–6, *H. Herm.* 143–5.

222 βήματα: cf. 345 for βῆμα, which does not occur elsewhere in early hexameter poetry, and Sappho 16.17 L–P = 16.17 V, etc.

224 κενταύρου λασιαύχενος: the epithet appears first here and in *H.* 7.46, next in fifth-century drama. In Geometric and Archaic art the centaur is portrayed either as a horse with a human head and shaggy beard, or as a bearded man with human legs, joined to the back part of a horse (cf. *LIMC* s.v.

Kentauroi et Kentaurides). The footprints of the second type would be more distinctive.

225 Apollo recognises both the size and speed of these extraordinary steps. For τοῖα πέλωρα cf. 342 and 349.

βιβᾶι: in Homer the verb occurs only as a participle; cf. 149 προβιβῶν.

226 'Strange are the tracks on one side of the road, and still stranger on the other.' Cf. 357 ὁδοῦ τὸ μὲν ἔνθα τὸ δ' ἔνθα. This presumably all refers still to Hermes' steps, and is a way of saying that they go from side to side (cf. 210) and are totally incomprehensible.

227–92 Apollo came to Cyllene and entered Maia's cave. Hermes curled up in his blankets pretending to be asleep, and Apollo searched all the store-chambers of the cavern. He then ordered him to reveal the cattle at once, threatening to hurl him into Tartarus otherwise. Hermes denied all knowledge, claiming that he could have nothing to do with such things, since he was only just born, and offering to swear an oath to confirm his innocence. Apollo laughed at his deceit, saying that he would become an expert in burglary and rustling. He ordered him to get out of his cradle and declared that his divine privilege would be to become the prince of thieves.

In this scene Apollo's anger and impatience are deflated by Hermes' blatant sophistry, and he cannot help laughing indulgently at his tricks (281), and admiring him for them. The scene thus foreshadows their reconciliation and Hermes' reception among the Olympians, and has a burlesque quality which undermines Apollo's usual seriousness and dignity. On two vases of *c.* 530 and 490 BC (for details see 21n.) Hermes is shown in his cradle, with the stolen cattle nearby. On the first of these Apollo and Maia are depicted, together with a third bearded figure (possibly Zeus). The second shows what is probably Maia and Apollo.

227–34 Apollo's arrival and entry to the cave follow a typical pattern, with mention of divine fragrance, sheep grazing outside, and crossing of the stone threshold. Cf. however especially Hermes' arrival at Calypso's island (*Od.* 5.55–77) ἀλλ' ὅτε δὴ τὴν νῆσον ἀφίκετο... | ἤϊεν, ὄφρα μέγα σπέος ἵκετο, τῶι ἐνὶ νύμφη | ναῖεν ἐϋπλόκαμος... | πῦρ μὲν ἐπ' ἐσχαρόφιν μέγα καίετο, τηλόθι δ' ὀδμὴ |... ἀνὰ νῆσον ὀδώδει [followed by description of the wood around the cave and birds nesting there, etc.]... αὐτίκ' ἄρ' εἰς εὐρὺ σπέος ἤλυθεν. For other links with this episode cf. 4, 154nn. Cf. also *Od.* 9.181–4, where Odysseus and his men find sheep and goats grazing round the cave of Polyphemus. Van Nortwick (1975) 110–15 and (1980) 1–5 detects a pattern of vocabulary in 227–51, involving divine fragrance, radiance, and wealth, which he finds in Homeric scenes of deception or seduction.

229 βαθύσκιον: first here, later in Theocritus 4.19 etc.

230 ἀμβροσίη: this is not used of persons elsewhere in early epic (whereas ἄμβροτος is).

ἐλόχευσε: the verb occurs only here before Attic tragedy.

231–2 Cf. *H. Dem.* 277–8 ὀδμὴ δ' ἱμερόεσσα θυηέντων ἀπὸ πέπλων | σκίδνατο, of Demeter's epiphany. Fragrance is a sign of divinity: see Richardson on *H. Dem.* 275ff. (p. 252). Here it is most probably due to the presence of Maia, as a feminine deity.

234 ἑκατηβόλος αὐτὸς Ἀπόλλων 'far-shooting Apollo in person'. Cf. *H. Aph.* 151 ἑκηβόλος αὐτὸς Ἀπόλλων. αὐτός is often applied especially to Apollo: see *H. Ap.* 140n.

236 χωόμενον περὶ βουσίν: cf. Hes. *Sc.* 12 χωσάμενος περὶ βουσί.

237–9 The simile resembles and may be inspired by *Od.* 5.488–93, where Odysseus heaps leaves over himself as a man hides a brand under a heap of ashes (σποδιῆι μελαίνηι) to keep it alight, and then Athene sends him to sleep (cf. *H. Herm.* 240–1).

238 πρέμνων: πρέμνον is only found here in early poetry; cf. Pindar etc.

239 ἀνέειλε' ἓ αὐτόν 'rolled himself up', from ἀνειλέω, which does not recur before Thucydides. The reading of the MSS ἀλέεινεν ἓ αὐτόν has been explained as meaning 'concealed himself': cf. perhaps 85, and *LfgrE* s.v., but it is less easy to extract this meaning here with ἓ αὐτόν than it is at 85 with ὁδοιπορίην.

240 ἐν δ' ὀλίγωι συνέλασσε 'and he huddled together in a small (bundle)'.

241 φή ῥα νεόλλουτος: φή ('like') is an emendation. It was read by Zenodotus at *Il.* 2.144, 14.499, and adopted there by modern editors, but Aristarchus held it to be post-Homeric (Schol. A *Il.* 14.499) and quoted examples from Antimachus (fr. 121) and Callimachus or his followers (frr. 260.58, 737). It may occur in Hes. fr. 204.138. See also Janko on *Il.* 14.499–500. νεόλλουτος, if correct, means 'newly washed', and recurs in Hippocrates (νεόλουτος) of a woman after childbirth (1.535 etc.). Hermes curls up like a baby after it has been washed and is ready for sleep: cf. 267–8, where he includes sleep and warm baths among his concerns. The variant θῆρα νέον λοχάων is hard to explain. AHS suggest νεολλοχέων, meaning 'newborn', which occurs nowhere in surviving literature.

ἥδυμον ὕπνον: cf. 249. In Homer the form νήδυμος is normally used, with ἥδυμος as an occasional variant reading. Both occur in later poetry. ἥδυμος is actually the original form of the word: cf. *H. Aph.* 170–2n., and Chantraine, *Dict.* s.v. νήδυμος.

242 Martin's conjecture ἐγρήσσων ἐρατήν τε would make the verse closer to 153 χέλυν ἐρατὴν ἐπ' ἀριστερὰ χειρὸς ἐέργων. AHS compare Hipponax fr. 177 West Ἑρμῆ μάκαρ, <σὺ γὰρ> κατ' ὕπνον οἶδας ἐγρήσσειν.

μασχάληι 'arm-pit': only here in early poetry, then in Aeschylus etc.

243 γνῶ δ' οὐδ' ἠγνοίησε: cf. Hes. *Th.* 551 γνῶ ῥ' οὐδ' ἠγνοίησε δόλον, of Zeus seeing through the deception of Prometheus.

244 νύμφην τ' οὐρείην: cf. Hes. fr. 123.1 οὔρειαι νύμφαι.

245 δολίηις εἰλυμένον ἐντροπίηισι 'wrapped in cunning tricks'. εἰλύω and εἰλυμένος are used elsewhere in a purely physical sense, and ἐντροπίη recurs only in Hippocrates (*Decent.* 2), where it means 'concern', like ἐντροπή. The metaphor is perhaps suggested by the description of Hermes wrapped in his σπάργανα (235–42 etc.). For a similar transference cf. Archil. fr. 191.1 West ἔρως ὑπὸ καρδίην ἐλυσθείς ('love curled up beneath my heart'), with Silk (1974) 131–3.

246–51 Here the cave is like a great house or temple with store-chambers full of wealth, in contrast to Hermes' complaints at 167–81. Cf. for example *Il.* 6.289–311, where Hecabe takes a precious robe from a storeroom and offers it to Athene, or the storerooms of *Od.* 2.337–47. The spectacle of Apollo hastily and vainly rifling through the possessions of Maia is somewhat ludicrous. Like a police officer with a search warrant he does not stop to question Maia or Hermes until he has been through everything.

246 ἀνά: this reading suits the context better than ἄρα, since παπταίνω with accusative is used in Homer of looking for someone (*Il.* 4.200, 17.115).

247 ἀδύτους: elsewhere in early epic the gender is uncertain, but later ἄδυτον is neuter in Hdt. 5.72, E. *Ion* 938.

248 νέκταρος . . . ἠδ' ἀμβροσίης ἐρατεινῆς: cf. *Il.* 19.347, 353, *H. Ap.* 124 νέκταρ τε καὶ ἀμβροσίην ἐρατεινήν.

ἐμπλείους: the variant reading ἐκπλείους is possible, but this form does not occur otherwise before Euripides and Xenophon.

250 φοινικόεντα καὶ ἄργυφα εἵματα: the first epithet is used of a cloak in Homer (*Il.* 10.133, *Od.* 14.500, 21.118), the second of a robe, in the form ἀργύφεος (*Od.* 5.230, 543); cf. ἄργυφος of sheep.

252 ἐξερέεινε 'searched'. Cf. *Od.* 12.259 πόρους ἁλὸς ἐξερεείνων.

254–9 Apollo's speech of interrogation is brusque and peremptory: a single-verse command plus highly emphatic runover word (θᾶσσον: 'and quick!'), followed by a more extensive description of the dire consequences of failure to obey, culminating in a sentence with two consecutive examples of integral enjambment (257–9): cf. Van Nortwick (1975) 92–3. Imprisonment in Tartarus is a typical punishment for unruly deities, usually administered by Zeus. Cf. especially *Il.* 8.12–13, where Zeus threatens the gods with either a beating or Tartarus: πληγεὶς οὐ κατὰ κόσμον ἐλεύσεται Οὔλυμπόνδε· | ἤ μιν ἑλὼν ῥίψω ἐς Τάρταρον ἠερόεντα (and 8.40 resembles *H. Herm.* 466). Other examples are Hes. *Th.* 868 (Typhoeus), fr. 30.22 (Salmoneus), and 54(a) + 57 (Apollo himself). Vox (1981) suggests that there is a specific echo here of Hes. frr. 54(a) and 57, where Zeus threatens this fate for Apollo because he killed the Cyclopes, and Apollo's mother Leto intercedes to save him. On this theme of divine punishment see also Harrell (1991).

254 Ὦ παῖ: the abruptness of the address is increased by the rare metrical shortening of παῖ. Contrast the more relaxed tone of 282, 436, and 514.

μήνυε: the verb occurs first here and at *SLG* 5323.15 (Simonides?); cf. 264 μήνυτρον. It is the standard legal term later for disclosing information.

255 θᾶσσον: the MSS read θᾶττον (the Attic or Boeotian form) here, but θᾶσσον at 212. It seems more likely that the usual epic form has been corrupted at 255 than vice versa.

ἐπεί 'for otherwise'.

διοισόμεθ' οὐ κατὰ κόσμον: an ominously euphemistic way of describing the quarrel which would ensue. διαφέρειν ('to differ') does not occur elsewhere in early epic; cf. Heraclitus 72 (with the same sense) etc. οὐ κατὰ κόσμον is used in the context of a quarrel at *Il.* 2.214; cf. also *Il.* 8.12, quoted in 254–9n.

256 Cf. 374 ἠπείλησε βαλεῖν ἐς Τάρταρον εὐρύν. Ilgen proposed λαβών, but the duplication of ῥίψω with βαλών is not unusual.

257 εἰς ζόφον αἰνόμορον καὶ ἀμήχανον: αἰνόμορος is used of persons in Homer (*Il.* 22.481, *Od.* 9.53, 24.169). The phrase is new and suitably awe-inspiring.

257–9 οὐδέ σε μήτηρ | ... οὐδὲ πατὴρ ἀναλύσεται, ἀλλ'... | ἐρρήσεις: for this type of threat cf. *Il.* 21.123–5 οὐδέ σε μήτηρ | ... γοήσεται, ἀλλὰ Σκάμανδρος | οἴσει..., *Od.* 24.292–6 οὐδέ ἑ μήτηρ | κλαῦσε περιστείλασα πατήρ θ'... | οὐδ' ἄλοχος... | κώκυσ'... See also *H. Ap.* 362–70n.

259 ἐρρήσεις: this has a double implication, of wandering vainly (e.g. *Od.* 4.367), and of going to one's ruin or death.

ὀλίγοισι μετ' ἀνδράσιν ἡγεμονεύων 'as leader among the people of small importance', i.e. the souls of the dead. Cf. the Homeric ἀμενηνὰ κάρηνα. ὀλίγος means 'slight' in early Greek poetry: cf. (e.g.) *Od.* 14.492 ὀλίγῃ ὀπί, and Moorhouse (1947) 31–45. Cf. also later *AP* 9.334 κἀμὲ τὸν ἐν σμικροῖς ὀλίγον θεόν, of a minor deity. There may be irony in the fact that Hermes will indeed become a leader for the dead, in his capacity as ψυχοπόμπος (cf. 572–3). AHS take ὀλίγοισι μετ' ἀνδράσιν as 'among little men', and West translates 'among human children'. But with ἀνδράσιν it can hardly refer to children.

260–77 Hermes' reply is a parody of a defence speech in miniature, fully worthy of this god of rhetoric. He begins by expressing his surprise with a rhetorical question, and denying his guilt or any knowledge of the crime (261–4). He then uses arguments from probability, claiming that he does not resemble a thief, corroborated by appeal to his lifestyle and character as a baby, and suggesting that such an accusation is shocking and improper (269–73). Finally he offers to swear an oath that he is innocent of all complicity, adding (in contradiction to 263) that he only knows of it by hearsay (274–7).

This is the first of Hermes' two defence speeches; the second, to Zeus, is at 368–86. Görgemanns (1976, 113–19) shows how they fit the patterns of later rhetorical theory. For example, the type of argument that Hermes does not resemble a cattle-rustler because he is not strong enough (265) was said to have been discussed by the early fifth-century BC rhetorician Teisias, as an example of the use of τὸ εἰκός (cf. Pl. *Phdr.* 273B3–C4), and by his contemporary Corax (cf. Arist. *Rhet.* 1402a17–20). But the way these arguments are used and developed further in these two passages indicates that the point which Hermes makes was already a traditional one before the time of these two theorists, even if we do not have earlier examples. Stylistically also the speech is highly crafted, with the double rhetorical question (261–2), the use of tricolon crescendo in 263 and 273, the emphatic repetition of negatives in 263–6 and 275–6, the variation of μηνύσαιμ'... μήνυτρον ἀροίμην (264), the emotive catalogue of 267–8, and the exclamatory expressions of 269–72, ending in a staccato half-line (272), a device used again in the concluding lines (275–7). See Eitrem (1906) 269, Radermacher ad loc., and Kennedy (1963) 40–1.

Van Nortwick (1975, 93–5) also discusses this speech, together with those by Hermes at 307–12 and 368–86. He notes a high frequency of short sentences, simple sentence-structure, and in 260–77 a repetitive pattern of verse-endings with a verb scanned ⏑ – – ⏑ , often preceded by a trochaic noun. Together with alliteration, assonance, and anaphora, these, he suggests, all give an effect of artfully childish speech.

261–2 There is a slight ellipse of a natural kind in 262: e.g. 'what is this harsh speech . . . and (why) have you come?'

261 τοῦτον ἀπηνέα μῦθον: cf. Iris to Poseidon at *Il.* 15.201–2 οὕτω γὰρ δή τοι . . . τόνδε φέρω Διὶ μῦθον ἀπηνέα τε κρατερόν τε . . . ;

ἔειπας: the Homeric forms are ἔειπες or εἶπας.

263–4 These lines are quoted by Apollo at 363–4.

263 Cf. *Od.* 23.40 οὐ ἴδον, οὐ πυθόμην, ἀλλὰ στόνον οἶον ἄκουσα, and *Od.* 3.94 = 4.324 ἄλλου μῦθον ἀκούσας.

264 οὐκ ἂν μήνυτρον ἀροίμην 'I could not gain a reward for information'. μήνυτρον recurs in Hipponax (fr. 102.4), and later in the plural in Attic writers. Cf. possibly Soph. *Ichneutai* fr. 314.87 Radt μηνυ[.

οὔτε: The sequence οὐ . . . οὔτε . . . is common in epic and later (Denniston, *GP*² 509–10). There is no need to alter this to οὐδέ (as Baumeister and Allen do).

266 Again οὐκ (the MSS' reading) is better here than οὔτ' (Gemoll) or οὐδ' (Allen). The asyndeton is dramatic and effective: 'this is not my business'.

269 'I hope that no one will learn how this quarrel arose!'

271 Cf. 158 διὲκ προθύροιο περήσειν. Hermes is answering Apollo's original assumption that the cows might be hidden somewhere in the cave.

272 τὸ δ' ἀπρεπέως ἀγορεύεις: this is the first appearance of ἀπρεπ(έ)ως, and the adjective first occurs in Hippocrates and Thucydides. The concepts of τὸ πρέπον and τὸ ἀπρεπές will later become standard terms of rhetorical theory.

273 An effective tricolon in its brevity and the contrast of the second and third elements.

χθές: only here in literature before the fifth century, but its derivative χθιζός is common in Homer, where χθιζόν and χθιζά are used adverbially.

274–7 Hermes offers to swear an oath, but both here and at 378–84 he cunningly avoids perjuring himself (see 275–7n.). Hermes is the expert in the art of swearing oaths: cf. *Od.* 19.394–8, where Autolycus is said to have learnt this from him. As a means of settling a dispute oath-taking is already attested in the *Iliad*, 23.581–5: cf. Richardson on *Il.* 23.566–85. Callaway (1993, 22–4) argues that both here and at 378–84 Hermes only offers an oath, but does not actually swear one. εἰ δ' ἐθέλεις in 274 does leave it somewhat open as to whether he is really doing so or not, since it is a conditional clause.

274 εἰ δ' ἐθέλεις: the form ἐθέλω is normal in Homer and Hesiod, although θέλω does occur at *H. Ap.* 46, and so could possibly be correct here (see also Richardson on *H. Dem.* 160).

πατρὸς κεφαλήν: at *Il.* 15.36–40 Hera swears by Zeus's head, together with various other witnesses, and Zeus himself says that when he nods his head this is the greatest guarantee (τέκμωρ) he can give to the gods (*Il.* 1.524–7).

275–7 Hermes repeats his denial at 309–11, where 311 = 277. 275 can mean 'I do not profess to be guilty myself', a clever way of avoiding an outright lie.

275–6 The indicative is used here as it is in oaths of denial: cf. *Il.* 10.330–1, 15.41–4, 19.261–2, and Chantraine, *GH* II. 331.

276 **κλοπόν:** only here, and at Opp. *C.* 1.517.

277 **αἵ τινες αἱ βόες εἰσί:** cf. 209 ὅς τις ὁ παῖς, for this kind of throwaway expression.

τὸ δὲ κλέος οἷον ἀκούω: cf. *Il.* 2.436 ἡμεῖς δὲ κλέος οἷον ἀκούομεν.

278–80 'Thus he spoke, and flashing frequent glances from his eyes he kept signalling with his eyebrows up and down, looking to one side and the other, with a long dismissive whistle, as if listening to a pointless story.' West (2003) and Vergados (2007a) take ὀφρύσι with what precedes, and ῥιπτάζεσκεν as 'he tossed and turned', as in later uses of this verb (Hippocrates etc.). This is closer to Hes. *Th.* 826–7 ἐκ δέ οἱ ὄσσων | . . . ὑπ' ὀφρύσι πῦρ ἀμάρυσσεν, and could be right, although ὀφρύσι without ὑπό is slightly awkward in this case.

Hermes' reactions are described in great detail. Cf. 387 where he winks at Zeus, and 415 where again his flashing eyes are described. The general effect is one of mischievous insolence and contempt for Apollo's claims.

278 **ἀμαρύσσων:** see 45n. (ἀμαρυγή).

279 **ὀφρύσι ῥιπτάζεσκεν:** for signals with the eyebrows cf. *Od.* 9.468, 12.194, etc.

ὁρώμενος ἔνθα καὶ ἔνθα: cf. Hes. fr. 294, where this is applied to the many-eyed Argos, Hermes' enemy (with ὁρώμενον).

280 **ἀποσυρίζων:** this compound recurs in Lucian (*VH* 2.5); cf. Homeric σῦριγξ. It may indicate contempt (cf. ἐκσυρίζω, of hissing in the theatre), or indifference.

ἅλιον ὡς μῦθον ἀκούων: ὡς seems necessary here, and τόν in some MSS may be due to expressions like ἅλιον τὸν μῦθον ὑπέστημεν (*Il.* 5.715).

281–92 Apollo's tone changes dramatically to relaxed and friendly amusement and admiration, and the warning at 289 cannot be taken seriously.

281 **ἁπαλὸν γελάσας:** cf. *Od.* 14.465 ἁπαλὸν γελάσαι. Zeus likewise smiles at Hera's deceptive speech, at *Il.* 15.47, and at Hermes' speech at *H. Herm.* 389–90.

282 **Ὦ πέπον:** nearly always a term of endearment. But it is also used by Zeus of Prometheus, when deceived by him over the division of sacrificial meat, at Hes. *Th.* 544, 560.

ἠπεροπευτά is used of Paris at *Il.* 3.39, again in a series of vocative epithets.

δολοφραδές: first here; cf. Pi. *N.* 8.33.

283 **ἀντιτοροῦντα:** see 178n.

284 Literally, 'in the night-time you would not make only one person sit upon the ground'. Sitting on the ground is a sign of grief or despair (see Richardson on *H. Dem.* 197–201), but here it may imply that Hermes has stolen all the furniture.

285 **σκευάζοντα** 'packing things up': the verb possibly occurs at Arch. fr. 140.2 West, then in Herodotus and fifth-century Attic literature.

ψόφου: the word is attested first in Sappho (twice).

οἷ' ἀγορεύεις '(to judge by) the way you talk'.

286–8 The only other use of the word μηλοβοτήρ is at *Il.* 18.529, in the description of a raid on sheep and cattle on the shield of Achilles. Cf. *Il.* 18.528–9 τάμνοντ' ἀμφὶ βοῶν ἀγέλας καὶ πώεα καλὰ | ἀργεννέων οἰῶν, κτεῖνον δ' ἐπὶ μηλοβοτῆρας. If our poet had this in mind, this would support the reading of the MSS at 288 ἀντήσηις ἀγέληισι βοῶν καὶ πώεσι μήλων, as opposed to the marginal variant ἄντην (for ἄντηις?) βουκολίοισι καὶ εἰροπόκοις ὀΐεσσιν. βουκόλιον otherwise does not occur before Herodotus. This marginal reading could have arisen as a genuine rhapsodic variant.

289 **πύματόν τε καὶ ὕστατον:** this occurs adverbially at *Od.* 20.116, in the context of the impending death of the suitors; cf. also *Il.* 22.203. Apollo's words, however, as addressed to an immortal, are an empty threat.

290 **μελαίνης νυκτὸς ἑταῖρε:** cf. 15, 67, 577–8, and 436 δαιτὸς ἑταῖρε of Hermes.

291–2 Already one aspect of Hermes' honours is announced, confirming his own boast at 166–75. For γὰρ οὖν ('for indeed', in Homer always with a backward reference) see Denniston, *GP*² 445–6. Here this final statement refers back to 282–8. For Hermes as 'leader of thieves' cf. 175, and see 67n.

293–321 Apollo picked up Hermes, but the child farted and sneezed, and Apollo dropped him at these ominous sounds, but told him that he must lead the way to the cattle. Hermes again denied being to blame and demanded that the case be brought before Zeus. They set off for Olympus, with Hermes leading.

293–303 Hermes interrupts Apollo's attempt to seize him by two unexpected and startling actions, which were usually involuntary and so could be regarded as ominous, although here he does them on purpose (294). The first (a fart) is comically treated as an omen in Ar. *Eq.* 638–42, and could be seen in comedy as a parody of Zeus's thunder (Ar. *Nub.* 392–4). The second (sneezing) was commonly viewed as ominous. These reactions may be intended to confirm Apollo's prediction at 292, but they also have the effect of making him drop Hermes. Apollo retaliates by saying that he will use them as aids in finding his cattle (302–3). There is an echo at 295–7 of 213–15 (οἰωνὸν . . . ἐσσυμένως δέ), where Apollo sees a bird-omen and at once rushes off towards Pylos. See also Katz (1999) 315–19.

295–6 **οἰωνὸν . . . ἀγγελιώτην** 'let fly an omen, as he was lifted in Apollo's hands, an insolent servant of the belly, an impudent messenger'. The description is riddling and comically personifies this physical emission in a pseudo-honorific way. Cf. Eubulus, *PCG* fr. 106.1–10, where οἰκείων ἀνέμων ταμίας in a riddle is interpreted as πρωκτός. Theoretically 296 could also refer to a burp, but this is less probable. τλήμων is best taken as 'insolent' here, rather than 'wretched' (Katz (1999) 317). ἔριθος ('hired servant') is occasionally used metaphorically later. ἀγγελιώτης occurs only here in early Greek, later in Callimachus and Nonnus. For further discussion of the way in which early epic and other 'high' genres of poetry refer to words relating to bodily functions cf. Bain (2007), especially 51–2 on this passage.

297 **ἐπέπταρε:** cf. *Od.* 17.545 ἐπέπταρε πασὶν ἔπεσσιν, where Penelope treats Telemachus' sneeze as a confirmatory omen.

299–300 Despite his eagerness to find his cattle Apollo sits down in order to continue his verbal sparring-match (κερτομέων).

301 **θάρσει:** perhaps like our colloquial 'don't worry!', i.e. whatever you do, you can't stop me.

σπαργανιῶτα: this word occurs nowhere else, and was perhaps invented ad hoc. As in 282 the tone is presumably affectionately mocking. Cf. ἀγγελιώτην (296), μηχανιῶτα (436), etc.

302 **καὶ ἔπειτα** 'in the end', or 'after all'.

304–5 In contrast to Apollo it is Hermes who now shows haste to move on and end this argument. σπουδῆι here means 'hastily' (cf. *Od.* 13.279, 15.209). For Κυλλήνιος Ἑρμῆς cf. *Od.* 24.1 Ἑρμῆς . . . Κυλλήνιος, and *H.* 18.1.

305–6 **ἄμφω . . . ἐελμένος:** lit. 'he thrust with his hands along both his ears, with his blanket wrapped round his shoulders', i.e. he stopped his ears from hearing any more, whilst still maintaining his position as a mere baby. This interpretation of 305 seems more natural than taking it as 'pushed his ears back' with παρεώθει as a *tmesis* (AHS), or reading ἐελμένον and taking σπάργανον as the object of ἐώθει (Càssola). For σπάργανον . . . ἐελμένος cf. 151–3, where this characterises Hermes as a baby, and similarly 235–42.

307–12 Hermes maintains his pretence of injured innocence with a further protest, which skilfully leads up to his demand for a trial before their father Zeus. This marks a major turning point in the narrative, diverting Apollo from his original aim of finding the cattle directly, and thereby engineering Hermes' entry to Olympus and ultimate reception as a member of the divine family.

307 **ζαμενέστατε** 'most furious'. The epithet occurs first here, then in Pindar and later literature, but cf. Hes. *Th.* 928 ζαμένησε.

308–11 The four-fold repetition of different forms of the plural of βοῦς within four lines emphasises the absurdity of this whole quarrel over mere cattle. 309–11 echo Hermes' earlier denials at 263–77, especially 275–7. 311 is a variation of 277, and 309 ὢ πόποι . . . γένος expresses exasperation: 'to hell with all the race of cattle!'

308 **ὀρσολοπεύεις:** literally 'flay the arse', from ὄρσος (rump) and λέπειν, i.e. 'persecute, give me a hard time'. This coarse expression suits Hermes' comic style. Cf. Anacreon fr. 393 P. ὀρσολόπος of Ares, A. *Pers.* 10 ὀρσολοπεῖται θυμός metaphorically, Max. Tyr. 107 ὀρσολοπεύει μύθωι ὀνειδείωι, and *LfgrE* s.v.

312 **δὸς δὲ δίκην καὶ δέξο:** i.e. submit your case to arbitration, a legal expression, with the alliteration and brevity of this phrase effectively indicating the reciprocal character of the process. For δίκας διδόναι καὶ δέχεσθαι cf. *IG* I^3 6.A 41–2, Thucydides, etc., and similarly δίκας διδόναι καὶ λαμβάνειν (Hdt. etc.). δίκην διδόναι already occurs in Anaximander (fr. 1).

313–21 This passage sums up the stalemate which the two gods have reached with a lengthy preamble (313–19), in which the first subordinate clause (αὐτὰρ ἐπεί) is left suspended at 315, and then resumed after a parenthesis (315–18) with a second αὐτὰρ ἐπεί (319). The unresolved balance of the conflict is expressed throughout by contrasting phrases, and then neatly encapsulated in the anaphora of 319 (πολύμητις . . . πολυμήχανον). Finally 321–2 move the narrative forward, with the comic picture of the infant Hermes leading the way to Olympus, followed by his adult brother. Hermes has by implication won this round of their contest, but he is still Apollo's prisoner (cf. 330).

313 διαρρήδην 'expressly, explicitly'. This occurs first here, and is later used above all in legal contexts (of treaties, laws, etc.) from the late fifth century onwards.

314 οἰοπόλος: in Homer this is used of wild or solitary places (*Il.* 13.473 etc.), as if connected with οἶος ('alone'), but an alternative ancient etymology connected it with οἶς, as if meaning 'sheep-haunted' (cf. Schol. *Il.* 13.473, Schol. A.R. 4.1322), and it may have this sense sometimes in later poetry (e.g. Colluthus 15, and cf. οἰοπολέω in *AP* 7.657). Elsewhere when applied to deities it probably means 'solitary' (Pindar *P.* 4.28, fr. 70b.19, A.R. 4.1322, 1413). It is impossible to know for sure whether our poet intended it to mean 'who haunts the wilds' or 'shepherd' (as most scholars assume). Either way it anticipates his future role as guardian of animals (567–71), as 331 does for his role as herald. See also Janko (1982) 136.

315 ἀμφὶς θυμὸν ἔχοντες 'with divided hearts'. Cf. *Il.* 13.345 ἀμφὶς φρονέοντε etc.

315–16 ὁ μὲν νημερτέα φωνῶν | οὐκ ἀδίκως ἐπὶ βουσὶν ἐλάζυτο κύδιμον Ἑρμῆν 'Apollo, speaking the truth, was not unjustly apprehending glorious Hermes on account of his cattle'. The simple verb φωνεῖν is only used in the aorist in Homer. The transmitted reading φωνήν would have to be an internal accusative, as at S. *Ai.* 1107–8 τὰ σεμνʼ ἔπη κόλαζʼ ἐκείνους, and *OT* 339–40 ἔπη . . . ἃ νῦν σὺ τήνδʼ ἀτιμάζεις πόλιν, but this seems very awkward here. ἐπὶ βουσίν represents the subject of the charge, as at A. *PV* 196 ποίῳ λαβών σε Ζεὺς ἐπʼ αἰτιάματι. The language continues to echo that of a lawsuit.

316 ἐλάζυτο: in Homer the form λάζεσθαι is used. λάζυσθαι is Ionic (Hippocrates) and Attic.

319 This sounds like a proverbial expression for a trickster meeting his match. πολύμητις must refer to Hermes, the subject of 317–18 and 320–1.

320–1 Once again the journey is described as over sandy terrain, a very abbreviated way of referring to the whole way from Cyllene to Olympus, and the gods walk on the ground, whereas in Homer they usually fly. To do so here would have ruined the comic effect.

322–96 They arrived at Olympus, where the gods were assembled, and stood before Zeus, who asked Apollo who this child he had captured could be. Apollo described the theft, the mysterious footprints, the old man who saw Hermes, and how he had hidden the cattle, returned to his cradle again, and denied all knowledge of the crime. Hermes pleaded that Apollo had come in search of his property without any witnesses and threatened him, and argued on grounds of probability that he could not have done the crime, claiming correctly that he had not driven the cattle to his home or crossed the threshold, and threatening vengeance against Apollo. Zeus laughed at his clever denials. He ordered them both to be reconciled, and Hermes to lead Apollo to the hiding-place of the cattle, and Hermes agreed.

This episode can be seen as an elaborate variation on the traditional motif in the *Hymns* of a new deity's introduction to Olympus and the society of the gods. Cf. 504–7, where Apollo and Hermes return to Olympus, and Zeus rejoices and reconciles them.

The trial scene has a simple and balanced structure:

322–8 Arrival of the two parties to the dispute
328–32 Zeus interrogates Apollo about the nature of the case
333–65 Apollo's accusation
366–88 Hermes' defence speech
389–96 Zeus gives his verdict.

Apollo's speech is longer than Hermes', because it contains an extensive narrative section. Hermes' reply repeats several of the motifs of his earlier defence (260–77), and in both cases is accompanied or followed by significant eye-movements and other physical gestures (278–80, 387–8). Both speeches provoke laughter from their addressees (281, 389–90).

322 τέρθρον 'summit'. This rare word occurs first here and was later used especially of the end of a sail-yard. It recurs in the late sixth-century lyric poet Apollodorus (*PMG* 701), Empedocles, etc. The variant reading αἶψα δ' ἵκοντο κάρηνα may derive from κάρηνα as a gloss on τέρθρον.

θυώδεος Οὐλύμποιο: cf. *H. Dem.* 331.

323 Διὸς περικαλλέα τέκνα: they are here joined for the first time in a single complimentary phrase, perhaps anticipating their impending reconciliation: cf. 397, 504.

324 'For there the scales of justice were set in place for them both.' The line resembles and may be influenced by *Il.* 18.507 κεῖτο δ' ἄρ' ἐν μέσσοισι δύω χρυσοῖο τάλαντα, in the trial scene on Achilles' shield, where τάλαντα refers to golden talents, and κεῖτο has more point than in the hymn. The origin of the idea of the scales of justice probably lies in the scales of Zeus, which weigh the fates of men and nations in the *Iliad* (8.69 etc.). Cf. Bacchyl. 4.12, 17.25 for Δίκας τάλαντον, A. *Ag.* 250 Δίκα . . . ἐπιρρέπει, *AP* 6.267.4 ἐκ Διὸς ἰθείης οἶδε τάλαντα δίκης. Here too the scales of justice are in the power of Zeus as arbiter.

325 West's εὐωχίη (with synizesis) would give a possible sense ('feasting, good cheer', in Aristophanes etc.), but the true text remains uncertain. For Ὄλυμπον ἀγάννιφον cf. *Il.* 1.420 etc., *H. Herm.* 505.

325–6 ἀθάνατοι . . . | ἄφθιτοι: for the repetition cf. *Od.* 3.3 θνητοὶ βροτοί etc.

326 μετὰ χρυσόθρονον ἠῶ: the gods assemble in the morning at *Il.* 1.493–5, *Od.* 5.1–4, and the variant ποτὶ πτύχας Οὐλύμποιο is weak after 322 and 325. Dawn came already at 184–5, but the time-scale is now vague.

327–8 The two contestants stand 'before the knees of Zeus' seeking justice, in the manner of suppliants.

330–2 Zeus rarely speaks directly in the *Hymns*. Apart from this three-line speech, there is no other instance except in *H.* 1. His words are reported indirectly, e.g. at *H. Herm.* 391–4, and several times in *H. Dem.* This is in marked contrast with the Homeric epics, and it accords with his presentation in the *Hymns* as a more distant figure. Zeus's interrogation is ironic and bantering. For πόθεν ταύτην μενοεικέα ληΐδ' cf. 32 πόθεν τόδε καλὸν ἄθυρμα (again ironic). Hermes has 'the form of a herald', i.e. in some way he already appears like what he is soon destined to become (528–32), the patron of heralds (cf. also 314n.).

332 σπουδαῖον τόδε χρῆμα 'this (is) a serious matter': again ironic. σπουδαῖος occurs first here and in Theognis (64–5 χρῆμα σπουδαῖον etc.), χρῆμα in Hesiod (*Op.* 344, 402).

334–64 Apollo's speech is simple in structure and content, and the language is quite repetitious (335 κερτομέων, 338 κέρτομον, 340 ἐλαύνων, 342 ἐλάων, 342, 349 πέλωρα, 347, 350 διὰ ψαμαθώδεα χῶρον, 352 στίβον, 353 στίβος).

334 μῦθον . . . οὐκ ἀλαπαδνόν 'no feeble tale', i.e. a truly serious matter.

335 Apollo was evidently sensitive to criticism for being greedy: see 176–81, 494–5, 549nn. φιλολήϊος ('fond of plunder') is a *hapax legomenon*, which echoes ληΐδα in 330, just as ἐλαύνων (340) and ἐλάων (342) echo ἐλαύνεις (330).

336–9 The opening of Apollo's *narratio* already characterises his opponent as a downright master-thief and trickster, and is full of vivid language. παῖδά τινα is somewhat derogatory ('some mere child'). διαπρύσιος means 'piercing', and so 'through and through, utter', with a possible secondary allusion also to the thief's activity as a piercer of walls (178, 283). κεραϊστής (from κεραΐζω, 'plunder'), occurs only here in literature, but is listed by Hesychius, with the sense 'baneful comet', which suggests that it was used in another source.

337 Cf. Hes. *Op.* 635 πολὺν διὰ πόντον ἀνύσσας.

338 κέρτομον: the form κέρτομος occurs first in Hesiod (*Op.* 788).

339 λησίμβροτοι 'deceivers of men': another *hapax*, similar in form to τερψίμβροτος.

ἐπὶ γαῖαν: for the accusative without an idea of motion cf. *Od.* 4.417, 7.332, 17.386.

342 εὐθὺ Πύλονδ' ἐλάων: cf. 355 εἰς Πύλον εὐθὺς ἐλῶντα. εὐθύ for Homeric ἰθύ occurs first here, but εὐθύς is found in archaic poetry and then in Attic and later Greek (cf. Janko (1982) 147). At 215–17 Apollo sets off in the general direction of Pylos, perhaps (by implication) having learnt this from the bird-omen of 213–14.

342–55 After the initial statement of the theft comes a much more detailed section devoted to the all-important theme of the physical evidence (i.e. the footprints) and the verbal testimony of the old man.

342–9 Cf. 219–26, where the two sets of prints are distinguished. In 225 and 349 πέλωρα refers only to Hermes' prints, but with δοιά in 342 it must refer to both sets. δῖα is a possible variant, but δοιά introduces the description in 344–9 (τῇσιν μὲν γὰρ . . . αὐτὸς δ' . . .).

344–5 'For in the case of the cattle, the black dust which held the footprints showed them facing backwards towards the meadow of asphodel': cf. 220–1. For κόνῑς cf. A. *PV* 1084, *Supp.* 180, 783, in contrast to Homeric κόνῐς, κόνῐν (*Il.* 13.335, 18.23, 23.764).

346 αὐτὸς δ' οὗτος ἄδεκτος ἀμήχανος 'but as for himself, this unacceptable, impossible fellow'. For ἄδεκτος cf. Hesychius s.v. ἄδεκτον· ἄπιστον. Later (Theophrastus etc.) it is used to mean either 'incapable of' or 'unacceptable', and the latter sense is perfectly possible. This reading gives a suitably emphatic reduplication of epithets with alpha privative (cf. 80n.). West's οὔθ' ὁδοῦ ἐκτός ('without either leaving the road') is ingenious, but the word order is awkward, with this phrase separating οὗτος from ἀμήχανος, and the sense does not add much, in terms of Apollo's general expression of puzzlement about the footprints.

347 χερσὶν ἔβαινε: i.e. 'walked on all fours', as in A. *Eum.* 37 τρέχω δὲ χερσίν.

348–9 ἀλλ' . . . βαίνοι 'but he had some other scheme, and was rubbing such monstrous tracks as if one were walking on slender tree trunks'. In Homer vowels are normally scanned long before -τρ-. For the scansion διἔτριβε cf. 394 ἀπἔκρυψε, *Od.* 5.488 ἐνἔκρυψε, and other examples in Chantraine, *GH* I 108.

350–5 Apollo is like a detective following the tracks as far as they are visible, and then when they vanish picking up the trail by other means. Cf. 353 ἄφραστος contrasted with 354 ἐφράσατο.

352–3 στίβον . . . στίβος: 'track' in the sense of 'trodden way' and 'footmarks'. The word occurs first here, then in fifth-century and later prose and poetry.

355 εἰς Πύλον εὐθὺς ἐλῶντα: strictly speaking the old man did not tell Apollo this fact, and the narrative is slightly compressed here (see on 342).

356 κατέερξε: this compound occurs first here, then in Herodotus and later.

357 καὶ . . . ἔνθα 'and had juggled his lightning tricks on one side of the road and the other'. διαπυρπαλαμᾶν occurs only here, and could well have been invented ad hoc. πυρπάλαμος ('fire-fashioned') is used as an epithet of the thunderbolt by Pindar (*O.* 10.80), and πυρπαλάμης is said by Hesychius s.v. to be applied to 'those who can devise something quickly', and τοὺς ποικίλους τὸ ἦθος; cf. Photius s.v. πυρπαλάμην 'one who manages something cleverly (παλαμώμενος) like fire'. Eustathius (*Hom.* 513.30) explains πυρπαλαμᾶσθαι as 'to perform evil tricks, and as it were go through fire in one's trickery'. Perhaps the idea is of Hermes' cleverly and quickly concealing all traces, as he actually does after the sacrifice at 138–41. Apollo's phrase is derogatory and vague. Cf. 226 αἰνὰ μὲν ἔνθεν ὁδοῖο, τὰ δ' αἰνότερ' ἔνθεν ὁδοῖο.

358–60 Apollo strongly emphasises Hermes' attempt to hide himself, as a further indication of his guilt (cf. 235–42). μελαίνῃ νυκτὶ ἐοικώς suggests both invisibility and deceitfulness or evil intention, and perhaps echoes *Il.* 1.47 ὁ δ' ἤϊε νυκτὶ ἐοικώς, of Apollo's own deadly journey to send plague on the Greeks. ἄντρωι ἐν ἠερόεντι κατὰ ζόφον repeats this motif of impenetrable darkness, and οὐδέ κεν . . . ἐσκέψατο is a vivid exaggeration of the same idea.

360 αἰετὸς ὀξὺ λάων 'keen-sighted eagle'. Cf. Hesychius s.v. λάετε· σκοπεῖτε, βλέπετε, and two manuscripts have βλέπων as a gloss on λάων in this verse; cf. *Il.* 17.675, where an eagle is said to be 'keenest in sight of all the birds under heaven', *Od.* 19.229 (with Russo's discussion of λάω), and *Il.* 13.344, where γηθήσειε λάων is a papyrus variant for γηθήσειεν ἰδών.

360–1 Apollo cites another of Hermes' childlike gestures, by which he pretends to have been asleep, as at 240–2.

361 αὐγὰς: αὐγαί meaning 'eyes' occurs first here, later in Attic tragedy.

ὠμόργαζε: ὀμοργάζειν occurs only here, but cf. Homeric ὀμόργνυμι, and *Od.* 18.199–200 τὴν δὲ γλυκὺς ὕπνος ἀνῆκε, | καὶ ῥ' ἀπομόρξατο χερσὶ παρείας.

δολοφροσύνην ἀλεγύνων: cf. 476 ἀγλαΐας ἀλέγυνε, *H. Aph.* 11 ἀγλαὰ ἔργ' ἀλεγύνειν. In the *Odyssey* ἀλεγύνω is used only of preparing a meal.

362 μῦθον ἀπηλεγέως ἀγόρευεν: cf. *Il.* 9.309 τὸν μῦθον ἀπηλεγέως ἀποειπεῖν, *Od.* 1.373.

363–4 A direct quotation of Hermes' outright denial at 263–4 (with οὐδέ κε for οὐκ ἄν in 364), dramatically closing Apollo's speech.

365 Cf. *Od.* 16.213 ὣς ἄρα φωνήσας κατ' ἄρ' ἕζετο (again with double ἄρα), and similarly *Il.* 1.68 etc.

366–88 Hermes' second defence speech is another masterpiece of special pleading and injured innocence (cf. 260–77 with comments). To begin with he makes a gesture with his right hand towards Zeus as president of the assembly, like an accomplished orator (367). His opening gambit is the standard assertion of truthfulness, underscored by reference to his own sincerity and lack of expertise in falsehood (a variant of the disclaimer to expertise in public speeches). 370–7 are a *narratio*, emphasising Apollo's disturbance of Hermes' peace at an early hour of the day, his lack of witnesses, and his violent and threatening behaviour towards one so young and helpless. 377 repeats the argument from τὸ εἰκός made at 265, about the implausibility of the charge. 378–84 then appeal to Zeus for parental support, with a skilful and literally truthful denial of the charge (379–80), an assertion of his respect for the gods (381–2), especially Helios (whom he has not offended, as he worked at night), and an offer again to swear an appropriate oath (383–4 ~ 274–7). His conclusion includes a threat to be avenged against Apollo, showing the emotion of righteous indignation suitable to a peroration, and a final appeal to Zeus to support the younger and weaker party (385–6). On Hermes' use of standard techniques of rhetoric see Görgemanns (1976), 113–19. For the childish aspects of style of the speech see Van Nortwick (1975, 93–5): cf. 260–77n.

366 Neither of the two variant lines is traditional as a formula of response, although they are made up of formulaic elements. Manuscript variation in such formulae is common in the Homeric poems (cf. Allen (1895) 302). For ἄλλον μῦθον cf. *Il.* 7.358 = 12.232 οἶσθα καὶ ἄλλον μῦθον ἀμείνονα τοῦδε νοῆσαι. ἄλλον μῦθον refers here specifically to Hermes' speech as a whole.

367 **δείξατο δ' εἰς Κρονίωνα** 'he pointed towards the son of Cronos': cf. Hdt. 4.150 ἅμα τε ἔλεγε καὶ ἐδείκνυε ἐς τὸν Βάττον.

θεῶν σημάντορα πάντων: cf. Hes. *Sc.* 56.

368–9 Hermes' insistence on the fact that he is by his very nature unable to lie may also allude ironically to Apollo's claim to veracity as a mantic god. If so, it would be a kind of counter to 335, where Apollo throws back at him the charge of rapacity. False tales are introduced by an assertion of veracity at *Od.* 14.192, 16.61, *H. Dem.* 120–1. Here, however, Hermes does strictly speaking avoid telling any direct lies in what follows.

368 **ἀληθείην ἀγορεύσω:** cf. 561 ἀληθείην ἀγορεύειν. The variant reading καταλέξω could have been suggested by the common Homeric formula ἀληθείην/ἀτρεκέως καταλέξω/-ον/κατέλεξα.

369 **νημερτής** 'unerring': used of persons at *Od.* 4.349 etc. (Proteus) and Hes. *Th.* 235 (Nereus).

370 Hermes deliberately does not name Apollo throughout his speech, and the introduction to the narrative is abrupt: 'he entered our home...' Similarly in Attic drama, omission of a person's name in a speech may be a sign of anger or dislike. Forceful irruption into someone's home is described in Demosthenes, *Against Meidias* 78 εἰσεπήδησαν ἀδελφὸς ὁ τούτου καὶ οὗτος εἰς τὴν οἰκίαν.

ἐς ἡμετέρου: this form, for ἐς ἡμέτερον, must be due to analogy with ἐς πατρός etc. ('to the house of...'). It is a variant with ἐς ἡμέτερον at *Od.* 2.55, 7.301, 17.534, and had Aristarchus' support. It is described as Attic by Schol. *Od.* 2.55, 7.301, but occurs also in Herodotus (1.35, 7.8δ).

371 **ἠελίοιο νεὸν ἐπιτελλομένοιο:** this is an un-Homeric expression for sunrise. ἐπιτέλλομαι is the term used by Hesiod (*Op.* 383, 567) and later (in the active) for the rising of a constellation or heavenly body. The variant νεόν γ' is possible, as the unsociable time of day could be stressed, but equally γ' may have been added *metri gratia*. Cf. 197 ἠελίοιο νεὸν καταδυομένοιο, again un-Homeric.

372 Apollo had cited the old man as an eyewitness (354–5), but failed to bring with him any divine witnesses to justify his assault on Hermes. In Homer the form μάρτυρος is used. μάρτυς occurs first in Hesiod (*Op.* 371), and κατόπτης first here (cf. Aeschylus etc.). μάρτυς/-υρος is used in cases where someone is actually invoked or called as a witness to a fact or a statement (e.g. an oath), whereas a κατόπτης or αὐτόπτης is someone who happens to have been present at an event (cf. Nenci (1958) 221–41).

373 'But he insisted on disclosure with much duress' (West). The language again has a legal tone: for μηνύειν cf. 254, and ἀνάγκη is used later of torture, punishment, etc. (LSJ s.v. 1.3).

373–4 **ἀναγκαίης ὕπο πολλῆς, | πολλὰ δέ μ' ἠπείλησε:** the anaphora with variation of πολλῆς and πολλά is a common device.

375 Cf. Hes. *Th.* 988 τέρεν ἄνθος ἔχοντ' ἐρικυδέος ἥβης. φιλοκυδής occurs only here and at 481, but later as a proper name Φιλοκύδης. In this line ἐρικυδής would not scan. Cf. also *Il.* 13.484 ἥβης ἄνθος, *H. Dem.* 108 κουρήϊον ἄνθος ἔχουσαι.
376 τὰ δέ τ' οἶδε καὶ αὐτός is parenthetical. Cf. 382–3 οἶσθα καὶ αὐτὸς | ὡς οὐκ αἴτιός εἰμι.
377 Cf. 265.
378 Cf. *Od.* 9.519, 529 πατὴρ δ' ἐμὸς εὔχεται (εὔχεαι) εἶναι, and formulae such as υἷος . . . εὔχομαι εἶναι. Hermes seems to be taking something for granted, since Zeus has not yet explicitly admitted paternity in his case and the affair was secret (cf. 5–9).
379–80 **ὡς . . . ἔλασσα . . . ἔβην** is dependent on πείθεο, with ὣς ὄλβιος εἴην parenthetical, 'so may I prosper', i.e. the prayer or wish for prosperity is dependent on the truth of what he claims. Strictly speaking Hermes had crossed his threshold at line 23, but 380 can be taken as referring to the same event as in 379, and on his return he slipped through the keyhole (145–7). Cf. *Il.* 15.36–46, where Hera swears a solemn oath that she had not prompted Poseidon directly to help the Greeks, again strictly true, but totally misleading (see Janko's comments ad loc.).
381–2 The three verbs are carefully chosen: due respect for the Sun-god as all-seeing witness and guardian of justice, love for his father, and awe or reverence for his elder brother. In Homer and Hesiod ὀπίζομαι or ἐποπίζομαι are especially used of awe or dread for the anger of a god or powerful mortal, and ὄπις normally of divine vengeance (cf. *LfgrE* s.v.). Hermes can show respect for Helios, since he has not directly offended him, the whole crime having occurred at night.
383 **μέγαν δ' ἐπιδώσομαι ὅρκον** 'I shall offer in addition a great oath'. This reading gives a future tense, which might be taken as an offer to swear rather than an actual oath (cf. 274–7n.).
384 εὐκόσμητος is a *hapax legomenon*, but εὐκόσμως occurs at *Od.* 21.123, Hes. *Op.* 628. προθύραια (perhaps 'porticoes') is also a *hapax* as a noun: cf. Homeric πρόθυρον, and later προθύραιος as an epithet of deities. This extraordinary form of oath may be inspired by Hermes' own role as προπύλαιος or gate-keeper (see 15n. on πυληδόκον). Cf. Men. fr. 884 K–A μαρτύρομαι, | < . . . .> τὸν Ἀπόλλω τουτον<ὶ> καὶ τὰς θύρας, where someone swears by Apollo Agyieus and the doors near which his statue stands.
385 'And some day I shall repay him in addition for his pitiless search.' Text and interpretation are uncertain. This reading assumes that ποτί is adverbial, and φωρή refers to Apollo's investigation: cf. Hesychius s.v. φώρην· τὴν ἔρευναν, LSJ s.v. φωρά II 'detection, discovery', and 134–7n. The legal term used for searching to recover stolen property is φωρᾶν. For καί ποτε cf. *H. Ap.* 305, *H. Aph.* 48. τίνω normally means 'pay' or 'repay', whereas the middle means 'take vengeance for', but τείσω could be ironic, i.e. 'recompense' in a bad sense. It is possible also (as Gemoll suggests) that the words have the secondary meaning 'I

shall repay the cruel theft', i.e. Hermes could be hinting that in the end he *will* recompense Apollo, as he does by his gift of the lyre. Cf. 385–6 with 417–18 ῥεῖα μάλ' ἐπρήϋνεν . . . | καὶ κρατερόν περ ἐόντα.

386 καὶ κρατερῶι περ ἐόντι: cf. *Il.* 15.195 καὶ κρατερός περ ἐών, *Od.* 8.360.

σὺ δ' ὁπλοτέροισιν ἄρηγε: Hermes ends with a last appeal. Apollo may be the stronger party (and due for more respect as the older one), but Hermes is the younger. Zeus himself was the youngest child (Hes. *Th.* 468–84).

387 ἐπιλλίζων 'winking': cf. *Od.* 18.11 οὐκ ἀΐεις ὅτι δή μοι ἐπιλλίζουσιν ἅπαντες; ἰλλός means 'squinting', and ἐπιλλίζω is later used of looking askance or mockingly (AR 1.486, 3.791, 4.389). Hermes invites Zeus's complicity in his deceit.

388 Hermes has been holding his σπάργανον over his (left) arm throughout his speech, partly to conceal the lyre, and partly also perhaps as the visible sign of his infancy. ὠλένη occurs nowhere else in early epic, but cf. λευκώλενος.

389–96 The quarrel is resolved painlessly by Zeus, whose reaction to Hermes' speech resembles Apollo's at 281, a mixture of admiration and amusement, and Hermes needs no further inducement to comply. He still has up his sleeve (or rather, under his arm) his greatest trick of all to win Apollo's favour.

389 κακομηδέα: another *hapax legomenon.*

390 εὖ καὶ ἐπισταμένως: cf. *Il.* 10.265, *Od.* 20.161, 23.197, Hes. *Op.* 107.

391 ὁμοφρόνα θυμὸν ἔχοντας: cf. *Il.* 22.263 (ἔχουσιν), *H. Dem.* 434 (ἔχουσαι), Theognis 81, 765.

392 ζητεύειν . . . ἡγεμονεύειν: a neatly balanced pair of verbs. For ζητεύειν (a poetic form of ζητέειν) cf. *H. Ap.* 215, Hes. *Op.* 400.

διάκτορον: Hermes is the guide here, as in his later role.

393 ἐπ' ἀβλαβίηισι νόοιο 'without malicious intent'. Zeus lays down as a condition that Hermes should act properly from now on. The phrase, as part of his verdict, has a legal ring to it. Cf. 524 ἐπ' ἀρθμῶι καὶ φιλότητι, A. *Ag.* 1024 Ζεὺς ἀπέπαυσεν ἐπ' ἀβλαβείαι (with Fraenkel's note), E. *Hipp.* 511 οὔτ' ἐπὶ βλαβῆι φρενῶν, and ἀβλαβῶς, ἀβλαβής in treaties (Th. 5.18, 47, *IG* I 33). ἀβλαβίη occurs first here; cf. the personified Ἀβλαβίαι in *SIG* 1014.67, Cretan ἀβλοπία (*GDI* 4986, 5125), and *H. Herm.* 83 ἀβλαβέως.

394 δὴ αὖτ': with synizesis, as at *Il.* 1.340 etc.

ἀπέκρυψε: for this scansion cf. 348–9n.

395 nicely balances the nod of Zeus and Hermes' agreement. ἀγλαὸς Ἑρμῆς (only here, but cf. 432 Διὸς ἀγλαὸς υἱός) is a variant with initial vowel for κύδιμος Ἑρμῆς. In 314 and 500 it is Apollo who is Λητοῦς ἀγλαὸς υἱός.

396 This line closes the whole episode with a reference to the persuasive power of Zeus's will, and the characteristic ease with which divinity achieves its purpose.

397–512 The two brothers went to the ford of the Alpheios, where the cattle were hidden, and Hermes drove them out of the cave. Apollo was amazed to see that Hermes had killed two of the cows. He began to make bonds of withy (to tie them), but Hermes made them grow into the ground and twine themselves round the cattle, again to Apollo's amazement. But he placated Apollo easily, for he delighted him by playing the lyre, and he sang about the origin of the gods and how they were allotted their honours. Apollo was astonished at this new sound, asked him how he had discovered it, and promised to reward him with fame and prosperity.

Hermes in answer promised to share his skill with Apollo, and reminded him that he had received from Zeus the powers of omniscience and prophecy. He should play and sing as he wished. If one played with skill the lyre would easily respond, if not it would sound discordantly. Hermes ended by asking Apollo to share with him his role as patron of cattle, and to give up his anger.

Apollo took the lyre, gave Hermes his goad and the care of cattle, and began to play the lyre and sing. The cows returned to their sacred meadow, the two gods went back to Olympus, and Zeus was glad and made them friends. So Hermes has loved Apollo ever since, having taught him how to play the lyre, whilst he in turn invented the panpipes for himself to play.

In this scene of reconciliation the two leading themes of the earlier part of the hymn are interwoven, the creation of the lyre and the theft of the cattle. The lyre is the instrument of harmony and appeasement, by which Apollo's favour is won and strife is ended (cf. Pindar, *Pythian* 1). In return for this gift Hermes receives a share in Apollo's care of cattle (and other animals: cf. 567–71), thus regaining as a free gift what he had originally won by theft. As in the legend of Archilochus' meeting with the Muses (where he receives a lyre in exchange for his cow), lyre and cattle are the elements in a complex process of exchange between the two brothers (cf. 437): Hermes the thief has become Hermes the god of commerce (cf. 516–17). At the same time Hermes emphasises Apollo's own gift of prophecy, a counterpart of musical skill (cf. 466–74, 489, 533–5), and this motif will be resumed in the final part of the hymn, where Apollo grants him a special type of prophecy at Delphi, separate from his own (533–66).

398 For Pylos and the ford over the Alpheios see 128–9, 216nn., and *H. Ap.* 398, 423.

400 ἠχοῦ ('where') occurs nowhere else, though cf. Hesychius s.v. ἤχου [*sic*]· ἐνθάδε. ἦχι ('where') is Homeric, and ἠχοῖ is a dialect form (Oropus, *IG* VII 235.16). The form, however, is comparable to common Greek ἀλλαχοῦ, πανταχοῦ, etc., and therefore gives no indication of the hymn's provenance: Janko (1982) 148.

τὰ χρήματ' 'livestock': in the plural this word can refer to any kind of goods or property (literally 'useable things'), e.g. *Od.* 2.78, 203, etc., but is not used elsewhere in early Greek poetry of livestock; it probably has this sense in Xenophon *An.* 5.2.4, 7.8.12; cf. Hesychius s.v. χρήματα· κτήματα, βοσκήματα.

ἀτάλλετο 'were being cared for', or 'were feeding'. The normal epic form for this would be ἀτιτάλλετο (cf. *Il.* 5.271 etc.), but this is unmetrical here, although most MSS read it. ἀτάλλω means 'foster' at Hom. *Epigr.* 4.2 (= *Vita Herodotea Homeri* 174 Allen), and is used in a similar sense metaphorically at Pi. fr. 214.2

Snell–Maehler, S. *Ai.* 559, whereas it means 'play' at *Il.* 13.27, Hes. *Op.* 131 (cf. ἀταλός).

401 κιὼν παρὰ λάϊνον ἄντρον 'going the length of the rocky cavern' (West). ἐς (M's reading) is probably a conjecture, παρά being the more difficult reading.

402 εἰς φῶς: in Homer φάος or φόως are always used, and so normally in Hesiod and the *Hymns*. But cf. Hes. fr. 204.150 ἐς φῶς. Otherwise φῶς recurs in Attic and later Greek. In this hymn there is no need to change it to φάος.

403 ἀπάτερθεν ἰδών 'looking aside'. Cf. Theognis 1059 ἀπάτερθεν ὁρῶντι.

405 ἐδύνω: this contracted form of the imperfect (cf. ἐδύνασο) is not found elsewhere in early poetry (cf. Xen. *An.* 1.6.7, 7.5.5). For similar cases cf. Chantraine, *GH* I 52–3.

δειροτομῆσαι: literally 'cut the throat of', and so not strictly true in this case, but virtually equivalent to 'slaughter'.

406 ὧδε νεογνὸς . . . καὶ νήπιος 'such a newborn infant as you are', with emphatic alliteration and duplication of sense. For νεογνός cf. *H. Dem.* 141 etc.

αὐτὸς ἐγώ γε 'I myself indeed'. Cf. 473, and for αὐτός of Apollo see 234n.

407 θαυμαίνω κατόπισθε τὸ σὸν κράτος 'I wonder at your strength in the future'.

407–8 οὐδὲ . . . ἀέξεσθαι 'you had better not go on growing much taller'.

409–19 The sequence of events is unclear, and it is possible that a line or lines have dropped out (e.g. after 415 or 416). Apollo plaits bonds of withy, but these (410 ταί = the withies) take root in the ground and entwine themselves around all the cattle, to Apollo's amazement. Hermes looks at the place with flashing eyes, 'eager to hide (it)' (?). But then he easily pacifies Apollo, by playing on the lyre. It is not clear whether Apollo wants to bind Hermes or the cattle. But it is a bit late for him to do the former, since Hermes has done as he was told by Zeus, and there is no indication as yet that Apollo fears any further thefts (as he does at 514–20). More probably he is preparing to bind his cattle, before taking them home (although at 503–4 they seem to return of their own accord). Withies were commonly used to bind livestock: cf. for example *Od.* 9.427, E. *Cyc.* 224–5, Verg. *G.* 3.166–7, Columella 6.2.3. There is no need for a lacuna after 409, as ταί can refer to the δεσμὰ ἄγνου, i.e. ἄγνοι. Hermes then performs a miracle which stops the cattle from leaving, and in his usual mischievous way (415) seems intent on covering the whole place with bushes (see 410–13, 416nn.). Then, somewhat abruptly, he turns his attention to the more essential task of winning over his brother by the power of music. The episode of the bound cattle seems to be forgotten, but in the end Hermes gains a wider share in βουκολίαι (497–8).

409 χερσί 'with his [i.e. Apollo's] hands'. Cf. *Il.* 19.131 χειρὶ περιστρέψας.

410 ἄγνου: first here, whereas Homer uses λύγος. It recurs in Hippocrates, and in Attic and later Greek.

410–13 ταὶ δ' . . . κλεψίφρονος: possibly there is an aetiological point to Hermes' miracle, i.e. some bushes or trees may have been identified as those he had created. Eitrem (1909, 333–5) compared Paus. 2.31.10, which describes a statue of Hermes Polygios (= πολυ-λύγιος ?), against which Hermes leaned his club of wild olive wood: this took root, and was still growing there in Pausanias' day. Other aetiological legends told of various statues of deities which were bound with withies, or found in a withy bush: cf. Paus. 3.16.11 (Artemis Lygodesma), 7.4.4, and Menodotus of Samos, *FGrH* 541 F 1 (Hera of Samos), quoted in Athenaeus' discussion of withy-wreaths (671E–4B). Cf. also Paus. 1.27.1 (the wooden image of Hermes in the temple of Athena Polias on the Acropolis of Athens was hidden in myrtle boughs), Merkelbach (1970–1) 549–65. In *Hymn* 7 the pirates bind Dionysus with withies, but these fall away from his hands and feet (11–15), and then a vine grows along the top of the sail and ivy twines itself around the mast (38–41).

410 αἶψα φύοντο: suddenness is typical of such miracles. Cf. *H.* 7.38 αὐτίκα, and similarly when ivy grows at once (εὐθύς) round the newborn Dionysus in E. *Ph.* 651–4.

411 ἐμβολάδην: only here, and perhaps meaning that they grew into one another 'like grafts'. Cf. later ἐμβάλλω (LSJ s.v. 1.8), ἐμβολάς, ἔμβολος (LSJ s.v. 7), of grafting.

412 'Easily, and over all the cattle': these are two separate qualifications of φύοντο. Ease is also a feature of the miraculous, or divine activity. Cf. for example Hes. *Op.* 5–8, with West's comments.

413 Hermes and Apollo frame this line, in contrast.

κλεψίφρονος: only here and in late authors (Manetho, Gregory of Nazianzus).

414 θαύμασεν: the aorist is used first here.

415 χῶρον ὑποβλήδην ἐσκέψατο πῦρ ἀμαρύσσων 'eyed the place askance, flashing fiery glances'. Cf. Hes. *Th.* 827 ὑπ' ὀφρύσι πῦρ ἀμάρυσσεν (of Typhoeus), *H. Herm.* 278 πυκνὸν ἀπὸ βλεφάρων ἀμαρύσσων, and 45. For ἀμαρύσσω used transitively cf. Q.S. 8.29. ὑποβλήδην ἐσκέψατο is like ὑποβλέπειν, ὑπόδρα ἰδεῖν. In *Il.* 1.292 ὑποβλήδην seems to mean 'interrupting', and in later epic 'in reply'.

416 ἐγκρύψαι μεμαώς: if the text of 415–16 is correct, the object must be χῶρον, i.e. Hermes covers the area where the cattle are with the withy branches. This, however, does not necessarily imply that he wants to hide the cattle again from Apollo. The miracle seems to be rather just another demonstration of the mischievous powers of this Puck-like creature.

417 ὡς ἔθελ' αὐτός 'just as he himself wanted'.

418 καὶ κρατερόν περ ἐόντα: see 386n.

418–26 The preparations for Hermes' musical display are described at length, as befits this momentous occasion. He begins to play, and Apollo's reactions of laughter, delight, and desire are portrayed (cf. also 434, and 436–55). He then stands confidently on Apollo's left side and begins the prelude of his song. Throughout this passage there is a constant emphasis on the power of this new music to evoke desire, and this theme is developed later in the scene: cf. 434, 448–9, 478–88, and Introduction 3(b).

418 λύρην: this conjecture supplies an object for ἐπειρήτιζε. The lyre is not actually called λύρη before this point in the hymn, but cf. 423, and 47–51n. The alternative is to posit a lacuna after 416 or 418.

419–20 Cf. 53–4, and also 501–2 where M's reading ὑπὸ νέρθεν is probably right. The repetition of χειρός in 418–19 is due to the 'formular' character of the phrasing. For 420 cf. also *Od.* 17.542 σμερδαλέον κονάβησε, γέλασσε δὲ Πηνελόπεια, and Hes. *Th.* 40 where in reaction to the Muses' song on Olympus γελᾶι δέ τε δώματα πατρός (etc.).

421 ἐρατὴ δὲ διὰ φρένας ἤλυθ' ἰωή: cf. *Il.* 10.139 περὶ φρένας ἤλυθ' ἰωή, *Od.* 17.261–2 περὶ δέ σφεας ἤλυθ' ἰωὴ | φόρμιγγος γλαφυρῆς.

422 The omission of this line in all MSS except M may be due to a scribe's eye jumping from 421 ἐρατή to 423 ἐρατόν.

θεσπεσίης ἐνοπῆς: cf. *H. Ap.* 360 θεσπεσίη δ' ἐνοπή, and for ἐνοπή of the music of pipes *Il.* 10.13, *H. Herm.* 512; also *Il.* 2.599–600 ἀοιδὴν | θεσπεσίην.

καί μιν γλυκὺς ἵμερος ἥιρει: cf. *Il.* 3.446, 14.328 καί με γλυκὺς ἵμερος αἱρεῖ (of love), and *Od.* 23.144–5, of the singer, ἐν δέ σφισιν ἵμερον ὦρσε | μολπῆς etc.

423 θυμῶι ἀκουάζοντα: West's θυμόν would be parallel to 434 (double accusative with ἥιρει), but is not absolutely necessary.

λύρηι δ' ἐρατὸν κιθαρίζων: cf. 455, and *H. Ap.* 515 ἐρατὸν κιθαρίζων.

424–5 Hermes is encouraged by Apollo's response and so takes up his stand beside him, with Apollo on his right (the more honorific position).

427–33 Hermes' song is a cosmogony or theogony like Hesiod's, and the poet seems to have the song of the Muses at the opening of Hesiod's *Theogony* particularly in mind throughout this episode. Cf. also 420 with *Th.* 40. 427–8 and 431–2 resemble the themes of *Th.* 43–6 (and 105–13), and the prominence of Mnemosyne as mother of the Muses recalls *Th.* 53–5. Cf. also 423 ἐρατὸν κιθαρίζων and 426 ἐρατὴ . . . φωνή with *Th.* 65 ἐρατὴν . . . ὄσσαν, 70 ἐρατὸς δοῦπος. Moreover, Hermes' song has the effect of appeasing Apollo: cf. the power of the Muses to effect reconciliation and to relieve sorrow, at *Th.* 80–93, 98–103. Radermacher (p. 149) suggested that the poet might have in mind an actual *Theogony* attributed to Hermes, since the late antique *Corpus Hermeticum* contains such theogonic poetry. Hermes' second song has a broader and more ambitious theme than his first (54–61), as it concerns divine society in general, to whose company he now aspires after his exploits: cf. Johnston (2002) 124.

426 ἀμβολάδην 'as a prelude'. Cf. *Od.* 1.155, 8.266 φορμίζων ἀνεβάλλετο καλὸν ἀείδειν (and 17.261), Pi. *N.* 10.31 ἀμβολάδαν. In *Il.* 21.361 ἀμβολάδην is used of water 'bubbling up'.

ἐρατὴ . . . φωνή is a parenthesis.

427 κραίνων 'honouring'. Cf. Hesychius s.v. κραίνειν· τιμᾶν (etc.). The verb does not seem to be used in exactly this sense elsewhere, but in some of its Homeric uses it could be interpreted as 'give due honour to', as well as 'accomplish', e.g. *Il.* 1.41, 504 τόδε μοι κρήηνον ἐέλδωρ. In *H. Herm.* 531 and 559 it perhaps means 'authorise, give due authority to'. West (2003) translates here 'he spoke authoritatively of'. Jaillard (2007, 199–204) argues that it actually means 'authorise' here, and that Hermes' song promotes the existence of the gods, but this surely gives him too much power.

γαῖαν ἐρεμνήν: cf. *Od.* 24.106 ἐρεμνὴν γαῖαν, although there this refers to descending to the Underworld.

428 These are major themes of Hesiod's *Theogony*, as announced in the proem: *Th.* 108 εἴπατε δ' ὡς τὰ πρῶτα θεοὶ καὶ γαῖα γένοντο, and 112 καὶ ὡς τιμὰς διέλοντο. For the latter cf. *Th.* 383–403 (Styx and her children), 411ff. (Hecate), 885, etc. Cf. also the division of the world between the three sons of Cronos at *Il.* 15.187–93, where Poseidon says that ἕκαστος δ' ἔμμορε τιμῆς, and ἤτοι ἐγὼν ἔλαχον πολίην ἅλα, etc.

429–30 For a god to begin his song with praise of Mnemosyne is perhaps rather like a mortal singer beginning with the Muses (as Hesiod does in the *Theogony*). But here she is also said to have been assigned to Hermes as his patron. For this type of expression cf. *Il.* 23.78–9 κὴρ . . . ἥ περ λάχε γιγνόμενόν περ. This suits Hermes' roles as god of speech and interpretation in later literature. Cf. also Hes. *Th.* 94–5 (Apollo and Muses as patrons of singers), and Call. *H. Ap.* 43 κεῖνος ὀϊστευτὴν ἔλαχ' ἀνέρα, κεῖνος ἀοιδόν.

431 **κατὰ πρέσβιν** 'according to seniority'. Cf. Pl. *Lg.* 855D, 924C, for this phrase.

433 **κατὰ κόσμον** 'in due order', often applied to speech or song, e.g. 479, *Od.* 8.489, etc.

ὑπωλένιον κιθαρίζων 'playing the lyre beneath his arm'. Cf. 510, where the MSS have ὑπωλένιον. The instrument was supported by a strap or sling looped round the player's left wrist and attached to the arm of the lyre: cf. Maas and Snyder (1989) 98, West (1992) 65. Consequently ὑπωλένιον seems more likely to be right than ἐπωλένιον in the MSS here. It recurs at Theocr. 17.30 of a quiver.

434 **ἔρος . . . ἀμήχανος** 'helpless longing'. Cf. 447 μοῦσα ἀμηχανέων μελεδώνων.

436–95 Apollo's speech expresses his admiration and amazement, hints at an exchange of cattle for lyre (437), and ends with a solemn promise of fame and favour for his brother. The hint is taken up by Hermes (464–5, 475–95), who couples it with a request that Apollo should honour his promise (477), and an emphasis on Apollo's prophetic omniscience, which hints in turn at his desire for a share in this skill.

436 The structure of this verse, with its accumulated epithets, resembles *Il.* 13.769 Δύσπαρι, εἶδος ἄριστε, γυναιμανές, ἠπεροπευτά. βουφόνος is new, but cf. βουφονέων at *Il.* 7.466. It recurs in Simonides and Aeschylus, and as the title of the priest in the Attic ritual of the Bouphonia at Paus. 1.24.4. μηχανιώτης is unique, but on the same model as ἀγγελιώτην (296), σπαργανιῶτα (301), etc. πονεύμενε ('busy') shows the kind of use of a participle as an epithet which is commoner in later hymns and Nonnus: cf. Orph. *H.* 14.7–8 ὀβριμόθυμε | ψευδομένη, σώτειρα, 51.7 φαινόμεναι, ἀφανεῖς (etc.), Nonnus *D.* 2.570 ψευδόμενε, σκηπτοῦχε. δαιτὸς ἑταῖρε gives Hermes the same phrase he had applied to the tortoise (31).

437 This plays with the literal sense of oxen (i.e. Apollo's stolen cattle) and their use as a measure of value (ἑκατόμβοιος etc.). Cf. Leduc (2005) 163–4.

μέμηλας 'you have contrived': μέλω is used only here with an (internal) object, usually with genitive. μέμηδας is a possible correction.

438 The asyndeton gives dramatic emphasis to this important statement.

ἡσυχίως: first here; cf. Pl. *Tht.* 179e, and ἡσύχιον *Il.* 21.598, ἡσυχίη *Od.* 18.22.

439–42 Apollo's question reflects the kind of thing one might ask a human musician, and indeed might be traditional in that context: were you born with this skill, or did you have a divine or mortal teacher? It seems rather incongruous for the god of music to ask another god if he was taught by a mortal.

440 **ἐκ γενετῆς:** cf. *Il.* 24.535 (of gifts given by the gods), *Od.* 18.6.

442 **δῶρον ἀγαυόν:** in Homer ἀγαυός is only used of persons (heroes etc.). Cf. Pi. *Paean* 9, fr. 52 k. 36 Snell–Maehler (with θρόος, of song), and later Greek verse and prose.

θέσπιν ἀοιδήν: cf. *Od.* 1.328, 8.498 (with θεὸς ὤπασε).

443 'For wonderful is this newly spoken voice which I hear': νεήφατος occurs only here, but cf. Homeric παλαίφατος.

447–8 Apollo's second question concerns the nature of this skill itself, and is divided into three parts (τέχνη, μοῦσα, τρίβος), which are counterbalanced by the triad of gifts which it offers (449). Just as at 440–2 he had distinguished innate ability and learning, so here he speaks of skill, inspiration (μοῦσα), and practice or experience (τρίβος).

447 **μοῦσα ἀμηχανέων μελεδώνων** 'music which inspires [*or possibly* expresses] irresistible passions'. Cf. 434 ἔρος . . . ἀμήχανος, and 422, 449. This seems a better interpretation than 'music to cure overwhelming cares'. This would resemble Hes. *Th.* 98–103, and cf. also Soph. fr. 314.323–4 καὶ τοῦτο λύπης ἐστ᾿ ἄκεστρον καὶ παραψυκτήριον κείνωι μόνον. But it reads a lot into the single word μοῦσα. For μοῦσα as a common noun cf. *H.* 19.15 μοῦσαν ἀθύρων etc., and especially E. *Ion* 757 τίς ἥδε μοῦσα; and *Tr.* 609 μοῦσά θ᾿ ἣ λύπας ἔχει. The central caesura mitigates the effect of the hiatus. ἀμηχανέων is probably feminine genitive plural from ἀμήχανος, treated as a three-termination adjective, as often in early epic (cf. Janko (1982) 139).

448 **τρίβος** 'practice, study'. The word occurs first here and (from the sense 'worn or beaten way') usually means 'track' later. But cf. τριβή, which is used of study or practice in the classical period. Plato contrasts τριβή with τέχνη, meaning 'mere routine', and couples it with ἐμπειρία, to describe unscientific procedures or abilities: cf. *Phdr.* 260C, 270B, *Grg.* 463B, *Phil.* 55E, *Lg.* 938A.

τρία πάντα: for this use of πᾶς with numerals cf. *Il.* 19.247 δέκα πάντα τάλαντα etc. (LSJ s.v. C).

449 For this kind of enumeration of goods cf. for example the English 'wine, women, and song'. For εὐφροσύνη cf. 480–2 in the context of music and festivities. The accusative form ἔρωτα occurs first here and at Sappho fr. 23.1.

ἤδυμον ὕπνον: see 241n. For music's power to produce calm sleep in a divine context cf. Pi. *P.* 1.6–12.

450 Μούσῃσιν . . . ὀπηδός: ὀπηδός is not Homeric (cf. Pindar etc.), but ὀπηδέω is. Cf. phrases such as Μουσάων θεράπων, of a poet: Hes. *Th.* 100, *H.* 32.20, *Margites* fr. 1.2, etc. But Apollo himself is usually called the Muses' leader, rather than 'companion' or 'follower'.

451 οἶμος ἀοιδῆς 'path of song'. Cf. Homeric οἴμη, and Pi. *O.* 9.47 ἐπέων οἶμον, Call. *H.* 1.78 λύρης . . . οἴμους; also προοίμιον.

452 μολπή 'music' or 'play'. According to Aristarchus, this word and μέλπεσθαι in early epic referred to play in general as well as music specifically, but to music alone in later poetry: see Janko on *Il.* 13.636–9.

ἱμερόεις βρόμος αὐλῶν: for βρόμος αὐλῶν cf. *H.* 14.3. Apparently Apollo is still only familiar with flute-music and not any stringed instrument, whereas in the *Hymn to Apollo* he claims the *kitharis* after he has been born (131). Cf. *H. Herm.* 509–10 where Hermes' gift of the lyre is equated with the *kitharis*, and see 47–51n. On Helicon Pausanias saw a bronze statue group showing Apollo and Hermes fighting for the lyre (9.30.1).

453–4 'But never yet was anything else so dear to me in my heart, such as are the exploits of young men at feasts, passing from left to right': Apollo seems to be saying both (a) that he has never heard anything which he cared about so much before, and (b) that it reminds him of young men's songs at banquets. For the latter cf. 54–6, with comments on 55–61. In Homer the neuter plural ἐνδέξια is used of things being passed round from left to right (e.g. wine etc.), or of favourable omens ('on the right'). Here it surely refers to the practice of singing or speaking in turn at symposia or feasts. Later, a lyre was passed round from left to right (ἐπὶ δέξια), or a drinking-cup, or branch of myrtle, to each speaker or singer in turn: cf. Dionysius Chalcus frr. 1, 4 West, Eupolis, *PCG* frr. 354, 395, Pl. *Symp.* 177D3, Anaxandrides, *PCG* fr. 1, with Reitzenstein (1893) 31, 40. Cf. *H. Herm.* 424–5, where Hermes gives Apollo the honorific position on his right while he is singing.

455 This rounds off Apollo's passage in praise of Hermes as musician, with a *reprise* of the theme of wonder, emphasised at 440 and 443. The honorific Διὸς υἱέ sets the seal on this.

456–62 Apollo now moves on to his promise of fame and fortune. There is a slight implication here of the elder brother reasserting his position of authority (457), which might help to explain his use of ἡγεμονεύσω in 461, if the text is correct there.

456 οἶδας: this form is an Ionic innovation, which recurs at 467 and once in Homer (*Od.* 1.337), instead of the older and more usual οἶσθα which is metrically guaranteed at 382. Cf. also for οἶδας Hes. *Aspis* 355, Hipponax fr. 177 West, Hdt. 3.72.1, and Janko (1982) 148, S. West on *Od.* 1.337.

457 'Sit down, dear fellow, and assent to the advice of your elders!' Cf. *Il.* 4.412 τέττα σιώπηι ἧσο ἐμῶι δ' ἐπιπείθεο μύθωι, 7.115 ἀλλὰ σὺ μὲν νῦν ἵζευ, and for μῦθον ἐπαίνει πρεσβύτεροισι cf. *Il.* 2.335 μῦθον ἐπαινήσαντες Ὀδυσσῆος, 18.312 Ἕκτορι . . . ἐπῄνησαν κακὰ μητιόωντι.

458–62 This fulfils Hermes' prediction to his mother at 166–73.

460 **ναὶ μὰ τόδε κρανάϊνον ἀκόντιον** 'yes indeed, by this cornel-wood javelin'. Cf. Achilles' oath by the sceptre at *Il.* 1.234–9 (with 7.411–12, 10.321–31), and Parthenopaeus' oath by his spear, A. *Sept.* 529–30. The form κρανάϊνον (first here) is closer to the MSS readings than κρανέϊνον: both occur in later Greek. ἀκόντιον is also new, but is common in fifth-century and later literature.

460–1 **ἦ μὲν ἐγώ σε . . . ἡγεμονεύσω** 'I shall indeed introduce you among the immortals as honoured and prosperous'. ἡγεμονεύω does not take a direct object elsewhere, and is possibly corrupt, but no satisfactory alternative has been proposed.

462 **καὶ ἐς τέλος οὐκ ἀπατήσω** 'and I shall never deceive you'. Apollo's final insistence on his veracity makes an ironic contrast with Hermes' past duplicity (cf. also 514–20).

463–4 Hermes' reply is described as crafty (or gainful) because of its implied suggestion that he should have a share in Apollo's prophetic skill as well as in his pastoral role, in return for the gift of the lyre. Equally, περιφραδές (most probably vocative) alludes to Apollo's veiled request for a share in Hermes' skill. περιφραδέως is Homeric; the adjective occurs here and at S. *Ant.* 348.

464–89 There is a very strong emphasis throughout this part of Hermes' speech on knowledge and skill, prophetic and musical. Forms of the verb δάω are particularly prominent, along with τέχνη, οἶδα, ἐπίσταμαι, σοφίη, διδάσκω, and νῆϊς. Such expertise comes through different forms of speech, the utterances of the gods, and the voice of the lyre, which is described as responding to questioning (483–4, 487–8) just as the gods do in prophecy. The parallel between musical and mantic communication is emphasised by the close resemblance of 482–8 with what Apollo says of prophecy at 533–49, where again good and bad use of this art is contrasted, and at 552–66, where the bee-maidens can also utter true or false oracles.

464–7 Hermes at once assents, regaining the initiative in his rather lordly opening words.

465 **τέχνης ἡμετέρης ἐπιβήμεναι:** cf. 166 τέχνης ἐπιβήσομαι, and 173.

466–7 **ἐθέλω δέ τοι ἤπιος εἶναι | βουλῆι καὶ μύθοισι:** given Hermes' subordinate position this might seem particularly assertive. The second half of 466 is used by Zeus at *Il.* 8.40 and 22.184.

467 **σὺ δὲ φρεσὶ πάντ' εὖ οἶδας:** somewhat ironically Hermes reminds Apollo of his reputed omniscience, as again at 474 = 489. Cf. Pi. *P.* 9.29–49, where

Chiron responds to Apollo's embarrassed questions about Cyrene, reminding him gently that he ought to know everything (44–5 κύριον ὃς πάντων τέλος οἶσθα καὶ πάσας κελεύθους etc.).

468–72 Blatant flattery, in preparation for his request for favour.

470 **ἐκ πάσης ὁσίης** 'as is wholly right and proper'. Here ὁσίη refers to what is divinely sanctioned: see also 130, 173nn.

470–2 **ἔπορεν . . . πάντα** 'and he has given you fine gifts and privileges: and they say that by the utterance of Zeus you know oracles, Far-Shooter, all the divine revelations that come from Zeus'. Punctuation and text are not certain. It seems best, however, to take τιμάς as object of ἔπορεν together with δῶρα, with a colon after τιμάς, rather than putting a colon after δῶρα and making τιμάς object of δαήμεναι (with σὲ δέ or σέ γε). δαήμεναι will then govern μαντείας (with τε omitted), with θέσφατα πάντα in apposition, and Διὸς πάρα echoing ἐκ Διὸς ὀμφῆς.

471 **ἐκ Διὸς ὀμφῆς:** ὀμφή is always used of a divine voice in Homer, and cf. 532, 566. It refers to an oracle at Theognis 808 and elsewhere.

472 **μαντείας:** first here in early epic, and in the singular at 533, 547, for Homeric μαντοσύνη. It is often used in the plural of prophecies or oracles: cf. Tyrt. fr. 4.2 etc.

473 This line does not make sense as it stands, although all of it except παῖδ' is metrically possible. The corruption has not been satisfactorily healed. We expect a request by Hermes for a share in prophecy (e.g. τῶν νῦν αὐτὸς ἔγωγε . . . ἐθέλοιμι δαῆναι), which would then be contrasted with 474 (σοὶ δὲ . . .), but it is difficult to suggest a suitable whole line, or to explain the corruption.

474 This line is repeated again at 489, marking off the intervening passage in which Hermes speaks in detail about the art of lyre-playing, i.e.: 'You do not really need to ask my help over this skill, but since you do, I will give it to you.' For αὐτάγρετον (= αὐθαίρετον) cf. *Od.* 16.148 εἰ γάρ πως εἴη αὐτάγρετα πάντα βροτοῖσι.

476 **ἀγλαΐας ἀλέγυνε** 'have a care for festivities'. Cf. Hes. *Sc.* 272 ἐν ἀγλαΐαις τε χοροῖς τε, 284–5 θαλίαι τε χοροί τε | ἀγλαΐαι τ'. In *Od.* 17.244 ἀγλαΐαι refers to arrogant behaviour. There is strong alliteration in this phrase, as at *H. Aph.* 11 ἀγλαὰ ἔργ' ἀλεγύνειν.

477 **σὺ δ' ἐμοὶ φίλε κῦδος ὄπαζε:** this picks up Apollo's promise at 458–62, and might be seen as a veiled request for a share in prophecy, although it is not really specific.

478–88 The description of the lyre resembles that of a hetaera whom one embraces, who has a clear voice and is an eloquent speaker, and who can respond to one's advances if she is properly handled. See also 31n.

478 **εὐμόλπει** 'be a fine musician' (West): the verb occurs only here. Cf. Εὔμολπος as a name at *H. Dem.* 154, and Εὐμολπία as title of a poem by Musaeus (fr. 11 Diels, Paus. 10.5.6): see Richardson on *H. Dem.* 154.

479 **κατὰ κόσμον:** see 433n.

480 εὔκηλός μιν . . . φέρειν 'take her confidently'. Cf. Hes. *Op.* 671–2 εὔκηλος τότε νῆα . . . | ἑλκέμεν, again with infinitive for imperative.
481 φιλοκυδέα κῶμον: for φιλοκυδής cf. 375. κῶμος occurs only here in early epic. Cf. Theognis 829, 940, Pindar, etc., and κωμάζω in Hes. *Sc.* 281 etc.
482 εὐφροσύνην 'a source of good cheer': probably in apposition to μιν in 480, or possibly to ἐς δαῖτα . . . κῶμον. Cf. 449, where this is one of the results of music.
482–8 Hermes describes the differences between the skilled and unskilled lyre-player, in two balanced and contrasted sentences: 482–6 ὅς τις ἂν αὐτὴν . . . ἐξερεείνηι . . . , 486–8 ὃς δέ κεν αὐτὴν . . . ἐρεείνηι . . . The ease and lack of painful effort of the good player is contrasted with the violence and senseless sounds of the ignorant one. The process is seen as a dialogue, or question and answer, between player and instrument, and the lyre continues to be personified (as at 478–9). She is able to give instruction as well as pleasure to the good player, but her answers to the bad one make no sense. Cf. the good and bad uses of prophecy, at 541–9 (with comments). The lyre is addressed in invocation by Sappho (fr. 118; see *H. Herm.* 24n.), and later cf. Pi. *P.* 1.1, *N.* 4.44, Bacchyl. fr. 20 B. 1, etc.
482 ὅς τις ἂν αὐτήν: the asyndeton is typical of this hymn (cf. 17, 25, etc.).
483 σοφίηι 'expertise': often applied to musical or poetic skill in early Greek literature. Cf. also 511 ἑτέρης σοφίης . . . τέχνην.
484 νοῶι χαρίεντα 'to charm one's fancy'.
485 ῥεῖα συνηθείηισιν ἀθυρομένη μαλακῆισιν 'easily played with gentle intimacy'. συνηθεία (first here; cf. Hippocrates, and classical prose) can mean 'intimacy' or 'intercourse', as well as 'habit' or 'custom', and in this context, where the lyre is personified as a ἑταίρη, the first sense is surely relevant. It is also used of musical practice by Plato, *Laws* II 656D. μαλακός is later used sometimes of musical harmony or pitch (LSJ s.v. III.2(e)). For ἀθύρειν of music or song cf. *H.* 19.15, Pi. *I.* 4.39, *Anacreont.* 41.11.
486 ἐργασίην φεύγουσα δυήπαθον 'avoiding painful labour'. ἐργασίη occurs first here, then in fifth-century and later literature. It may be relevant that it can also be used of sexual intercourse (Arist. *Pr.* 876a39), or applied to the trade of a courtesan (Hdt. 2.135.1, D. 18.129). δυήπαθος is a *hapax*; cf. δυηπαθής and δυηπαθία in Apollonius Rhodius and later.
487 ἐπιζαφελῶς 'violently, roughly': used of anger in Homer.
488 μάψ . . . θρυλίζοι 'She would then, vainly and uselessly, utter empty discordant sounds.' For the combination μάψ αὔτως cf. *Il.* 20.348, *Od.* 16.111, *H. Dem.* 83. μετήορος (cf. μετέωρος) occurs first here, then in Herodotus and later. It is not apparently elsewhere applied to music. Cf. perhaps μετεωροκοπέω, μετεωρολογέω (etc.) in Aristophanes and Plato, used in a derogatory sense of pretentious scientific talk (together with ἀδολεσχία). θρυλίζω is another *hapax*; cf. θρυλέω in Attic Greek, etc. θρυλιγμός or θρυλισμός are used of false musical notes in late Greek: cf. D.H. *Comp.* 11 (of a flute-player) θρυλιγμὸν ἢ τὴν καλουμένην ἐκμέλειαν ηὔλησε, and similarly Porph. *in Harm.* p. 204 W.

489 = 474 (see comment).
490–5 Hermes concludes his speech with his bargain (lyre for cattle). In 491 ἡμεῖς may mean 'I' in contrast to Apollo, but is more likely to be a genuine plural. Hermes associates himself with Apollo as Νόμιος, and emphasises at 493–5 how much Apollo stands to gain by this new arrangement. For this role of Apollo see *H. Ap.* 21n., and for Hermes as god of the fertility of herds and flocks cf. Hes. *Th.* 444–7, Farnell, *Cults* v 9–11.
491–2 'And we in turn, Far-Shooter, shall graze the pastures of the mountain and horse-feeding plain with the cattle which live in the fields.'
493 ἅλις 'in plenty'.
494 **μίγδην:** first here, for μίγδα (*Od.* 24.77, *H. Dem.* 426); cf. A.R. 3.1381, Orph. fr. 223.
494–5 'And so (οὐδέ) there is no need for you, acquisitive as you are, to be furiously angry': a slight sting in the tail, reminding Apollo again of his reputation for acquisitiveness (cf. 176–81, 335, 549nn.). This is ironic here, in view of Hermes' own aims (464 μύθοισιν . . . κερδαλέοισιν). περιζαμενῶς (or -ής) occurs only here and at Hes. fr. 204.126 in early epic.
496–502 The exchange of lyre and goad seals the pact, and Apollo at once begins to use his new instrument.
496 **ὤρεξ', ὁ δ' ἐδέξατο:** the lyre should be understood as object of these verbs.
497 ἔχων 'which he had'. If correct, this stresses that the goad was Apollo's by right. But ἔχειν or ἑκών are possible conjectures. For the former cf. *Il.* 11.192–3 κράτος ἐγγυαλίξω | κτείνειν, for the latter A.R. 2.55–6 ἐγγυαλίξω | αὐτὸς ἑκών.
498 **βουκολίας:** cf. Hes. *Th.* 445 (βουκολίας), of Hecate's and Hermes' care for cattle, as here.
499–502 Cf. 53–4, 418–20. In 501 we have ὑπὸ νέρθεν instead of ὑπὸ χειρός (418), and in 502 ἱμερόεν (if right) is a variant of σμερδαλέον (54, 420). Cf. *Il.* 18.570 ἱμερόεν κιθάριζε· λίνον δ' ὑπὸ καλὸν ἄειδεν. In 502 the aorist ἄεισεν is appropriate, whereas in 54 the imperfect is better ('began to sing').
500 Apollo is given a whole-line denomination to mark this highly significant moment.
503–12 The return of the cattle to their home and of the gods to Olympus gives a charmingly bucolic closure to the main story of the theft, and Zeus cements the reconciliation already effected at 389–96, which becomes a permanent bond. At the same time, to compensate for Hermes' loss of the patronage of one instrument he promptly invents another, the shepherd's syrinx.
503–4 With βόας (M) it is Apollo and Hermes who send the cattle back, and the dual ἐτραπέτην suits the context well. βόες . . . ἐτραπέτην would make them return of their own accord, with ἐτραπέτην as intransitive aorist dual used instead of a plural. The former seems clearly preferable. M's καί ῥα (for ἔνθα) in 503 is also possible: cf. *Od.* 12.233 καί ῥα ἔπειτα etc.

504–7 Entry or return to Olympus, and joyful reception there, are typical motifs of these hymns: cf. *H. Dem.* 483–6, *H. Ap.* 186–206, *H.* 6.14–18, 15.7–8, 19.42–7. See also 322–96n., and Introduction 1(c).

505–6 Cf. Apollo's journeys to Pytho and Olympus, playing the *phorminx* and dancing, at *H. Ap.* 183–8 and 513–19, and Zeus's delight with Apollo's music at *H. Ap.* 205–6. (ἐπι)ρώομαι is used of dancing at *Il.* 24.616, Hes. *Th.* 8, *H. Aph.* 261, etc.

508 διαμπερὲς ὡς ἔτι καὶ νῦν: i.e. he has continued to love him ever since. Cf. 125 ὡς ἔτι νῦν τὰ μέτασσα etc.

508–9 As the text stands in the MSS it is difficult to explain σήματ᾽. West marks a lacuna, and his suggested supplement means '<and Leto's son acknowledged his brother's love> tokens'. This also gives a δέ clause to answer τὸ μέν in 507, which otherwise would only be answered by 511 αὐτὸς δ᾽. The loss of the line could be due to repetition of Λητοΐδην/Λητοΐδης.

510 δεδαώς: it is better to take this with what precedes ('expert as he was') than to put a comma after ἱμερτήν, as some editors have done.

ὑπωλένιον: see 433n.

511–12 The invention of the syrinx (first mentioned at *Il.* 10.13 and 18.526) is very briefly described, almost as an afterthought. Hermes invents the syrinx or panpipes also in Euphorion fr. 182 Van Groningen. In Apollodorus (3.10.2) Apollo offers him the golden wand (cf. *H. Herm.* 528–32) in exchange for this new invention, and Hermes then receives the gift of divination by pebbles (cf. *H. Herm.* 552–66). Hermes is several times represented in art with the syrinx from *c.* 580/570 BC, and sometimes together with Apollo as citharode. It is significant that all the examples belong to the sixth century, whereas from *c.* 500 onwards it is Pan who is shown with the syrinx: see Haas (1985) 50–2, 60–2, 72–4, and for Hermes cf. also *LIMC* V.1 s.v. Hermes nos. 327–9. Pan plays the pipes in *H.* 19.15 (δονάκων ὕπο). The story of his love for Syrinx and her transformation first occurs in Ovid *Met.* 1.689–712.

511 ἐκμάσσατο 'sought out, devised'. This compound is only found here.

512 The asyndeton is due to the fact that 512 explains 511.

τηλόσ᾽ ἀκουστήν is an effective description of a herdsman's pipes, heard far away over the hills. ἀκουστός occurs first here, then in fifth-century and later literature.

513–78 Apollo says that he is afraid lest Hermes may steal both his lyre and his bow and arrows, and asks him to swear an oath. Hermes swears never to steal from him again, and Apollo promises that Hermes will be his dearest friend, and that he will give him a three-branched golden wand, to keep him unharmed. He cannot give him a share in his own prophetic art, as he alone of the gods is allowed to know Zeus's will. As for mortals, he will deceive some and help others by his prophecies, depending on whether they come with favourable omens or not. But he does offer Hermes a special prophetic gift, three winged virgin sisters, who live in a cave under Mt Parnassus. When these have eaten honey they are willing to speak the truth, but if they have not done so they utter lies. Hermes also will have the care of all domestic and wild animals, and will be the only messenger to Hades.

Thus did Apollo show his love for Hermes, and Zeus added his favour. He associates with all men and gods, seldom giving profit and generally deceiving mankind at dead of night.

For discussion of this final episode and its place in the poem see Introduction 3(a).

514–15 The theft of Apollo's bow and arrows (or quiver) was described in Alcaeus' hymn to Hermes (fr. 308 LP = V, with S 264.11–19 *SLG* = fr. 306c Campbell (Loeb)). The scene was popular later: cf. Hor. *Odes* 1.10.9–12, Philostr. *Imag.* 1.26, Lucian *D. Deor.* 11 (7). 1, Schol. AB *Il.* 15.256, and Page (1955) 252–8.

515 ἀνακλέψῃς 'steal back' or 'steal again'. This rare compound is more likely to have been changed to ἅμα κλέψῃς than vice versa. It recurs in Theocr. 5.9, and in one or possibly two inscriptions (*SEG* 34.1019, sixth century BC, ἀνακλε<π>τέτω, and *GDI* 1586).

κίθαριν καὶ καμπύλα τόξα: cf. *H. Ap.* 131 κίθαρις ... καὶ καμπύλα τόξα, which this may echo.

516 ἐπαμοίβιμα ἔργα 'acts of barter'. Hermes becomes god of commerce as well as theft, here ironically viewed as themselves interchangeable concepts. The epithet is found only here (cf. ἐπημοιβός in Homer). This is the first indication that Hermes has now received this privilege from Zeus (cf. 291–2).

518–20 Apollo does not specify the nature of the oath, but this is made clear by 521–3.

518 Cf. *Od.* 5.178 = 10.343 εἰ μή μοι τλαίης γε, θεά, μέγαν ὅρκον ὀμόσσαι, and *H. Ap.* 79 ἀλλ' εἴ μοι τλαίης γε, θεά, μέγαν ὅρκον ὀμόσσαι. In *Od.* 2.377 θεῶν μέγαν ὅρκον is an oath invoking the gods, whereas here it is presumably the oath sworn by gods, as at *Od.* 10.299.

519 The oath is confirmed either by a nod of the head, as in the case of Zeus's promise at *Il.* 1.524–9, or by invoking the river Styx, the usual formula for divine oaths. In early epic, and often later, the object by which one swears is in the accusative with ὄμνυμι, whereas various prepositions are used in later prose examples.

521–6 Once again a mutual pact is sealed with promises, in two balanced clauses: ... Μαιάδος υἱὸς ... κατένευσεν | μή ποτ' ... | μηδέ ποτ' ... αὐτὰρ Ἀπόλλων | Λητοΐδης κατένευσεν ... | μή τινα ... | μήτε ... μήτ' ...

521–2 Cf. Hermes' earlier threat to ransack Apollo's temple at Delphi (178–81).

523 ἐμπελάσειν: first here and at Hes. *Sc.* 109.

524 ἐπ' ἀρθμῶι καὶ φιλότητι 'in a bond of friendship'. This legal formula (with ἀρθμός first used here) recurs in A. *PV* 191–2 εἰς ἀρθμὸν ἐμοὶ καὶ φιλότητα ... ἥξει, and Call. fr. 497a (Pfeiffer (1949–53) II p. 122) ἀρθμὸν δ' ἀμφοτέροις καὶ φιλίην ἔταμες. Cf. also *Il.* 7.302 ἐν φιλότητι διέτμαγεν ἀρθμήσαντε, and for ἄρθμιος coupled with φίλος cf. Theognis 326, 1312.

526 μήτ' ἄνδρα Διὸς γόνον: i.e. a mortal son of Zeus, such as Heracles.

526–8 ἐκ δὲ τέλειον . . . τίμιον 'And I shall make an authoritative contract [*or* guarantee] between immortals, and at the same time one which will be altogether trustworthy and honoured by my heart.' Assuming that there is no lacuna after 527, we have here the kind of change from indirect to direct speech which occurs occasionally in Homer: cf. especially *Il.* 4.301–9 (after ἀνώγει), 15.346–51 (after ἐκέκλετο . . . ἀΰσας), 23.854–8 (after ἀνώγει τοξεύειν). For some other possible examples cf. Janko on *Il.* 15.346–7. *Il.* 23.855–6 is unique among Homeric instances, in that (as here) the transition occurs within the verse (see Richardson ad loc.). In the hymn, the speech is anticipated by the verb κατένευσεν, and it gives dramatic emphasis to the solemnity of Apollo's promise. As at 524 we are here in the realm of legal terminology: τέλειος (and related words) is used of fully constituted or authoritative decrees, laws, etc. (LSJ s.v. I.1(b)). For σύμβολον see 30n. and especially Gauthier (1972) 69–70 on this passage. Here it may mean either a guarantee (e.g. LSJ s.v. I.3) or a contract (e.g. Theognis 1150, and LSJ s.v. II.3, 4). For σύμβολον πιστόν cf. Pi. *O.* 12.7–8 σύμβολον δ' οὔπω τις ἐπιχθονίων | πιστὸν ἀμφὶ πράξιος ἐσσομένας εὗρεν θεόθεν, and Isoc. 4.49 σύμβολον τῆς παιδεύσεως πιστότατον.

526–7 ἐκ . . . ποιήσομαι: a *tmesis*, with ἐκποιέω meaning 'fully make', emphasising again the validity of the action. This compound (first here) has this sense in fifth-century BC and later literature.

527 πάντως: this makes better sense than the transmitted reading πάντων.

528–32 The gift of the golden wand (Hermes' κηρύκειον or *caduceus*) seals the compact, just as material tokens or σύμβολα were exchanged in commercial transactions. It has remarkable properties: it will be the bearer of wealth and prosperity, and a protection from harm, and it will 'accomplish [*or* authorise] all the ordinances' (if θεμούς is correct) 'of good words and actions' which Apollo has learned from the voice of Zeus. Hermes is called χρυσόρραπις in the *Odyssey* (5.87 etc.) and will now be so addressed (*H. Herm.* 539). In Homer he uses his wand to put men to sleep and wake them (*Il.* 24.343–4, *Od.* 5.47–8), and to lead souls down to Hades (*Od.* 24.1–10): see also Richardson on *Il.* 24.343–5. Here, however, for the first time, it is called τριπέτηλον ('trefoil'): this is usually taken as indicating a branch which forks at the top in a V-shape, i.e. the basic form of the κηρύκειον as it was portrayed in art. The earliest example, in the scene of the Judgement of Paris on the Chigi vase (*c.* 630 BC), shows the top of the wand apparently having a chi-shape (cf. *LIMC* VIII.1 s.v. Kerykeion, and I s.v. Alexandros no. 5). See also Chittenden (1947) 100 for a seventh-century BC *pinax* on which Hermes' *caduceus* has a tip from which spring two three-leafed shoots, one above the other, like two clover plants: the most literal representation of τριπέτηλον. The curved branches take the form of snakes from at least the fifth century BC (*LIMC* s.v. Dionysus no. 706), and the role of the wand as bringer of luck and averter of harm may be connected with this, snakes being both symbolic of wealth and apotropaic. It has also been compared to the divining-rod. For further discussion and bibliography cf. *LIMC* VIII.1 728–30, and De Waele (1927).

530 **τριπέτηλον:** this recurs in Call. *H.* 3.165, Nic. *Th.* 522 as a noun meaning 'clover'.

ἀκήριον ἥ σε φυλάξει: cf. *Od.* 20.47 διαμπερὲς ἥ σε φυλάσσω.

531–2 Hermes will thus be a minister responsible for putting the will of Zeus, mediated by Apollo, into effect. The wording of 532–4 echoes 471–2: cf. δαήμεναι ἐκ Διὸς ὀμφῆς | μαντείας . . . θέσφατα . . . In other words, Apollo is offering his brother a significant, though still subsidiary, role in relation to the major prophetic one which he alone is allowed to exercise.

531 **θεμούς** 'dispositions' or 'ordinances'. The word is a conjecture, recurring only in Hesychius s.v. θεμούς· διαθέσεις, παραινέσεις.

533 **διοτρεφές:** M's variant διαμπερές is read by Radermacher and Vergados (2007a). διοτρεφής is normally used of human beings in early epic, but cf. *Il.* 21.223 of Scamander. The combination of φέριστε and another epithet is unusual (Orph. *H.* 13.9, 64.13), but seems quite possible.

ἣν ἐρεείνεις 'which you ask about'. Cf. *Il.* 6.145 τίη γενεὴν ἐρεείνεις; (etc.). ἐρεείνω does not mean 'ask for', but Apollo assumes that Hermes wants a share in his art (unless 473 made this explicit).

534 Cf. *Od.* 4.561 σοὶ δ' οὐ θέσφατόν ἐστι.

535–8 Once again there is strong emphasis on a promise guaranteed by a solemn oath, as at 518–28. πιστόω is used especially in the context of oaths: e.g. *Od.* 15.436, S. *OC* 650, Th. 4.88, etc. For the specially close bond between Zeus's will and Apollo's prophecies cf. A. *Eum.* 616–18.

535 **τὸ γὰρ οἶδε Διὸς νόος** 'for that (i.e. the subject matter of prophecy) is known by the mind of Zeus'.

538 **πυκινόφρονα:** in early poetry only here and at Hes. fr. 253.1.

539 **χρυσόρραπι:** see 528–32n. Apollo diplomatically honours Hermes with his newly gained attribute, when denying him what he wanted.

541–9 Oracles were proverbially ambiguous and liable to misinterpretation, and the god here disclaims responsibility for any possible deception. It is a question of whether the omens are valid or invalid, i.e. whether what is desired or requested of the gods accords with divine favour. In the similar case of Hermes' oracular gift, truth or deception depends on whether the proper sacrificial offerings have been made (558–63). Cf. Hes. fr. 240.9–11 (of Zeus's oracle at Dodona): ἔνθεν ἐπιχθόνιοι μαντήϊα πάντα φέρονται, | ὃς δὴ κεῖθι μολὼν θεὸν ἄμβροτον ἐξερεείνηι | δῶρα φέρων <τ'> ἔλθηισι σὺν οἰωνοῖς ἀγαθοῖσιν. See also Amandry (1950) 58–9. 541–2 are paralleled by Hermes' own functions as summed up by 577–8. There is in addition an analogy with Hermes' discourse on the lyre, which responds well or badly to a player's questioning (482–8: see 464–89n.).

541 **ἀνθρώπων δ'** 'but as for mankind'. This is in contrast with 535 ἀθανάτων.

542 πολλὰ . . . ἀνθρώπων 'leading about in all directions the tribes of miserable mankind'. Cf. *Od.* 9.465 πολλὰ (i.e. μῆλα) περιτροπέοντες ἐλαύνομεν. The implication is that mortals are helpless creatures in the hands of the gods, and also easily misled.

544–9 For the distinction between birds which have valid significance and others cf. *Od.* 2.181–2 ὄρνιθες δέ τε πολλοὶ ὑπ' αὐγὰς ἠελίοιο | φοιτῶσ', οὐδέ τε πάντες ἐναίσιμοι, and Call. *H.* 5.123–4 γνωσεῖται δ' ὄρνιχας ὃς αἴσιος, οἵ τε πέτονται | ἤλιθα, καὶ ποίων οὐκ ἀγαθαὶ πτέρυγες.

544 φωνῆι . . . οἰωνῶν 'with the cry or flights of valid birds'. Cf. Hes. fr. 240.10–11 (quoted above on 541–9). τελήεντων implies that what the birds appear to portend is accomplished, as opposed to ὄρνιθες μαψιλόγοι. Cf. αἰετὸν . . . τελειότατον πετεηνῶν (*Il.* 8.247, 24.315), of a bird 'most capable of bringing fulfilment' (see Richardson on *Il.* 24.314–16), and Tyrtaeus fr. 4.2 West τελέεντ' ἔπεα.

545 This line emphasises the point by repetition after 543.

546–9 If one tries to obtain something against the gods' will, relying on omens and prophecy, this is tantamount to thinking oneself cleverer than the gods and will lead to failure. Cf. E. *Ion* 373–80, where Ion advises Creusa not to try to force the gods to utter what they do not want, with sacrifices and interpretation of omens, since this will not bring any benefits.

546 μαψιλόγοισι 'vainly speaking': only here. Homer has μάψ, μαψιδίως, Hesiod (*Th.* 872) μαψαῦραι.

549 φήμ': this is emphatic, in parenthesis.

ἁλίην ὁδὸν εἶσιν: cf. *Od.* 2.273, 318 οὐ τοι ἔπειθ' (or οὐδ') ἁλίη ὁδὸς ἔσσεται. Omens and prophecy are often associated with journeys or expeditions, e.g. Pi. *N.* 9.18–20 καί ποτ' ἐς ἑπταπύλους | Θήβας ἄγαγον στρατὸν αἰσιᾶν | οὐ κατ' ὀρνίχων ὁδόν, and A. *Eum.* 770 ὁδοὺς ἀθύμους καὶ παρόρνιθας πόρους.

ἐγὼ δέ κε δῶρα δεχοίμην: cf. *Il.* 2.420 (Zeus) ἀλλ' ὅ γε δέκτο μὲν ἱρά, πόνον δ' ἀμέγαρτον ὄφελλε. This is a general rule for the gods in Homer, if what is requested is against their will. In the case of Apollo, this appears to be an answer to more specific accusations of φιλοκέρδεια (see on 176–81, 335, 494). The offerings of a sacred cake and animal sacrifice were both essential prerequisites for entry to the temple of Apollo and consultation of the oracle (cf. E. *Ion* 226–9), but in no way guaranteed success. For details of procedure cf. Amandry (1950) 86–114, Parke and Wormell (1956) 32, Parke (1967a) 83–4.

550–1 The two-line honorific address to Hermes acts as a prelude to the special prophetic gift which Apollo is offering.

551 θεῶν ἐριούνιε δαῖμον 'swift messenger-deity of the gods': an unusual vocative phrase, since δαίμων in Homer is not normally used of a particular god; cf. however *Il.* 3.420 ἦρχε δὲ δαίμων (Aphrodite). Although Hesiod uses δαίμονες of the spirits of men of the golden age (*Op.* 122), and later it comes to be used of subordinate spiritual beings, it need not have this connotation here.

552–66 'There are certain august maidens, who are sisters, glorying in their swift wings: they are three, and their heads are sprinkled with white barley meal. They have their homes under a fold of Parnassus, and are teachers, set apart, of a prophetic skill which I practised when I was still a boy, whilst tending my cattle: but my father was not concerned with this. From there then they fly hither and thither, to feed on honeycombs, and make all their authoritative pronouncements. When they have eaten pale honey and are inspired, they are favourable, and willing to speak the truth: but if they have been deprived of the sweet food of the gods, then indeed they utter falsehoods, swarming amongst themselves. These then I grant you, and you should question them accurately and delight your own heart; and if you should teach a mortal man, he will often listen to your voice, if he is lucky.'

Apollo is surely being deliberately mysterious in this description, which lends these characters an awesome dignity. The poet appears to be describing a triad of three virgin sisters, who were associated with Apollo as a boy and taught him their mantic art, which was separate from the prophetic skill he has from Zeus. Their home is under Parnassus (probably in a cave), and they are like bees, for they feed on honey, which gives them inspiration, and swarm in a confused way (δονέουσαι) if they are deprived of this. Their utterances may be true or false, depending on whether they are properly fed or not. Hermes is to use them as a source of prophecy for his own pleasure, and he can also benefit mortals if he wishes by passing on this information. It is not clear whether the poet envisages this triad as having anthropomorphic shape but behaving like bees, or whether they are actually bees, which are seen as having human or divine characteristics. The myth about the origins of the oracle at Dodona reflects a similar ambiguity as to whether the instigators were women or doves with a human voice (Hdt. 2.54–7). They may also be a mixed form of 'bee-maidens', like the winged woman with a bee's body from the waist, depicted on two late Geometric gold plaques from Camiros in Rhodes (cf. Cook (1895) 11–12). Given that there are only three of them and they are not actually called bees, they are most probably envisaged as nymphs with bee-like characteristics. Since they are said to live 'under a fold of Parnassus' it seems probable that a particular cult of Hermes, associated with a triad of mountain nymphs in a cave beneath this mountain, is in mind here. A plausible suggestion is that these are the Corycian Nymphs, whose cult was located under Parnassus. A very large double cave, thought to be sacred to them, has been excavated high up on the mountain's foothills, about 3 miles from Delphi. Dedications to the nymphs begin there in the seventh century BC, and later they are often associated with Pan. But at least one fragment of an Attic relief from the cave shows Hermes leading three nymphs, and in another fourth-century BC relief from Delphi itself a mountain is shown with three seated nymphs, Apollo, and Hermes. The cave also contained some 25,000 *astragaloi* (knucklebones), which may have been used for divination, as they were in some other sanctuaries. See Amandry *et al.* (1984) especially 347–78, 394–425, and Larson (1995) 341–57. Larson also collects evidence for the close association between nymphs and bees in antiquity (352–4).

In Apollodorus' version of the myth of Hermes and Apollo (3.10.2) Apollo gives Hermes the art of divination by means of pebbles, in exchange for Hermes' syrinx. Consequently, the triad of sisters has also been identified with the Thriai, three nymphs of Parnassus who were said to have nursed Apollo, and invented the art of divination by pebbles (called ϑριαί). This *aition* derives from Philochorus (cf. *FGrH* 328 F 195, with parallel texts and helpful discussion by Jacoby). Various versions reflect the idea that this form of divination was regarded as less reliable, or less reputable, than Apolline prophecy. If Thriai is another name for these 'bee-maidens', this would fit the implications of the hymn, that Apollo's gift to Hermes is on a lower level of inspiration, and that it is not a direct representation of the will of Zeus (cf. Jacoby, *FGrH* III. B Supplement p. 560). The hymn does not mention divination by either *astragaloi* or pebbles, but it is possible that there is a connection between the bee-maidens, the Corycian nymphs, and these mantic techniques. Offerings of honey may have been made to the nymphs of the cave, who were thought to be a source of inspiration, and then the visitor could have used the throw of either dice or pebbles in order to find out the gods' will. Hermes as god of luck would have been seen as the mediator for this knowledge (cf. 565–6). For divination by pebbles at Delphi and elsewhere cf. Call. *H.* 2.45 (with F. Williams's comments), Amandry (1950) 29–30 and 72, Fontenrose (1978) 219–24, Scheinberg (1979) 8–9; and for divination by *astragaloi* see Frazer on Paus. 7.25.6, and Larson (1995) 347 n. 19. See also on this passage Sourvinou-Inwood (1991) 192–216, especially 196–201.

552–61 There is some verbal similarity here with *H. Dem.* 485–7 ναιετάουσι . . . σεμναὶ . . . προφρονέως; cf. *H. Herm.* 552 σεμναὶ . . . 555 ναιετάουσιν . . . 561 προφρονέως (Scheinberg (1979) 15).

553 ἀγαλλόμεναι πτερύγεσσιν: cf. *Il.* 2.462 ἔνϑα καὶ ἔνϑα ποτῶνται (cf. *H. Herm.* 558) ἀγαλλόμενα πτερύγεσσιν.

554 τρεῖς: in Indo-European mythology female deities, nymphs, etc. are often triads of virgin sisters. They can also be winged, or take animal or bird form (e.g. the winged Gorgons of A. *PV* 798–9, or swan-like Graiai, A. *PV* 794–5). In art nymphs are regularly portrayed as a triad (e.g. with Hermes, Pan, etc.). Cf. Scheinberg (1979) 2–7.

κατὰ δὲ κράτος πεπαλαγμέναι ἄλφιτα λευκά: various explanations have been proposed for this odd feature:

(1) They are like the κανηφόροι, who powdered their hair with flour or white barley: cf. especially Hermippus, *PCG* fr. 25 ὥσπερ αἱ κανηφόροι | λευκοῖσιν ἀλφίτοισιν ἐντετριμμένος, Ar., *PCG* fr. 553 ἀλφιτόχρωτος κεφαλῆς, and Ar. *Eccl.* 732, etc.
(2) It is a metaphor for their white hair (Matthiae; cf. Allen & Sikes p. 312).
(3) It refers to bees covered with pollen (Ilgen; Cook (1895) 7; Radermacher).

(4) Wilamowitz (1931–2, I 381) identified them with the 'white maidens' who are mentioned as allies of Apollo against the Gauls at Delphi, in the oracle ἐμοὶ μελήσει ταῦτα καὶ λευκαῖς κόραις (cf. Cic. *de Div.* 1.81, with Greek passages in Pease's comments). But these were identified as meaning either snowflakes or Athena and Artemis by ancient authors.

(5) They have been compared to ἀλφιτομαντεῖς, who used barley for divination (Cook (1895) 7, Amandry (1950) 60–1).

The closest analogy seems to be with the κανηφόροι.

555 ὑπὸ πτυχὶ Παρνησοῖο: cf. *H. Ap.* 269. Here this suggests a cave in the mountainside.

556 ἀπάνευθε 'apart'. This seems to mean that they live in a secluded place, away from mankind, or from Apollo's sanctuary at Delphi. It would fit with their location in the Corycian cave, some distance from Delphi and higher up the slopes below Parnassus.

διδάσκαλοι: first here; cf. Aeschylus etc. μαντείης ... διδάσκαλοι go together.

556–7 ἣν . . . μελέτησα: the pastoral setting for Apollo's education in prophecy reminds one of the theme of the poet or prophet who receives his gift of inspiration as a shepherd or herdsman on a mountain: cf. West on Hes. *Th.* 22–34, pp. 159–60. Hesiod's Muses could also speak truth or falsehood, like these women.

557 πατὴρ δ' ἐμὸς οὐκ ἀλέγιζεν: ἀλέγιζεν is a conjecture, but seems necessary. Cf. 361 where ἀλεγύνων, ἀλεγίζων and ἀλεείνων are variants. This suggests that this form of divination was not directly derived from Zeus's will, as Delphic prophecy was. Cf. the account of the Thriai in *FGrH* 328 F 195, where Zeus causes their authority to be doubted.

558 ἄλλοτε ἄλλῃ: for the hiatus (as corrected by Schneidewin) cf. *Od.* 4.236 ἄλλοτε ἄλλωι, Hes. *Op.* 713 ἄλλοτε ἄλλον, and other examples in West's comment.

559–63 Honey was used in wineless libations (e.g. Soph. *OC* 481; cf. Schol. Soph. *OC* 100, and Porph. *de Abstin.* 2.20), and could be offered to both the nymphs and Hermes (cf. Paus. 5.15.10, Larson (1995) 355). The seer Iamus was fed on honey by snakes as a baby (Pi. *O.* 6.45–7). Porphyry (*Antr.* 15–19) discusses possible associations of honey and bees with nymphs, and calls honey 'the food of the gods' (cf. *H. Herm.* 562), saying that some have identified it with nectar and ambrosia. Cf. also Ransome (1937), especially 119–39, Waszink (1974) especially 11–14. For the contrast in these lines cf. Plato, *Ion* 534A: αἱ βάκχαι ἀρύτονται ἐκ τῶν ποταμῶν μέλι καὶ γάλα κατεχόμεναι, ἔμφρονες δὲ οὖσαι οὔ.

559 καί τε κραίνουσιν ἕκαστα 'they make all their ordinances' or 'their authoritative pronouncements' (cf. West). κραίνειν can be used of oracular pronouncements, e.g. at E. *Ion* 464 (cf. A. *Ag.* 1255 τὰ πυθόκραντα). It is also used of true dreams at *Od.* 19.567, as opposed to ἔπε' ἀκράαντα (560). Cf. Fraenkel on A. *Ag.* 368 (II p. 193), 'to pronounce and establish in binding and valid form with the guarantee of fulfilment in the future'. Possibly there is word-play or an implied connection here between κήρια and κραίνουσιν. Cf. *Od.* 19.562–7, for word-play between κέρας and κραίνειν.

560 θυίωσιν: θυίειν is used in early epic especially of elements or people raging or in high excitement, and θυιάς is later used like μαινάς of an inspired woman or Bacchant (A. *Th.* 498, 836, *Supp.* 564, etc.; cf. Θυῖαι in S. *Ant.* 1151 etc.). The implication here also is probably that they are inspired. The spelling θυίειν is likely to be original in this verb: cf. Chantraine, *GH* I 372. It occurs in a number of older MSS at *Il.* 11.180, Hes. *Th.* 131, 848, 874; cf. also Anacreon, *PMG* fr. 2.17.

562 θεῶν ἡδεῖαν ἐδωδήν: cf. Porph. *Antr.* 16 θεῶν τροφῆς ὄντος τοῦ μέλιτος. There was a belief in antiquity that honey 'falls from the air': cf. Arist. *HA* 553b29, and Verg. *G.* 4.1 *aerii mellis caelestia dona.*

563 The two alternative lines are both possible, and look as if they could be rhapsodic variants. But δι' ἀλλήλων δονέουσαι fits well with the bee-like character of the women. Cf. Choerilus, *SH* 318.2–3 μύρια φῦλ' ἐδονεῖτο πολυσμήνοισι μελίσσαις | <εἴκελα. . . >. The confused noise, like bees buzzing, would make their message impossible to interpret correctly.

564–6 What is for Hermes a source of entertainment (like his music) will be more serious for mortals who may profit from these prophecies.

565 εἰ βροτὸν ἄνδρα δαείης: in Homer the reduplicated aorist δέδαε means 'he taught' (*Od.* 6.233 etc.), and in Apollonius Rhodius δάε, ἔδαε also have this sense (1.724, 3.529, 4.989). δαείης may be used with this sense here. The normal meaning would be 'learn', but this hardly fits the present context.

566 For ὀμφή of a prophetic voice cf. 471, 532. αἴ κε τύχῃσι suggests Hermes' role as the god who brings luck.

567–73 In 567–8 Apollo continues to address Hermes and gives him the care of various domestic animals. In 569–73 the construction changes to accusative and infinitive, with Hermes as the subject of the verbs. If this text is correct one should translate 569–71 as 'and over fierce lions and white-tusked boars, and dogs and sheep, all that the broad earth nourishes, and in the case of all grazing animals, their lord is to be the glorious Hermes'. On this view the infinitives are 'jussive', and we have a construction which is especially used in prescriptions, laws and treaties: see Bers (1984) 166–82. The shift from second-person imperative to accusative and infinitive may seem unusual, but cf. for example the prescriptions at Hes. *Op.* 722–60, where we have accusative and infinitive at 735–6 and 748–54, in the middle of a series with nominative and infinitive, or second-person future indicative (729). In 571 πᾶσι δ' ἐπὶ προβάτοισιν is best taken as a general summarising phrase, rounding off the previous list: hence the change to δέ rather than another καί. Apollo's speech began by stressing the formality of his compact with Hermes, and on this view it also closes in a more formal style, concluding at 572–3 with Hermes' solemn role as sole messenger to Hades.

Editors have usually marked a lacuna after 568, and assumed a switch to indirect speech, with either Apollo or Zeus as subject. This would be awkward in the middle of the list of animals, and there is no need for a change of speaker to Zeus, since Apollo is fully empowered to express the wishes of his father (cf. 468–72 and 533–8). In 575 χάριν δ' ἐπέθηκε Κρονίων refers to the approval of Zeus, rather than actual speech. In defence of the transmitted text see also Brioso (1990) and Vergados (2007a) on 568–71. For Hermes as god of flocks and herds see 490–5n. But originally his associations with the natural world were much wider, and he is often depicted in art with dogs or horses, various wild animals, and (in Archaic art) monsters such as sphinxes, and he was associated with hunting and hunters: cf. Chittenden (1947) 89–114, especially 102–5, and *LIMC* v.1 287, 380–1.

568 **ἡμιόνους ταλαεργούς:** cf. (in various cases) *Il.* 23.654, 662, 664, and with ἵπποι . . . θήλειαι *Od.* 4.636 = 21.23.

569–71 A colourful list of creatures, noted by Notopoulos (1962, 367–8) for its 'patterns of sibilant assonances'. For 569 cf. *Od.* 11.611 ἄρκτοι τ' ἀγρότεροί τε σύες χαροποί τε λέοντες, Hes. *Sc.* 177 χλοῦναί τε σύες χαροποί τε λέοντες, and *Od.* 14.532 (etc.) σύες ἀργιόδοντες. For the sense of χαροπός see 194n.

572 **τετελεσμένον** 'fully empowered, authorised'. Cf. τέλος meaning 'power, authority'.

573 'And he who receives no gift will grant a privilege which is far from the least': this must surely refer to Hades, who was traditionally ἀμείλιχος (*Il.* 9.158), i.e. could not be appeased by offerings, and who yet will give Hermes this unique privilege. Cf. also A. *Niobe* fr. 161.1–3 Radt μόνος θεῶν γὰρ Θάνατος οὐ δώρων ἐρᾶι, | οὐδ' ἄν τι θύων οὐδ' ἐπισπένδων ἄνοις, | οὐδ' ἐστὶ βωμός, οὐδὲ παιωνίζεται, and Schol. AbT *Il.* 9.158 ἀνελεής ἐστιν· ὅθεν ἐν οὐδεμιᾶι πόλει Ἅιδου βωμός ἐστιν (quoting the Aeschylean verses). Pausanias tells us that the Eleans alone worship Hades and have a sanctuary and temple to him, which they open only once a year, in gratitude for his help for the Pylians against Heracles (6.25.2–3). The exception proves the rule. This special accolade for Hermes makes an effective climax for the narrative section of the hymn. Hermes alone is *superis deorum gratus et imis* (Hor. *Od.* 1.10.19). It is also possible to take ἄδοτος as active (cf. Càssola, Vergados), i.e. Hades usually does not give anything, but will do so for Hermes.

574–8 With these transitional lines we move from the narrative mode to the present time: cf. *H. Dem.* 483–9, 15.7–8, and other parallels in Richardson on *H. Dem.* 483–9.

574–5 echo 506–510, 523–6. 576–8 are a generalising summary of Hermes' ubiquitous powers (cf. for example *H. Ap.* 19–24), qualified by a final ironic allusion to his chief attribute as the unpredictable god of deception.

577 **τὸ δ' ἄκριτον** 'continually'. Cf. 126 δηρὸν δὴ μετὰ ταῦτα καὶ ἄκριτον. It could also mean 'indiscriminately'. For the article cf. Hes. *Op.* 596 τρὶς . . . τὸ δὲ τέτρατον . . . , Hdt. 3.104 τὸ ἑωθινόν.

578 **νύκτα δι' ὀρφναίην:** cf. *Il.* 10.83 = 386, *Od.* 9.143.

579–80 For these two formulaic closing lines see *H. Ap.* 545–6n.

To Aphrodite

1–44 *Prelude: Aphrodite's universal power and its exceptions.* Aphrodite has power over all living things, except for Athene, Artemis, and Hestia. She can even influence Zeus, the greatest of all gods, so that he forgets his own wife Hera.

The opening is unusual, because it develops into a smaller 'hymn' in praise of the three goddesses who are not subject to Aphrodite, and concludes with a further passage in praise of Hera (40–4). But the *Hymn to Apollo*, for example, also includes in its proem a small hymn to Leto (5–18), and the effect is rather like that of the *priamel*-type catalogues of possible themes of praise at *H. Ap.* 19ff., 207ff. (cf. Miller (1986) 29–30). Here, however, there is a dramatic contrast: the poet immediately suggests that Aphrodite is not after all quite so powerful as one might suppose, a motif which anticipates the theme of 45ff., where Zeus turns the tables on her. At the same time he skilfully pays tribute to four other major goddesses at the outset. The opening section is particularly indebted to Hesiod: cf. 1, 5, 8, 9–11, 14, 21–32, 29–32nn. with Solmsen (1968), 55–67, and Faulkner (2008) 35–8.

The prelude is also unusual in that it proclaims the poem's theme not as the deity herself (as in the other *Hymns*), but as her 'works'. The word ἔργον or ἔργα is emphasised throughout the opening section, recurring six times in 2–21, in relation also to Athena and Ares (cf. Clay (2006) 155–7).

1–6 The poet asks the Muse to sing in praise of 'Aphrodite's works'. 6 echoes the opening line in ring-form. Aphrodite's power is elegantly described by three pairs of antitheses: gods and men, birds and beasts, those both of land and sea. There is also artful variation in πολυχρύσου Ἀφροδίτης . . . Κύπριδος (1–2) and ἐϋστεφάνου Κυθερείης (6), naming two of her chief epic cult-epithets (cf. Hes. *Th.* 192–9, *H.* 6.2 and 18, 10.1). There are similar descriptions of the power of love in Soph. fr. 941 Radt, Eur. *Hipp.* 1268–81, and cf. the opening of Lucretius' poem.

1 Μοῦσα μοι ἔννεπε resembles *Od.* 1.1, but in early hexameter poetry the placing of Μοῦσα first is less usual in such opening invocations: cf. Hes. *Th.* 1 Μουσάων, *Op.* 1 Μοῦσαι Πιερίηθεν . . .

ἔργα: cf. Hes. *Op.* 521 οὔπω ἔργα ἰδυῖα πολυχρύσου Ἀφροδίτης, where 519 is echoed by *H. Aph.* 14, 531 by 6: see Introduction 4(b). 'Aphrodite's works' means primarily sexual love, and all that goes with this.

πολυχρύσου Ἀφροδίτης is a Hesiodic formula (6× in the Hes. corpus): cf. Boedeker (1974) 26–7, and see also 87–90n.

2 **Κύπριδος:** in Homer this epithet of Aphrodite, due to her cult in Cyprus, is confined to *Iliad* 5; cf. Hes. fr. 124.2 M–W, and Kirk on *Il.* 5.327–30.

3 For ἐδαμάσσατο of Aphrodite cf. 251, *Il.* 14.198–9.

4 We shall see Aphrodite's effect on the animals when she visits Mt Ida at 68–74.

διιπετέας ought to mean 'flying through the sky' here, though its original sense is debated (cf. Janko on *Il.* 16.173–5). In Homer it is always used as an epithet with ποταμός, and is usually assumed to mean 'fallen from the sky'.

5 Cf. Hes. *Th.* 582 κνώδαλ' ὅσ' ἤπειρος πολλὰ τρέφει ἠδὲ θάλασσα.

6 πᾶσιν δ' ἔργα μέμηλεν: cf. Hes. *Op.* 531 πᾶσιν (of wild beasts) ἐνὶ φρέσι τοῦτο μέμηλεν.

ἐϋστεφάνου Κυθερείης: this formula (cf. 287, 175?) also occurs in the *Odyssey* (2×) and *Theogony* (2×). Cf. *Cypria* fr. 5 Allen, where Aphrodite weaves garlands with Nymphs and Charites, and Boedeker (1974) 27–8. Κυθερείης was understood by the Greeks as referring to Aphrodite's connection with Cythera, where she emerged from the sea foam (Hes. *Th.* 198) and had a famous shrine, founded by the Phoenicians like her cult in Cyprus (Hdt. 1.105, Paus. 3.23.1; cf. Hunter (1999) 126 on Theoc. *Id.* 3.46). The form of the word (if it is from Κυθήρα with metrical shortening) may be due to influence from epithets such as εὐπατέρεια.

7–33 These lines form a complete section, marked off like 1–6 by ring-composition. 7 and 33 introduce the theme of deceit, so crucial to the narrative to come.

7 τρισσάς occurs first here and at Hes. fr. 233.2 M–W.

τρισσὰς . . . φρένας is best taken as a double accusative, with θεάς understood with τρισσάς.

8–15 Athene is honoured as the virgin goddess of war and the crafts of both men and women.

8 = Hes. *Th.* 13, where the MSS read γλαυκῶπιν, which makes it likely that M's reading is correct here. Both γλαυκῶπιν and γλαυκώπιδα occur elsewhere in MSS of early epic.

9–11 The neglect of digamma in γάρ οἱ (cf. Hes. *Op.* 526, and West ad loc.) is unusual in early epic, and led to Matthiae's οἱ ἅδεν. But the poet probably wanted variation between οὐ γάρ οἱ εὔαδεν ἔργα . . . and ἀλλ' ἄρα οἱ πόλεμοί τε ἅδον καὶ ἔργον . . . He is echoing Hes. *Th.* 926 here, where Athene is πότνιαν, ἧι κέλαδοί τε ἅδον πόλεμοί τε μάχαι τε. For ἁδεῖν in such contexts cf. also *Th.* 917, *H. Aph.* 18, 21, etc.

The contrast between love and war is emphasised by the positioning of ἔργα . . . Ἀφροδίτης and ἔργον Ἄρηος at the ends of 9 and 10. Cf. *Il.* 5.428–30 (Zeus to the wounded Aphrodite) οὔ τοι, τέκνον ἐμόν, δέδοται πολεμήια ἔργα, | ἀλλὰ σύ γ' ἱμερόεντα μετέρχεο ἔργα γάμοιο, | ταῦτα δ' Ἄρηι θοῶι καὶ Ἀθήνηι πάντα μελήσει. (The love story of Ares and Aphrodite in *Od.* 8 also alludes to the contrast of Strife and Love.) For ὑσμῖναί τε μάχαι τε cf. *Od.* 11.612, Hes. *Th.* 228. But in ἀγλαὰ ἔργ' ἀλεγύνειν we move to the more creative work of craftsmanship: hence the asyndeton in 12.

11–12 resemble *H.* 20.2–3, where Hephaestus with Athene ἀγλαὰ ἔργα | ἀνθρώπους ἐδίδαξεν ἐπὶ χθονός.

13 σατίνας: σατίναι (only in plural) is probably a Thracian or Phrygian loan word, used elsewhere of waggons or carriages for women (Sappho fr. 44.13 L–P = V, Anacr., *PMG* fr. 388.10, Eur. *Helen* 1311); see Leumann (1959) 206–7. Here it is coupled with war-chariots as also in Sappho fr. 44.13–17 (note also 15 παρθενίκαν τ' [ἀπαλο]σφύρων with *H. Aph.* 14). σατίνας τε may be right, avoiding hiatus after καί: cf. (τε) καὶ ἅρματα ποικίλα χαλκῶι 3× *Il.* The incidence of hiatus in this hymn is very low (Janko (1982) 36).

14 παρθενικὰς ἀπαλόχροας: cf. Hes. *Op.* 519 παρθενικῆς ἀπαλόχροος. Hesiod is describing a young girl staying at home in winter with her mother, οὔπω ἔργα ἰδυῖα πολυχρύσου Ἀφροδίτης (521), i.e. implying a similar contrast to that expressed here.

16–20 Artemis is praised as the virgin goddess of hunting and dancing, and as a deity both of the countryside and also of 'the city of just men'. Cf. *H.* 27, where she is first a huntress and then leads the dancing; a fragmentary poem assigned to either Sappho or Alcaeus (Sappho fr. 44(A) V = Alc. fr. 304 L–P), where she swears to remain a virgin huntress for ever; Anacr., *PMG* fr. 348, where she watches over θρασυκαρδίων ἀνδρῶν . . . πόλιν, and citizens who are 'not savage'. Call. *H.* 3 echoes both our hymn and Sappho fr. 44(A) V: cf. Call. *H.* 3.1–3 Ἄρτεμιν . . . τῆι τόξα λαγωβολίαι τε μέλονται | καὶ χορὸς ἀμφιλαφὴς καὶ ἐν οὔρεσιν ἑψιάασθαι; 6–40, where she asks Zeus for perpetual virginity, hunting, and dancing, all mountains, and (somewhat casually) 'whatever city you wish', but he grants her many cities; 121–35, where she attacks 'a city of unjust people', and favours the just with prosperity. Her association with cities and justice is far less prominent than her other aspects, but cf. Anacr., *PMG* fr. 348 (above), Libanius *Or.* 5.34 (Artemis rewards and punishes the just and unjust), Farnell, *Cults* II 467–70, Nilsson, *GGR* I³ 498.

16 Ἀρτέμιδα χρυσηλάκατον κελαδεινήν: for this formula cf. *Il.* 16.183 (genitive, in a passage similar to *H. Aph.* 117–21) etc. χρυσηλάκατος means 'with golden arrows', and κελαδεινή refers to the din of the hunt (cf. Janko on *Il.* 16.183, Edwards on *Il.* 20.70–1).

17 Cf. *Il.* 14.198–9 (Hera to Aphrodite) δὸς νῦν μοι φιλότητα καὶ ἵμερον, ὧι τε σύ πάντας | δαμνᾶι . . .

φιλομμειδής: probably originally 'lover of smiling', rather than connected with μήδεα, 'genitals', as in Hes. *Th.* 200; cf. Chantraine, *Dict.* s.v. μειδιάω.

18 M reads πουλύχρυσα δὲ τόξα, which may be the result of a conjecture to repair a corrupted exemplar, as the form πουλύχρυσος occurs nowhere else.

οὔρεσι θῆρας ἐναίρειν: cf. *Il.* 21.458 (κατ' οὔρεα), of Artemis.

19 διαπρύσιοί τ' ὀλολυγαί: ὀλολυγή and related words are normally used of women crying aloud in invocation of the gods, sometimes also of goddesses. It is used in the context of the birth of Apollo at *H. Ap.* 119 (see comment), and cf. Call. *H.* 4.258 διαπρυσίην ὀλολυγήν in the same context. Here, however, there is no reason to see a reference to Artemis' role as patron of childbirth. διαπρύσιος is always used adverbially in Homer (*Il.* 8.227 etc.), of a piercing cry or of a bull (?) running out into the plain. Cf. *H. Aph.* 80, of lyre-playing, *H. Herm.* 336–9n.

20 ἄλσεά τε σκιόεντα: cf. *H. Ap.* 76 etc. ἄλσεα δενδρήεντα, *Il.* 9.157 οὔρεα τε σκιόεντα, *H.* 27.4.

δικαίων τε πτόλις ἀνδρῶν: this phrase occurs only here in early epic. πτόλις seems to be used as a collective singular here. Cf. Call. *H.* 3.122 ἀλλά μιν εἰς ἀδίκων ἔβαλες πόλιν, of Artemis, echoing this line.

21–32 Hestia receives a more extensive passage of praise, which really is a mini-hymn, since it contains a brief narrative, both of her birth (22–3) and of her refusal of proposals from Poseidon and Apollo (24–8), followed by an account of her special place among the gods and in mortal cult (29–32). θεῶν πρέσβειρα in 32 forms a neat ring-motif with ἣν πρώτην τέκετο in 22.

Hestia is the subject of *Hymns* 24 and 29, and of a few later hymns (Aristonous, in Powell, *CA* 164–5, Simias fr. 9 Powell, Orph. *H.* 84), but she never really acquired a mythological life of her own. The poet follows Hesiod here in making her the eldest child of Cronos (*Th.* 453–4, where she is named first), and also the youngest, since he disgorged his children in reverse order (*Th.* 493–7). The story of her wooing may well be an invention, and recurs nowhere else. The fact that two such august gods wished to marry her both adds to her status and also underlines her determination in refusing. Zeus's gift to her of special privileges (29–32) is another Hesiodic motif: cf. especially Hesiod's 'hymn' to Hecate (*Th.* 411–52), and the special honours given by Zeus to Styx and her children (*Th.* 383–403). But Hestia's virginity is presumably fundamental to her nature, and it recurs in the case of Vesta, whether because of an association of fire with purity, or for other reasons.

21 αἰδοίηι: perhaps not only 'reverend', but also because of her own display of αἰδώς in the face of marriage.

22 Ἱστίηι: most MSS read the Ionic form here, rather than Ἑστίηι, which frequently occurs as a variant elsewhere in early texts.

22–3 Her two births are juxtaposed and contrasted, as are 'crooked-counsellor Cronos' and 'the plan of Zeus'. Cornutus (first century AD) connects this birth-legend with the practice of making libation and prayer to Hestia at the beginning and end of a feast (*ND* 28, p. 53.12–16 Lang), and this is probably what is meant by *H.* 29.4–6. The opening libation is well known, but there is no other Greek evidence for a final one. In *Od.* 7.136–8 the Phaeacians make their last libation before sleeping to Hermes, with whom Hestia is sometimes associated (cf. *H.* 29). Cicero, however, in discussing Vesta and Hestia, does say that she is the subject of both first and last prayer and sacrifice (*ND* 2.27.67), and this was normal Roman practice. Cf. also *RE* VIII 1271–7.

24–8 The pursuit of Hestia has been compared to the story of the pursuit of Thetis by Zeus and Poseidon (cf. Jouan (1956) 290–302, and Dornseiff (1931) 203–4). Poseidon and Apollo may be chosen as two major gods (after Zeus). Hestia is also associated with Apollo because of her place at Delphi (*H.* 24, Aristonous, Powell, *CA* 164–5, etc.). Poseidon is sometimes portrayed next to her in art and cult (Paus. 5.26.2, at Olympia, *LIMC* V.1 s.v. Hestia nos. 11, 15, 17), but this connection seems more casual.

25 στερεῶς ἀπέειπεν: cf. *Il.* 9.510; the adverb ('fixedly') suits Hestia's character.

26–8 Hestia's great oath resembles that sworn by Artemis in Sappho fr. 44(A) V (= Alc. fr. 304 L–P: cf. *H. Aph.* 16–20n.) 4–5 μέγαν ὄρκον ἀπώμοσε . . . | . . . ἄϊ πάρθενος ἔσσομαι, and this is confirmed by Zeus. Cf. also Call. *H.* 3.6, 26–8. Hestia and Zeus were closely associated: cf. *Od.* 14.158–9 etc., *H.* 24.4–5, *RE* VIII 1300f. Cf. also *Il.* 1.524–7 for the idea of certain accomplishment of an oath guaranteed by Zeus's head (and 15.36–40, *H. Herm.* 274). It was customary to touch the object by which one swore (*Il.* 1.233–4 etc.).
28 πάντ' ἤματα occurs only here in early hexameter poetry for ἤματα πάντα, but is common in Hellenistic and later poetry.
29–32 The phrasing of 29 resembles Hes. *Th.* 585 τεῦξε καλὸν κακὸν ἀντ' ἀγαθοῖο. The scansion κᾰλόν (cf. *H. Aph.* 261) occurs at *Th.* 585 and *Op.* 63 (cf. West, *Theogony* p. 82). Hestia sits at the centre of the house, as in Orph. *H.* 84.2 ἣ μέσον οἶκον ἔχεις πυρὸς ἀενάοιο; cf. Orph. *H.* 27, Simias fr. 9 Powell. For her special position and privileges cf. also *H.* 29.1–5. Here too the implication seems to be that she has a share in all feasts, both in men's houses and in the gods' temples, and πῖαρ ἑλοῦσα presumably means that she enjoys the fat of the sacrifices offered to the gods.
31–2 These lines are similar in expression and structure, stressing the parallelism of divine and human honours. Cf. *H. Dem.* 268–9 εἰμὶ δὲ Δημήτηρ τιμάοχος, ἥ τε μέγιστον | ἀθανάτοις θνητοισί τ' ὄνεαρ καὶ χάρμα τέτυκται, probably influenced by *H. Aph.* (cf. Richardson on *H. Dem.* 268–9). πρέσβειρα may imply both Hestia's primogeniture, and also her special honour. This form (for Homeric πρέσβα) does not recur before fifth-century Attic drama (E. *IT* 963, Ar. *Ach.* 883 parodying Aeschylus, and Ar. *Lys.* 86).
33 This line echoes 7, rounding off this episode, and 34–5 resume the theme of 1–3. 36–44 then add as a further development the final proof of Aphrodite's power, over Zeus himself.
35 = *Od.* 9.521, *H. Herm.* 144.
36–44 Aphrodite's deception of Zeus is expressed by aorists (36, 39), which are probably generic (or 'gnomic'), rather than referring only to the past. The generalising καί τε (36, 38) indicates recurrent events. For this reason, M's ἐθέλῃ is more likely to be correct in 38 than the variant ἐθέλοι. For the subjunctive in such cases cf. *Il.* 1.218, *Od.* 20.85–6. See also Faulkner (2008) on 38, and (2005) for a broader discussion of such aorists.
36 Here παρέκ must go with ἤγαγε, with νόον as object, whereas in the *Iliad* παρὲκ νόον means 'beyond reason' at 20.133 and probably also at 10.391 πολλῇσίν μ' ἄτῃσι παρὲκ νόον ἤγαγεν Ἕκτωρ.
37 Ironically in this context, the greatness of Zeus is emphatically expressed, with the unusually marked repetition of μ and στ, as well as the duplication of the superlative (cf. Porter (1951) 39). On alliteration in Greek see Silk (1974) 173ff., 224ff.
38 Cf. the language of Hera's deception of Zeus in *Il.* 14, e.g. 160 ὅππως ἐξαπάφοιτο Διὸς νόον αἰγιόχοιο, 217 πάρφασις, ἥ τ' ἔκλεψε νόον πύκα περ φρονεόντων, 294 ὡς δ' ἴδεν, ὥς μιν ἔρως πυκινὰς φρένας ἀμφεκάλυψεν.

39 The common motif of divine 'ease' is extended to cover even Aphrodite's power over Zeus. The idea of the 'mixing' of gods and mortals is a main theme of the hymn (see 45–52n.), and μείγνυμι implies not only sexual intercourse but also the blurring of the normal boundary between these two spheres. The feminine form καταθνήτη occurs only in this hymn (50, 110, 250), with the masculine as a variant.
40 **Ἥρης ἐκλελαθοῦσα** 'causing him to forget Hera'. Cf. *Il.* 2.600 ἐκλέλαθον κιθαριστύν.
41–4 These lines develop into a passage praising Hera, as if the poet did not want to be accused of neglecting this goddess also. In *Il.* 4.57–61 Hera claims respect both as Zeus's wife and as the eldest daughter of Cronos, whereas here she is μέγα εἶδος ἀρίστη (μέγα is probably adverbial), and κυδίστη among his children, Hestia being the eldest. 42 seems to echo *Il.* 4.59 καί με πρεσβυτάτην τέκετο Κρόνος ἀγκυλομήτης. Cf. also *H.* 12 Ἥρην ἀείδω χρυσόθρονον, ἣν τέκε Ῥείη, | ἀθανάτων βασίλειαν, ὑπείροχον εἶδος ἔχουσαν, | Ζηνὸς ἐριγδούποιο κασιγνήτην ἄλοχόν τε | κυδρήν . . . In the legend of the double birth (cf. 22–3n.) Hera could also claim to be eldest daughter when the goddesses were reborn.
43 The formula Ζεὺς . . . ἄφθιτα μήδεα εἰδώς occurs only once in Homer (*Il.* 24.88), but five times in Hesiod, and also at *H. Dem.* 321. There may be a touch of irony here, as at 37, although in what follows Zeus again shows that he has the upper hand.
45–52 In revenge, Zeus causes Aphrodite herself to fall in love with a mortal.

This passage both rounds off the prelude to the hymn and introduces the main theme of its narrative part. It contains a great deal of artful repetition, especially of the idea of the mixing of gods and mortals: words for mortal occur five times, for god four times (cf. Porter (1949) 263–6). Aphrodite has delighted in causing confusion in the order of the world, but she must not be allowed to escape unpunished, and it is Zeus who has the last laugh. This theme is echoed at 247–55.
45 **γλυκὺν ἵμερον ἔμβαλε θυμῶι:** cf. *H. Aph.* 53, 143, and *Il.* 3.139, where Iris fills Helen with desire for her former husband Menelaus and her homeland.
46 **ὄφρα τάχιστα** suggests Zeus's eagerness to retaliate.
47–8 The sequence of optative εἴη followed by the more vivid subjunctive εἴπηι occurs at *Il.* 14.163–5, 24.582–6, 653–5, etc.; cf. Janko on *Il.* 14.162–5.
48 **καί ποτ':** the force of the negative is continued here. This occurs nowhere else in early epic with καί ποτε.
49 This line plays on the traditional sense of φιλομμειδής (cf. 17n.).
γελοιήσασα: γελοιάω for γελάω occurs only here, and as a variant at *Od.* 20.347, 390. Cf. *Od.* 18.111 ἡδὺ γελώοντες, and discussion by Hoekstra (1969) 45, Janko (1982) 156.
50–2 Aphrodite created unions both of gods and mortal women, leading to the race of heroes (the subject of the Hesiodic *Catalogue*), and of goddesses and mortal men (the theme of Hes. *Th.* 965–1020). The latter tended

to be problematic, as Calypso says (*Od.* 5.118–29). The variation θεοὺς συνέμειξε... θεὰς ἀνέμειξε avoids repetition (Porter (1949) 265). In 50–2 we also have a double chiasmus: θεοὺς... καταθνητῇσι γυναιξὶ... καταθνητοὺς υἱεῖς... ἀθανάτοισιν,... θεὰς... καταθνητοῖς ἀνθρώποις.

51 υἱεῖς: if sound, this Attic form of the accusative plural occurs only here in early epic. It could be due to Attic transmission of the text: cf. Faulkner (2008), who reads υἷας.

53–74 Zeus makes Aphrodite fall in love with Anchises, who is a cowherd on Mt Ida. She goes to Paphos to prepare herself, and then flies to Mt Ida, where the wild beasts greet her and she makes them couple together.

53–7 It is only now that we learn the name of Aphrodite's future husband. The second half of 53 repeats 45, after the intervening excursus (cf. δ' ἄρα, resuming the narrative 'and so'). For ἐν ἀκροπόλοις ὄρεσιν cf. *Il.* 5.523, *Od.* 19.205 ἐν ἀκροπόλοισιν ὄρεσσιν (at line-end), of which this is a modification. The o-stem form πολυπιδάκου, instead of πολυπίδακος, is probably correct here and at Cypria fr. 5.5 Allen (= 5.5 Davies): cf. also Janko on *Il.* 14.157–8. These passages have thematic links with ours: Ida is the scene of Hera's seduction of Zeus in *Iliad* 14; cf. (58–67n. below) the parallels for Aphrodite's toilette. The *Cypria* passage refers to the Judgement of Paris, which took place when Paris was a herdsman on Mt Ida (*Il.* 24.29, *Cypria* summary, p. 102 Allen = fr. 31 Davies), and the motif of the Trojan prince as herdsman is typical in such stories (cf. Richardson on *Il.* 24.29, and Theocr. *Id.* 1.105–7, Griffin (1992) 189–211). For Anchises and Aphrodite cf. the brief references in *Il.* 2.820–1, 5.313, Hes. *Th.* 1008–10.

55 Anchises (though a cowherd) is a fit partner because of his godlike beauty, a feature common to his family (*H. Aph.* 200ff.). For Anchises as herdsman in the same context cf. *Il.* 5.213.

βουκολέεσκεν βοῦς: the rhythm is unusual, and βουκολέεσκε βόας would have been possible.

57 ἐκπάγλως: Aphrodite uses ἔκπαγλα φίλησα of her fondness for Helen at *Il.* 3.415, when she wants her to return to Paris, and the same expression recurs at 5.423, in mockery by Athene of Aphrodite for her fondness for the Trojans, after her wounding by Diomedes. All these passages have thematic links with the Judgement of Paris (see 53–7n., and Kirk on *Il.* 5.422–5). These are the only places in early epic where the word is used in the context of strong love or desire.

58–67 Aphrodite's toilette is a typical motif in such divine seduction stories. Cf. Hera's preparations at *Il.* 14.161–89, where 169 = *H. Aph.* 60 and 172 = 63. Hera enters her chamber and shuts the doors, cleans and anoints herself with ambrosia, combs her hair, dresses and puts on her jewellery, and then goes to Aphrodite, who gives her the special κεστὸς ἱμάς which contains all the power of love (188–223); cf. Janko on *Il.* 14.153–353 (pp. 170–1). Cf. also the end of the song of Ares and Aphrodite, where the goddess returns to Paphos after their detection (*Od.* 8.362–6), and where 363–5 = *H. Aph.* 59 + 61–2. Here she is washed and anointed by the Charites, and clothed by them (cf. *Il.* 5.338, for her robe made by the Charites). The same scene recurs, with variations, in *Hymn* 6, where the Horai dress her and adorn her with jewellery before bringing her to join the other gods; and she is again dressed by the Charites and Horai, with clothes dyed in spring flowers, and accompanies the nymphs and Charites over Mt Ida, in *Cypria* frr. 4 and 5, presumably in connection with the Judgement of Paris (see Stinton (1965) 33, 61). Cf. also Pandora's adornment (Hes. *Op.* 72–6). These motifs are picked up again in the elaborate description of Aphrodite's dress and jewellery (cf. 65) at 84–90, when Anchises first sees her, and at 161–6, where he undresses her. Behind the present passage lies the Homeric typical scene of bathing, which describes female attendants washing, anointing, and clothing guests (*Od.* 3.464–8 etc.); cf. Arend (1933) 124ff., Ginouvès (1962) 156–62.

58–9 Aphrodite's cult at Paphos and elsewhere in Cyprus was originally Phoenician (Hdt. 1.105.3). For excavation of the sanctuary see Maier and Karageorghis (1984). A fundamental aspect of her cult was the fragrance of the incense, again brought by the Phoenicians (cf. Burkert (1985) 62, Sappho fr. 2 L–P = V). Cf. here 58 θυώδεα νηόν, 59 βωμός τε θυώδης, 63 τεθυωμένον, 66 εὐώδεα, although such epithets are applied also to other gods.

61–3 The Charites are closely associated with Aphrodite in art and literature. Cf. especially the scene where Athene beautifies Penelope in order to arouse desire in the suitors (*Od.* 18.192–4): κάλλεϊ μέν οἱ πρῶτα προσώπατα καλὰ κάθηρεν | ἀμβροσίωι, οἵωι περ ἐϋστέφανος Κυθέρεια | χρίεται, εὖτ' ἂν ἴηι Χαρίτων χόρον ἱμερόεντα. For ἐπενήνοθε ('covers') see Richardson on *H. Dem.* 279. The repetition in 62–3 is similar to that in *Il.* 14.170–8 ἀμβροσίηι . . . ἀμβροσίωι . . . ἀμβροσίους . . . ἀμβρόσιον . . . ; cf. also *H. Aph.* 58–9, 97–8 (νυμφάων . . . νυμφῶν), etc. The plural οἷα presumably means 'such (oils) as . . .' ἑδανῶι was understood as meaning 'sweet' in antiquity. The MSS reading ἑανῶι is a variant at *Il.* 14.172, where it has been taken as meaning 'for her robe' (cf. 178), but this is out of place in both contexts: see Faulkner (2008) 146–8.

64–7 After dressing, Aphrodite sets off for Mt Ida. Her journey has a typical form (65–91): 66 departure; 68–75 arrival; 76 discovery of person visited; 81–3 approach; 84–90 reaction to this; 91ff. conversation. See Arend (1933) 28ff. 64 is echoed at 171–2, after the Seduction scene. The genitive ἐπὶ Τροίης is preferable to the accusative, meaning 'in the direction of' (*Il.* 3.5 etc.).

66 Κύπρον: some editors have preferred M's reading κῆπον, since Aphrodite's cult at Paphos was associated with sacred gardens (Strabo 683–4), as elsewhere (cf. Langlotz (1954), especially 34). Càssola compared Ar. *Birds* 1067 κήπους εὐώδεις. κῆπον is the *lectio difficilior*, but it has not been referred to before and its mention here seems less natural. We need the place-name in this journey scene, echoing 58.

66–8 Aphrodite's swift aerial journey to Troy and Ida is a miniature version of Hera's in *Iliad* 14 (225–30, 280–5), which may be the direct model for this passage. Cf. especially 67 with 14.282 ῥίμφα πρήσσοντε κέλευθον and 68 with *Il.* 14.283 Ἴδην ἱκέσθην πολυπίδακα, μητέρα θηρῶν. See also Faulkner (2008) 32 and 149, on the possible connection with *Iliad* 14 here.

67 M's reading ὕψι μετὰ νέφεσιν ῥίμφα πρήσσουσα κέλευθον is preferable, as closer to *Il.* 14.282 and also 23.501, *Od.* 13.83 than the variant reading νεφέεσσι θοῶς.

69–74 The traditional description of Ida as 'mother of wild beasts' is given a special point here, with the reaction of the animals to the arrival of the goddess. Behind this lies a typical motif: cf. *Il.* 13.27–30, where sea beasts play as Poseidon crosses the sea, *Od.* 14.29–30, where Eumaeus' dogs bark at Odysseus on arrival, 16.3–5, where they fawn on Telemachus (σαίνοντας), and 17.291–323, where Argos recognises and greets Odysseus (οὔρηι . . . ἔσηνε 302). Closer still is *Od.* 10.210–19, where Circe's wolves and lions fawn on Odysseus' men like dogs. But Aphrodite's power over animals (4–5) is shown by the way in which they all respond to her presence. For nature's response to an epiphany cf. Aphrodite's first appearance from the sea at Hes. *Th.* 194–5, where the earth flowers below her feet, and *Il.* 14.347–9, where this happens when Zeus and Hera sleep together. Delos bursts into flower after Apollo's birth (*H. Ap.* 133–9), and wine flows and a vine entwines the mast of the ship on which Dionysus is held prisoner at *H.* 7.34–42. In the context of Mt Ida, Aphrodite may be portrayed here as a 'Mistress of Animals' (πότνια θηρῶν, used once in Homer, of Artemis, *Il.* 21.470), like Cybele, with whom she was identified in Phrygia and Lydia (Charon of Lampsacus, *FGrH* 262 F 5; cf. Hesychius s.v. Κυβήβη). The wild beasts resemble those associated with Cybele: cf. *H.* 14.3–4, where the Mother of the Gods takes pleasure in λύκων κλαγγὴ χαροπῶν τε λεόντων, *PMG* 935.17–18 for her χαροποὶ λέοντες and πολιοὶ λύκοι, and A.R. 1.1144–5, where such beasts greet Rhea. Ishtar also has the title 'Mistress of Animals' (West (1997) 56), and Aštarte is portrayed in a similar way (Budin (2000) 350–2). See Faulkner (2008) 152–3, Rose (1924) 11–16, and also Malten (1931) 33–59, Nilsson, *GGR* I^3 522–3.

70–1 Cf. *H. Herm.* 223 οὔτε λύκων πολιῶν οὔτ᾽ ἄρκτων οὔτε λεόντων, *Il.* 10.334 πολιοῖο λύκοιο. For χαροπός see *H. Herm.* 194n.

71 προκάδων: προκάς for πρόξ (*Od.* 17.295) occurs only here, but is paralleled by the double form δόρξ, δορκάς.

74 σύνδυο . . . ἐναύλους: for σύνδυο cf. *Il.* 10.224 σύν τε δύ᾽ ἐρχομένω, *Od.* 9.429 σύντρεις, etc. ἔναυλος in Homer means 'torrent, stream-bed'; the sense 'dwelling, haunts' (cf. αὐλή) occurs at Hes. *Th.* 129, *H.* 14.5 (Mother of the Gods), 26.8. κατὰ σκιόεντας ἐναύλους recurs at *H. Aph.* 124, again of wild beasts.

75–90 Aphrodite finds Anchises alone and playing the lyre, and appears to him disguised as a young girl. He is amazed at her beauty, her radiant dress and jewellery.

75 This poet likes εὐποίητος: cf. 161, 173; cf. κλισίην εὔτυκτον 2× *Il*, 1× *Od.*

76–80 Anchises' isolation is emphasised by the repetition of 76 and 79. Epiphanies in a natural setting tend to take place when someone is alone, especially in the case of herdsmen. Cf. for example the Judgement of Paris, Hesiod's meeting with the Muses, or Teiresias' encounter with Athena and Chariclo (Call. *H.* 5.70–8).

77 Ἀγχίσην ἥρωα: cf. Hes. *Th.* 1009 in the context of Anchises' union with Aphrodite.

θεῶν ἄπο κάλλος ἔχοντα: cf. 55. The formula is usually applied to women (*Od.* 8.457; cf. also *Od.* 6.18, Hes. fr. 215.1, and perhaps 171.4).

79–80 Anchises walks up and down, playing on his lyre, like Achilles in his hut at *Il.* 9.186–9. Similarly, Paris plays his pipes in Euripides' description of the Judgement story at *IA* 573–8 (cf. *Helen* 358, Colluthus 110ff.), and on vase-paintings he is shown playing the lyre (Stinton (1965) 28–9). Cf. *Il.* 3.54 κίθαρις τά τε δῶρ' Ἀφροδίτης, of Paris. For διαπρύσιον see 19n. It is used of the sound of cymbals at E. *Helen* 1308–9. Here it probably describes the sharp, clear sound of plucked strings.

81–90 Aphrodite's appearance in disguise resembles other scenes of meeting with a disguised deity (see Richardson on *H. Dem.* 98ff., and pp. 339–41).

81–3 Athene is disguised as a young girl at *Od.* 7.19–20. *H. Aph.* 82 resembles *H. Dem.* 145–6 παρθένος ἀδμής . . . εἶδος ἀρίστη, and 275 μέγεθος καὶ εἶδος ἄμειψε (Demeter's self-revelation); cf. *Od.* 6.109, 228 (παρθένος ἀδμής of Nausicaa). In Homer the form ἄδμητος is only applied to animals, and εἶδός τε μέγεθός τε is the usual Homeric formula (5×), but cf. φυὴν καὶ εἶδος (4×).

83–5 Fear and wonder are normal reactions to an epiphany (see Richardson on *H. Dem.* 188–90, 275ff.). Here Aphrodite naturally does not want Anchises to feel fear, but he does experience wonder, and addresses her as a goddess (92–106). Cf. especially *H. Dem.* 188–90, where Metaneira experiences reverence, awe, and fear at the appearance of Demeter in disguise. In 83 ἐν ὀφθαλμοῖσι means 'before his eyes, in his field of vision' (see LSJ s.v. ἐν A III.1). Cf. 179 ἐν ὀφθαλμοῖσι νοήσας.

84 θάμβος or τάφος denotes a strong reaction of astonishment, and is often used in epiphanies (cf. Richardson on *H. Dem.* 188–90, §3), whereas θαῦμα and its cognates seem often to be less strong ('admiration'). The rarer form θάμβαινεν (*varia lectio* at Pi. *O.* 3.32 also) seems better here than θαύμαινεν, as the *lectio difficilior.*

85 For εἵματα σιγαλόεντα at line-end cf. 164 and *Il.* 22.154. There and at *Od.* 6.26 the epithet is used in the context of washing clothes, whereas here it is explained by 86, and has a special point.

86–90 Here we have a more detailed description of Aphrodite's dress and jewellery (cf. 64–5). The emphasis on their radiance is another feature which this scene shares with epiphanies, which sometimes speak of a deity's shining robes (see Richardson on *H. Dem.* 188–90, 275ff.): in the *Hymns* cf. 31.13–14, 32.8 (of the Moon: cf. *H. Aph.* 89–90).

86 Cf. *Il.* 18.610, where Achilles' divine breastplate is φαεινότερον πυρὸς αὐγῆς, and *Il.* 5.315 πέπλοιο φαείνου of Aphrodite's robe.

87–90 For 87 cf. *Il.* 18.401 (= *H. Aph.* 163) πόρπας τε γναμπτάς θ' ἕλικας κάλυκάς τε καὶ ὅρμους (made by Hephaestus for Eurynome and Thetis). ἕλικας must be 'spirals', but it is not clear what they are for, whether for the hair, or as bracelets or something else. ἑλικτήρ is later used of an earring, but these need not be the same. ἐπιγναμπτός ('curved') is only found here; cf. ἐπιγνάμπτω, ἐπικαμπύλος, etc. κάλυκας ('buds') are usually thought to be rosettes, probably designed as earrings (cf. *H.* 6.9 ἄνθεμα, of earrings). ὅρμοι are necklaces, in this case golden and very elaborately made. ἐλάμπετο is probably best taken as meaning 'it shone, there was a radiance'; cf. Richardson on *Il.* 22.319 ἀπέλαμπε. For the comparison cf. *Od.* 24.148 where Laertes' shroud is ἠελίωι ἐναλίγκιον ἠὲ σελήνηι, *Od.* 18.295–6 (Penelope's necklace is like the sun), and *Od.* 4.45 (Menelaus' palace). The most famous early Greek example is Sappho fr. 96.6–11 L–P = V, of the beauty of a girl, like the moon among the stars. θαῦμα ἰδέσθαι echoes 84 θάμβαινεν, closing this passage.

Aphrodite's jewellery resembles that of some of the parallel passages mentioned in 58–67n. Hera's ornaments include golden clasps for her robe, elaborate earrings, and a headdress shining like the sun (*Il.* 14.180–5). In *Hymn* 6 Aphrodite has a golden crown, earrings of orichalc and gold, and golden necklaces (7–13). The emphasis on the richness of her dress and ornamentation may well reflect Oriental traditions about the goddess of love. In Cyprus, for example, some statuettes have elaborate jewellery of a similar kind. These are similar to statues from other parts of the Near East (see Karageorghis (1977) 58–60, 196, Maier and Karageorghis (1984) 363–5). Moreover, there are literary parallels in the Sumerian and Akkadian versions of the Descent of Inanna (or Ishtar), the goddess of love, to the Underworld. These include long catalogues of the fine clothing and jewellery which she puts on, only to have these removed again piece by piece by the Gatekeeper of the Underworld (*ANET* 52ff., 106ff.; cf. Dalley (1989) 156f.). Thematically closer is a passage from a Sumerian cult-song, describing Inanna's preparations for rescuing her beloved Dumuzi, where she bathes, anoints herself with oil, dresses in a special way, arranges the lapis lazuli about her neck, and finally appears to him 'like the light of the moon' (*ANET* 639; see West (1997) 204–5). See also Richardson (1991).

91–106 Anchises is seized by love and addresses Aphrodite as a goddess, promising her a cult and asking for her favour.

Anchises' speech has all the basic characteristics of a prayer: greeting the deity by whatever name is proper, promise of cult, and request for prosperity in return. Here the motif of uncertainty over names is extended into an elaborate catalogue. Odysseus' speech to Nausicaa at *Od.* 6.149–85 is similar in structure (and *H. Aph.* 98–9 resembles *Od.* 6.123–4), although Odysseus professes to be unsure whether she is a goddess or not, whereas Anchises appears certain that she is, in spite of her disguise (cf. 185–6). Anchises' response to Aphrodite's appearance (prayer and promise of cult) is the proper one for an epiphany (see Richardson on *H. Dem.* 188–90, 268ff.). For promise of sacrifice in prayer in Homer cf. *Il.* 6.305–10, 10.284–94, *Od.* 3.380–4, 13.356–60.

91 Ἀγχίσην δ' ἔρος εἷλεν: the same phrase is repeated at 144, after Aphrodite's speech of persuasion.

92 For this common formula of address to a deity whose identity or proper name is unknown cf. *Od.* 4.376, 5.445, A. *Ag.* 160, Pl. *Crat.* 400e, and Norden (1913) 144ff.

93–9 The list begins with major deities, and progresses to the immortal Charites, and then to the nymphs, who are said to be mortal at 257–72. Cf. *H.* 7.17–21 for a shorter catalogue of gods, in a similar context.

93–4 For these five goddesses cf. the list in Hes. *Th.* 11–20.

94 ἠΰγενής (for εὐγενής) occurs only here; cf. Homeric εὐηγενής (see *H. Aph.* 229n.). Themis is καλλιπάρηιος at *Il.* 15.87, αἰδοίη Hes. *Th.* 16.

95–6 In *Il.* 5.338–42 a reference to the Charites (338) is followed at 342 by καὶ ἀθάνατοι καλέονται.

97–9 97 resembles *Il.* 20.8 (οὔτ᾽ ἄρα νυμφάων...); 98 resembles *Od.* 6.123 νυμφάων αἳ ἔχουσ᾽ ὀρέων αἰπεινὰ κάρηνα; 99 = *Il.* 20.9, *Od.* 6.124. Ruhnken thought that 98 was an interpolation from *H. Aph.* 258 and 285, and Hermann that 97 and 98 were rhapsodic variants. But the variation is not dissimilar to 61–3 (see n.) and 98 links the nymphs specifically to Mt Ida, anticipating 256–8. There is marked alliteration in 99.

100–2 There is very slight evidence for actual cult of Aphrodite on Ida (*RE* I 2752.34ff.), but more in the Troad as a whole (*ibid.*). If the myth is based on one about Cybele, then the reference to cult might be more significant. But this hymn is not concerned primarily with the aetiology of Aphrodite's cult, which is taken as already established in Cyprus.

For 100–1 cf. *Od.* 1.426 etc. περισκέπτωι ἐνὶ χώρωι, 5.476 ἐν περιφαινομένωι, *Il.* 13.179 ὄρεος... περιφαινομένοιο. Altars are often elevated, and in prominent or high places: e.g. *Il.* 8.47–8, *H. Dem.* 272, 297–8.

102 ὥρηισιν πάσηισι 'in every due season'. Cf. *H. Dem.* 265 ὥρηισιν, with Richardson's note.

σὺ δέ responds to ἐγώ in 100: 'and do you in return...'

εὔφρων means 'well-disposed, kindly' here, whereas elsewhere in early epic it is always 'cheerful' or 'cheering'. For its sense here cf. Pi. *O.* 4.12–13 and later examples.

103 Cf. *Il.* 6.476–7 (Hector's prayer) δότε δὴ καὶ τόνδε γενέσθαι | παῖδ᾽ ἐμόν, ὡς καὶ ἐγώ περ, ἀριπρεπέα Τρώεσσιν etc.

104 Anchises asks her to grant that his offspring may flourish, but ποίει δ᾽... γόνον could mean 'create, produce a flourishing son', which is what Aphrodite will in fact do.

εἰσοπίσω ('in time to come') occurs first here and in Solon fr. 27.10 West; cf. Homeric ἐξοπίσω (with γένος, Tyrtaeus fr. 12.30 West), ἔς περ ὀπίσσω *Od.* 18.122. It could also imply the prosperity of his family in later times, which Aphrodite will grant as well (196–7).

105 For ἐῢ ζώειν cf. *Od.* 19.79 εὖ ζώουσι (and ὄλβιος 76). The rest of the verse is a Homeric formula (3× *Il.*, 5× *Od.*).

106 Cf. Teiresias' prophecy to Odysseus of a gentle death after a prosperous old age, ἀμφὶ δὲ λαοὶ | ὄλβιοι ἔσσονται (*Od.* 11.134–6).

γήραος οὐδόν probably means 'the threshold consisting of old age', i.e. old age as a transitional stage between life and death (cf. *Od.* 15.246, 23.212, and Richardson on *Il.* 22.60). At *Od.* 15.348 however ἐπὶ γήραος οὐδῶι is contrasted with ἐν ὠμῶι γήραϊ θῆκεν (357), suggesting the sense 'at the beginning of old age' in that context. Anchises' request contrasts with his prayer not to be harmed after he discovers the truth (185–90). Aphrodite promises him flourishing descendants (195–7), but his life is still at risk (286–8).

107–42 Aphrodite replies that she is the daughter of Otreus, king of Phrygia, and was carried away by Hermes from a group of dancing girls. He promised that she would become Anchises' wife and bear him children. She now asks Anchises to take her home and introduce her to his family, to ask her parents to send her a rich dowry, and then to hold a marriage feast.

True to her nature as a goddess of deception, Aphrodite spins a false tale which has all the necessary ingredients to tempt Anchises: she is a princess, the gods have sanctioned her marriage and arranged it, and she promises him wealth. It is a fairy-tale story, but Anchises does not really need much persuasion. For such false tales by a deity to mortals cf. *H. Dem.* 119–34, and also Hera's lies at *Il.* 14.200ff., 301ff.

108–10 As often there is strong emphasis on the contrast of mortal and immortal here. For the non-Homeric χαμαιγενέων ἀνθρώπων see Richardson on *H. Dem.* 113. It is often used in contexts where the human and divine are contrasted or juxtaposed in some way.

109–10 Cf. *Od.* 16.187–8 οὔτίς τοι θεός εἰμι· τί μ' ἀθανάτοισιν ἐΐσκεις; | ἀλλὰ πατὴρ τεός εἰμι.

110 τε... δέ is a common sequence (Denniston, *GP*² 513). Here δέ may be explanatory of the previous phrase, as at *Il.* 23.277, and *H. Aph.* 130.

111–12 Otreus is a chief of the Phrygians with whom Priam once fought the Amazons (*Il.* 3.184–9). He is later said to be the maternal grandfather of Priam (Apollod. 3.12.3), or son of Dymas, and so Hecuba's brother (Schol. T *Il.* 3.189). The name may be related to the town of Otroia on the border of Phrygia and Bithynia or the Phrygian town Otrus, whose location is unknown.

111 εἴ που ἀκούεις (i.e. 'as you may well have heard') picks up its echo from ὄνομα κλυτός; cf. *Od.* 15.403.

112 εὐτειχήτοιο: εὐτείχητος is a variant for Homeric εὐτείχεος and εὐτειχής, and occurs only here, perhaps meaning 'well-equipped with fortresses'.

113–16 In the *Iliad* the Trojans and their allies are said to speak several languages (2.803–4, 437–8), and the Carians are specifically called βαρβαρόφωνοι (2.867), and cf. *Od.* 19.175 for different languages in Crete, again in a false tale. But it is a new thing for the poet to draw attention to a difference of language or dialect between Trojans and neighbouring Phrygians and to explain how Aphrodite can speak both ('bilingualism'), and this has been thought to indicate that he himself comes from an area near the Troad. The explanation given by Aphrodite 'gilds her lie with a degree of pseudo-realism which is quite devastating' (Walcot (1991) 145).

113 ὑμετέρην τε: Wolf's addition of τε avoids the hiatus which is rare after καί.

114 διάπρο in Homer means 'right through' spatially, whereas here (uniquely, as it would seem) it must mean 'continually'; cf. διαμπερές for a similar development.

117–21 This is a variation on the motif typified by *Il.* 16.179–86, where Hermes falls in love with Polymele, ὀφθαλμοῖσιν ἰδὼν μετὰ μελπομένῃσιν | ἐν χορῶι Ἀρτέμιδος χρυσηλακάτου κελαδεινῆς, and she bears Eudorus as a result. Abduction by a god from a chorus or company of girls or nymphs is a traditional motif (see Richardson on *H. Dem.* 5, and cf. Moschus, *Europa* 28ff.), although usually the god is acting on his own behalf. See also on 262–3, where Hermes mates with the mountain nymphs. Thus Aphrodite artfully alludes to the theme of seduction or rape, whilst insisting on marriage (126–7), thereby arousing Anchises' eagerness for a more immediate union.

119–20 νύμφαι are here young married women (or brides on the verge of marriage), as opposed to παρθένοι; cf. *Od.* 11.38–9, where they are coupled with παρθενικαί, Hunter on Theocr. 3.8–9, and Chantraine (1946–7) 228–9. This passage echoes the dancing scene at *Il.* 18.590–606: cf. 593f. ἔνθα μὲν ἠΐθεοι καὶ παρθένοι ἀλφεσίβοιαι | ὠρχεῦντ', and 603 πολλὸς δ' ἱμερόεντα χορὸν περιίσταθ' ὅμιλος. ἀλφεσίβοιος occurs nowhere else in early epic (see Edwards ad loc.). For 120 cf. also *Od.* 10.195 νῆσον, τὴν πέρι πόντος ἀπείριτος ἐστεφάνωται, and Hes. *Sc.* 204.

121–5 Such divine journeys are often elaborated in this way; cf. especially *H. Dem.* 33–9 (Rape of Persephone), and 380–3, where Hermes carries Persephone by air over land and sea.

123 ἄκληρον 'unallotted (land)'; whereas at *Od.* 11.490 it means 'without a portion of land'.

ἄκτιτον ('uncultivated') occurs only here in classical Greek, but cf. Linear B *a-ki-ti-to* with the same sense, Homeric ἐΰκτιτος, ἐϋκτίμενος, and Chantraine, *Dict.* s.v. κτίζω. For γῆν understood with both epithets cf. *Il.* 18.308 etc. 124 echoes 74, referring to the wild beasts coupling together in their mountain haunts.

125 'Nor did I seem to touch the life-giving earth with my feet.' The present ψαύειν makes better sense here than M's future: Aphrodite is describing her impressions of the actual journey, not her expectations (cf. Smith (1979) 32–4). Cf. also *Il.* 14.228, of Hera travelling over the mountains: οὐδὲ χθόνα μάρπτε ποδοῖιν.

ἐδόκουν: the contracted form is not found elsewhere in early epic. It could be due to Attic transmission: see Faulkner (2008) ad loc. Both he and West (2003) read δόκεον.

126–7 παραί is adverbial, 'alongside him, in his bed'. Cf. *Od.* 1.366 (= 18.213) πάντες δ' ἠρήσαντο παραὶ λεχέεσσι κλιθῆναι, where παραί goes with κλιθῆναι. This kind of expression has here been modified, and combined with formulae of the type φίλη κεκλήσηι ἄκοιτις (*Il.* 3.138), (σὴν) κεκλῆσθαι ἄκοιτιν (*Il.* 14.268

etc.; cf. *H. Dem.* 79), and κουριδίην ἄλοχον. καλέεσθαι and τεκεῖσθαι are future. τεκεῖσθαι is an abnormal form, derived from τεκέσθαι, similar to πεσέεσθαι, ἐσσεῖται. Cf. *Od.* 22.324 σοὶ δ' ἄλοχόν τε φίλην σπέσθαι καὶ τέκνα τεκέσθαι.

128 'But when he had shown me (the way) and told me (all this) . . .'

130 **κρατερὴ δέ μοι ἔπλετ' ἀνάγκη** = *Od.* 10.273 (~ *Il.* 6.458). δέ is explanatory here (cf. Denniston, *GP*² 169–70).

131–2 Cf. 187 ἀλλά σε πρὸς Ζηνὸς γουνάζομαι αἰγιόχοιο. For supplication in the name of parents cf. *Il.* 15.661–6 etc. and Richardson on *Il.* 22.338. This combination with Zeus does not occur in Homer. For 132 cf. *Od.* 4.64 ἐπεὶ οὔ κε κακοὶ τοιούσδε τέκοιεν, and see Richardson on *H. Dem.* 213ff.

133–5 Aphrodite maintains the pretence that she wants a proper marriage, with the consent of Anchises' family.

133 **ἀδμήτην . . . καὶ ἀπειρήτην:** such co-ordinated epithets with negative prefix are common in Greek; see Richardson on *H. Dem.* 200 (p. 221).

135 **ὁμόθεν** means 'from the same stock' here, as at Hes. *Op.* 108 (see West), and often in later Greek.

136 Cf. *H. Dem.* 83–4 οὔ τοι ἀεικὴς | γαμβρός, and *H. Dem.* 363–4. For parallels in later Greek and Latin literature see Richardson on *H. Dem.* 83ff.

137 **Φρύγας αἰολοπώλους** 'Phrygians with rapid steeds'. Cf. *Il.* 3.185 Φρύγας ἀνέρας αἰολοπώλους, and 19.404 πόδας αἰόλος ἵππος.

138 **κηδομένηι περ** 'anxious as she is', with περ intensifying, as at *Il.* 24.104.

139–40 Cf. *Od.* 13.136, 16.231 χαλκόν τε χρυσόν τε ἅλις ἐσθῆτα θ' ὑφαντήν. For κεν + future cf. Chantraine, *GH* II 225–6.

In epic ἄποινα normally means 'ransom, compensation', but here we would expect Aphrodite to hold out the hope of a rich 'dowry'. K. Rüter (*LfgrE* s.v.) suggests that she has been captured by Hermes and put in the possession of Anchises, but asks him to accept a ransom from her parents, so that she can marry him as a free woman, but this is unconvincing, and Aphrodite is surely referring to the material advantages which her marriage will bring. The giving of dowries has been considered a post-Homeric practice, but even in Homer gifts from the bride's family seem to be envisaged (see Richardson on *Il.* 22.49–51). Keaney (1981, 261–4) argues that the whole of this scene of meeting between Aphrodite and Anchises is influenced by that of Odysseus and Nausicaa, and that the reference to 'compensation' here is due to the fact that Aphrodite is posing as a suppliant before Anchises (as Odysseus supplicates Nausicaa).

141 **δαίνυ γάμον** 'hold a marriage feast'. Cf. *Il.* 19.299 δαίσειν δὲ γάμον, *Od.* 3.309 δαίνυ τάφον Ἀργείοισι, 4.3 τὸν δ' εὗρον δαίνυντα γάμον. Normally one would expect the bride's father or family to give the feast, as in later Greek practice (cf. *Od.* 1.277–8, 2.52–4, 23.133–6, 143–51). But in Aphrodite's tale her family are far away, and the situation is completely unusual.

143–67 Aphrodite arouses Anchises' love, and he replies that if her story is really true then no one will stop him from sleeping with her at once, even if he should die as a result. He leads her to his bed and undresses her, and they are united in intercourse.

The sequence of events follows the pattern of such scenes of seduction. Cf. *Il.* 14.312ff., where Zeus expresses his love and urgent desire to sleep with Hera now, and, after her speech expressing fear of being seen, he wraps her in a golden cloud as they lie together. Paris too expresses his desire before going to bed with Helen at 3.441ff., as does Ares to Aphrodite at *Od.* 8.292ff. Cf. Janko on *Il.* 14.153–353 (pp. 170–1), Sowa (1984) 67–94.

143 = *Il.* 3.139 (of Helen), and cf. *H. Aph.* 45, 53, of Zeus casting desire for Anchises into Aphrodite's own heart.

144 This line echoes 91, with variation of the speech formula.

145–54 The structure of Anchises' speech of resolution is effective. It begins with a four-line protasis ('if indeed...'), which is climactic: two balanced half-lines (145), a whole-line clause (146), and two more clauses with a runover word (147–8), all repeating what Aphrodite has said. The apodosis (149–52) is composed of two clauses with emphatic runover at αὐτίκα νῦν, and a rhetorical progression with οὔ τις... οὐδ' εἴ κεν...; cf. Achilles' rhetoric at *Il.* 9.379–87, 22.346–53, for this kind of device. The implication is that Anchises is being very careful to rehearse all the details given him by this girl, in order to be sure that he risks nothing by acting as he does. Finally a two-line sentence with asyndeton expresses Anchises' feelings in the most emphatic way.

147 ἀθανάτου δὲ ἕκητι: in Homer and Hesiod the digamma of ἕκητι is observed, and only at *H.* 26.5 is it neglected. The contracted genitive in -ου is also used elsewhere in this poem (cf. Janko (1982) 51–4), whereas digamma is rarely neglected (Janko (1982) 47). It seems best therefore to follow the reading of M here, rather than the variant of other MSS.

διακτόρου: see *H. Herm.* 392n.

149–51 ἐνθάδε usually means 'here' or 'hither' in Homer, but occasionally implies 'here and now', e.g. *Il.* 21.92, *Od.* 16.246, 371. It is emphatic at the beginning of the line, and αὐτίκα νῦν with enjambment underlines the point still more clearly. For οὔ τις... σχήσει πρὶν... cf. *Il.* 17.502–4 οὐ γὰρ ἔγωγε | Ἕκτορα... σχήσεσθαι ὀΐω, | πρίν γ'... βήμεναι... σῇ in σῇ φιλότητι is the equivalent of an objective genitive, as in *Il.* 19.321 σῇ ποθῇ ('desire for you') etc.

151 ἑκηβόλος 'far-shooting' (as it was usually understood in antiquity) anticipates the point of 152.

αὐτός is emphatic here ('even Apollo'), but it is quite often used of Apollo to emphasise his dignity (see *H. Ap.* 140n.).

153–4 The asyndeton is highly effective. Cf. Longinus 19.2: 'for phrases both disconnected and at the same time hurried convey an impression of an agitation which both halts the reader and drives him on'. ἔπειτα means 'in this case' here. This form of expression ('I should be ready to die, if only...') is found already in Homer: cf. *Il.* 24.224–7 εἰ δέ μοι αἶσα | τεθναμέναι... | βούλομαι· αὐτίκα γάρ με κατακτείνειεν Ἀχιλλεύς (etc.), *Od.* 7.224–5, and see Garvie on A. *Cho.* 438. But its use in an erotic context occurs first here. Later it became a conventional motif of erotic literature: cf. Musaeus 79 αὐτίκα τεθναίην λεχέων ἐπιβήμενος Ἡροῦς, and also Ter. *Eun.* 550–1, Heliodorus 4.6, and Nonnus *D.* 4.146ff. In Homer the closest parallel is *Od.* 8.334–42, where Hermes is willing to endure being enchained, like Ares, in order to sleep with Aphrodite.

153 γύναι εἴκυῖα θεῇισι carries great weight: Anchises senses that he really does have the opportunity of union with someone who is 'godlike'. The irony here is increased by the risk he is running of really dying (cf. 187–90n.).

155 λάβε χεῖρα: cf. *Od.* 8.291, of Ares and Aphrodite.

155–7 Aphrodite goes with him to his bed, turning her face away and casting down her lovely eyes. For an artful appearance of αἰδώς cf. *Il.* 3.217 κατὰ χθονὸς ὄμματα πήξας, and for κατ' ὄμματα καλὰ βαλοῦσα cf. *H. Dem.* 194 (common later as an erotic motif: see Richardson ad loc.). Cf. also Hera's shame at *Il.* 14.330–40.

157 ἐς λέχος εὔστρωτον: the epithet occurs first here and at *H. Dem.* 285 ἀπ' εὐστρώτων λεχέων. Here it is glossed by 157–60. The phrase recurs at Alc. fr. 283.8 L–P = V εὔστρωτον λέχος, one of several parallels between this hymn and Lesbian poetry: see Introduction 4(b).

157–60 Normal bedding (cf. *Il.* 24.643–6 etc.) is replaced here by the skins of wild animals killed by Anchises (cf. *H. Aph.* 69–74, 123–4, and also 18), as Eumaeus' bed is covered with sheep and goat skins (*Od.* 14.519). Here the motif symbolises Anchises' prowess.

159 βαρυφθόγγων occurs first here, later in Pindar etc. (*Od.* 9.257 φθόγγον . . . βαρύν). Homeric lions are silent, whether because the poet or his audience had only seen them in art, or more probably because lions do not roar when hunting prey. Cf. Janko on *Il.* 15.586–8 and Lonsdale (1990) 44–5.

160 Cf. *Od.* 11.574 τοὺς αὐτὸς κατέπεφνεν ἐν οἰοπόλοισιν ὄρεσσι.

ἐν οὔρεσιν ὑψηλοῖσιν: this recurs at 266, and cf. ὑψηλῶν ὀρέων (1× *Il.*, 3× *Od.*, 3× *Hymns*).

161–7 161–6 are really one sentence, with enjambment, creating a slow build-up of expectation. The subject is unusually postponed to the very end, to be picked up in the final sentence (166–7), the key-point and centrepiece of the whole poem. The detailed description of Aphrodite's undressing resembles the scenes in the Near-Eastern Descent of Inanna (or Ishtar) (see 87–90n.), but this is the first description of its kind in Greek literature. Homer is (as always) more reticent, and the most he gives us is the simple λῦσε δὲ παρθενίην ζώνην at *Od.* 11.245 (cf. *H. Aph.* 164).

163 = *Il.* 18.401, and see *H. Aph.* 87–90n.

πόρπαι are brooches or pins for clothing: cf. Janko on *Il.* 18.401, and E. Bielefeld, *Arch. Hom.* C 6–8, 38–40, 49–52, S. Marinatos, *Arch. Hom.* A 36–8.

165 ἐπὶ θρόνου ἀργυροήλου: cf. *Il.* 18.389 etc.

166–7 This crucial statement is very carefully composed. θεῶν ἰότητι καὶ αἴσηι underlines that fact that the action is divinely willed and fated: cf. θεῶν ἰότητι 1× *Il.*, 6× *Od.*, Διὸς αἴσηι *Il.* 9.604 (~ 17.321, *Od.* 9.52), δαίμονος αἴσηι *H. Dem.* 300. The combination of the two phrases is unique, adding emphasis. ἀθανάτηι παρέλεκτο θεᾶι βροτός sums up the central theme; for this vivid juxtaposition of deity and mortal cf. *Il.* 2.821 θεὰ βροτῶι εὐνηθεῖσα, of Aphrodite and Anchises again, 16.176 γυνὴ θεῶι εὐνηθεῖσα (see *H. Aph.* 117–21n.), Hes. fr. 30.33 φιλότητι θεὸς βροτῶι, and West on Hes. *Th.* 380. Finally οὐ σάφα εἰδώς expresses with powerful brevity the dangerous ignorance of which Anchises is the victim; cf. *Il.* 15.632 νομεὺς οὔ πω σάφα εἰδώς (~ *Od.* 1.202 etc.).

168–90 Towards the evening Aphrodite sends Anchises to sleep (cf. Zeus at *Il.* 14.352–3), and puts on her clothes. She resumes her appearance as a goddess, and wakens him. He is afraid, and begs her not to do him any harm.

At the end of such Seduction scenes comes 'the rude awakening': cf. Janko on *Il.* 14.153–353 (p. 171), with *Il.* 15.4f., *Od.* 8.296ff. Here this takes the form of an Epiphany scene (see 172–5n.).

168–9 At 78–9 Anchises' fellow herdsmen had all gone off to pasture the cattle, and now it is the time for them to start bringing the herd home. The poet is giving a special direction to what is a typical way of expressing time in early epic, reflecting the pastoral or agricultural basis of early Greek society: cf. *Il.* 16.779 (= *Od.* 9.58) ἦμος δ' ἠέλιος μετενίσετο βουλυτόνδε, 11.86–9 ἦμος δὲ δρυτόμος περ ἀνὴρ ὡπλίσσατο δεῖπνον. *Od.* 12.439–41 is a similar marker of time, taken from the life of the poet's own day. ἀποκλίνουσι means 'turn back' here.

170–2 Cf. *Od.* 2.395 ἐπὶ γλυκὺν ὕπνον ἔχευεν etc. νήδυμος ('sweet') is probably originally from ἥδυμος with a mobile nu attached by misdivision of a previous word, as in *Il.* 2.2 ἔχεν ἥδυμον ὕπνον. Cf. *Od.* 13.79–80 νήδυμος ὕπνος ... | νήγρετος ἥδιστος for the repeated sense. 171–2 echo 64, but here δῖα θεάων is introduced, at the point when Aphrodite resumes her divine form.

172–5 The epiphany is marked by supernatural stature (her head reaches the rafters) and divine beauty radiating from her face. Cf. *H. Dem.* 188–9 ἡ δ' ἄρ' ἐπ' οὐδὸν ἔβη ποσὶ καί ῥα μελάθρου | κῦρε κάρη, πλῆσεν δὲ θύρας σέλαος θείοιο, and the more extended epiphany at *H. Dem.* 275–80 (with parallels in Richardson on *H. Dem.* 188–90, 275ff.).

173–4 'She stood then in the hut, her head touched the well-built roof-beam, and beauty shone from her cheeks.' Here we have an unusual and dramatic asyndeton combined with hiatus in 173, and if one assumes that κάρη is the subject of κῦρε (rather than being an internal accusative), the subject changes twice in 173–4. This type of asyndeton ('A, B, and C') is rare in Greek: cf. Denniston, *GP*² 164. There is only one example in Homer (*Od.* 8.322–3 ἦλθε ... ἦλθ' ... ἦλθεν δὲ ...), where the repetition makes the effect quite different. The late position of ἄρα also seems unusual in early epic: Denniston's examples (*GP*² 41–2) are all from classical Greek. All these features combine to underline the awe-inspiring character of Aphrodite's transformation.

175 M's ἰοστεφάνου, 'violet-crowned', is applied to Aphrodite at *H.* 6.18 (again with ἐϋ- as variant), Solon fr. 19.4 West, and also in a Laconian inscription (*c.* 500 BC) ϝιοστεφάνοι Ἀφροδίται (*Arch. Delt.* 23.2 (1) (1968) 153).

176 The first τε connects the sentence to the previous one (cf. *Il.* 1.459–60 etc.). This is better than assuming another asyndeton here, with τε looking forward.

177–9 Aphrodite's slightly reproachful tone ('Why do you sleep?') is typical of scenes of wakening (see Richardson on *Il.* 23.69–92). There is also mockery in her question at 178–9, emphasised by the ironic use of δή, common after οἷος (cf. Denniston, *GP*² 220–1, who wrongly classes this as an exception). For νήγρετον ὕπνον ἰαύεις cf. *Od.* 13.74 ἵνα νήγρετον εὕδοι, 13.79–80 νήδυμος ὕπνος . . . | νήγρετος ἥδιστος. For ἰνδάλλομαι ('seem, appear') in this context cf. *Od.* 3.246 ὥς τε μοι ἀθάνατος ἰνδάλλεται εἰσοράασθαι. Aphrodite (unusually in an epiphany) does not identify herself, but Anchises presumably recognises who she is, as Helen does in *Iliad* 3 (see 181–2n.).

179 τὸ πρῶτον: in Homer τό/τά is always scanned long before πρῶτον/πρῶτα (as in 185 below). Cf. however *Od.* 3.320 ὅν τινα πρῶτον, 17.275 ἠὲ σὺ πρῶτος.

180 Cf. *Il.* 10.162 ὣς φάθ'· ὁ δ' ἐξ ὕπνοιο μαλὰ κραιπνῶς ἀνόρουσε, and *Od.* 14.485 ὁ δ' ἄρ' ἐμμαπέως ὑπάκουσεν of someone waking from sleep.

181–90 Fear is a normal reaction to an epiphany: see *H. Aph.* 83–5n., and Richardson on *H. Dem.* 188–90, 190, 275ff.

181–2 This resembles Helen's recognition of Aphrodite, despite her disguise, at *Il.* 3.396–8 καί ῥ' ὡς οὖν ἐνόησε θεᾶς περικαλλέα δειρὴν | στήθεα θ' ἱμερόεντα καὶ ὄμματα μαρμαίροντα, | θάμβησέν τ' . . . , and cf. 427 (Helen with Paris) ὄσσε πάλιν κλίνασα. Cf. also *Od.* 16.178–9, where Telemachus sees Odysseus after his transformation by Athene: θάμβησε δέ μιν φίλος υἱός, | ταρβήσας δ' ἑτέρωσε βάλ' ὄμματα μὴ θεὸς εἴη. Before (156) it was Aphrodite, now it is Anchises who averts his gaze.

183 Cf. *Od.* 8.83–5 where Odysseus covers his head with his cloak to hide his tears (85 κάλυψε δὲ καλὰ πρόσωπα), and similarly *Il.* 24.162–3, of Priam in his grief.

χλαίνῃς ἐκαλύψατο: this conjecture removes τε, which is awkward at this point, after ἂψ δ' αὖτις has preceded the noun.

185–6 Anchises' opening words are a reproach to Aphrodite for her deception of him, in preparation for his plea for mercy. Cf. *Il.* 22.9–10 οὐδέ νύ πώ με | ἔγνως ὡς θεός εἰμι. This parallel may help to explain the use of θεός in 186 ('a deity') immediately after the feminine θεά in 185.

187–90 187 echoes 131, where the disguised goddess was the suppliant, an ironic reversal of normality, which is reinstated here with Anchises' plea to her. For ἀμενηνός ('strengthless') see Richardson on *H. Dem.* 352. As it is applied to the souls of the dead in the Odyssey (4×) there is a deliberate contrast with ζῶντ';

cf. *Il.* 5.887 ἤ κε ζὼς ἀμενηνὸς ἔα χαλκοῖο τυπῇσι. There is a similar fear that Circe may 'unman' Odysseus, if he sleeps with her (*Od.* 10.301 ~ 341): μή σ' ἀπογυμνωθέντα κακὸν καὶ ἀνήνορα θήῃ. Anchises' words leave open just what form of damage he fears. Aphrodite reassures him (192–5), but later threatens him with Zeus's thunderbolt if he boasts of their union (286–8). The idea that those who openly marry goddesses do not have a long or happy life is expressed by Calypso in her complaint at the jealousy of the gods, who begrudge men such fortune (*Od.* 5.118–29, where 119 resembles *H. Aph.* 190). She mentions Orion, loved by Dawn and killed by Artemis, and Iasion, who was slain by Zeus's thunderbolt after he had slept with Demeter. Gilgamesh expresses similar fears of Ishtar, recalling how all her lovers came to grief (*ANET* 83–5, Dalley (1989) 77–9). In the case of paramours of such goddesses, impotence is one possible consequence (cf. Rose (1924) 11–16). Later tradition has Aphrodite's warning (at 286ff.) come true: cf. Soph. *Laocoon* fr. 373.2–3 Radt ('Anchises' back struck by the thunderbolt'), and Verg. *A.* 2.647–9 *iam pridem inuisus diuis et inutilis annos | demoror, ex quo me diuum pater atque hominum rex | fulminis adflauit uentis et contigit igni* (cf. Austin ad loc.). Other versions have him blinded (Servius on *Aen.* 1.617, 2.35, 687), or even killed (Hyginus *Fab.* 94). In art from the mid-sixth century BC onwards Aeneas carries his old father out of Troy on his shoulders, as in Sophocles, and this suggests that the theme of his punishment with physical incapacity goes back to the *Iliou Persis* (cf. Pearson on S. *Fr.* 373.2f.). Consequently we may infer that this story was probably already known to the poet of our hymn. At *Il.* 13.465–6 Aeneas was 'looked after as a child' by his brother-in-law Alcathous, but this does not necessarily imply that Anchises was already dead or disabled: see Janko ad loc.

189 βιόθαλμιος 'hale and hearty'. This occurs only here; cf. Soph. *Tr.* 235 ζῶντα καὶ θάλλοντα, and the similar form ζωθάλμιος ('life-enhancing'), used of Charis at Pi. *O.* 7.11.

191–290 Aphrodite reassures Anchises. He will come to no harm, and will have a son, Aeneas, who will rule Troy, and a long line of descendants. She then tells the stories of Ganymede and Tithonus, to show that Anchises' family has always been closest to the gods in beauty. But like Tithonus Anchises too will grow old, to her distress, and her affair with him will be a scandal among the gods. Their son will be brought up by the mountain nymphs, who are between immortals and mortals, and whose lives are bound up with that of the trees. They will bring the young child back to Anchises, and he will take him to Troy. Finally he is ordered to keep their affair a secret and say that Aeneas is the son of a nymph, or else Zeus will strike him with his thunderbolt.

This remarkable speech of a hundred lines occupies virtually all the rest of the hymn. Much of it is taken up with the paradigmatic stories of Ganymede (202–17) and Tithonus (218–38), and the lengthy passage about the nature of the wood nymphs (256–73). The rest is focused mainly on Aeneas, the fruit of their union.

Two main themes help to articulate this material, the ancestors and descendants of Anchises, and the contrast of mortality and immortality. The speech may be seen as a much expanded version of Poseidon's address to Tyro at *Od.* 11.248–52: χαῖρε, γύναι, φιλότητι, περιπλομένου δ' ἐνιαυτοῦ | τέξεις ἀγλαὰ τέκνα, ἐπεὶ οὐκ ἀποφώλιοι εὐναὶ | ἀθανάτων· σὺ δὲ τοὺς κομέειν ἀτιταλλέμεναί τε. | νῦν δ' ἔρχευ πρὸς δῶμα, καὶ ἴσχεο μηδ' ὀνομήνῃς· | αὐτὰρ ἐγώ τοί εἰμι Ποσειδάων ἐνοσίχθων. There we have encouragement (248), promise of offspring, instructions about upbringing, command for secrecy, and self-revelation. Cf. also the structure of Zeus's speech in Moschus, *Europa* 154–61.

192–9 Aphrodite answers Anchises' plea at 187–90, but she is also responding to his prayer at 102–9, for honour, prosperity, and fine offspring. 191–2 recall Aphrodite's reply at 107–8, and 196 seems to echo 103.

193 Cf. *Od.* 4.825 (dream figure) θάρσει, μηδέ τι πάγχυ μετὰ φρεσὶ δείδιθι λίην. This kind of reassurance is typical of such Epiphany scenes: cf. *H.* 7.58, *Il.* 24.171 θάρσει . . . μηδέ τι τάρβει, and see Richardson on *Il.* 21.288, 24.153–4, 171–4.

194 οὐ γάρ τοί τι δέος: cf. *Il.* 1.515 οὔ τοι ἔπι δέος, *Od.* 5.347 οὐδέ τί τοι παθέειν δέος. Aphrodite's promise is somewhat undermined by her final warning (286–8), but presumably the point is that he will be unharmed if he obeys her instructions. For the idea of 194–5 cf. *Il.* 20.347 (Aeneas rescued because dear to gods), 24.61, 422–3, 748–50, etc.

196–7 Cf. *Il.* 20.307–8 νῦν δὲ δὴ Αἰνείαο βίη Τρώεσσιν ἀνάξει | καὶ παίδων παῖδες, τοί κεν μετόπισθε γένωνται. The Homeric prophecy, made by Poseidon, says that both Aeneas and his descendants will rule the Trojans. Aphrodite, however, says that Aeneas will rule among the Trojans, and that his line will continue in future generations. ἐκγεγάονται appears to be an anomalous third-person form of the perfect ἐκγέγαα, treated as if it were a future; cf. the similar anomaly of τεκεῖσθαι (127). This seems more likely than a 'prophetic present' (Hoekstra (1969) 39–40), since it accompanies future verbs in 196 and 198. See Chantraine (1935) 131–2. West (2003) adopts Baumeister's conjecture ἐκγεγάοντες. This would make the prophecy closer to Poseidon's in the *Iliad*, but the form would itself be unique, and it seems unnecessary to change the text.

It is quite possible that these prophecies reflect an actual historical situation in which a ruling family in the Troad claimed descent from Aeneas in the time of the *Iliad* or the hymn. Among the many later traditions about Aeneas were some which did make his descendants, together with those of Hector, rulers of either Troy (Hellanicus, *FGrH* 4 F 31, Dion. Hal. *AR* 1.47.5 and 53.4–5) or Scepsis, south-east of Troy (Strabo 13.1.52). Strabo reports, relying probably on Demetrius of Scepsis, that the families of Ascanius and Scamandrius were said to have reigned in Scepsis for a long time, and adds that this tradition disagrees with the prophecy in the *Iliad*, which points to Aeneas remaining in Troy and handing on the kingship to his descendants (13.1.53). By contrast, those who believed that Aeneas had migrated to Italy could argue that he was still ruling over the Trojans, whom he had taken with him (Dion. Hal. *AR* 1.53.5). Re-examination of the archaeological evidence for Troy in the period between 1100 and 700 BC suggests that after the destruction of Troy VIIb2 (in the eleventh century BC) the site was immediately reoccupied, and continued to be so throughout the following centuries: cf. Hertel (1991) 131–44. Such continuity would fit in with the traditions of a local dynasty claiming descent from Aeneas in this area. The historical basis of the traditions about Aeneas' family has been questioned: cf. Smith (1981b). But it does appear that there were ruling families in the Troad in later times who claimed descent from Aeneas and also Hector. It has been suggested that the change of wording between the two prophecies might be due to a political change, if Aeneas' family had lost the kingship by the time of the hymn, as happened (for example) at Scepsis at some date which cannot be precisely determined; cf. Hoekstra (1969) 39–40. But the change can be explained simply by the different context in the hymn. Aphrodite reassures Anchises about his future, prophesies the birth of a son, and promises that his line will continue for generations to come. The main point is the prosperity and continuity of his race, in contrast to his fears. On *H. Aph.* 196–7 cf. also Edwards on *Il.* 20.75–155 (pp. 298–301), and Faulkner (2008) 3–18, 256–7.

198–9 Aeneas' name is introduced for the first time, and given an etymology, with emphatic positioning and enjambment of αἰνὸν | ἔσχεν ἄχος; cf. *Il.* 13.481–2 δείδια δ' αἰνῶς | Αἰνείαν, and the connection of Odysseus and ὀδύσσομαι at *Od.* 1.62, 19.407–9 (with S. West on 1.62). Aphrodite's affair will be a great cause of pain and embarrassment to her, as she explains later: 241–55 return to the theme of 198–9 (cf. 243 ἄχος), after the passages on Ganymede and Tithonus.

199 ἕνεκα must be a conjunction ('because'). This sense of ἕνεκα (= οὕνεκα) is rare in early poetry: cf. possibly Hes. fr. 180.10 M–W (εἵνεκα), Pi. *I.* 8.32 where εἵνεκεν means 'that'. It is commoner in Hellenistic poetry: Call. fr. 1.3, 6, 75.6, A.R. 4.1523, Bion 12.7.

For the rest of 199 cf. *Il.* 18.85 ἤματι τῶι ὅτε σε βροτοῦ ἀνέρος ἔμβαλον εὐνῆι (of Thetis and Peleus).

200–38 The general statement in 200–1 picks up the theme of 194–5 and introduces the two *exempla* of Ganymede and Tithonus. These represent two different ways of bridging the gap between men and gods: both have immortality, but Ganymede has eternal youth as well, whereas Tithonus does not. Aphrodite goes on to say that Anchises is not fated to escape old age or death (239–46). The progression of thought changes, but by a natural development, moving from the closeness to the gods of the family to the restriction imposed on Tithonus, and hence to the mortality of Anchises, the point from which she began (199). Walcot (1991, 148–9) suggests that with these stories of divine love for Trojan princes Aphrodite is also excusing her own weakness in falling for Anchises.

200 ἀγχίθεοι: the Phaeacians are called ἀγχίθεοι at *Od.* 5.35, because of their unusually close familiarity with the gods (6.203, 7.201–6). Here Anchises' family resembles the gods in physical appearance and beauty (203, 219), and both

Ganymede and Tithonus have become literally ἀγχίθεοι as a result of divine favour.

202–17 In the *Iliad* Ganymede's abduction is referred to at 20.232–5: καὶ ἀντίθεος Γανυμήδης, | ὃς δὴ κάλλιστος γένετο θνητῶν ἀνθρώπων. | τὸν καὶ ἀνηρείψαντο θεοὶ Διὶ οἰνοχοεύειν | κάλλεος εἵνεκα οἷο, ἵν' ἀθανάτοισι μετείη. The language is similar to that of *H. Aph.* 202–4, but in the *Iliad* he is carried off by the gods to be the cupbearer of Zeus, whereas here these roles of Zeus and the gods are reversed. The story, however, is likely to be the same in both cases, and the motif of Zeus's love is surely implied, although typically not stressed in Homer. Moreover, at *Il.* 5.265–72 the horses of Tros are mentioned, which Zeus gave him in recompense for Ganymede (cf. *H. Aph.* 210–17), again in connection with Anchises and Aeneas, since Anchises is said to have used them as sires to produce his own horses and those of his son. In the *Ilias Parua* (fr. 6 Allen = 6 Davies) Ganymede is son of Laomedon, and Zeus gives the father a golden vine in compensation for the loss of his son. Later poets elaborated the erotic theme: Ibycus told the story of the rape, together with that of Tithonus by Dawn, in his poem to Gorgias (fr. 289; see Barron (1984) 16ff.); cf. Theognis 1345–8, Pi. *O.* 1.44–5, 10.103–5, etc. For other literary and artistic versions see *LIMC* IV.1 154–69 s.v., and 207n. below. In this description of Ganymede's rape the visual and ornamental aspects are constantly stressed: ξανθὸν . . . ὃν διὰ κάλλος . . . θαῦμα ἰδεῖν . . . χρυσέου . . . ἐρυθρόν, with an artful juxtaposition of colours in 206. The cheerfulness of all this contrasts sharply with the grief of Tros which follows (207–9). This double theme recurs again at the end of the story (215–17), where grief and joy are contrasted.

202 ἦ τοι μέν emphasises the truth of what has just been said ('truly, indeed').

203 Cf. *Od.* 15.250 (see *H. Aph.* 218–19n.).

204 ἐπιοινοχοεύοι: the compound does not recur elsewhere, but cf. ἐπιοίνιος Theognis 971, and forms such as ἐπιβουκόλος (*Od.* 3.422, etc.).

205 The phrasing is traditional, but cf. especially *H. Dem.* 397 ναιετάοις πάντεσσι τετιμ[ένη ἀθανάτοι]σιν, of Persephone on Olympus, followed at 403 by μέγα θαῦμα θεοῖς θνητοῖς τ' ἀνθρώποις.

206 Cf. *Il.* 1.598 (Hephaestus on Olympus) οἰνοχόει γλυκὺ νέκταρ ἀπὸ κρητῆρος ἀφύσσων, 23.219–20 χρυσέου ἐκ κρητῆρος . . . | οἶνον ἀφυσσόμενος, *Od.* 5.93 νέκταρ ἐρυθρόν.

207 Τρῶα . . . φρένας is a double accusative.

208 θέσπις ἄελλα only occurs here, but when people disappear the storm-winds (ἄελλαι, θύελλαι, or ἅρπυιαι) are often said to have carried them off: cf. *Il.* 6.345–8 (Helen wishes a κακὴ ἀνέμοιο θύελλα had carried her off at birth), *Od.* 1.241–2 (where it is the gods who have made Odysseus vanish at 234–6), 4.727–8, 20.63–79. In early Greek art Zeus himself is usually the pursuer of Ganymede, sometimes Hermes or Iris. The first evidence we have of the eagle carrying him off is in a work by the fourth-century BC sculptor Leochares (Pliny *NH* 34.79), and this is common later; in literature cf. Apollod. 3.12.2, Verg. *A.* 5.252–7, etc. Occasionally in fourth-century art the swan takes over this role. Cf. *LIMC* s.v., and on rape scenes and winged predators in general see Vermeule (1979) 145–77.

210–11 Cf. *Il.* 5.265f., where the horses are υἷος ποινήν, *Ilias Parua* fr. 6 Allen (= 6 Davies) οὗ παιδὸς ἄποινα. ἵππους ἀρσίποδας ('prancing horses') is a new adaptation of the formular ἵπποι ἀερσίποδες (*Il.* 3.327 etc.).

212 εἶπέν τε: a single connective is not unusual in early epic where there is no change of subject. Cf. Denniston, *GP*[2] 497. There is therefore no need to read δέ.

212–14 εἶπέν τε ἕκαστα | . . . ὡς ἔοι . . . : the ὡς clause can be taken as an indirect question ('to tell in detail how . . .'): cf. Heubeck on *Od.* 24.237.

213 ἐφημοσύνῃσι: ἐφημοσύνη is always singular in Homer (1× *Il.*, 2× *Od.*), but the plural recurs in Hellenistic poetry; cf. A.R. 1.33 etc.

214 ἶσα θεοῖσιν (cf. *Il.* 21.315 etc.) is clearly preferable to the variant ἤματα πάντα, which is due to the formular ἀθάνατον καὶ ἀγήραον ἤματα πάντα (*Od.* 5.136 etc.); cf. also 209, 221.

ἀγήραος: for ἀγήραος/ἀγήρως see Richardson on *Dem.* 242.

215–17 The story ends on a happy note, with Tros riding his immortal steeds: but we may still wonder if this is really sufficient recompense for the loss of a beloved son (cf. Smith (1981a) 71–7).

216 This line echoes and contrasts with 209, and γόασκε, γεγήθει δέ are in strong opposition, with alliteration, emphasised further by the anaphora γεγήθει . . . γηθόσυνος. Cf. *Il.* 11.683 γεγήθει δὲ φρένα Νηλεύς, and *Od.* 11.337 etc. φρένας ἔνδον ἐΐσας.

217 ἀελλοπόδεσσιν: ἀελλόπος is used of Iris in Homer (3× *Il.*); cf. ἀελλοπόδων θύγατρες ἵππων Simon, *PMG* 515, Pi. *N.* 1.6, etc.

218–38 So too Tithonus was carried off by Dawn, who asked Zeus for immortality for him, but did not think of asking for eternal youth. While he was young they lived together happily, but when he began to grow old she left his bed, though still looking after him. When he was really old, however, she locked him away in a room, where he lives on, unable to move but with his voice still flowing incessantly.

The story of Tithonus first occurs here. In Homer (*Il.* 11.1–2, *Od.* 5.1–2) Dawn rises from Tithonus' bed at daybreak, and he is mentioned in Aeneas' genealogy as a son of Laomedon and brother of Priam (*Il.* 20.237). In Hes. *Th.* 984–5 she bears him Memnon and Emathion. In Tyrtaeus he is a model of exceptional beauty (fr. 12.5 West), and Mimnermus (fr. 4 West) says that he was given eternal old age, worse even than death. Sappho cites him as an example of the inevitability of old age in a poem which has several close links with the version in the hymn. Cf. the new text by West (2005) 5, of fr. 58.11–22 L–P = V:

Υ̓́μμες πεδὰ Μοίσαν ἰ]ọκ[ό]ḷπων κάλα δῶρα, παῖδες,
σπουδάσδετε καὶ τὰ]ṿ φιλάοιδον λιγύραν χελύνναν·
ἔμοι δ' ἄπαλον πρίν] ποτ̣' [ἔ]ọντα χρόα γῆρας ἤδη

ἐπέλλαβε, λεῦκαι δ' ἐγ]ένοντο τρίχες ἐκ μελαίναν·
βάρυς δέ μ' ὁ [ϑ]ῦμο̣ς̣ πεπόηται, γόνα δ' [ο]ὐ φέροισι,
τὰ δή ποτα λαίψηρ' ἔον ὄρχησϑ' ἴσα νεβρίοισι.
τὰ <μὲν> στεναχίσδω ϑαμέως· ἀλλὰ τί κεν ποείην;
ἀγήραον ἄνϑρωπον ἔοντ' οὐ δύνατον γένεσϑαι.
καὶ γάρ π̣[ο]τ̣α̣ Τίϑωνον ἔφαντο βροδόπαχυν Αὔων
ἔρωι φ̣ . . α̣ϑ̣εισαν βάμεν' εἰς ἔσχατα γᾶς φέροισα[ν,
ἔοντα̣ [κ]α̣λ̣ο̣ν καὶ νέον, ἀλλ' αὖτον ὔμως ἔμαρψε
χρόνωι π̣ό̣λ̣ι̣ο̣ν̣ γῆρας, ἔχ[ο]ν̣τ̣' ἀϑανάταν ἄκοιτιν.

[You for] the fragrant-bosomed Muses' lovely gifts
[be zealous,] girls, [and the] clear melodious lyre:
[but my once tender] body old age now
[has seized;] my hair's turned [white] instead of dark;
my heart's grown heavy, my knees will not support me,
that once on a time were fleet for the dance as fawns.
This state I oft bewail; but what's to do?
Not to grow old, being human, there's no way.
Tithonus once, the tale was, rose-armed Dawn
love-smitten, carried off to the world's end,
handsome and young then, yet in time grey age
o'ertook him, husband of immortal wife.

Lines 3–5 resemble *H. Aph.* 228–9 and 233–4, and 10 is similar to 227. See Introduction 4(b).

Tithonus' endless ageing process stands in ironic contrast with Dawn's eternally youthful freshness, as in Tennyson's *Tithonus*. In one version he becomes a cicada (cf. *Il.* 3.150–3, where the garrulous old men of Troy are like cicadas): Hellanicus, *FGrH* 4 F 140, Schol. *Il.* 11.1, etc. Kakridis (1930, 25–38) argues that this story lies behind the hymn's version, but it is probably a later development. See also King (1986), Segal (1986), and Clay (2006) 193–6. The motif of divine regret for an ageing mortal lover is paralleled by Thetis and Peleus (cf. *Il.* 18.428–35), and the story of Tithonus acts as a contrast to the happy ending of Ganymede's tale. Aphrodite will not make the same mistake as Eos, and Anchises will eventually die like other mortals.

218–19 Eos made a habit of falling for attractive young men: Orion (*Od.* 5.121–4), Cleitus (*Od.* 15.250–1 ἀλλ' ἤτοι Κλεῖτον χρυσόϑρονος ἥρπασεν Ἠὼς | κάλλεος εἵνεκα οἷο, ἵν' ἀϑανάτοισι μετείη), Cephalus (E. *Hipp.* 455–8 etc.); cf. Vermeule (1979) 162–5.

218 **χρυσόϑρονος** is used only of goddesses in early epic, and especially of Dawn (*Odyssey*, *Hymns*). It may have originally meant 'with golden flowers' (cf. Hainsworth on *Od.* 5.123).

220–1 The usual Homeric formula ἀϑάνατον καὶ ἀγήραον ἤματα πάντα (as Calypso promises to make Odysseus: *Od.* 5.136 etc.) is here deliberately altered to suit the story of Eos' lapse. Cf. *H. Aph.* 240.

222 This is not a Homeric formula for Zeus's consent, but cf. Zeus's famous nod (*Il.* 1.524–30, 15.75–7), and *H. Dem.* 466.

223–4 Cf. *Il.* 20.264 νήπιος, οὐδ' ἐνόησε κατὰ φρένα, and 22.445. One can treat this as an emphatic asyndeton ('Fool, for she did not think...'), or else regard 222 as a parenthesis. For 224 cf. *Il.* 9.446 γῆρας ἀποξύσας θήσειν νέον ἡβώοντα, and *Nostoi* fr. 6 Allen (= 6 Davies). ξῦσαί τ' ἄπο goes together, for ἀποξῦσαι. 'The image is of scraping away calluses and wrinkles to restore the smoothness of youth... Related is the idea of old age as a skin which, ideally, we could slough off, as snakes do (a cast snakeskin is called γῆρας)...' (Griffin (1995) 128, on *Il.* 9.446).

225–7 Dawn naturally lives on the borders of the world (cf. *Od.* 12.3–4), as she rises from her bed in the far east. Cf. Sappho's poem, quoted in 218–38n., lines 9–10.

228 **κατέχυντο** suggests his long grey locks and beard flowing down from his head (cf. Call. *H.* 6.5 κατεχεύατο χαίταν).

ἔθειραι is used only of a horse's mane or helmet-crest in Homer, but of human hair in later poetry.

229 **εὐηγενέος** ('noble') is a variant form of εὐγενής (cf. *Il.* 11.427, 23.81, and Richardson on 23.81). Heitsch (1965, 31) suggests that it could be influenced by ἠϋγένειος ('well-bearded'). There may in any case be word-play in εὐηγενέος τε γενείου.

230–2 There is a strong contrast between εὐνῆς μὲν and αὐτὸν δ' αὖτε. In Homer ἀτίταλλεν is always used of nursing children (cf. *H. Aph.* 115). The wider sense occurs in Theocritus (15.111, 17.58). But the implication may be that Dawn treats him like a baby, old age being often seen as a second childhood (cf. Schol. Lycophron, *Alexandra* 18, where she keeps him in a cradle). The combination of human food and ambrosia (contrasted at *Od.* 5.195–9) may also reflect his intermediary status between mortal and immortal.

233–6 At this point presumably Dawn no longer feeds Tithonus, who grows weaker and weaker. 236 suggests the idea of shutting something away in a storeroom.

234 Cf. *Od.* 8.298 οὐδέ τι κινῆσαι μελέων ἦν οὐδ' ἀναεῖραι.

237 Cf. *Il.* 18.403 ῥέεν ἄσπετος of Oceanos, 1.249 ῥέεν αὐδή (of old Nestor), Hes. *Th.* 39, 84. ἄσπετος presumably means 'incessant' here (cf. *LfgrE* s.v.). It originally meant 'unspeakable', and so 'immeasurable'. It is used of loud noises at *Od.* 14.412, *H. Ap.* 360.

237–8 Cf. *Od.* 11.393–4 οὐδ' ἔτι κῖκυς, | οἵη περ πάρος ἔσκεν ἐνὶ γναμπτοῖσι μέλεσσιν, 21.282–3, and *Il.* 11.668–9. In the formula ἐνὶ γναμπτοῖσι μέλεσσι the epic poets probably saw a contrast between the supple limbs of youth and those of old age (see Hainsworth on *Il.* 11.669, Richardson on 24.358–60).

239–55 Aphrodite returns to the present situation. The *paradeigmata* of Ganymede and Tithonus originally illustrated the godlike qualities of Trojan princes, but now the theme is the misery of old age, inevitable for Anchises, and (as at 198–9) her grief and shame over a mortal love affair. This progression of thought resembles the way in which extended Homeric similes sometimes develop from one to another point of comparison. The implication of 239–46 seems to be that Aphrodite cannot make Anchises both immortal and ageless like Ganymede, because this is only in the power of Zeus to grant (cf. Clay (2006) 189–91).

239–40 The asyndeton is emphatic: 'I myself certainly would not choose such a fate for you!' τοῖον implies 'like Tithonus', and 240 = 221.

241–6 The structure of this passage, contrasting the unattainable ideal with reality, resembles that of *Il.* 12.322–8 (in Sarpedon's famous speech to Glaucus about heroism) ὦ πέπον, εἰ μὲν γὰρ . . . | αἰεὶ δὴ μέλλοιμεν ἀγήρω τ' ἀθανάτω τε | ἔσσεσθ'· οὔτε κεν αὐτὸς ἐνὶ πρώτοισιν μαχοίμην . . . νῦν δ' ἔμπης γὰρ κῆρες ἐφεστᾶσιν θανάτοιο . . . There it is death, here old age which is inevitable.

241 τοιοῦτος means 'such as you now are', i.e. young and beautiful.

242–3 For 242 cf. 126–7, *Od.* 6.244 αἲ γὰρ ἐμοὶ τοιόσδε πόσις κεκλημένος εἴη, *Il.* 2.260 πατὴρ κεκλήμενος εἴην. 243 echoes 198–9, and cf. *Il.* 8.124 ἄχος πύκασε φρένας, 14.294 ἔρως πυκινὰς φρένας ἀμφεκάλυψεν.

244–6 For γῆρας ὁμοίιον cf. *Il.* 4.315. ὁμοίιος is also used of war, strife, and death in Homer. It was disputed in antiquity whether this was a variant form of ὁμοῖος, meaning 'common to all' (as Hesiod apparently supposed, *Op.* 182), or a separate word altogether, meaning 'evil, hateful'. Cf. Russo on *Od.* 18.264, in favour of 'levelling' as the translation.

The repetition of the verb at the end of 243 and 244 emphasises the parallelism between Aphrodite's grief and Anchises' fate. The expanded description of old age in 245–6 also underlines Aphrodite's extreme revulsion at the prospect, and the contrast between men and gods. The form νηλειής ('pitiless', cf. νηλής) occurs at Hes. *Th.* 770. The idea of old age personified as a divine force 'standing near' men is paralleled by expressions about death and fate (cf. 269 etc.).

245 ἔπειτα must mean here 'in time to come'.

246 καματηρόν: καματηρός occurs only here in early poetry; cf. Herodotus, Aristophanes, etc.

247–51 Aphrodite's main concern is her shame. 249–51 have been taken as implying that she will no longer have power to cause unions of gods and mortals (cf. Clay (2006) 192–3), but this is not a necessary interpretation of the text. For 247–8 cf. *Il.* 16.498–9 κατηφείη καὶ ὄνειδος | ἔσσομαι ἤματα πάντα διαμπερές. ὀάρους is used in the context of love at Hes. *Th.* 205, and in later poetry. 249–50 recall 50–2 (here abbreviated), and δάμνασκε is used of Aphrodite as at 2–5.

252 στόμα τλήσεται: this conjecture gives the best sense. It has been objected that 'στόμα as an organ of speech . . . does not occur in early epic', and 'the στόμα speaking itself is not found before Pind. *Nem.* X.19' (van Eck 86–7); but cf. *Il.* 2.489–90, 14.91, etc. There is no certain parallel elsewhere in early epic for the scansion στόμᾰ τλ-, in the case of this particular combination of mute plus liquid (τλ), but final vowels in thesis usually remain short in epic before such mute-plus-liquid combinations: cf. Chantraine, *GH* I 108–9, and *H. Aph.* 114, 131, 179, 187.

253 πολλὸν ἀάσθην: cf. *Il.* 19.113, of Zeus deceived by Ate.

254 οὐκ ὀνομαστόν: cf. *Od.* 19.260 etc. Κακοΐλιον οὐκ ὀνομαστήν, and Hes. *Th.* 148 οὐκ ὀνομαστοί.

255 This line is echoed by 282.

256–80 The nymphs of Ida will nurse Aeneas. Divine or semi-divine nursing of gods or heroes is a common theme of early Greek mythology: cf. for example Dionysus' nurses in *Il.* 6.132–5 (identified as nymphs in *H.* 26.3–6), *H. Ap.* 123–5 (Themis nurses Apollo), *H. Dem.* 98–274 (Demeter and Demophon, with Richardson on *H. Dem.* 231–55), Hes. fr. 145.1–2 (nymphs of Ida and Minos), Pi. *P.* 4.102–3 (Chiron's daughters and Jason), 9.59–65 (Aristaeus given to Seasons and Earth by Hermes), and see Jeanmaire (1939) 283–96. For the nymphs as κουροτρόφοι in general cf. Hes. *Th.* 346–8, West ad loc.

256–8 256 is echoed at 274 and 278. Normal epic usage (*Il.* 5.150 etc.) suggests that the subject of ἴδηι should be Aeneas, rather than φάος ἠελίοιο. For the repetition of the pronoun in 257 (μιν) cf. *Od.* 16.78–9 ἀλλ' ἤτοι τὸν ξεῖνον . . . ἕσσω μιν . . .

ὀρεσκῷιος ('with mountain lairs') is used of the Centaurs (Φῆρες) at *Il.* 1.268, and other animals elsewhere in the *Hymns*. At *Od.* 9.154–5 nymphs disturb αἶγας ὀρεσκώιους; cf. *Il.* 6.420 νύμφαι ὀρεστιάδες. For the sense cf. Chantraine, *Dict.* s.v., Heubeck on *Od.* 9.155. The Oceanids are βαθύκολποι at *H. Dem.* 5, and the epithet is suitable for nursing deities: cf. *H.* 26.3–4 ὃν τρέφον . . . νύμφαι . . . δεξάμεναι κόλποισι . . . , and *H. Dem.* 231. 258 recalls 98 and is echoed with variation at 285; cf. Hes. *Th.* 2 (Muses) αἵ θ' Ἑλικῶνος ἔχουσιν ὄρος μέγα τε ζάθεόν τε.

259–72 are a discursive expansion on the nature and life of the mountain nymphs, the first on this topic in Greek literature. The boundaries of mortality and divinity have already been blurred in the stories of Ganymede (immortal and ageless) and Tithonus (immortal but not ageless). The nymphs are mortal, but in their length of lives approach immortality most closely. In Homer the sea nymphs are called ἀθάναται (*Il.* 18.86, *Od.* 24.47), and nymphs are θεαί at *Il.* 24.615, *Od.* 12.131–3, *H.* 26.7, Hes. *Th.* 129–30, fr. 123. But Hes. fr. 304 agrees with our hymn: nymphs themselves claim to live for 9,720 generations. Plutarch quotes this in his discussion of beings intermediary between men and gods (*Mor.* 415ff.), and also Pindar fr. 165 Snell–Maehler ἰσοδένδρου | τέκμαρ αἰῶνος θεόφραστον λαχοίσα of Hamadryads whose life-span is that of the trees. Cf. also Eumelus fr. 15 Kinkel (= 15 Bernabé), Charon of Lampsacus, *FGrH* 262 F 12, Call. *H.* 4.79–85, A.R. 2.476–83, etc., and see Süss, *RE* VII 2287–92 s.v. Hamadryaden.

259 αἵ ῥ': for this introduction to a discursive passage cf. (e.g.) *Od.* 17.292–3 Ἄργος . . . ὃν ῥά ποτ' αὐτὸς | θρέψε μὲν . . .

ἕπονται is used here to mean 'belong with'. Cf. LSJ s.v. ἕπω B II.4.

261 For the scansion of καλόν with short alpha cf. 29–32n. χορὸν ἐρρώσαντο means 'moved nimbly in the dance'. ἐρρώσαντο is used of the movement of nymphs around the river Achelous at *Il.* 24.616. Cf. also Hes. *Th.* 7–8 χοροὺς ἐνεποιήσαντο | καλοὺς ἱμερόεντας, ἐπερρώσαντο δὲ ποσσίν, which is perhaps in this poet's mind (cf. 256–8n.), and would help to explain the unusual internal accusative χορόν with this verb. The *Theogony* passage also combines present and 'timeless' past tenses in a similar way to 258ff. (cf. West on *Th.* 7 and 10, and see *H. Ap.* 1–8n.).

262 Σιληνοί: the name occurs here for the first time in literature. In early vase inscriptions this, rather than Σειληνός, is the form. Later Silenoi and Satyrs are often treated as closely related or identical beings. Satyrs are first mentioned in literature in the Hesiodic *Catalogue of Women*, frs. 10(a) 17–19 and 10(b) in *Hesiodi opera* (Oxford 1990, 3rd edn with new Appendix of fragments, ed. R. Merkelbach and M. L. West). They and the mountain nymphs are probably children of the five daughters of Dorus and a daughter of Phoroneus. The Satyrs are described in this passage as γένος οὐτιδανῶν Σατύρων καὶ ἀμηχανοέργων, in other words a race of idle and mischievous layabouts. From Pindar onwards Silenus is a specific individual (frs. 156–7 Snell–Maehler etc.), and in Attic satyr-plays he is the leader or father of the Satyrs.

In art we first meet Silenoi by name on the François Vase (*c.* 570 BC), where three of them accompany Dionysus and Hephaestus, together with women labelled as nymphs. A singular Silenus is first identified by name on a vase by the same potter Ergotimos, led captive by a man with a wineskin. Satyrs and Silenoi are usually depicted in early Greek art as naked, shaggy, and bearded men with large *phalloi*, and equine features (horses' ears, legs, and/or tails). The earliest example of a 'proto-satyr' is said to belong to a vase *c.* 650–25 BC: *LIMC* VIII.1 s.v. Silenoi no. 29(c). They often accompany nymphs (or women), sometimes pursuing them. See Carpenter (1986) 76–97, Lissarague (1990) 228–36, *LIMC* VIII.1 s.v. Silenoi, *OCD*[3] s.v. satyrs and silens.

The name of one of Dorus' daughters in the Hesiodic fragment quoted above is Iphthime (fr. 10(a) 13), and she appears in Nonnus (14.105–19) as the mother of the Satyrs by Hermes. In *H. Aph.* 262–3 we again meet Hermes, and here he and the Silenoi both mate with nymphs. For nymphs and Hermes in art see M. Halm-Tisserant and G. Siebert, *LIMC* V.1 316–18 s.v. Hermes. Cf. also on *H. Aph.* 117–21 (where Hermes is said to carry off a girl from a chorus dancing in honour of Artemis), *H.* 19.32ff. (Hermes and nymph as parents of Pan), Hes. fr. 64 (Hermes and Philonis parents of Autolycus), and *Od.* 14.435–6 (sacrifice to Hermes and nymphs).

εὔσκοπος Ἀργειφόντης: cf. *H. Ap.* 200–1n.

263 Cf. *Od.* 5.225–6 μυχῶι σπείους γλαφυροῖο | τερπέσθην φιλότητι, of the nymph Calypso and Odysseus. The epithet ἐρόεις does not occur in Homer, but is common in the *Theogony* (of nymphs, 245 etc.) and *Hymns*; cf. *Od.* 13.103–4 ἄντρον ἐπήρατον ἠεροειδές, | ἱρὸν νυμφάων, αἳ νηϊάδες καλέονται.

264–72 This idea of nymphs as coeval with trees (see on 259–72) may be implied or foreshadowed by Hes. *Th.* 187 (nymphs called Meliai from μελίη, 'ash tree', i.e. tree nymphs), and especially *H. Dem.* 22–3, where immortals, mortals, and ἀγλαόκαρποι Ἐλαῖαι all fail to hear Persephone's cries (implying that they are intermediary between gods and men: cf. Humbert 42, 146). Cf. also *Il.* 6.419–20, where mountain nymphs grow elm trees around a tomb. Here the picture of the growth and dying of the trees is described in elaborate detail: cf. *Il.* 6.146–9, the famous comparison of the generation of men to that of leaves, especially 147–8 φύλλα τὰ μέν τ' ἄνεμος χαμάδις χέει, ἄλλα δέ θ' ὕλη | τηλεθόωσα φύει, ἔαρος δ' ἐπιγίγνεται ὥρη, and 21.662–6. Callimachus may have had our hymn in mind at *H.* 4.82–5, when he asks if nymphs are truly coeval with trees, and gives the Muses' reply that they rejoice when the trees grow, and weep when their leaves are gone.

264–6 It is probably best to punctuate with full stop at end of 266, and take 267–8 as a dramatically effective sentence in asyndeton, expanding the point of 266. Alternatively, one could begin the second sentence at 266, as West does.

264–5 There may be an echo of Hes. *Op.* 509–10 πολλὰς δὲ δρῦς ὑψικόμους ἐλάτας τε παχείας | οὔρεος ἐν βήσσῃς πιλνᾷ χθονὶ πουλοβοτείρῃ (cf. Introduction 4(c)).

267 ἠλίβατοι: originally perhaps 'inaccessible' (cf. Chantraine, *Dict.* s.v.), but the word was often used to mean 'tall, steep' (cf. Hes. *Th.* 786–7 πέτρης . . . ἠλιβάτοιο | ὑψηλῆς). ἠλίβατος is always used of rocks in Homer (although at *Od.* 13.196 πέτραι τ' ἠλιβάτοι are combined with δένδρεα τηλεθόωντα), but also of a cave at Hes. *Th.* 483, and a falling tree at Hes. *Sc.* 421–2.

267–8 τεμένη . . . | ἀθανάτων 'and men call them precincts of the immortals'. This presumably means that they are considered as sacred to the gods in general, not the nymphs, who have been defined as mortal. Cf. for example the grove of Demeter, haunted by nymphs in Call. *H.* 6.32ff., Ov. *M.* 8.741ff. For the expression cf. *Od.* 4.355 Φάρον δέ ἑ κικλήσκουσιν. This seems to be the only case where ἑ is certainly used as a plural (cf. Leaf on *Il.* 2.197). Latin *se* however can be plural or singular, and cf. ἑ-αυτούς (etc.). For κείρουσι σιδήρωι cf. *H. Herm.* 109 ἐπέλεψε σιδήρωι.

269–72 Cf. *Il.* 16.853 = 24.132 ἄγχι παρέστηκεν θάνατος καὶ μοῖρα κραταιή, and see *H. Aph.* 244–6n. The verb ἀζάνεται is a *hapax legomenon*, for epic ἄζεσθαι (*Il.* 4.487 etc.), but cf. καταζήνασκε (*Od.* 11.587). ἀμφιπεριφθινύθει is also a unique compound, if regarded as a single word. As often δέ τε adds a further generalising statement to those already made (cf. Smith (1979) 37–9, and Denniston, GP^2 520ff.).

273 This line recalls 256–7, closing this excursus on the nymphs.

274–91 When the nymphs bring Aeneas to his father, he must take him to Troy and say that he is the son of a nymph of Mt Ida. If he tells the truth Zeus will strike him with a thunderbolt.

The narrative closes with Aphrodite's return to heaven.

274–7 These two couplets are evidently variant versions. 274–5 have been suspected because the nymphs are called θεαί, despite their mortality. But the word is applied to them elsewhere in early epic (see 259–72n.). These verses agree much better with the usual practice elsewhere of upbringing of gods or heroes by nymphs. For the repetition in 274 and 278 (echoing 256) cf. 225, 230, and 237, and also the endings of 243 and 244. AHS retained both couplets, holding that ἥβη in 274 refers to the moment when a child begins to walk, or is weaned, and that two presentations are envisaged. But ἥβη in epic refers to the beginning of manhood, even if Solon (fr. 27 West) sets it at seven years. Van Eck also keeps the whole passage, arguing that '276–7 should be regarded as a correction of what Aphrodite said at 274–5', perhaps added by the poet to harmonise with *Il.* 13.465–6, where Aeneas while still a child was brought up by his brother-in-law Alcathous. It is, however, most improbable that the poet himself should have added such a correction, although 276–7 could possibly have been inserted later for this reason. The text of 276 is unmetrical as it stands, and μετὰ φρεσί does not make sense with ταῦτα . . . διέλθω. The whole style of 276 is banal and unsuitable for a speech by a goddess to a mortal. The comparison which has been made with the Persian custom of leaving children with their mothers until they are five years old and then showing them to their fathers (Hdt. 1.136.2) also seems irrelevant in this context. Finally, it is inappropriate for Aphrodite herself to bring the child to Anchises, given her embarrassment about the whole affair.

278 For θάλος of a child or young person cf. *Il.* 22.87, *Od.* 6.157, etc.

279 μάλα γὰρ θεοείκελος ἔσται: this resembles *H. Dem.* 159 δὴ γὰρ θεοείκελός ἐσσι, which may be an echo of this phrase (cf. Introduction 4(b)). Aeneas will resemble the members of his family in godlike appearance (200–1).

280 μιν: MSS give Doric νιν, but μιν is the standard early epic form.

281–90 True to her nature to the last, Aphrodite orders Anchises to lie about his affair with her. This motif of secrecy, which is here explained by her embarrassment (247–55), is common in such stories of love affairs between gods and mortals: cf. *Il.* 2.512–15 (Ares sleeps with Astyoche λάθρηι), 16.179–86 (Hermes and Polymele), *Od.* 11.235–53 (Poseidon and Tyro). The last story closely resembles the present myth in several respects: see 191–290n., and cf. here *H. Aph.* 290 with *Od.* 11.251 ἴσχεο μηδ᾽ ὀνομήνηις. Secrecy or reticence in the case of affairs between gods is also (understandably) a common theme: cf. for example Call. fr. 75.4ff. Pfeiffer (cf. *Il.* 14.294–6, 329–45), and *H. Herm.* 3–9 (Zeus and Maia's secret love, unknown to Hera; cf. *H. Ap.* 105–6). See also Janko on *Il.* 14.295–6 for other examples of 'secret sex' as a *topos*. This motif is here combined with the hymnic theme of a final warning against transgressing the god's command: cf. the solemn injunction about the secrecy of the Mysteries at the end of the *Hymn to Demeter* (478–9), and Apollo's final warning to his Delphic priests not to misbehave (*H. Ap.* 540–4, where 544 resembles *H. Aph.* 289–90).

284 φασίν is at first sight odd in the mouth of Anchises himself. Cf. *Il.* 20.105–6, where Apollo in disguise says to Aeneas καὶ δέ σέ φασι Διὸς κούρης Ἀφροδίτης | ἐκγεγάμεν . . . The point may be that Anchises should profess uncertainty about just who it was that he encountered, as at 92–9. The implied subject of φασίν is presumably the nymphs who will nurse Aeneas. Matthiae's φάσθαι is unnecessary, since we already have the imperative μυθεῖσθαι in 283.

καλυκώπιδος: this epithet is used of Persephone and an Oceanid nymph at *H. Dem.* 8, 420: 'with eyes like buds' (see Richardson on *H. Dem.* 8).

285 This line resembles 98 and 258. ὄρος καταειμένον ὕλῃ occurs at *Od.* 13.351, *H. Herm.* 228, and is a formulaic doublet of *H. Aph.* 258 ὄρος μέγα τε ζάθεόν τε.

286–8 Aphrodite's warning comes true in later versions, and perhaps already in the *Iliou Persis*: see 187–90n.

289–90 Cf. *H. Ap.* 544 εἴρηταί τοι πάντα, σὺ δὲ φρεσὶ σῇσι φύλαξαι, *Od.* 11.251 ἴσχεο μηδ' ὀνομήνῃς, *Od.* 5.146 Διὸς δ' ἐποπίζεο μῆνιν, 14.283.

290 **ὀνόμαινε:** the present imperative form, conjectured by Hermann, replaces aorist ὀνόμηνε, the MSS reading, which is anomalous as one would expect ὀνόμηνον. Elsewhere in early epic the present form ὀνομάζω is used, but ὀνομαίνω occurs in other tenses.

291 closes the narrative in a typical way with the return of the deity to heaven: cf. *Il.* 24.694, *Od.* 6.41–7; *H. Dem.* 483–4, where Demeter and Persephone go to Olympus at the end of their hymn, and similarly *H.* 15.7–8, where Heracles now dwells on Olympus. It is, however, surely significant that here Aphrodite is not said to return to the company of the other gods. The ending of the narrative is also extremely abrupt, and after Aphrodite's final warning this adds to our sense of her potential for retaliation. For 291 cf. *Il.* 23.868 ἤιξε πρὸς οὐρανόν (of an arrow). The usual epic formula is οὐρανὸν ἀστερόεντα: cf. *Il.* 15.371 etc. It could have been replaced because the epithet is unsuited to daytime (van Eck ad loc.), but it might also be an instance of variation, influenced by ποτὶ/πρὸς/ Ἴλιον ἠνεμόεσσαν (*H. Aph.* 280 etc.). In any case, this phrase accords well with Aphrodite's rapid and sudden departure. Contrast the windless calm of the gods' abode in heaven at *Od.* 6.42–5.

292–3 The hymn closes with a typical expression of greeting or farewell to the goddess, and the usual transition to another song (see Richardson on *H. Dem.* 490–5). χαῖρε is common in the closing greeting of the *Hymns* (and cf. similarly *H. Aph.* 92 etc.). Here there is no final request for favour, as at *H. Dem.* 494 etc., but the word χαῖρε in itself suggests that the deity should be well-disposed: cf. *H. Aph.* 102–3 σὺ δ' εὔφρονα θυμὸν ἔχουσα | δός..., Hes. *Th.* 104 χαίρετε... δότε δ'..., *H.* 10.4–5, etc. 292 also typically refers again to Aphrodite's chief place of worship: cf. (to Aphrodite) *H.* 10.4–5 (closing address) χαῖρε θεὰ Σαλαμῖνος ἐϋκτιμένης μεδέουσα | εἰναλίης τε Κύπρου..., and *H. Aph.* 1–2, *H.* 6.1–3; also *H. Herm.* 2 = *H.* 18.2 (μεδέοντα).

293 = *H.* 9.9, 18.11. ὕμνος here can mean simply another song (e.g. in praise of heroes), not necessarily a hymn to a god. This accords with the general view of these hymns as originally preludes (cf. Introduction 1(a)). For σεῦ δ' ἐγὼ ἀρξάμενος in this context cf. also *H.* 31.18–19, 32.18–19 (to be followed in both cases by heroic narrative). μετάβηθι is used by Odysseus in asking Demodocus to move on to a new song at *Od.* 8.492.

BIBLIOGRAPHY

Abramowicz, S. (1937) *Études sur les Hymnes Homériques*. Wilna
Allen, T. W. (1895) 'The text of the Homeric Hymns: II', *JHS* 15: 251–313
(1931) 'Miscellanea – VIII', *CQ* 25: 146–50
Aloni, A. (1989) *L'aedo e i tiranni: ricerche sull' inno omerico a Apollo*. Rome
Amandry, P. (1950) *La mantique apollinienne à Delphes*. Paris
Amandry, P. *et al.* (1981) *L'antre Corycien* I, *BCH* Suppl. 7. Paris
(1984) *L'antre Corycien* II, *BCH* Suppl. 9. Paris
Andrisano, A. (1978–9) 'La datazione di [Hom.] Hymn. Pan', *MCr* 13–14: 7–22
Arend, W. (1933) *Die typischen Scenen bei Homer*. Berlin
Bain, D. (2007) 'Low words in high places', in P. J. Finglass, C. Collard and N. J. Richardson, edd., *Hesperos: studies in ancient Greek poetry presented to M. L. West on his seventieth birthday* (Oxford) 40–57
Baltes, M. (1982) 'Die Kataloge im homerischen Apollonhymnus', *Philologus* 125: 25–43
Barchiesi, A. (1999) 'Venus' masterplot: Ovid and the Homeric Hymns', in P. Hardie, A. Barchiesi, and S. Hinds, edd., *Ovidian transformations* (Cambridge) 112–26
Barron, J. P. (1984) 'Ibycus: GORGIAS and other poems', *BICS* 31: 13–24
Bean, G. E. (1971) *Turkey beyond the Maeander*. London
Bean, G. E. and Cook, J. M. (1952) 'The Cnidia', *BSA* 47: 171–212
Beazley, J. D. (1948) 'Hymn to Hermes', *AJA* 52: 336–40
(1950) 'Some inscriptions on vases, V', *AJA* 54: 310–22
Ben, N. van der (1980) 'De homerische Aphrodite-hymne I – De Aeneas – passages in de Ilias', *Lampas* 13: 40–77
(1981) 'De homerische Aphrodite-hymne II – Een Interpretatie van het Gedicht', *Lampas* 14: 67–107
(1986) 'Hymn to Aphrodite 36–291 – Notes on the pars epica of the Homeric hymn to Aphrodite', *Mnemosyne* 39: 1–41
Bergren, A. L. T. (1982) 'Sacred apostrophe: re-presentation and imitation in the Homeric Hymns', *Arethusa* 15: 83–108
(1989) 'The Homeric hymn to Aphrodite: tradition and rhetoric, praise and blame', *ClAnt* 8: 1–44
Bers, V. (1984) *Greek poetic syntax in the classical age*. New Haven
Bickerman, E. J. (1976) 'Love story in the Homeric hymn to Aphrodite', *Athenaeum* 54: 229–54
Bing, P. (1993) 'Impersonation of voice in Callimachus' Hymn to Apollo', *TAPhA* 123: 181–98
(1995) 'Callimachus and the *Hymn to Demeter*', *Syllecta Classica* 6: 29–42

Bittlestone, R., Diggle, J., and Underhill, J. (2005) *Odysseus unbound: the search for Homer's Ithaca.* Cambridge

Bloomfield, M. (1923) 'The art of stealing in Hindu fiction', *AJP* 44: 97–133

Blumenthal, A. von (1927–8) 'Der Apollontempel des Trophonios und Agamedes in Delphi', *Philologus* 83: 220–4

Boardman, J. (2002) *The archaeology of nostalgia: how the Greeks re-created their mythical past.* London

Bodson, L. (1971) 'Hymne homérique à Apollon, 209–13: un "locus desperatus"?', *AC* 40: 12–20

Boedeker, D. (1974) *Aphrodite's entry into Greek epic.* Leiden

Bommelaer, J.-F. (1991) *Guide de Delphes: le site.* Paris

Borthwick, E. K. (1959) 'κατάληψις – a neglected technical term in Greek music', *CQ* 53: 23–9

Breuning, P. S. (1929) *De Hymnorum Homericorum memoria.* Utrecht (Traiecti ad Rhenum)

Brioso, M. (1990) 'Himno Homerico a Hermes 567ss: una supuesta laguna', *Habis* 21: 7–14

Bruneau, P. (1970) *Recherches sur les cultes de Délos à l'époque hellénistique et à l'époque impériale.* Paris

Bruneau, P. and Ducat, J. (2005) *Guide de Délos*, 4th edn. Paris

Budin, S. L. (2000) *The origins of Aphrodite.* Bethesda, MD

Bulloch, A. W. (1977) 'Callimachus, Erysichthon, Homer and Apollonius Rhodius', *AJPh* 98: 97–123

Bundy, E. L. (1972) 'The quarrel between Kallimachos and Apollonios', *CSCA* 5: 39–94

Burkert, W. (1972) *Homo necans: Interpretationen altgriechischer Opferriten und Mythen.* Berlin

(1975) 'Rešep-figuren, Apollon von Amyklai und die Erfundung des Opfers auf Cypern', *GB* 4: 51–79

(1979a) 'Kynaithos, Polycrates and the Homeric hymn to Apollo', in G. W. Bowersock, W. Burkert, and M. C. J. Putnam, edd., *Arktouros: Hellenic studies presented to B. M. W. Knox* (Berlin) 53–62

(1979b) *Structure and history in Greek mythology and ritual.* Berkeley

(1984) 'Sacrificio – sacrilegio: il "trickster" fondatore', *StudStor* 4: 835–45

(1985) *Greek religion, archaic and classical.* Oxford

(2001) *Kleine Schriften I: Homerica*, ed. C. Riedweg. Göttingen

Calame, C. (1995) 'Variations énonciatives, relations avec les dieux et fonctions poétiques dans les hymnes homériques', *MH* 52.1: 2–19

Callaway, C. (1993) 'Perjury and the unsworn oath', *TAPhA* 123: 15–25

Carey, C. (1980) 'Homeric Hymn to Apollo, 171', *CQ* 30: 288–90

Carpenter, T. H. (1986) *Dionysian imagery in archaic Greek art.* Oxford

(1991) *Art and myth in ancient Greece.* London

Casson, L. (1971) *Ships and seamanship in the ancient world.* Princeton

Chamoux, F. (2000) 'Hermès à la tortue', in Ἀγαθὸς δαίμων: *mythes et cultes. Études d'iconographie en l'honneur de Lilly Kahil*, *BCH* Suppl. 38 (Paris), 93–9
Chantraine, P. (1935) 'Grec ἐκγεγάονται (Hymne homérique à Aphrodite, 197)', *BSL* 36: 131–2
(1946–7) 'Les noms du mari et de la femme, du père et de la mère', *REG* 59–60: 219–50
Chappell, M. (2006) 'Delphi and the *Homeric Hymn to Apollo*', *CQ* 56: 331–48
Chittenden, J. (1947) 'The master of animals', *Hesperia* 16: 89–114
Clarke, M. (2001) 'Homeric "heart-cutting" talk', *CQ* 51: 329–38
Clay, J. S. (2006) *The politics of Olympus: form and meaning in the major Homeric hymns*, 2nd edn. London
(2009) 'The silence of the Pythia', in L. Athanassaki, R. P. Martin, and J. F. Miller, edd., *Apolline politics and poetics* (Athens) 5–16
Clinton, K. (1986) 'The author of the Homeric Hymn to Demeter', *OAth* 16: 43–9
Cook, A. B. (1895) 'The bee in Greek mythology', *JHS* 15: 1–24
Courbin, P. (1980) *L'Oikos des Naxiens*. Paris
Crudden, M. (1994) 'Studies in the Homeric Hymn to Hermes'. PhD, Trinity College, Dublin
Currie, B. (2007) 'Heroes and holy men in early Greece: Hesiod's *Theios Aner*', in A. Coppola, ed., *Eroi, eroismi, eroizzazioni della Grecia antica a Padova e Venezia*, Atti del Convegno Internazionale Padova, 18–19 Settembre 2006 (Padova), 163–203
Cusset, C. (1997) 'Entre le vol et le festin, à propos de la correction du vers 136 de l'*Hymne Homérique à Hermes*', *RPh* 71: 39–43
Dalley, S. (1989) *Myths from Mesopotamia*. Oxford
Danielewicz, G. (1973) 'Hymni Homerici minores quanam arte conscripti sint', *SPhP* 1: 7–17
Danielewicz, J. (1976) *Morfologia hymnu antycznego*. Poznan (English summary: pp. 116–25)
Davies, J. K. (1994) 'The tradition about the First Sacred War', in S. Hornblower, ed., *Greek historiography* (Oxford) 193–212
Davies, M. (1982) Review of P. G. Maxwell-Stuart, *Studies in Greek colour terminology*, *CR* 32: 214–16
Defradas, J. (1972) *Les thèmes de la propagande delphique*. Paris
De la Génière, J. (1998) 'Claros: bilan provisoire de dix campagnes de fouilles', *REA* 100: 235–56
De Martino, F. (1980) 'ΑΛΛΗ ΑΟΙΔΗ (in coda all'inno omerico ad Apollo, 545–6)', *AC* 49: 232–40
Detienne, M. (1998) *Apollon le couteau à la main*. Paris
Deubner, L. (1941) *Ololyge und verwandtes*, Abhandlungen der preussischen Akademie der Wissenschaften 1. Berlin
Devlin, N. (1995) 'The hymn in Greek literature: studies in form and content'. DPhil, Oxford
De Waele, F. J. M. (1927) *The magic staff or rod in Graeco-Roman antiquity*. Gent

Dihle, A. (2002) 'Zu den Fragmenten eines Dionysos-Hymnus', *RhM* 145: 427–30
Dittenberger, W. (1906) 'Ethnika und Verwandtes', *Hermes* 41: 161–219
Dornseiff, F. (1931) 'Der homerische Aphroditehymnos', *ARW* 29: 205–6
(1938) 'Zum homerischen Hermeshymnos', *RhM* 87: 80–4
Dumoulin, D. (1994) *Antike Schildkröten*. Würzburg
Edwards, G. P. (1971) *The language of Hesiod in its traditional context*. Oxford
Eitrem, S. (1906) 'Der homerische Hymnus an Hermes', *Philologus* 65: 248–82
(1909) 'Hermes πολύγιος', *RhM* 64: 333–5
Evans, S. (2001) *Hymn and epic: a study of their interplay in Homer and the 'Homeric Hymns'*. Turku
Fantuzzi, M. and Hunter, R. (2004) *Tradition and innovation in Hellenistic poetry*. Cambridge
Faulkner, A. (2005) 'Aphrodite's aorists: attributive sections in the *Homeric Hymns*', *Glotta* 81: 60–79
(2008) *The Homeric Hymn to Aphrodite: introduction, text and commentary*. Oxford
(2009) 'Callimachus and his allusive virgins', *HSCP* 105
Fontenrose, J. (1959) *Python*. Berkeley
(1960) 'The cult and myth of Pyrrhos at Delphi', *University of California Publications in Classical Archaeology* 4.3: 191–260
(1978) *The Delphic oracle*. Berkeley
Ford, A. (2002) *The origins of criticism*. Princeton
Forderer, M. (1971) *Anfang und Ende der abendländischen Lyrik*. Amsterdam
Forrest, G. (1956) 'The first Sacred War', *BCH* 80: 33–52
Forssmann, B. (1964) 'περ' ἰγνύσι, *hy. Merc.* 152', *Zeitschrift für vergleichende Sprachforschung* 79: 28–31
Förstel, K. (1979) *Untersuchungen zum homerischen Apollonhymnos*. Bochum
Frazer, J. G. (1930) *Myths of the origin of fire*. London
Freed, G. and Bentman, R. (1954) 'The Homeric Hymn to Aphrodite', *CJ* 50: 153–9
Friedrich, P. (1978) *The meaning of Aphrodite*. Chicago
Fröhder, D. (1994) *Die dichterische Form der homerischen Hymnen: untersucht am Typus der mittelgrossen Preislieder*. Hildesheim
Furley, W. D. and Bremer, J. (2001) *Greek hymns*. 2 vols. Tübingen
Gallet de Santerre, H. (1958) *Délos primitive et archaique*. Paris
Garcia, J. F. (2002) 'Symbolic action in the Homeric Hymns', *ClAnt* 21: 5–39
Garland, R. (1990) *The Greek way of life: from conception to old age*. London
Gauthier, P. (1972) *Symbola*. Nancy
Gelzer, Th. (1987) 'Bemerkungen zum Homerisches Ares-Hymnus (Hom. Hy. 8)', *MH* 44: 150–67
(1994) 'Zum *Codex Mosquensis* und zur Sammlung der Homerischen Hymnen', *Hyperboreus* 1: 113–37
Georgoudi, S. (1996) 'Les douze dieux des grecs: variations sur un thème', in S. Georgoudi and J.-P. Vernant, edd., *Mythes grecs au figuré de l'antiquité au baroque* (Paris) 43–80

Ginouvès, R. (1962) *Balaneutike: recherches sur le bain dans l'antiquité grecque*. Paris
Görgemanns, H. (1976) 'Rhetorik und Poetik im homerischen Hermeshymnus', in H. Görgemanns and E. A. Schmidt, edd., *Studien zum antiken Epos* (Meisenheim am Glan) 113–28
Graf, F. (1979) 'Apollon Delphinios', *MH* 36: 2–22
Graziosi, B. (2002) *Inventing Homer: the early reception of epic*. Cambridge
Griffin, J. (1992) 'Theocritus, the *Iliad*, and the east', *AJP* 113: 189–211
ed. (1995) *Homer: Iliad book nine*. Oxford
Gruben, G. (1997) 'Naxos und Delos', *JDAI* 112: 261–416
Guarducci, M. (1943–6) 'Creta e Delphi', *SMSR* 19–20: 85–114
Guida, F. (1972) 'Apollo arciere nell' inno omerico ad Apollo Delio', *Studi Omerici ed Esiodei* 1: 7–25
Guillon, P. (1943) *Les trépieds de Ptoion*. Paris
(1963) *Le bouclier d'Héraclès et l'histoire de la Grèce centrale dans la période de la première guerre sacrée*. Aix-en-Provence
Gutzwiller, K. (2006) 'The bucolic problem', *CPh* 101: 380–404
Haas, G. (1985) *Die Syrinx in der griechischen Bildkunst*. Vienna and Graz
Harrell, S. E. (1991) 'Apollo's fraternal threats: language of succession and domination in the *Homeric Hymn to Hermes*', *GRBS* 32: 307–29
Harrison, J. E. (1903) 'Mystica vannus Iacchi', *JHS* 23: 292–324
Haubold, J. (2001) 'Epic with an end: an interpretation of *Homeric Hymns* 15 and 20', in F. Budelmann and P. Michelakis, edd., *Homer, tragedy and beyond: essays in honour of P. E. Easterling* (London) 23–41
Head, B. V. (1911) *Historia nummorum*. Oxford
Heitsch, E. (1965) *Aphroditehymnos, Aeneas und Homer*. Göttingen
Helbig, W. (1887) *Das homerischen Epos aus den Denkmälern erläutert*, 2nd edn. Leipzig
Henrichs, A. (1996) 'Dancing in Athens, dancing on Delos: some patterns of choral projection in Euripides', *Philologus* 140: 48–62
Hertel, D. (1991) 'Schliemanns These vom Fortleben Troias in den "Dark Ages" im Lichte neuer Forschungsergebenisse', *ST* 1: 131–44
Higgins, R. A. (1961) *Greek and Roman jewellery*. London
Hinds, S. (1987) *The metamorphosis of Persephone: Ovid and the self-conscious Muse*. Cambridge
Hoekstra, A. (1965) *Homeric modifications of formulaic prototypes*. Amsterdam
(1969) *The sub-epic stage of the formulaic tradition*. Amsterdam
(1986) Review of R. Janko, *Homer, Hesiod and the Hymns*, *Mnemosyne* 39: 158–63
Holland, R. (1926) 'Battos', *RhM* 75: 156–83
Hope Simpson, R. and Lazenby, J. F. (1970) *The catalogue of the ships in Homer's Iliad*. Oxford
Hopkinson, N. (1982) 'Juxtaposed prosodic variants in Greek and Latin poetry', *Glotta* 60: 162–77
Hunter, R. (1992) 'Writing the god: form and meaning in Callimachus, *Hymn to Athena*', *MD* 29: 9–34

(1996) *Theocritus and the archaeology of Greek poetry*. Cambridge
(1999) *Theocritus, a selection*. Cambridge
(2003) *Theocritus: encomium of Ptolemy Philadelphus*. Berkeley
Hunter, R. and Fuhrer, T. (2002) 'Imaginary gods? Poetic theology in the *Hymns* of Callimachus', in F. Montanari and L. Lehnus, edd., *Entretiens de la Fondation Hardt: Callimaque* (Geneva) 143–87
Huxley, G. (1975) 'Cretan paiawones', *GRBS* 16: 119–24
Immerwahr, H. (1964) 'Book-rolls on Attic vases', in C. Henderson Jr., ed., *Studies in honour of B. L. Ullmann* (Rome) 17–48
Jacoby, F. (1933) *Der homerische Apollonhymnos*. Berlin
Jacquemin, A. (1993) 'Repercussions de l'entrée de Delphes dans l'amphictionie sur la construction à Delphes à l'époque archaique', in J. des Courtils and J.-C. Moretti, edd., *Les grands ateliers d'architecture dans le monde égéen du VIe siècle avant J.C.* (Paris), 217–25
Jaillard, D. (2007) *Configurations d'Hermès. Une 'théogonie hermaïque'*. Liège
Janko, R. (1979) 'ΒωΣΕΣΘΕ revisited', *CQ* 29: 215–16
(1981) 'The structure of the Homeric Hymns: a study in genre', *Hermes* 109: 9–24
(1982) *Homer, Hesiod, and the Hymns*. Cambridge
(1991) Review of J. S. Clay, *The politics of Olympus*, *CR* 105: 12–13
Jeanmaire, H. (1939) *Couroi et Courètes*. Lille
Johnston, S. I. (2002) 'Myth, festivals and poet: the *Homeric Hymn to Hermes* and its performative context', *CPh* 97: 109–32
Jong, I. J. F. de (1989) 'The biter bit: a narratological analysis of *H. Aphr.* 45–291', *WS* 102: 13–26
Jouan, F. (1956) 'Thetis, Hestia et Athéna', *REG* 69: 290–302
Kahn, L. (1978) *Hermès passe ou les ambiguités de la communication*. Paris
Kaimio, M. (1974) 'Music in the Homeric Hymn to Hermes', *Arctos* 8: 29–42
Kakridis, J. T. (1930) 'Tithonos', *WS* 48: 25–38
(1937) 'Zum homerischen Apollonhymnos', *Philologus* 92: 104–8
Kamerbeek, J. C. (1967) 'Remarques sur l'hymne à Aphrodite', *Mnemosyne* 20: 385–95
Karageorghis, J. (1977) *La grande déesse de Chypre et son culte*. Lyon
Katz, J. T. (1999) '*Homeric Hymn to Hermes* 296: τλήμονα γαστρὸς ἔριθον', *CQ* 49: 315–19
Kauer, S. (1959) *Die Geburt der Athena im altgriechischen Epos*. Würzburg
Keaney, J. (1981) 'Hymn. Ven. 140 and the use of "ΑΠΟΙΝΑ"', *AJP* 102: 261–4
Kennedy, G. A. (1963) *The art of persuasion in Greece*. Princeton
Kerkhecker, A. (1999) *Callimachus' book of iambi*. Oxford
King, H. (1986) 'Tithonus and the tettix', *Arethusa* 19: 15–35
Kleiner, G. (1968) *Die Ruinen von Milet*. Berlin
Knoepfler, D. (1988) 'Sur les traces de l'Artemision d'Amarynthos près d'Érétrie', *CRAI* 382–421

Koettgen, L. (1914) 'Quae ratio intercedat inter Indagatores fabulam Sophocleam et hymnum in Mercurium qui fertur Homericus'. Diss. Bonn

Kolk, D. (1963) *Der pythische Apollonhymnos als aitiologische Dichtung*, Beiträge zur klassischen Philologie 6. Meisenheim am Glan

Kowalzig, B. (2007) *Singing for the gods: performances of myth and ritual in archaic and classical Greece*. Oxford

Kroll, J. (1956) 'Apollon zum Beginn des homerischen Hymnus', *SIFC* 27–8: 181–91

Kumpf, M. M. (1984) *Four indices of Homeric hapax legomena*. Hildesheim

Landels, J. (1999) *Music in ancient Greece and Rome*. London

Langlotz, E. (1954) *Aphrodite in den Gärten*. Heidelberg

Larson, J. (1995) 'The Corycian nymphs and the bee maidens of the Homeric Hymn to Hermes', *GRBS* 36: 341–57

Latacz, J. (1966) *Zum Wortfeld 'Freude' in der Sprache Homers*. Heidelberg

Latte, K. (1968) *Kleine Schriften*. Munich

Lawler, L. B. (1948) 'A necklace for Eileithyia', *Classical Weekly* 42: 2–6

(1951) 'Krêtikôs in the Greek dance', *TAPhA* 82: 62–70

Leclerc, M.-C. (2002) 'Cheminements vers la parole: notes sur l'Hymne homérique à Apollon', *Pallas* 59: 151–65

Leduc, C. (2005) '"Le pseudo-sacrifice d'Hermès". *Hymne homérique à Hermès* 1, vers 112–42: poésie rituelle, théologie et histoire', *Kernos* 18: 141–66

Lefèvre, F. (1998) *L'amphictionie pyléo-delphique: histoire et institutions*. Paris

Lehrs, K. (1882) *De Aristarchi studiis homericis*, 3rd edn. Leipzig

Lenz, L. H. (1975) *Der homerische Aphroditehymnus und die Aristie des Aeneas in der Ilias*. Bonn

Leumann, M. (1950) *Homerische Wörter*. Basel

(1959) *Kleine Schriften*. Zurich

Liberman, G. (1999) *Alcée: fragments*. Paris

Lissarague, F. (1990) 'Why satyrs are good to represent', in J. J. Winkler and F. I. Zeitlin, edd., *Nothing to do with Dionysos? Athenian drama in its social context* (Princeton) 228–36

Lloyd, M. (2004) 'The politeness of Achilles: off-record conversation strategies in Homer and the meaning of *Kertomia*', *JHS* 124: 75–89

Lloyd-Jones, H. (2003) *Sophocles: fragments*. Cambridge, Mass.

Long, C. L. (1987) *The twelve gods of Greece and Rome*. Leiden

Lonsdale, S. (1990) *Creatures of Speech: lion, herding and hunting similes in the Iliad*. Stuttgart

Maas, M. and Synder, J. M. (1989) *Stringed instruments of ancient Greece*. New Haven

Maier, F. G. and Karageorghis, V., edd. (1984) *Paphos: history and archaeology*. Nicosia

Malkin, I. (2002) 'La fondation d'une colonie apollinienne: Delphes et l'*Hymne homérique à Apollon*', in A. Jacquemin, ed., *Delphes cent ans après la grande fouille: essai de bilan*, *BCH* Suppl. 36 (Paris) 69–77

Malten, L. (1931) 'Aineias', *ARW* 29: 33–59

Marx, F. (1907) 'Der blinde Sänger von Chios und die delischen Mädchen', *RhM* 62: 619–20

Matthews, V. J. (1996) *Antimachus of Colophon: text and commentary*. Leiden

Maurizio, L. (1995) 'Anthropology and spirit possession: a reconsideration of the Pythia's role at Delphi', *JHS* 115: 69–86

Maxwell-Stuart, P. G. (1981) *Studies in Greek colour terminology* II. Leiden

Mazon, P. (1937) 'Une formule homérique', in *Mélanges offerts à A.-M. Desrousseaux* (Paris) 319–25

McNamee, K. (1992) *Sigla and select marginalia in Greek literary papyri*. Brussels

Merkelbach, R. (1970–1) 'Gefesselte Götter', *Antaios* 12: 549–65. Reprinted in W. Blümel, B. Krämer, J. Krämer, and C. E. Römer, edd., *Hestia und Erigone: Vorträge und Aufsätze* (Stuttgart, 1996) 17–30

Meuli, K. (1946) 'Griechische Opferbräuche', in O. Gigon *et al.*, edd., *Phyllobolia für Peter von der Mühll* (Basel) 185–288

Miller, A. M. (1986) *From Delos to Delphi: a literary study of the Homeric hymn to Apollo*. Leiden

Moorey, R. (1985) *Materials and manufacture in ancient Mesopotamia: the evidence of archaeology and art*. Oxford

Moorhouse, A. C. (1947) 'The meaning and use of μικρός and ὀλίγος in the Greek poetical vocabulary', *CQ* 41: 31–45

Morgan, C. (1990) *Athletes and oracles: the transformation of Olympia and Delphi in the eighth century* BC. Cambridge

Morgan, M. H. (1890) 'De ignis eliciendi modis', *HSCP* 1: 13–64

Morrison, J. S. and Williams, R. T. (1968) *Greek oared ships 900–322* BC. Cambridge

Müri, W. (1931) ΣΥΜΒΟΛΟΝ, *Wort- und sachgeschichtliche Studie*. Bern

Murr, J. (1890) *Die Pflanzenwelt in der griechischen Mythologie*. Innsbruck

Nenci, G. (1958) 'Il μάρτυς nei poemi omerici', *PP* 13: 221–41

Neugebauer, O. (1963) 'Decem tulerunt fastidia menses', *AJP* 84: 64–5

Newton, C. T. (1865) *Travels and discoveries in the Levant* II. London

Nilsson, M. P. (1906) *Griechische Feste der religiöser Bedeutung*. Leipzig

Norden, E. (1913) *Agnostos Theos*. Leipzig

Notopoulos, J. A. (1962) 'The Homeric Hymns as oral poetry: a study of the post-homeric oral tradition', *AJP* 83: 337–68

Nünlist, R. (2004) 'The Homeric Hymns', in I. de Jong, R. Nünlist, and A. Bowie, edd., *Narrators, narratees, and narratives in ancient Greek literature* (Leiden) 35–42

Olivieri, A. (1897) *Mythographi Graeci*. Leipzig

Page, D. L. (1955) *Sappho and Alcaeus*. Oxford

Papadopoulou-Belmehdi, I. and Papadopoulou, Z. D. (2002) 'Culte et musique: le cas des Déliades', *Religions méditerranéennes et orientales de l'antiquité*, Institut français d' archéologie orientale, Bibliothèque d' étude 125: 156–76

Parke, H. W. (1967a) *Greek oracles*. London

(1967b) *The oracles of Zeus*. Oxford

(1985) *The oracles of Apollo in Asia Minor*. London
Parke, H. W. and Wormell, D. E. W. (1956) *The Delphic oracle*. 2 vols. Oxford
Parker, R. (1983) *Miasma*. Oxford
(1991) 'The Hymn to Demeter and the Homeric Hymns', *G&R* 38: 1–17
(1996) *Athenian religion: a history*. Oxford
(2005) *Polytheism and society at Athens*. Oxford
Parry, H. (1992) *Thelxis*. Lanham
Pearson, A. C. (1917) *The fragments of Sophocles* I. Cambridge
Penglase, C. (1994) *Greek myths and Mesopotamia: parallels and influence in the Homeric hymns and Hesiod*. London
Peponi, A.-E. (2009) '*Choreia* and aesthetics in the Homeric *Hymn to Apollo*: the performance of the Delian maidens (lines 156–64)', *ClAnt* 28.1: 39–70
Pfeiffer, R. ed. (1949–53) *Callimachus*. 2 vols. Oxford
Picard, Ch. (1938) 'Les allées de trépieds apolliniennes', *RA* 112: 97–9
Picard, O. (1992) 'Recherches récentes autour du temple d'Apollon à Délos', in *La Magna Grecia e i grandi santuari della madrepatria*, Atti del trentunesimo Convegno di Studi sulla Magna Grecia, Taranto, 4–8 Ottobre 1991, 232–47
Porter, H. N. (1949) 'Repetition in the Homeric hymn to Aphrodite', *AJP* 70: 249–72
(1951) 'The early Greek hexameter', *YCS* 12: 3–63
Pulleyn, S. (2000) *Homer: Iliad book one*. Oxford
Pye, D. W. (1964) 'Wholly spondaic lines in Homer', *G&R* 11: 2–6
Radin, P. (1956) *The trickster: a study in American Indian mythology*. London
Ransome, H. (1937) *The sacred bee in ancient times and folklore*. London
Reitzenstein, R. (1893) *Epigramm und Skolion*. Giessen
Richardson, N. J. (1981) 'The contest of Homer and Hesiod and Alcidamas' Mouseion', *CQ* 31: 1–10
(1991) 'Homer and Cyprus', in V. Karageorghis, ed., *The civilizations of the Aegean and their diffusion in Cyprus and the eastern Mediterranean, 2000–600* BC. (Larnaca) 124–7
(2007) 'The Homeric Hymn to Hermes', in P. J. Finglass, C. Collard, and N. J. Richardson, edd., *Hesperos: Studies in ancient Greek poetry presented to M. L. West on his seventieth birthday* (Oxford) 83–91
Roberts, H. (1981) 'Reconstructing the Greek tortoise-shell lyre', *World Archaeology* 12: 303–12
Robertson, N. (1978) 'The myth of the First Sacred War', *CQ* 28: 38–73
Rolley, C. (1977) *Fouilles de Delphes* V.3 *(Les trépieds à cuve clouée)*. Paris
Rose, H. J. (1924) 'Anchises and Aphrodite', *CQ* 18: 11–16
Roux, G. (1964) 'Sur deux passages de l'Hymne homérique à Apollon', *REG* 77: 1–22
(1966) 'Testimonia Delphica I. Note sur l'hymne homérique à Apollon, vers 298', *REG* 79: 1–5
(1976) *Delphes: son oracle et ses dieux*. Paris

Rubensohn, O. (1962) *Das Delion von Paros*. Wiesbaden
Ruijgh, C. J. (1971) *Autour de* τε *épique*. Amsterdam
Rutherford, I. (2001) *Pindar's paeans*. Oxford
Sale, W. (1961) 'The Hyperborean Maidens on Delos', *HThR* 54: 75–89
Samter, E. (1911) *Geburt, Hochzeit und Tod*. Leipzig
Sanchez, D. (2001) *L'amphictionie des Pyles et de Delphes*. Stuttgart
Schachter, A. (1967) 'A Boeotian cult type', *BICS* 14: 1–16
(1976) '*Homeric Hymn to Apollo*, lines 231–238 (the Onchestos Episode): another interpretation', *BICS* 23: 102–13
(1981–94) *Cults of Boeotia. BICS* Supplement 38.1–4. London
Schefold, K. and Auberson, P. (1972) *Führer durch Eretria*. Bern
Scheinberg, S. (1979) 'The bee maidens of the Homeric *Hymn to Hermes*', *HSCP* 83: 1–28
Schliemann, H. (1878) *Mycenae*. London
Schulze, W. (1885) 'Zum Dialect der ältesten Ionischen Inschriften', *Hermes* 20: 491–4
Schwabl, H. (1986) 'Zum Problem der Themenwahl in den homerischen Götterhymnen', in I. Vaslef and H. Buschhausen, edd., *Classica et mediaevalia: studies in honour of Joseph Szövérffy* (Washington and Leiden) 147–59
Seaford, R. (1984) *Euripides: Cyclops*. Oxford
Segal, C. (1974) 'The Homeric hymn to Aphrodite: a structuralist approach', *CW* 67: 205–12
(1986) 'Tithonus and the Homeric hymn to Aphrodite: a comment', *Arethusa* 19: 37–46
Settis, S. (1966) *Saggio sull'Afrodite Urania di Fidia*. Pisa
Shelmerdine, S. C. (1981) 'The Homeric Hymn to Hermes: a commentary (1–114) with introduction'. PhD dissertation, University of Michigan
(1984) 'Hermes and the tortoise: a prelude to cult', *GRBS* 25: 201–7
(1986) 'Odyssean allusions in the fourth Homeric Hymn', *TAPhA* 116: 49–63
Sherwin-White, S. M. (1978) *Ancient Cos*. Göttingen
Silk, M. S. (1974) *Interaction in poetic imagery, with special reference to early Greek poetry*. Cambridge
Skorda, D. (1992) 'Recherches dans la vallée du Pleistos', in J.-F. Bommelaer, ed., *Delphes: centenaire de la 'grande fouille' réalisée par l'École française d'Athènes (1892–1903)* (Leiden) 39–66
Smith, P. M. (1979) 'Notes on the text of the fifth Homeric hymn', *HSCP* 83: 29–50
(1981a) *Nursling of mortality: a study in the Homeric hymn to Aphrodite*. Frankfurt
(1981b) 'Aineiadai as patrons of *Iliad* xx and the Homeric hymn to Aphrodite', *HSCP* 85: 17–58
Sokolowski, F. (1960) 'On the episode of Onchestus in the Homeric *Hymn to Apollo*', *TAPhA* 91: 376–80
Solmsen, F. (1968) *Kleine Schriften* I. Hildesheim

Sourvinou-Inwood, C. (1991) *'Reading' Greek culture: texts and images, rituals and myths.* Oxford

Souza, P. de (1999) *Piracy in the Graeco-Roman world.* Cambridge

Sowa, C. A. (1984) *Traditional themes and the Homeric hymns.* Chicago

Steffen, V. (1960) *Sophokleous Ichneutai.* Warsaw

Stehle, E. (1997) *Performance and gender in ancient Greece.* Princeton

Stengel, P. (1910) *Opferbräuche der Griechen.* Leipzig

(1920) *Die griechischen Kultusaltertümer.* Munich

Stinton, T. C. W. (1965) *Euripides and the judgement of Paris.* London

Strunk, K. (1959) 'Frühe Veränderungen in der griechischen Literatur', *Glotta* 38: 74–89

Teffeteller, A. (2001) 'The chariot-rite at Onchestos: Homeric hymn to Apollo 229–38', *JHS* 101: 159–66

Thomas, O. R. H. (2007) 'Charting the Atlantic with Hesiod and Hellanicus', *ZPE* 160: 15–23

(forthcoming) 'Sacrifice and the *Homeric Hymn to Hermes* 112–41', in S. S. Hitch and I. C. Rutherford, edd., *Animal sacrifice in the ancient Greek world.* Cambridge

Torres-Guerra, José B. (2003) 'Die Anordnung der homerischen Hymnen', *Philologus* 147: 3–12

Tréheux, J. (1946) 'Ortygie', *BCH* 70: 560–76

(1953) 'La réalité historique des offrandes hyperboréennes', in G. E. Mylonas and D. Raymond, edd., *Studies presented to David Moore Robinson* (St Louis, Missouri) 758–74

Turkeltaub, D. W. (2003) 'The God's radiance manifest: an examination of the narrative pattern underlying the Homeric divine epiphany scenes'. Diss. Cornell

Vamvouri-Ruffy, M. (2004) *La fabrique du divin.* Liège

Van der Valk, M. (1976) 'On the arrangement of the Homeric Hymns', *AC* 45: 419–45

Van Groningen, B. A. (1958) *La composition littéraire archaique grecque.* Amsterdam

Van Nortwick, T. (1975) 'The Homeric Hymn to Hermes: a study in early Greek hexameter style'. PhD dissertation, Stanford University

(1980) 'Apollônos apatê: associative imagery in the *Homeric Hymn to Hermes* 227–92', *CW* 74: 1–5

Verdenius, W. J. (1969) 'Νόστος', *Mnemosyne* 22: 195

Vergados, A. (2007a) 'A commentary on the Homeric Hymn to Hermes'. Diss. Virginia

(2007b) 'The *Homeric Hymn to Hermes* 51 and Antigonus of Carystus', *CQ* 57: 737–42

Vermeule, E. (1979) *Aspects of death in early Greek art and poetry.* Berkeley, Los Angeles and London

Vos, H. (1956) *Themis.* Assen

Vox, O. (1981) 'Apollo irato nell'inno ad Ermes', *Prometheus* 7: 108–14

Walcot, P. (1958) 'Hesiod's hymns to the Muses, Aphrodite, Styx and Hecate', *SO* 34: 5–14
(1991) 'The Homeric hymn to Aphrodite: a literary approach', *G&R* 38: 137–55
Wallace, P. W. (1979) *Strabo's description of Boeotia*. Heidelberg
Walsh, G. B. (1984) *The varieties of enchantment*. Chapel Hill
Waszink, J. H. (1974) *Biene und Honig als Symbole des Dichters und der Dichtung in der griechisch-römischen Antike*. Opladen
Watkins, C. (1995) *How to kill a dragon: aspects of Indo-European poetics*. New York
Weniger, L. (1920) 'Die monatliche Opfer in Olympia', *Klio* 16: 1–39
West, M. L. (1970) 'The eighth Homeric Hymn and Proclus', *CQ* 20: 300–4
(1974) *Studies in Greek elegy and iambus*. Berlin
(1975) 'Cynaethus' hymn to Apollo', *CQ* 25: 161–70
(1983) *The Orphic poems*. Oxford
(1989) 'An unrecognized injunctive usage in Greek', *Glotta* 67: 135–8
(1992) *Greek music*. Oxford
(1995) 'The date of the *Iliad*', *MH* 52: 203–19
(1997) *The east face of Helicon*. Oxford
(1999) 'The invention of Homer', *CQ* 49: 364–82
(2001a) 'Some Homeric words', *Glotta* 77: 118–35
(2001b) 'The fragmentary Homeric Hymn to Dionysus', *ZPE* 134: 1–11
(2002) 'The view from Lesbos', in M. Reichel and A. Rengakos, edd., *Epea pteroenta: Beiträge zur Homerforschung. Festschrift für Wolfgang Kullmann zum 75. Geburtstag* (Stuttgart) 207–19
(2003) *Homeric Hymns, Homeric apocrypha, lives of Homer*. Cambridge, Mass.
(2005) 'The new Sappho', *ZPE* 151: 1–9
(2007) *Indo-European poetry and myth*. Oxford
Wiechers, A. (1961) *Aesop in Delphi*. Meisenheim am Glan
Wilamowitz-Moellendorff, U. von (1916) *Die Ilias und Homer*. Berlin
(1931–2) *Der Glaube der Hellenen*. 2 vols. Berlin
Wills, J. (1996) *Repetition in Latin poetry: figures of allusion*. Oxford
Wortmann, D. (1968) 'Die Sandale der Hekate–Persephone–Selene', *ZPE* 2: 155–60
Yalouris, N. Ph. (1953–4) 'Ἑρμῆς βούκλεψ', *AEph* 1953–4, part 1: 162–84
Zanetto, G. (1996) *Inni omerici*. Milan
Zumbach, O. (1955) *Neuerungen in der Sprache der homerischen Hymnen*. Winterthur

INDEXES

Italic numerals refer to pages of the Introduction. Non-italic references are to line numbers in the commentary, using the traditional numbering of the individual hymns, i.e. 3 for Apollo, *4 for* Hermes, *and 5 for* Aphrodite. *Thus 3.1* = Hymn to Apollo, *line 1, etc.*

1 SUBJECTS

2 GREEK WORDS

3 PASSAGES DISCUSSED

Lightning Source UK Ltd.
Milton Keynes UK
UKOW01f0827300717
306296UK00013B/158/P

9 780521 457743